# Adolescence and Youth

# Adolescence and Youth

## PSYCHOLOGICAL DEVELOPMENT IN A CHANGING WORLD

### FIFTH EDITION

## John Janeway Conger
University of Colorado School of Medicine

## Nancy L. Galambos
University of Victoria

An imprint of Addison Wesley Longman, Inc.

New York • Reading, Massachusetts • Menlo Park, California • Harlow, England
Don Mills, Ontario • Sydney • Mexico City • Madrid • Amsterdam

ACQUISITIONS EDITOR: REBECCA DUDLEY
DEVELOPMENTAL EDITOR: RICHARD MOREL
SUPPLEMENTS EDITOR: DONNA CAMPION
PROJECT COORDINATION: ELECTRONIC PUBLISHING SERVICES INC.
COVER DESIGNER: KAY PETRONIO
COVER PHOTOGRAPH: TONY FREEMAN/PHOTOEDIT
ART STUDIO: ELECTRONIC PUBLISHING SERVICES INC.
PHOTO RESEARCHER: ROSEMARY HUNTER
ELECTRONIC PRODUCTION MANAGER: VALERIE L. ZABORSKI
MANUFACTURING MANAGER: HELENE G. LANDERS
ELECTRONIC PAGE MAKEUP: ELECTRONIC PUBLISHING SERVICES INC.
PRINTER AND BINDER: R.R. DONNELLEY & SONS COMPANY
COVER PRINTER: PHOENIX COLOR CORP.

For permission to use copyrighted material, grateful acknowledgment is made to the copyright holders on pp. 441–442, which are hereby made part of this copyright page.

**Library of Congress Cataloging-in-Publication Data**
Conger, John Janeway
  Adolescence and Youth : psychological development in a changing world / John Janeway Conger, Nancy L. Galambos.—5th ed.
        p.   cm.
    Includes bibliographical references and indexes.
    ISBN 0-673-99262-4
    1. Adolescence.   I. Galambos, Nancy L.   II. Title.
HQQ796.C76   1996
305.23'5—dc20                                                                95-49010
                                                                                    CIP

0-673-99262-4

1234567890—DOW—99989796

I have sent forth my prayers.

Our children,

Even those who have erected their shelters

At the edge of the wilderness,

May their roads come in safely,

May the forests

And the brush

Stretch out their water-filled arms

To shield their hearts;

May their roads come in safely;

May their roads all be fulfilled,

May it not somehow become difficult for them

When they have gone but a little way.


May all the young boys,

All the young girls,

And those whose roads are ahead,

May they have powerful hearts,

Strong spirits;

On roads reaching to Dawn Lake

May they grow old.


—Zuñi Indian Prayer



For Trista, Steven, David, and Christopher

For Roger and Gillian

# Brief Contents

# Detailed Contents

# Preface

## Our Perspective

In the past decade, the world in which young people are coming to maturity has changed dramatically. As the last edition of this book was being completed, "people's revolutions" were spreading across the face of Europe and much of the rest of the world, with long-term consequences that are still shrouded in uncertainty. What is clear, however, is that these revolutions, like all revolutions, have already had their own share of victories and victims, of new hope and opportunity for some and disappointment or despair for many others.

Today, as the world nears a new millennium, we are engaged in still another kind of revolution: a knowledge-based, technological revolution. This latest revolution is taking place in the context of a global economy that is increasingly independent of national boundaries, and in which success will come only to those prepared to meet its challenges. Moreover, all of these challenges are coming at a time when our society is becoming ever more polarized—politically, socially, and economically.

If young people are to be ready to meet the challenges of new realities—in work, in their personal lives, and as citizens—they will need to be emotionally mature, well-educated, socially responsible, and sure of their own goals and values. This will require enlightened support and encouragement from families, schools, the business community, and government.

Success will not come easily. The challenges confronting the family as a social institution have increased and become still more complex. If young people are to function successfully in a rapidly changing global economy, many will need to raise their vocational sights and to shift away from traditional occupations to newly emerging ones. Our educational institutions must play a major role in helping them to do so. American youth cannot continue to be so poorly informed about their own history and culture, and to rank near the bottom among industrialized nations in mathematical and scientific skills. Yet reduced budgets, ideological differences regarding the fundamental purposes of education, and the disintegration of previously stable families and neighborhoods have created increasingly critical problems for our schools. Changing sex roles, particularly for women, are leading to changes in educational and vocational opportunities and, in many instances, to reappraisals of personal and social goals.

The challenges of meeting the developmental demands of adolescence are most acute for the increasing number of young people—currently more than one in five—who are growing up in poverty, whether in deteriorating inner-city neighborhoods plagued by gangs, crime, and drugs; at the social fringes of suburbia; in rural slums; or on reservations. Often lacking a stable family life, supportive peers, safe and nurturing neighborhoods, adequate schools, health care, or prospects of securing a decent job, many poor and minority youth are in danger of becoming a new underclass—excluded not only from productive employment, but from hope for the future and meaningful participation in the mainstream of society.

Although many young people are affected in one way or another by recent massive cutbacks in federal and state funding for social, educational, nutritional, health, mental health, rehabilitative, and other youth programs, it is this vulnerable minority, whose needs are greatest, who are being hit hardest by this sea change in social policy.

All these changes, and others, have affected the adolescent's development and the challenges he or she faces in the search for a stable, workable sense of identity. Much of the new material in this edition reflects the influence of these changes.

This edition also reflects the remarkable progress that has been made in research on adolescent development in the last fifteen years. There has been a virtual explosion in the number of studies on adolescence in areas as diverse as biological influences on behavior, sex roles, patterns of family interactions, ethnic influences on development, peer relations, and the influence of the social and economic context on adolescent develop-

ment. The current coverage of topics in this text reflects this new material and provides detailed bibliographic references to it.

# What is New in This Edition?

Although a focus on the changes adolescents experience as they develop has been a feature of this text since its initial edition, for the first time we introduce explicitly the *life-span developmental perspective*. This theoretical perspective offers a set of assumptions about the course of human development, including the view of development as a lifelong process that occurs as a result of a continuing interaction between individuals and their environment. This perspective guides us in our exploration of adolescent development because it focuses attention on how the naturally unfolding physical and intellectual changes of adolescence combine with the adolescent's social world—the family, school, peer settings, neighborhoods, and political and economic systems—to shape the person who is in the process of becoming an adult.

Two of the most prominent social issues in today's world concern gender roles and multiculturalism. Although this text has always been sensitive to gender and cultural issues, this edition brings with it an *enhanced focus on gender and ethnicity* that is spread throughout the chapters. Given that there has been a concerted effort in the last decade to consider gender and ethnic issues systematically in research on adolescent development, it was not difficult to find examples of research that expand our understanding of the multiple worlds of adolescents. These issues are discussed both in the text and in supplementary boxes.

There is a *new focus on adolescents at risk,* reflecting the growing body of research in the field of adolescence on the nature, sources, and consequences of a variety of problem behaviors such as binge drinking, unprotected sexual intercourse, and conduct problems. In the first of three chapters devoted to examining adolescents at risk (Chapter 11) we introduce a global perspective on problem behavior in order to set the stage for the topics and chapters to follow. The remaining portion of Chapter 11 focuses on substance use, Chapter 12 focuses on alienation and delinquency, and Chapter 13 examines psychological disorders in adolescence.

*New boxes* to accompany the text have been added to every chapter. These boxes serve multiple purposes, including the presentation of new and exciting research that provides examples of how best to study a particular aspect of adolescent development. Some boxes focus on an important social issue, challenging the reader to consider alternative ways to view a social problem. Other boxes focus on stories written by or about real-life people who have experienced the joys and pains of adolescence.

The artwork has changed dramatically in this edition. You will notice that *color photographs* depict in exciting images the many faces of adolescence. Every effort was made to find the most effective photographs of adolescents engaging in relevant activities. There are also significant changes in the tables and figures in this text. This edition has been revised to contain *easily accessible and visually appealing tables and figures in full color* to supplement important points made in the text. These changes ensure that the first-time student of adolescence will be able to grasp easily the information presented in the tables and figures.

*Fully updated references* have been incorporated extensively into the text, bringing with them the latest research findings from the many journals that now specialize in adolescent development, as well as those dealing with human development in general, in order to bring the student up to date on current issues and recent research in the field of adolescence.

# Highlights from This Fifth Edition

**Chapter 2,** Viewing Development: Principles of Change, contains a new section devoted to exploring the features, usefulness, and implications of the *life-span developmental perspective* for considering adolescent development. Other major changes include a new focus on the latest research on stress and coping and an expanded discussion of sex roles.

**Chapter 3,** Biological Changes in Adolescence, contains many new studies from the burgeoning area of research on the psychological experiences associated with pubertal maturation. There are updated discussions of the effects of pubertal timing on adolescents' relations with peers and parents.

**Chapter 4,** Intelligence and Cognitive Development, has been reorganized to focus explicitly on three approaches to cognitive development: psychometric, Piagetian, and information-processing. The section on information processing has been expanded to include new results pertaining to adolescents' cognitive abilities.

**Chapter 5,** The Family and Parent–Adolescent Relations, combines two chapters from the previous edition in an extensive regorganization that now describes the changing face of today's families, and pre-

sents the latest research on parental responsiveness and demandingness, parent–adolescent conflict, father involvement, and adolescent functioning in working, economically stressed, and divorced families.

**Chapter 6,** Adolescent Sexuality, contains the most recent statistics available on adolescents' sexual attitudes and behavior. The discussion of AIDS and sexual orientation has been extended considerably, reflecting the increased amount of research available on these issues in the last five years.

**Chapter 7,** Adolescents and Their Peers, has been generally updated with new references and findings on adolescent friendships, relations with opposite-sex peers, peer acceptance, neglect, and rejection. New boxes explore the links among parenting practices, peer relations, and adolescent behavior and the issues of date rape and harassment by peers.

**Chapter 8,** Adolescents and Schools, presents the most recent findings on what and how well adolescents are learning in school. There is an expanded discussion of research on school transitions, and new boxes highlighting research on ethnicity and school achievement, school tracking, and single-sex schools.

**Chapter 9,** Adolescents, Work, and Careers, has been generally updated, presenting the most recent research on the effects of work on adolescents' psychological health and well-being, sex differences in occupational choices and values, and the influence of mothers' and fathers' work on adolescent development and behavior. A fully updated section describes the most recent trends in career values.

**Chapter 10,** Moral Development and Values, presents new research on the course of moral development in adolescence, including the influences of family interactions, parenting styles, and adolescent personality characteristics on moral reasoning and the development of conscience. The chapter ends with an in-depth exploration of adolescents' current social, political, and economic values.

**Chapter 11,** Adolescents at Risk I: Drugs and Behavior, is the first of three chapters devoted to examining adolescents at risk. This chapter opens with an entirely new discussion of adolescent problem behavior, followed by a presentation of the most up-to-date findings on adolescents' use of tobacco, alcohol, marijuana, and other drugs, and on parental and peer influences on substance use.

**Chapter 12,** Adolescents at Risk II: Alienation and Delinquency, has been extensively revised to present the newest information on incidence of, sex differences in, and causes of delinquency. New sections on violence, homicide, and gangs explore the significant social problem of serious crime among youth.

**Chapter 13,** Adolescents at Risk III: Disorders in Development, has been thoroughly updated and includes new findings on the etiology, diagnosis, and treatment of anxiety disorders, depression, schizophrenia, and eating disorders. There is also a new section on conduct disorders. Particular attention is paid to sex differences and the role of adolescent developmental changes in these disorders.

## Pedagogical Features

A number of features have been included in this edition to help students to organize and learn the material, to start to think about issues, and to encourage students to pursue some topics in depth.

- Each chapter has a *detailed outline* in the table of contents and at the beginning of the chapter.
- Chapter *summaries* are comprehensive and written to help students integrate the contents.
- *Key terms* in each chapter are printed in boldface type, accompanied by a *glossary* of these terms at the back of the book.
- As mentioned above, *boxes* appear throughout the text dealing with important social issues, case studies, or particularly interesting and important research.
- *Review questions* appear at the end of each chapter, and are designed to help students think actively about the major topics covered.
- At the end of each chapter a short list of *recommended readings* has been updated for those wishing to pursue chapter topics in greater depth.
- Over 1800 *references* are cited at the back of the book, with the names of the authors in bold face to facilitate easy searching. This bibliography should prove useful to students in preparing term papers and to investigators in gaining a broad overview of particular areas of research.

## Supplementary Materials

A number of high quality supplements have been carefully developed to accompany this text and provide additional teaching support.

*Instructor's Resource Manual.* For each chapter of the text this helpful teaching resource features outlines, overviews, learning objectives, key words and concepts, teaching tips and activities, lecture and discussion sections, lists of audiovisual resources, additional references, and suggested readings.

*Test Bank.* Written by Rebecca L. Slaton, this resource contains over 1,000 test items including multiple choice, short answer, true/false, matching, and essay questions. Each question is referenced to a specific page number, topic, and skill in the text.

*Computerized Test Bank.* The Testmaster Computerized Testing System is a flexible easy-to-master testing system that includes all questions found in the printed test bank. The Testmaster software allows you to edit existing questions and add your own items. Tests can be printed in several different formats and can include figures such as graphs and tables. Testmaster is available in Macintosh- and IBM-compatible formats.

*Student Study Guide.* Written by Rebecca Slaton, this valuable student resource contains outlines, overviews, key terms and definitions, review questions, mix and match exercises, multiple choice, true/false, and fill-in-the-blank questions for each chapter. Answers to practice test items are also provided at the end of each chapter. Single authorship of the Test Bank and Study Guide ensures consistency in testing and studying objectives.

## Acknowledgments

Many people have made important contributions to the preparation of this book. We especially want to thank Pamela K. Turner for her tireless efforts in conducting literature searches and seeking permissions from colleagues for the reprinting of their materials. We also want to thank Tristin M. Wayte for the skill and energy she devoted to searching the literature, gathering references, and integrating, correcting, and organizing the multitude of references that accompany this text. Dorothy R. Townsend also assisted with typing part of the manuscript and making helpful editorial suggestions.

For carefully reviewing all of the chapters, and for valuable suggestions aimed at improving the readability of the text and making it more accessible to students, and for helpful comments on simplifying tables and figures, as well as his interest and encouragement, we wish to thank our developmental editor, Richard Morel. We also wish to thank Rosemary Hunter, our senior photo researcher, for her unflagging enthusiasm and her excellent work in finding and helping to select the many new color photographs that accompany the text of this edition.

We also want to express our gratitude to Lloyd Johnston, Jerald Bachman, and Joyce Buchanan of the University of Michigan's Institute for Social Research for providing access to as yet unpublished data from Monitoring the Future, their ongoing national survey of high school and college students. Thomas J. Crowley generously supplied expert advice during our review of current drug research.

For reviewing the manuscript as a whole and making valuable suggestions, we would like to thank the following colleagues: Daniel Lynch, University of Wisconsin-Oshkosh; Stephanie Clancy Dollinger, Southern Illinois University; Seth Kalichman, Georgia State University; Mary Lou Arnold, University of Toronto; Richard Smith, University of New Mexico; Janice Stapley, Monmouth College; Narina Nunez Nightingale, University of Wyoming; Gregory Fouts, University of Calgary; Patrick S. Williams, University of Houston-Downtown; Robert Wunderlin, Old Dominion University; Susan McFadden, University of Wisconsin-Oshkosh; Stephanie Broderick, University of California-Irvine; Alan Butler, University of Maine; and Marvin Berkowitz, Marquette University.

Finally, a book such as this inevitably reflects not only the current status of an area of scientific investigation but, at least to some extent, the outlook of the authors—their own values, hopes and fears, perceptions, and blind spots. To the extent that the hopes outweigh the fears and that, despite the blind spots, there is some understanding, our greatest debt is to our families. They have provided not only pleasure and love, but, equally important, a meaningful link between the best of the past, present, and future.

JOHN JANEWAY CONGER
NANCY LYNN GALAMBOS

Adolescence and Youth

# Introduction

## 1

h umankind has long been preoccupied with its youth. In the collective life of societies, each new generation has been perceived as a fragile vessel by which the best of the past is transmitted into the present. In the faces of each new generation we see written the future of nations and cultures—the future of humanity itself. Despite the decline in political and governmental support for solving the problems of children and adolescents during the 1980s and 1990s (Conger, 1981, 1988), most of us recognize that much of human history is the story of successive generations of young people.

There is also a personal and subjective side to our fascination with youth. Over the centuries, from the time of the ancient Egyptians to the present, adults have considered their own lives from the perspective of what they learned, hoped for, and anticipated during their adolescent years. Most of us perceive our childhood as a period of becoming, whereas adolescence is remembered as the time when our identities became more coherent and when our potential for accomplishment—though not the accomplishments themselves—was at its height. For many, adolescence is remembered as the time when one was most alive: "a flick of sunshine upon a strange shore, the time to remember, the time for a sigh" (Conrad, 1902, p. 843). The friendships we formed in these years, our first loves, the music we enjoyed, and the activities we participated in all have a certain permanence in our minds.

When we think about whether we have changed over the years, whether we have lived up to our expectations and dreams, whether we have realized our potential, the inevitable comparison is with the hopes we had in our youth. We may no longer wish to be young, but we may look back fondly at some of the memories.

Adolescence is remembered by many as a time of being most alive.

## 1.1 One Teen's View of Adolescence
### AGAINST ALL ODDS, I'M JUST FINE

What troubled times the American teenager lives in! Ads for Nike shoes urge us to "Just do it!" while the White House tells us to "Just say no." The baby boomers have watched their babies grow into teens and history has repeated itself: the punk teens of the '80s have taken the place of the hippie teens of the '60s. Once again, the generation gap has widened and the adults have finally remembered to remember that teenagers are just no good. They have even coined a name for their persecution of adolescents: "teen-bashing."

If what is being printed in the newspapers, viewed on television and repeated by adults is correct, it is against all odds that I am able to write this article. Adults say the average teenager can't write complete sentences and has trouble spelling big words. Their surveys report that I can't find Canada on a map. According to their statistics, my favorite hobbies are sexual intercourse and recreational drug use. It's amazing that I've found time to write this; from what they say, my time is spent committing violent crimes or just hanging out with a gang. In fact, it is even more amazing that I'm here at all, when you consider that the music I listen to is supposedly "warping" my mind and influencing me to commit suicide.

Nonetheless, here I am. I write this article to show that a teenager can survive in today's society.

Actually, I'm doing quite well. I haven't fathered any children, I'm not addicted to any drugs, I've never worshiped Satan and I don't have a police record. I can even find Canada on a map along with its capital, Ottawa. I guess my family and friends have been supportive of me, for I've never been tempted to become one of those teenage runaways I'm always reading about. Call me a rebel, but I've stayed in school and (can it be true?!) I enjoy it. This month, I graduate from high school and join other graduates as the newest generation of adults. I'm looking forward to four years of college and becoming a productive member of society. I may not be America's stereotypical teen, but that only proves there is something wrong with our society's preconceived image of today's teenager.

My only goal in writing this article is to point out the "bum rap" today's teenager faces. I feel the stereotypical teen is, in fact, a minority. The true majority are the teenagers who, day in and day out, prepare themselves for the future and work at becoming responsible adults. Our time is coming. Soon we will be the adults passing judgment on the teenagers of tomorrow. Hopefully, by then, we will have realized that support and encouragement have a far more positive effect on teenagers than does "bashing" them.

SOURCE: Newsweek Special Issue: "The New Teens," June 1990. Reprinted by permission of author.

Consequently, when we look at adolescents we see not merely a necessary generational link between the past and the future, but also ourselves. In many ways, we react to adolescents in much the same way that we react to projective personality tests such as the Rorschach inkblots. We see in youth not merely what is actually there but the mirror of our own desires, hopes, satisfactions, frustrations, fears, and disappointments.

## A New Generation

Some observers believe that today's young people are more rootless, more emotionally troubled, and more self-centered and materialistic than their counterparts of earlier generations. In support of this view, they cite high rates of juvenile crime, drug use, and adolescent suicide; high rates of adolescent pregnancy; and young people's apparent preoccupation with self-fulfillment at the expense of societal concerns (Conger, 1988; Takanishi, 1993). Others argue that adolescents today are better informed about the world than their predecessors were; that they are no less idealistic, though more pragmatic and less sentimental; and that they are more open, honest, and tolerant, and less given to viewing others in terms of simplistic stereotypes. Indeed, the authors of a survey of Canadian adolescents argued that "Today's young people are the best informed teenagers in . . . history. When it comes to a basic awareness of what's happening in the world, they leave their counterparts of the past three generations in the dust" (Bibby & Posterski, 1992, p. 65).

Still others observe that presumed differences—good or bad—between today's adolescents and those of earlier generations are largely illusory and more a matter of form than of substance, or that they stem from unwarranted generalizations based on the behavior of a small number of atypical young people.

If you are confused about what to conclude, you might want to know that all of these observations contain a kernel of truth. Some social indicators (such as suicide rates) suggest that some things are worse now than in recent history. Other indicators, however, point to the fact that things are getting better for youth (such as the rates at which young people are obtaining higher education). On many characteristics (such as the importance of the peer group), adolescents of today may not look so different from their predecessors.

One of the aims of this book, then, is to examine the evidence for or against such contrasting views and to attempt to arrive at a balanced judgment about the problems and opportunities confronting today's adolescents. We will examine the social, biological, and cognitive changes that occur in adolescence; these changes will be discussed within the context of the family, peer group, school, and the larger culture of which the adolescent is a part. Only by examining the bigger picture can we begin to understand the adolescent experience. In the process of looking at what we know about adolescents, we may also learn a little more about ourselves.

# Historical Roots of the Concept of Adolescence

Although concern with adolescents became especially intense during the "youth revolution" of the 1960s (when college students questioned and demonstrated against many of the decisions and actions of those in authority), the years surrounding puberty have long received attention as a noteworthy period in the life span. Ancient Egyptian writings commented on the distinctive characteristics of youth many centuries before the emergence of Christianity. Then as now, such comments often served as a basis for dire predictions regarding the likely behavior of adolescents.

## Views of Adolescence in Ancient Times

Reflecting the early Greek philosophers' interest in human nature, Plato (1953) offered advice on the socialization of children from their earliest years through adolescence and young adulthood. He pointed out that during the developmental years adolescents "are subject

to many changes in the course of their lives" (p. 359). He noted that adolescents are prone to argument for its own sake. In their enthusiasm they would "leave no stone unturned, and in their delight at the first taste of wisdom, they would annoy everyone with their arguments" (quoted in Muus, 1988, pp. 5–6).

Another observer characterized the period that we now recognize as adolescence in these words:

> The young are in character prone to desire and ready to carry any desire they may have formed into action. Of bodily desires it is the sexual to which they are most disposed to give way, and in regard to sexual desire they exercise no self-restraint. . . .
>
> They are passionate, irascible, and apt to be carried away by their impulses. They are the slaves, too, of their passion, as their ambition prevents their ever brooking a slight and renders them indignant at the mere idea of enduring an injury. . . .
>
> They are charitable rather than the reverse, as they have never yet been witnesses of many villainies; and they are trustful, as they have not yet been often deceived. . . . They have high aspirations; for they have never yet been humiliated by the experience of life, but are unacquainted with the limiting force of circumstances. . . .
>
> If the young commit a fault, it is always on the side of excess and exaggeration for they carry everything too far, whether it be their love or hatred or anything else. They regard themselves as omniscient and are positive in their assertions; this is, in fact, the reason of their carrying everything too far (quoted in Kiell, 1967, pp. 18–19).

Although these words sound as though they might have been written by a twentieth-century social critic, they were written by Aristotle 2300 years ago. In Aristotle's view, children and animals alike were under the control of what today would be called Freud's pleasure principle ("children and brutes pursue pleasures") and although they had the capacity for voluntary action, they did not have the capacity for choice ("acts done on the spur of the moment we describe as voluntary, but not as chosen") (Aristotle, 1941, pp. 967–968).

The development of the ability to choose was seen as an important characteristic of adolescence. Aristotle's emphasis on voluntary and deliberate choice as necessary for the attainment of maturity is not unlike that of some contemporary social critics, who believe that "with prolonged education and prolonged dependency we

Aristotle.

have reduced choices for adolescents to the extent that we interfere with their attainment of maturity" (Muus, 1988, p. 8).

Much of the astute reasoning and empirically based observation that characterized Aristotle and other Greek philosophers was obscured by the impact of early Christian theology. However, discussion of the "ages of life" reappeared in the pseudoscientific treatises of the Middle Ages (Ariès, 1962). Consider the following passage from *Le grand propriétaire de toutes choses,* a kind of encyclopedia of "scientific" knowledge published in 1556:

> Afterward [i.e., after infancy and childhood] follows the third age, which is called adolescence, which ends according to Constantine in his viaticum in the twenty-first year, but according to Isidore it lasts until twenty-eight . . . and it can go on until thirty or thirty-five. This age is called adolescence because the person is big enough to beget children, says Isidore. In this age the limbs are soft and able to grow and receive strength and vigour from natural heat (quoted in Ariès, 1962, p. 21).

## Adolescence in Early Modern History

Although the above treatise recognized the word *adolescence,* historians note that it was not a widely used term before the nineteenth century. In fact, in the sixteenth and seventeenth centuries, agrarian society demanded that children learn how to perform work-related tasks; their ability to fulfill their economic roles in the family was of primary importance. In essence, children of all but the youngest ages were considered miniature adults. Such a view of children is *not* concordant with a focus on the successive stages of life or with the notion of an extended period of time during which youth explore their future roles (Modell & Goodman, 1990). Indeed, "some historians have denied that early modern Europeans had any conception of adolescence" (Smith, 1975, p. 493).

As part of the training for children's economic roles in western Europe and parts of colonial America, girls and boys between the general ages of 12 and 15 years were "fostered out." This practice, which was seen as a crucial part of the youth's education and experience, meant that he or she lived and worked with another family in the same community as an apprentice or domestic. This sort of service was common, although some adolescents were sent to boarding schools to achieve the same goal. Essentially, this fostering out was a rite of passage—a ritual that marks a significant transition in the adolescent's movement toward adulthood. As a result of the fostering-out experience and of the very clear expectations for the roles men and women were to fulfill in adulthood, "transitions to adulthood were relatively unmarked by psychological traumas and personal crises" (Modell & Goodman, 1990, p. 96).

Although thoughts about adolescence as a stage of development may not have been prominent in the early modern era (up to the nineteenth century), examinations of sermons have revealed that religious leaders preached specifically to youth (Smith, 1975). "Sermons given by religious leaders reveal a view of young people as both a threat to the social order and a means of maintaining that order" (Modell & Goodman, 1990, p. 97). The principal danger to youth was thought to be sinfulness, with sexuality a key concern. Religious conversion (usually after age 20) was seen as the antidote (Smith, 1975). The dominant theme of seventeenth-century writings by members of the clergy and others was the need to help undependable youth master their unruly impulses (Spacks, 1981). The romantic preoccupation with the psychological complexities and special needs of adolescence that we see today was still largely absent. Young people were not yet important enough to be taken as seriously as older and wiser adults.

Not until the late nineteenth century do we encounter precursors of the contemporary concern with adolescence as a socially significant and psychologically complex period. The reasons are both demographic and cultural. The perception of adolescence as a truly distinctive stage of development depends at least in part on the existence of communities of young people who share similar experiences at about the same age and are isolated to some extent from the adult world. It is not surprising, therefore, that much of the so-called youth culture of the late 1960s and early 1970s centered on schools and universities, where large numbers of young people congregate in age-segregated groups.

Such conditions did not exist before about 1890. The idea of a large city school with 500 or more tenth-grade students living, studying, and interacting in relative isolation from younger children and older adults would have seemed incomprehensible before this time. For one thing, in the United States and other Western countries most of the population lived in rural areas or in small towns and cities. Moreover, there was far less separation between adolescents and adults because most children were involved in the world of work early, whether on the family farm, in other households, as helpers or apprentices to skilled craftspersons and shopowners, or as workers in mills and small factories. In many instances, it was necessary to send children away from home at an early age because there were too many

mouths to feed or because one or both parents had died. (In the first half of the nineteenth century, only 20 percent of mothers survived their youngest child's maturity.) Even among the upper classes, the practice of

Before the late 1800s, the idea of a large city high school with hundreds of students in one grade, isolated from younger children and adults, would have seemed incomprehensible.

sending young children away from home was not uncommon (Kett, 1977).

Few children continued their education into the adolescent years. Even for those who did, the experience was far different from that of a junior high or high school student today. School attendance was generally sporadic; for example, at Pinkerton Academy in Massachusetts, of thirty students enrolled for the winter term in 1850 only ten were in attendance for the spring term. Moreover, there was little of the age grading that is typical of modern schools. In 1812 the age range at Exeter Academy was 10–28; the age range of students in public district schools was equally broad (Kett, 1977). Many students wandered casually back and forth between school and work throughout childhood and adolescence.

Such circumstances of work and education did little to encourage the development of a youth culture or a perception of adolescence as a distinct stage of development. As historian Joseph Kett comments, "If adolescence is defined as the period after puberty during which a young person is institutionally segregated from casual contacts with a broad range of adults, then it can scarcely be said to have existed at all, even for those young people who attended school beyond age 14" (1977, p. 36).

## The Impact of Industrialization

In the late nineteenth century, the situation began to change, largely as a result of industrialization and migration to the cities. Although the majority of young people continued to work, the nature of work was changing. The practice of apprenticeship declined, with youth becoming increasingly marginalized; many were left by the wayside as opportunities for close guidance from a mentor decreased (Modell & Goodman, 1990). The relationship between an individual craftsperson, shopkeeper, or mill owner and the young helper or apprentice was qualitatively different from that between a factory owner and the scores of "bobbin" boys and girls working in the factory.

In addition, with the mechanization of many tasks, the division between dead-end jobs and those offering the possibility of advancement became more sharply defined. Young people—both boys and girls—soon learned that the least skilled jobs carried little hope of advancement. Even worse, they often discovered that when they reached the usual "adult" age of 17 or 18 and began asking for adult wages, they were replaced by younger children. In contrast, fewer young people were available to fill the growing number of more complex, higher-level jobs, and those who did qualify were more richly rewarded. The better jobs, however, required greater maturity and more education.

Consequently, increased education and delayed entrance into the work force became more highly valued. But for most families these goals were unattainable. Many needed the earnings of their young to survive, and the generational cycle of poverty and despair, a bitter fruit of the industrial revolution, gained momentum.

For the upper classes and the emerging middle classes, however, the story was different. Greater wealth and a marked decrease in average family size allowed them to make what they perceived as an investment in the future by providing more education for their children. Parental attitudes toward children were altered in the process.

The relation of an individual craftsperson or shopkeeper to a younger helper or apprentice was much more personal and direct than that of a factory owner employing scores of "bobbin boys."

Increasingly, each child was treated (according to sex) without prejudice to his or her place in the birth order. "Give the boys a good education and a start in life," wrote J. E. Panton in 1889,

> and provide the girls with £150 a year, either when they marry or at your own death, and you have done your duty by your children. The girls cannot starve on that income, and neither would they be prey of any fortune hunter; but no one has a right to bring children into the world in the ranks of the upper middle class and do less" (quoted in Gillis, 1974, p. 99).

The result was a rapid increase in the number of schools, academies, and colleges. These institutions quickly became less casual, more tightly organized, and more academically demanding, with a sharp narrowing of the age ranges included at each educational level. In addition, institutions such as the Boy Scouts and settlement houses arose in response to the need to prepare children for the "new corporate and bureaucratic world" (Modell & Goodman, 1990, p. 100). The preconditions were set for the delineation of adolescence as a distinct stage of development: age segregation, a specific set of expectations for—and demands on—youth, and increased isolation from adults and the world of work. As we have noted, this phenomenon was initially restricted to young people from economically advantaged backgrounds, but it established a model that would eventually be democratized and considered normal for young people generally.

## The "Era of Adolescence"

Once broad economic and social conditions had begun to create a visible category of segregated youth, the time was ripe for speculation about the psychological nature of youth, for concerns about how it should be controlled, and for prognoses for its future. Each of these areas of speculation would vary over time as society changed. The important fact, however, is that by 1900 the "era of adolescence" in the modern sense of the term had begun.

Although middle- and upper-class youth were the initial beneficiaries of the new concept of adolescence (which included the idea that adolescents are still developing and require special nurturance), gradually poorer youth began to benefit as well. Incredible as it may seem, in America in 1904 only seventeen states had any age limits on employment in coal mining, and in those that

did, the highest minimum age was 14. Even in those states, however, desperate 12-year-olds lied about their age in order to work 10 to 12 hours a day in the mines for 35 cents a day. The 1900 U.S. Census found over three-quarters of a million children aged 10 to 13 employed in sweatshops, factories, mines, and other work settings. In England around the same time, only 9 percent of young people were still in school at age 14. The child labor laws and later school-leaving ages of subsequent decades were an outgrowth of a new view of the nature of childhood and adolescence, as well as social and religious pressures and a more enlightened view of the value of human life generally.

Widespread popular awareness of youth really came into its own, however, only after World War I, when young people became conscious of themselves as a group. A foreshadowing of the generational conflict of the 1960s could be seen in the solid opposition of young veterans to the older generations who had been spared the fighting. From that point on, popular notions of, and preoccupation with, adolescence occupied an increasingly important place in social thought. As Philippe Ariès commented, "It is as if, to every period of history, there corresponded a privileged age and a particular division of human life: youth is the privileged age of the seventeenth century, childhood of the nineteenth, adolescence of the twentieth" (1962, p. 32).

## The Scientific Study of Adolescence

Although serious literary concern with the phenomenon of adolescence had already developed, North American scientific study of adolescence as a separate and distinct phase of human development really began with the work of G. Stanley Hall, who published his two-volume work *Adolescence* in 1904. Hall was a remarkable person: He obtained America's first Ph.D. in psychology, was the founder of the American Psychological Association, and initiated the child study movement in the United States. Although Hall and his students did much to introduce scientific techniques into the study of adolescence and to delineate it as a separate field of study, Hall's interests were far more global—some would say grandiose.

Enchanted by Darwin's concept of evolution and by the related notion that ontogeny recapitulates phylogeny (i.e., individual development parallels the evolutionary development of the human race), Hall developed a psychological theory of **recapitulation** (Hall, 1904, 1923; Muus, 1988). According to this theory, during its devel-

G. Stanley Hall (front row, center) began the modern scientific study of adolescence. He is shown here with Sigmund Freud (lower left) and other early psychoanalysts during the only visit Freud made to America.

opment the individual organism passes through stages comparable to those that occurred during the history of humankind, "from early animal-like primitivism, through periods of savagery [i.e., later childhood and prepubescence], to the more recent civilized ways of life which characterize maturity" (Muus, 1988, p. 21).

Partly because of his Germanically inspired romanticism (he was influenced by the poetic works of Schiller and Goethe) and partly because of his lofty expectations for adolescents, Hall formulated what was probably his most controversial concept regarding adolescent development, namely, that adolescence is a period of extreme **storm and stress** (Sturm und Drang).

Contrary to popular perceptions, Hall believed that cultural influences played at least as large a role as maturational factors in the oscillations of behavior that, in his view, were characteristic of adolescence: energy alternating with lethargy, exaltation with depressive gloom, childish selfishness with altruistic selflessness, conceit with humility, tenderness with cruelty, curiosity with apathy. As we shall see in some detail in this book, the presumed bases for adolescent storm and stress and the extent of the phenomenon itself have generated considerable controversy.

## Issues in Adolescent Development

However anachronistic some of Hall's notions may seem today, they set the stage for the development of a scientific psychology of adolescence. They also led to a clear-er delineation of the most important theoretical and empirical issues to be addressed by researchers in the field of adolescent development. Among those issues are the following:

1. What is the relative importance of biological and environmental influences on adolescent development (the nature versus nurture issue), and how do they interact?

2. Should adolescent development be viewed as basically continuous with earlier and later development, or is adolescence a separate, distinct stage, indicative of discontinuity in biological, cognitive, and psychosocial development?

3. Is adolescence a relatively placid time characterized by a smooth transition or is it characterized by storm and stress?

In the remainder of this section we will take a closer look at each of these issues.

### Issue #1: Biological Versus Environmental Influences

Biologically oriented views of adolescent behavior emphasize the unfolding of a biologically programmed process called **maturation.** According to some theorists, individual differences in adolescent adjustment are due largely to biologically determined, usually genetic differences in basic temperament (Muus, 1988). Some theorists emphasize the psychological changes required to adjust to the physiological changes of

puberty, including increases in sex hormones and changes in body structure and function (Paikoff & Brooks-Gunn, 1991).

In contrast, other theorists view differences in adolescent adjustment as primarily environmental in origin. They emphasize the many demands society makes on youth during this period—for independence, for peer and heterosexual adjustments, for educational and vocational preparation, and for the development of a workable set of personal and social values. They assert that in cultures in which these demands are less complex and are not limited to a specific age range, adolescence is not viewed as a particularly difficult period (Mead, 1928; Schlegel & Barry, 1991).

**On the Biological Side.** Classic psychoanalytic theory emphasized genetic programming and the enduring effects of early childhood experiences. There was relatively little emphasis on social and cultural influences. Psychoanalytic theory can be viewed as a theoretical system that is primarily historical in orientation. However, later analytic theorists such as Erik Erikson and some psychoanalytically oriented "ego psychologists"—and even Freud himself to some extent in his later years— gave increasing importance to cultural and situational determinants of behavior and noted that personality could be modified in important ways well beyond childhood. Erikson's discussions of the development of **identity** in adolescence pointed out that the adolescent's chances of establishing a stable identity and finding meaning in life depended on the ethical soundness, credibility, and rational consistency of his or her social environment as well as on his or her psychological assets and liabilities (Erikson, 1968). Furthermore, Anna Freud (1968) made an important contribution by emphasizing the opportunities adolescence may sometimes provide for undoing the effects of prior adverse experiences.

Arnold Gesell, a pioneer in the systematic study of infant and child development, favored a biological orientation, although he did not deny the role of culture. "The culture inflects and channelizes," he wrote, "but it does not generate the progressions and trends of development" (Gesell, Ilg, & Ames, 1956, p. 19). For Gesell, development involved maturationally determined, recurring cycles of "innovation, integration, and equilibrium." In other words, each major advance in development disturbs a previously existing equilibrium and requires a period of integration—often characterized by awkwardness and partial regression—until a new equilibrium is established.

Gesell's descriptions of modal or "normal" behaviors at various ages—descriptions that served as a kind

of bible for middle-class parents before the publication of Benjamin Spock's *Pocket Book of Baby and Child Care* (1946)—reflect this rather reassuring view of development. Whether a particular age promises to be a difficult or placid experience for parent and child depends on the child's position in one of these recurring cycles of equilibrium and disequilibrium. In periods of innovation and incomplete integration, greater difficulty can be expected; in periods of equilibrium, on the other hand, both parent and child experience a respite from the maturational struggle.

Thus, in Gesell's view, "Ten [is a year of] consummation as well as of transition—an amiable, relatively relaxed interlude in which the organism assimilates, consolidates, and balances its attained resources" (1956, p. 37). In contrast, "Eleven, like Five-and-a-half to Six, is 'loosening up,' 'snapping old bonds.'" The child is restive, investigative, talkative, argumentative; moods are likely to be intense and to fluctuate rapidly—gay and enthusias-

In Gesell's view, 11-year-olds are "snapping old bonds": They are likely to be restive, investigative, and talkative, with rapidly changing moods.

# 1.2 The Mead–Freeman Controversy
## THE NATURE–NURTURE DEBATE IN ACTION

Cultural anthropologist Margaret Mead published her first and most controversial book, *Coming of Age in Samoa,* in 1928. This book has since sold millions of copies around the world. In it, Mead summarized the findings of her research on adolescent girls on the Island of Ta'u in Samoa, research that was based on her observations of and discussions with these girls while she lived in the center of their community. Although many scholars believed that storm and stress typified the adolescent experience everywhere, Mead argued that adolescent girls in Samoa moved through adolescence with a minimal amount of difficulty, largely because the traditions, practices, and attitudes of their culture facilitated coming of age. Aspects of life on the island of Ta'u that seemed to make this passage easier included the existence of unambiguous and uniform roles for adolescents—roles that gave adolescents a clear path to follow, thereby mitigating against the development of identity crises; and a casualness in Samoan culture that limited the amount of concern with girls' develop-

ing sexuality, as well as the general level of conflict and competition among community members. Mead's arguments challenged the notion of universal storm and stress and provided evidence in favor of the "nurture" side of the nature–nurture debate (Côté, 1992).

In 1983, Derek Freeman published *Margaret Mead and Samoa: The Making and Unmaking of an Anthropological Myth.* By publishing this book, Freeman sought to refute Mead's evidence and conclusions, taking a position that sides with the "nature" side of the nature–nurture debate (Côté, 1992). The charges made against Mead in this book (including questions about the credibility of her informants and the logic of her arguments) created a scientific controversy marked by a flurry of commentaries by scholars taking one side or another. One recent entrant into this debate is James Côté, a sociologist who published *Adolescent Storm and Stress: An Evaluation of the Mead–Freeman Controversy* (1994). In this book, Côté takes a careful and compelling

tic at one moment, gloomy or angry the next. But peace gradually returns, and "Twelve [becomes] more positive in mood, smoother in relationships." And so it goes: "Thirteen pulls inward; Fourteen thrusts out; Fifteen specifies and organizes; Sixteen again achieves a more golden mean" (p. 19).

Gesell made valuable contributions to developmental psychology by insisting on careful and detailed observations of behavior (as opposed to reliance on anecdotal or clinical impressions) and by developing some ingenious techniques for studying infant and child development. Although his observations were often perceptive, his theoretical model is somewhat simplistic, implying that periods of equilibrium and disequilibrium may be uniquely tied to specific ages. Such broad and inclusive generalizations fail to account adequately for deviations from established norms. More importantly, his model does not provide a means for conceptualizing the processes through which biological, psychological, and cultural factors may interact to produce deviant as well as normative behavior.

It seems likely that a more fruitful biological approach to development is represented by current research into the complex interactive effects of hormones and other influences on physical and psychological development, both prenatally and throughout the life span (Buchanan, Eccles, & Becker, 1992; Paikoff & Brooks-Gunn, 1991; Petersen, 1988). We need to know much more, for example, about the possible effects of rapidly changing levels of sex hormones on affective (i.e., emotional) states during puberty, as well as on sexual, aggressive, and other behaviors. For example, there is evidence that levels of pubertal hormones are related in boys (but not girls) to acting-out behavior and to "emotional dispositions" such as sadness and anxiety (Susman et al., 1987). This example illustrates the potentially important influences of biological factors on psychological and behavioral indicators. Among girls, patterns of intense exercise, together with restricted food intake, can alter growth patterns and body shape, demonstrating the influence of behavior on physical development (Brooks-Gunn & Warren, 1985). Pubertal

look at the evidence and arguments of both Mead and Freeman. He claimed that Mead may have mishandled some matters (overgeneralizing from her sample, for example), but the arguments and interpretations of Freeman were flawed in critical respects. In this regard

> With respect to Mead's conclusion that coming of age on the island of Ta'u in 1925–1926 was accomplished with relative ease, there is little in Freeman's critique that constitutes an actual refutation. Not only are Freeman's arguments regarding adolescence easily refuted themselves, there is also sufficient corroboration of Mead's conclusion from other sources (Côté, 1992, pp. 521–522).

On the basis of all the evidence, Côté concludes that Mead's findings on the ease of coming of age in Samoa were essentially correct.

timing, which is biologically driven, also appears to be related to intellectual functioning, with early maturers having a small but consistent advantage on intelligence tests (Newcombe & Dubas, 1987; Petersen, 1988).

**On the Environmental Side.** Some theorists— including cultural anthropologists and social psychologists—emphasize the importance of cultural influences on adolescent behavior (see Box 1.2). Using comparative studies of preliterate cultures, historical accounts of social change, and clinical observations of adolescents in our own society, these theorists have demonstrated that human personality and behavior may vary over an extremely wide range. Often these variations are a function of the social structure of a culture, especially its child-rearing practices.

Many different behavior patterns may be considered normal and adaptive within the context of a particular culture. Sometimes, however, the social structure of a culture may produce neurotic or destructive personali-

ties. For example, culturally oriented psychoanalysts such as Erich Fromm, author of *Escape from Freedom* (1941), and Karen Horney, author of *The Neurotic Personality of Our Time* (1937), emphasized the maladaptive consequences of societal and family structures in which love is lacking; in which a sense of community is absent; in which individuals are emotionally isolated, deprived of roots, and treated impersonally; and in which competition is stressed at the expense of cooperation. Such conditions, they believed, violate humanity's "essential nature" and are likely to lead to neurotic distortions in relations with the self and others (Fromm, 1941, 1955; Horney, 1937, 1950). Long before the youth revolution of the 1960s, Horney and Fromm called attention to the internal contradictions inherent in much of contemporary society: the contradiction between rewards for "competition and success on the one hand and brotherly love and humility on the other"; the conflict between the stimulation of desires through marketing and the frustration often encountered in trying to satisfy those desires; the contradiction between the concepts

## 1.3 Examining Environmentally and Biologically Based Influences

The work of Glen Elder, a family sociologist, has provided evidence for the delicate interplay between environmental and biological influences on the development of children and adolescents. To document these influences, Elder and colleagues (Elder, 1974; Elder, Caspi, & Van Nguyen, 1986; Elder, Van Nguyen, & Caspi, 1985) used longitudinal, archival data from two studies of families who lived through the Great Depression of the early 1930s: The Oakland Growth Study observed young adolescents and their parents as they moved through the Depression; the Berkeley Guidance Study followed preschool children and their parents during the Depression years.

In general, this research shows that the financial losses experienced by many families during the Depression created a great deal of family stress. Hard times were particularly difficult for fathers, who were frustrated by their inability to fulfill their role as economic provider. (At that time, there was a clear delineation between the socially sanctioned roles of fathers and mothers.) Marital relations and father–child relations suffered as fathers became more explosive, irritable, and punitive. This behavior on the part of fathers was linked to social and psychological adjustment problems among children and adolescents. This research, then, demonstrated how a macroeconomic event (an environmental influence) affected the lives and behavior of children.

The research did not stop there, however. Elder and colleagues carefully documented the fact that not all fathers with financial difficulties become more explosive. Rather, fathers who were explosive *before* the Depression became more explosive, whereas others did not. Thus, it can be argued that personality characteristics such as explosiveness, which are in part biologically based, interacted with environmental forces to shape the behavior of fathers.

The picture that emerges from comparing how children (in the Berkeley study) and adolescents (in the Oakland study) experienced the Depression is even more complicated. Young boys from economically deprived families in the Berkeley sample generally showed poorer psychosocial adjustment as adolescents, scoring low on measures such as self-adequacy and social competence. Income loss seemed to have an enduring impact on boys who lived their earliest years during the Depression—an impact that can be traced in part to the parenting behavior of fathers.

of individual freedom and equal opportunity, on one hand, and the fact that for the majority of people opportunities are quite limited.

A theoretical system that has given rise to a thoughtful and sophisticated exploration of situational determinants of behavior is the **field theory** of Kurt Lewin (1935, 1951). Lewin, one of the most innovative psychologists of this century, came to the United States from Germany, where he had studied at the University of Berlin (Morrow, 1969; Muus, 1988). Undoubtedly he was influenced by the Gestalt school of psychology, with its assertion, derived largely from studies of perception, that the dynamic unity of the whole is greater than the sum of its parts. He probably was also affected by his observation of the rise of Hitlerism in Europe, which revealed how easily, often tragically, human behavior can be swayed by the social climate of the times.

As a core concept of his theory, Lewin proposed the following formula: Behavior ($B$) is a function ($f$) of the person ($P$) and his or her environment ($E$), or $B = f(PE)$. In this formula $P$ and $E$ are viewed as interdependent variables—"An unstable psychological environment during adolescence brings about instability in an individual" (Lewin, 1951, p. 8). Therefore, to understand the behavior of a child or adolescent one must consider both the individual and his or her environment as a constellation of dynamically interacting, interdependent factors. Lewin's concepts, along with his breadth of vision, curiosity, charm, and infectious enthusiasm, had a significant impact on the development of social psychology. They moved social-psychological research toward "real-life experiments" in the field—from studies of racial prejudice to the effects of authoritarian, democratic, and laissez-faire leadership on individual and group behavior in boys' clubs (Lewin, 1951; Muus, 1988).

Less well known, however, is the extent to which

environmental and biological forces can interact.

Among adolescents from deprived families (the Oakland sample), girls were generally at a greater disadvantage psychologically and socially than boys, as evidenced by their moodiness, lower social competence, and feelings of inadequacy. This was largely a result of the rejecting behaviors of fathers in deprived families. Girls may have been more vulnerable to mistreatment by their fathers because of their smaller size or greater presence in the home. Among these girls, however, vulnerability was related to physical attractiveness. Girls who were judged by independent observers to be more unattractive physically were more likely to be rejected and exploited by their fathers; attractive girls, on the other hand, were more likely to experience benign treatment.

Adolescent girls from economically deprived families were also at a social disadvantage compared to nondeprived girls because of a lack of material resources, such as adequate clothing, that were needed for participation in social activities.

Overall, Elder's program of research provides convincing evidence of the complex ways in which the unique blend of circumstances to which individuals are exposed and their personal strengths and weaknesses interact to influence their development.

Arbitrary and punitive fathering, however, was not universal; boys who showed early behavioral problems (such as temper tantrums and negativism) were more likely to receive punitive treatment. To the extent that such early behavior problems might have a biological component, we see again how

Lewin proposed a relatively integrated and specific theory of adolescent development. In Lewin's view, many American adolescents know that it is important for them to get somewhere in a hurry, but they know only roughly where they need to go and have an even poorer idea of how to proceed. Moreover, they have no real status in our society during this period. The adolescent has renounced childhood but has not yet been fully accepted as an adult. Partly accepted and partly rejected by the privileged group (i.e., adults), the adolescent is in a position somewhat similar to that of what sociologists call the marginal man. Lewin noted that behavior that is characteristic of the marginal man can often be found in the adolescent as well, who "is oversensitive, easily shifted from one extreme to the other, and particularly sensitive to the shortcomings of [younger peers]" (1939, pp. 882–883).

Lewin's emphasis on the importance of under-

standing the dynamic interaction between the growing person and his or her environment laid the theoretical groundwork for what is now known as **ecological psychology.** This term was first used by Roger Barker and H. F. Wright (1955) to describe the study of how children's surroundings affect their behavior and development. Barker and his colleagues have shown, for example, how behavior is influenced by the social setting, such as a school, in which it occurs (Barker & Wright, 1955). More broadly, the work of ecological psychologists "focuses on the progressive accommodation, throughout the life span, between the growing human organism and the changing environments in which it actually lives and grows" (Bronfenbrenner, 1977, p. 513). Those environments include not only smaller settings such as the home, family, or peer group but also larger social and economic systems. Urie Bronfenbrenner, in particular, has been interested in the effects of urban liv-

ing, poverty, current welfare policies, and employment practices on family life and parent–child relationships (Bronfenbrenner, 1979). He and other ecological psychologists are also interested in the question of whether society can find better alternatives to current policies in these areas (Garbarino, 1985).

Environmental perspectives on development point to the possibility that the individual's history—his or her experiential past—is an important determinant of behavior, sometimes more important than the particular situation in which he or she is functioning at any given time. Such a historical approach might be used to understand how an individual who suffered a great deal of abuse as a young child might evidence violent episodes as an adolescent or adult.

**A Synthesis of Biology and Environment.** As we shall see in later chapters, many aspects of development—from the individual's academic achievement to behavior with peers—can be traced to both biology and environmental influences. The focus now is not on whether biology or environment is more important; this was yesterday's question. The burning question today is "How do organisms and environments combine to produce human development?" (Scarr, 1992). The emphasis is now on the relative influence of nature and nurture. This question will have many answers depending on the characteristics under consideration, the individual involved, and his or her biological and cultural heritage.

## Issue #2: Continuity Versus Discontinuity

Still another important theoretical and empirical question is whether adolescence should be viewed as a distinct *stage* in development. Discontinuity implies the existence of stages of growth or the emergence of new qualities. For example, evidence that adolescents engage in abstract thinking, quite unlike the concrete thinking of children, suggests discontinuity in cognitive development—a different form of thinking has emerged. To the extent that development is viewed as steady, continuous, and gradual, a concept of adolescence as a stage of development appears misleading. For example, if the major cognitive change that occurs is that adolescents think more efficiently and quickly than children, then this change is more quantitative (continuous) than qualitative (discontinuous). As we will see in Chapter 4, there is evidence of continuity and discontinuity in cognitive development.

**Theories That Favor Continuity.** A view of adolescence as continuous, rather than discontinuous, was expressed by Leta Hollingworth (1928), a progressive educator, who took sharp exception to Hall's concept of adolescence as a period of dramatic storm and stress: "A child grows by imperceptible degrees into an adolescent, and the adolescent turns by gradual degrees into the adult. . . . The widespread myth that every child is a changeling, who at puberty comes forth as a different personality, is doubtless a survival in folklore of the ceremonial rebirth, which constituted the formal initiation of our savage ancestors into manhood and womanhood" (pp. 16–17).

Among contemporary psychologists, social-learning theorists such as Albert Bandura also tend to view development as a continuous process without abrupt changes at any one age level (Bandura, 1977b; Muus, 1988). In Bandura's view, much of the "storm and stress, tension, rebellion, dependency conflicts, [and] peer-group conformity" commonly associated with the adolescent transition are not widespread (Bandura, 1964, p. 224). When they do occur, they are more likely to result from external social experiences than from age-related maturational forces (Bandura, 1967). **Information-processing** theory, which focuses on the mental processes underlying cognitive development, favors continuity. Although there may be advances in the adolescent's ability to process, store, and retrieve information, these changes in mental functioning represent improvements in the basic apparatus that exists. Information-processing theorists have not suggested that new qualities or new types of thought emerge in adolescence (Kail & Bisanz, 1992).

To the degree that such views emphasize that there are important continuities in development that might otherwise be ignored, they may perform a useful function. For example, **longitudinal** research (in which the same individuals are assessed repeatedly over time, often over many years of their lives) has shown that there are some basic personality characteristics (such as passive withdrawal from stressful situations, dependency, and involvement in intellectual mastery) that show a remarkable degree of stability and consistency from the early school years through adolescence (Kagan, Reznick, & Snidman, 1988a, 1988b; Plomin, 1986).

**Theories That Favor Discontinuity.** Although most theorists do not deny the existence of significant continuities in development, many have been impressed with what they perceive as crucial changes during puberty and the years immediately thereafter. Proponents of stage theories posit qualitative changes in terms

of personality organization and defense mechanisms, the emergence of new needs and new developmental tasks, and the development of more advanced forms of thinking and reasoning. Within such theories, the concept of adolescence as a distinct **developmental stage** is considered useful because it focuses attention on the importance of these perceived changes. However, the nature of adolescence as a stage of development varies from one theorist to another, depending on what each considers to be the essential aspects of this developmental period.

Under the psychoanalytic theory of Sigmund Freud, adolescence was a stage of development characterized by a breakthrough of sexual impulses, which occurred largely as a result of the physiological changes accompanying puberty (Freud, 1953). This phase of development (which was preceded by the oral, anal, and phallic stages) was referred to as the genital stage. Among other things, it involved a revival of earlier oedipal attachments and rivalries within the family, along with the need to resolve them in the direction of greater independence from parents and a shifting of the adolescent's attachments to new love objects.

Erik Erikson, while acknowledging his debt to Freud's biologically oriented ("historical") views, stressed the unique psychological tasks of the adolescent. Strongly influenced by the findings of cultural anthropology and by his own background as an artist, writer, and educator of young people as well as a psychoanalyst, Erikson believed that the quintessential task of adolescence is to establish a sense of self as a unique person (to develop one's identity).

For Peter Blos—a psychologist and a psychoanalyst—the onset of puberty, accompanied by increased sexual drive, disturbs the relative equilibrium of middle childhood. The resulting "instinctual tensions" lead to **regression**—a reactivation of infantile needs and behavior, such as messiness, bathroom humor, restless activity, impulsiveness, and sudden episodes of childish dependency. This occurs most conspicuously in boys, but it can also be observed in girls.

According to Blos, this regression, far from being negative in its effects, is not only positive but necessary: "Adolescent development progresses via the detour of regression" (1979a, p. 58). By revisiting earlier experiences and conflicts (such as a distorted perception of the parents) with a more mature ego and greater cognitive ability, the adolescent reworks and resolves long-standing, inappropriate ways of responding that may be impeding his or her further development. This opens the way to what Blos calls a "second individuation," an effort to define who and what one is and is not, often through

such "adolescent" means as opposition to parental dictates, trying out different roles, or developing sudden and transitory loves and hates. The process of individuation—which may be accompanied by feelings of isolation, loneliness, and confusion—is consistent with Erikson's concept of the development of a stable sense of identity (Blos, 1971a, 1971b, 1979b; Conger, 1981).

Piagetian theory, the theory of cognitive development put forth by distinguished Swiss psychologist Jean Piaget, also favors a discontinuous view of development (see Chapter 4). In Piaget's view, adolescence is characterized by development of the capacity to think abstractly and to generate alternative hypotheses and test them against evidence; this is the stage of "formal operations," which replace the "concrete operations" of middle childhood.

Lawrence Kohlberg's theory of moral development was strongly influenced by Piaget's work. Kohlberg conducted extensive studies of moral development in childhood and adolescence. In his view, adolescence involves reaching what he called **postconventional** stages of moral development, which are characterized by "a major thrust toward autonomous moral principles which have validity and application apart from authority of the groups or persons who hold them and apart from the individual's identification with those persons or groups" (Kohlberg & Gilligan, 1971, pp. 1066–1067) (see Chapter 10).

All such descriptions of adolescence as a stage of development have a certain arbitrary quality. Although some theorists tend to view their formulations as having a kind of independent existence, in reality each represents only the theorist's judgment (often astute) of what is *most* important about a particular developmental period. It is also important to recognize that some characteristics that may appear to be an inevitable accompaniment of an adolescent stage of development may in fact reflect to an important degree the effects of social change. The proverbial alien from Mars, if asked to bring back a report of what earthly adolescents were like, would probably have brought back rather different reports in 1950, 1968 (at the height of the youth revolution), and 1995.

In a recent book that examined continuity and discontinuity in several domains across adolescence, the authors concluded that adolescence is marked by both continuity and discontinuity. Adolescents *may be* different from children physiologically, socially (e.g., friendships deepen and become more important), behaviorally (e.g., aggression among males increases), and cognitively (e.g., they think more abstractly)—all evidence of discontinuity. Because many of these characteristics begin to be evident in childhood and emerge gradually, how-

ever, some continuity in development is suggested (Montemayor & Flannery, 1990). In other words, the individual who emerges in adolescence may be different in some respects, but we do not see an entirely new person.

## Issue #3: Smooth Transition Versus Storm and Stress

Most behavioral scientists agree that in our society adolescence generally represents a more difficult developmental period than middle childhood. In contrast to more stable periods in the life cycle, such as middle childhood and adulthood, adolescence is characterized by accelerated physical, physiological, and cognitive development as well as by new and changing social demands. As a consequence, some adolescents, in their efforts to deal with change, may display alterations of mood, distressing and unpredictable thoughts, manifestations of anxiety and exaggerated defenses against anxiety, and impulsive, inappropriate, or inconsistent behaviors. How much of this turmoil (or **storm and stress**) does the average young person actually experience? Is the transition through adolescence rough, with the adolescent showing signs of inner disturbances, behavior problems, and large variations in mood? Or is it a relatively smooth transition, consisting of nothing more than the normal ups-and-downs encountered throughout life?

**Roots of the Storm and Stress Hypothesis.** The issue of whether most adolescents experience a high degree of turmoil has been prominent since G. Stanley Hall first posited his view of adolescent storm and stress. More recent formulations of adolescence as a disturbed, maladjusted (but temporary) state stem primarily from psychoanalytic conceptualizations of adolescence. Anna Freud, for example, in discussing the normality (and desirability) of "adolescent upheaval," remarks:

> We all know individual children who as late as the ages of 14, 15, or 16 show no such outer evidence of inner unrest. They remain as they have been during the latency [i.e., middle childhood] period, "good" children, wrapped up in their family relationships, considerate sons of their mothers, submissive to their fathers, in accord with the atmosphere, ideas, and ideals of their childhood background. Convenient as this may be, it signifies a delay of normal development and, as such, is a sign to be taken serious-

ly. The first impression conveyed by these cases may be that of a quantitative deficiency of drive endowment, a suspicion which will usually prove unfounded. . . . These are children who have built up excessive defenses against their drive activities and are now crippled by the results, which act as barriers against a normal maturational process of phase development. They are perhaps, more than any others, in need of therapeutic help to remove the inner restrictions and clear the path for normal development, however "upsetting" the latter may prove to be (1968, p. 14).

Similarly, Irene Josselyn (1968), a prominent psychoanalyst experienced in the treatment of adolescents, stated that although adolescents have a greater "ego capacity" than they had at an earlier age, this new-found resource is likely to be exhausted by the difficulty of integrating stronger sexual, aggressive, and other impulses, the demands of conscience, and the demands of reality: "Adolescence, as is equally true of the neuroses and psychoses, is characterized by the relative failure of the ego" (1954, p. 225). Despite the apparent severity of this description, Josselyn differentiates this state of relative "ego failure" from psychopathology: "The normal adolescent is inevitably a mixed-up person, but not at all in the sense of being a psychologically sick person." Most adolescents, she maintains, actually have "sufficient inherent personality strengths to emerge from their confusion as relatively healthy adults" (1959, p. 43).

Anna Freud and Irene Josselyn developed their theories of normal adolescent development on the basis of clinical populations with which they worked. Thus, it is not surprising that they viewed upheaval as normal. Equating adolescent disturbance with normal adolescent development has some interesting implications. Some analytic theorists have asserted that adolescent disturbance is sufficiently normal that its *absence* may be a greater source of concern than its presence (Weiner, 1970).

Whether it is useful to label normative adolescent upheavals as a disturbed state is debatable. To the extent that transient variations in mood, thought, and action do occur in the "normal" course of adolescence, and to the extent that they resemble more serious psychiatric symptoms in adults, it may be valuable to identify those similarities and then to note explicitly the differences in their significance for adolescents and adults.

On the other hand, there is the inherent danger that, in identifying upheavals as normal adolescent phenomena, we may be tempted to view serious disorders as normal when in fact they may require prompt atten-

Anna Freud at age 16 and at age 85 with her puppy.

tion. Less skilled clinicians than Anna Freud or Irene Josselyn may be tempted to ignore or dismiss signs of psychopathology on the assumption that they represent normal adolescent turmoil and will pass. The findings of a number of investigators who followed up samples of adolescents who had been initially diagnosed as suffering from "transient situational personality disorder" or "situational adjustment reaction of adolescence" (adjustment problems that were assumed to be temporary) attest to this potential danger. In a significant number of cases (approximately 50 percent in one study), these young people either ended up in psychiatric treatment or showed continued, and in some instances more serious, problems several years later (Graham & Rutter, 1985; Parry-Jones, 1985).

**Do Most Adolescents Experience Storm and Stress?** Studies suggest that the extent of adolescent turmoil is exaggerated. A large body of data (Ebata, Petersen, & Conger, 1990; Petersen, 1988) is accumulating to suggest that "the modal [typical] teenager is a reasonably well-adjusted individual whose daily functioning is minimally marred by psychological incapacity" (Weiner, 1970, p. 48). This is not to say that some normal adolescents may not undergo considerable turmoil during this period; indeed, this is clearly the case. What is questioned is the presumed universality of adolescent turmoil.

A longitudinal investigation of middle-class midwestern adolescent boys revealed little evidence of a high degree of turmoil or chaos in the life of the average boy (Offer & Offer, 1974, 1975). In this study, only about one subject in five displayed tumultuous growth—the kind of adolescent turmoil (anxiety, depression, distrust, extreme mood swings, and lack of self-confidence) that some consider typical. Many of these subjects were sensitive and introspective people who took great interest in exploring their inner world. About one-third of them had received some form of therapy or counseling. For the parents of this group, separation from their sons (when they went away to school or college) tended to be painful, and many of those parents appeared unsure of their own values and, hence, unable to present well-defined values to their children.

Most of the remaining subjects fell into one of two groups: a continuous-growth group and a surgent-growth group. Members of the continuous-growth group (about 25 percent) had strong egos, "were able to cope well with internal and external stimuli, and had mastered previous developmental stages without serious setbacks. They had accepted general cultural and soci-

## 1.4 Studying the Daily Emotional States of Children and Adolescents

Reed Larson and Claudia Lampman-Petraitis (1989) studied the daily emotional states of a large number of midwestern children and adolescents ages 9–15. They used electronic pagers or "beepers" to signal the participants to report on their subjective emotional experiences at random times during the day and evening. At the sound of the beeper, the participant was asked to stop and rate his or her present emotional state or mood on six scales (including happy–unhappy, cheerful–irritable, and excited–bored). Possible responses ranged from −3 (most negative) to +3 (most positive). The frequency of self-reported states by grade is presented in Figure B1.1.

The investigators found few age differences in the variability of moods throughout the day (although the moods of adolescent girls were somewhat more variable than those of younger girls). However, significant age trends in average daily emotional states were found. The average state, or emotional baseline, was lower among older subjects than among younger ones. For example, among both boys and girls, fifth graders used the most positive score (+3) to describe their emotional states twice as often as ninth graders. In a similarly designed earlier study comparing high school students and adults, average mood levels were similar for the two groups, but adolescents reported more occasions of both positive and negative extremes (Larson, Csikszentmihalyi, & Graef, 1980).

What accounts for the fact that adolescents had more negative moods than younger children and a higher frequency of extreme emotions—both positive and negative—than adults? Possibilities include increasingly stressful events during adolescence (Brooks-Gunn & Warren, 1989), hormonal changes (Petersen, 1988), and a higher degree of conflicts over independence and dependence (Larson & Lampman-Petraitis, 1989). Further research is needed to determine the relative importance of these and other factors.

etal norms, and felt comfortable within their context" (Offer & Offer, 1974, p. 212). Although they had reasonably active fantasy lives, subjects in this group tended to be oriented toward reality and action. "The balance between the intensity of the drives and the ego capacity to tolerate new impulses was good. They had a realistic self-image, a sense of humor, and were relatively happy human beings" (Offer & Offer, 1974, p. 212). Parents of these subjects were generally able to tolerate their children's growth and gradual assumption of independence, and there was mutual respect, trust, and affection between the generations. Adolescents in this group moved through adolescence relatively smoothly.

Members of the surgent-growth group (about 35 percent), although reasonably well adjusted and capable of meeting the developmental demands of adolescence, tended to have somewhat greater difficulty dealing with unexpected stresses. They tended to use projection, anger, and regression at such times. Among parents of this group, there were more likely to be value conflicts between mother and father and maternal difficulty in separating from children. Although their transition through adolescence was not entirely smooth, adolescents in this group did not display the turmoil consistent with the storm and stress hypothesis.

A similar study of adolescent girls and boys has found that about 11 percent of young adolescents have serious chronic difficulties; 32 percent have more intermittent, probably largely situational difficulties; and 57 percent show basically positive, healthy development during adolescence (Petersen, 1988; Petersen & Ebata, 1987). These figures suggest, again, that adolescent turmoil is not a normative experience. An earlier study of 3000 adolescents also suggested an absence of turmoil in most adolescents. Indeed, the researchers expressed some dismay at the relative absence of turmoil in many adolescents, attributing much of it to "premature identity consolidation, ego and ideological construction, and a general unwillingness to take psychic risks" (Douvan & Adelson, 1966).

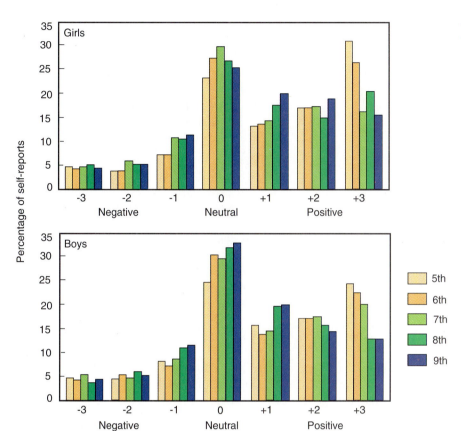

Figure **B1.1**
Frequency of self-reported states by grade: (top) girls; (bottom) boys. From R. Larson & C. Lampman-Petraitis (1989). Daily emotional states as reported by children and adolescents. *Child Development*, **60,** 1250–1260. By permission.

It appears from these and other studies that the stresses adolescence imposes on the individual do not, in the majority of cases, lead to the high degree of emotional turmoil, violent mood swings, and threatened loss of control suggested by some theorists. Although many adolescents face occasional periods of uncertainty and self-doubt, loneliness and sadness, and anxiety and concern for the future, they are also likely to experience joy, excitement, curiosity, a sense of adventure, and a feeling of competence as they master new challenges.

## Plan of the Text

As will be apparent throughout this book, many of the issues discussed in this chapter are still subjects of active research and debate. In many instances, however, the recent expansion of research on adolescence has succeeded in reducing the areas of uncertainty and in better defining some of the questions that remain to be

Although many adolescents have periods of uncertainty and self-doubt, they also experience joy, excitement, and a sense of adventure.

answered. One goal of this text is to point to relevant research that sheds light on these issues as they apply to dimensions of adolescent development, such as pubertal maturation, the changing nature of parent–adolescent relations, sexuality, and friendship. A second goal of this text is to discuss and examine theories as they apply to these dimensions. Armed with such a theoretical and empirical grounding in adolescent development, students will be in a better position to think about, approach, and work with adolescents.

# Summary

Some observers believe that today's young people are more rootless, more emotionally troubled, and more self-centered and materialistic than their counterparts of earlier generations; as evidence, they cite high rates of drug use, violent crime, and adolescent pregnancy. Others maintain that today's youth are better informed, more pragmatic, and more open and honest. Still others believe that presumed differences between present and past generations of adolescents are largely illusory. One aim of this book is to arrive at a balanced view of adolescents today.

Concern with adolescence and youth is not new; it dates back at least as far as Plato and Aristotle, whose views about adolescents seem remarkably contemporary. A preoccupation with the "ages of life," including adolescence, was evident in the pseudoscientific treatises of the Middle Ages. Seventeenth-century writings focused on helping "undependable" youth to master their "unruly" impulses. But not until the end of the nineteenth century do we encounter the precursors of the modern concern with adolescence as a socially significant and psychologically complex period. By the turn of the century, urban migration and industrialization had led to the creation of large numbers of more complex, better-paying jobs requiring greater maturity and more education. Although these goals were beyond the reach of most families, those in the upper and middle classes came to regard education—and the time it requires—as an investment in the future.

Once economic and social conditions had begun to create a visible group of segregated youth, the time was ripe for speculation about the psychological nature of adolescents. By 1900 the "era of adolescence" had begun, although in the absence of child labor laws a majority of adolescents were still working full-time, often under deplorable conditions. Only after World War I did concern with adolescence as a privileged age become widespread.

The scientific study of adolescence began with the work of G. Stanley Hall, who viewed adolescence as a period of storm and stress. However anachronistic some of his views may seem today, Hall set the stage for the development of a scientific psychology of adolescence and a clearer definition of many of the most important theoretical and empirical issues to be addressed by researchers in the field. One issue is the relative importance of biological and environmental influences on adolescent development. The biological emphasis is exemplified by the work of Arnold Gesell, who described modal behavior for each age period; in contrast, cultural anthropologists, social psychologists, and others (including Erich Fromm, Karen Horney, and Margaret Mead) emphasized the consequences of environment, including the culture and the family, for individual behavior.

A second important issue is whether adolescent development is continuous or discontinuous with earlier development. Theories that emphasize a continuous view (such as social-learning and information-processing theories) imply that individual development is steady, continuous, and gradual whereas stage theories (such as Piagetian and Kohlbergian theory) emphasize the emergence of new qualities or characteristics in the individual.

Finally, a third issue is whether adolescence should be viewed as a relatively smooth transition or one that is marked by a high degree of turmoil, as Hall and other theorists asserted. Although many adolescents experience ups and downs, the bulk of the evidence suggests that most adolescents do not experience a great deal of turmoil; storm and stress is not normative.

As will become apparent, many of the issues raised in this chapter are still with us, although recent research on adolescence has greatly increased our knowledge and succeeded in reducing the areas of uncertainty.

# Review Questions

1. What are the arguments in favor of and against the view that today's adolescents are more troubled than ever before?

2. What did Aristotle think about adolescence?

3. What was the view of adolescence in early modern history? How was that view related to the social and economic circumstances of the time?

4. What role did industrialization play in the delineation of adolescence as a distinct stage of development?

5. Discuss G. Stanley Hall's theory of recapitulation and his concept of storm and stress.

6. Name three basic issues in the study of adolescent development, and discuss each briefly.

7. Where do Sigmund Freud, Kurt Lewin, and Margaret Mead fit in to the nature versus nurture controversy?

8. Name several stage theorists. How do they differ in their views regarding the key characteristics of adolescence as a stage of development? Who are some proponents of continuity in development? What does the evidence say about continuity versus discontinuity?

9. What do recent research findings tell us about the extent of adolescent turmoil? Has the idea of adolescent turmoil been exaggerated in the research literature on adolescence and in the popular press?

# Recommended Readings

Conger, J. J. (1981). Freedom and commitment: Families, youth and social change. *American Psychologist, 36,* 1475–1484.

Côté, J. E. (1992). Was Mead wrong about coming of age in Samoa? An analysis of the Mead/Freeman controversy for scholars of adolescence and human development. *Journal of Youth and Adolescence, 21,* 499–527.

Modell, J., & Goodman, M. (1990). Historical perspectives. In S. S. Feldman & G. R. Elliot (Eds.), *At the threshold: The developing adolescent* (pp. 93–122). Cambridge, MA: Harvard University Press.

Montemayor, R. R., Adams, G. R., & Gullotta, T. P. (Eds.). (1990). *From childhood to adolescence: A transitional period?* Newbury Park, CA: Sage.

Muus, R. E. (1988). *Theories of adolescence* (5th ed.). New York: Random House.

# Viewing Development: Principles of Change

## 2

a

dolescence can be many things: a time of irrepressible joy and inconsolable sadness, gregariousness and loneliness, altruism and self-centeredness, insatiable curiosity and boredom, confidence and self-doubt. It can be an exciting and hopeful time, filled with promise and opportunity, a time when, in the words of the English poet Matthew Arnold, the world stands before us "so beautiful, so various, so new." But it can also be a time of apathy, anger, or despair—especially for those who have felt the pain of parental neglect and abuse, rejection by peers, or societal discrimination.

More than anything else, however, adolescence is a period of rapid change—physical, sexual, emotional, and cognitive changes within the young person and changes in the adolescent's world and in the demands placed on him or her by society. Indeed, at no time between the age of 2 and the onset of puberty does a person undergo as many, and as rapid, changes as occur during adolescence. It should hardly seem surprising, then, that many adolescents, faced with a changing physical image and conscious of new, sometimes strange feelings and thoughts, may ask themselves what that person in the mirror is all about (Conger, 1979).

As we shall see in subsequent chapters, the maturational changes of puberty—the growth spurt in height and weight, changing physical proportions, hormonal changes, the development of primary and secondary sexual characteristics, and accelerated cognitive development—provide adolescence with its uniqueness as a transitional period during which new challenges are faced, identity is explored, and the route to adulthood is negotiated.

## The Life-Span Developmental Perspective

In Chapter 1 we explored three issues that are critical to the study of adolescent **development:** the relative influence of biology and environment on behavior, the extent to which continuity or discontinuity characterizes ado-

Studies of genetic influences on personality characteristics often compare identical twins with nonidentical twins and nontwin siblings.

lescent development, and whether the transitional period of adolescence is relatively smooth or stormy and stressful. How we approach the scientific investigation of these questions depends in part on the assumptions we make about how human development proceeds—about what are the essential principles of development.

A set of coherent principles or assumptions constitutes a theoretical perspective. The significance of following a given theoretical perspective on adolescent development can be likened to the significance of a road map on a long automobile trip. You may know what your final destination is, but you need a map to guide you there, illuminating the most practical and efficient route while eliminating choices that will take you in the wrong directions. So it is with the **life-span developmental perspective,** a perspective on human development that we believe will help guide us to our final destination: an understanding of the complexities of adolescent development.

Emerging in the 1970s, the life-span perspective (which may be most properly defined as a *family* of per-

spectives sharing some common principles about development) gained prominence as psychologists sought to merge and synthesize other perspectives, each of which seemed to capture only a part of the complicated moving picture that is development (Baltes, 1987; Baltes, Reese, & Lipsitt, 1980; Lerner, Hultsch, & Dixon, 1983). Since that time, there has been continuing discussion of the crucial assumptions of the life-span approach. What are some of these assumptions and how do they inform our understanding of adolescence?

## Development Is a Lifelong Process

Explicit in the life-span approach to development is the concept of development as a lifelong process: Individuals continue to develop from the time they are conceived until their death (Baltes, Reese, & Lipsitt, 1980). Moreover, the effects of events occurring at any one stage of development depend on and proceed from earlier developmental events and will, in turn, influence the individual's

Development may be viewed much like a growing tree: Even into old age, the tree shows new growth.

responses to future events. These relationships may be called **antecedent–consequent relationships** (Conger, 1991a). If one considers the notions of development as a lifelong process and of antecedent–consequent relationships, development may be viewed much like a growing tree: Even into old age, the tree shows new growth. The possibilities of present and future growth, however, are still dependent on and limited by the nature of the tree, by patterns of prior growth, and by present environmental conditions.

Consider the popular view that the early childhood years are all-important in determining future adjustment—that, as one worried mother remarked, "the game is over by the age of 6." The assumption of lifelong development clearly contradicts this notion. Research shows that the adolescent years present important opportunities for continued growth and development and for repairing the damaging effects of adverse prior experiences (Blos, 1979a; Hartup, 1983). For example, a supportive, understanding, nonexploitive friend may play a significant, sometimes crucial, role in helping a boy or girl gain a clearer concept of self, a feeling of personal worth, and renewed hope for the future. Similarly, adolescents who were sexually abused as children can often be helped a great deal by appropriate treatment, although they may carry the psychological scars of their experiences throughout their lives.

The readiness of adolescents to cope with the increased demands of their adolescent years depends to a large extent on the whole array of intellectual, physical, and social competencies they bring to their lives and the feelings of security, confidence, and self-esteem they have acquired since infancy. In turn, the amount of success they have in mastering the tasks of the adolescent period and developing a stable, clearly defined sense of their own identity affects their chances of leading a rewarding, fulfilling adult life, whether as worker, lover, spouse, parent, or citizen.

In this connection it is important to stress that, although the chances of achieving these goals are strongly influenced by the young person's inherent resources and by the facilitating or inhibiting effects of prior experience, these factors need not constitute insurmountable barriers.

## Individuals and Environments Interact

A fundamental assumption of the life-span perspective is that the kind of person an individual becomes is the result of the continuing and continuous interaction between a growing, changing biological organism and its physical, psychological, and social environment. This concept of **reciprocal interactions** between individual and environment rests on the assumption that individuals and environments are constantly changing, with changes in one leading to and sometimes causing changes in the other (Lerner & Busch-Rossnagel, 1981).

Even in the earliest stages of prenatal development, when the future poet, executive, or scientist is represented by only a few, seemingly simple and identical cells, the individual's genetic inheritance is already interacting with a physical environment that can have a variety of nurturant or harmful effects. For instance, future development may be affected by the adequacy or inadequacy of the mother's nutritional status, by the effects of any drugs she may take, by certain diseases she may contract (such as rubella, or German measles), and even by her emotions, which can liberate soothing or irritating chemicals into her bloodstream (Guttmacher & Kaiser, 1986; Illingworth, 1987; Plomin, 1986). The problems associated

A supportive, understanding friend can often play a significant role in helping a boy or girl to repair the damaging effects of earlier adverse experiences.

## 2.1 Childhood Risk Factors and Adolescent Outcomes

The assumptions of development as a lifelong process and of antecedent–consequent relations are illustrated in a longitudinal study of 367 subjects conducted by Nadine Lambert (1988). Two research questions guided this study. First, how well could the educational and mental health outcomes, conduct problems, and substance use patterns of adolescents at ages 17–18 be predicted from their biological, cognitive, and social characteristics in early and middle childhood? Second, to what extent could these outcomes in adolescence be predicted by prior aspects of the home environment (such as family stability and parenting behaviors)? One focus, then, was on factors in childhood that could place the child at risk for later problems in development. Another focus was on the timing of these factors. Was the locus of risk for a particular adolescent problem to be found in early

childhood (the infancy and preschool years) or in middle childhood (the elementary school years)?

This study found that with respect to predicting mental health outcomes (such as depression), risk factors present during early childhood were more important than those present in middle childhood. On the other hand, Lambert found that risk factors present in the elementary school years were more predictive of poorer educational outcomes (such as dropping out of high school) than risk factors in early childhood. Adolescent substance use and conduct problems (such as running away and delinquency) were predicted by risk factors in early *and* middle childhood. This study demonstrates how a life-span perspective can help to pinpoint particular features of the environment and of the child that may create later developmental problems.

with infants exposed to cocaine before birth provide a good but regrettable example of reciprocal interactions between the environment and individual. Cocaine-exposed infants tend to evidence high-pitched and excessive crying (the prenatal environment provided by the mother influenced the infant's behavior). The extent to which the caregiving environment (the parent) can respond appropriately to this potentially hard-to-handle behavior has implications for the infant's later behavior and development (Lester et al., 1991).

As growth and development proceed, the biological organism becomes increasingly complex as a function of both maturation and prior interactions between organism and environment. The environment also becomes more complex, first within the womb and later in the ever-expanding world outside it. Initial encounters with the mother and father and a relatively simple world of sight, sound, and touch are soon augmented by interactions with family, peers, and community. Eventually, of course, the individual exists within, and interacts with, a far wider world. These days, he or she may be affected immediately, through satellites and television, by events occurring on distant continents. In later chapters we will examine in some detail the importance of environmental influences such as peers, parents, school, and the world of work on an adolescent's development.

## Development Proceeds in Multiple Directions

This concept of **multidirectionality** states that the course of development is not destined to proceed in one direction or toward one endpoint, but may follow any one of multiple possible paths (Baltes, 1987). As an illustration, consider the storm and stress hypothesis discussed in Chapter 1. If we believe that individuals will experience a great deal of turmoil in adolescence, then we have assumed that development inevitably proceeds in a particular direction: a path in which one inevitably experiences many difficulties. We now know, however, that such storm and stress does *not* typify the adolescent experience (Petersen, 1993). For *some* adolescents the course of development is stormy and stressful; for others it is relatively smooth and trouble-free. Still others fall in between, experiencing some ups and downs but no major difficulties. The fact that there are multiple ways to move through adolescence attests to the multidirectionality of development.

The life-span view of development becomes even more complex when we consider specific domains of development, such as biological change, peer relations, or academic achievement. Each of these domains may

| ADOLESCENT OUTCOME | LOCUS OF RISK | EXAMPLE OF RISK FACTOR |
|---|---|---|
| Mental health problems | Early childhood | Serious accidents |
| | | Moodiness |
| | | Family instability |
| Low educational attainment | Middle childhood | Poor parental discipline |
| | | Hyperactivity |
| | | Interpersonal problems in school |
| Conduct problem | Early childhood | Family instability |
| | Middle childhood | Poor parental discipline |
| | | Aggressive behavior |
| Substance use | Early childhood | Premature birth |
| | | Low birth weight |
| | Middle childhood | Poor self-concept |
| | | Interpersonal problems in school |

proceed in a different direction or at a different pace. For example, an adolescent may maintain an average level of academic achievement throughout junior high and high school, undergo rapid physical maturation in which the body changes dramatically, and evidence a slow, steady accumulation of friendships across adolescence. All aspects of development, then, do not proceed in lockstep along the same path.

Moreover, because of multidirectionality the developmental *pattern* of changes differs from individual to individual. Nonetheless, various aspects of development are likely to be related to each other in some manner. For example, rapid physical maturation may lead to a heightened awareness of the other sex and may press the adolescent to move further into the world of peers. Movement into peer networks may, in turn, affect other behaviors, such as smoking or drinking.

## Individuals Are Active in Their Own Development

Children and adolescents do not simply respond passively to biological and environmental forces. A life-span developmental perspective assumes that individuals play an active role in determining their own development

(Lerner & Busch-Rossnagel, 1981). This may be seen in the evocative influence of the adolescent: that is, the adolescent influences others in a social context—parents, teachers, and peers—through his or her physical or behavioral characteristics. These responses from others then feed back to influence the adolescent (Kendall, Lerner, & Craighead, 1984; Scarr, 1992; Scarr & McCartney, 1983).

For example, consider physical attractiveness as an attribute with the potential to influence reactions from others. In a study of sixth-grade adolescents, Lerner et al. (1991) found significant positive correlations between adolescents' physical attractiveness (as indicated by college students' ratings of facial photos), and perceptions of these adolescents by their classroom peers. Physically attractive adolescents were seen as possessing more positive qualities, such as being happy or likeable, and fewer negative ones, such as being sloppy or unpopular, than were their more physically unattractive classmates. Parents and teachers also had more positive impressions of the competence and behaviors of physically attractive adolescents. On some dimensions (for example, social acceptance), physically attractive adolescents rated themselves more positively than did less physically attractive adolescents. These findings are consistent with the notion that adolescents evoke responses from others through their personal attributes; responses from others

## 2.2 Understanding the Biological Bases of Behavior

Behavioral geneticists are scientists who investigate the degree to which cognitive, personality, and behavioral differences among individuals are attributable to genetic and environmental origins (Goldsmith, 1994). Because of the remarkable differences among individuals in personality, much behavioral genetic research has focused on the biological and environmental foundations of personality characteristics (Plomin et al., 1991). What do we know from these studies?

To investigate these issues, behavioral geneticists conduct comparative studies of **monozygotic twins,** who are genetically identical, and **dizygotic** or "fraternal" **twins,** who are no more closely related genetically than other brothers and sisters (Plomin, 1986; Scarr & Kidd, 1983). In general, it appears that genetic influences are strongest for basic temperamental characteristics such as activity level, emotional reactivity, and extraversion. They appear to be weakest for characteristics that are highly dependent on learning and social experience, such as ethical and social values (Buss & Plomin, 1984; Kagan, Reznick, & Snidman, 1988a, 1988b; Matheny, 1983; Plomin, 1990).

From infancy to adolescence, monozygotic (MZ) twins resemble each other significantly more than dizygotic (DZ) twins do on many temperamental dimensions, including activity, attention, task persistence, irritability, emotionality, sociability, and impulsiveness (Buss & Plomin, 1984; Cohen, Dibble, & Grawe, 1977; Goldsmith, 1984; Matheny, 1983; Torgersen & Kringlen, 1978). In addition, at later ages MZ twins resemble each other more than DZ twins do on such characteristics as extraversion and neuroticism, although twins in general (MZ and DZ) become less similar over time (Floderus-Myrhed, Pedersen, & Rasmuson, 1980; McCartney, Harris, & Bernieri, 1990; Plomin, 1986; Scarr & Kidd, 1983).

may, in turn, have an impact on adolescents' own self-perceptions.

Adolescents also influence their own development in a more active way, by shaping and selecting their environments (Kendall, Lerner, & Craighead, 1984; Scarr, 1992; Scarr & McCartney, 1983). The shaping and selection of environments occurs when individuals respond selectively to particular aspects of the environment and seek environments that appear to be compatible with their own personalities, interests, and goals (Scarr & McCartney, 1983). The young person who is socially oriented may be more likely than less socially oriented peers to attend parties or join sports teams. The academically oriented adolescent may choose to spend more time in the library or doing homework or in discussions with other adolescents who enjoy talking about intellectual issues. As a result, adolescents are influenced by the unique set of social contacts and experiences to which they actively expose themselves.

**Biological Influences.** The role of biological influences in determining an individual's effect on his or her environment is important to developmental psychologists. As we have seen, physical characteristics, such as attractiveness, which are largely genetically determined, can affect the responses of others. Personality characteristics and behaviors may have a genetic component (see Box 2.2). The extent to which an individual seeks out environments that fit with his or her physical, temperamental, social, and intellectual characteristics determine the degree of match or goodness-of-fit between the individual's characteristics and the environment. A higher goodness-of-fit is more likely to be associated with a higher level of adjustment (Lerner & Lerner, 1983).

## The Role of Learning in Development

The life-span perspective provides us with general principles of developmental change, but we also need to understand the specific processes that govern the continuing interaction between the individual and his or her environment, and that help to shape the course of development. These processes are commonly referred to as principles, or laws, of **learning.**

Jerome Kagan.

Although these studies suggest that genetic factors have a significant influence on **temperament,** it should be kept in mind that virtually all personality characteristics are influenced by both genes and environment. Moreover, the relative effects of genetic and environmental forces might differ across different developmental periods. For example, change in personality across childhood has been attributed more to genetic influences, whereas personality changes that occur in adolescence and adulthood have been attributed more to environmental influences (Loehlin, 1992; McGue, Bacon, & Lykken, 1993; Plomin & Nesselroade, 1990).

How might environmental influences operate to limit or reinforce the expression of genetically linked personality characteristics? Studies of shyness help to shed light on this question. Kagan (1989) argued that environmental stressors such as marital conflict and family illness might activate a genetic predisposition to shyness. This predisposition, under less stressful conditions, would be less likely to be expressed. Another study found high stability of shyness (shyness was maintained) from early childhood to adolescence among girls, but not among boys. The authors suggested that cultural expectations for gender-appropriate behavior limited change in girls' shyness because shyness was seen as acceptable (Kerr et al., 1994).

To the average person, *learning* means something done in school or while acquiring a vocational skill (such as "learning" to be a schoolteacher or an airline pilot). As the term is used by psychologists, however, its connotations are far broader. Stated in its simplest form, *learning is the process by which behavior or the potential for behavior is modified as a result of experience.* Behaviors that are subject to learning can be as varied as thoughts and images, motor acts (such as driving a car), and physiological responses—even so-called involuntary responses such as changes in heart rate, blood pressure, or electrical activity of the brain.

## Learning and Innate Responses

Not all of the behaviors—even complex behaviors—that seem to require learning are in fact learned. Ethologists have demonstrated that in animals, highly specific external stimuli can "release" complex patterns of behavioral response in the absence of any opportunity for prior learning (Lorenz, 1981). In a male stickleback fish, for example, the sight of the red underbelly of another stickleback provokes complex fighting behavior. Even models that look very little like sticklebacks provoke the response as long as the essential elements of the key stimulus are present (Lorenz, 1981). In many instances, complex maternal behavior takes place without prior experience. Animals ranging from rats to birds build nests in preparation for their young, even though they may never have witnessed such activities themselves.

It is far more difficult to isolate and study complex human behaviors that may have been innately programmed and not learned. It appears that complex behavior in humans is generally much more dependent on learning and much less dependent on innate response tendencies. It is possible, however, that some types of human behavior that were previously assumed to be learned may turn out to depend at least in part on such tendencies.

Consider the complex psychological responses of adults to a "baby-faced" appearance in children (large eyes, round face). Baby-faced people are seen as more childlike, kinder, warmer, more affectionate, and more desirous of being hugged than are more mature-faced individuals (Zebrowitz, Kendall-Tackett, & Fafel, 1991;

## 2.3 Dealing with Aggressive or Delinquent Children and Youth

Gerald Patterson and his colleagues compared families of children who were highly aggressive and unruly, both at home and at school, with a control group of families that were similar in age, socioeconomic status, and number of children, but whose children were not excessively aggressive. They identified some significant differences: Unlike the families in the control group, the families of highly aggressive children were found to be unwittingly rewarding aggressive behavior. For example, members of those families were five times as likely to respond to the child's actions in ways that tended to maintain aggression. A sister who teased her brother after he yelled increased the likelihood that the brother would respond in a hostile manner, such as hitting, often setting in motion an escalating exchange.

The parents of the problem children tended to be inconsistent in their handling of aggressive responses. At times they reinforced those actions by approving, paying attention, or complying with the child's wishes; at other times they threatened the child with punishment, although they often failed to back up their threats (Patterson, 1982; Patterson, DeBaryshe, & Ramsey, 1989; Snyder & Patterson, 1987). In contrast, the parents in the control group tended to be evenhanded and consistent in their use of punishment.

On the basis of such findings, Patterson and his colleagues concluded that parents can control a child's aggressive behavior if they apply certain techniques when interacting with the child. They explained the basic principles of learning to the parents and showed them how to identify undesirable aggressive behaviors and keep accurate records of their occurrence and the conditions surrounding them. Modeling and role-playing procedures were used to teach the parents how to reinforce appropriate behavior with warmth and affection, and to reduce deviant behavior by not giving in to the child's aggression and not allowing their own coercion to escalate. Techniques of control using rewards for desirable responses and calm forms of punishment such as "time-out" (removing the child from an activity until he or she stops using coercive tac-

---

Zebrowitz & Montepare, 1992). Some investigators have argued that such responses may be innately programmed and that they serve an important evolutionary purpose: helping to ensure the infant's survival by attracting caretakers and maintaining their interest in feeding, caring for, and sheltering their young (Bowlby, 1969; Clarke-Stewart & Friedman, 1987; Hess, 1970).

### Kinds of Learning

**Classical Conditioning.** Probably the most basic category of learning is **classical conditioning,** in which a reflexive response (one that is automatically elicited by a specific, or "unconditioned," stimulus) becomes associated with a previously neutral stimulus (one that would not normally elicit the reflexive response). The response can be an overt action (such as withdrawing one's hand from a hot stove) or a physiological reaction (such as a change in heart rate in response to an electric shock). In either case the response is a naturally occurring reaction to an existing stimulus.

In a pioneering experiment, the great Russian physiologist Ivan Pavlov demonstrated that a dog can be taught to salivate in response to the previously neutral stimulus of a buzzer through repeated pairings of the sound of the buzzer with the presentation of food (an unconditioned stimulus). Eventually, the buzzer alone becomes capable of eliciting the salivation response. The buzzer thus is a conditioned stimulus.

Similar conditioning takes place in humans. For example, within a few weeks after birth the infant's sucking reflex, an innate (unconditioned) response to a nipple in the mouth, is readily conditioned to previous neutral stimuli such as the sight, smell, and sound of the mother as she prepares to feed the infant. Through association with the unconditioned stimulus of the nipple, these previously neutral stimuli come to elicit sucking. Consider an adolescent whose questions in class are criticized by his teacher. This criticism leads to an increased

tics) were substituted for more severe forms of punishment, such as hitting.

The effectiveness of this approach was tested systematically over a twelve-month period in twenty-seven families with boys between the ages of 5 and 15 who were considered to show excessive aggression. The program was highly successful. After the treatment, approximately three-fourths of the boys showed significant reductions in amount of aggression expressed and in number of "bursts" of aggressive behaviors. Moreover, when the program was completed, *all* members of the family showed less aggression and provided fewer of the kinds of stimuli that had originally provoked the problem child's aggressive behavior.

Learning-based techniques were also used in an experimental intervention designed to reduce offense rates among chronic delinquents (Bank et al., 1991). Parents of 28 male adolescents (younger than age 17) who were repeat offenders participated in sessions in which parents were trained to identify and track the behaviors of their sons, including attendance at school, homework completion, associations with deviant peers, substance use, and defiance toward adults. Parents in this experimental treatment were encouraged to communicate daily with their sons and with the school, behavior contracts were completed jointly by parents and youth (agreements about the behaviors expected of the youth and what consequences would result from behaving or not behaving as agreed), and reinforcers (such as receiving an allowance or privileges such as watching TV) were given as consequences for prosocial behavior. In short, parents were trained to monitor and take more responsibility for their sons' behavior.

Boys in this experimental group were compared over a two-year period to those in a control group of chronic offenders who received community-based intensive family therapy, drug counseling, and monitoring of activities by a therapist or probation officer. Relative to the control group, the experimental group showed a quicker drop in status offenses (offenses that are dependent on the offender's age, such as curfew violation) and nonstatus offenses (illegal for youth and adults). They also spent less time in institutional confinement. Although the control group after two years reached the same relatively low rate of offending, the package provided to the experimental group was less expensive overall, and because it was more effective initially, there were fewer costs to society.

heart rate (a reflexive response). Now the adolescent's heart races whenever he asks a question in class because of the previous pairing of question-asking (a conditioned stimulus) with a rapid heartbeat.

**Operant or Instrumental Conditioning.** Many instances of learning in older children and adolescents cannot be explained by simple classical conditioning. A more complex kind of learning is involved, called **operant** or **instrumental conditioning.** Here the response to be learned is not automatically elicited by a known stimulus but must be developed gradually. A familiar example is teaching a dog to play dead, roll over, or shake hands. In essence, this technique involves rewarding appropriate responses whenever they happen to occur.

In operant conditioning, the subject's own response is instrumental in producing the reward—it operates to bring about the reward; hence the term *instrumental* or *operant conditioning.* Through operant or "shaping" procedures, animals can be taught surprisingly complex sequences of behaviors. For example, operant-conditioning procedures have been used to teach dolphins to deliver equipment to divers in undersea explorations. An activity that is very important to most adolescents—learning to drive a car—is also learned through operant conditioning. The experience of simply getting behind the wheel may be rewarding to adolescents, who then progress to turning the motor on, turning the wheel, and pushing the gas pedal.

**Behavior Modification.** Similar techniques are being applied to humans in what is known as **behavior modification** or **behavior therapy.** Gerald Patterson and his associates at the Oregon Social Learning Center have had remarkable success in helping parents learn to deal with excessive aggression and delinquency in children and adolescents through identification and consistent reinforcement of appropriate responses (Bank et al., 1991; Patterson, 1982; Snyder & Patterson, 1987). Their approach is described in Box 2.3.

In other studies, behavior modification procedures have been used to overcome social withdrawal and increase social interaction in children. Such procedures have also been used to treat disorders such as enuresis (bed-wetting) and insomnia, to discourage smoking or drug use, and to treat bulimia (Leitenberg & Rosen, 1988; Graziano & Diament, 1992; Hersen, Eisler, & Miller, 1990; Lewis & Sugai, 1993).

**Observational or Vicarious Learning.** Not all learning depends on conditioning. Many human activities, especially complex responses, are acquired by observing the behavior of others. A student will learn how to solve a difficult problem by observing the teacher demonstrating the correct approach. Adolescents in par-

Social learning theorists have found that children and adolescents are more likely to imitate the behavior of prestigious models, such as tennis great Arthur Ashe, than of nonprestigious individuals. Until his untimely death, Ashe headed the Safe Passage Foundation, whose mission is to help provide safe passage for young people into productive adult lives.

ticular are likely to observe the behavior of their peers carefully in order to learn which ways of dressing, talking, and acting lead to approval and which ones have the opposite effect. Social-learning theorists such as Albert Bandura emphasize the importance of **observational learning** and the factors that influence the likelihood that a person will repeat responses acquired through observation (Bandura, 1977b; Muus, 1988). Observational learning seems to affect smoking among adolescents. Adolescents are more apt to smoke if their parents and friends do (Chassin et al., 1986).

Social-learning theorists have found that subjects are more likely to imitate the behavior of prestigious models (people who have characteristics that they look up to) than that of nonprestigious models. An adolescent, for example, might imitate the behavior of peers who are popular, if popularity is highly regarded by the adolescent. Other adolescents might imitate athletic or achievement-oriented peers. In addition, models who are similar to the subject have a greater effect on behavior than models who do not resemble the subject. An adolescent is more likely to imitate the behavior of a peer with similar interests and abilities and who belongs to the same social clique or group than to imitate that of a peer with different interests and talents.

**How Important Is Reinforcement?** You have probably noticed that in several of the examples of learning discussed in this chapter, the subject was given a reward or **reinforcement** whenever the desired response was made. How important is such reinforcement in facilitating learning? Psychologists differ in their answers to this question. Some argue that reinforcement is not a necessary condition for learning and that its apparent importance in some cases is only incidental—it helps motivate the individual and ensures that the appropriate response will occur in the presence of the stimulus and not under other conditions (Atkinson et al., 1987; Bower & Hilgard, 1981). In contrast, other psychologists assert that reinforcement is always necessary for learning and that instances in which learning appears to take place without reinforcement are deceptive.

Still other psychologists—perhaps a majority—maintain that although reinforcement may not be a necessary condition for all learning (including some conditioned responses that involve the autonomic nervous system), it is important for many and perhaps most forms of learning, particularly social learning (Atkinson et al., 1987; Bower & Hilgard, 1981). For example, they note that a child or adolescent who finally makes the correct response in a complicated learning problem is more likely to repeat it the next time if he or she is rewarded for it and is not rewarded for incorrect

responses. The reward may be a piece of candy, a grade of A, or simply a congratulatory statement such as "very good"—as long as the reward actually is rewarding to that particular child. In our view, although reward or reinforcement may not be necessary for all learning, it plays an important role in many kinds of social learning that we shall be concerned with throughout this book.

**The Principle of Generalization.** If an individual could profit from past learning only when he or she encountered *exactly* the same situation again, opportunities for continued development would be severely limited. Fortunately, this is not the case. When a young girl has been trained to avoid a particular hot radiator or stove, she will tend to avoid similar radiators or stoves in other locations. But how does that happen? If the stimuli (cues) presented are not identical, why doesn't the child have to learn all over again to make the appropriate response in the new situation?

The answer to this question is found in an additional learning principle: **stimulus generalization.** This principle states that when a response to one stimulus has been learned, it is likely to occur in the presence of similar stimuli. The greater the degree of similarity between the original stimulus and the new one, the greater the likelihood that the response will occur, and the stronger it will be. This is called the **gradient of generalization** (Miller, 1984).

Initially, generalization is likely to be extensive. A young boy who has learned to attach the label *dog* to the family pet is likely to extend that label to all four-footed animals he meets, including sheep, cows, and horses. Gradually, through a process called **discrimination,** he learns to limit the label to dogs. Similarly, the adolescent girl who feels anxious whenever she asks a question in *any* class (a generalized response resulting from her negative experiences with *one* teacher) may learn through discrimination to limit her anxiety in the presence of teachers who respond positively to question-asking.

Whereas generalization involves "reaction to similarities," discrimination is "reaction to differences" (Atkinson et al., 1987, p. 219). Discrimination is brought about by selective reinforcement of responses that have been appropriately generalized and by the elimination, or **extinction,** of incorrectly generalized responses.

## Cognition and Learning

Social-learning theorists tend to place greater emphasis on cognitive processes than learning theorists, whose primary interest is in basic conditioning. They point out that because humans can think and represent situations symbolically, they can foresee the probable consequences of their actions and alter their behavior accordingly: "Anticipated consequences, represented symbolically in one's thoughts, can motivate behavior in much the same way that actual consequences can" (Hilgard, Atkinson, & Atkinson, 1979, p. 318). Children and adolescents therefore are more likely to imitate the behavior of models who are rewarded for their actions than that of models who are punished or not rewarded.

Cognitive psychologists view the individual as an active seeker of knowledge and processor of information (Klatzky, 1980). They view learning as "the step in which we acquire information that we then modify, manipulate, store, and use in various ways" (Kagan & Segal, 1988, p. 181). Because of the complexity of human mental processes, much human learning cannot be adequately understood without an understanding of cognitive development, including the ways in which individuals at different stages of development acquire and process information, use problem-solving strategies, store information and solutions in short-term ("working") and long-term memory, and retrieve stored information for later use (Siegler & Richards, 1982). In Chapter 4 we will discuss current theories of cognitive development and information processing in some detail.

# The Role of Motivation in Development

An understanding of underlying motivations is essential if we are to understand properly adolescent behavior. In general, the term **motivation** refers to the needs, goals, and desires that provoke a person to action. More specifically, there are basic biological needs, commonly called primary needs, that must be met if the person is to survive; these include the needs for food, water, warmth, and oxygen.

There are, of course, many other sources of motivation besides primary needs. There is nothing innate about an adolescent's need for social status, security, love from parents, money, or acceptance by friends. These needs are *learned* (Bower & Hilgard, 1981; Miller, 1984). In common with primary needs, however, learned needs, also called motives, may serve to motivate future learning. Moreover, as with primary needs, the individual has to learn a set of behaviors to gratify the learned needs. One common source of tension and anxiety in human beings is the chronic presence of a learned need without a means of gratifying it (for example, living beyond one's financial means because of an acquired need for an array of material goods).

Learned needs or motives may play an important role in the acquisition of other motives. For example, if

a mother gives love to her daughter only if she is orderly and conscientious, the child may develop needs for orderliness and conscientiousness that will be manifested even when the mother is not around. She may even learn to perform numerous behaviors, such as always putting her toys away, never getting her clothes dirty, washing her hands frequently, and always doing what she is told, in order to satisfy those needs.

One of the important characteristics of needs or motives (both primary and learned) is that they energize behavior. When a person is hungry or thirsty, or anxious or in need of nurturance, he or she tends to become active and to engage in a variety of behaviors, some of which may be reinforced and lead to further learning.

## The Complexity of Adolescent Needs and Motives

The newborn's repertoire of needs is largely restricted to primary needs, such as the needs for food, sleep, physical contact, environmental stimulation, and protection from extremes of heat or cold. In contrast, the adolescent has had many years in which to develop an elaborate set of learned needs or motives—for social approval, friendship, love from parents and others, independence (or dependence), nurturance of others, achievement, self-esteem, and a sense of identity. Even the adolescent's biologically based needs are likely to be more numerous and more inextricably intertwined with socially learned motives (e.g., tastes for special foods rather than simply food per se).

It should be emphasized that the individual need not be, and probably never is, fully aware of all his or her motives. Many motives remain at least partially unconscious. For example, the adolescent who astounds himself and his parents by suddenly "blowing up" at his mother and is unable to provide any reason for his behavior may be motivated by unconscious aggressive or control needs. Many adolescents are puzzled or alarmed by such evidence of unconsciously motivated behaviors. Some may be led to wonder if they are "losing their minds" because of what may appear, even to themselves, to be irrational, unmotivated thoughts or acts.

## The Role of Stress in Behavior

In addition to understanding motivations as a source of adolescent behavior, we need to consider the effects of stress. It is common these days to hear about the stressfulness of living in contemporary society. As one writer

in the popular press declared, "today's teenagers face more adult-strength stresses than their predecessors did" (Gelman, 1990, p. 10). Regardless of the truth of this particular claim, we do know that stress helps to shape the lives of adolescents. What is stress?

Although there has been much debate about the exact meaning and nature of **stress,** typically, it has been defined as the response of the individual (conscious or unconscious) to noxious conditions. Stress may be observed physiologically (in increased heart rate or perspiration), symptomatically (in poor physical health), or psychologically, in terms of anxiety, depression, or fear (Pearlin et al., 1981).

Stress is a major determinant of human behavior because it is associated with strong physiological responses and because it may conflict with the satisfaction of other needs or motives. For example, an adolescent wants to do well on an examination, but the anxiety makes her unable to order her thoughts and concentrate on the task at hand. Speaking in front of groups is a common source of anxiety and fear that may limit many people from following careers such as teaching that require this skill.

Anxiety involves both a physiological component and a cognitive component (Barlow, 1988). The physiological component of anxiety is part of the constitutional make-up of the individual; it is not learned. What is learned is an association between a person, object, or situation and the combined feelings, images, and physiological reactions that characterize anxiety. In other words, the *arousal* of anxiety is learned (Miller, 1984).

How do anxiety and stress begin? What produces the feelings of discomfort, perspiration, trembling, exaggerated startled response, dryness of the throat and mouth—the general anxiety? Feelings of stress follow the same principles of learning that apply to other behaviors. For example, if an adolescent has had humiliating experiences with the first few attempts at dating, and has learned to fear such experiences, this reaction may be generalized to dating in general, even though some dating experiences would be more comfortable. At a more profound level, an adolescent who as a child learned to fear a physically abusive father may generalize this fear to other adult males, such as a teacher. Such fear could ultimately limit the adolescent's chances of academic success.

## Sources of Stress in Adolescents

Use of the term *stress* without stipulating the source of the stress is not helpful in understanding or predicting behavior. Clearly, we have a better chance of under-

A high level of anxiety can make performance of tasks such as doing well on an examination or speaking before a group more difficult.

standing adolescent development if we can identify specific sources of stress in adolescents' lives. Researchers have put a great deal of effort into identifying and measuring situations and events that can lead to feelings of stress. Initially, most research was conducted on adults, but stress in adolescence is now a burgeoning field of research (Masten, Neemann, & Andenas, 1994).

The earliest research on sources of stress focused on **negative life events** such as loss of a parent, parental separation or divorce, or a sudden serious illness. This research focused typically on discrete (occurring over a short period of time), uncontrollable, and undesirable occurrences in the lives of adolescents. The studies based on this approach generally indicate a link between negative life events and adolescent stress. Negative events are associated with depression, anxiety, and conduct problems (Compas et al., 1986; Friedrich, Reams, & Jacobs, 1982; Holahan & Moos, 1987; Newcomb, Huba, & Bentler, 1981; Swearingen & Cohen, 1985). Negative life events, then, are connected in predictable ways to aspects of adolescent functioning.

As much as negative life events help to shed light on adolescent behavior, these events are less predictive of the behaviors of adolescents than are **ongoing life stressors** such as difficulties with peers, academic problems in school, or conflict with parents (Daniels & Moos, 1990). The importance of ongoing life stressors for adolescent behavior may be attributable to the continual strain that chronic or frequently occurring difficulties place on the adolescent's psychological resources. It is easy to imagine how an adolescent who is bullied repeatedly at school or who lives in a dysfunctional family would build up feel-

ings of anxiety or depression. This accumulation of daily stresses inhibits healthy functioning (Compas et al., 1989; DeLongis et al., 1982). What are the possible ongoing life stressors that can affect adolescents?

Most scholars who examine stress in adolescence discuss family, school, and peers as potential sources of life stress in adolescence. Other stressors might arise from the pubertal process (such as concern with appearance or timing of maturation) or from societal expectations (such as for more mature behavior) or opportunities (educational and occupational) (Petersen & Spiga, 1982). Denise Daniels and Rudolf Moos (1990) developed a measure of ongoing life stressors in adolescence that focused on eight types of stressors that are common in adolescence:

- *Parent stressors,* which involve interpersonal difficulties between parents and adolescents, difficulties in the parents' marital relationship, and parental health problems
- *Home/money stressors,* which have to do with the living conditions at home and the financial status of the family
- *Physical health stressors,* which are physical conditions and problems that arise among youth
- *Sibling stressors,* which are interpersonal problems between the adolescents and siblings as well as health problems in siblings
- *Extended family stressors,* which involve interpersonal stress between relatives and the adolescent
- *School stressors,* which include difficulties in dealing with teachers, counselors, coaches, or other students

- *Friend stressors,* which have to do with interpersonal difficulties (such as peer pressure) with friends
- *Boyfriend/girlfriend stressors,* which are interpersonal difficulties in boyfriend/girlfriend relationships

This set of stressors is not exhaustive but it does point to major areas in the adolescent's life that could be sources of chronic stress. In their research, Daniels and Moos found that youth who experienced more of these stressors were more likely to be depressed or anxious, display conduct problems, or exhibit a lower level of self-confidence. Moreover, although negative life events were also associated with depression, anxiety, conduct problems, and lower self-confidence, the ongoing stressors were more important than negative life events in explaining adolescent functioning.

## Coping with Stress: Unconscious Defense Mechanisms

To build a better understanding of adolescent behavior, we need not only to identify sources of stress, but to know what coping strategies adolescents use to deal with stress. Psychoanalytic theory postulates a variety of largely unconscious techniques, termed **defense mechanisms,** that may help to defend an individual against stress, often by distorting reality in some way (Freud, 1966; Horowitz, 1988; Swanson, 1988). Many of these defenses were originally conceptualized in an effort to make sense of otherwise inexplicable psychological phenomena such as amnesia, phobias, severe obsessions and compulsions, and apparent physical disabilities for which no organic impairment could be found. In many instances the source of these symptoms seemed to lie in unconscious thoughts, feelings, or impulses that the individual could not admit without experiencing painful increases in anxiety or sometimes even panic. The seemingly senseless symptoms protected or defended the individual from such awareness. A painful episode may not be remembered precisely *because* it was so painful.

According to psychoanalytic theory, *the basic function of defense mechanisms is to help the individual avoid painful feelings of anxiety* without being consciously aware of doing so; however, some defense mechanisms have the additional advantage of allowing the gratification of unconscious needs or impulses. In effect, such defense mechanisms are doubly reinforcing. A classic example (of reaction formation) is censors of pornographic literature or films who are able to reassure themselves that they have no unacceptable sexual impulses. Simultaneously, however, they may gain secret satisfaction from reading the suspect books or viewing the films in order to "protect" others.

Psychoanalytic theorists believe that many of the symptoms of psychological disorders reflect the presence (or the failure) of defense mechanisms, and that most of these mechanisms also play a role in the development and functioning of normal individuals (Horowitz, 1988; Swanson, 1988). The kinds of defense mechanisms used by any given individual will vary depending on personality, learning experiences, age, and level of cognitive development. Some defense mechanisms, such as regression or withdrawal, may be most easily seen in children because of their relative lack of sophistication and the immaturity of their egos. Others, such as intellectualization and rationalization, may depend on the attainment of a fairly advanced level of intellectual and cognitive functioning, and for that reason they are most likely to become evident during adolescence.

Table 2.1 summarizes twelve different defense mechanisms. In considering these defense mechanisms, it is important to remember several points based on psychoanalytic theory. First, the defense mechanism of repression is hypothesized to serve as a basis for many other defenses (e.g., reaction formation or displacement). Second, to the extent that a defense mechanism is effective in reducing anxiety, its use may be reinforced, thereby leading to increased use of that defense. This might sometimes work to the individual's disadvantage, as when withdrawal leads the individual to "run away" from all stressful situations without ever learning to handle crises. Third, when taken to extremes, defense mechanisms are maladaptive and can evidence themselves as forms of pathology.

## Coping with Stress: Problem- and Emotion-Focused Coping

Because stress is an uncomfortable state of heightened tension that markedly disturbs psychological equilibrium, responses that lead to a reduction in stress tend to be learned. In the course of the individual's development, he or she acquires a variety of strategies for coping with, or defending against, the anxiety generated by stressful situations. Coping takes two primary forms: **problem-focused coping** and **emotion-focused coping** (Compas, Malcarne, & Fondacaro, 1988; Lazarus & Folkman, 1984).

**Problem-Focused Coping.** In problem-focused coping, the person confronts and evaluates the stressful situation and then takes steps to deal with it. This may involve efforts to change the situation or to change one's own behavior, or a mixture of the two (Kagan & Segal, 1988). A young man who discovers that he is in danger of failing a course may evaluate the reasons for his dif-

# Table 2.1 An Overview of Defense Mechanisms

| DEFENSE MECHANISM | DEFINITION | EXAMPLE |
| --- | --- | --- |
| Repression | Anxiety-producing thoughts, impulses, and memories are kept from conscious awareness involuntarily. | Child represses memory of violent fight between parents. |
| Suppression | Voluntary effort is made to exclude thoughts from conscious awareness. | Adolescent suppresses thoughts of unpleasant stressors (e.g., deadline for a term paper). |
| Denial | Obvious realities are treated as if they do not exist. | Abused child insists that abusive parent is kind, loving, and not hostile. |
| Projection | One's own undesirable thoughts or actions are ascribed to another person. | Adolescent engrossed in thoughts about sex sees another adolescent as promiscuous despite evidence that this is not so. |
| Displacement | Appropriate emotional reaction is too painful to acknowledge, so source of emotion is attributed to other symbolic substitute. | Fear of abusive parent is not consciously acknowledged but emerges in fear of monsters. |
| Rationalization | One provides socially acceptable reasons for one's behavior or attitudes when the real reason is not acceptable to one's conscience. | Adolescent blames test failure on a headache rather than on a lack of studying. |
| Reaction formation | A repressed idea is replaced by a focus on the opposite. | Adult who is fascinated with sexuality becomes a censor of pornographic films. |
| Withdrawal | Person directly avoids, or flees from threatening situations or people. | Student with fear of public speaking withdraws from all classes requiring oral reports. |
| Regression | Person readopts a response that was characteristic of an earlier phase of development. | A spouse displays temper tantrums to get his or her way with partner. |
| Asceticism | One attempts to deny one's bodily needs and impulses, possibly to gain control over inner world. | Adolescent refuses to eat favorite foods, deprives self of sleep, or tests capacity to withstand pain. |
| Intellectualization | Person avoids emotional implications of a topic by dealing with it on a purely ideational level. | Person discusses military and political strategies of war impersonally and philosophically, instead of learning how to handle aggressive feelings. |

ficulty and then take remedial actions such as cutting back on extracurricular activities, developing a regular work schedule, or finding a tutor (Atkinson et al., 1987; Cohen, 1984). After seeking counseling, a premedical student may realize that she is having difficulty with the required course work, not because of lack of ability but because her heart is not in the work. She may discover that she has been attempting, albeit unconsciously, to sat- isfy the hopes of her physician father rather than her own artistic talents and interests. She may then change her major to fine arts. In these examples, the individuals involved confronted and evaluated the stressful problem situation and then took action to resolve it. The emphasis is on objectivity, flexibility, logical analysis, and active problem solving (Haan, 1977; Horowitz, 1988; Lazarus & Folkman, 1984; Swanson, 1988).

**Emotion-Focused Coping.** In contrast, emotion-focused coping centers on emotional responses to the problem; "the individual tries to reduce anxiety without dealing directly with the anxiety-producing situation" (Atkinson et al., 1987, p. 475). As such, emotion-focused techniques include unconscious defense mechanisms (Cohen, 1987). Although emotion-focused coping techniques may be used in a wide variety of situations, they are most likely to occur in stressful problem situations that are, or appear to be, insoluble. These techniques can be relatively straightforward and adaptive, or they can be maladaptive. Engaging in physical exercise to reduce tension, seeking support from friends, or temporarily putting a problem aside may be adaptive (Horowitz, 1988). At a more complex level, one may cope with an overwhelming loss, such as the death of a loved one, by only gradually coming to accept the full impact of the tragedy. In contrast, an individual may resort to emotion-focused or avoidant coping techniques that, although they may reduce anxiety at the time, are ultimately maladaptive and self-defeating (Holahan & Moos, 1987). Consider a woman who ignores the early warning signs of possible cancer by telling herself that they mean nothing or a young man who denies that he is in serious trouble in his academic work or in his job, despite every sign to the contrary; both are courting disaster (Horowitz, 1988).

In general, research suggests that adolescents who more frequently use problem-focused coping show better psychosocial adjustment than those who use emotion-focused methods (Compas, Malcarne, & Fondacaro, 1988; Ebata & Moos, 1991; Glyshaw, Cohen, & Towbes, 1989; Hanson et al., 1989; Kurdek & Sinclair, 1988). Moreover, specific types of problem-focused coping, such as logical analysis (understanding and mentally preparing for a stressor) and positive reappraisal (putting the stressor in a positive, though realistic, light), increase with age across adolescence. This suggests that the increased cognitive capabilities of adolescents enable them to cope in a more problem-focused manner (Ebata & Moos, 1994).

## The Role of Personal and Social Resources

The effects of negative life events and of ongoing life stressors on the adolescent depend not only on his or her coping efforts but also on personal or social resources that affect how the stressor is experienced and managed. Broadly speaking, individuals have access to two types of resources that may influence their reaction to stressors: personal resources, which are resources that the individual possesses, and social resources, which are resources in the individual's social network that he or she can access when necessary. Personal resources include personal characteristics such as a high self-esteem, an internal locus of control (a feeling of personal control over one's life), an adaptable temperament, a high level of intelligence, and a high level of social skill. Social resources include family members or friends who can be relied on for emotional or instrumental (e.g., financial) support. The more resources, personal and social, that the individual can draw on, the better he or she is able to respond when faced with a challenge or threat (DeLongis, Folkman, & Lazarus, 1988; Ensel & Lin, 1991; Luthar, 1991; Pearlin & Schooler, 1978).

Scientists have postulated several ways in which the availability of personal and social resources is likely to influence the individual's functioning with respect to stress. First, the availability of resources may decrease the likelihood of experiencing a stressful event. For example, in one study adolescents who were psychologically healthier before their entrance into college later reported experiencing fewer stressful life events (Compas et al., 1986). Second, in the face of a stressor, people who have more resources are less psychologically impaired by it than those who have fewer resources. In this regard, the adolescent with an adaptable temperament or a supportive parent may feel less distressed when her parents divorce than the adolescent with fewer resources (Garmezy, Masten, & Tellegen, 1984). Third, resources can be used to help individuals cope with stress once it is experienced. In this case, resources are pulled into play as part of the coping process. For example, a distressed adolescent who has lost a best friend in an accident may enlist the social support available from relatives and friends in order to help cope with the loss (Ensel & Lin, 1991; Garmezy, Masten, & Tellegen, 1984).

Studies of adolescents find that personal resources such as an active temperament or high intelligence are linked to more effective coping strategies. Social resources such as supportive relationships with siblings and friends are just as important in coping with stress (Daniels & Moos, 1990; East & Rook, 1992; Ebata & Moos, 1994; Holahan & Moos, 1987; Luthar, 1991).

# Developmental Tasks of Adolescence

Although most stressors in adolescents' lives are unique to their particular situations, some challenges that adolescents must cope with are nearly universal, or at least universal for adolescents living in the same culture. These challenges, which must be mastered if adolescents are to function suc-

Young people work together to prepare a building site for Habitat for Humanity.

cessfully in adult society, are called **developmental tasks.** The task of establishing an occupational or vocational identity is an example. Developmental tasks vary considerably from one society to another. Among the Mountain Arapesh of New Guinea, for example, there is a very gradual transition from a high degree of dependence in infancy and early childhood to increasing independence as the child grows older. In that culture, unlike much of the industrialized world, there is no discernible "spurt" during puberty or adolescence. Developmental tasks also vary from one era to another. The sexual, social, and vocational roles of men and women that contemporary American adolescents are expected to master are very different, and in some ways much more complex, than was the case in the 1940s and 1950s.

Despite such variations in developmental tasks, there are some important commonalities. First, if an adolescent is to become truly adult, and not just physically mature, he or she must gradually achieve independence from parents. Second, the adolescent must make a psychological adjustment to pubertal maturation, including feeling comfortable with one's changed body and new

sexually related interests. A third important developmental task is the establishment of cooperative and workable relations with peers, marked by an ability to resist undue peer pressure. Fourth, the adolescent must decide on and prepare for a meaningful vocation. A fifth developmental task is that young people must also gradually develop a philosophy of life and establish a set of guiding moral beliefs and standards that, however simple, are "nonnegotiable." A basic philosophy gives order and consistency to the many decisions and actions the individual must carry out in a diverse and changing world (Conger, 1979, 1981; Havighurst, 1953). Finally, as we shall see, the young person must also develop a sense of **identity.** Before adolescents can successfully abandon the security of childhood dependence on others, they must have some idea of who they are, where they are going, and what the possibilities are of getting there (Erikson, 1956, 1968).

## Identity: A Central Task of Adolescence

A central task of adolescence is to find a workable answer to the question, "Who am I?" Although this question has preoccupied humankind for many centuries and has been the subject of innumerable poems, novels, and autobiographies, only in recent decades has it become an important concern of psychologists, beginning with the writings of Erik Erikson (Erikson, 1968).

Adolescents and adults with a strong sense of their own identity see themselves as separate, distinct individuals. The very word *individual,* as a synonym for *person,* implies a need to perceive oneself as somehow separate from others, no matter how much one may share with them. Closely related is the need for self-consistency, a feeling of wholeness. When we speak of the integrity of the self, we imply both separateness from others and unity of the self—a workable integration of the person's needs, motives, and patterns of responding.

In order to have a clear sense of identity, an adolescent or adult also needs a sense of continuity of the self over time. In Erikson's words, "the younger person, in order to experience wholeness, must feel a progressive continuity between that which he has come to be during the long years of childhood and that which he promises to become in the anticipated future" (Erikson, 1956, p. 91). In addition, according to Erikson, a sense of identity requires psychosocial reciprocity—consistency "between that which he conceives himself to be and that which he perceives others to see in him and expect of him" (Erikson, 1956, p. 94). Erikson's asser-

A central task of adolescence is finding a workable answer to the question, "Who am I?"

tion that one's sense of identity is tied at least partly to social reality is important; it emphasizes the fact that rejection can seriously impair the individual's chances of establishing a strong, secure sense of identity.

## Developing a Sense of Identity

The development of a sense of identity—**identity achievement**—does not begin in adolescence. The elements of an individual's identity are already being shaped during early childhood, beginning, in Erikson's view, with the infant's basic trust or mistrust of the people and the world (see Box 2.4). Nor does identity development end with adolescence. Many adults, for example, question who they are and who they want to be, how they might improve in their social relationships, or how they might get more satisfaction from their vocational or leisure pursuits. In contemporary society we see much evidence of later identity development, as mature adults return to school, retrain and change vocations, and reassess their marital and family situations.

The search for a sense of identity is most obvious during adolescence, however. As we have already noted, during the adolescent years, the young person is confronted with a host of psychological, physiological, sexual, and cognitive changes, as well as new and varied intellectual, social, and cognitive demands. Adolescents may at times feel like spectators observing their chang-

ing selves, or as one young poet put it:

Standing in front of the mirror,
I'm wondering what that person is all about.
Tony Hall, age 16

Adolescents need time to integrate the rapid changes of body and mind into a gradually emerging sense of identity.

## Identification and Identity

Erikson believed that adolescent identity development had its roots in childhood identifications. **Identification** refers to the process by which one is led to think, feel, and behave as though the characteristics of another person belonged to oneself (Freud, 1953; Kagan, 1964; Mussen et al., 1990). Although identification may involve imitation (a boy who identifies with his father may imitate his father's habit of reading the sports page), the two terms are not synonymous. Identification is a more complex process than simple imitation. It involves responding as though one *were* the other person. A young girl who identifies with her mother is likely to feel pleasure when her mother receives a promotion at work. Whereas simple imitative responses are likely to involve conscious awareness, identification responses often occur unconsciously and may have an emotional intensity that is lacking in simple imitation (Bronfenbrenner, 1960; Horowitz, 1988).

Erik Erikson.

ings. Not only do they find themselves playing roles that shift from one situation or one time to another, and worry about "which, if any, is the real me," but they also self-consciously try out different roles in the hope of finding one that seems to fit.

Achieving a clear sense of identity depends partly on cognitive skills. The young person must be able to conceptualize herself or himself in abstract terms. As we shall see in Chapter 4, an increased capacity for abstract thinking, along with the ability to take a future time perspective, aids the adolescent in the search for an individual identity but at the same time makes the search more difficult. As Erikson put it, "From among all possible and imaginable relations, [the adolescent] must make a series of ever-narrowing selections of personal, occupational, sexual, and ideological commitments" (1968, p. 245).

Any developmental influences that contribute to one's perception of oneself as separate and distinct from others, as reasonably consistent and integrated, as hav-

Identification is not an all-or-none phenomenon. Children and adolescents identify to varying degrees with both parents, and they identify with adults and peers outside the family as their social contacts and cultural awareness expand. As Erik Erikson observed, the successive and interrelated identifications of childhood can provide a child with "a set of expectations as to what he is going to be when he grows older" (Erikson, 1968, p. 159). Patterns of childhood identifications, though essential, are not by themselves capable of providing adolescents with a coherent, reasonable, stable, and consistent image of the self—that is, a sense of identity. Also needed is the capacity to synthesize successive identifications into a coherent, consistent, and unique whole.

Consider the following example: When one adolescent girl was asked why she had three distinctly different handwriting styles, she replied, "How can I only write one way till I know who I am?" (Conger, 1979, p. 495). Although she had a number of identities, as indicated by her varied handwriting styles, she had not yet synthesized them into a coherent whole that was uniquely her own. Many adolescents have similar feel-

Identification is a far more complex process than simple imitation: It involves responding as though one *were* the other person.

## 2.4 Erikson's Eight Stages of Development

Erik Erikson, a psychoanalytic theorist who lived to age 91, proposed major revisions in Freud's ideas about stages of development. Erikson thought that Freud had overemphasized the biological and sexual determinants of developmental change while underemphasizing the importance of childhood experiences, social relationships, and cultural influences on the development of ego or self. He also believed that major developmental changes occur after childhood and adolescence.

Erikson proposed eight stages of development stretching over the entire life span. Each stage is defined by a developmental task or crisis that needs to be resolved if the individual is to continue a healthy pattern of development (see below a summary of the stages and their corresponding period in the life span). Erikson's theory stimulated little research on young children, but it has been influential in generating research on adolescent and adult development.

The major concern of the first stage is establishment of trust. Erikson believed that infants develop trust when their world is consistent and predictable—when they are fed, warmed, and comforted in a consistent manner.

The second stage is described as a conflict between autonomy and shame and doubt. In the toddler period children begin to assert independence—they say no, and they can walk and run where they choose. Toilet training, often begun during this period, can become a battlefield where the child refuses to do what the parent wishes. Erikson believed that it is important to give children a sense of autonomy and not to be harsh or punitive during this period. Parents who shame their children for misbehavior could create basic doubt about being independent.

The third stage entails a conflict between initiative and guilt. The child in this stage begins to be task oriented and to take initiative in planning new

ing continuity over time, and as being similar to the way others perceive one to be foster an overall sense of identity.

### Identity Foreclosure and Identity Confusion

Erikson (1968) pointed out two important ways in which the search for identity can go wrong: It may be prematurely foreclosed (i.e., crystallized too early) or it may be indefinitely extended. These two pitfalls are called **identity foreclosure** and **identity confusion** (Archer & Waterman, 1990).

**Identity Foreclosure.** Identity foreclosure is an interruption in the process of identity formation, a premature fixing of the adolescent's self-image that interferes with the development of other possibilities for self-definition. Young people whose identities have been prematurely foreclosed are likely to be highly approval oriented. They base their self-esteem largely on recogni-

tion by others, usually have high respect for authority, and tend to be more conforming and less autonomous than other youth. Compared to adolescents who have not experienced identity foreclosure, they are more interested in traditional religious values, less thoughtful and reflective, less anxious, and more stereotyped and superficial, as well as less intimate in their personal relationships (Dellas & Jernigan, 1990; Marcia, 1980; Orlofsky, Marcia, & Lesser, 1973).

Although they do not differ from their peers in overall intelligence, identity-foreclosed youth have difficulty being flexible and responding appropriately when confronted with stressful cognitive tasks, and are less open to experience; they seem to have a greater need for structure and order in their lives. They tend to have close relationships with their parents (perhaps especially with fathers) and to adopt their parents' values. Their parents, in turn, generally appear to be accepting and encouraging while at the same time exerting considerable pressure for conformity to family values (Benson, Harris, & Rogers, 1992; Clancy & Dollinger, 1993; Marcia, 1980).

activities. It is a period when masturbation and sexual curiosity are often noticed by parents. The danger in this period, according to Erikson, is that the child may develop excessive guilt about his or her actions.

During middle childhood children need to solve the conflict between industry and inferiority. Children become industrious in the sense that they enter school, begin to perform tasks, do homework, and acquire important skills. Achievement and a sense of competence become important; a child who has no particular competencies or who experiences repeated failure may develop strong feelings of inferiority.

The major conflict in adolescence is between identity formation and identity confusion. The young person attempts to solidify many elements of his or her childhood identity and to form a clear vocational and personal identity. Failure to solve this conflict can result in confusion about one's roles.

In young adulthood the major conflict is between intimacy and isolation. Deep, enduring personal relationships must be formed. A person who does not form such relationships may be psychologi-

cally isolated from others and have only superficial social relationships. The most important intimate relationship, according to Erikson, is a committed sexual relationship with a partner of the other sex. This view has been challenged as unnecessarily narrow; some people have argued that many kinds of intimate relationships are important and rewarding.

In middle adulthood the conflict is between generativity and stagnation. Generativity involves satisfactions gained from contributing to the development of others—particularly the young—or from dedication to other forms of altruism or creativity that transcend the self. Without generativity, Erikson argued, an adult stagnates and ceases to grow.

The final conflict is between ego integrity and despair. People with ego integrity have a sense of order and meaning in life and a feeling of satisfaction with what they have accomplished. There is a sense of being part of a larger culture or world. Despair can occur when people become afraid of death or do not accept the life they have led as satisfying or worthy (Erikson, 1968, 1985; Mussen et al., 1990).

*box continues*

**Identity Confusion.** Other adolescents may go through a prolonged period of identity confusion. Some never develop a strong, clear sense of identity; these are adolescents who cannot "find themselves," who keep themselves loose and unattached (Douvan & Adelson, 1966). Such a person may exhibit a pathologically prolonged identity crisis, never achieving any consistent loyalties or commitments. Young people experiencing identity confusion often have low underlying self-esteem and immature moral reasoning. Typically, they are impulsive, are disorganized in their thinking, and have difficulty taking responsibility for their own lives. They tend to be focused on themselves, and their relationships are often superficial and sporadic. Although they are generally dissatisfied with their parents' way of life and may experience less closeness to their mothers, they have difficulty fashioning a life of their own (Adams, Abraham, & Markstrom, 1987; Benson, Harris, & Rogers, 1992; Dellas & Jernigan, 1990; Marcia, 1980).

Young people exhibiting identity confusion seem to have adopted a negative stance toward life. They tend to score high in terms of negative emotions, low on agree-

ableness, and low on conscientiousness. They may also perform at a lower level in school and feel more negatively about school, teachers, and academic activities (Clancy & Dollinger, 1993; Vondracek, 1994).

**Psychosocial Moratorium and the Search for Identity.** Many adolescents, especially privileged adolescents, go through a period of what Erikson called a **psychosocial moratorium** (a period relatively free of major responsibilities and commitments) during which they actively search for a workable identity. The searching is often marked by career indecision and uncertainty and there may be changes in clothing and inappropriate social relationships. Not surprisingly, this searching may be accompanied both by autonomous striving and by increased anxiety, as well as by vulnerability, depression, self-consciousness, and impulsiveness (Clancy & Dollinger, 1993; Dellas & Jernigan, 1990; Marcia, 1980; Wallace-Broscious, Serafica, & Osipow, 1994).

Adolescents who are firmly attached to their mothers are less likely to undergo a psychosocial moratorium, perhaps because a close relationship to the mother may

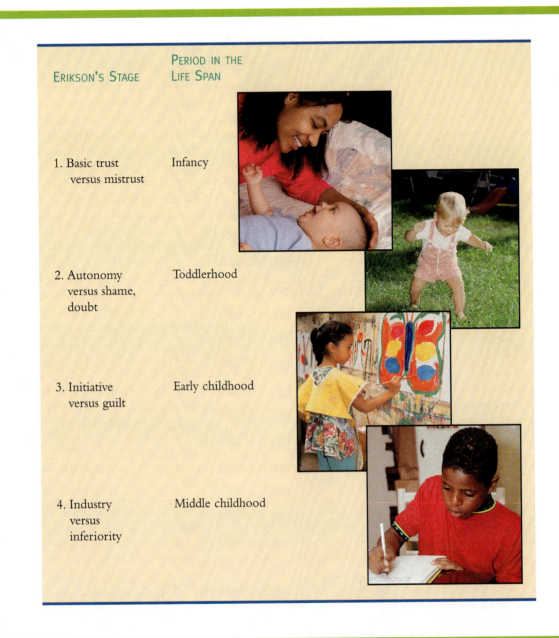

| ERIKSON'S STAGE | PERIOD IN THE LIFE SPAN |
|---|---|
| 1. Basic trust versus mistrust | Infancy |
| 2. Autonomy versus shame, doubt | Toddlerhood |
| 3. Initiative versus guilt | Early childhood |
| 4. Industry versus inferiority | Middle childhood |

provide a young person with the psychological resources necessary to make commitments (Benson, Harris, & Rogers, 1992).

**Identity Achievement.**   People who have achieved a strong sense of identity, especially after a period of active searching, are likely to be more autonomous, creative, and complex in their thinking; more open, less self-conscious, and less self-absorbed; and more resistant to pressure for conformity than adolescents who have not achieved a clear sense of identity. They manifest greater

control over their impulses. They also exhibit greater capacity for intimacy, tend to be happy and extroverted, and experience a more confident sexual identity, a more positive self-concept, and more mature moral reasoning. Although their relationships with their parents are generally positive, they have typically achieved considerable independence from their families (Adams, Abraham, & Markstrom, 1987; Clancy & Dollinger, 1993; Cooper & Grotevant, 1987; Dellas & Jernigan, 1990; Marcia, 1980).

Young women and men who have achieved a clear sense of identity usually have weighed a variety of occu-

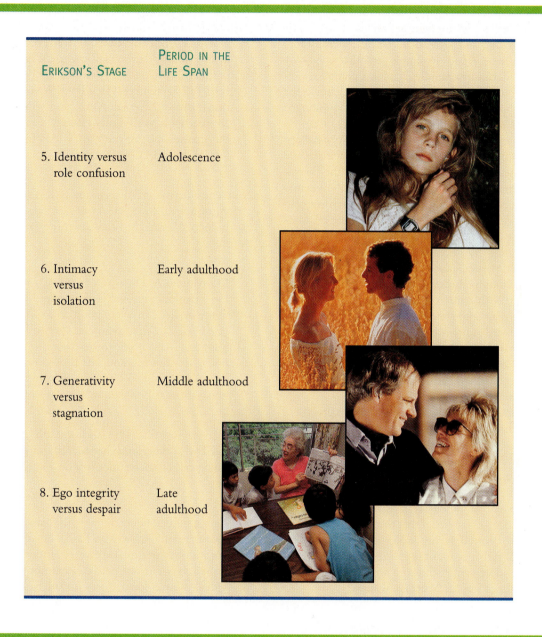

| Erikson's Stage | Period in the Life Span |
|---|---|
| 5. Identity versus role confusion | Adolescence |
| 6. Intimacy versus isolation | Early adulthood |
| 7. Generativity versus stagnation | Middle adulthood |
| 8. Ego integrity versus despair | Late adulthood |

pational and ideological options and arrived at conclusions to which they are committed. They feel positively about school and have higher grades (Vondracek, 1994; Wallace-Broscious, Serafica, & Osipow, 1994).

## Variations in Identity Formation

Thus far we have discussed identity formation as though it were a single task at which a young person either suc-

ceeds or fails. In reality the matter is more complex. One's identity status may change over time. Indeed, in early adolescence there may be a preponderance of identity foreclosures and identity confusions that eventually result in moratorium or identity achievements (Marcia, 1980). We all know examples of adults who have achieved identities through their careers or family lives, only to question their choices and lifestyles later on.

Patterns of identity formation may vary widely as a result of influences that range from parent–child relationships to cultural pressures and the rate of social

change (Archer & Waterman, 1990; Mussen et al., 1990). In a simpler society, where there are only a limited number of adult roles and little social change, identity formation may be a relatively simple task that is quickly accomplished. But in a rapidly changing, complex society such as our own, where there is so much choice, the search for identity can be difficult and prolonged (Conger, 1979; Erikson, 1968; Mussen et al., 1990).

Some authors have suggested that identity development may proceed somewhat differently for females and males. Whereas Erikson (1968) argued that the formation of intimate relations occurs only after the identity crisis has been resolved, some recent research suggests that among females, the formation of intimate relationships is more likely to accompany identity development (Dyk & Adams, 1990; Schiedel & Marcia, 1985).

Within a particular society, identities may be typical or deviant: Individuals may seek personal, social, and vocational roles that are expected and approved by society, or they may adopt more idiosyncratic roles. Some unusual roles are positive and constructive, as in the case of the artist or poet who marches to a different drummer; others are negative, as in the case of the long-term drug addict or career criminal (Conger & Petersen, 1984; Erikson, 1968).

It is important to keep in mind that the process of identity formation varies from one person to another. The popular stereotype of an acute and prolonged "identity crisis" is probably exaggerated. Indeed, Erikson himself was moved to ask, "Would so many of our youth act so openly confused and confusing if they did not *know* they were supposed to have an identity crisis?" (1968, pp. 18–19). The belief that the absence of a period of intense turmoil during adolescence portends later emotional disturbance is not supported by research findings; many adolescents achieve a strong sense of ego identity without serious "storm and stress."

**Self-Concept and Identity.** Adolescents have a much more sophisticated view of what is involved in a sense of self than younger children have. Whereas the self-descriptions of younger children tend to center on concrete characteristics, those of adolescents are likely to be more abstract and to include psychological characteristics, interpersonal relationships, self-evaluations, and conflicting feelings (Damon & Hart, 1988; Harter, 1990; Hill & Palmquist, 1978; Selman, 1980). Self-conceptions also become more differentiated and better organized during adolescence (Harter, 1992).

For example, note the concrete flavor of this 9-year-old boy's self-description, emphasizing his age, sex, physical characteristics, and likes and dislikes:

My name is Bruce C. I have brown eyes. I have brown hair. I have brown eyebrows. I'm nine years old. I LOVE! Sports. I have seven people in my family. I have great! eye site. I have lots! of friends. I live on 1923 Pinecrest Dr. I'm going on 10 in September. I'm a boy. I have a uncle that is almost 7 feet tall. My school is Pinecrest. My teacher is Mrs.V. I play Hockey! I'am almost the smartest boy in the class. I LOVE! food. I love fresh air. I LOVE School.

Now consider the self-description of this 11½-year-old girl. Although she, too, speaks of her likes, she stresses psychological characteristics and interpersonal relationships:

My name is A. I'm a human being. I'm a girl. I'm a truthful person. I'm not pretty. I do so-so in my studies. I'm a very good cellist. I'm a very good pianist. I'm a swimmer. I try to be helpful. I'm always ready to be friends with anybody. Mostly I'm good, but I lose my temper. I'm not well-liked by some girls and boys. I don't know if I'm liked by boys or not.

Finally, note how this 17-year-old twelfth-grader is preoccupied with describing her identity in terms of her psychological characteristics, moods, and ideological concerns:

I am a human being. I am a girl. I am an individual. I don't know who I am. I am a Pisces. I am a moody person. I am an ambitious person. I am a very curious person. I am not an individual. I am a loner. I am an American (God help me). I am a Democrat. I am a liberal person. I am a radical. I am a conservative. I am a pseudoliberal. I am an atheist. I am not a classifiable person [i.e., I don't want to be].

The authors of the study from which these descriptions are taken add, "Children describe where they live, what they look like, and what they do. Their self-concept seems somewhat shallow and undifferentiated, both from other people and from their environment. Adolescents, however, describe themselves in terms of their beliefs and personality characteristics, qualities which are more essential and intrinsic to the self and which produce a picture of the self that is sharp and unique" (Montemayor & Eisen, 1977, p. 318).

## The Role of the Family in Identity Development

An adolescent's freedom to explore a variety of possibilities in forming an individual identity is significantly influenced by relationships within the family (Cooper & Grotevant, 1987; Cooper, Grotevant, & Condon, 1983; Grotevant & Cooper, 1983, 1985; Kamptner, 1988; Marcia, 1980; Youniss & Smollar, 1985). One study of family interactions found that adolescents who scored high on a measure of identity exploration (they were actively considering a variety of options in terms of occupations, relationships, and political views) were more likely to come from families in which self-assertion and freedom to disagree (*separateness*) were encouraged along with *connectedness* to the family, including openness or responsiveness to the views of others (*plurality*) and sensitivity to and respect for the ideas of others (*mutuality*). In the words of one high-scoring participant, "I have a say but not a deciding vote in family decisions" (Cooper, Grotevant, & Condon, 1983, p. 54).

Adolescents who scored lower in identity exploration were more likely to come from families in which individuality was not encouraged and mutual support and agreement were emphasized. One low-scoring young woman, referring to her efforts to choose a career, said, "I'm having a hard time deciding what to do. It would be easier if they would tell me what to do, but of course I don't want that" (Cooper, Grotevant, & Condon, 1983, p. 55).

The findings of studies like this one are consistent with Erikson's view that people with a strong sense of identity perceive themselves as separate, distinct individuals. They also support the idea that openness and responsiveness to the views of others are important "because identity function requires the consideration, selection, and interpretation of possible sources of information about the self and others" (Cooper, Grotevant, & Condon, 1983, p. 53). These characteristics of family interaction facilitate access to such information.

## Gender Identity and Sex-Role Identity

An important aspect of identity is **gender identity,** an awareness and acceptance of one's basic biological nature as a male or a female. Most people acquire gender identity early in life (Huston, 1983; Mussen et al., 1990). With the notable exception of transsexuals (who typically report having felt, even as children, that they were trapped in a body of the wrong sex), the great majority of people, including most homosexuals, appear to be content with being male or female and have no desire to change (Green, 1987; Spence, 1985).

But for those who resent their gender—who are uncomfortable about their sexual nature and procreative capabilities or are hostile toward members of their own or the other sex—adolescence can be a particularly stressful and confusing period. Rapid sexual maturation calls dramatic attention to the fact that one's gender is a biological fact. Conflicts about gender identity are difficult to deal with and are likely to create significant problems in the development of a confident, secure overall identity.

Adolescents who are actively involved in pursuit of an individual identity are more likely to come from families that encourage self-assertion and the freedom to disagree, as well as respect for the ideas of others.

Another aspect of identity, **sex-role identity,** pertains to one's perceptions of oneself as masculine or feminine. Masculinity encompasses the characteristics (physical attributes, behaviors, feelings, attitudes, and beliefs) that typically are associated with maleness in a culture (such as being competitive) and femininity reflects the characteristics associated with femaleness (such as being caring). One's sex-role identity, then, is a reflection of the extent to which the individual adheres to **sex roles,** which are *societal* expectations regarding the appropriate behaviors for females (the feminine sex role) and males (the masculine sex role).

Sex roles, however, are currently in flux, thereby making the 1990s an interesting time in history for adolescents to be developing their sex-role identities. Challenges to traditional sex roles pervade North American culture, with issues such as women in the workplace, sexual harassment, and violence against women receiving much media attention. Indeed, nationally representative surveys conducted in Canada showed an *increase* from 1984 to 1992 in the percentage of teenagers viewing violence against women as a very serious concern. The level of concern was highest among adolescent women, even more than among adult women (see Table 2.2). This same survey found that 69 percent of female teens and 36 percent of male teens thought that women had "too little power" in the nation's affairs (Bibby & Posterski, 1992). These figures demonstrate the high degree of awareness of gender issues among adolescents, particularly females.

At the same time that there is a high level of awareness of these issues among teens, however, images in the media (e.g., on MTV) continue to promote stereotypes of males as aggressive and dominant and females as submissive and as sexual objects. How these conflicting images come to be represented in adolescents' definitions of masculinity and femininity and in their assumption of masculine and feminine characteristics is an issue of great interest.

Before the 1970s, many developmentalists believed that healthy psychological development was based on the assumption of traditional roles: Females should acquire culturally defined feminine characteristics to the exclusion of masculine characteristics and males should acquire only masculine characteristics. Psychologists in the 1970s, however, promoted the notion of **sex-role flexibility,** which is the ability to change one's behavior, regardless of gender, to meet the demands of differing situations (Bem, 1975; Hefner, Rebecca, & Oleshansky, 1975; Spence, 1985). In order to be flexible, one needs both socially valued masculine and feminine attributes, a sex-role identity that may be described as **androgynous.** Access to positive feminine *and* masculine behaviors enables one to function most effectively (Bem, 1975). The idea here is that the adolescent girl who feels comfortable not only in babysitting but in competing in math and science courses has access to a wider range of behaviors, choices, and options in life than does the girl who is not androgynous. The same principle applies to adolescent boys who might show sensitivity and concern in interpersonal relationships (traditionally feminine qualities) as well as competition on the baseball diamond (a traditionally masculine quality). As the distinction between feminine and masculine sex roles becomes more blurred because of changes at the societal level, presumably it will be easier for both adolescent girls and boys to behave more flexibly.

Interestingly, although contemporary writing in the sex-role literature places a high value on the acquisition of both feminine and masculine qualities, research suggests that from the perspective of the adolescent boy's psychosocial well-being, having masculine attributes is more important than is having feminine attributes (Markstrom-Adams, 1989). In adolescent boys, high

## Table 2.2 Growing Concern for Violence Against Women: Percentage Viewing Issue as "Very Serious"

| | TEENS | | ADULTS |
| --- | --- | --- | --- |
| | 1984 | 1992 | 1990 |
| Total | 46 | 58 | 38 |
| Females | 55 | 70 | 48 |
| Males | 36 | 44 | 28 |

SOURCE: R. W. Bibby, & D. C. Posterski (1992). *Teen trends: A nation in motion.* Toronto: Stoddart. By permission.

masculinity, but not high femininity, is related to high self-esteem and high peer acceptance. The results for girls are more in tune with contemporary theorizing about sex-role flexibility. Among girls, high levels of masculinity and femininity are important for self-esteem and peer acceptance; femininity alone is not associated with high adjustment (Lamke, 1982; Massad, 1981). Many people do vary from one situation, task, or setting to another in the extent to which they exhibit one or another gender-related psychological characteristic (Spence, 1985). *Positive* masculine attributes, such as independence and self-confidence, are the most important and adaptive components of androgyny, especially for females (Huston, 1983; Mullis & McKinley, 1989).

Further evidence of the salience of masculinity in boys' development was found in a longitudinal study examining how sex-role identity changes across early ado-lescence (Galambos, Almeida, & Petersen, 1990). In this study, while girls' *and* boys' femininity and masculinity increased from the sixth through the eighth grades, the increase in boys' masculinity was most noticeable. This increasing divergence between girls and boys in mascu-line characteristics provides support for the notion of **gender intensification.** The gender intensification hypothesis proposes that behavioral, attitudinal, and psy-chological differences between boys and girls increase across adolescence and are the result of strong socializa-tion pressures to conform to traditional masculine and feminine sex roles (Hill & Lynch, 1983). Although other research provides some support for the notion of gender intensification (Petersen, Sarigiani, & Kennedy, 1991; Roberts et al., 1990) much work is needed to elucidate the behaviors on which girls and boys become dissimilar and the processes by which this occurs.

# Summary

Adolescence is a period of rapid change—physical, sex-ual, and cognitive changes within the young person and changes in the adolescent's world and the demands of society. To help us understand these changes, we follow a *life-span developmental perspective* on human develop-ment. This perspective focuses attention on development as a *lifelong process,* a process in which the individual is open to change at any point in the life cycle. Another fundamental principle of the life-span perspective is that a person evolves as a result of *reciprocal interactions* between a growing, changing biological organism and its physi-cal, psychological, and social environment; that interac-tion begins in the earliest stages of prenatal development. Implicit in this principle is the concept of *antecedent–con-sequent relations*—the idea that events occurring at one stage of development depend on prior developmental events and, in turn, influence responses to future events. Because development is lifelong and takes place as a result of reciprocal interactions, the life-span perspective also leads us to consider development as *multidirectional.* That is, development may follow any one of multiple possible paths. Of course, the direction that is followed depends in part both on how the active individual evokes responses from his or her environment and how he or she shapes and selects environments.

The continuing interaction between the growing, changing individual and his or her environment is not random. It is governed by specific principles known as principles, or laws, of learning. *Learning* is the process by which behavior or the potential for behavior is modi-fied as a result of experience. Not all behaviors are learned, however; even some complex behaviors, such as nest building, are innately programmed.

Two basic kinds of learning are *classical conditioning* and *operant (instrumental) conditioning.* Among the more complex human applications of the latter are *behavior modification* and *behavior therapy.* Not all learning depends on conditioning; many human activities are acquired vicariously through observation of the behavior of oth-ers (*observational learning*), a fact that is stressed by social-learning theorists. Although some kinds of learning may not require a reward or *reinforcement,* reinforcement appears to play a significant role in many kinds of social learning. The principle of *generalization* states that when a response to one stimulus has been learned, it is likely to be evoked by similar stimuli.

Cognitive psychologists stress the importance of cognitive processes in learning; these include processing information, using problem-solving strategies, and stor-ing information in memory and retrieving it.

Insight into adolescent behavior also requires an understanding of *motivation,* which refers to the needs, goals, and desires that provoke an individual to action (including both *primary* and *learned* needs). Adolescents' needs and motives are far more complex than the basic biological needs of the infant, and in some instances they may be unconscious or only partially conscious.

We need to consider also the effects of *stress* on ado-lescent behavior. Manifested in psychological (e.g., depression, anxiety), physiological (e.g., increased heart

rate), or symptomatic (e.g., illness) responses, stress arises from *negative life events,* such as a parental divorce, and *ongoing life stressors.* Sources of ongoing life stress in adolescence may include troubled relations with parents, financial difficulties, problems with physical health, difficult relations with siblings, interpersonal problems with extended family, difficulties in school, trouble with friends, and difficulties in relations with a boyfriend or girlfriend. In order to cope with stress, adolescents may resort to *emotion-focused* and *problem-focused coping.* Emotion-focused techniques are attempts to reduce anxiety in an indirect manner, and include unconscious *defense mechanisms* such as repression and denial. Problem-focused coping is when the individual deals directly with the stressful situation by analyzing and confronting it. Adolescents who more frequently use problem-focused coping show better psychosocial adjustment than those who use emotion-focused methods. Of course, the ability to cope depends in part on the availability of *social* and *personal resources.*

Some challenges that adolescents must cope with are nearly universal. These challenges, which must be mastered if adolescents are to function successfully, are called *developmental tasks.* One of the central developmental tasks is to develop a sense of *identity*—to answer the age-old question, "Who am I?" Individuals with a strong sense of identity perceive themselves as separate from others, they possess self-consistency or a feeling of wholeness, and they have a sense of continuity of the self over time. The development of identity is aided by *psychosocial reciprocity,* or consistency between one's self-perceptions and the way one is perceived and treated by others.

Identity has its roots in childhood identification, but patterns of childhood identifications are not by themselves sufficient to provide adolescents with a clear, stable sense of identity. Something more is needed: *the capacity to synthesize successive identifications into a coherent, consistent, and unique whole*—a capacity aided by the adolescent's more advanced cognitive skills. As the ability to think more abstractly increases, self-conceptions become more differentiated and better organized during adolescence.

Identity formation is significantly influenced by relationships within the family. Adolescents who score high on measures of *identity exploration* are likely to come from families in which self-assertion and freedom to disagree (*separateness*) are encouraged along with *connectedness* to the family. Two important ways in which identity development can go wrong are *identity foreclosure,* in which identity development is prematurely cut short, and *identity confusion,* in which the development of a clear sense of identity is delayed, in some cases permanently. Individuals who have achieved a strong sense of identity (*identity achievement*) are likely to be more autonomous, creative, resistant to pressure for conformity, and capable of intimacy than those who experience identity foreclosure or identity confusion.

An important aspect of identity is *gender identity,* which is awareness and acceptance of one's basic biological nature as a male or a female. Sex-role identity pertains to one's perceptions of oneself as masculine or feminine. Individuals who have both positive masculine and positive feminine characteristics are *androgynous.* Androgyny contributes to *sex-role flexibility,* which is the ability to change one's behavior, regardless of gender, to meet the demands of varied situations. In adolescence, behavioral, attitudinal, and psychological differences between boys and girls may increase as a result of strong socialization pressures to conform to traditional masculine and feminine sex roles, a developmental pattern called *gender intensification.*

# Review Questions

1. What are the key assumptions of the life-span developmental perspective?

2. What kinds of learning are there? How might the principles of learning be applied to changing behaviors?

3. What is stress, and what are the important sources of stress in adolescence?

4. Describe two main types of coping techniques. Which category includes defense mechanisms?

5. What is meant by the term *identity*? Distinguish between identity foreclosure, identity confusion, and identity achievement. What is meant by a psychosocial moratorium?

6. What kinds of parent–adolescent relations foster a sense of identity?

7. Distinguish between gender identity and sex-role identity. What is the gender intensification hypothesis?

# Recommended Readings

Baltes, P. B. (1987). Theoretical propositions of life-span developmental psychology: On the dynamics between growth and decline. *Developmental Psychology, 23,* 611–626.

Block, J. H. (1984). *Sex role identity and ego development.* San Francisco: Jossey-Bass.

Compas, B. E. (1987). Coping with stress during childhood and adolescence. *Psychological Bulletin, 101,* 393–403.

Erikson, E. H. (1968). *Identity: Youth and crisis.* New York: Norton.

Harter, S. (1990). Self and identity development. In S. S. Feldman & G. R. Elliott (Eds.), *At the threshold: The developing adolescent* (pp. 352–387). Cambridge, MA: Harvard University Press.

Miller, N. E. (1984). Learning: Some facts and needed research relevant to maintaining health. In J. Matarazzo, S. W. Weiss, J. A. Herd, N. Miller, & S. M. Weiss (Eds.), *Behavioral health: A handbook of health enhancement and disease prevention* (pp. 199–208). New York: Wiley.

# Biological Changes
# 3 in Adolescence

adolescence, it has been said, begins in biology and ends in culture. The biological changes that accompany adolescence are inevitable and dramatic. They include rapid increases in height and weight, maturation in the reproductive system, changes in body proportions, and the emergence of secondary sex characteristics such as pubic hair. These biological changes and the young person's need to adjust to them differentiate adolescence from earlier periods of development. In contrast, culture determines whether adolescence is long or short and whether its social demands represent an abrupt change or only a gradual transition from earlier periods of development.

The culture of a society may facilitate or hinder the young person's adjustment to the biological changes of puberty. It also influences whether these changes are a source of pride or of anxiety and confusion. But culture cannot change the fact that these changes occur and must be coped with somehow. Moreover, were it not for the biological maturation that occurs during adolescence, young people would not be able to meet many of the demands made on them in most cultures— whether the demands are for academic competence, for physical or vocational skills, or for heterosexual relationships, marriage, and parenthood.

For all of these reasons, as well as the fact that development results from the interaction between a biological organism and its environment, it is important to consider in some detail the nature of the biological changes that accompany adolescence and their effects on the individual. In this chapter we are concerned primarily with physical and physiological development—the external and internal aspects of biological development. Later we will consider intellectual and cognitive development (Chapter 4) and the psychological and behavioral consequences of sexual maturity (Chapter 6).

## Puberty

The term **puberty** refers to a process of change in the first phase of adolescence, when sexual maturation becomes evident. Strictly speaking, puberty begins with hormonal increases and their manifestations, such as

gradual enlargement of the ovaries in females and testicular cell growth in males. Because these changes are not outwardly observable, the onset of puberty is often measured by observing the development of secondary sex characteristics (visible bodily changes) such as the emergence of pubic hair in boys and girls, the beginning of elevation of the breasts in girls, and growth of the penis and testicles in boys. Another major aspect of puberty is an accelerated increase in height and weight that usually lasts about four years.

## Hormonal Factors in Development

As we shall see, the timing and course of the various developmental phenomena that surround puberty—such as the so-called growth spurt and sexual maturation—are closely related (Tanner, 1991). This is not surprising in view of the fact that hormones from the endocrine glands are among the principal agents "for translating the instructions of the genes into the reality of the adult form" (Tanner, 1970, p. 112; also see Kulin, 1991a). The actions of these hormones in stimulating physical growth, sexual maturation, and other physiological aspects of development are themselves interrelated.

The **pituitary gland,** located immediately below the brain, is critical to the orderly regulation of growth. When the cells of the hypothalamus, a central regulating nerve center in the brain, mature, signals are sent to the pituitary gland to begin releasing certain **hormones** (Higham, 1980; Petersen, 1988; Petersen & Taylor, 1980). These hormones, in turn, stimulate other endocrine glands, including the thyroid and adrenal glands and the testes and ovaries, to release specific growth- and sex-related hormones. The latter include **androgens** (masculinizing hormones), **estrogens** (feminizing hormones), and **progestins** (pregnancy hormones). These and other hormones interact in complex ways to stimulate the orderly progression of physical and physiological development during puberty and adolescence. For example, the development of pubic and other body hair is linked to the production of adrenal androgens, and the development of fluctuating levels of estrogen and progesterone is involved in **menarche** (the onset of menstruation) (Bell, 1988; Money & Ehrhardt, 1972).

## The Timing of Puberty

Exactly *when* puberty begins depends on a variety of factors, not all of which are understood. Genetic influences obviously play a role; for example, the onset of puberty and subsequent events, such as menarche, occur closer together among identical (monozygotic) twins than among nonidentical (dizygotic) twins. Within the limits set by heredity, environmental influences—especially nutrition and health—are also important. Puberty occurs earlier among young people who have been well nourished throughout their development; chronic illness and hazardous living conditions are also associated with delayed puberty (Eveleth & Tanner, 1990).

There are also some geographic and ethnic differences in the timing of puberty; for example, African girls living in Africa experience menarche later than do girls living in the United States who are either of European or African descent. However, when variations in general health and nutrition between and within countries are taken into account, such differences are significantly reduced or eliminated (see Figure 3.1) (Eveleth & Tanner, 1978, 1990; Tanner, 1991).

## Sex Differences in Hormones

In the early days of sex hormone research, when sex differences were thought to be absolute, it was assumed that females produce only female sex hormones and males only male sex hormones. In reality, however, the hormones of both sexes are present in both men and women (Petersen & Taylor, 1980). These hormones, which are similar in chemical structure, are produced in the ovaries or testes, the cortex of the adrenal gland, or other glands or tissues. The hormonal differences between the sexes, and corresponding differences in sexual characteristics, are actually differences in the proportions of masculinizing and feminizing hormones present in males and females. As puberty proceeds, the ratio of estrogen to testosterone increases in girls and decreases in boys.

## The Adolescent Growth Spurt

**Height and Weight.** The **adolescent growth spurt** is the accelerated rate of increase in height and weight that accompanies the onset of adolescence. This increase varies widely in intensity, duration, and timing from one child to another, even among entirely normal children—a fact that is often poorly understood by adolescents and their parents and, hence, too often a source of needless concern.

In both boys and girls, the growth spurt takes about 4½ years (Malina, 1991; Tanner, 1991; Thissen et al., 1976). For the average boy in the United States, peak growth occurs at age 13; in girls it occurs about two years earlier, at age 11. Whereas in the average boy the adolescent growth spurt begins a few months before his eleventh birthday, it may begin as early as age 9; the spurt usually ends shortly after age 15, but it may continue

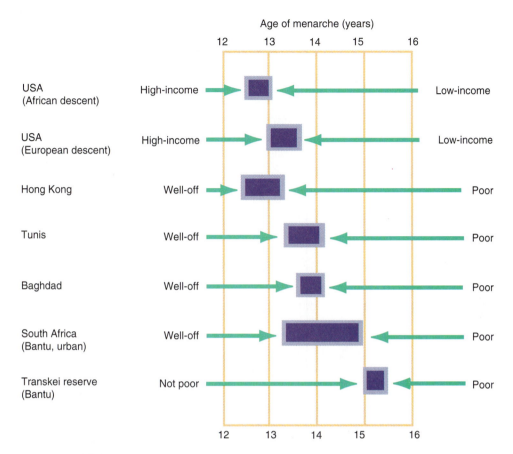

# Figure 3.1

Median ages of menarche in well–off and poor population samples. Shaded areas show difference between median ages in each geographic area. From P. B. Eveleth & J. M. Tanner (1978). *Worldwide variation in human growth.* Cambridge: Cambridge University Press. Reprinted with the permission of Cambridge University Press.

until age 17. In girls the entire process begins, and ends, about two years earlier. Further slow growth may continue for several years after the spurt has ended (see Figure 3.2).

The timing of the growth spurt is so variable that some adolescents complete the spurt before others have begun. Figure 3.3 illustrates how widely the onset, pattern, and end of the growth spurt can vary among normal adolescent girls; the early maturer's spurt ended a year before the late maturer's began. Clearly, *normal* includes large differences in timing.

Events occurring within the normal growth spurt are not independent of one another. For example, girls with an early growth spurt tend to reach menarche earlier than those with a later growth spurt (Faust, 1977; Petersen, 1979). Similarly, in boys the period of most rapid growth tends to be closely related to the development of secondary sex characteristics such as underarm hair and pubic hair.

Timing of the adolescent growth spurt varies widely from one young person to another. Some adolescents complete the growth spurt before others have begun.

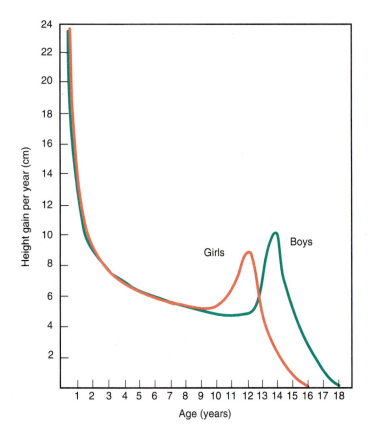

## Figure 3.2

The growth spurt in height in boys and girls. These curves represent the velocity of the typical boy or girl at any given instant. From J. M. Tanner, R. H. Whitehouse, & M. Takaishi (1966). Standards from birth to maturing for height velocity, and weight velocity: British children, 1965. *Archives of Disease in Childhood,* **41,** 455–471. By permission.

One matter that is likely to generate concern in adolescents and their parents is ultimate height (Conger, 1979). This may be especially true of boys who are short and girls who are tall. Much of this concern is exaggerated, however. Height before the growth spurt is correlated with ultimate height, which means, for example, that a young person who is in the twenty-fifth percentile in height before the growth spurt is likely to be in the twenty-fifth percentile after puberty. Girls who are early maturers tend to be somewhat shorter at the onset of puberty than late maturers, but they also grow more rapidly during the growth spurt and their growth spurt tends to be longer. Conversely, late maturers tend to be somewhat taller at the beginning of the growth spurt, but they also tend to have shorter, less intense periods of growth. The net result is that early maturers as a group do not end up any taller or shorter than girls who mature later. Once an early-maturing girl and her late-maturing peers have passed the period of rapid growth, their comparative heights are most likely to resemble those of the period before adolescence. Similar developmental phenomena occur in boys (Faust, 1977; Tanner, 1970, 1991).

Increases in weight tend to follow the general curve for height in both males and females, but there are some differences. Although increased weight obviously reflects skeletal growth, it also reflects increases in muscle and fat tissue and in the size of various internal organs. Because weight is so subject to the effects of diet and exercise, it is not as informative a measure of physical maturation as height. Genetic factors appear to play a major role in determining height and weight, but environmental conditions such as malnutrition, disease, and severe psychological stress also affect growth rate, final height, and (to a lesser extent) body shape (Eichorn, 1975; Eveleth & Tanner, 1990).

**Skeletal Changes.** Rapid acceleration in height and weight is accompanied by changes in body proportions in both males and females. Although changes in the skeletal and muscular systems are part of the growth spurt, they develop according to different timetables. The parts of the body that reach adult size and form earliest are the head, hands, and feet. Increases in the length of arms and legs reach their peak before increases in body width (including shoulder width). Adult trunk length is achieved last, although it accounts for the greatest proportion of the total increase in height during the growth spurt. The effect is that "a boy stops growing out of his trousers (at least in length) a year before he stops growing out of his jackets" (Tanner, 1970, p. 94).

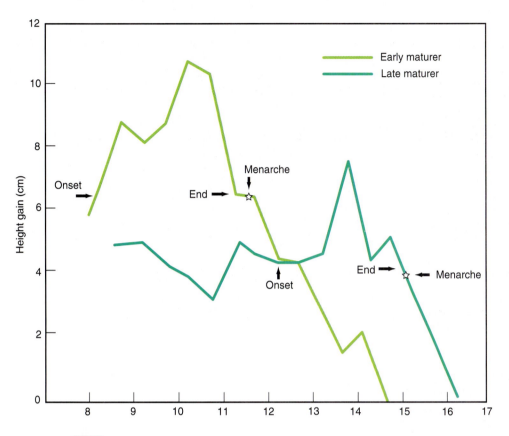

## Figure 3.3

Differences in timing of the pubertal growth period in height. The early-maturing girl reached the end of the pubertal period before the late-maturing girl reached onset. From M. S. Faust (1977). Somatic development of adolescent girls. *Monographs of the Society for Research in Child Development,* **42,** 1, Serial No. 169. By permission.

The disparate rates of growth in the various parts of the skeletal structure (which are even more varied in some atypical young people) often produce feelings of awkwardness. Adolescents may feel at times that their hands and feet are too big or that they are "all legs."

More subtle changes in physique also occur during this period. The last traces of the baby face of childhood disappear. The forehead becomes higher and wider; the mouth widens, and the relatively flat lips of childhood become fuller; the slightly receding chin of earlier years begins to jut out (Mussen, Conger, & Kagan, 1979; Tanner, 1991). Of course, as head growth diminishes while other parts of the skeletal system continue to grow, the large head that is characteristic of childhood becomes smaller in relation to total body size (see Figure 3.4).

Changes such as those just described reflect the fact that as skeletal structures increase in length they also change in width, proportions, and composition. Bone width, as well as length, increases during this period. The composition of the skeletal structure also changes. During early childhood the bones have relatively more cartilage and fibrous tissues and less mineral matter than they have later. This makes the bones somewhat spongy and soft as well as more flexible. But as the skeletal structures increase in size, the cartilage begins to calcify, making the bones harder, denser, and more brittle (Eveleth & Tanner, 1990).

Another change occurs in the ratio of shoulder width to hip width. Before puberty this ratio is higher for girls than for boys, but the picture reverses dramatically soon after the beginning of the growth spurt. The extent of this difference continues to increase until adult height is reached. However, variability in hip width is significantly greater among girls than among boys at all stages of development (Faust, 1977; Eveleth & Tanner, 1990).

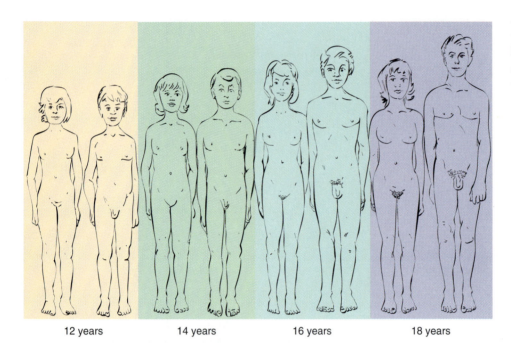

Figure **3.4**
Body growth and
development from age
12 to age 18.

12 years        14 years        16 years        18 years

During the adolescent growth spurt, boys experience a more rapid rate of muscular development than girls. Consequently, their overall gain in muscle tissue is greater than that of girls.

**Muscle and Fat.** Changes in adolescent physique reflect changes in the development of muscle and body fat as well as changes in skeletal structure. In both boys and girls muscular development proceeds rapidly as height increases, reaching a peak rate of growth slightly after the peak in the rate of increase in height. Boys experience a more rapid rate of increase than girls do, with the result that their overall gain in muscle tissue during this period is greater than that for girls, a difference that is maintained throughout the adult years (Neinstein, 1984; Tanner, 1970, 1991).

Conversely, in both boys and girls there is a decline in the *rate* of development of fat during the growth spurt—a decline that reaches its maximum velocity at the point of maximum increase in height. In girls the decline is not enough to offset a modest absolute gain in fat during this period. In boys, however, the rate of decline is so great that it produces an actual (though temporary) loss of fat in the months preceding and following the point of peak increase in height.

Although both muscle and fat are influenced by the sex hormones, they are also influenced by exercise, an activity that may differ in boys and girls. Studies that control for amount of exercise still find male–female differences in the percentage of body weight due to fat, but the differences are much smaller than those found in the population as a whole (Woods et al., 1977).

**Strength and Tolerance for Exercise.** The acceleration of muscular development that takes place during

In the past some of the greater strength and tolerance for exercise found among boys were due to more physical exercise among boys than among girls, as a result of cultural pressures.

adolescence is, not surprisingly, accompanied by increases in strength, as measured by such indices as hand grip and pulling and pushing strength in the arms (Faust, 1977). On average, the greatest overall increase in strength occurs about one year after the peak increase in height and weight. The relative increases are much greater for boys than for girls, although the distribution of overall strength scores (arm pull, arm thrust, hand grip) of boys and girls overlaps at every point in development. For the most part, prepubescent boys and girls are similar in strength, but after adolescence boys are much stronger. This greater strength is primarily a function of greater muscular development; however, it is probably due partly to certain related factors as well. Relative to their size, boys develop larger lungs and heart, higher systolic blood pressure, greater capacity for carrying oxygen in the blood, lower heart rate while at rest, and greater ability to neutralize the chemical products of muscular exercise, such as lactic acid, which is felt as fatigue (Tanner, 1970, 1991). It seems likely that some of the greater increase in strength and tolerance for exercise among boys is due to more physical exercise, since there may be cultural pressure on girls to decrease such "masculine" activity at adolescence (Freedland & Dwyer, 1991). A recent report of the U.S. Centers for Disease Control and Prevention found that only 25 percent of females in their senior year in high school exercised regularly, whereas 50 percent of

male high school seniors did so. Such poor rates of physical activity may well pose health problems in adulthood, and the outlook for adolescent women is particularly dim (Steinhauer, 1995).

Exercise to maintain physical fitness is extremely important for adolescents of both sexes. Unfortunately, adolescents in the United States today may be less fit than their counterparts of only a decade ago. One study found that in 1984, about two-thirds of adolescents exercised vigorously. By 1990, this figure had dropped to just over a third (Steinhauer, 1995). Additionally, through the 1970s the percentage of overweight adolescents in the United States, ages twelve to nineteen, held steady at about fifteen percent. By 1991, however, that rate increased to twenty-one percent (National Center for Health Statistics, 1994). Too much time spent in front of the television, the failure of schools to provide enough vigorous physical exercise, the wide availability of high-fat food, and poor examples set by parents may share in the blame for decreasing levels of adolescent fitness at a time when public awareness of the importance of good health, nutrition, and exercise may be at an all-time high (Parcel et al., 1987; Steinhauer, 1995; Tucker, 1987).

## Other Aspects of Adolescent Growth

While the visible aspects of the growth spurt, such as increased height and weight and changes in muscle and fat, are taking place, other less readily apparent but equally important changes are also occurring. As already noted, a number of these changes, though related to the onset and course of the rapid increase in height, have their own timetables within the overall developmental sequence.

**Growth of the Heart.** During the adolescent years, the heart's transverse diameter increases by about half and its weight almost doubles. The total growth is not as great for girls as it is for boys, however, so that by late adolescence boys have significantly larger hearts than girls do (Litt & Vaughn, 1987). The heart rate in boys and girls falls gradually during the entire period of growth, with the decline during adolescence slightly faster for boys, so that by age 17 the average boy's heart rate is about 5 beats per minute slower than the average girl's (Eichorn, 1970; Neinstein, 1984).

Conversely, systolic blood pressure rises steadily throughout childhood, accelerating rapidly during the years immediately before puberty and for about six

months thereafter. It then tends to settle at a somewhat lower level; sexual maturity apparently stabilizes the upward trend of blood pressure. The pulse rate also increases during the prepubescent years, reaching a maximum before puberty and declining thereafter (Behrman, Vaughn, & Nelson, 1987).

**Growth of the Lungs.** Lung growth is similar to heart growth. The steady, gradual increase of the childhood years gives way to a rapid acceleration during the years of maximum growth in boys and girls; the greatest growth occurs in boys. On measures of vital capacity (the amount of air that can be exhaled after a deep breath), boys exceed girls up until about 10 years of age, at which point there is no significant difference between the two. However, beginning at about 11½, boys again exceed girls, and the difference continues to increase throughout the growth years as a function both of boys' larger hearts and of their typically greater amount of exercise (Ferris, Whittenberger, & Gallagher, 1952; Litt & Vaughn, 1987).

**Development of the Brain.** In contrast to the marked increases in the heart and lungs that accompany adolescence, there is little further growth in the size of the brain during this period. Whereas the average child has acquired only about 50 percent of total adult weight by the age of 10, he or she has acquired 95 percent of adult brain weight (Litt & Vaughn, 1987; Neinstein, 1984).

Neural changes continue to occur, however (Graber & Petersen, 1991). **Myelination** (the development of a fatty sheath around certain nerve fibers) facilitates rapid transmission of neural impulses. This process continues at least to puberty and may be lifelong (Yakoler & Lecours, 1967). Recent evidence suggests that overproduction of neural pathways occurs from age 5 to age 10, with a significant decline from age 10 to age 15; this decline is thought to reflect fine-tuning of the neurological system (Feinberg, 1987).

**Basal Metabolism.** Another change occurring during this period is a rather sudden decline in basal metabolism (the energy turnover of the body at a standard low level of activity). Although both boys and girls show a continuous decrease in metabolic rate following puberty, boys retain a higher rate than girls do, probably partly as a function of greater muscular development, which requires greater consumption of oxygen, and perhaps also because of hormonal differences between boys and girls (Tanner, 1971, 1991).

**Nutritional Needs.** The nutritional needs of the young person during the years of accelerated growth increase considerably, although there is a wide variation from one individual to another. On the average, young people gain 50 percent of their adult weight, 20 percent of their adult height, and 50 percent of their adult skeletal mass during adolescence (Litt & Vaughn, 1987; Neinstein, 1984). For this reason, and because dietary habits formed in adolescence are likely to continue into adulthood, it is important for adolescents to learn sound nutritional practices. As can be seen in Table 3.1, the nutritional needs of the average boy consistently exceed those of the average girl, although sex differences are far greater following the growth spurt owing primarily to size differences (Neinstein, 1984).

Severe undernutrition in infancy has been found to have long-term effects on development that continue through adolescence (Eveleth & Tanner, 1990). Interestingly, effects on physical growth can be corrected, but

## Table 3.1 Recommended Daily Dietary Allowances (Calories)

|         | AGE   | WEIGHT (LB.) | HEIGHT (IN.) | CALORIES |
|---------|-------|--------------|--------------|----------|
| Boys    | 11–14 | 99           | 61           | 2700     |
|         | 15–18 | 145          | 69           | 2800     |
|         | 19–22 | 154          | 69           | 2800     |
| Girls   | 11–14 | 101          | 61           | 2200     |
|         | 15–18 | 121          | 64           | 2200     |
|         | 19–22 | 121          | 64           | 2200     |

SOURCES: National Academy of Sciences, National Research Council (1980). *Recommended dietary allowances* (9th ed.). Washington, DC: Author; Alton, 1982; Neinstein, 1984.

behavioral and cognitive effects persist even after adequate nutrition has been restored (Lozoff, 1989; Petersen, Susman, & Beard, 1989).

# Sexual Maturation

The adolescent growth spurt is accompanied by sexual maturation in both boys and girls. The rapidity of all these changes—most of which take place within a period of only about four years—may give young people a feeling of being spectators of their own growth and development. Many adolescents seem to be waiting, sometimes self-consciously, to find out what will happen next.

## Sexual Maturation in Boys

Although testicular cell growth and secretion of male sex hormones begin earlier—typically about 11½ (Litt & Vaughn, 1987; Neinstein, 1984)—the first outward sign of impending sexual maturity in boys is usually an increase in the rate of growth of the testes and scrotum (see Table 3.2). Growth of pubic hair may also begin at about the same time or shortly thereafter. Approximately

# Table 3.2  Maturation in Boys and in Girls

Although there may be some individual—and perfectly normal—variations in the sequence of events leading to physical and sexual maturity in boys, the following sequence is typical:

1. Testes and scrotum begin to increase in size.

2. Pubic hair begins to appear.

3. Adolescent growth spurt starts; the penis begins to enlarge.

4. Voice deepens as the larynx grows.

5. Hair begins to appear under the arms and on the upper lip.

6. Sperm production increases, and nocturnal emission (ejaculation of semen during sleep) may occur.

7. Growth spurt reaches peak rate; pubic hair becomes pigmented.

8. Prostate gland enlarges.

9. Sperm production becomes sufficient for fertility; growth rate decreases.

10. Physical strength reaches a peak.

Although, as in the case of boys, there may be normal variations in the sequence of physical and sexual maturation in girls, a typical sequence of events is as follows:

1. Adolescent growth spurt begins.

2. Downy (nonpigmented) pubic hair makes its initial appearance.

3. Elevation of the breast (the so-called bud stage of development) and rounding of the hips begin, accompanied by the appearance of downy axillary (armpit) hair.

4. The uterus and vagina, as well as the labia and clitoris, increase in size.

5. Pubic hair grows rapidly and becomes slightly pigmented.

6. Breasts develop further; nipple pigmentation begins; areola increases in size; axillary hair becomes slightly pigmented.

7. Growth spurt reaches peak rate and then declines.

8. Menarche (onset of menstruation) occurs.

9. Pubic hair development is completed, followed by mature breast development and completion of axillary hair development.

10. Period of "adolescent sterility" ends; girl becomes capable of conception (up to a year or so after menarche).

a year later an acceleration in the rate of growth of the penis accompanies the beginning of the growth spurt in height. Body hair (underarm) and facial hair usually make their first appearance about two years after the beginning of pubic-hair growth, although the relationship between the two is variable and in a few boys body hair actually appears first (Neinstein, 1984; Tanner, 1971, 1991). The ultimate amount of body hair developed by both males and females appears to depend largely on genetic factors.

Although the process begins earlier, a definite lowering of the voice usually occurs fairly late in puberty. In some boys this voice change is rather abrupt and dramatic, whereas in others it occurs so gradually that it is hardly perceptible. During this process the larynx (Adam's apple) enlarges significantly and the vocal cords (which it contains) approximately double in length, with a consequent drop in pitch of about an octave. It may take two or more years for a boy to achieve control of his voice in the lower register, and during that time the instability of his vocal tones may become a source of embarrassment.

The insensitivity of adults who tease boys about these changes, even in a friendly manner, is obvious. The first shave may be a welcome sign of adulthood or an embarrassing experience for a boy, depending on whether his parents treat it as a matter of course or poke fun at him (Conger, 1979).

During adolescence the male breast also undergoes changes. The diameter of the areola (the area surrounding the nipple) increases considerably (although not as much as in girls) and is accompanied by elevation of the nipple. In some boys (perhaps 20–30 percent) there may also be a distinct enlargement of the breast about midway through adolescence (Bell, 1988; Tanner, 1970); this usually disappears within a year or so. Although this enlargement is usually temporary and is quite normal, its superficial resemblance to female breast development can be a source of needless anxiety to the boy and his parents.

## Sexual Maturation in Girls

Although hormonal stimulation of the sex glands begins earlier, at about age 9 or 10 the appearance of unpigmented, downy pubic hair is usually the first outward sign of sexual maturity in girls (Harlan, Harlan, & Grillo, 1980). However, in about 20 percent of girls the beginning of elevation of the breasts (the so-called bud stage of breast development) may precede the appearance of pubic hair (Brooks-Gunn & Reiter, 1990). Budding of the breasts is accompanied by the emergence of downy, unpigmented body hair and by increases in estrogen

secretion. In the following year the uterus and vagina show accelerated growth; the labia and clitoris also enlarge (Petersen & Taylor, 1980). Pubic hair becomes moderately well developed, and vaginal secretion begins. By age 12 the nipples show pigmentation and the breasts show further development toward their mature form. At about 12½ (i.e., fairly late in the developmental sequence) the first menstruation occurs. By this time, most girls are in the final stages of pubic-hair development and are approaching the final stages of breast and axillary-hair development.

Often there is a period that may last up to a year and a half following the beginning of menstruation, during which the adolescent girl is not yet physiologically capable of conception. Similarly, boys are able to have intercourse long before the emergence of live spermatozoa (Kulin, 1991b). However, because of significant individual differences, sexually active adolescents cannot assume that they are "safe" from conception because of their age. Some girls are capable of conception within the first year after menarche.

## Normal Variations in Development

It should be emphasized that the average developmental sequences for boys and girls discussed here are just that: *average*. Among normal boys and girls there are wide variations in the age of onset of the developmental sequence, as well as significant, though generally much smaller, variations in the interrelationships among events within the sequence (Eichorn, 1975). For example, whereas maturation of the penis may be complete in some boys by age 13½, for others it may not be complete until 17 or even later. Pubic-hair development may vary even more. The bud stage of breast development may occur as early as age 8 in some girls and as late as 13 in others (Tanner, 1970, 1991). Age of menarche may vary from about 9 to 16½ (see Box 3.1). The great differences in rates of development that occur among normal boys and girls are illustrated in Figure 3.5, which shows the differing degrees of pubertal maturity among three normal boys, all aged 14¾, and three normal girls, all aged 12¾.

As we have noted, the age of onset of the developmental sequence may vary widely. There is also some variation within individual sequences in the order in which various developmental changes occur. For example, in most girls, breast-budding begins before the appearance of pubic hair. This sequence is reversed, however, in 20 percent of girls. Such variations in sequencing also occur in boys (Petersen & Taylor, 1980; Brooks-Gunn & Reiter, 1990).

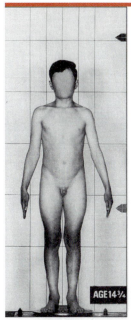
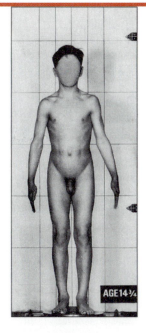
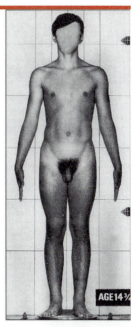
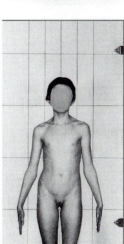
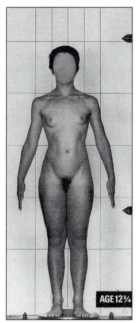
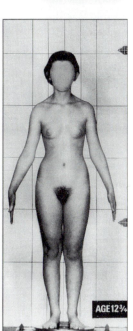

## Figure 3.5

Different degrees of pubertal development at the same chronological age.
Upper row: three boys, all age 14¾.
Lower row: three girls, all age 12¾.
From J. M. Tanner (1975). Growth and endocrinology of the adolescent. In J. J. Gardner (Ed.), *Endocrine and genetic diseases of childhood* (2nd ed.). Philadelphia: Saunders.
By permission.

# Psychological Aspects of Adolescent Growth and Development

As discussed in Chapter 2, a central problem of the adolescent period is the development of a sense of identity. This requires, among other things, a feeling of consistency over time—of being similar to, and having consistent links with, the person one was yesterday and will be tomorrow. The adolescent is faced with rapid increases in height, changing body proportions, and the objective and subjective changes related to sexual maturation. All of these changes threaten the feeling of self-consistency, and the adolescent needs time to integrate them into a positive, self-confident personal identity.

Developmental changes and the need to adjust to them cause adolescents to focus on physical aspects of the self. However, the nature of that concern is influenced by a number of other factors. With the onset of

# 3.1 Will Age at Menarche Continue to Decrease?

During the past century there has been a trend toward earlier physical and sexual maturation among both boys and girls (see Figure B3.1). Does this mean, as a number of social scientists have concluded, that a relentless evolutionary trend is at work and that we can expect the average girl in the next century to begin menstruation at 9 or 10?

Fortunately, the answer is no. When age of menarche is compared across generations reared under nearly identical conditions, no dramatic downward trend in menarcheal age is found. Rather than being due to a continuing evolutionary trend, earlier maturation appears to be a result of general health and nutrition throughout the entire developmental period. For example, during World War II the age of menarche was significantly retarded in a number of European countries with temporarily inadequate diets.

Moreover, although good nutrition and health care and an optimal physical environment may accelerate maturation, it appears that they can do so only within the ultimate, genetically determined limits for a particular population. Current estimates of the biological limit for age of menarche for the *average* girl are around 12¼ years. Although we should be concerned about the recent "epidemic" of adolescent pregnancies, we are not likely to have to set up prenatal classes for 9-year-olds.

SOURCES: *A history of the study of human growth.* Cambridge, England: Cambridge University Press, 1981; A. F. Roche (Ed.). (1979). Secular trends in human growth, maturation, and development. *Monographs of the Society for Research in Child Development,* Serial No. 179; V. L. Bullough. (1981). Age at menarche: A misunderstanding. *Science,* **213,** 365–366.

adolescence and the shift from the family to the peer group as a major source of security and status, conformity to the behavior, appearance, and physical skills of peers becomes increasingly important. Like any group that is concerned about where it stands and where it is going, the adolescent peer group tends to be more harshly critical of deviation than groups that are more secure and confident in their social identity. Although there are signs of somewhat greater tolerance for diversity among some groups of young people today, deviance in rate of development and physical appearance can still be an agonizing experience for many adolescents, particularly younger ones (Conger, 1979).

In addition to feeling that they must conform to the norms of their peer group, adolescents tend to have idealized norms of physical appearance and skills that are based on cultural stereotypes of masculinity and femininity. Advertisements in popular magazines, for example, reflect stereotypes that bear little relationship to real people, yet adolescents yearn to resemble the bulky athletic men or the slim, usually underweight women portrayed. This is a difficult enough ideal for boys to obtain, but it is an impossible one for girls (Brooks-Gunn, 1988, 1991). As we have seen, among boys adolescent weight gain occurs primarily in muscle and lean tissue; in girls, however, the gain is mainly in fat tissue. Before puberty girls have 10–15 percent more fat than boys, but after puberty they have nearly twice as much (Marino & King, 1980). Thus, "whereas physical maturation brings boys closer to the masculine ideal, for most girls it means a development away from what is currently considered beautiful" (Striegel-Moore, Silberstein, & Rodin, 1986, p. 250).

Not surprisingly, both boys and girls are sensitive to, and often critical of, their changing physical selves (Petersen, 1988). Girls are more likely than boys to be dissatisfied with their appearance and body image—particularly in the early adolescent years (Brooks-Gunn, 1988; Striegel-Moore, Silberstein, & Rodin, 1986). Moreover, for girls, outward appearance and inner self-image are more closely linked than for boys. Girls are more likely than boys to interpret remarks about appearance such as

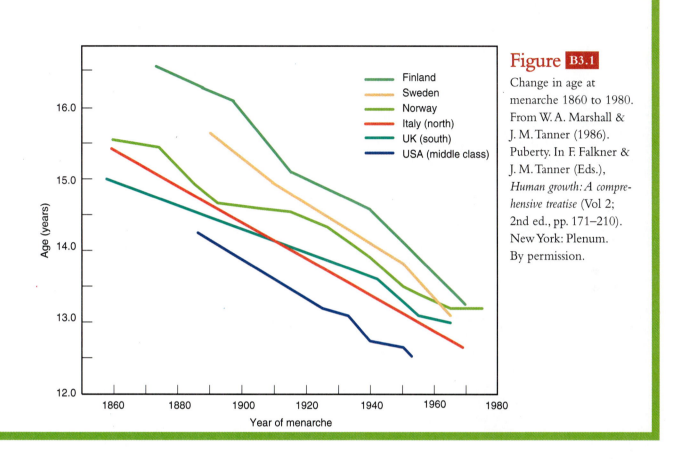

**Figure** **B3.1**

Change in age at menarche 1860 to 1980. From W. A. Marshall & J. M. Tanner (1986). Puberty. In F. Falkner & J. M. Tanner (Eds.), *Human growth: A comprehensive treatise* (Vol 2; 2nd ed., pp. 171–210). New York: Plenum. By permission.

"You look awful" to mean "You are awful." Despite recent changes in sex role concepts, which have resulted in more flexibility and greater allowance for individual differences, the average girl's self-esteem is still more anchored to interpersonal relationships than is the case for boys (Petersen, 1988). These findings may help explain why girls are somewhat more likely than boys to go through a period of lower self-esteem and more depressed feelings during early to middle adolescence, when maturational changes are greatest (Brooks-Gunn, 1988; Petersen, 1988; Simmons, Blyth, & McKinney, 1983).

It is important to note that self-perceptions are not always a result of objective realities. Adolescents' body image may be influenced by prior experiences that have led them to view themselves as attractive or unattractive, strong or weak, masculine or feminine—regardless of their actual appearance and capabilities. Thus, a boy with low self-esteem who is of average overall size and strength may view himself as smaller and weaker than he really is. A girl who is attractive in terms of cultural stereotypes may view herself as unattractive because she

has been told for years that she looks like a parent or other relative whom she resents or whom others have denigrated.

Whereas adolescents' perceptions of their physical appearance can be influenced by their general image of themselves as people—that is, their overall self-esteem or lack of it—the reverse can also occur. Unfair as it may seem, a young person who meets cultural standards of physical appearance and ability, and receives approval from peers and adults for these characteristics, may gain a better self-image in other respects as well (Lerner et al., 1991).

Finally, although conformity to cultural stereotypes regarding appearance may be a social asset, it may also present problems (Conger, 1979). Extremely attractive adolescents may receive special treatment that they have not earned; as a result, they may fail to recognize the need to establish competence in other areas of life. Being a high school queen or king, for instance, may be a very pleasant experience, but it does little to prepare one for the demands and stresses of adult life.

Illustrations of young people in popular magazines tend to reflect idealized cultural stereotypes of physical appearance (the broad-shouldered, athletic male and the slim, willowy female) that are difficult, if not impossible, for most adolescents to achieve.

## Psychological Aspects of Menstruation

To the adolescent girl, menstruation is much more than a physiological readjustment. It is a symbol of sexual maturity, of her future status as a woman. Because a girl's reaction to menstruation may generalize so broadly, it is vital that her initial experiences be positive (Brooks-Gunn & Ruble, 1983).

Increasing numbers of girls view the onset of menstruation calmly, and some look forward to it as a symbol of increased status (Brooks-Gunn & Ruble, 1983; Ruble & Brooks-Gunn, 1982). In the words of one adolescent girl, "It seemed that all my friends had gotten their period already, or were just having it. I felt left out. I began to think of it as a symbol. When I got my period, I would be a *woman*." Unfortunately, however, many other girls react negatively to this normal—and

inevitable—development. One study found that a majority of preadolescent and adolescent American girls view the effects of menstruation as either negative or at best neutral; only 39 percent of those surveyed expressed the view that it was something to be happy about. Most felt that menstruation "is something women just have to put up with" (Ruble & Brooks-Gunn, 1977).

Why do many adolescent girls react negatively to the onset of menstruation? One reason is the negative attitude of others. If a girl's parents and friends act as though she requires sympathy for her "plight"—an attitude that is reflected in euphemisms such as "the curse"—the girl is likely to react in a similar fashion. Another reason is lack of adequate preparation for menarche (Brooks-Gunn & Ruble, 1983; Rierdan, Koff, & Stubbs, 1989). If a mother or other caretaker waits until menstruation has actually begun before explaining its functions, the girl may be surprised and shocked by the sudden appearance of menstrual blood, believing that she has injured herself. Some girls have actually thought that they were dying:

> I didn't know what was happening. I had these cramps and a headache, so I went to the bathroom, but it wasn't like I had the flu or anything. I didn't know what I had. When I got up from the toilet I noticed this blood in there and then I saw some blood on my thigh, so I started to scream. I thought I was bleeding to death. Nobody told me about periods, nobody told me about anything (Bell, 1988, p. 32).

Fortunately, such events are much rarer today as a result of greater openness regarding sexual matters. However, researchers have found that premenarcheal girls still *expect* more menstrual difficulties than postmenarcheal girls of the same age actually *experience* (Brooks-Gunn & Ruble, 1983; Petersen, 1983).

Attitudes toward menstruation are also likely to be influenced by the time at which menarche occurs relative to peers (Brooks-Gunn, 1988). In one study, college women were asked to recall their age at menarche, estimate the percentage of their peers who reached menarche before them, and describe their initial experience of menstruation (Rierdan & Koff, 1985b). Those who perceived themselves as reaching menarche early relative to their peers had more negative memories of menarche than those who perceived themselves as either on time (similar to other girls) or late.

In view of the concern of adolescents (especially younger ones) with conformity and belonging, these findings should not be surprising. Girls who perceive themselves as maturing early may have a sense of being off time. In contrast, girls who see themselves as on time can feel

assured of their normality (Petersen, 1983). The girl who experiences menarche late is, like the early maturer, also off time. In her case, however, the onset of menstruation ends her status as socially deviant. Menarche, again, provides reassurance of normality. Thus, "the late-maturing girl, like the on-time girl, can respond to menarche with relatively positive feelings" (Rierdan & Koff, 1985b, p. 242).

Some reactions to menstruation are, of course, related to the actual experience of negative side effects. These may include headaches, backaches, skin problems, cramps, nausea, and water retention (Bell, 1988). Some young women experience none or only some of these effects. Gini, a 16-year-old swimmer and lacrosse player, reports:

> My period is no problem and it never really was. When I first got it, I got it when I woke up one morning, and even now, four years later, it still usually comes in the morning, so I almost always know I have it before I go to school. . . . My period doesn't affect my life at all (Bell, 1988, p. 35).

Ruth, also 16, reports quite a different experience:

> I hate my period. I almost always get really bad cramps. . . . I never know when it's coming,

and even now, after I've had it for three years, it's so irregular that sometimes I skip a whole month. . . . For me it's the biggest problem of my life (Bell, 1988, p. 36).

In a National Health Examination survey conducted in the early 1980s, approximately 60 percent of a sample of American female adolescents reported having experienced some dysmenorrhea, or cramps, before or during menstruation (Klein & Litt, 1983). Contrary to the popular belief that cramps and other menstrual symptoms are worse during the early postmenarcheal years, reports of at least mild pain increase from 31 percent to 78 percent over the first five years after menarche and then level off at about 70 percent. Only 14 percent of those who experience pain describe it as severe.

In addition to experiencing physical symptoms, some adolescent girls report mood changes and negative or depressed feelings that appear during the premenstrual period. Such symptoms may be linked to monthly variations in levels of estrogens (such as estradiol) and progesterone (see Figure 3.6). Other adolescents report no such effects or even experience an increase in positive feelings (Bell, 1988; Brooks-Gunn & Ruble, 1983). Although there is no doubt that some girls and women

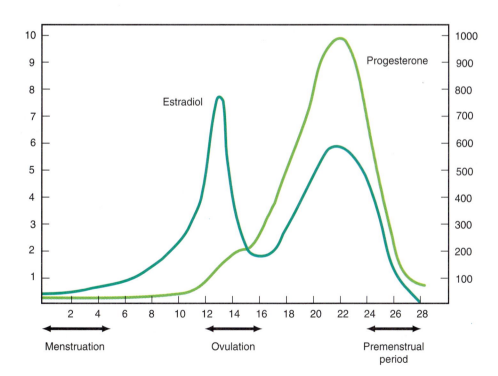

## Figure 3.6

Variations in hormonal levels during the menstrual cycle. Adapted from L. Speroff & R. L. Van de Wiele (1971). Regulation of the human menstrual cycle. *American Journal of Obstetrics and Gynecology,* **109,** 234–247. By permission.

do experience physiologically based psychological effects of menstruation, the popular conception about such effects has tended to exaggerate the prevalence and perhaps the intensity of those effects (Brooks-Gunn & Ruble, 1983; Ruble, 1977).

Educational materials for boys and girls, such as *Changing Bodies, Changing Lives* (Bell, 1988), describe the changes accompanying menarche and menstruation more accurately than earlier publications did. But accurate educational materials cannot do the job alone; parents play an essential role. Many negative reactions to menstruation could be avoided or alleviated if parents took a wise and understanding approach. By explaining to the girl the naturalness of the phenomenon, by seeing that she receives adequate medical care in case of any physical difficulties, and by showing pride and pleasure in her maturity, parents can help make the onset of menstruation a rewarding, rather than a feared or hated, event.

## Erection, Ejaculation, and Nocturnal Emission

Just as the onset of menstruation may cause concern in a pubescent girl, so may uncontrolled erection and initial ejaculation cause surprise and worry in a pubescent boy. The penis is capable of erection from birth on, and erection is often seen in male infants during bathing or before elimination. Most often it results from local stimulation or related physical events (such as a full bladder). Although genital stimulation (as well as other forms of bodily stimulation) is clearly pleasurable for male (and female) infants and children, neither erection nor genital stimulation usually carries with it the sense of sexual urgency that arises during puberty; moreover, erection is much less frequent in earlier years.

Before puberty boys may produce an erection and are capable of penetration, though without ejaculation. During puberty, however, the penis begins to tumesce very readily, either spontaneously or in response to a variety of stimuli: "provocative sights, sounds, smells, language, or whatever—the [younger] male adolescent inhabits a libidinized life-space where almost anything can take on a sexual meaning" (Stone & Church, 1973, p. 424). Although boys may be proud of their capacity for erection, they may also be worried or embarrassed by an apparent inability to control this response. They may become apprehensive about dancing with a girl or even about having to stand up in class to give a report. They may wonder whether other boys experience a similar apparent lack of control.

The adolescent boy's first ejaculation is likely to occur within a year of the beginning of the growth spurt (around age 13 or 14, although it may occur as early as 11 or as late as 16) (McCoy & Wibbelsman, 1984). First ejaculation may occur as a result of masturbation or nocturnal emission (ejaculation of seminal fluid during sleep), or even as a result of spontaneous waking orgasm. A boy who has previously masturbated, with accompanying pleasant sensations but without ejaculation, may wonder whether the ejaculation of seminal fluid is harmful or an indication that something is physically wrong with him.

Today the first ejaculation is far less likely to be a source of concern and more likely to be a source of positive feelings than was the case in earlier times (Bell, 1988). In one limited survey, 73 percent of early adolescents reported being excited by this event; 55 percent felt more grown up, and 36 percent felt happy and proud. However, a minority felt somewhat embarrassed, and nearly half reported feeling "a little scared" (Gaddis & Brooks-Gunn, 1985).

Approximately 83 percent of males report experiencing nocturnal emissions, or "wet dreams" at some time in their lives, usually beginning a year or two after the onset of puberty (Kinsey, Pomeroy, & Martin, 1948). Often, these emissions are accompanied by erotic dreams. Nocturnal emissions occur more commonly among youth without other sexual outlets such as masturbation, petting to orgasm, or intercourse. The female equivalent of nocturnal emissions, nocturnal dreams with orgasm, is far less common (probably under 10 percent of females) and tends not to occur at all until after adolescence (Kinsey, Pomeroy, & Martin, 1953; Money & Ehrhardt, 1972).

Contemporary adolescents are generally better informed and less likely to be concerned about developmental events such as menstruation or nocturnal emission than those of earlier generations (Bell, 1988). Nevertheless, many boys and girls, especially in the early years of adolescence, do not receive proper instruction from parents, schools, or peers and may torture themselves with unnecessary fears.

## Hormonal Influences on Adolescent Behavior

**Sexual Interest and Activity.** The hormonal changes accompanying puberty, particularly increases in **testosterone,** play an important but by no means exclusive role in fostering increased sexual interest and activity during this period, most clearly for males (Udry et al., 1985; Udry, Talbert, & Morris, 1986). In males, increased sex drive (manifested in nocturnal emissions and masturbation) and such behaviors as dating and

falling in love correspond with the rapid rise in testosterone levels between the ages of 12 and 14 (Higham, 1980). A decline in the frequency of sexual activity with age during the adult years also tends to parallel decreasing testosterone levels (Money & Ehrhardt, 1972).

In females, the relationships between hormonal levels and psychosexual functioning are more complex and are not completely understood (Petersen & Taylor, 1980; Susman et al., 1985). Androgen (testosterone) levels increase in girls during puberty, but much less than in boys (see Figure 3.7). Nevertheless, androgens appear to play some role in the female sex drive, as evidenced in masturbation and thinking about sex (Udry et al., 1985; Udry, 1988).

Although hormones may play a direct role in sexual interest and arousal, the behavioral expression of these feelings is also determined by environmental factors such as how the adolescent was taught to view and deal with sexuality.

**Aggression.** Psychoanalytic theory emphasizes an upsurge in both sexual and aggressive impulses at the onset of adolescence, particularly in males (Freud, 1958). Social and clinical observers also call attention to the restlessness of younger adolescent boys, as well as to their greater preoccupation with sexual activity. The magnitude of the sex difference in testosterone levels following puberty, along with the fact that testosterone level is related to activity levels and aggressive (including sexual) behavior, may help account not only for relatively greater aggressiveness of adolescent males but also for the

more imperious and less easily suppressed quality of the male sexual drive during adolescence (Inoff-Germain et al., 1988; Olweus et al., 1988; Petersen, 1988; Susman et al., 1985). However, in discussing the greater aggressiveness of adolescent males it is important to note that this does not mean that females are either angelic or weak. Studies show that some women are as capable of showing aggression as men (Maccoby & Jacklin, 1974).

**Mood.** In addition to influencing adolescent sexuality, hormonal changes during pubertal development may have some direct temporary relationship to depressed feelings and other adjustment problems. However, any such effects appear slight compared with the effects of social and psychological factors, including negative life events (Brooks-Gunn & Warren, 1989; Buchanan, Eccles, & Becker, 1992; Richards & Larson, 1993; Susman et al., 1985).

## Early and Late Maturation: The Issue of Timing

As we have already seen, young people vary widely in the age at which they reach puberty. At age 15 one boy may be small, with little evidence of pubertal development. Another boy of the same age may look like and sound like a grown man. Even though such variations in adolescent males and females are normal and do not either promote or hinder the eventual achievement of full physical and sexual maturity, they can affect the way adoles-

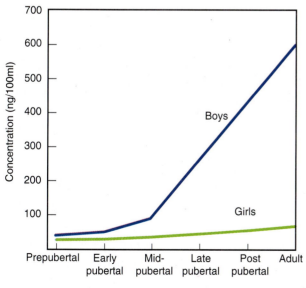

## Figure 3.7

Trends in testosterone concentrations related to pubertal developmental stages. From D. Gupta, A. Attanasio, & S. Raaf (1975). Plasma estrogen and androgen concentrations in children during adolescence. *Journal of Clinical Endocrinology and Metabolism,* **40,** 636–643. © The Endocrine Society. By permission.

## 3.2 The Social Context of Pubertal Timing

The effects of maturational timing depend, at least in part, on the social context in which it occurs. In activities and occupations such as gymnastics and ballet, in which there is a professional emphasis on leanness and a more "prepubertal" figure, late maturation may be more adaptive (and normative) than early or even average maturation. Dancers with delayed menarche are different physically: They weigh much less than dancers for whom menarche is on time, and they appear to have greater control over their eating habits. They also tend to have longer limbs (Brooks-Gunn & Warren, 1985; Frisch et al., 1981).

In a comparative study of private-school students and students in a ballet school, girls between the ages of 14 and 18 were classified as early, on-time, or late maturers on the basis of age at menarche (Brooks-Gunn & Warren, 1985). The dancers were far more likely to be late maturers than the private-school students (55 percent versus 29 percent). Among dancers, those who were on time in their development had significantly higher scores than late maturers on measures of psychopathology, perfectionism, and bulimic tendencies, and lower scores on measures of body image, family relationships, and education. (There were too few early-maturing dancers to provide useful comparisons.) In contrast, and in accordance with other studies, being on time presented no such problems among private-school students. Indeed, on-time maturers in this group had a more positive body image than either early or late maturers.

The importance of social context was also demonstrated in a pioneering study of students in Milwaukee schools (Simmons et al., 1979; Simmons, Blyth, & McKinney, 1983). The investigators found that the effects of maturational timing

varied as a function of school context and of transition from one kind of school to another. Among seventh-graders, those who had moved into junior high school had more difficulty adjusting and demonstrated lower self-esteem and more negative changes than girls who remained in a K–8 system (Simmons et al., 1979). However, changing schools was harder on early-maturing than on late-maturing girls: "In seventh grade, girls were more likely to

cents view themselves and the way they are viewed by others. The issue of **pubertal timing** is a crucial one for adolescents. Pubertal timing is the adolescent's position in terms of pubertal development *relative to peers*. Girls and boys who are more advanced with respect to pubertal maturation than the majority of their same-age and same-sex peers are called early maturers. Girls and boys

who are behind most of their peers in terms of pubertal maturation are called late maturers. Both of these groups differ from those in the middle, who are on time.

**Early Versus Late Maturation in Males.** In general, the psychological effects of early or late maturation appear to be more direct and easier to understand

exhibit lower self-esteem if they incurred these life changes simultaneously—change in school type, early pubertal change, and early assumption of dating behavior" (Simmons, Blyth, & McKinney, 1983, p. 265). The same finding was obtained for both boys and girls in a second study (Petersen, Kennedy, & Sullivan, 1991).

Finally, a recent study compared the effects of early, on-time, and late maturation in a sample of adolescent girls attending either mixed-sex or all-girl secondary schools in New Zealand. As in previous research, early maturation was associated with higher levels of norm-breaking or delinquent behavior at ages 13 and 15 and more association with peers who

engaged in delinquent behaviors. (On-time and late maturation were not linked with delinquency.) The association between early maturation and delinquency, however, was found *only among girls who attended mixed-sex schools* (see Figure B3.2). The authors concluded that "at least two factors are necessary for the initiation and maintenance of female delinquency: puberty and boys" (Caspi et al., 1993, p. 26). The authors also discovered that early maturation exacerbated behavior problems that were evident before adolescence. Specifically, early maturation was linked most strongly to delinquency in girls who had a history of behavior problems in childhood (Caspi et al., 1993; Caspi & Moffitt, 1991).

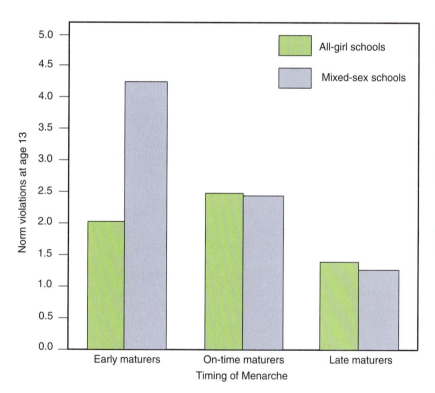

Figure B3.2

Norm violations in early adolescence as a function of age at menarche and school type. From A. Caspi, D. Lynam, T. E. Moffitt, & P. A. Silva (1993). Unraveling girls' delinquency: Biological, dispositional, and contextual contributions to adolescent misbehavior. *Developmental Psychology, 29*, 19–30. © 1993 by the American Psychological Association. Reprinted with permission.

among boys than among girls. Adults and other adolescents tend to think of the 14- or 15-year-old boy who looks 17 or 18 as older than he actually is. They are likely to expect more mature behavior from him than they would from a physically less developed boy of the same age (Conger, 1979; Steinberg & Hill, 1978). Because there is less difference in height between an early-maturing boy and most girls his own age (owing to the earlier growth spurt in females), he may become involved in boy–girl relationships sooner and with more self-confidence than his later-developing peers. Moreover, a physically more developed male has an advantage in many activities, especially athletics. Although a boy who matures much faster than most of his peers may feel

somewhat different, he is not likely to feel insecure about the difference. After all, with his more rugged physique, increased strength, and greater sexual maturity, he can assure himself that he is simply changing in the direction society expects and approves (Mussen et al., 1990; Richards & Larson, 1993; Tobin-Richards, Boxer, & Petersen, 1983).

In contrast, the late-maturing boy is more likely to be treated like a child. He is likely to have a harder time excelling in athletic and other activities and establishing relationships with girls. He may wonder when, if ever, he will reach full physical and sexual maturity.

These differences tend to produce certain differences between the personalities of early and late maturers. Extensive long-term studies at the University of California found that males who matured late tended to be less poised, more tense and talkative, and more self-conscious. They were also likely to be more restless, overeager, impulsive, bossy, and attention seeking. Although there were exceptions, late maturers tended to be less popular with peers and less likely to be leaders. Early maturers, on the other hand, appeared more reserved, self-assured, and matter-of-fact, and were more likely to engage easily in socially appropriate behavior. They were also better able to laugh at themselves (Clausen, 1975; Jones, 1957; Mussen & Jones, 1957; Simmons et al., 1983).

Research has found an essentially linear relationship (for boys) between timing of puberty and positive feelings about oneself (Crockett & Petersen, 1987; Tobin-Richards, Boxer, & Petersen, 1983). Adolescent boys who perceived themselves as early maturers had a more positive body image and mood and a greater sense of their own attractiveness. In contrast, those who perceived themselves as late maturers had a more negative body image and a decreased sense of attractiveness; those who perceived themselves as maturing on time fell between the two extremes. Other studies have found that early pubertal development in boys was related to more positive body image and higher self-esteem (Alsaker, 1992; Blyth et al., 1981).

Although early-maturing boys generally have an advantage over those who mature late, the picture is not entirely one-sided. When early- and late-maturing groups were compared at or after (but *not* before) the beginning of puberty, late-maturing boys were found to be more intellectually curious and more likely to engage in exploratory behavior and social initiatives (Livson & Peskin, 1980; Peskin, 1973). In contrast, early maturers tended to avoid problem solving or new situations unless urged. "The early maturers appeared to approach cognitive tasks cautiously and timidly, with a preference for

rules, routines, and imitative action" (Livson & Peskin, 1980, p. 73).

A far-ranging follow-up study of the participants in the University of California studies makes clear that differences between early and late maturers—both positive and negative—can persist into adulthood. As adults (age 38) the early-maturing males were found to be more responsible, cooperative, sociable, and self-contained, but also more conventional, conforming, moralistic, humorless, and concerned with making a good impression. On the other hand, the late maturers remained less controlled, less responsible, and more impulsive and assertive, but also "more insightful, perceptive, creatively playful, and able to cope with the ambiguity of new situations" (Livson & Peskin, 1980, p. 71).

Much can be done by parents, teachers, and others to minimize the anxiety and other negative psychological effects of late maturation. Adults can make a conscious effort to avoid treating a late maturer as younger than he actually is (Mussen et al., 1990). They can help him realize that his slower maturation is normal—that he will indeed "grow up" and be as physically and sexually masculine as his peers. They can help him achieve success in activities in which his lesser size and strength are not a handicap. For example, whereas immaturity and smaller size can be a handicap for a football player, they may be assets for a diver or a tumbler.

Conversely, parents and others can assist early maturers by not having unrealistic expectations of maturity based on physical appearance. They can also encourage early-maturing boys—and, as we shall see, girls—to take the time to catch up psychologically and socially with their physical development instead of rushing headlong into adult activities.

**Early Versus Late Maturation in Females.** Although early maturation is generally advantageous to boys, among girls early maturation may be more stressful than either on-time or late maturation (Caspi et al., 1993; Caspi & Moffitt, 1991). Initially, compared to later-maturing girls, early maturers tend to be less satisfied with their body image; more easily disorganized under stress; more restless, listless, moody, and complaining; and less popular with same-sex peers (Alsaker, 1992; Blyth et al., 1981; Crockett & Petersen, 1987; Faust, 1983; Peskin, 1973; Tobin-Richards, Boxer, & Petersen, 1983). They are more likely to perform poorly in school, to exhibit problem behaviors in school, to have lower academic aspirations, and to show more delinquent behavior. Early maturers also emerge as more independent, more popular with opposite-sex peers, more interested in dating, and more sexually experienced (Flannery, Rowe, &

Gulley, 1993; Jones & Mussen, 1958; Magnusson, Stattin, & Allen, 1986; Silbereisen et al., 1989; Simmons, Blyth, & McKinney, 1983). Very early maturers (menarche occurred by grade 6) are significantly more depressed than their premenarcheal counterparts (Rierdan & Koff, 1991). In terms of their feelings about pubertal timing, girls who report that they are on time have more positive reactions to their timing than girls who are early or late (Dubas, Graber, & Petersen, 1991).

Of particular interest is the clear difference in body image between early-maturing boys and girls. While the early-maturing boy is steadily developing in the direction of favored adult norms, the same is not the case for early-maturing girls, who tend initially to be bigger, heavier, and fatter than their more "petite" late-maturing peers (Crockett & Petersen, 1987; Petersen, 1988; Richards et al., 1990; Richards & Larson, 1993). Our society's emphasis on being tall and slim may help explain the finding that the heavier a girl is—or thinks she is—the more dissatisfied she is with her weight and body shape. Body dissatisfaction is a significant factor in the development of adolescent girls' eating disorders (Attie & Brooks-Gunn, 1989; Leon et al., 1993; Phelps et al., 1993).

In contrast to early-maturing girls, late maturers initially are more gregarious, poised, assertive, and active; more popular with peers; and less concerned about and more satisfied with their body image. They also do better academically and exhibit fewer behavior problems in school, and have higher academic aspirations (Petersen, 1988; Petersen & Crockett, 1985; Simmons et al., 1983).

By late adolescence and adulthood the picture may be less negative for early maturers. Earlier studies indicated that the formerly stress-ridden early-maturing girl became more popular with peers of both sexes than did the late-maturing girl, as well as more self-possessed and self-directed cognitively, socially, and emotionally (Livson & Peskin, 1980; Peskin, 1973). Similarly, a long-term look at girls who were early maturers found that their higher levels of delinquent behavior in adolescence did not persist into adulthood. They did not achieve as high a level of education in adulthood, however, compared to their later-maturing peers (Magnusson, Stattin, & Allen, 1986). To some extent, then, early-maturing girls may later recover from the difficulties that they experienced earlier in adolescence, although more longitudinal research is needed to support this conclusion.

Why is early maturation clearly a more favorable situation for boys? Society favors early maturity in adolescent males more clearly and less ambiguously than early maturity in females. In young men, early maturity means greater strength and physical prowess and, eventually, active sexual behavior (Flannery, Rowe, & Gulley, 1993). Among girls, early maturity may mean being temporarily bigger and heavier than female peers and taller than boys of the same age; in our society it may also mean being subjected to more conflicting sexual messages than males are.

For instance, parents worry that a girl who is sexually mature at an early age will attract the attention of older boys. If she dates boys who are considerably older than she is, she may not form strong relationships with girls and boys her own age or develop as an independent individual in her own right. She may also come to feel that she is gaining attention merely as a sex object rather than as a complete person (Mussen et al., 1990). On the other hand, her attractiveness can add to her prestige in her peer group, thereby making her social relationships more positive.

In the case of an early-maturing female, parents and other adults should be careful to avoid pressing her into sexual relationships, such as dating, too early. They can help her develop her own interests and maintain her friendships with peers her own age, assuring her that the other girls will soon catch up.

Adults need to assure a late-maturing girl that she will ultimately attain physical and sexual maturity. If they can help her realize that there is no need to rush things, that in fact gradual maturation can be useful in that it allows her to devote her energies to other developmental tasks, much unnecessary concern can be avoided (Conger, 1979).

# Puberty and Parent–Adolescent Relations

Are the changes of puberty associated with changes in the nature of the parent–adolescent relationship? This question has intrigued many researchers who believe that the physiological events of puberty and the accompanying psychological and behavioral changes might influence how parents and adolescents respond to each other. For example, the adolescent who looks more and more like an adult is likely to expect to be treated more like an adult, to desire some independence from parents, and to have a greater say in family decision-making.

There is evidence to suggest some emotional distancing between parents and adolescents as the adolescent matures pubertally. This distancing may take the form of higher parent–adolescent conflict (particularly with mothers), greater expression of negative feelings such as criticism or anger, and somewhat less warmth and closeness between

# 3.3 Why is Father Absence Linked to Girls' Earlier Menarche?

Most studies of pubertal maturation have considered the pubertal process as a series of events that affect adolescent behavior—in essence, puberty is believed to influence adolescents to behave in particular ways. A recently proposed sociobiological (evolutionary) theory, however, turned this approach around and considered how adolescents and their families may influence the pubertal process (Belsky, Steinberg, & Draper, 1991). This theory asserts that when families are stressed (for example, when there is marital discord or fathers are absent due to separation or divorce), the adolescent is more likely to experience behavior problems, and that these adjustment problems on the part of the adolescent trigger earlier pubertal maturation than would have occurred under normal, nonstressful family conditions.

According to the authors of this theory, the evolutionary function of earlier maturation, which is generally associated with earlier sexual activity and (in the natural course of things) earlier childbearing, is to maximize the opportunities for reproduction (producing offspring). This may be necessary in an environment where the adolescent may not have the psychological and behavioral resources to achieve these goals through a stable, long-term marital relationship (Belsky, Steinberg, & Draper, 1991).

To what extent is there empirical support for this theory? Several themes seen in human and primate research suggest the occurrence of earlier pubertal maturation and sexual activity when fathers are absent. For example, a retrospective study of over 1000 adolescents found that girls whose biological fathers were absent before puberty experienced a significantly earlier menarche (onset of menstruation) than girls whose fathers were present in the home (Surbey, 1990).

Only one study, however, has tested the major propositions of the theory put forth by Belsky and colleagues (Moffitt et al., 1992). In this study, as predicted by the theory, family stress (father absence and family conflict) was associated with girls' behavior problems in childhood. Family stress was also associated with earlier menarche. Contrary to the theory, however, earlier menarche in stressed families was *not* the result of girls' behavior problems. The authors of this study concluded that the sociobiological theory was not confirmed.

Rather, the results were more suggestive of a genetic transmission model. This genetic transmission model, for which there is some empirical support, assumes that the timing of maturation is genetically based, passed from mother to daughter; early maturity is linked with early sexual relations, early childbearing, and early marriages; early marriages are more likely to end in divorce; and, therefore, daughters of early-maturing mothers are more likely themselves to mature early *and* to experience father absence. In other words, the link between father absence and early menarche may be due to the correlation between mothers' and daughters' age at menarche, and the consequences of early menarche for early marriage and subsequent marital instability (Moffitt et al., 1992). Although both the sociobiological and the genetic transmission theories are provocative in terms of explaining the link between father absence and early menarche, it is much too soon to tell whether either of these theories provides an adequate explanation for this interesting relationship.

parents and adolescents. These kinds of behaviors are seen more often in families with adolescents who are further along in the pubertal process compared to families in which the adolescents are prepubertal or in the earliest stages of puberty (Montemayor, Eberly, & Flannery, 1993; Paikoff & Brooks-Gunn, 1991; Steinberg, 1988).

Although we may expect adolescents and parents to show signs of emotional distancing, this does not mean necessarily that the relationship is suffering or that the adolescent does not need the support of parents. Rather, some distancing in adolescence is a natural part of growing up, and as long as the conflict is not severe and the adolescent does not feel alienated from parents, this greater distance may help the adolescent to accomplish the developmental tasks of achieving independence from parents and establishing a sense of identity.

# Health Care for Adolescents

Because adolescence is a unique developmental period involving rapid physical, psychological, and social change, adolescents have special health care needs (Dryfoos, 1990; Hurrelmann & Losel, 1990). It is estimated that in the United States, about 20 percent of adolescents aged 10 to 18 have at least one serious health problem (Dougherty, 1993). Adolescents seek professional care and treatment for a wide range of concerns and problems, including acne or allergies; diet and exercise; headaches or fatigue; delayed puberty or very rapid growth; sexual activity, contraception, or pregnancy; menstrual difficulties or worries about sexually transmitted diseases such as AIDS; problems with parents, peers, or teachers; feelings of acute self-consciousness, anxiety, or depression; and, increasingly, injuries inflicted in violent assaults.

Adolescents may be concerned about multiple physical health problems at the same time. In some cases, the primary source of these problems may be mental health difficulties (Dougherty, 1993; Hammond & Yung, 1993). Not infrequently, adolescents seek treatment for a set of complaints that are really of secondary concern as a way of "testing the water" (consciously or unconsciously) to see whether it is safe to explore more pressing and painful psychological or physical problems.

All of this requires that the physician or other health-care professional be sensitive not only to the unique physical and medical needs of adolescents but to their psychological and social situations as well. Consequently, it is desirable that physicians and others involved in caring for and treating adolescents receive special training in adolescent medicine. Although the number of health-care professionals who specialize in adolescence is still relatively small, it is increasing.

It is also desirable for adolescents to have easy access to a health-care facility where they are treated with understanding and respect, their privacy is protected, and a variety of services are readily available. A promising development in the past decade has been the growth of hospital-based comprehensive-care clinics for adolescents in the United States and Canada. These clinics are staffed by physicians, nurses, and other health-care professionals, including psychologists and social workers, who have special training in the physiology and psychology of adolescents. They offer a wide variety of services at low cost, usually based on ability to pay (Earls et al., 1989).

Another important development is the growth of school-based clinics. School-based clinics are intended to capitalize on many of the features to which adoles-

Adolescents should have easy access to a health-care facility, such as a school- or hospital-based clinic, where a variety of services are readily available, and where they are treated with understanding and their privacy is respected.

cents are likely to respond, including convenience, comfort, confidentiality, and low cost. Located in the school building or on school grounds, most clinics operate during school hours and do not require appointments. Because they are visible entities in the school, clinic staff become familiar to students and vice versa. In addition, because the programs are geared to the needs of adolescents, and students are aware that their friends use the services, school-based clinics seem more approachable to many young people than doctors' offices, hospitals, or freestanding adult clinics (Dryfoos & Klerman, 1988; Hayes, 1987; Robert Wood Johnson Foundation, 1990).

School-based clinics vary in the range of family-planning services they provide. At a minimum, most provide counseling and referrals to family-planning clinics, such as Planned Parenthood, or private physicians, and follow-up after referrals. Although less than one-third dispense contraceptives, those that do have had considerable success in reducing rates of teenage pregnancy (Dryfoos & Klerman, 1988; Hayes, 1987).

Other clinics that provide comprehensive health care to adolescents are community based. One such clinic on the Lower East Side of New York City provided the following services: routine medical care; management of acute and chronic illnesses; assistance in coping with social, psychological, family, peer, or school prob-

lems; counseling related to health care and nutrition; and family-planning services. A one-year study found that family-planning education significantly increased contraceptive use among the 35 percent of adolescents who were sexually active when they entered the clinic (Kyman, Berger, & Perez, 1987). Among active females, contraceptive use increased during the course of the year from 22 percent to 70 percent; among males, the increase was from 33 percent to 83 percent. Among adolescents who were not sexually active when they first visited the clinic, only 3 percent became active during this period—far fewer than would generally be expected. In addition, possibly because the clinic provided continuous and comprehensive services in an atmosphere of trust and caring, most adolescent clients were responsible about keeping appointments and complying with treatment procedures.

## Health and Behavior

Advances in medicine and public-health practices during the last fifty years have led to a dramatic decline in mortality from infectious diseases. As a consequence, most health problems are now related to "aspects of individual behavior, especially long-term patterns of behavior referred to as 'lifestyle'" (Hamburg, Elliott, & Parron, 1982, p. 3). As much as 50 percent of the ten leading causes of death in the United States (including cardiovascular disease, cancer, and accidents) can be traced to aspects of lifestyle (Hamburg, Elliott, & Parron, 1982; *Healthy people,* 1979; Matarazzo, 1984).

Among the largest threats to adolescents today, however, is assaultive violence and homicide. Indeed, homicide is now the second leading cause of death among children and adolescents in the United States, with homicide rates the highest and increasing most rapidly among African-American males (Fingerhut, Ingram, & Feldman, 1992; Rodriguez, 1990). All in all, considering the statistics on the numbers of adolescents who are involved in fighting or carrying weapons, and who are victims of violent crime, we may conclude that *all* adolescents are vulnerable to assaultive injury (see pages 335-344). The level of violence among adolescents clearly calls for a concerted response at all levels of society (government, community, school, family) (Hammond & Yung, 1993).

Adolescents may not have much control over the environments in which they live and, to some extent, the violent situations to which they are exposed, but some health-damaging behaviors are under their control. If a young person can avoid behaviors such as smoking, excessive alcohol or drug use, sexual acting out, or disturbed eating patterns during the adolescent period, he or she is markedly less likely to engage in these behaviors in subsequent years. This is one of the principal reasons that smoking and other prevention programs have focused on the preadolescent and early adolescent years (Evans, 1984a, 1984b; Hamburg, Elliott, & Parron, 1982; Jessor, 1984; Millstein & Litt, 1990). Similarly, the estab-

If young people can avoid health-damaging behaviors, such as smoking, during adolescence, they will be much less likely to engage in these behaviors as adults.

lishment of healthful patterns of exercise and nutrition, a positive attitude toward health, and adaptive mechanisms for coping with stress are also likely to yield continued future benefits (Conger, 1987).

At the same time, however, adolescents are more vulnerable than adults to the adoption of health-damaging behaviors. In part, this reflects their openness to change, their uncertain sense of self, their need to define themselves as separate from parents, their greater dependence on peers, the greater risks to which they are exposed, and their relatively limited time perspective. But it also reflects the effects of social changes that have increased adoles-

cents' vulnerability to maladaptive behaviors. For one thing, opportunities to become involved in drug use, associating with gangs, unplanned pregnancy, and other problem behaviors abound. For another, contemporary adult society, lacking a strong, coherent, unified set of moral and social values of its own, provides at best a fragmented, inadequate model for young people. In the final analysis, success in creating a growth-enhancing, health-promoting climate, both for young people and for society itself, will require far greater commitment to meeting the needs of children and youth than our society has shown up to now (Conger, 1987, 1988).

# Summary

Adolescence is a period of rapid physical, sexual, and psychological changes. *Puberty* is the biological changes of adolescence, including sexual maturation and the *adolescent growth spurt*. It is initiated by the release of certain activating hormones by the pituitary gland. Those hormones stimulate other endocrine glands to begin releasing growth- and sex-related hormones, including *androgens, estrogens,* and *progestins.* The hormonal differences between the sexes are actually differences in the proportions of masculinizing and feminizing hormones present in each sex.

The age of onset and the duration of the adolescent growth spurt—an accelerated rate of increase in height and weight—vary widely among normal young people. However, the average age at which the growth spurt begins is about 11 in girls and 13 in boys; the period of rapid growth lasts about 4½ years, with the peak rate of growth occurring about a year after onset.

Changes in height and weight are accompanied by changes in body proportions. Sex differences in body shape also are magnified during early adolescence. Changes in physique reflect changes in the development of muscle, body fat, and skeletal structure and help account for differences in strength and tolerance for exercise.

In males, sexual maturation begins with an increase in the growth of the testes and scrotum, followed by an acceleration in growth of the penis, the appearance of underarm hair, and lowering of the voice. In females, the first sign of sexual maturity is the appearance of pubic hair and "budding" of the breasts. These changes are followed by accelerated growth of the reproductive organs and finally by *menarche* (onset of menstruation).

For adolescent girls, the onset of menstruation is a symbol of womanhood. However, a majority of American girls react negatively—or at best neutrally—to menarche, partly because of the negative attitudes of others and partly because of associated physical discomfort. For adolescent boys, uncontrolled erection and initial ejaculation may be sources of worry and embarrassment.

Early-maturing males face higher expectations for mature behavior and have an advantage in many activities, especially athletics. Late-maturing males are more likely to be treated like children and are likely to have more difficulty excelling in athletics and other activities. These differences result in personality differences that initially favor early-maturing boys, who tend to be more self-assured and able to engage easily in socially appropriate behavior, although in the long run, late maturers emerge as more intellectually and socially curious.

Although early maturation is generally advantageous to boys, among girls early maturation may be more stressful than either on-time or late maturation. Early maturation in girls is associated with more body dissatisfaction, more problem behaviors in school and delinquent behaviors, lower academic aspirations, and earlier engagement in dating and sexual activities. However, these effects may diminish with age.

There is evidence to suggest some emotional distancing between parents and adolescents as the adolescent matures pubertally. This distancing may take the form of higher parent–adolescent conflict, greater expression of negative feelings, and less warmth and closeness between parents and adolescents. Some dis-

tancing, as long as it is not severe, may help the adolescent to accomplish developmental tasks.

Because adolescence is a unique developmental period, adolescents have special health-care needs ranging from concerns about diet or problems with parents or peers to concerns about sexual activity, anxiety, or depressed feelings. This requires that health-care professionals be sensitive not only to the unique physical and medical needs of adolescents, but also to their psychological and social needs. The health-care needs of young people can best be met in adolescent clinics that provide comprehensive health care, whether they are located in schools, hospitals, or the community.

As much as half of current mortality can be traced to lifestyle patterns. Among the largest health threats to adolescents today, however, is assaultive violence and homicide. If a young person can develop adaptive ways of responding to the stresses of life while avoiding health-damaging behaviors, he or she is likely to continue to respond in these ways in adulthood.

# Review Questions

1. Briefly describe the role of hormonal factors in pubertal development.

2. Briefly discuss the age of onset and duration of the adolescent growth spurt in boys and girls, and describe the resulting changes in height, weight, and other physical characteristics.

3. How does sexual maturation progress in adolescent males and females?

4. What are the effects of maturation, especially early or late maturation, on the psychological adjustment of adolescent boys and girls?

5. What factors influence whether the onset of menstruation will be a positive, neutral, or negative experience for girls?

6. Discuss briefly the effects of pubertal hormones on adolescent behavior.

7. Describe how puberty might have some impact on the parent–adolescent relationship.

8. Why do adolescents have special health-care needs? How can those needs best be met?

9. Why is it especially important to learn adaptive ways of responding to stress and avoiding health-damaging behaviors during the early adolescent years?

# Recommended Readings

Bell, R. (1988). *Changing bodies, changing lives: A book for teens on sex and relationships* (rev. ed.). New York: Random House.

Brooks-Gunn, J., & Reiter, E. O. (1990). The role of pubertal processes. In S. S. Feldman & G. R. Elliott (Eds.), *At the threshold: The developing adolescent* (pp. 16–53). Cambridge, MA: Harvard University Press.

Hurrelmann, K., & Losel, F. (Eds.). (1990). *Health hazards in adolescence.* Berlin: Walter de Gruyter.

Paikoff, R. L., & Brooks-Gunn, J. (1991). Do parent–child relationships change during puberty? *Psychological Bulletin,* **110,** 47–66.

Stattin, H., & Magnusson, D. (1990). *Pubertal maturation in female development.* Hillsdale, NJ: Erlbaum.

Tanner, J. M. (1971). Sequence, tempo, and individual variation in the growth and development of boys and girls aged twelve to sixteen. *Daedalus,* **100** (4), 907–930. Also in J. Kagan and R. Coles (Eds.). (1972). *12 to 16: Early adolescence.* New York: Norton.

# Intelligence and Cognitive Development

# 4

t he impressive gains in physical and physiological development that are made during adolescence are accompanied by equally impressive gains in intellectual and **cognitive development.** For example, if asked why we should keep away from bad company, a 15-year-old might say, "To keep from being influenced by them." A younger child might say, "Cause they're bad," or, "My mother wouldn't like it." The response of the 15-year-old demonstrates a deeper understanding of the issue and an ability to reason at a higher level than that of the younger child. When asked to listen to a series of numbers and then repeat them, the average 15-year-old will be able to remember more numbers in the correct order than will the average younger child. Similar results are found on a variety of indices of mental ability, ranging from measures of general information, abstract verbal reasoning, and commonsense understanding of everyday events to tests of arithmetic skill and mechanical ability. Although parents may express consternation about the apparent inability of adolescent children to follow instructions for such simple tasks as straightening up a bedroom, taking out the garbage, or putting the cap back on the toothpaste tube, the fact is that adolescents are much more advanced cognitively than their younger sisters and brothers.

The cognitive gains of adolescence can be viewed quantitatively—there are increases in the individual's existing cognitive capacities. As intelligence tests demonstrate, the adolescent becomes capable of accomplishing more easily, more quickly, and more efficiently intellectual tasks, such as adding, that he or she previously was able to accomplish only slowly, inefficiently, and with difficulty. Cognitive gains can also be viewed qualitatively—significant changes occur in the nature of the adolescent's mental processes. For example, relative to the child's problem-solving and reasoning abilities, the adolescent's ability to reason is more abstract, thorough, and systematic. The scientific reasoning that emerges in adolescence is distinctly different from the concrete thinking displayed in childhood. Without these quantitative and qualitative gains in their cognitive capability, young people would be unable to confront and deal successfully

with many of the important demands made on them during adolescence. This may appear obvious in the case of demands for educational achievement and the development of vocational skills, but as we shall see in later chapters, it is equally true in the case of nonacademic tasks such as the development of personal, social, and political values.

In this chapter, we will discuss three common approaches to the understanding of intellectual development and cognitive change in adolescence. The first, the **psychometric approach,** has the longest tradition, and relies heavily on intelligence testing to discover individual and age-related differences in intellectual ability (Berg, 1992). The second, the **Piagetian approach,** focuses on qualitative changes in reasoning ability, as exemplified by the developmental psychology of Jean Piaget and others (Flavell, 1985; Neimark, 1975a, 1975b). Because Piaget emphasized the attainment of abstract thought as the hallmark of change in adolescent reasoning, this and related approaches have dominated our understanding of cognitive development in adolescence (Keating, 1980). A third approach, the **information-processing approach,** gained popularity among researchers in the 1970s and 1980s. Here "the focus is on what occurs between the input of information and the output of specific intellectual responses, and how this changes across development" (Berg, 1992, p. 7). Research from the information-processing perspective may lead to a better understanding of the specific mechanisms underlying cognition. Although these three perspectives have different foci and emphases, they complement rather than compete with each other; each contributes pieces to the complex jigsaw puzzle of cognitive development in adolescence.

# The Psychometric Approach to Cognitive Development

The psychometric approach to intellectual development dates from the pioneering work of Alfred Binet, a French psychologist who originated the modern intelligence test. In 1904 the French government, concerned about the many nonlearners in the schools of Paris, asked Binet to develop a test to determine which children would be unable to profit from ordinary schooling. In collaboration with another French psychologist, Theodore Simon, Binet set about devising a test that would distinguish children of adequate educability from those who were less capable of learning. Their responsibility was not to devise a measure of intellectual achievement but to create a way of measuring **intelligence,** or intel-

lectual ability. That is, they were to assess not what students had accomplished (achievement) but what they *might be able to* accomplish (potential). This is not a simple task, and it requires the adoption of a number of assumptions about the nature of intelligence and how it develops. To understand what Binet and Simon faced, it is necessary to explore what is actually meant by the term *intelligence* and to distinguish tests of intelligence from tests of achievement.

## The Meaning of Intelligence

What do we actually mean by intelligence? The answer may seem obvious, for we think we understand what is meant by phrases such as, "He is not very bright," or "As any normally intelligent person can see. . . ." However, the matter is more complex than it may appear. In attempting to clarify the issue we must first understand that intelligence is one example of what we call a hypothetical construct.

To explain, some words stand for concrete, observable, tangible things. When someone mentions the words *tree* or *chair,* the listener immediately understands what is meant. Other words, however, do not symbolize objects; these words are simply hypothetical constructs, or phenomena that are hypothesized or believed to exist, but cannot be seen, touched, or heard. Concepts such as time and force illustrate the notion of hypothetical constructs. In the same way, no one has ever seen, heard, or touched intelligence. It is a hypothetical construct invented to help explain and predict behavior. Because intelligence is hypothetical, there is no single correct definition of the term, although one definition may be more useful for some purposes than another. Over the years a number of psychologists have defined *intelligence,* and although the terminology differs, most experts agree that intelligence involves the ability to benefit from experience and to learn new ideas or new sets of behaviors easily. For example, David Wechsler (1981), who developed the widely used Wechsler Intelligence Scales for children, adolescents, and adults, defines intelligence as the aggregate or global capacity of the individual to comprehend the world and to deal effectively with its challenges. Another expert, Robert Sternberg, refers to intelligence as "goal-directed adaptive behavior" (Sternberg, 1985).

It is generally assumed that every individual has a "ceiling," a point above which he or she cannot profit from experience in a particular activity, and that the ceiling is set by hereditary factors. How nearly any individual approaches the ceiling, and the rate at which he or she does so, is determined by a variety of factors,

including his or her rate of physiological maturation and the richness of the environment to which he or she is exposed.

A person's potential ceiling may be lowered in the course of development by a variety of external and internal events. Examples include the trauma of brain injury or disease, nutritional deficiency, or maternal drug use during pregnancy. Less obviously, it is possible that if the developing biological organism does not receive the appropriate amount of psychological and physical stimulation from its environment during certain critical periods, it will be limited in its ability to profit from subsequent learning opportunities.

## Is Intelligence Multidimensional?

Early on, intelligence was considered to be a general competence—an ability that is developed across a wide variety of tasks (Mussen et al., 1990; Sternberg, 1985). Over time, however, psychologists began to challenge this view. Some argued that what is called general intelligence actually consists of a variety of intellectual skills that do not necessarily vary together. Others argued that individuals possess not only a general intelligence factor but also a variety of specific factors, or abilities, that may vary independently of one another (Gardner & Clark, 1992; Spearman, 1927).

Although disputes about the relative importance of general and specific factors in intellectual functioning have not been fully resolved (Berg, 1992), most psychologists agree that patterns of ability differ among individuals. For example, some adolescents have outstanding verbal skills but have difficulty in mathematics or in visualizing spatial relationships; for others the reverse may be true.

## Dimensions of Intelligence

Most scientists agree that intelligence is multidimensional, involving a variety of abilities, but they are less likely to agree on the nature and number of these dimensions (Guilford, 1982; Mussen et al., 1990). L. L. Thurstone, a pioneer in the study of intelligence, concluded that in addition to a general intelligence factor, intelligence involves seven primary mental abilities: verbal comprehension, word fluency, ability to manipulate numbers, ability to visualize spatial relationships, associative memory (the ability to memorize quickly and correctly), perceptual speed, and general reasoning ability (Thurstone, 1938). A majority of currently used intelligence tests mea-

sure performance in most of these abilities (Gardner & Clark, 1992; Spreen & Strauss, 1991).

More recently, psychologist Howard Gardner has proposed six distinct kinds of intelligence: linguistic ability, logical mathematical reasoning, spatial ability, musical ability, bodily kinesthetic skills (which are involved in controlling bodily movements such as dancing, playing the piano, and performing surgery), and personal intelligence (Gardner, 1983, 1989, 1993). Personal intelligence, in turn, has two components that can be viewed as distinct: intrapersonal intelligence, which includes the ability to monitor one's own feelings and emotions, and interpersonal intelligence, which includes the ability to notice and understand the feelings, needs, and intentions of others. Gardner's first three abilities are familiar aspects of intelligence and are typically included in intelligence

Howard Gardner proposed six distinct kinds of intelligence: linguistic ability, logical mathematical reasoning, spatial ability, musical ability, bodily kinesthetic skills controlling bodily movements (as in dance or playing the piano), and personal intelligence.

tests; the latter three are more novel and more difficult to measure. Nevertheless, it would be hard to argue that they are unimportant.

Robert Sternberg (1985, 1990; Sternberg, Wagner, & Okagaki, 1993), a prominent cognitive psychologist at Yale University, also takes a broader view of the nature of intelligence. He has developed a "triarchic" (three-part) theory of intelligence in which intelligence has three major components: cognitive processes (e.g., planning and problem-solving) and knowledge acquisition; the ease with which one deals with new experiences (i.e., how rapidly one learns); and the ability to adapt to and influence one's social and cultural environment. Although most traditional intelligence tests are reasonably effective in measuring problem-solving skills and the acquisition of knowledge, they are generally not very helpful in assessing broader aspects of intellectual functioning, such as interpersonal intelligence and the ability to influence others. New methods must be devised to accurately assess the broader, more novel aspects of intelligence proposed by Gardner and Sternberg (Atkinson et al., 1987).

## Is an Intelligence Test a "Pure" Measure of Intelligence?

It is important to stress that there is no way to measure directly an individual's intellectual potential (i.e., his or her ultimate "ceiling"). We can only measure what a person can do currently, whether the task is verbal or psychomotor. A child who was raised in silence in a dark room from birth would not be able to perform any of the tasks on a standard intelligence test, but this does not mean that his or her intellectual potential is zero. One of the purposes of an intelligence test, as distinguished from an achievement test, is to *estimate* a child's or adolescent's intellectual potential. This estimate is often called the IQ score.

Intelligence tests attempt to control for the potentially distorting effects of differing environmental influences, on the assumption that differences in individuals' performances will then reflect differences in intellectual potential rather than differences in environmental experiences. But because we can never be certain that we have succeeded in controlling for the effects of all environmental influences or other relevant factors, such as motivation or transient physical or psychological states, we can never be sure than an IQ actually represents a person's full intellectual potential. A practical guideline is that people are unlikely to be *less* capable than their IQ score indicates but, depending on circumstances, they may well be *more* capable.

## Constructing Intelligence Tests

The manner in which the creators of intelligence tests take into account the potentially distorting effects of environmental influences can be illustrated by considering an example of intelligence-test construction. Here we return to the task confronting Alfred Binet at the turn of the century. Binet assumed that children who had difficulty learning were like normal children except for their retarded mental growth. He reasoned, then, that less capable learners would perform on tests like normal children of a younger age. He therefore decided to scale intelligence as the kind of change that occurs in the course of a child's maturation.

Accordingly, Binet set about constructing a scale of units of **mental age** (MA). In a child of average intelligence, the MA would be equal to his or her chronological age (CA) (i.e., age determined by date of birth). A bright girl's MA would be higher than her CA; a retarded boy would have an MA lower than his CA. The men-

Alfred Binet.

tal-age scale could easily be interpreted by teachers and others who deal with children of differing mental abilities.

**Item Selection.** Because Binet conceived of intelligence as an individual's global capacity to profit from experience, he attempted to sample a wide range of mental abilities. Included were measures of verbal ability, perceptual–motor coordination, memory, perception, and logical reasoning. Scores on these individual measures could be combined to form an estimate of overall ability.

Because he was attempting, albeit indirectly, to measure intellectual ability or potential rather than achievement, Binet tried to select tasks that would not unduly favor individuals with specific training or unduly penalize those without it. His assumption was that if the kind of task selected did not favor a child with specific training, then differences in children's levels of performance would be more likely to reflect differences in their basic potential. There are two ways to find items on which success is not influenced by special training. One is to choose *novel items* that presumably are unfamiliar to all children (Atkinson et al., 1987). Figure 4.1 illustrates such items. In this example the child is directed to select figures that are alike.

The second way is to select *familiar items,* on the assumption that those for whom the test is designed have the necessary experience to deal with them. To illustrate, the Wechsler Adult Intelligence Scale-Revised (WAIS-R), which is widely used in assessing adolescents and adults, contains an information subtest that asks the individual to supply facts (naming the author of a classic book, for example). It is assumed that virtually all chil-

dren in our society (for whom the test was designed) would have been exposed to this information. Whether they have incorporated it into their store of knowledge is assumed to depend on their underlying level of mental ability. Unfortunately, we cannot be certain that all individuals taking the test were indeed exposed to the required information.

In some respects the intelligence test is a crude instrument because its assumptions can never be strictly met. "The language spoken in one home is never exactly the same as that spoken in another; available reading matter and the stress on cognitive abilities also vary. Even the novel items depend upon perceptual discriminations that may be acquired in one culture and not in another" (Atkinson et al., 1987, p. 390). As an example, Kpelle rice farmers in Nigeria perform better than American adults when asked to estimate the amounts of rice in bowls of different sizes, but more poorly when asked to estimate the lengths of objects; Kpelle culture has a standardized system for measuring volume (used in buying and selling rice) but not for measuring length (Laboratory of Comparative Human Cognition, 1983; Mussen et al., 1990). Despite these difficulties, test items can be chosen that work reasonably well for many purposes.

Once a large number of items have been selected for possible use, construction of the test can begin. Binet and his immediate successors selected items by noting the changes in the proportions of children of different ages who answered a particular item correctly. They reasoned that unless older children were more successful than younger ones in answering the item, the item was unsatisfactory for a test based on the concept of mental devel-

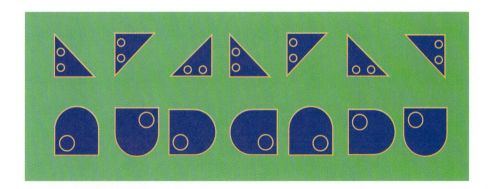

**Figure** 4.1

Novel items used in an intelligence test. The following instructions accompany the test: "Here are some cards for you to mark. In each row mark every card that is like the first card in the row." From L. L. Thurstone & T. G. Thurstone (1941). Factorial studies of intelligence. *Psychometric Monographs* [No. 2]. Chicago: University of Chicago Press. By permission.

opment. On other tests, such as the Wechsler scales for children and adults, difficulty is determined by the percentage of subjects in a given population, without respect to age, who can answer a particular item correctly. Within each of the subtests included in the Wechsler test, the items answered correctly by almost all subjects are presented first and those answered correctly by almost none are presented last. The assumption is that the more items a person answers correctly, the greater his or her ability.

**Determining IQ.** The test items originally developed by Binet were adapted by Lewis Terman of Stanford University and subsequently revised to create what is now known as the Stanford–Binet Intelligence Scale (Terman & Merrill, 1960; Thorndike, Hagen, & Sattler, 1986). To standardize the test for American schoolchildren, items were administered to a representative sample of children of different ages (a somewhat easier task when children were not as diverse in terms of ethnic and national background as they are today). Each item was assigned to an age level on the basis of the youngest age at which a majority of children answered it correctly. A child's mental age could be determined by adding up the number of items answered correctly at each age level. An **intelligence quotient,** or **IQ,** could then be computed by dividing the child's mental age by his or her actual age:

$$IQ = 100 \times \frac{\text{Mental age (MA)}}{\text{Chronological age}}$$

The most recent version of the Stanford–Binet scale differs from earlier versions in two important ways:

1. In accordance with current views of intelligence as multidimensional, scores on the 1986 revision are determined for four broad categories of intellectual functioning: verbal reasoning, quantitative reasoning, abstract/visual reasoning, and short-term memory (Thorndike, Hagen, & Sattler, 1986).

2. Like other recently developed tests of intelligence, such as the WAIS-R, the revised Stanford–Binet determines IQ on the basis of the percentage of subjects in the standardization group falling above or below a certain score. The higher an individual's IQ, the smaller the percentage of his or her contemporaries who perform at or about this level (see Table 4.1). As can be seen in Figure 4.2, the distribution of IQs takes the form of a curve that is typical of many differences among individuals (e.g., differences in height). This is known as the bell-shaped normal curve, in which most people cluster around the midpoint and only a few score at either extreme.

## The Stability of IQ

The practical utility of an intelligence test score depends partly on its stability or constancy—that is, its capacity to predict scores on future tests. How confidently can we predict that a child or adolescent who attains a superior score at one age will attain a comparable score at a later age? Whereas tests given to infants under 2 years of age have little value for the prediction of future intelligence scores, tests given to older children and adolescents are more highly predictive (Sternberg & Powell, 1983).

## Table 4.1 Intelligence Classifications

| IQ | CLASSIFICATION | PERCENT INCLUDED |
|---|---|---|
| 130 and above | Very superior | 2.2 |
| 120–129 | Superior | 6.7 |
| 110–119 | High average | 16.1 |
| 90–109 | Average | 50.0 |
| 80–89 | Low average | 16.1 |
| 70–79 | Borderline | 6.7 |
| 69 and below | Mentally retarded | 2.2 |

SOURCE: D. Wechsler (1981). *WAIS-R Manual: Wechsler Adult Intelligence Scale, Revised.* New York: Copyright © 1981, 1955 by The Psychological Corporation. Reproduced by permission. All rights reserved.

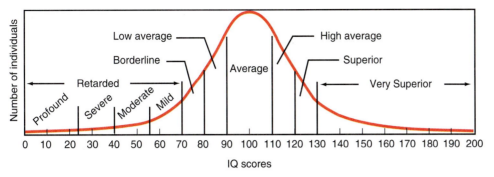

# Figure 4.2

The distribution of IQ scores. Subclassifications of the retarded group are based
on criteria adopted by the American Association on Mental Deficiency.

Table 4.2 presents the **correlations**[1] between intelligence test scores at ages 2, 7, 10, 14, and 18. Clearly, IQ at age 2 is not a strong predictor of later IQ. However, tests given at ages 7 and 10 are fairly good predictors of intellectual status in middle and later adolescence (ages 14 and 18). Nevertheless, despite the fact that the IQ becomes more stable at later ages, we must be cautious in using test scores for predicting the future status of individual children because the correlations are not high enough to preclude the possibility of marked changes in individual IQs. Indeed, repeated testing of large groups of children between the ages of 6 and 18 years found that the IQs of over half the children varied by 15 points or more at some time during the school years, and one-third varied by as much as 20 points (Honzik, 1973; Honzik, Macfarlane, & Allen, 1948; Sontag, Baker, & Nelson, 1958). With respect to adult intelligence test scores, adolescent test scores are fairly good predictors (Siegler & Richards, 1982). In one study, the correlation between preschool and adult IQs was .65 (Stanford–Binet), whereas adolescent and adult IQs correlated at .85 (Stanford–Binet) and .80 (Stanford–Binet and WAIS) (Bayley, 1949).

IQ scores beyond early childhood are generally quite stable. Among people whose IQ scores change, we must ask what circumstances might be responsible for such change. In general, children and adolescents whose IQ scores increase with age are likely to come from socioeconomically favored environments, whereas those whose scores decrease are likely to come from culturally isolated environments (remote rural mountain villages) or disadvantaged families and settings (inner-city ghettoes) (McCall, Applebaum, & Hogarty, 1973; Roberts, 1971; Sameroff et al., 1993).

A wide range of more specific factors have also been found to be related to changes in IQ during the course of development. For example, parents who display interest in their child's educational achievement during the preschool years are more likely to have children who show gains in IQ. One study, however, strongly suggests that parental encouragement is less effective if it is combined with either very harsh or very weak and ineffective discipline. In contrast, "parents of children who show gains in IQ provide their children with acceleration and encouragement for intellectual tasks and take a moderate, rationally structured approach to discipline" (McCall, Applebaum, & Hogarty, 1973, p. 73).

Earlier studies found that children whose IQ scores increase are more independent, competitive, and verbally aggressive than those whose scores decrease (Kagan et al., 1958; Sontag, Baker, & Nelson, 1958). They also worked harder in school, showed a strong desire to master intellectual problems, and were unlikely to withdraw from difficult problem situations. Apparently, children and adolescents who attempt to master challenging problems are more likely to show increases in IQ than those who withdraw from such situations.

More individual, idiosyncratic influences, which can be detected only through detailed case histories, may

---

[1]A correlation is a measure of the relationship between two characteristics. A positive correlation means that high levels on one variable tend to be associated with high levels on the other. For example, height and weight are positively correlated. A negative correlation means that high levels on one variable tend to be associated with low levels on the other. For example, education is negatively correlated with the amount of television people watch. A zero correlation means that the two variables are not related. Correlations can range from +1.00 to −1.00. The + or − sign indicates the direction of the correlation (positive or negative) and the number describes the magnitude of the relationship. The greater the number, whether it is positive or negative, the stronger the association.

## Table 4.2 Correlations Among Intelligence Test Scores at Different Ages

| AGE (YEARS) | AGE (YEARS) | | | |
| --- | --- | --- | --- | --- |
| | 7 | 10 | 14 | 18 |
| 2 | .46 | .37 | .28 | .31 |
| 7 | | .77 | .75 | .71 |
| 10 | | | .86 | .73 |
| 14 | | | | .76 |

NOTE: Table entries show correlation between IQs obtained from the same individuals at different ages.

SOURCE: Table from *Educability and group differences* by Arthur R. Jensen. Copyright © 1973 by Arthur R. Jensen. Reprinted by permission of HarperCollins Publishers, Inc.

also result in IQ changes upward or downward. Figure 4.3 shows the results of repeated tests of three subjects from the longitudinal Guidance Study at the Institute of Human Development at the University of California, Berkeley (Honzik, Macfarlane, & Allen, 1948). As can be seen, these subjects showed markedly different patterns of change between the ages of 2 and 18. Their individual histories suggest some of the factors that may have been involved:

> Case 783 changed very little in IQ through the years, although he had poor health, was insecure, did poorly in school, and had a number of symptoms of emotional disturbance. Case 946 scored as low as 87 and as high as 142. She was the daughter of unhappily married immigrant parents who were divorced when the girl was seven. When she was nine her mother remarried but the girl was very insecure and unhappy at home. When she became better adjusted in her family, her IQ scores rose. Case 567 showed consistent improvement. In her early years she was sickly and shy, but after age 10 her social life expanded and she became very much involved in music and sports. These changes were reflected in her improved test scores (Mussen et al., 1973, p. 365).

## How Useful are IQs?

What do we actually know when a child or adolescent obtains an IQ of, for example, 119 on the Wechsler Adult Intelligence Scale? At the very least, we know that he or she can complete the items on that test better than

approximately 90 percent of people the same age on whom the test was standardized. But is a score based on tasks such as putting a manikin together or assembling blocks useful to teachers or potential employers who are interested in predicting how well the person will perform in school or at work?

The only way to settle this question is to examine the actual relationship between IQ and school and occupational success. In general, IQ scores have been found to be fairly good predictors of academic performance (Atkinson et al., 1987; Carroll, 1982; Siegler & Richards, 1982). Of course, the fairly high correlation between school success and IQ scores may be attributed partly to the fact that similar kinds of behavior are measured in both cases. Indeed, when it comes to predicting success in less related fields, such as mechanical trades, music, and art, the intelligence test does a far less adequate job, although *on average* there are IQ differences between people who hold different kinds of jobs (Harrel & Harrel, 1945). For example, accountants, lawyers, and physicians have average IQ scores in the superior range (over 120), whereas farm hands, laborers, and truck drivers all score in the average range.

Interestingly, in both academic and vocational performance the spread in IQs is greater at lower levels than at higher levels (Bodmer & Cavalli-Sforza, 1970). Thus, although the mean IQ of unskilled workers is below 90, individual unskilled workers may score in the very superior range. On the other hand, among physicians and other professionals whose mean scores are in the superior or very superior range, one does not find individuals scoring in the 80s. The obvious implication is that although certain tasks—academic or vocational—require a certain minimum level of intellectual capability, intelligence alone does not guarantee placement in a presti-

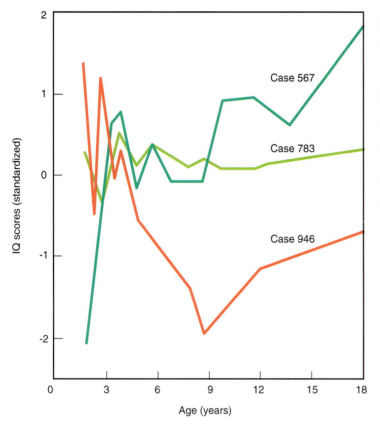

**Figure** `4.3`

IQ scores of three children assessed repeatedly over time. Scores represent their standing relative to children in the overall sample. From M. P. Honzik, J. W. McFarlane, & L. Allen (1948). The stability of mental test performance between 2 and 18 years. *Journal of Experimental Education,* **17,** 309–324. Adapted by P. H. Mussen & M. R. Rozensweig et al. (1973) in *Psychology: An Introduction.* Lexington, MA: Heath. By permission.

gious occupation; other factors, ranging from motivation and personality characteristics to environmental stimulation and opportunity, may be necessary as well.

## Intellectual Development in Adolescence and Beyond

Although the average person's IQ remains fairly stable as he or she grows older, mental ability does not. This is a frequent source of confusion. The explanation is that a mental ability score is an *absolute* measure (i.e., an average 15-year-old can pass more and harder items than an average 5-year-old). IQ, on the other hand, is a *relative* measure; it is based on the individual's ability *in relation to that of his or her contemporaries.* Thus, both the 5-year-old and the 15-year-old may have the same IQ, but the 15-year-old can do many tasks that the 5-year-old cannot; the older child's mental ability is greater.

It is clear from any number of investigations that mental ability, as distinguished from IQ, increases rapidly from birth through adolescence (see Figure 4.4) (Bayley, 1970; Honzik, 1973; Siegler & Richards, 1982). Moreover, certain components of overall mental ability appear to mature more rapidly than others. Thus, **fluid** intelligence, which is best represented in measures of reasoning and speed of information processing (inductive reasoning, spatial reasoning, and perceptual speed) tends to develop more rapidly than **crystallized** intelligence, which is represented by measures of the breadth and depth of acquired knowledge (vocabulary, general information, and verbal comprehension). By age 12, the average young person's score on perceptual speed (a measure of fluid intelligence) has reached 80 percent of his or her ultimate peak; in contrast, the 80 percent level for verbal comprehension (a measure of crystallized intelligence) is not reached until age 18. In general, the peak of fluid intelligence occurs in the twenties, with a decline thereafter, whereas crystallized intelligence remains stable or increases at least through the sixties (Carroll, 1989; Cattell, 1963; Horn & Hofer, 1992).

Studies of *overall* intelligence might indicate a leveling off during young adulthood, with a slight decline in middle age and a more rapid decline in old age, but these results can be deceptive because they mask differences in fluid and crystallized intelligence. For example, in the Berkeley Growth Study, which involved repeated measurements of the same subjects over time, scores on crystallized measures from the Wechsler intelligence test, such as vocabulary and verbal comprehension, were still improving at age 36. In contrast, scales that appear to depend more on fluid abilities, such as object assembly (the individual must put together a jigsaw puzzle of an object such as an animal without any prior knowledge about what the object is) and

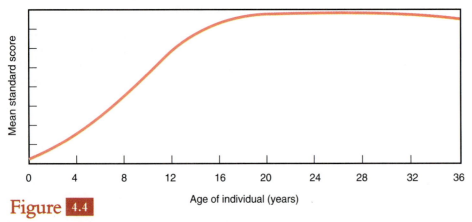

## Figure 4.4

Theoretical curve of the average growth of intelligence based on repeated examination of the same individuals in the Berkeley Growth Study with infant and preschool intelligence tests, the S–B, W–B, and WAIS. $N = 61$ cases; the number of cases tested at each of 42 ages averaged 54 per age. Adapted from N. Bayley (1970). Development of mental abilities. In P. H. Mussen (Ed.), *Carmichael's manual of child psychology* (Vol. 1). New York: Wiley. p. 1176, Fig. 3 (3rd ed.). Copyright © 1970 by John Wiley & Sons, Inc. Reprinted by permission.

block design (presented with a drawing of a geometric pattern, the individual must arrange a set of multicolored blocks to match the pattern), peaked in early adulthood and then began to decline (see Figure 4.5) (Bayley, 1966, 1971). Such tasks demonstrate the individual's response speed, speed of perception, and the ability to conceptualize objects in space.

Research on cognitive aging continues to show that performance on crystallized measures (particularly vocabulary) is maintained at a relatively high level until late in life (Dixon, Kramer, & Baltes, 1985; Perlmutter, 1988; Schaie, 1983). Although some aspects of intelligence do decline, particularly fluid reasoning, it is clear that there is a great deal of variability in older adults' performances. What enables some adults to maintain or even improve their intellectual skills well into their old age? One line of recent research is examining the notion of compensation, the possibility that some aspects of intelligence that do not decline may actually compensate (or substitute) for those that do. For example, although many older adults experience memory difficulties, the practical use of memory aids (such as written reminders) or reliance on other people (spouses, friends) are intellectual strategies that can counter some of those difficulties (Dixon, 1992). Undoubtedly, future research will turn up examples of the ways in which individuals can compensate for possible losses in cognitive functioning. We already know that the intellectual performance of older adults on some tasks can be improved through training and practice (Baltes & Willis, 1982; Schaie & Willis, 1986).

In sum, researchers are pursuing an understanding of the course of development of various cognitive abilities, and the ways in which these abilities can be expressed. It seems clear, however, that the level of intellectual functioning achieved by late adolescence and the extent to which that capacity is exploited during this period largely determine cognitive functioning in adulthood. As Alfred North Whitehead once remarked, "the imagination is most active between the ages of 19 and 35 and we must keep going thereafter on whatever fizz we have experienced then" (quoted in Elkind, 1968, p. 132).

## Sex Differences in Cognitive Development

There are a number of consistent differences in intellectual functioning between male and female children and adolescents (Deaux, 1985; Linn & Hyde, 1991; Linn & Petersen, 1985). Beginning at about age 10 or 11, girls outperform boys on a variety of measures of verbal ability, including language production, creative writing, comprehension of difficult written material, and verbal fluency, although currently, differences in verbal ability appear to be narrowing (Applebee, Langer, & Mullis, 1986; Hyde, 1993; Mullis et al., 1994). In contrast, by adolescence, boys perform better than girls on some measures of spatial and mathematical ability (Benbow, 1992; Linn & Hyde, 1991; Linn & Petersen, 1985; Scarr & Carter-Saltzman, 1982).

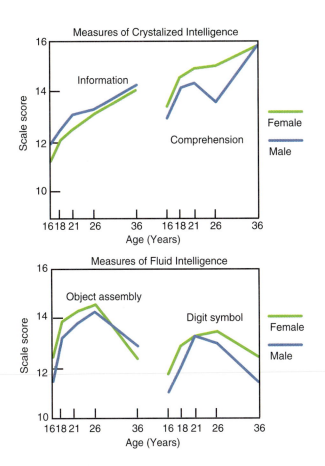

## Figure 4.5

Curves of mean scores by sex and age for four Wechsler subtests, Berkeley Growth Study. From N. Bayley (1966). Learning in adulthood: The role of intelligence. In H. J. Klausmeier & C. W. Harris (Eds.), *Analysis of conceptual learning.* New York: Academic Press. By permission.

Spatial ability requires skill in visual transformations. This ability has been studied a great deal, using many different measures (Law, Pellegrino, & Hunt, 1993; Linn & Petersen, 1985; Sanders, Soares, & D'Aquila, 1982). All of the measures are interrelated, but most investigators conceive of three types of spatial ability: *mental rotation*—the ability to conceptualize a transformed visual arrangement, such as imagining how an object in space would look from a different angle, or deducing from a set of gears how movement in one gear would affect the direction and speed of movement in another gear (see Figure 4.6); *spatial relations* or *spatial orientation*—comprehension of the arrangements of elements within a visual stimulus pattern (e.g., looking at complex designs to determine whether they are the same or, if not, how they differ); and *spatial visualization*—the ability to plan and carry out multiple-step procedures in solving visual tasks (e.g., mentally unfolding a piece of paper). Such tasks may involve mental rotation or spatial orientation. Visual spatial tasks, such as those involved in architecture, engineering, and graphic arts use these three abilities to varying degrees. The principal and most consistent sex differences in spatial ability have been found on tasks requiring mental rotation (Law, Pellegrino, & Hunt, 1993; Linn & Petersen, 1985; Scarr & Carter-Saltzman, 1982).

During adolescence, boys begin to perform better, on average, than girls on mathematics tests. Much recent research has focused on sex differences in mathematics ability in an effort to determine why such differences exist (Board on Mathematical Sciences, 1989; Dossey et al., 1988; Lapointe, Mead, & Askew, 1992; Linn & Hyde, 1991; Mullis et al., 1994). Some studies have found that sex differences disappear when the number of mathematics courses the adolescent has taken is considered; girls may elect to take fewer courses, thereby reducing their experience with math (Board on Mathematical Sciences, 1989). However, more boys than girls are identified as mathematically precocious *before* the time that mathematics courses become elective (Benbow, 1992; Benbow & Stanley, 1980).

It should be stressed that where sex differences in cognitive abilities exist, they are not large; moreover, there is much overlap in the performances of girls and boys (Benbow, 1992; Hyde, 1993). Many boys are proficient in verbal skills, and many girls do very well at spatial reasoning and mathematics. It is important to note also that although there may be sex differences in some aspects of intellectual functioning, these differences do not explain the different numbers of men and women found in certain occupations. For example, even if we

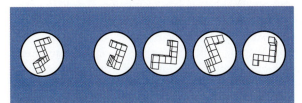

Which two drawings of the four on the right show the same object as the one on the left?

## Figure 4.6

Sample item from Vandenberg and Kuse's Mental Rotation Test. The answer is 1 and 4. Reproduced with permission of the authors and publisher from: S. G. Vandenberg & A. R. Kuse (1978). Mental rotations, a group test of three-dimensional spatial visualization. *Perceptual and Motor Skills,* **47**, 599–604. © 1978 by Perceptual and Motor Skills.

# 4.1 Social Expectations and Math Performance

## WHAT DOES BARBIE SAY?

Many researchers argue that one reason girls may sometimes perform more poorly on mathematics tests than boys do is because of social expectations. One study showed that although adolescent boys and girls had performed equally well in math class and on standardized math tests, the parents of girls, when compared to the parents of boys, believed that math was harder for their daughters and that their daughters had to work harder to do well. Moreover, parents of sons were more likely to believe that math was more important for them than other school subjects. Parents' attitudes toward their children's math abilities were linked to the children's own attitudes. Parents who thought their children had to work hard in math had children who had low self-concepts of their math ability (Parsons, Adler, & Kaczala, 1982).

Such expectations for girls may not be passed on solely through parents. In 1992, Mattel distributed a talking Barbie doll ("Teen Talk Barbie") that, among other messages, said "Math class is tough." Not every doll communicated this message because a computer chip inside the doll determined which messages the doll would provide. Initially, after an uproar by educational organizations and demands that the doll be withdrawn from the market, Mattel agreed only to offer replacements for the dolls carrying the offensive messages. When the furor did not subside, Mattel agreed to change the computer chips so that new dolls coming off the production line would not contain this potentially harmful message.

---

assume that a very high level of spatial ability (ninety-fifth percentile) is required for engineering—and this is true in only a few areas of engineering—the ratio of men to women in that occupation on the basis of spatial ability would be 2:1 rather than 17:1, as it is at present (Hyde, 1981; U.S. Bureau of the Census, 1993).

Where sex differences do exist, the reasons for these differences have been debated vigorously. Because sex differences tend to increase during adolescence, some investigators have concluded that these differences are due primarily to differences in training and social expectations (Board on Mathematical Sciences, 1989). Indeed, boys are more often expected to be interested in, and to do well in, mathematics and mechanical tasks; girls are more often encouraged to pursue and excel in the arts, languages, and literature, but in recent years such gender-oriented expectations have diminished. It is arguable that this difference in experience may be linked with the differential development of cognitive skills. "Given clear gender-differentiated preferences in activities leading to different experiences, socialization patterns rather than sex per se would be more influential in explaining cognitive gender differences" (Graber & Petersen, 1991, p. 269) (see Box 4.1).

It is also possible that biological factors play a role in determining some of the sex differences that become more apparent during adolescence. From early childhood,

the toy preferences and play activities of boys and girls show different patterns, and girls and boys segregate themselves into same-sex social groups. Eleanor Maccoby (1991), a pioneer in the field of sex differences in behavior, argued that this segregation of girls and boys develops naturally, and probably not as a result of socialization. The suggestion of a biological influence emerges from studies showing that late maturers of both sexes tend to outperform early maturers on visual–spatial tasks (McGee, 1979a, 1979b; Petersen, 1981; Sanders & Soares, 1986; Scarr & Carter-Saltzman, 1982). Late maturers are also more likely to have higher spatial than verbal scores, whereas among early maturers the reverse is true (Newcombe & Bandura, 1983; Waber, 1977, 1979; Waber et al., 1985). In one extensive study, later-maturing girls outperformed male peers of the same age on tests of mathematical ability, whereas early-maturing boys had better verbal skills than late maturers (Carlsmith, Dornbusch, & Gross, 1983). In brief, early maturation appears to favor verbal ability, whereas late maturation appears to favor visual–spatial and mathematical skills.

Despite these findings, some investigators have argued that the bulk of the evidence does not support a strong link between the timing of maturation and cognitive skills. First, an analysis of multiple studies found that the relationship between maturational timing and cog-

## 4.2 Minorities and IQ Tests
### ARE ALL PEOPLE TREATED EQUALLY?

A number of investigations have indicated that the average IQ scores of members of some minority groups tend to be lower than the average scores of socioeconomically advantaged whites and of the U.S. population as a whole (Baughman, 1971; Dreger & Miller, 1968; Roberts, 1971). These findings have led some people to conclude that members of certain groups, on average, are genetically limited in intellectual capacities compared with advantaged whites, and that their IQ scores are lower at least partly because they have less potential (Eysenck, 1981; Herrnstein & Murray, 1994; Jensen, 1969, 1980). Others have argued that any differences in average IQ scores are due to environmental factors such as poor prenatal nutrition, poor health, less stimulating early environments, inferior schools, and racial discrimination (Botwinick, 1977; Bradley, Caldwell, & Elardo, 1977; Nichols, 1984). When efforts are made to equalize some of these factors, IQ differences are reduced (Bodmer & Cavalli-Sforza, 1970; Kamin, 1981; Lazar & Darlington, 1982).

Whether proper control of all relevant environmental factors would eliminate differences in intellectual functioning has not been demonstrated conclusively. But even if a definitive study could be conducted, should the results be used as a basis for viewing and treating members of minority and majority groups differently? No. Even under present social conditions, variations in IQ *within* any racial or ethnic group are far larger than any differences that might exist *between* groups; there is wide overlap in their distribution curves. Therefore, it is impossible to predict an individual's IQ from the color of his or her skin (Baughman, 1971; Fraser & Nora, 1986). This will always be the case, regardless of the findings of any future genetic research. As long as racial and ethnic discrimination persist, attempts to apply comparative IQ data inappropriately must be resisted while we seek to create social conditions that provide every opportunity for every individual.

nitive skills was relatively small (Newcombe & Dubas, 1987). Second, sex differences in cognitive skills appear before puberty, thus suggesting that if there are biological determinants of sex differences, they are not related to puberty per se but to other biological influences (such as prenatal hormone levels and a recessive gene located on the X chromosome) (Newcombe & Baenninger, 1989; Vandenberg & Kuse, 1979). Third, reasoning ability in general increases in early adolescence, so there is not a generally disruptive effect of puberty on cognitive functioning (Graber & Petersen, 1991). It seems likely that both environmental and biological influences play a part in determining sex differences in some cognitive abilities.

## Genetic Determinants of Mental Ability

If the measures used in intelligence tests reflect underlying ability and not merely the results of specific learning opportunities (at least for the average individual in the population on which the test was standardized), and if the potential ceiling on an individual's ability is, as

assumed, set by heredity, then we might expect to find evidence of genetic influences on intelligence test performance. To what extent are the kinds of abilities measured by intelligence tests influenced by heredity? This is a controversial topic, as some authorities assert that genetic influences play a dominant role in determining intellectual abilities whereas others claim that the evidence to support such an assertion is slight at best. How can these conflicting views be resolved?

If genetic factors do play a significant role in determining an individual's intellectual abilities, we would expect to find that a child's or adolescent's IQ is more highly correlated with the IQs of his or her parents and other immediate relatives than with those of randomly selected nonrelatives. This is indeed the case. However, the matter is not so simple. Parents who may have provided their children with a superior genetic endowment may also be providing them with other advantages that may be related to intellectual ability: good health, a stimulating home environment, and superior educational opportunities. Thus, if we are to isolate the potential contributions of heredity, a way must be found to control for the potential effects of such environmental variables (see Box 4.2).

## Twin Studies

The investigation of the effects of heredity on intellectual ability is greatly aided by comparing **monozygotic** (MZ) twins (who have identical genetic makeups) with ordinary brothers and sisters and with **dizygotic** (DZ) twins. (Dizygotic twins are no more alike genetically than siblings). If genetic influences play an important role in the determination of intellectual ability, we would expect the IQs of monozygotic twins to be more highly correlated than those of dizygotic twins or nontwin siblings.

This turns out to be true. A review of many studies comparing the intelligence and abilities of monozygotic and dizygotic twins of the same sex found average correlations of .86 for monozygotic twins and .60 for dizygotic twins (Bouchard & McGee, 1981). The correlation for nontwin siblings raised in the same family was .47, suggesting that dizygotic twins share a more similar environment than nontwin siblings. Both of these, in turn, are substantially higher than the correlation for unrelated individuals raised in the same family (Loehlin, Willerman, & Horn, 1988; Plomin, 1986; Plomin & Neiderhiser, 1992; Segal, 1985).

One fascinating investigation has found that even the patterns of developmental change at early ages may have a genetic component. In one longitudinal study, repeated measurements of mental and motor develop- ment were conducted during the first two years of life. When the scores of 261 pairs of twins (MZ and DZ) were analyzed, the profiles of their developmental spurts and lags were very similar (see Figure 4.7). Apparently "the developmental sequence is an expression of timed gene action which may produce spurts or lags between ages" (Wilson & Harpring, 1972, p. 280). The finding that the pattern of development among MZ twins was even more similar than among DZ twins suggests further the strength of genetic influences. In a follow-up study of the same subjects during the preschool and school years, similar results were found; indeed, the correlations between IQs in MZ twins rose slightly with age, whereas those for DZ twins showed a significant decrease (Wilson, 1975, 1977, 1983).

Although twin studies comparing monozygotic and dizygotic twins can be extremely valuable in the search for genetic influences, some qualifications should be kept in mind. For one thing, it is often assumed that because they have the same genetic makeup, monozygotic twins are *physically* identical at birth. This is not necessarily so. For example, one twin usually weighs slightly more than the other, perhaps because the two fetuses shared un- equally in intrauterine blood circulation. It has been shown that even small differences between identical twins at birth can interact with the environment to produce larger differences in behavior (Smith, 1976).

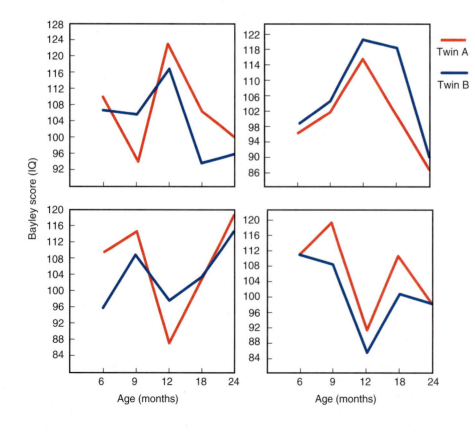

**Figure** 4.7

Bayley score profiles for four pairs of twins illustrating con- cordance in developmental sta- tus at each age and congruence for the pattern of changes over age. From R. S. Wilson & E. B. Harpring (1972). Mental and motor development in infant twins. *Developmental Psychology,* **7,** 277–287. Copyright © 1972 by the American Psychological Association. Reprinted by per- mission.

Another inaccurate assumption is that the environmental influences to which DZ twins are exposed are as similar as those to which MZ twins are exposed (Plomin, 1986). It is true that both DZ and MZ twins grow up in the same family and share many experiences. However, several studies have found that compared with fraternal twins, identical twins spend more time together, have more similar reputations, and are more likely to be in the same classrooms, have similar health records, and in many other respects share a nearly identical physical and social environment (Jones, 1946, 1954). MZ twins may also be treated in more similar ways by parents, siblings, peers, and others than DZ twins, partly because they look alike and partly because their behavior is more similar to begin with (Scarr & Carter-Saltzman, 1979). Even in twin studies, then, environmental influences cannot be fully controlled.

## Adoption Studies

Another useful way to investigate genetic influences on intelligence is to study children and adolescents who have been raised by adoptive parents from a very early age and to compare their IQs with those of their biological and adoptive parents (Loehlin et al., 1988; Plomin, 1986). Because these children have had little or no contact with their biological parents, any similarity to those parents is assumed to reflect genetic influences. The correlation between the IQs of children and their adoptive parents is assumed to indicate environmental influences.

Across adoption studies, the correlation between adoptive parents' intelligence test scores and those of their adopted children is about .16. In contrast, the correlation between those children's scores and those of their biological parents is about .36 (Vandenberg & Vogler, 1985). The correlation between parents' and children's scores for children raised by their biological parents was .61, thereby suggesting that both heredity *and* environment make important contributions (Reed & Rich, 1982).

A French adoption study examined children who had been born to unskilled parents and raised in upper-income professional families (Schiff et al., 1982). The investigators found that the IQs of the adopted children were similar to those of natural children from the same socioeconomically advantaged group, and 14 points higher than those of children of unskilled workers in general. Similar results were found in a study of black and interracial children who had been adopted in infancy by middle-class white families (Scarr & Weinberg, 1976).

In sum, similarities in IQ are highest between people who are closely related genetically (i.e., monozygotic twins) and lowest between people who are unrelated. It seems clear that an individual's genetic inheritance is an important determinant of IQ. However, there are also similarities between the IQs of adoptive parents and their adopted children. Although some of these similarities could be due to selective placement by adoption agencies (i.e., placement in homes similar to the biological parent's), they also reflect the importance of the home environment (Scarr & Kidd, 1983; Willerman, 1979). Environmental as well as genetic factors are important in raising or lowering a child's level of intellectual performance. However, environmental forces are effective only within the ultimate limits set by heredity.

## Creativity

Although it is difficult to define objectively, *creativity* impresses us as an important concept. We all know people, including adolescents, whom we acknowledge to be intelligent but who appear to lack creativity. Similarly, we know people who appear to be highly creative even though they may not attain particularly high scores on an intelligence test. What exactly do we mean by creativity? One definition of creativity is:

> The purposeful transformation of a body of knowledge, where that transformation is so significant that the body of knowledge is irrevocably changed from the way it was before. This kind of transformation can be accomplished conceptually, as in the case of proposing a new theory, or by making new products or representations, developing new technologies, or proposing innovative practical techniques. This notion of creativity emphasizes high-level functioning brought to bear on specialized problems (Feldman, 1989, p. 241).

We might see examples of creativity in successful artists, dancers, scientists, musicians, writers, and others in professions that require an "unusual set of talents" enabling something new to arise from "existing bodies of knowledge" (Feldman, 1989, p. 241). Among adolescents, choreographing a ballet show, winning an art or drama competition, writing short stories or children's books, placing high at a science fair, and other such activities are taken to be signs of creativity (Dacey, 1989).

Some studies of creativity have sought to determine whether creativity could be differentiated from intelligence per se. In one such study (Wallach & Kogan, 1971), the subjects (fifth-grade boys and girls) were given standard intelligence tests as well as tests of creativity. The creativity measures asked subjects to generate as many

School science fair contestants working on their entry.

answers as possible to a question, which gives an indication of divergent thinking. For example, subjects were asked to: name as many objects as they could that had a particular characteristic (e.g., "Name all the things you know that are *sharp*"); think up various uses for objects (e.g., "Tell me all the different ways that you would use a *newspaper*"); think of all the things some patterns might be (see Figure 4.8 *a* and *b*); and enumerate all the things that nonsense line drawings (see Figure 4.8 *c* and *d*) made them think of.

In this study, subjects were considered to be creative if they gave many answers, some of which were unique compared with those given by other children. The four measures of creativity correlated highly with one another, but they showed little correlation with the measures of intelligence. These findings suggest that creativity and intelligence can be meaningfully differentiated from each other. Other studies have indicated that a moderately high level of intellectual ability is essential for creativity (MacKinnon, 1983; Wallach, 1985).

Studies have found that among gifted adolescents there are personality differences between those who score higher on originality (creativity) than on intellectual mastery (intelligence) and those who score higher on intellectual mastery than on originality (Hogan, 1980; Horowitz & O'Brien, 1985). The former tend to be more sociable, impulsive, and nonconforming; their thinking is generally less precise and more fantasy based. In contrast, the latter tend to be more shy and guarded and more conventional; their thinking is more deliberate, logical, and narrowly analytical—it focuses more on individual trees than on the forest as a whole (Hogan, 1980).

In one study, the attitude patterns of high school seniors who scored high on measures of creativity were compared with those of adolescents who were *unselected* for creativity but similar in age, socioeconomic status, and parental occupation (Torrance & Dauw, 1966). The creative seniors emerged as far more intuitive, willing to experiment, and less hostile, as well as more resistant to social pressures. In contrast, seniors in the unselected comparison group were oriented much more toward rules and tradition, planfulness, and passive compliance.

Other studies have yielded similar results (Sternberg, 1988). Depending somewhat on the area of talent, such as mathematics or art, creative adolescents have been found to be more independent, unconventional, self-reliant, and imaginative, and more spontaneous and energetic. They appear to be better able to tolerate the tension that comes from holding strongly opposed values, as well as more capable of reconciling them; they are more flexible, intuitive, and capable of tolerating ambiguity; more open to feelings; and generally more socially poised and self-confident than their less creative peers (Albert & Runco, 1989; Csikszentmihalyi, Rathunde, & Whalen, 1993; Janos & Robinson, 1985).

## Promoting Creativity in Adolescents

Whether creative thinking can be promoted among adolescents appears to depend on a variety of external as well as internal factors, including family influences and the attitudes and behaviors of teachers and school adminis-

Tell me all the things you think each drawing (pattern) could be.

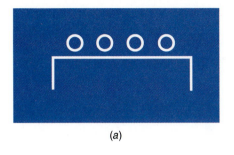

(a)

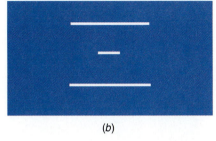

(b)

Tell me all the things it (the whole line) makes you think of.

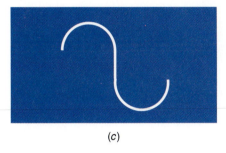

(c)

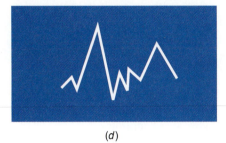

(d)

trators. Creativity appears to be fostered in direct proportion to the extent that parents and the schools value creative thinking, curiosity, and unusual questions and interests; recognize and reward unusual skills and talents; and try to provide a rich and varied cultural and educational atmosphere, one that includes opportunities for self-initiated learning (Bloom, 1985; Csikszentmihalyi, Rathunde, & Whalen, 1993; Hogan, 1980).

One investigation found that parents of high-intelligence/low-creativity adolescents tend to emphasize grades, conformity, cleanliness, and manners. In contrast, parents of high-intelligence/high-creativity adolescents are less critical of their children and encourage openness, enthusiasm, and interest in new experiences (Wallach & Kogan, 1971). Similarly, another study found that parents of creative adolescents were

keenly interested in their children's behavior, but they seldom proscribe rules to govern it. These parents were found to average one specific rule, such as the number of study hours, bedtimes, or sexual activity. . . . Parents in the creative families do not rely on rigid sets of rules to control their child's behavior. Instead, by modelling and family discussions, they espouse a well-defined set of values, and expect their child to make personal decisions based on these values (Dacey, 1989, pp. 266–267).

Other interesting features of families that foster creativity were also noted. For example, highly creative adolescents had a large number of collections (such as campaign pins) and were provided with a wide variety of opportunities (such as lessons and equipment). There was a great deal of humor in the family as well, with plenty of "fooling around" (Dacey, 1989).

Adolescence is the stage in development when the individual, with newly expanded cognitive skills, is most open to exploration and a sense of adventure, intellectually as well as in other areas. For this reason, it is an optimal time in which to encourage curiosity and creative potential.

## The Piagetian Approach to Cognitive Development

As noted earlier, for many years the psychometric approach, which focused on individual differences in intelligence, dominated the field of intellectual development. This approach, however, has not "contributed greatly to our understanding of adolescent cognitive development" (Keating, 1980, p. 239). The work of Jean Piaget, on the other hand, has contributed greatly to what we know about changes in the thinking and reasoning abilities of adolescents.

The emphasis on cognitive development owes more to Swiss psychologist Jean Piaget than to any other theorist. Piaget is shown here with his longtime collaborator, Barbel Inhelder.

Jean Piaget was a Swiss psychologist who argued that the individual proceeds through a series of stages of development. Each stage represents a qualitative shift in the way that the individual reasons. Piaget argued that, regardless of the age at which a given child or adolescent reaches a particular stage, he or she cannot enter that stage without having first demonstrated the cognitive achievements that are hallmarks of the earlier stages (Fischer & Silvern, 1985). Piaget viewed human cognition as "a specific form of biological adaptation of a complex organism in a complex environment" (Flavell, 1985, p. 4). The focus of Piaget's concern was not on individual differences in intelligence, as seen in the psychometric approach, but rather on the sequence of cognitive stages children pass through on their way to mature logical reasoning.

According to Piaget, there are four major stages of cognitive development: (1) the **sensorimotor** stage (birth to 18 months), (2) the **preoperational** stage (18 months to 7 years), (3) the stage of **concrete operations** (7 to 12 years), and (4) the stage of **formal operations** (from about age 12 on) (Piaget, 1954, 1970). In this stage theory, thought is viewed as developing through the gradual internalization of action (Inhelder & Piaget, 1958). During the sensorimotor stage (the period before the acquisition of language), the child is developing rather simple generalized responses, or schemas of action, to objects and people in the world around him or her. He or she may discover that already-acquired responses may be applied to new objects (i.e., shaking or banging an unfamiliar toy), a process called *assimilation*. However, in addition to incorporating new objects into existing schemas or response systems, the young child is also learning to modify existing respons-

es to adjust to the unique characteristics of new objects; this process is called *accommodation*.

> The 2-year-old child who has never been exposed to a magnet may initially assimilate it to prior schemata and act toward the magnet as he or she does toward a familiar toy. The child may bang it, bounce it, throw it, or try to make it produce a noise. But once the child discovers the unique quality of the magnet, that it attracts metal, he or she will now accommodate to that quality and begin to apply the magnet to a variety of objects to see if they will adhere to it (Mussen, Conger, & Kagan, 1979, p. 17).

Unless the young child is capable of accommodation as well as assimilation, progress in mental development would not be possible. Assimilation provides for continuity in development and enables the child to profit from his or her past experience; accommodation provides for meaningful growth and change. Much of a child's mental development, in Piaget's view, involves the resolution of tensions between the processes of assimilation and accommodation. Moreover, assimilation and accommodation are not confined to childhood; these processes occur continuously throughout life (see Box 4.3).

During the preoperational stage, children's mental growth advances significantly, for they now have the tool of language and can manipulate meanings as well as objects. They can deal with objects as symbols for other objects (pretending that a block of wood is a toy car, or that a doll is a baby girl, for example). But their conceptual ability is still relatively rudimentary, although recent research indicates that when dealing with rela-

## 4.3 Assimilation and Accommodation
### AN EXAMPLE FROM THE MOVIES

Assimilation (the process in which a person applies already learned responses to unfamiliar objects) and accommodation (the process in which existing schemas or ways of responding are modified to adapt to the unique characteristics of new objects) are two complementary processes that operate throughout life. A 1984 movie titled *The Gods Must Be Crazy* provides a perfect example of these two processes. The movie takes place in the Kalahari desert. The main character, Xi, is a bushman who has not been exposed to the ways and means of life in industrialized nations. Suddenly one day, Xi observes a jeep driving across the desert. Having never seen a moving vehicle, he interprets this object as an animal with four round legs. This response illustrates assimilation in that the unfamiliar object (jeep) is incorporated (assimilated) into the class of objects (i.e., animals) that is familiar to the bushman. Later on in the movie, we see Xi grinning and driving the jeep at a fast speed. Clearly, he has accommodated; his understanding of the concept of "jeep" has changed.

tively simple and familiar events and objects, preschool children are likely to display greater cognitive ability than Piagetian theory would predict (Keating, 1980; Mussen et al., 1990).

## The Stage of Concrete Operations

In middle and late childhood (about ages 7–11), the child's thought shows impressive advances over the preoperational period. The preoperational child functions largely in terms of "the phenomenal, before-the-eye-reality" (Flavell, 1963, p. 203). Even when the child is treating an object symbolically (pretending that a block of wood is a toy car), he or she is still dealing with it primarily in terms of the here and now. For example, the child does not mentally explore the various situations in which the "car" might logically become involved. In contrast, in the period of concrete operations the child begins to extend thought from the *actual* toward the *potential* (Elkind, 1970; Flavell, 1985). This extension is aided by the development of concrete operational cognitive structures. Unlike preoperational children, who are basically limited to responding directly to the properties of objects themselves, 7- to 11-year-olds become increasingly capable of dealing not only with the properties of objects but also with the relationships among them.

The concrete operational child begins to use a new set of rules, called *groupings,* for dealing with these relationships. Those rules greatly increase the flexibility and power of the child's thinking. One such rule is the rule of equivalence: If A is equal to B in some way (e.g., length)

and if B is equal to C, then it must be true that A is equal to C. Given this information, the child does not have to measure A and C to know that this is the case.

Another rule that the child recognizes is that there are certain fixed relationships among objects or properties of objects. For example, the concrete operational child can appreciate that if A is longer than B and B is longer than C, then A must be longer than C. The child at this stage also realizes that objects (or their qualities) can belong to more than one category or class (for example, a chocolate bar can belong both to a class of objects that are sweet and to a class of objects that are brown). In addition, he or she begins to recognize that classes can be hierarchical. For example, the concrete operational child can accept the idea that an orange belongs to the class *fruit,* which, in turn, belongs in the larger class *food.*

An important point is that the concrete operational child is able to engage in intellectual operations that are reversible. For example, the child recognizes that if four poker chips are removed from a pile of six chips and those four chips are further subdivided into two piles of two each, after which the whole procedure is reversed, the final pile must contain the original number of chips. Concrete operational children can also decenter; that is, "they can focus their attention on several attributes of an object or event simultaneously and understand the relations among dimensions or attributes" (Mussen et al., 1990, p. 276).

For example, faced with choosing between a long, thin popsicle and a shorter but very wide popsicle (in fact, the one with greater quantity) the preoperational child might very well choose the long popsicle, believ-

The concrete operational child can order and classify real objects, but is not yet ready to engage in abstract reasoning.

and five yellow blocks and asked whether there are more red blocks or more blocks, they are likely to reply that there are more red blocks. They cannot conceive that a particular object can belong to two classes at the same time. A 6- or 7-year-old child, on the other hand, can view red blocks as included in the more general class *blocks,* and will give the correct answer.

Another important operation that is mastered by the concrete operational child is conservation—the understanding that liquids and solids can change in shape without changing in volume or mass. For example, it is not until about age 6 or 7 that the child is able to grasp the fact that an amount of liquid poured from a large glass into two smaller glasses remains the same. A 4- or 5-year-old believes that if one changes the shape of an object one also changes its quantity; the child does not realize that its quantity is conserved.

> The concrete operational child solves the problem by taking account of both the width of the container and the levels of the liquids at the same time. He thus comes to realize that for every change in the level of the liquids there is a corresponding change in the widths of the containers which exactly compensates for change in level. The awareness of reversibility, thanks to the concrete operational system, allows the child to discover the conservation of quantities (Elkind, 1968, p. 141).

ing that it is bigger (contains more popsicle) than the shorter one. This is because the preoperational child focuses on only one dimension (length) and not the other (width). Concrete operational children, because of their ability to decenter, will not have any difficulty accurately determining which popsicle will give them the biggest bite.

The development of this system of concrete operations makes possible a kind of reasoning that does not appear in the preschool years: Children become increasingly able to think in relational terms. Where previously, they might have been able to describe an object in absolute terms (e.g., "the object is dark") they now become able to think relatively as well, so that they can also describe the object as darker or lighter than another object. Because they are less limited by the absolute properties of objects, concrete operational children can also deal with class inclusion: They can reason simultaneously about part of the whole and the whole. For example, if younger children are shown ten red blocks

Similarly, having gained the ability to depart from the absolute properties of objects, the concrete operational child becomes capable of serialization (or serial ordering)—the ability to arrange objects along some dimension such as height, weight, or brightness (e.g., to arrange a series of dolls from shortest to tallest). The child is able to do this because he or she can comprehend that doll B must be viewed *both* as taller than doll A *and* as shorter than doll C if it is to fit into its proper place. Younger children fail at such tasks because they cannot recognize that an element can simultaneously stand in two different relations with other elements. Piaget notes that the concrete operational child's ability to move from the actual to the potential is a logical consequence of just such processes as these. For example, once a child can view doll A as shorter than doll B, which, in turn, is shorter than doll C, it is a short step to thinking about the *possibility* of a doll D that would be taller than doll C (Inhelder & Piaget, 1958).

The child's thought clearly makes many significant advances during the concrete operational period, and those advances continue to play an important role

throughout life. However, the child's thinking is still limited when contrasted with that of the adolescent. As Piaget and Inhelder noted, "concrete thought remains essentially attached to empirical reality. . . . Therefore, it attains no more than a concept of 'what is possible,' which is a simple (and not very great) extension of the empirical situation" (Inhelder & Piaget, 1958, p. 250).

In other words, the starting point for concrete operational children is always the real rather than the potential, and they can reason only about things with which they have had direct personal experience. Moreover, they have difficulty as soon as they have to deal with a hypothetical or contrary-to-fact proposition. Although they can deal simultaneously with two classes, relations, or quantitative dimensions, such as size and color, that is about the limit of their capabilities. As soon as more than two variables have to be taken into account, they run into trouble (Elkind, 1968).

## The Stage of Formal Operations

During the stage of formal operations—usually beginning around age 12 but with marked individual variations—the adolescent gains a number of important capabilities that were not present in the middle childhood years. In Piaget's view, the most basic of those capabilities is a shift of emphasis from the *real* to the *possible,* from *what is* to *what might be.* The concrete operational child mentally manipulates objects and events; the formal operational child can manipulate ideas about hypothetical situations. For example, if a 7-year-old is asked, "If all creatures from outer space have yellow feet, and this creature has yellow feet, is it from outer space?" he or she may say, "I never saw a creature from outer space" (Mussen et al., 1990). The 7-year-old has trouble reasoning about unreal or improbable events. When asked the same question, an adolescent can reach a conclusion based solely on logic. "The child usually begins with reality and moves reluctantly, if at all, to possibility; in contrast, the adolescent or adult is more apt to begin with possibility and only subsequently proceed to reality" (Flavell, 1985, p. 98).

**Hypothetico–Deductive Reasoning.** The subordination of the real to the possible is reflected in the way adolescents approach problems (Flavell, 1985). Unlike the concrete operational child, the adolescent is able to approach a problem by trying to imagine all the possible relationships among items in a given body of data. Then, through a process that combines logical analysis and experimental verification, he or she can determine

which of the possible relationships actually holds true. In short, the adolescent becomes more capable of hypothetico–deductive thinking, which is much like the reasoning of the scientist. The process of deduction is no longer confined to perceived realities but extends to hypothetical statements.

The development of hypothetico-deductive thinking and related aspects of formal operations makes adolescent thought much richer, broader, and more flexible than that of the concrete operational child. Although the latter is capable of a rudimentary form of hypothesis formation closely linked to concrete experience, the limits of this capability are readily apparent. For example, once they have thought of one possible explanation for a problem situation, younger children are likely to immediately accept it as true. In contrast, adolescents are likely to recognize the arbitrary nature of hypotheses. Consequently, they tend to consider all possible explanations, even those that may be rather fanciful, and to examine the evidence for or against each, before adopt-

Adolescents are more capable than younger children of engaging in hypothetico-deductive reasoning, much as a scientist does.

ing one of them. Even then, as we shall see, they may hesitate to commit themselves.

This fundamental difference in approach between the younger child and the average adolescent was clearly demonstrated in an experiment by David Elkind. Two groups of subjects, children 8–9 years old and adolescents 13–14 years old, were given a concept-formation problem involving pictures of wheeled and nonwheeled tools and wheeled and nonwheeled vehicles. The pictures were presented in pairs, with each pair including both a wheeled object and a nonwheeled object. In each case the subject was asked to choose one member of the pair. Choosing a wheeled object always made a light go on whereas choosing a nonwheeled object did not. The subject was asked to determine the kind of picture that would make the signal light go on every time.

Adolescents and younger children handled the task in very different ways:

> Only half of the children were able to arrive at the notion that it was the choice of wheeled objects which made the light go on. Furthermore, it took those children who did succeed almost all of the allotted 72 trials to arrive at a correct solution. On the other hand, *all* of the adolescents solved the problem and many did so in as few as 10 trials (Elkind, 1966, p. 145).

The tendency of adolescents to consider a series of alternative hypotheses, testing each against the facts and discarding those that prove to be wrong, was apparent in their spontaneous verbalizations during the experiment ("Maybe it's transportation. . . . No, it must be something else, I'll try. . . "). In this fashion, adolescents quickly solved the problem. The children, on the other hand, appeared to become fixated on an initial hypothesis that was strongly suggested by the data (e.g., tool versus nontool or vehicle versus nonvehicle). They clung to that hypothesis even though they continued to fail most trials. Although the adolescents also might have considered such hypotheses initially, they quickly discarded them when they were not verified by experience. It appears that an important part of the child's lack of flexibility is an inability to differentiate hypotheses from reality. Once a hypothesis was adopted, it became "true" and the child felt no need to test it further. "Indeed, [the child] seems unaware of the hypothetical quality of his [or her] strategy and seems to feel that it is imposed from without rather than constructed from within" (Elkind, 1966, p. 146). In Piaget's view, it is the adolescent's awareness of possibility that enables him or her to distinguish thought from reality (Inhelder & Piaget, 1958).

Other related differences distinguish the thought of an adolescent from that of a concrete operational child. Unlike the child, the adolescent can take his or her own thought as an object and reason about it. Formal thinking is, above all, propositional thinking (Flavell, 1985). As Inhelder and Piaget (1958) commented, "When verbal statements are substituted for objects, a new type of thinking—propositional logic—is imposed on the logic of classes and relations relevant to these objects" (p. 253). This capability may lead adolescents to search for inconsistencies or fallacies in their own thought. Thus, a 14-year-old girl may become preoccupied with the following propositions:

1. God loves humanity.
2. There are many suffering human beings (Mussen et al., 1990, p. 281).

The apparent incompatibility of these propositions may lead her to try to resolve the tension, either by finding a way to reconcile the propositions or by questioning the validity of one or the other.

At times adolescents may feel almost like spectators at the creation of their own thoughts. One adolescent remarked, "I found myself thinking about my future, and then I began to think about why I was thinking about my future, and then I began to think about why I was thinking about why I was thinking about my future." This preoccupation with thought itself is characteristic of the emergence of the stage of formal operations.

## Other Characteristics of Adolescent Thought

In addition to the aspects of adolescent thought that were emphasized by Piaget, there are a number of other changes to which psychologists have recently called attention. Compared with younger children, adolescents are more likely to be aware of the distinction between simply perceiving something and storing it in memory; they are also more likely to be aware of their own memory capacities and limitations, and to use sophisticated techniques (mnemonic devices) to help them remember, such as dividing a long number into "chunks." "The common thread is the individual's awareness and knowledge about cognitive activity itself and about the mechanisms that can make it more or less efficient" (Keating, 1980, p. 215).

Adolescents are also more likely to use efficient problem-solving strategies in approaching a wide variety of tasks. A good example is the game of "Twenty Questions," in which one player has to determine what the other

player is thinking of, using as few questions as possible. An adolescent or adult is far more likely than a younger child to adopt an overall strategy that involves asking a series of increasingly narrow categorical questions ("Is it alive?" "Is it an animal?"). In contrast, the younger child is more likely to adopt the more concrete and considerably less efficient procedure of asking specific questions from the outset ("Is it a dog?") (Flavell, 1985).

The future time perspective of adolescents is greater than that of younger children (Keating, 1980). Adolescents begin to think about what they will be doing with their lives—whether they will go to college, what kind of work they may be doing, whether they will marry, what the world will be like in five or ten years. To the younger child, the prospect of three months of summer vacation may seem like an eternity; his or her attention is likely to be focused on an upcoming birthday party or a trip to the zoo.

In general, adolescents and adults are more likely than younger children to have what John Flavell calls "a sense of the game"—an awareness that much of life consists of anticipating, formulating, and developing strategies for dealing with problems, whether they involve developing a household budget to avoid financial crisis or estimating the interactions and probable behavior of other people (Flavell, 1985; Ford, 1982).

A number of other characteristics of adolescents appear to be related at least in part to their level of cognitive development. The adolescent's frequent use of irony—of the "put-on" or "put-down"—though clearly serving other motivations as well, can be understood partly as an exercise of his or her newfound talents for thinking at the symbolic level of metaphor, the "as if," and the manifestly absurd (Elkind, 1970, 1984).

## The Generality of Formal Operations

Many experts agree that there is a level of cognitive development beyond that of the concrete operational child, and that it conforms generally to the description of formal operational thinking (Flavell, 1985; Keating, 1990). There is less agreement, however, about how universal and age-specific that level of development may be. Doubts have also been raised about the extent to which the specific competencies that reflect the development of formal operational thinking develop together and represent a distinct departure from earlier modes of thinking (i.e., a new stage), as the theory suggests (Flavell, 1985; Ginsburg & Opper, 1979; Mussen et al., 1990).

Investigators have found some aspects of formal operational thinking in highly intelligent younger chil-

dren (Keating, 1975, 1980). Conversely, many adolescents and adults (perhaps as many as 50 percent) never attain true formal operational thought because of limited ability or cultural limitations, in our own society and in others (Flavell, 1985; Keating, 1980; Kohlberg & Gilligan, 1971). Even very bright adolescents and adults do not always use their capacity for formal operational thinking. This may occur, for example, when a problem seems too far removed from reality or when they are bored, tired, frustrated, or overly involved emotionally (Mussen et al., 1990; Neimark, 1975a, 1975b). Take the familiar example of an intelligent person searching for a favorite pen or a set of missing keys. Frustrated by the failure to find it, he or she is likely to end up looking in the same place repeatedly, despite the certain knowledge that it is not there. Even supposedly objective scientists may be inclined to look for evidence that will confirm their hypotheses while ignoring equally solid evidence that is contradictory (Neimark, 1975a).

# Effects of Cognitive Growth on Adolescents' Lives

## Social Cognition

If deviations from formal operational thinking often occur in dealing with intellectual problems, what can we expect when the far more elusive and emotion-laden problems of human affairs are involved? The scientific investigation of this kind of problem solving is called **social cognition.** It implies attempts to understand in what manner, to what extent, and how accurately people of different ages and differing levels of ability are able to infer what others are thinking or feeling, what they are like psychologically, how they view the world, what their intentions are, and the nature of their relationships with others (e.g., friendship, love, power, fear, admiration) (Lapsley, 1990; Selman, 1980; Shantz, 1983).

Research has shown that children tend to improve in all of these capabilities as they grow older. Preschoolers can identify certain simple emotions in others through facial and other cues, but they appear to be unable to anticipate another person's thoughts, and they tend to describe others in terms of their physical appearance, their behavior, where they live, their family, their possessions, or shared activities rather than in terms of their psychological or social characteristics (Livesley & Bromley, 1973; Shantz, 1983; Selman, 1980).

During middle childhood dramatic advances occur in the child's social understanding. Children describe others less in terms of outward characteristics such as

Social cognition continues to develop during adolescence, as young people become increasingly oriented toward and skillful in inferring the thoughts, intentions, and feelings of others. This girl's peers congratulate her for winning a student election.

appearance, possessions, and behavior and more in terms of inner attributes—attitudes, abilities, and interests. They begin to attend less to the physical aspects of interpersonal interactions and more to the inferred inner experiences and social relations of the participants. They understand that their "thoughts, feelings, and intentions can be the object of another's thinking. . . . In addition, the child shows an ability to infer the feelings of others" (Shantz, 1975, p. 312).

Social cognition continues to develop during adolescence. Adolescents extend their perspective to include the self, the other person, the inner experiences of each, and the relationship between the self and the other as an observer might understand it (Lapsley, 1990; Shantz, 1983). "In social episodes, the adolescent is much more oriented toward and accurate in making inferences about the thoughts, intentions, and feelings of each participant in the episode" (Shantz, 1975, pp. 312–313).

Adolescents are also likely to go beyond merely describing thoughts and feelings, both of the self and others, and try to explain them. They become increasingly likely to extend their efforts to understand thoughts, feelings, and motives beyond those of individuals to those of social groups and people in general (Collins, 1980; Flavell, 1985; Shantz, 1983).

Despite these remarkable advances in cognitive capacity, both adolescents and adults can, and often do, fail to perceive accurately the thoughts, feelings, and intentions of others and the nature of their interactions with them (Higgins & Bargh, 1987). This may occur for a variety of reasons, including lack of relevant information on which to base inferences. Most often, however, it is likely to result from egocentrism—failure to distinguish sufficiently clearly between one's own point of view and that of others (Lapsley, 1990; Shantz, 1975).

## Views of Self, Parents, and the Social System

We should appreciate the critical role that cognitive changes play in helping the adolescent deal with increasingly complex educational and vocational demands. It would be virtually impossible to master such subjects as calculus or the use of metaphor in poetry without the ability to engage in abstract thinking. Further reflection should make it clear that many other aspects of adolescent development also depend on the cognitive advances occurring during this period. Changes in the nature of parent–child relationships; establishment of educational and vocational goals; mounting concern with social, political, and personal values; even a developing sense of ego identity—all are strongly influenced by these cognitive advances.

As we have noted, one of the most important aspects of the emergence of formal operational thought is the ability to entertain hypotheses or theoretical propositions that depart from immediately observable events. In contrast to the child, who for the most part is preoccupied with learning how to function in the here and now, the adolescent is able not only to grasp the immediate state of things but also the state they might or could assume (Elkind, 1968). The implications of this change are vast.

For example, many adolescents exhibit a newfound talent for discovering their previously idealized parents'

feet of clay—questioning their values, comparing them with other, "more understanding" parents, and accusing them of hypocritical inconsistencies between professed values and behavior. All of these changes appear to depend on changes in the adolescent's cognitive ability: "The awareness of the discrepancy between the actual and the possible also helps to make the adolescent a rebel. . . . [They are] always comparing the possible with the actual and discovering that the actual is frequently wanting" (Elkind, 1968, p. 152).

The tendency of some adolescents to criticize existing social, political, and religious systems and their attempts to construct alternative systems depends on the emerging capacity for formal operational thought. The fact that much of an adolescent's concern with the deficiencies of parents and the social order turns out to be more a matter of word than of deed may reflect the fact that this kind of formal operational thinking is still relatively new and not yet fully integrated into the adolescent's adaptation to life.

At the same time, however, it is important to recognize the positive aspects of the adolescent's newly acquired ability to conceptualize and reason abstractly about hypothetical possibilities (Conger, 1979; Elkind, 1984). Although younger adolescents may seem to be playing a game of ideas, this is nonetheless an important and productive exercise. What may appear to an adult to be "vain rehashing or sterile questioning of old worn-out problems" is, for the young person, "youthful explorations and true discoveries" (Osterrieth, 1969, p. 15).

As already noted, preoccupation with thought itself, particularly with one's own thoughts about oneself, is characteristic of formal operations. An adolescent girl or boy is likely to become more introspective and analytical. Many adolescents are concerned about such issues as whether the world they perceive actually exists, and indeed whether they themselves are real or a product of consciousness.

### The Imaginary Audience and Personal Fable

Thoughts and behavior during adolescence may appear to be egocentric. Elkind (1966, 1968) argued that this egocentrism accompanies the attainment of formal operational thought and is a natural consequence of the adolescent's new focus on his or her own thoughts and behaviors. Egocentrism may be manifested in two ways: the imaginary audience and the personal fable. The **imaginary audience** refers to the adolescent's feeling of being on stage—that all eyes are focused on him or her. Much of the adolescent's time, then, is spent constructing, or reacting to, the imaginary audience. This audience is called imaginary because in reality the adolescent is not the object of such attention. In David Elkind's view, the construction of imaginary audiences helps account for a variety of adolescent behaviors and experiences, including the adolescent's sometimes excruciating self-consciousness. When the adolescent is feeling self-critical, he or she is likely to anticipate that the audience will be similarly critical.

Much of an adolescent's time is spent constructing or reacting to the "imaginary audience." This young woman may be dreaming of the impression she will make at her school prom.

By the same token, when the adolescent is in an ebullient, self-admiring mood, he or she may project these feelings onto peers or adults. Adolescents who stand before the mirror admiring their hair, faces, and bodies may be dreaming of the impression they will make on a date or at a party. It is a minor tragedy of adolescent life that when these young people actually meet, each is likely to be more preoccupied with himself or herself than with observing the other. "Gatherings of young adolescents are unique in the sense that each young person is simultaneously an actor . . . and an audience to others" (Elkind, 1966, p. 1030).

Although the concept of imaginary audience was theoretically linked to the emergence of formal operational thought, the research results do not support the existence of this link. The imaginary audience may be alive and well in the lives of adolescents, but it does not seem to require Piaget's highest level of reasoning (Lapsley et al., 1986; Lapsley, 1990; O'Connor & Nikolic, 1990).

The **personal fable,** which complements the imaginary audience, reflects the "belief in one's personal uniqueness and indestructibility" (Lapsley et al., 1986, p. 800). According to Elkind, adolescents, who tend to see themselves as so important to others (the imaginary audience), come to regard themselves and their feelings as very special and unique. Only he or she "can suffer with such agonized intensity, or experience such exquisite rapture" (Elkind, 1966, p. 1031). The personal fable has been used to explain common adolescent behaviors such as driving too fast or unprotected sexual intercourse, risk-taking behaviors that may be based in the belief that "it can't happen to me." Adolescents' intense interest in fads and fashion, idealism, and self-consciousness may also be attributable to the personal fable (Lapsley et al., 1986).

Although many of us can probably remember incidents from our own lives that illustrate the two facets of adolescent egocentrism (imaginary audience and personal fable), it is not at all clear *when* in adolescence egocentrism emerges. It probably begins to appear in early adolescence and to decline by late adolescence, but this conclusion is somewhat limited by inconsistent findings across a number of studies (Lapsley, 1990).

Daniel Lapsley (1990) has argued for a "new look" in our understanding of adolescent egocentrism. Rather than being tied specifically to formal operational thought, the imaginary audience and personal fable come into play when the adolescent has reached a relatively high level of interpersonal understanding. The imaginary audience and personal fable may assist in or arise out of the individuation process, in which the adolescent must establish a separate sense of self and uniqueness. From this perspective, the imaginary audience helps the young person to maintain a sense of connectedness to others whereas the personal fable allows for separateness (Lapsley et al., 1988, 1989); both connectedness and separateness are important dimensions of the individuation process (Grotevant & Cooper, 1985).

## The Information-Processing Approach to Cognitive Development

Although the Piagetian approach is more concerned with the mental processes underlying cognitive development than the psychometric approach, neither says much about the specific mechanisms involved in intellectual performance (Siegler & Richards, 1982; Sternberg, 1985). The **information-processing** approach attempts to do just that. It views cognition in terms of the ways in which people mentally represent and process information or stimuli that are presented to them (Sternberg & Powell, 1983). According to Robert Kail and Jeffrey Bisanz (1992):

> Information-processing theorists assume that *information* is represented internally and manipulated in real time by mental *processes*. Researchers seek to determine what types of information are represented, how information is coded, and how it is organized (p. 230).

Researchers and theorists who favor this approach may use computer simulation techniques to create models of human intellectual functioning. Both computers and humans are involved in attending to, and gaining information from, their environment, processing that information, using problem-solving strategies, storing information and solutions in short-term and long-term memory, and retrieving stored information for subsequent use (Siegler & Richards, 1982; Sternberg & Powell, 1983) (see Box 4.4).

Because the steps carried out by computers in dealing with information and solving problems are highly specific and detailed, they may help us understand the steps humans go through in performing similar tasks. For example, an information-processing analysis may show that an adolescent who is having difficulty solving a problem is using inappropriate strategies to attack the problem, is unable to retrieve information from memory, or is unable to transfer what was learned in a previous situation to the current problem (Campione, Brown, & Ferrara, 1982; Sternberg, 1985).

At the same time, it is important to recognize that computers and the human mind do not always function in the same ways. Table 4.3 presents some similarities and

## 4.4 Prospective Memory

### WATCHING THE CLOCK

The information-processing approach leads us to consider the strategies people use to perform cognitive tasks. Prospective remembering is one such task that we engage in every day and that requires some sort of strategy if the task is to be completed successfully. Prospective memory is remembering to attend to a future event. When we remember to take a particular book to school, or to pick up the dry cleaning on Friday, or to send a birthday card so that it reaches Uncle Mike on time, prospective remembering has occurred. Strategies that are used to enhance prospective memory may include writing notes to oneself, putting the book by the door, or having someone else serve as a reminder ("Remind me to pick up the dry cleaning").

In an investigation of prospective memory in children and adolescents, Stephen Ceci and Urie Bronfenbrenner (1985) set out to determine how efficiently 10- and 14-year-olds engaged in the strategy of time-monitoring, or "clock-watching," in order to remember to take cupcakes out of the oven after baking for 30 minutes. The subjects in the experiment played a video game during the 30 minutes, and every time that they turned around to

look at the clock, their movement was recorded. They were observed in order to determine to what extent they used a sophisticated cognitive strategy to remember. Use of a sophisticated strategy is demonstrated when, early on in the 30-minute interval, subjects engage in frequent clock-checking, ostensibly to calibrate their "psychological clocks"; then there is a waiting period with a low rate of clock-checking while they play the video game; and, finally, as the deadline approaches, there is frequent clock-checking. This particular strategy is an efficient one in that the total amount of time spent monitoring the clock is lower than when another strategy is used—watching the clock continuously.

Half of the sample participated in this study in their own kitchens at home and the other half participated in a laboratory on campus. In the home, the 10-year-olds were as efficient in their monitoring strategies as the 14-year-olds. In the laboratory, however, the 10-year-olds were not as efficient as the 14-year-olds. These results show that 10- and 14-year-olds can use sophisticated cognitive strategies to remember, but an unfamiliar setting hinders the efficiency of younger adolescents.

---

differences between human and computer memory, each of which has both advantages and disadvantages. For many tasks, the computer's speed of processing, storage, and retrieval capacities can be highly superior. For other tasks, however, the human mind functions in a far more complex, flexible, and creative way than even the most advanced computers (Miller, 1983). It is also important to emphasize that information-processing approaches to development, with their emphasis on the cognitive processes and strategies that children and adolescents actually use, extend well beyond the use of computer modeling (Sternberg & Powell, 1983).

### Developmental Changes in Information-Processing Abilities

The application of the information-processing approach to the study of cognitive development began seriously

in the 1960s and 1970s. In the 1990s "the information-processing perspective pervades the study of cognitive development, at least in the sense that the majority of researchers use some concepts, methods, and interpretations that carry an information-processing flavor" (Kail & Bisanz, 1992, p. 229).

The information-processing approach has generated a great deal of research on topics such as perception, memory, problem solving, language, and motor control (Kail & Bisanz, 1992; Schneider & Pressley, 1989). As a result, we know that adolescents are much better able than younger children to repeat a series of numbers, match two sets of abstract arrangements of letters, and respond more quickly to stimuli (Hale, 1990; Pascual-Leone, 1970). These results may be explained by developmental differences in attention span, speed in processing information, or the ability to use a variety of information-processing strategies such as increased knowledge, rehearsal, and mnemonic devices (aids to remembering) (Brown et al., 1983; Flavell, 1985; Siegler & Richards, 1982).

# Table  4.3  A Comparison of Human and Computer Memory[a]

|  | HUMAN MEMORY | COMPUTER MEMORY |
|---|---|---|
| Preferred method of storage | Time-oriented | List-oriented |
| Retention of information | Graded | All-or-none |
| Efficiency (bits of information per second) | Low | High |
| Capacity | Dependent on experience | Independent of experience |
| Retrieval |  |  |
| Relative to context | Strongly dependent | Independent |
| Relative to previous retrievals | Dependent | Independent |
| Purpose | General purpose: open set of functions | Special or general purpose: closed set of functions |

[a]The flexibility and adaptability to new problems and situations of human memory offset the greater precision and speed of computer memory.

SOURCE: From W. K. Estes (1980). Is human memory obsolete? *American Scientist,* **68,** 62–69. By permission of the Sigma Xi Scientific Research Society.

Robert Sternberg and his colleagues have used an information-processing approach to study age differences in problem solving (Sternberg, 1982; Sternberg & Nigro, 1980; Sternberg & Rifkin, 1979). In a study of analogical reasoning, they presented a number of different analogies to third-, sixth-, and ninth-graders and to college students. The type of problem used is illustrated in Figure 4.9. Elements A, B, and C are given; the task is to select the figure of the two on the right (1 or 2) that has the same relationship to C that A has to B (A:B::C:?). As can be seen, A and B have the same similarities (jersey, umbrella, and boots) and the same difference (hat) as C and figure number 1. Therefore, figure 1 is the correct choice. Arriving at the correct choice involves at least three mental processes: encoding (noting the attributes of each figure), inference (finding similarities and differences between A and B on each attribute), and application (finding a relationship between C and figure 1 that parallels the relationship between A and B). Although both children and adults generally used all of these operations, adults carried out each step exhaustively whereas younger children tended to cut the process short, presumably owing to inability to memorize all the attributes of each figure.

In another example of a study arising from the information-processing approach, speed of processing (the time it takes to execute a cognitive process such as mentally adding a series of numbers) was examined in a sample of 7.5- to 21-year-olds (Kail, 1991). Robert Kail noted that previous research had shown that processing time declined throughout childhood and adolescence on cognitive tasks as varied as mental addition, mental rotation, and memory search. Moreover, the decline in processing time was not linear (an even and steady downward trend) but rather exponential, meaning that there was a rather abrupt drop in processing time in late childhood, which leveled off by late adolescence. Given that this exponential function characterized performance on diverse cognitive tasks, Kail (1991)

Which picture on the right (1 or 2) is the same as and different from picture C in the same ways that picture B is the same as and different from picture A?

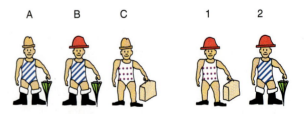

# Figure  4.9

A representative analogy item. The answer is 1 because only the hats differ (as in A and B). From R. J. Sternberg & B. Rifkin (1979). The development of analogical reasoning processes. *Journal of Experimental Child Psychology,* **27,** 195–232. Copyright © 1979 by Academic Press. Reprinted by permission.

argued for a common general mechanism that underlies processing time. Support for such a central mechanism would be found if the exponential change in processing speed were characteristic of not only cognitive tasks such as mental addition, but also of perceptual-motor tasks such as tapping (pressing a button as fast as possible).

To investigate the possibility of a central processing mechanism, children, adolescents, and adults completed three perceptual-motor tasks (tapping; simple reaction time, which called for releasing a button as rapidly as possible; and, pegboard, which required placing pegs in holes) and three cognitive tasks (mental addition; coding, which involved rapid duplication of lines drawn within geometric figures; and, name retrieval, which required judging whether two pictures had the same name). This study showed that an exponential function best described the relation between chronological age and processing time on most of these tasks (see Figure 4.10). Thus, Kail (1991) concluded that the results supported the existence of a general mechanism that controls processing speed. This mechanism can be described by drawing an analogy to computer hardware. "If two computers have identical software but one machine has a slower cycle time (i.e., the time for the central processor to execute a single instruction), that machine will execute all processes more slowly by an amount that depends upon the total number of instructions to be executed" (1991, p. 266). It appears that as the child approaches adolescence, the cycle time may speed up, resulting in faster processing time across all tasks.

As these examples suggest, the information-processing approach holds promise as a way to understand better the cognitive advances of adolescence. This approach does not compete with the Piagetian approach, but rather may complement it. Kail and Bisanz (1992) argued that

> Typical accounts of cognitive development during adolescence emphasize the emergence of powerful reasoning skills associated with formal operational thought. . . . These skills may emerge in adolescence because basic cognitive processes become functionally mature (i.e., achieving adultlike speeds), thus allowing mental resources to be allocated entirely to the "higher" processes typified by formal thought (p. 240).

Future research will undoubtedly tell us more about the link between the adolescent's advanced reasoning skills and the specific cognitive mechanisms that undergo change during the transition to adolescence.

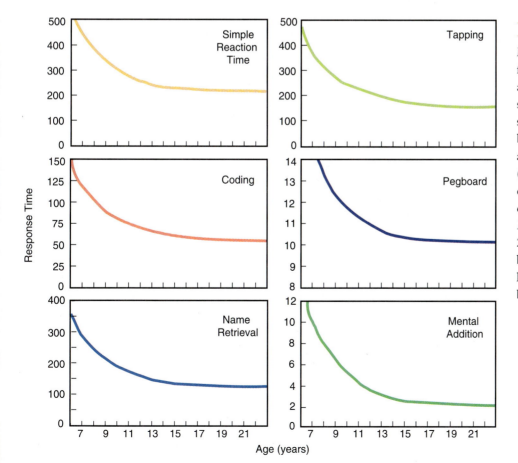

**Figure 4.10**

Mean processing time as a function of chronological age for six operations. (Response time is measured in seconds for coding and pegboard, and milliseconds for all others). From R. Kail (1991). Processing time declines exponentially during childhood and adolescence. *Developmental Psychology, 27,* 259–266. Copyright © 1991 by the American Psychological Association. Adapted by permission.

# Summary

The impressive gains in physical and physiological development that take place in adolescence are accompanied by equally impressive gains in intellectual development. These gains are quantitative (the adolescent becomes capable of accomplishing intellectual tasks more easily, more quickly, and more efficiently) and qualitative (changes occur in the ways in which the adolescent defines problems and reasons about them).

Our understanding of intellectual development in adolescence is guided by three major approaches. The first, the psychometric approach, relies on intelligence testing to discover individual and age-related differences in intellectual ability. The second approach, exemplified by Piagetian theory, focuses on the stages individuals pass through on their way to mature logical reasoning. The third approach, information processing, examines the mental processes that intervene between the input of information and the output of specific intellectual responses. Although these three perspectives have different foci and emphases, they complement rather than compete with each other.

The psychometric approach has led us to view intelligence as the aggregate or global capacity of the individual to comprehend the world and deal effectively with its challenges. It is generally assumed that every individual has an intelligence "ceiling" that is set by heredity, but how closely one approaches one's ceiling is determined by a variety of factors, including the richness of one's environment. Most psychologists believe that intelligence is multidimensional—that it involves a variety of abilities—but they are less likely to agree on the nature of those abilities.

Intellectual *potential* cannot be measured directly. We can only measure what a person can do currently. Thus, the IQ score is an indirect estimate of potential. Because one can never be sure that an IQ score represents a person's full intellectual potential, IQ tests should be used with caution. The practical utility of an intelligence test score depends partly on its stability over time. Although the prediction of adult intelligence is more reliable during adolescence than at earlier ages, some individuals show increases in IQ scores over time whereas others show decreases. Adoption and twin studies make it clear that an individual's genetic inheritance is an important determinant of IQ, although the home environment also plays a significant role.

*Mental ability* (as distinguished from IQ) increases rapidly from birth through adolescence. Moreover, certain components of overall mental ability appear to mature more rapidly than others. *Fluid* intelligence (i.e., reasoning; speed of information processing) reaches its peak in the twenties and declines thereafter, whereas *crystallized* intelligence (i.e., acquired knowledge, such as vocabulary) may increase through the sixties.

Some consistent sex differences in intellectual functioning become stronger in adolescence, with girls outperforming boys on verbal ability while boys overtake girls on some measures of spatial and mathematical ability. The reasons for these differences, biological or experiential, have been debated vigorously. Probably both environmental and biological influences play a part. There is evidence of a weak link between pubertal maturation and cognitive skills. At the same time, experiential factors (parental and social expectations) are associated with intellectual performance.

Although a moderately high level of intellectual ability is essential for creativity, beyond a basic "floor," which varies in different fields, there is little relationship between intellectual ability and creativity. Creative adolescents tend to be more independent, unconventional, self-reliant, perceptive, and rebellious than other young people.

The Piagetian approach to cognitive development outlines four major stages: the *sensorimotor* stage (birth to 18 months), the *preoperational* stage (18 months to 7 years), the stage of *concrete operations* (ages 7–12), and the stage of *formal operations* (from about age 12 on). The hallmarks of formal operational thought, which should be attained in adolescence, is the ability to think abstractly, to formulate and test hypotheses, and to consider what might be as well as what is. These advances in reasoning abilities may be associated with other aspects of adolescents' lives, including more advanced *social cognition* and changing perceptions of the self and others.

The *imaginary audience* and *personal fable* are forms of egocentrism that appear in adolescence. Rather than being tied specifically to formal operational thought, as originally hypothesized, adolescent egocentrism may be seen among people who have reached a relatively high level of interpersonal understanding.

Research conducted from the information-processing perspective has pointed out that adolescents are better able than younger children to repeat a series of numbers, to memorize, to process information more quickly, and to use more accurate strategies to rehearse and remember material. Future research will undoubtedly tell us more about the link between the adolescent's advanced reasoning skills and the specific cognitive mechanisms that undergo change during the transition to adolescence.

# Review Questions

1. In what ways do the three major approaches to intellectual development differ?

2. What do we mean by the term *intelligence*? Is intelligence multidimensional? How have different intelligence theorists dealt with this question?

3. How do intelligence tests attempt to control for environmental influences?

4. How constant are IQ scores over time?

5. Distinguish between fluid and crystallized measures of intelligence and discuss how each changes with age.

6. Discuss the current state of knowledge regarding sex differences in intellectual functioning, including possible reasons for these differences.

7. What methods are used to investigate genetic influences on intelligence? What are the main findings of this research?

8. How do creative adolescents differ from adolescents in general? How can creativity be promoted in adolescents?

9. What are the main characteristics of formal operational thought? Describe how these characteristics may influence the adolescent's view of self, parents, and the social system.

10. What relevance do the imaginary audience and personal fable have for adolescent behavior?

11. Describe the goals of the information-processing approach, and discuss what this approach has told us about adolescents' cognitive development.

# Recommended Readings

Graber, J. A., & Petersen, A. C. (1991). Cognitive changes at adolescence: Biological perspectives. In K. R. Gibson & A. C. Petersen (Eds.), *Brain maturation and cognitive development: Comparative and cross-cultural perspectives* (pp. 253–279). New York: Aldine de Gruyter.

Horowitz, F. D., & O'Brien, M. (1985). *The gifted and talented: Developmental perspectives.* Washington, DC: American Psychological Association.

Keating, D. P. (1990). Adolescent thinking. In S. S. Feldman & G. R. Elliott (Eds.), *At the threshold: The developing adolescent* (pp. 54–89). Cambridge, MA: Harvard University Press.

Shantz, C. U. (1983). Social cognition. In P. H. Mussen, J. H. Flavell, & E. M. Markman (Eds.), *Handbook of child psychology, Vol. 3. Cognitive development* (pp. 495–555, 4th ed.). New York: Wiley.

Sternberg, R. J. (1985). *Beyond IQ: A triarchic theory of intelligence.* San Diego, CA: Harcourt Brace Jovanovich.

Sternberg, R. J., & Berg, C. A. (Eds.). (1992). *Intellectual development.* Cambridge: Cambridge University Press.

# The Family and Parent–Adolescent Relations

5

d uring the past half century, rapid social change has had profound effects on the nature of the family in industrialized nations and on its relations with other social institutions and the community as a whole. In the process, the stresses of adolescence have increased for both parents and their adolescent daughters and sons. This is especially true for poor families—often single-parent families—living in the violent, drug-ridden, socially deteriorated inner cities of the United States. But it is also true in lesser measure for many middle-class families living in the prosperous, tree-shaded suburbs that dominate the North American landscape, and in many smaller cities and towns.

## The Changing Family

What are some of these changes and how have they affected the structure and functioning of today's families? Although the picture is complicated by socioeconomic, political, ethnic, religious, and other factors, some general trends are apparent.

### Urbanization and Mobility

Increasing urbanization, geographic mobility, and globalization of the world economy have altered the nature of modern life and the nature of social institutions (Bronfenbrenner, Moen, & Garbarino, 1984; Conger, 1981, 1988). A high degree of mobility tends to diminish personal, extended-family, and neighborhood ties, as well as the social support they can provide. A study of community life revealed the importance of continuity of residence in the maintenance of social relationships. A clear link was found between length of residence and the number of acquaintances people had, the number of relatives who lived nearby, and the proportion of their friends and relatives who lived in the local community (Kasarda & Janowitz, 1974). Having roots in a community appears to be especially important for low-income families, who are more depen-

## 5.1 | Families and Homelessness

At the most basic level, young people need a safe, dependable, nurturant environment in which to develop. In the United States, increasing numbers are growing up in deteriorated urban ghettos or rural slums, and an increasing percentage of homeless people are children and adolescents. Contrary to popular perception, families with children are now the fastest-growing subgroup of the homeless population (Children's Defense Fund [CDF], 1994).

A 1993 survey of 26 cities by the U.S. Conference of Mayors found that families with children accounted for 43 percent of the homeless population, up from 32 percent in 1992 and 20 percent in 1986 (CDF, 1992, 1994; Institute of Medicine [IOM], 1988). At a minimum, 100,000 children in the United States are homeless each night, and four to five times that number experience homelessness during the course of a year. These figures do not include runaway, abandoned, or abused children or adolescents on the streets or in institutions (CDF, 1994; IOM, 1988).

Homeless and badly housed children and adolescents suffer all the health, developmental, and nutritional risks that others growing up in poverty do, but even more so. They are often exposed to physical hazards such as lead poisoning, poor sanitation, and unsafe buildings. Their education is often disrupted because they move frequently or because shelters are located too far from schools. In one study of eight cities, only 57 percent of homeless children attended school regularly (IOM, 1988).

Homeless children often have significant health problems, but receive inadequate or even no health care at all (CDF, 1994; IOM, 1988). Chronic physical disorders are nearly twice as common among homeless children as among children generally (Wright & Weber, 1987). More than 50 percent lack proper immunization. Malnutrition is common. Developmental, emotional, and learning problems are all significantly more likely among homeless children than among poor but domiciled children (Bassuk & Rubin, 1987). Newly homeless children may regress to toddler-like behaviors or become depressed, anxious, or unusually attached to parents and siblings. In one study in Northern California, a homeless ten-year-old girl was asked what she liked most about herself. She answered, "That I haven't gone crazy yet" (CDF, 1992, p. 38).

Many young people living in shelters or welfare hotels are exposed to violence, deprived of nurturance, and often lack any successful adult—particularly male—role models. Not surprisingly, they learn early not to trust others. All too often, as adolescents the girls become pregnant and the boys become uncontrollable (Chavez, 1987; Conger, 1988).

Among the causes of the low-income family housing crisis (which results all too often in homelessness) are rising housing costs, falling incomes

dent on neighborhood sources of social support than those with higher incomes; "money enables people to reach beyond their own localities for their intimate ties, while the lack of money makes proximity important" (Fischer, 1977, p. 171).

Increased mobility and urbanization have reduced the number of opportunities for informal, direct communication between the family and other social institutions, including schools, churches, and agencies of local government; such communication is more likely to occur in small towns and cities with relatively stable populations (Bronfenbrenner, 1985; Harevan, 1984). The significance of this loss is accentuated because it paral-lels the transfer of many functions that were formerly carried out by the family—educational, vocational, social, economic, and religious—to other social institutions, largely as a consequence of industrialization (Coontz, 1992; Harevan, 1984).

These changes have weakened the stability and inter-dependence of communities, leaving the family more iso-lated from social support systems and more dependent on its own resources.

**Families at Risk.** The situation is particularly acute in the case of poor families living in inner cities. Plagued by low incomes, deteriorated housing, poor

(including those among previously middle-class workers), a steady decline in the availability of housing for the poor and near-poor as a result of sharply reduced government housing support over the past quarter century (see Figure B5.1), and gentrification, which displaces the poor from renovated neighborhoods without providing adequate alternatives. This situation is expected to continue for the remainder of this century.

In 1994, the Secretary of Housing and Urban Development called public attention to the growing levels of homelessness in the United States and has developed a series of federal–local collaborations to address the problem (CDF, 1994). To date, however, funding has been minimal, due at least in part to an increasing backlash against the homeless by a frustrated public, and future prospects in the current political climate appear bleak.

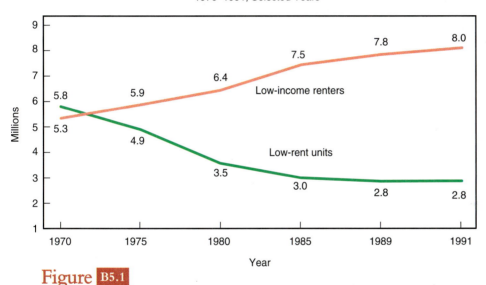

**Low-Income Renters Versus Low-Rent Units, 1970–1991, Selected Years**

**Figure** **B5.1**

Housing squeeze. Note: Low-income renters are the poorest 25 percent of households. Low-rent units rent for 30 percent or less of the income of low-income renters. SOURCE: Low Income Housing Information Service.

schools, and inadequate or nonexistent health care, poor families have more urgent needs than less disadvantaged families for informal support from friends and neighbors and for access to community services (Panel on High-Risk Youth, 1993; Reich, 1994; Schorr, 1988; U.S. Bureau of the Census, 1994). As psychologist James Garbarino and others have noted, social isolation cuts across class lines, but is worst in poor neighborhoods where everyone is stressed and few have the time or energy to be supportive to neighbors because their own needs are not being met (Garbarino & Sherman, 1980; Panel on High-Risk Youth, 1993; Schorr, 1988).

"Concentrated poverty neighborhoods" are much more stratified ethnically and racially and have much higher proportions of unmarried mothers, single-parent families, and unemployed young men than more affluent areas (Jargowsky & Bane, 1990; Panel on High-Risk Youth, 1993). Instead of a network of supportive neighbors, friends, or relatives, families in these neighborhoods are more likely to live in a climate of fear and isolation, surrounded by crime, violence, and drugs. Ominously, in recent years the number of individuals living in such neighborhoods in the United States has more than tripled (Panel on High-Risk Youth, 1993; Ricketts & Mincy, 1990) (see Box 5.1).

Social isolation cuts across class lines, but is worst in poor neighborhoods, where few have the time or energy to be supportive to neighbors because their own needs are not being met.

# The Changing Economy

Several major economic events in the past twenty years have had important consequences for families. Two of these are the accelerating shift from a manufacturing to a service-producing economy, and globalization of the world economy (see Chapter 9). The loss of manufacturing job opportunities has significantly reduced the wages available to less-educated workers because manufacturing has traditionally been a high-wage sector for blue-collar and skilled workers (Panel on High-Risk Youth, 1993; Reich, 1994; U.S. Bureau of the Census, 1994). Not only do many service sector jobs pay less and have fewer health and other benefits, but those that do pay well often require special skills, which may not be easily acquired. Globalization, though it may benefit consumers, has led corporations to export many low-skilled jobs to less-developed countries, and also to downsize and to restrict wages, in order to remain competitive in the world economy.

Although these shifts spurred economic expansion in the 1980s and early 1990s and provided increases in real per-capita income, the gains were highly concentrated in upper-income brackets and brought little real gain to the great majority of families, particularly young families with children (Panel on High-Risk Youth, 1993). In the United States, for families headed by 25- to 30-year-old parents, income in the past two decades has actually declined, with the greatest percentage losses occurring among those without college or high school degrees (Panel on High-Risk Youth, 1993; *The*

*Forgotten Half,* 1988). In 1992, almost a quarter of families in this age group had incomes below the poverty level—more than double the percentage twenty years ago (Children's Defense Fund [CDF], 1994; Panel on High-Risk Youth, 1993).

Most two-parent families have maintained their relative standard of living only because they have two wage earners. Without the added income provided by increased numbers of wives entering the workforce and working longer hours, incomes for 60 percent of two-parent families would actually have been lower in 1989 than in 1979. Though critical to maintaining family incomes, the additional effort families must make may "create stress for the family and problems in providing care and supervision of children" (Panel on High-Risk Youth, 1993, p. 42).

For families unable to earn enough to stay out of poverty, the consequences are likely to be severe. Economic hardship diminishes the emotional well-being and health of both parents and children, and leads to increases in family disintegration and in single parenthood (Simons, Finlay, & Yang, 1991; Huston, McLoyd, & Coll, 1994). Adolescents from low-income families are at greatly increased risk for health and behavioral problems, school failure, and becoming involved in criminal activities (Panel on High-Risk Youth, 1993).

Between 1970 and 1990, the number of households headed by single parents nearly doubled (see Table 5.1) and is still rising. In part, this is due to increased family disintegration leading to separation and divorce. In greater measure, however, it results from a dramatic increase in

## Table 5.1 U.S. Households with Children Under 18 (in 1000s)

| HOUSEHOLD TYPE | 1970 | 1980 | 1990 | PERCENT CHANGE, 1970–1990 |
|---|---|---|---|---|
| Married with children | 58,939 | 48,624 | 46,503 | −21.09 |
| Single parent | 8,199 | 12,466 | 15,867 | +93.52 |
| Single mother | 7,452 | 11,406 | 13,874 | +86.18 |
| Single father | 748 | 1,060 | 1,993 | +166.44 |
| Other | 2,024 | 2,337 | 1,768 | −12.64 |

SOURCE: Committee on Ways and Means, House of Representatives (1991). *1991 Green Book*. Washington, DC: U.S. Government Printing Office.

the percentage of never-married mothers (Panel on High-Risk Youth, 1993; Alan Guttmacher Institute [AGI], 1994). About half of all marriages now end in divorce, double the rate in 1960, and a quarter of all births today are to unmarried women. Although a majority of these births are to women over twenty, the greatest increase in childbearing outside of marriage has been among adolescents: In 1940, only 14 percent of adolescent mothers were unmarried; by 1991, nearly 70 percent of teenage mothers were unmarried (CDF, 1994) (see Figure 5.1).

Today, about a quarter of all adolescents ages 10 to 17 are living with only one parent; among Latino and black youth, the numbers are significantly higher (see Table 5.2). The dramatic rise in the number of single-parent families is troubling (CDF, 1994; Panel on High-Risk Youth, 1993; Schorr, 1988). Poverty rates for single-parent families are about six times greater than for two-parent families (U.S. Bureau of the Census, 1994). Because

most single parents (87 percent) are women, "other problems of single parenthood are often compounded by those of gender discrimination in employment and social welfare" (Panel on High-Risk Youth, 1993, p. 45). The National Commission on Children (1991) found that single parents are twice as likely as married couples to be worried about making ends meet and concerned that their children will be beaten up, get pregnant, not get a job, or drop out of school.

For adolescent mothers, the problems are particularly daunting. They are much more likely than their peers to drop out of school, less likely to gain employment, and more likely to be welfare recipients (Furstenberg, Brooks-Gunn, & Chase-Lansdale, 1989, 1990; Furstenberg, Brooks-Gunn, & Morgan, 1987; Panel on High-Risk Youth, 1993). Many still need mothering themselves and are ill-prepared to take on the psychological, social, and economic responsibilities of motherhood (CDF, 1994; Osofsky, 1987).

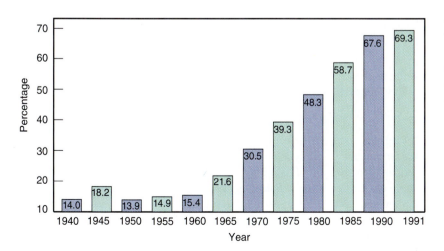

## Figure 5.1

Percentage of teen births that were to unmarried teens, 1940–1991, selected years.
SOURCE: National Center for Health Statistics, Children's Defense Fund, 1994.

# Table 5.2 Living Arrangements of Adolescents Ages 10 to 17

| AGE, LIVING ARRANGEMENT | TOTAL | WHITE | BLACK | LATINO* |
|---|---|---|---|---|
| **10–14** | | | | |
| Living with two parents | 72.8% | 78.5% | 41.9% | 67.7% |
| Living with one parent | 24.8 | 20.0 | 50.7 | 29.9 |
| Living with mother only | 21.6 | 16.8 | 47.3 | 26.8 |
| Living with father only | 3.2 | 3.2 | 3.3 | 3.1 |
| Living with neither parent | 2.4 | 1.5 | 7.5 | 2.4 |
| **15–17** | | | | |
| Living with two parents | 70.6 | 76.2 | 40.8 | 63.1 |
| Living with one parent | 24.8 | 20.5 | 48.4 | 31.2 |
| Living with mother only | 21.4 | 16.9 | 45.2 | 27.4 |
| Living with father only | 3.4 | 3.5 | 3.2 | 3.9 |
| Living with neither parent | 4.5 | 3.2 | 10.7 | 5.6 |

*Persons of Latino origin can be of any race.

SOURCE: U.S. Department of Commerce, Bureau of the Census (1990). *Current Population Reports,* Series P-20, no. 445, *Marital Status and Living Arrangements: March 1989,* Tables 4 and 5. Calculations by Children's Defense Fund.

## The Women's Movement

Perhaps the single most significant social change affecting the structure and functioning of families in the past two decades has been the rise of the women's movement. A logical extension of earlier struggles for individual and group rights, beginning with the civil rights movement in the early 1960s, the women's movement has produced major changes in contemporary society. Not only has it fundamentally altered the way women, particularly younger women, view themselves, but it has also changed the way men view women—and themselves. Traditional stereotypes of the psychological, social, and emotional characteristics of men and women have begun to break down, as have notions of what can properly be considered "women's (or men's) work," or the appropriate roles of men and women in society. Increasing numbers of women insist on being viewed as the equals of men and as individuals, each with her own unique set of talents, interests, and psychological and social needs.

The goal of equality is still far from being attained, and there remain strong pockets of resistance among both men and women. Nevertheless, an evolutionary process was set in motion in the 1970s that is unlikely to be reversed, despite slowdowns and occasional setbacks.

**Women's Participation in the Labor Force.** A closely related major change has been the increase in the number of women working outside the home. In the United States in 1950, only one-third of all women were employed outside the home; by 1970, the figure had increased to 43 percent; by 1980, it had reached 51 percent, and by 1992 it was approaching 58 percent. The largest increases have occurred among women with young children; since 1983 there has been a larger percentage of mothers with children under six in the labor force than out of it (see Figure 5.2), although this figure has declined slightly since 1991 in the United States and Canada (Statistics Canada, 1994; U.S. Bureau of the Census, 1993).

The reasons for the overall increases are varied. For some women, particularly those who were single parents or whose husbands were unemployed or underemployed, outside employment was an economic necessity. For others, it was a way of improving the family's living standards, coping with inflation, or remaining in contact with the world outside the home. For an increasing number of women, particularly those with interesting professions, it became a way of fulfilling vocational interests or career goals. Whatever the reasons for women's increased participation in the labor force, the implications for the family as a social institution, and for the quality of the lives of its members, are profound.

Balancing the pressures of work and family life is seldom easy, and leaves many couples starved for time (CDF, 1992; Coontz, 1992). Difficulties in gaining access to high-quality day care and health care, lack of flexibility in work schedules, long work hours, and poor parental leave arrangements are among the work-related problems that

Traditional stereotypes of "women's work" and "men's work," and of appropriate roles of men and women in society, are breaking down.

create pressures for young families. These pressures are most acute among poor families and single parents who cannot afford to solve some of these problems through financial means (by hiring a nanny, eating out more often, or paying for services such as housecleaning, laundering clothes, and gardening) (Coontz, 1992).

## Social Policy and Family Values

Not all of the problems confronting families result from such factors as urbanization, a rapidly changing economy, divorce, or even poverty. A major contribution has been

the erosion in social values that emerged in the 1980s, an erosion that had its roots in the failed promises of the 1960s and 1970s (Conger, 1988, 1991b; Edelman, 1987). This erosion was manifested in the retreat of political figures from candor, compassion, and concern for others in the direction of "narcissistic self-absorption, pious sloganeering, hypocrisy, and greed" (Conger, 1988, p. 298). It has led to a decline in the commitment of the United States to the needs of disenfranchised children, adolescents, and families.

Despite their proclaimed dedication to "family values" and to strengthening families, national leaders in the United States manifested their dedication in some surprising ways (CDF, 1991, 1994; Conger, 1988; Schorr,

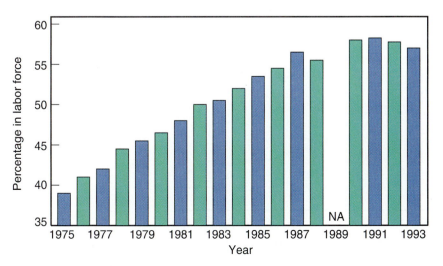

**Figure 5.2**

Labor force participation of mothers with children younger than six, 1975–1993.
SOURCE: U.S. Department of Labor, Bureau of Labor Statistics, 1994a.

1988). During the past decade and a half, the gap between the wealthy and the poor has widened steadily (see Figure 5.3). The share of all family income received by the poorest one-fifth of families shrank to 4.4 percent in 1992—the lowest since records began in 1947—while the share going to the wealthiest one-fifth hit 44.6 percent, a record high (CDF, 1994). This widening gap means that the richest 5 percent of all Americans received a greater share of total U.S. income than the poorest 40 percent.

Government policies facilitated this process. Tax cuts favoring the wealthy coincided with marked reductions in programs aimed exclusively at the poor; for example, there was a 25 percent reduction during the 1980s in Aid to Families with Dependent Children, but social programs such as Social Security, which aids a broader and more powerful group, were not cut (CDF, 1991, 1994; Moynihan, 1986; Passell, 1989). Many demonstrably successful and cost-effective services, ranging from prenatal and early postnatal nutritional and medical programs for low-income mothers and infants to health care, counseling, mental health, and job-training programs for adolescents, were eliminated or severely cut back (Conger, 1988, 1991b; Edelman, 1987; Hughes et al., 1989). At present, one child in four and more than one youth in five are living in poverty; indeed, children are currently the only age group overrepresented in the poverty population (CDF, 1995). This picture is not quite so gloomy everywhere. In Canada, for instance, one child in five is living in poverty—a lower, albeit discouraging, figure.

Contrary to popular perceptions, over half of the 13.3 million poor children and adolescents in the United States are white, less than one-third are black, and nearly one-fifth are Hispanic (CDF, 1994; U.S. Bureau of the Census, 1994).

Difficulty in gaining access to high-quality day care and inflexible work schedules often create problems for young families.

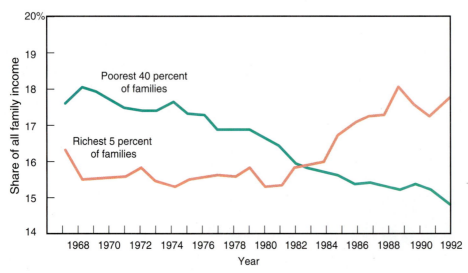

**Figure** 5.3

Growing income disparity. Percentage of total U.S. income received, by selected family income groupings, 1967–1992. SOURCE: U.S. Census Bureau, 1994. Calculations by the Children's Defense Fund.

In 1992, the new U.S. administration proclaimed its determination that, in the words of the Secretary of Housing and Human Services, "no child will be left behind," and a number of legislative initiatives, both federal and state, were launched, aimed at improving the lot of poor children, adolescents, and families. Some programs were implemented, including the Family and Medical Leave Act (which allows workers to take unpaid leave to care for children or other family members). Head Start was expanded modestly, although in 1993, it served only 36 percent of eligible children. Other initiatives included limited job training and employment programs for adolescents, such as AmeriCorps and the Jobs Corps; and expanded nutrition programs for children and for women and their infants during and after pregnancy (the WIC program) (CDF, 1994). In the closing days of 1995, however, all of these programs were under attack, and they face an uncertain future. In any event, there must be a greater recognition on the part of government and the public of the often desperate plight of many of today's families, and of the need for a greater sense of community in society as a whole, if the young are to achieve their birthright.

## Parents and Adolescent Development

As we have just seen, recent social changes have had important effects on the nature of the family and its relations with other social institutions. In the process, these changes have increased the stresses of adolescence, both for parents and for young people themselves. Despite the added difficulty, however, adolescents still must master the important developmental tasks of adolescence: adjusting to the physical and sexual changes of puberty, gaining autonomy from parents and other caretakers, establishing effective social and working relationships with same- and opposite-sex peers, preparing for a vocation, and developing a system of values and a sense of identity (Conger, 1971, 1979; Havighurst, 1953; Thomas, 1985). Given that each of these tasks is a critical and indispensable challenge for the adolescent, we must ask: What factors will increase the likelihood that a young person can accomplish these tasks successfully and get through the adolescent period without excessive turmoil and with a reasonable degree of resilience to psychological difficulties and external pressures?

We cannot look only to individual or familial factors for answers; social factors such as the geographical setting in which one lives are also important (Bronfenbrenner, 1985; Conger, 1977). For example, adolescents growing up in a relatively isolated and homogeneous small town—where values are largely shared by the community as a whole and generally acceptable models of adult identity may be found—will still face complex developmental demands. Their challenges may be different, however, from those of adolescents growing up in a heterogeneous urban area and markedly different from those of young people growing up in a socially disorganized ethnic ghetto—and usually far less stressful.

To accomplish successfully the confusing and sometimes daunting process of developing an identity, adolescents need support from all levels of society, including the mass media, the government, social policies and programs, neighborhoods, schools, and family members. An increasing body of data indicates that the single most important external influence on the average young person attempting to accomplish the developmental tasks of adolescence is his or her parents (Baumrind, 1991a, 1991b; Collins & Russell, 1991; Conger, 1991b; Paikoff & Brooks-Gunn, 1991). Because parents are so important, both as models and as nurturers, for preparing contemporary adolescents to cope with the largely unpredictable world of tomorrow, the remainder of this chapter is devoted to exploring the contributions parents make to adolescent development.

## Models of Parent–Child Interaction

In the case of adolescents, the question of what kinds of parents are most helpful involves the effects not only of current patterns of parent–child interaction but of a history of prior interactions extending back to early childhood. Parents may be loving or rejecting, calm or anxious, involved or uninvolved, rigid or flexible, controlling or permissive. All of these qualities have been found to influence the child's subsequent behavior and adjustment. Two major dimensions of parental behavior, **responsiveness** and **demandingness,** have consistently been identified as global indicators of the parent–child relationship that are critical to the child's development (Baumrind, 1991a, 1991b; Conger, 1991a; Elder, 1980; Maccoby & Martin, 1983; Schaefer, 1965).

### Responsiveness

Although we refer to the first dimension as *responsiveness,* the exact labels used vary from one investigator to another; examples include *love, warmth,* and *acceptance* (Maccoby & Martin, 1983; MacDonald, 1992; Parker,

Tupling, & Brown, 1979). Parents who are highly responsive are accepting, affectionate, understanding, child-centered, and reassuring. They use praise a great deal and punishment very little. Parents who are not responsive may show a lack of sensitivity toward their children, or even neglect. At worst, they may actively express hostility.

How does parental responsiveness affect the child? Unambiguous manifestations of love, as demonstrated by highly responsive parents, enable the child or adolescent to develop self-esteem, constructive and rewarding relationships with others, the ability to consider different perspectives, and a confident sense of his or her own identity (Bell et al., 1985; Eisenberg & McNally, 1993; Feldman & Wentzel, 1990; Kawash, Kerr, & Clewes, 1985). A lack of parental responsiveness is associated with cognitive and academic difficulties, impaired social relations, neurotic disorders, psychophysiological disturbances, and delinquency (Becker, 1964; Conger, 1991b; Mussen et al., 1984; Paulson, 1994; Rutter & Giller, 1984; Wentzel, Feldman, & Weinberger, 1991). As we will see later, parental unresponsiveness at its extreme is manifested in parents who abuse their children.

### Demandingness

The other critical dimension emerging from studies of parent–child relationships may be broadly termed *demandingness.* Here again, the label varies from one investigator to another, with the words *controlling* and *restrictive* often used synonymously with *demanding* (Baumrind, 1991a, 1991b; Becker, 1964; Maccoby & Martin, 1983; Schaefer, 1965). Parental behaviors defined as demanding are those that involve restrictions and strict enforcement of rules, including rigid insistence on neatness, orderliness, obedience, and inhibition of aggression (verbal or otherwise) toward parents, siblings, or peers. Parents who are highly undemanding allow the child to make his or her own decisions without parental input or guidance—they grant the child unregulated autonomy.

A balanced level of demandingness seems desirable. Specifically, parents who have clear expectations for socially appropriate behavior and who monitor the child's freedom to some extent actually encourage their children to develop capabilities and talents (Dornbusch et al., 1990; Paulson, 1994). However, one of the adjustments that must be made by parents of adolescents is to realize that their 16-year-old is no longer a child and needs to be trusted with progressively greater autonomy if he or she is to be prepared for the independence and responsibilities of adulthood (Conger, 1971, 1991a; Dornbusch et al., 1990; Youniss & Smollar, 1985). Excessive demandingness tends to foster inhibition not only in social behavior but also in creativity, initiative, and flexibility in approaching academic and practical problems (Baumrind, 1991a, 1991b; Maccoby & Martin, 1983).

## An Interactive Model of Parental Behavior

Diana Baumrind, whose studies have had a major impact on our understanding of parent–adolescent relations (1987, 1991a, 1991b), established that it is useful to combine the dimensions of responsiveness and demandingness into prototypes representing parental patterns of behavior. Four such patterns emerge when considering the possible combinations of responsiveness and demandingness (see Figure 5.4). As we shall see, such combinations of responsiveness and demandingness are better predictors of the child's social and academic competence than is either of these dimensions considered alone.

### Authoritative Parents

Tomorrow's adults will need self-discipline, but they will also need independence, self-reliance, adaptability, creativity, a strong sense of their own values, and the ability to distinguish between assertiveness and hostility—in addition to a sense of humor. These qualities are best fostered by **authoritative** parents—those who are both highly responsive and demanding. Authoritative parents show respect for their children, involve them in family affairs and decision making, and encourage the devel-

| | Responsive | Unresponsive |
|---|---|---|
| Demanding | Authoritative (high in two-way communication) | Authoritarian (power-assertive) |
| Undemanding | Permissive–indulgent (undemanding, responsive) | Permissive–indifferent (neglecting, uninvolved) |

**Figure 5.4**

A fourfold typology of parenting patterns. From E. E. Maccoby & J. A. Martin (1983). Socialization in the context of the family: Parent–child interaction. In M. Hetherington (Ed.), *Handbook of child psychology* (Vol. 4, pp. 1–101). Copyright © 1983 by John Wiley & Sons, Inc. Adapted by permission.

Authoritative parents show respect for their children, involve them in family affairs, and encourage age-appropriate independence, while still retaining ultimate responsibility.

opment of age-appropriate independence while retaining ultimate responsibility (Baumrind, 1991a, 1991b; Buri et al., 1988; Elder, 1980). The following description by a 16-year-old girl is typical of such parents:

> I guess the thing I think is great about my parents, compared to those of a lot of kids, is that they really listen. And they realize that eventually I'm going to have to live my own life—what I'm going to do with it. A lot of the time when I explain what I want to do, they'll go along with it. Sometimes, they'll warn me of the consequences I'll have to face if I'm wrong, or just give me advice. And sometimes, they just plain tell me no. But when they do, they explain why, and that makes it easier to take (Conger, 1979, p. 49).

Abundant evidence demonstrates that authoritative parenting promotes social, intellectual, and academic competence in children and adolescents (Baumrind, 1989, 1991a, 1991b; Feldman & Weinberger, 1994; Maccoby & Martin, 1983; Steinberg, Elmen, & Mounts, 1989). In a study of 10,000 high school students from ethnically diverse families, the advantages of authoritative parenting cut across ethnicity, class, and family structure (i.e., marital status of parents). Regardless of their backgrounds, when compared with adolescents from nonauthoritative homes, adolescents from authoritative homes showed the highest levels of competence and adjustment. They were psychosocially more competent, more self-reliant, and less likely to engage

in delinquent activities, and showed lower anxiety and depression (Lamborn et al., 1991; Steinberg et al., 1992; Steinberg et al., 1991).

## Authoritarian Parents

In contrast to the authoritative parent, the **authoritarian** parent simply tells the child what to do and feels no obligation to explain why ("Because I said so!"). Such parents are highly demanding and unresponsive. They favor obedience as an absolute virtue and tend to deal with any attempts at protest with forceful, punitive measures. Free discussion or two-way interaction between parent and child is discouraged out of the conviction that the young person should unquestioningly accept the parent's word about what is right (Baumrind, 1989; Buri et al., 1988; Lesser & Kandel, 1969).

Some parents may take this stance out of a feeling of hostility or simply because they do not wish to be bothered. Others may do so because they think that this is the way to develop "respect for authority." However, although they may suppress dissent they do not usually eliminate it and at the same time they may generate resentment. Authoritarian parenting is, in general, associated with a lack of social competence with peers, a tendency to withdraw instead of taking social initiative, a lack of spontaneity, low self-esteem, an external locus of control (a belief that fate or outside forces, rather than forces within the self, control one's destiny), and a moral orientation that is guided more by external than internal demands and standards (Baumrind, 1991a, 1991b;

Maccoby & Martin, 1983). Adolescents from authoritarian homes tend to be conforming and obedient (i.e., they report low levels of problem behavior) and they are academically competent. At the same time, they tend to have negative self-perceptions of their social and academic abilities. In short, this pattern "suggests a group of young people who have been overpowered into obedience" (Lamborn et al., 1991, p. 1062).

The distinction between authoritarian and authoritative parental behaviors takes on special significance in adolescence. This is so because adolescents are capable of taking greater responsibility for their own behavior and because they will need to do so if they are to become mature, self-reliant adults. Because adolescents can imagine viable alternatives to parental directives, parents must be ready to defend their directives on rational grounds (Baumrind, 1987). Parental authority based on rational concern for the young person's welfare is generally accepted well, whereas authority based on the adult's desire to dominate or exploit is rejected.

### Permissive–Indifferent and Permissive–Indulgent Parents

In sharp contrast to the authoritarian parent, the permissive parent allows the young person to disregard parental wishes (Elder, 1980). In general, permissive parents fail to provide the kind of support adolescents need (Baumrind, 1991a, 1991b; Conger, 1979, 1991a). Such parents "find it hard to make decisive value judgments that require the exercise of power over their children and prefer to escape from the obligation of being an authority figure" (Blum et al., 1972, p. 52). In so doing, they end up leaving their children to drift essentially alone in an uncharted sea without any dependable models of responsible adult behavior.

Research points to two different forms of permissiveness (Baumrind, 1991a, 1991b; Maccoby & Martin, 1983). One form of permissive parenting is called **permissive–indifferent,** which refers to parents who are unresponsive and undemanding. These parents are uninvolved with or neglectful of their children. The other form of permissiveness is called **permissive–indulgent,** which refers to parents who are undemanding but highly responsive. They exert little control over their children, but are loving. These two forms of permissiveness are associated with different outcomes for adolescents. One study found that adolescents who reported their parents to be permissive–indifferent were the least well-adjusted when compared to adolescents from authoritative, authoritarian, and permissive–indulgent homes. Specifically, adolescents with permissive–indifferent parents were least competent

academically and socially and showed the highest levels of problem behavior and internalized distress (such as depression). Adolescents from permissive–indulgent homes, on the other hand, showed a mixture of positive and negative characteristics. These adolescents saw themselves as self-reliant, academically competent, and socially competent (in essence, they were psychologically well-adjusted), but they were also likely to engage in a moderate level of deviant behavior, such as drug and alcohol use and misbehavior in school (Lamborn et al., 1991).

The general picture, then, arising from joint consideration of the dimensions of demandingness and responsiveness, indicates that adolescents from authoritative homes are likely to show the most optimal behaviors and self-perceptions, followed by those from permissive–indulgent and authoritarian homes. Adolescents with permissive–indifferent parents can be expected to show the poorest developmental outcomes.

## Parent–Adolescent Relations and Ethnicity

Although we seem to know a great deal about parenting practices and their influences on adolescent behavior, much of the research that has taken place over the years has been conducted on white, middle-class families. We know little about parent–child relations in African-American, Hispanic-American, and Asian-American families. Over a quarter of adolescents aged 14 to 24 years in the United States fall into these three ethnic categories (Schulenberg & Ebata, 1994). To what extent do the parenting patterns seen in white, middle-class families apply to minority families? Is authoritative parenting as important for the developing competencies of minority adolescents as it is for white adolescents?

Recent studies indicate that the full range of parenting styles is represented in Asian-, African-, and Hispanic-American samples, with authoritarian parenting more prevalent and authoritative parenting less prevalent than in white samples. Authoritative parenting is found least in Asian-American parents (Dornbusch et al., 1987; Steinberg, Dornbusch, & Brown, 1992). As to the importance of authoritativeness, in all ethnic groups authoritative parenting (when contrasted with nonauthoritative parenting) is linked to adolescents' higher social adjustment, lower psychological distress, and lower levels of problem behavior. An exception is found, however, in school performance. Among African- and Asian-American groups, authoritative parenting is not linked to better school performance. The reason for this may be that the peer group has more influence on attitudes about the value of schooling than do parents, with Asian-American

peer groups placing a high value and African-American peers placing a low value on achievement. Hence, Asian-American students tend to perform very well in school and African-American students tend to perform more poorly, regardless of parenting style (Steinberg, Dornbusch, & Brown, 1992). These findings illustrate the necessity of delving into the culture of different ethnic groups in attempting to understand the complexities of adolescent development.

## Parent–Adolescent Conflict

Although it is useful to characterize *parents'* behavior on the broad dimensions of responsiveness and demandingness, these dimensions say little about the qualities of the parent–adolescent relationship—how parents and adolescents interact. Given that this relationship is a partnership of two individuals, it makes sense to consider the characteristics of this partnership. The degree of parent–adolescent conflict is one characteristic that has received much attention (Collins & Russell, 1991). Although the degree of conflict between a parent and adolescent may range from no or mild conflict to severe conflict, it is more commonly the case that parent–adolescent conflict consists of "mild bickering, disagreements and conflicts over everyday issues" (Smetana, 1988b, p. 79). Figure 5.5 shows that most parent–adolescent conflicts center on details of family life such as household chores and interpersonal behavior.

Some conflict appears to be a normal part of most families, but high levels of conflict are harmful to ado-lescents and parents. Although many parents assume that conflict will increase as their children move into adolescence, it is not clear that this is usually the case. A recent study of parent–adolescent conflict in two-earner families (where both parents have paying jobs) followed adolescents and their parents from the middle of sixth grade to the summer following eighth grade (Galambos & Almeida, 1992). Contrary to the expectation of an increase in parent-adolescent conflict, mothers, fathers, and adolescents reported a *decline* in the overall level of conflict. Considering specific types of conflict, disagreement over finances was the only type of conflict that increased. Conflict over chores, appearance, and politeness (typical conflicts in adolescence) declined. Conflict over substance use remained low throughout early adolescence. Other research also suggests that overall levels of parent–adolescent conflict may not increase in the early teenage years (Laursen & Ferreira, 1994).

Parent–adolescent conflict may increase, however, when there are stresses in the family. One study found that changes in parent–adolescent conflict over a two-year period accompanied changes in the family's economic situation. Among families who experienced economic instability, the level of parent–adolescent conflict increased. In families whose economic situation was stable, parent–adolescent conflict did not change (Flanagan, 1990). Some research has found that in both girls and boys, changes in pubertal status (physical maturation) are associated with modest increases in mother–adolescent conflict (Steinberg, 1988). Whether these results apply to most adolescents is a matter of some debate (Laursen & Ferreira, 1994).

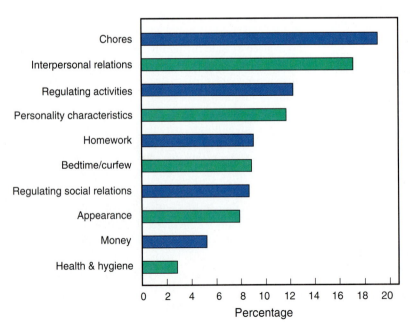

### Figure 5.5

Percentages of parent–adolescent conflicts surrounding different issues. Adapted from J. G. Smetana (1988). Concepts of self and social convention: Adolescents' and parents' reasoning about hypothetical and actual family conflicts. In M. R. Gunnar & W. A. Collins (Eds.), *Minnesota Symposium on Child Psychology* (Vol. 21, pp. 79–122). Hillsdale, NJ: Erlbaum. By permission.

# Parent–Adolescent Relations and the Development of Autonomy

The development of autonomy is a critically important task of adolescence. Before considering how parent–adolescent relations influence the way in which adolescents approach this task, it is important to clarify what we mean by **autonomy.** Autonomy is the adolescent's ability to self-govern and self-regulate (Ryan & Lynch, 1989). This self-reliance means that adolescents must learn to make their own decisions and to follow through on them (Greenberger & Steinberg, 1986). This is not a sudden occurrence. It is important that autonomy develop gradually and that it be age-appropriate. For instance, it is as inappropriate for an 11-year-old to be permitted complete freedom as it is for a 17-year-old to have no say in the matters that affect him or her. One study found that fathers who expected to grant early autonomy to their sons had sons who, by middle adolescence, performed and behaved more poorly in school than sons of fathers with more age-appropriate autonomy expectations (Feldman & Wood, 1994).

The development of autonomy is important but it is also closely related to the resolution of other tasks. An adolescent who does not resolve the conflict between continuing dependence on the family and the demands and privileges of independence will encounter difficulties in most other areas as well. Without the achievement of a reasonable degree of emotional separation and autonomy, an adolescent can hardly be expected to form mature friendships or intimate relations, confidently pursue a vocation, or gain a clear sense of identity—which requires a positive image of the self as separate, unified, and consistent over time.

As we have noted, North American adolescents and their counterparts in other advanced nations are likely to encounter greater stress while developing autonomy than young people in societies in which social roles are simpler and more clearly defined and in which there is a very gradual transition from childhood dependence to adult independence. Nevertheless, most contemporary adolescents make this transition successfully, though not always easily.

## Separation and Connectedness

What kinds of parent–child relationships facilitate this transition, and what kinds hinder it? Most theorists agree that the development of age-appropriate autonomy requires the dual processes of separation (achieving a sense of distinctiveness from others) and continued connectedness (being sensitive, responsive, and open to others) (Allen et al., 1994; Cooper, Grotevant, & Condon, 1983; Lamborn & Steinberg, 1993; Youniss & Smollar, 1985). As adolescence progresses, young people must be given sufficient freedom from parental authority and control in order to experience themselves as individuals with needs and feelings of their own, to make decisions about their own lives, and to take responsibility for the consequences of those decisions. At the same time, they continue to need their parents' guidance and support. "For parents to leave adolescents on their own would be irresponsible. For parents to seek to duplicate themselves in their sons and daughters would be equally dysfunctional" (Youniss & Smollar, 1985, p. 93).

Before puberty, interactions between children and parents are dominated by parents (Steinberg & Hill, 1978; Youniss & Smollar, 1985). During adolescence, however, there is a gradual shift away from unilateral parental authority toward more give-and-take in parent–child interactions. This does not mean that parental authority is abandoned. Under favorable circumstances adolescents still view their parents as having the right to monitor and direct their behavior, to set rules and require that they be followed, and to expect that schoolwork, household chores, and other responsibilities will be carried out properly. Research shows that parental monitoring of adolescents' activities continues to be important (Brown et al., 1993; Crouter et al., 1990; L. Steinberg, 1986).

However, there are some important changes in the nature of parental authority during adolescence. First, parental authority is increasingly restricted to particular areas of adolescents' lives. Much of the average adolescent's social and personal life, particularly with peers, takes place outside the family circle. Consequently, adolescents gain independence from parental authority in many more areas of their lives than is possible for younger children (Hill & Holmbeck, 1987; Youniss & Smollar, 1985).

Second, although parents can and do continue to assert unilateral authority at times, particularly with respect to basic social obligations such as schoolwork, in other areas they are perceived by their children as more ready to discuss differences and seek compromise. Especially when dealing with personal problems or concerns, "if parents are involved at all, they act less as unilateral authorities and more as advisors willing to listen, seeking to understand" (Youniss & Smollar, 1985, p. 73). Moreover, even when they are asserting unilateral authority, authoritative (though not authoritarian) parents are more likely to explain their actions.

## Perceiving Parents as Individuals

As the relationship between adolescents and their parents shifts away from unilateral parental authority, and as adolescents gain greater capacity for formal operational thinking, adolescents' perceptions of their parents undergo a corresponding shift. As James Youniss (1980) notes, childrens' and preadolescents' descriptions of parent–child interactions lack any perception of parents as complex individuals, with likeable and unlikeable traits, emotional ups and downs, and varying competencies. Children are likely to perceive their parents as "*figures* who have knowledge and power to get things done, especially those things children need or want" (Youniss & Smollar, 1985, p. 75). In a sense, parents *are* what parents *do*.

In contrast, as they develop cognitively and experience more complex give-and-take interactions with their parents, adolescents begin to view their parents as unique individuals. They are better able to differentiate parents as *persons* with their own needs and feelings, from the *roles* they play in carrying out their responsibilities as mothers or fathers. One older adolescent girl described her relationship with her mother as follows: "I'm more independent of her. Also, I am more free with my opinions even when I disagree. I realize she's not only my mother but an individual herself and I take her more on that level now. We still turn to each other when we have problems. We're still close" (Youniss & Smollar, 1985, p. 80).

## Authoritative Parenting and Autonomy

Granting adolescents greater freedom as they mature is not incompatible with maintaining elements of connectedness and control. For example, authoritative parents, who are loving yet demanding, are most likely to foster the development of autonomy in their adolescents. Authoritarian parents, on the other hand, tend to stifle the orderly acquisition of self-reliance and independence, whereas permissive–indifferent and permissive–indulgent parents may fail to encourage the development of responsibility (Baumrind, 1989; Buri et al., 1988). In a study of several thousand adolescents and their parents in the United States and Denmark (Kandel & Lesser, 1972; Lesser & Kandel, 1969), authoritative parents, who provided frequent explanations for their rules, were significantly more likely than either authoritarian or permissive parents to have adolescents who felt independent and viewed themselves as being treated in an adult manner by their parents.

Other studies have yielded similar results. Confidence and self-esteem appear to be highest among adolescents whose parents express strong interest in their opinions and activities and encourage the adolescents to behave autonomously and participate actively in family affairs (Baumrind, 1989; Buri et al., 1988; Eccles et al., 1991). Sanford Dornbusch and his colleagues have shown that in a large, ethnically diverse sample, adolescents who were granted early autonomy in family decision-making had lower grades, showed

Adolescents begin to view their parents not simply as *parents,* but also as *persons* with their own needs and feelings.

poorer academic effort, and engaged in more deviant behaviors than adolescents whose decisions were made jointly with their parents. Regardless of family structure, ethnicity, gender, or socioeconomic status, youth who made decisions alone seemed to be too self-directed for their own good (Dornbusch et al., 1990; Dornbusch et al., 1985).

It appears that authoritative practices, with frequent explanations of parental rules of conduct and expectations, foster responsible, autonomous behavior in several ways: by providing opportunities for increasing autonomy, guided by interested parents who communicate with the child and exercise an appropriate degree of control; by promoting positive identification with the parent, based on love and respect for the child; and by providing models of reasonable independence, that is, autonomy within a framework of democratic order. In contrast, a child of authoritarian, permissive–indulgent, or permissive–indifferent parents is not likely to be actively exposed to this set of experiences that promote the orderly assumption of responsible autonomy (Baumrind, 1991a, 1991b; Conger, 1977, 1991a).

The relation between age-appropriate autonomy and parenting practices is expressed in the words of a longtime fisherman and grandfather:

> Parenting is like fishing. You cast out the line and you start to pull in. If the tension is too tight and you pull in too much, the fish escapes. If you let out too much line, the fish gets away. Good parenting, like good fishing, requires a balance between freedom and control.

# The Adolescent in the Family

So far, we have focused primarily on how parental behaviors affect adolescent daughters and sons. This is the focus of most psychological research on parent–child relations. However, the interaction between parent and child is not a one-way street (Bell, 1979; Hartup, 1989; Mussen et al., 1990). Just as parental behavior affects the responses of children, the behavior of children and adolescents affects the responses of their parents. Both children and parents are members of a family system in which the behavior of individual members affects, and is affected by, all members of the family, often in complex ways (Belsky, Lerner, & Spanier, 1984; Silverberg & Steinberg, 1987).

## The Principle of Bidirectionality

The principle of **bidirectionality** states that parent–child influences go both ways—from parent to child and from child to parent. Parents and children both have behavioral, personality, and physical characteristics that shape their interactions with each other. Consequently, the development of children and adolescents is "a product of their own characteristics and those of the people who socialize [care for] them" (Mussen et al., 1984, p. 143). As an example, parents are more likely to smile, talk to, and play with a baby who is cuddly and smiles readily rather than one who is quieter, more sober, and more passive (Mussen et al., 1990). Consider the impulsive and thrill-seeking adolescent who elicits increasingly authoritarian behavior from her parents, as they become more and more controlling in an effort to stifle potentially harmful risk-taking behaviors, such as drinking. Their efforts to control her may actually increase distance in the parent–adolescent relationship and push her further toward the very behaviors they wish to inhibit.

The bidirectional nature of parent–child relationships puts adolescent parents, relative to older parents, at greater risk of abusing their children. Because they have not yet completed the transition to adulthood, adolescent parents are more likely to be poorly equipped socially and emotionally for the demanding task of being a parent. They are also more likely to have low-birthweight infants who are more irritable, less healthy, and more difficult to care for. The personal characteristics of the parent and the child, then, might lead the parent to lash out at the child, setting in motion a vicious cycle of potentially tragic events (Garbarino et al., 1986; Steele, 1987).

An example of the way in which adolescent characteristics influence parent–adolescent relations is seen in a study of pairs of adolescent siblings. The sibling who is psychologically better adjusted is likely to experience more maternal closeness and to be given a greater voice in family decision-making (Daniels et al., 1985). Given the existence of bidirectional influences, it is likely that the adolescent's closeness to the mother and participation in making decisions will shape further the nature of the parent–adolescent relationship.

## The Family as a System

Just as individuals differ in important ways, so too do families. Families may be organized or chaotic, close-knit or distant, communicative or uncommunicative, warm or cold, reserved or expressive, disturbed or essentially

normal. These factors can have profound effects on the interactions (or lack of them) among family members and people and institutions outside the family.

One of the most important dimensions of the family system is communication (Barnes & Olson, 1985; Grotevant & Cooper, 1985; Youniss, 1983). A large study found that families with more effective communication among parents and adolescents were also more cohesive (had strong emotional bonds) and more adaptable (were able to reorganize in the face of stresses), and family members were more satisfied with their families. They were also more satisfied with their overall quality of life, and were less likely to use passive appraisal—"they tended not to be fatalistic about problems but would reframe problems and see them as a challenge to be overcome" (Barnes & Olson, 1985, p. 445).

Family communication appears to be particularly important during the adolescent years. The onset of puberty and subsequent physical, cognitive, and social development requires a reappraisal of earlier relationships by both parents and their adolescent children. Changing

Families with effective communication among parents and adolescents are more cohesive, better able to handle stress, and more satisfied with the quality of family life.

long-established patterns of parent–child interaction in order to adapt to new realities is seldom easy for parents or their children, but the resolution of transitional difficulties and conflicts can be greatly facilitated by effective communication and openness in a family environment that provides both for separateness and connectedness (Cooper, Grotevant, & Condon, 1983; Youniss, 1983; Youniss & Smollar, 1985).

Effective communication plays a vital role in helping family members strike a balance between separateness from and connectedness to each other (Barnes & Olson, 1985; Grotevant & Cooper, 1983). Research indicates that effective family communication fosters adolescent identity formation and mature role-taking ability, both of which "require the adolescent to possess a viewpoint, to be aware of others' views, and both to integrate and to differentiate his or her own views from those of others" (Cooper, Grotevant, & Condon, 1983, p. 48). A recent study of university students found that this process of achieving greater mutuality in late adolescence was facilitated when adolescents were living in residence at the university rather than at home with parents (Flanagan, Schulenberg, & Fuligni, 1993).

## Communication Patterns in Troubled Families

Studies of parent–child interaction in troubled families, or in families with a mentally ill parent or child, have often found distortions in the capacity of parent and child to communicate with each other. For example, in one comprehensive study of adolescents on the Isle of Wight, altercations with parents, physical withdrawal (e.g., going to one's own room or staying out of the house), and communication difficulties all occurred more often in the families of adolescents with psychological disorders (see Figure 5.6) (Rutter, Graham, & Yule, 1976). In troubled families it often seems that family members are talking *past* each other (Goldstein, Baker, & Jamison, 1980; Rutter, 1980; Wynne et al., 1976). The failure of parents to respond in a meaningful way in such situations is well illustrated in the following excerpt from a family therapy session:

Daughter (the patient): Nobody will listen to me. Everybody is trying to still me.

Mother: Nobody wants to kill you.

Father: If you're going to associate with intellectual people, you're going to have to remember that still is a noun and not a verb (Wynne et al., 1976, p. 195).

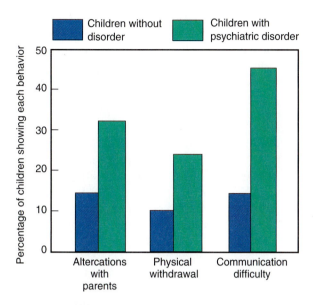

## Figure 5.6

Parent–child alienation at age 14. From M. Rutter, O. F. D. Graham, & W. Yule (1976). Adolescent turmoil: Fact or fiction? *Journal of Child Psychology and Psychiatry,* **17,** 35–36. By permission.

Troubled adolescents whose problems become more severe, or who fail to get better, are more likely to have at least one parent who says confusing things, is overly critical or hostile, and is intrusive (Goldstein et al., 1978). Families of delinquent boys have higher rates of communications in which the purpose is to defend oneself (Alexander, 1973; Hetherington, Stouwie, & Redberg, 1971; Rutter & Giller, 1984).

In families of disturbed adolescents, there is a greater frequency of communications revealing negative feelings, particularly critical evaluations of the adolescent (Fischer, 1980; Goldstein, 1987; Prinz, Rosenblum, & O'Leary, 1978; Tienari et al., 1987). For example, one study found that a negative emotional quality in verbal interactions between parent and child—such as harsh criticism, excessive intrusiveness, and guilt inducement—was related to lower self-esteem, a greater sense of isolation, and increased negative or contrary responses on the part of the adolescent (West, 1981).

Research clearly suggests a link between troubled communication and troubled adolescents; however, it is not clear that communication difficulties actually *cause* psychological disturbances. An equally likely explanation is that ineffective communication patterns might be a symptom or the result of repeated interactions with a disturbed child. The current view, based on longitudinal studies of families, is that poor communication does not necessarily cause adolescents to develop psychological problems. Rather, troubled communication increases the probability that a child who is vulnerable to a psychological disorder will express that disorder, or relapse following treatment (Goldstein, 1990).

## Role Relations in the Family

In addition to the overall characteristics that differentiate families from one another (such as effectiveness of communication and level of conflict), there are also differences in the roles played by individual family members. For example, in studies of the parent–child relationships of normal middle-class adolescents, compared to fathers, mothers have been found to be more open and communicative with their adolescent children and more involved in the details of their everyday lives (Almeida & Galambos, 1991; Montemayor & Brownlee, 1987; Richardson et al., 1984; Small, 1988; Youniss & Ketterlinus, 1987).

Fathers, on the other hand, tend to "administer authority indirectly and from a distance" (Youniss & Smollar, 1985, p. 78) and to focus on problem-solving (Hauser et al., 1987; Power & Shanks, 1989). They are also more likely to make demands without modifying them in light of adolescents' views. Youniss and Smollar (1985) assert that fathers, by virtue of their lesser degree of involvement and more impersonal standards, tend to encourage separateness, whereas mothers, with their greater degree of involvement and more open communication, tend to encourage family cohesion and connectedness. In brief, in these families, the roles played by the parents may complement each other in fostering a balance between age-appropriate behavior and a continuing sense of security and belonging.

## Father Involvement

As much as there may be a role-differentiation between mothers and fathers in many families, with the dramatic changes occurring at the societal level (increased labor-force participation of women and changes toward more egalitarian sex-role attitudes) the roles of mother and father are moving toward less differentiation. Fathers are spending time with their children in ways that they have not done before (Bronstein, 1988; Lamb, 1987). There is increasing evidence, for example, that fathers in two-earner families (where both mother and father have paid jobs) are more involved with their children than those in single-earner families. Specifically, when mothers are employed or increase the number of hours they work outside of the home, fathers spend more time in child-care duties (Almeida, Maggs, & Galambos, 1993;

Fathers who involve themselves more in the lives of their adolescent children become more accepting of their children than less-involved fathers.

Crouter et al., 1987). This represents a break from the traditional family of the 1950s, where in most families fathers were breadwinners and mothers were nurturers.

What does increased father involvement mean for adolescents? One study examined how father involvement was linked to changes in father–adolescent relations across a six-month period. This study found that fathers who were initially more involved with their adolescents (spent more time taking care of and doing things with the child) subsequently became more accepting of their adolescent children when compared to fathers who were initially less involved. More contact with adolescents apparently meant that fathers had more opportunity to demonstrate understanding and warmth. This study found that involved fathers were more similar to mothers in their levels of acceptance of the adolescent. Mothers typically score higher on measures of acceptance, but in families where fathers could be described as involved, mothers were no more accepting than fathers. The roles of mother and father were less differentiated than in many families (Almeida & Galambos, 1991). It will be interesting to observe in coming years to what extent mothers' and fathers' roles merge and how this change affects adolescents' development.

## Parental Attitudes Toward Adolescent Autonomy

As we have noted, there are likely to be contradictions in attitudes toward adolescent autonomy, not only in adult society but also within individual parents. Contradictions in the attitudes of a parent are likely to be most difficult for an adolescent to cope with. When parents proclaim that they want their adolescents to be independent but covertly behave in ways that prolong dependence, the result is likely to be confusing for adolescents. Consider the parents who, on dropping their 18-year-old daughter off at a college dormitory 50 miles away from home said, "Well, when we dropped your brother off at college, he returned home within a few days." Three days later, this unhappy adolescent girl packed her bags and her parents promptly came to take her home. It may be difficult for adolescents to deal rationally with such conflicting expectations and to develop a true sense of autonomy.

Inconsistency in parents' attitudes may simply reflect confusion about the roles society expects them to play. In a rapidly changing and deeply divided society, making appropriate decisions is seldom a simple matter. Parents may wonder: When should the child be permitted to go out on dates, and with whom? Should a child be allowed to go to parties where adults are absent and alcohol is used? Should a child have his or her own spending money, and if so, how much? When should the adolescent be told about sexuality and the risk of AIDS?

Often, parents' ambivalence toward autonomy stems from within—perhaps from contradictory needs. For example, many parents genuinely want their children to become able to handle their own affairs because they realize that ultimately this will be necessary. At the same time, however, they want to protect their children from the realities of life outside the protected family setting—an impossible task. Some parents who were very comfortable in their child-rearing role when their children were younger have difficulty deal-

ing with the fact that their adolescent son or daughter is no longer a child. One study found that parents' stress was related to issues of adolescent autonomy. Fathers of adolescent children who did not follow their father's advice felt more stress than those whose children went along with father's advice. Mothers were more stressed if their adolescents desired more, rather than less, autonomy in decision-making (Small, Eastman, & Cornelius, 1988).

## Sex-Role Socialization and the Development of Autonomy

Major societal changes in the last three decades have already had an impact on the development of autonomy and the resolution of conflicts over dependence and independence, particularly in adolescent girls (Conger & Petersen, 1984). Studies conducted in the 1960s and earlier indicated that girls experienced fewer and less stressful conflicts over the development of independence than boys. Moreover, girls were more likely than boys to consider their parents' rules to be fair, right, and lenient (Blos, 1971a; Coleman, 1961; Douvan & Adelson, 1966).

Since that time there have been important changes in the socialization and development of adolescent girls (Gilligan, 1979; Huston, 1983; Petersen, 1988). In one study of fifth- to ninth-graders, girls scored higher than boys on all measures of autonomy in their relations with parents; they also described themselves as more self-reliant (Steinberg & Silverberg, 1986). Moreover, girls were more resistant than boys to peer pressure. Other studies, though, have found few sex differences in attitudes related to autonomy and independence (Lerner, Sorrell, & Brackney, 1981; Offer, Ostrov, & Howard, 1981; Steinberg, 1987a).

A consistent finding of both earlier and more recent studies is that female adolescents and young women who are more independent, self-reliant, and achievement-oriented than their peers tend to have parents who, while fundamentally loving and caring, are not passively accepting of or overprotective toward their daughters. The parents of such adolescents make strong demands for maturity, self-reliance, and a reasonable level of achievement (Baumrind, 1989; Cooper & Grotevant, 1987; Eccles et al., 1991; Hauser et al., 1987). Adolescent girls and boys desire autonomy, and parents and teachers must strive to provide appropriate opportunities to exercise autonomy so that the transition through adolescence proceeds reasonably smoothly and successfully (Eccles et al., 1991).

# Parent–Adolescent Relations and Identity Formation

The ease with which adolescents are able to achieve a clear sense of identity depends on many factors, including the kinds of identifications with others that they have developed (see Chapter 2). Adolescents must integrate those identifications with their newfound sexual maturity, the aptitudes and skills they have developed, and the opportunities provided by changing social roles. Perhaps most importantly, however, identity formation depends on the kinds of relationships they have had and continue to have with their parents. Adolescents are more likely to establish a strong sense of identity if they have a rewarding, interactive relationship with their parents.

Adolescent identity development is also facilitated when parents provide models of competent problem-solving behavior, a confident sense of their own identity, and a mutually supportive relationship with each other (Block, 1973, 1984; Huston, 1983; Maccoby & Martin, 1983). In addition, adolescents who are further along in identity formation are more likely to have parents who encourage self-assertion and freedom to disagree (*separateness*) while at the same time encouraging *connectedness* to the family, including openness or responsiveness to the views of others (*plurality*) and sensitivity to and respect for the ideas of others (*mutuality*) (Cooper, Grotevant, & Condon, 1983; Ryan & Lynch, 1989; Youniss & Smollar, 1985).

## Sex-Typing and Parental Behavior

Parents play a role, too, in their children's **sex-typing,** which is the process by which children attain the attributes that are consistent with sex roles, or societal expectations for their gender. The results of this process are seen in traditionally masculine characteristics such as aggressiveness in males and traditionally feminine characteristics such as nurturance in females (Huston, 1983). As we saw in Chapter 2, exaggerated sex-typing can limit development in both sexes. The male who possesses only masculine characteristics and the female who possesses only feminine characteristics may be less prepared to meet the demands of a changing society or to sustain mature, intimate relationships. Having both masculine and feminine behaviors at one's disposal allows for flexibility in meeting the requirements of different situations (Bem, 1975; Huston, 1983). Moreover, among both males and females those who are most likely to be creative are those who combine

positive masculine and feminine traits (Spence, 1985; Spence & Helmreich, 1978).

The possession of positive masculine attributes in addition to positive feminine characteristics might be especially important for females. Among adolescent girls as well as boys, self-reported masculinity is an important correlate of self-esteem and peer acceptance (Allgood-Merten & Stockard, 1991; Huston, 1983; Lamke, 1982; Massad, 1981). A balance of masculine and feminine characteristics gives each adolescent, regardless of sex, the best chance to develop his or her unique potential as a human being.

Research shows that for both sexes, adolescents' identity development is influenced by the kinds of role models provided by parents; a strong sense of identity develops in adolescents whose parents are affectionate, praising, and supportive (Baumrind, 1991a, 1991b; Conger, 1977; Huston, 1983; Waterman, 1982). Although early research suggested that adolescents identify with same-sex parents, particularly when those parents are warm and nurturant, recent studies have also shown that adolescents may identify with the more powerful parent—mother or father. The parent who controls more of the rewards or resources in the family may have the strongest influence over the adolescent's behavior through imitation or modeling processes (McDonald, 1977, 1980). This may explain in part why girls with employed mothers are more achievement-oriented, have higher occupational and educational aspirations, and have more egalitarian attitudes toward the roles of men and women (Galambos, Petersen, & Lenerz, 1988; L. W. Hoffman, 1980). Presumably, by observing female models of competence, girls will come to see themselves as capable of carrying out many important responsibilities.

## Parental Identity Concerns in the Adolescent Years

Much is made of adolescent identity problems. But adults, too, may have identity crises, and for a majority most such crises are likely to occur during the period when their children are coming to maturity (Small, Eastman, & Cornelius, 1988). As one observer noted, one reason that the adolescent years tend to be difficult ones for the family is that everyone concerned is likely to be in a "dangerous" stage of development (Chilman, 1968). Not only are adolescent children going through many transitions; at mid-life, men and women may be re-evaluating their lives, wondering whether the educational, occupational, and marital choices they made earlier were the correct ones (Julian, McKenry, & Arnold,

1990). Parents' growing awareness of aging is likely to be heightened by the obvious contrasts between themselves and their adolescent young, who are approaching the height of their physical, sexual, and mental capabilities.

There is often a temporary dip in marital satisfaction during the child-rearing years (Gove & Petersen, 1980; Silverberg & Steinberg, 1987). In view of the stresses of this period, it is not surprising that parents may be more ambivalent in their attitudes toward their children's growing autonomy than might otherwise be the case. One study showed that mothers' intense mid-life crisis symptoms were linked to lower satisfaction with the parenting role (Koski & Steinberg, 1990). In another study, Silverberg (1992) assessed the mid-life concerns of mothers and fathers with adolescent children. More mid-life concerns among parents were linked to increases in parent–daughter conflict and decreases in the number of calm discussions over a one-year period. These studies support the notion that the stresses associated with parents' stage in life may well affect their satisfaction with parenting and the nature of the parent–adolescent relationship.

There is another side to this story as well. For many parents who have lived full lives and have been reasonably successful vocationally, socially, in their marriage, or as parents, the disadvantages of this stage are outweighed by greater security, other interests, and continuing contact with their children. Erik Erikson observed that whereas the stage of young adulthood centrally involves the search for intimacy, the proper concern of a mature middle-aged adult involves making the transition to what he calls generativity—satisfaction gained from contributing to the development and well-being of others, particularly the young (Erikson, 1963, 1968). Middle-aged adults who can gain satisfaction from using their experience, resources, security, and position in society and in the family in caring for others may have the best possible insurance against the disappointments and stresses of increasing age.

## Working Families

Earlier in this chapter we discussed the social changes of the previous few decades and indicated what they have meant for the structure and functioning of families today. With women's entrance into the labor force—a major social change since the 1950s—two-earner families (in which both parents have paid jobs) have become more common than one-earner families (in which only the husband or the wife works). In the absence of a traditional division of labor in which fathers supply the income and

## 5.2 Judy Blume as Adolescent and Parent

In the following excerpt from an article in *Newsweek,* Judy Blume, a prolific writer of fiction for adolescents, reveals her own difficulties both as an adolescent and as a parent of adolescents.

My own adolescent rebellion came late. Somewhere around the age of 35. I don't recommend waiting till then. Better to drag your parents through it than your kids. I was the *good* child in our family. My job was to be happy, to make up for my brother, who wasn't. Even as a teen, I gave my parents little trouble. I told them only what I thought they wanted to hear. I kept the rest to myself. . . .

[M]y friends envied me. Our house was a haven, a gathering place. Rules were simple and reasonable. My mother was always available . . . and my father was warm, funny, loving. He told me if I ever had problems, I should come to him. Other young people did. . . . But not me. I was his daughter!

My father died suddenly, when I was 21, and my life changed overnight. We never had the chance to know each other as adults. Until I began to write this piece it never occurred to me that I have taken my father's place, becoming a confidante to thousands of young people who write to me every year, in response to my books.

They write about their most immediate concerns—family, friends, love, loss, sex, school. The same concerns I had as a teenager. They wish their parents would acknowledge their feelings and take them seriously. They wish for unconditional love. . . .

So I certainly should have been prepared for my children's adolescence . . . [but] when the going got tough my daughter went to someone else. . . . And even though I knew her rejection was necessary to prove she could survive without me, it hurt!

I was feeling very fragile myself at that time, in the midst of my own late adolescence—confused about life, about where I belonged, trying to make up for what I had missed out on when I was young. . . . But the last thing my daughter needed was a parent in the same boat. . . . I felt alone and frightened.

How could this be happening? I wondered. After all, thousands of kids were writing to me every month. They trusted me. I knew how to listen without judging. (Yes, but it's so much easier when they're not *your* kids. And it's so much easier for them to tell someone other than *their* parents.)

The good news is, most of us survive our children's adolescent years. My only advice is to stay aware, listen carefully and yell for help if you need it. Somehow, with common sense and humor most of us manage to muddle through. And on the other side is a reward. A new relationship with adult children.

mothers supply the child care, two-earner families have had to negotiate how they accomplish the complicated tasks of combining work and raising children.

There are many tales about the difficulties parents in two-earner families face, particularly when children are young and need constant care and attention. Still, the bulk of the research examining whether children and adolescents differ in one- and two-earner families reveals a striking absence of findings overall, except in the area of sex-role socialization (Frankel, 1993; Hoffman, 1989; Lerner & Galambos, 1991). (As we will see

in Chapter 9, children with employed mothers differentiate less between women's and men's roles than do children with nonemployed mothers). This does not mean that parents' work environments and their work duties do not influence their children's development in any way. Rather, as in any family, what matters most is the quality of care that the child receives and the nature of the parent–adolescent relationship. Parents' work will influence adolescents' development only to the extent that it interferes with or enhances parenting and the parent–adolescent relationship.

Parents in two-earner families are faced with a time crunch. Does this mean that they spend less time with their adolescents? One study of fifth to ninth graders found that whereas adolescents with nonemployed mothers spent more time with their mothers in the afternoon, adolescents with employed mothers spent more time with their mothers in the evening. The *total* amount of time spent with mother did not differ in one- and two-earner families. The total amount of time adolescents spent with fathers did differ, however; adolescents in two-earner families spent more time alone with their fathers. This study also examined the kinds of activities adolescents engaged in. Adolescents with mothers employed full-time spent more time doing homework and less time in general leisure activities than did adolescents with nonemployed mothers (Richards & Duckett, 1994).

In thinking about how parents' work can affect family relations, some writers have discussed negative spillover. Negative spillover occurs when demands experienced by a parent on the job create stress for the parent, and these feelings of stress are brought home and spill over into behaviors with family members (Piotrkowski, 1979). Parents who are overloaded at work, for instance, may be irritable with their spouses or children.

One study of two-earner families with adolescent children found evidence of such spillover. Fathers and mothers who experienced work overload (too much to do at work) were more likely to report feelings of stress; these feelings of stress were related, in turn, to less accepting behaviors in mothers and more conflict between parents and adolescents. When parent–adolescent relations suffered, adolescents subsequently engaged in an increasing level of problem behavior. This study also found that parent–adolescent conflict was highest when *both* parents were stressed (Galambos et al., 1995). The other side of the coin is that positive spillover can occur as well. Parents whose jobs provide them with satisfaction and challenge are likely to bring a positive mood home to their families (Piotrkowski, 1979).

## Latchkey Adolescents

What children do after school is one concern resulting from the shift toward mothers' employment. Many jobs require parents to work in the afternoon. Adolescents who come home to an empty house after school are called latchkey adolescents because they must carry a key to gain entry. Younger children might attend supervised, structured programs after school when such programs are available, but such programs are not generally geared to adolescents. The concern that is raised is whether adolescents will get into trouble when they are without adult supervision.

Despite this concern, most studies have found few overall differences between latchkey children and adult-supervised children on measures indicating how they feel about themselves, their academic achievement, and peer relations (Galambos & Garbarino, 1985; Rodman, Pratto, & Nelson, 1985; Vandell & Corasaniti, 1988; Vandell & Ramanan, 1991). Laurence Steinberg (1986) argued that most important is *where* the child spends time after school and whether the parent *monitors* the child's activities from a distance. Steinberg's study demonstrated that latchkey adolescents who stayed home were no more likely to be influenced by peer pressure than adult-supervised adolescents. Latchkey adolescents who spent time away from home—at a friend's house or "hanging out"—were more likely to respond to peer pressure, but only if their parents did not monitor their activities and whereabouts. A similar study also found higher levels of misconduct among latchkey adolescent girls who spent time away from home and whose parents were less responsive and less demanding (Galambos & Maggs, 1991).

Although most latchkey adolescents who stay at home after school do not show adjustment problems, research examining this issue has focused on adolescents living in rural, suburban, or small-town settings. Children or adolescents living in urban environments may well be more at risk for experiencing negative consequences of being left unsupervised than those who are in safer environments (Galambos & Garbarino, 1985). In line with this reasoning, a large-scale study of eighth-grade adolescents living in a large metropolitan area found that the more time adolescents spent without adult supervision, the higher were their levels of substance use (Richardson et al., 1989). In an urban environment the opportunities for engaging in high-risk activities are likely to be greater than in places with a small-town or rural atmosphere.

## Economic Stress

As pointed out earlier in this chapter, many of today's families have a difficult time making ends meet. Loss of a parent's job may have the most dramatic consequences for family life, but financial stresses can exist in any family, due to circumstances such as poor pay, demotions, cutbacks in hours, business or investment losses, and poor money management.

Psychologists Constance Flanagan and Jacquelynne Eccles have demonstrated how changes in a parent's work situation can affect the nature of family relations and adolescent behavior. A large number of families with adolescents were followed over two years, and changes in parents' work situations across this period were used to character-

ize families as nondeprived (parents had stable employment situations), recovery (there was a layoff or demotion, but with reemployment by the end of two years), and deprived (there was a layoff or demotion with no recovery). In deprived families, adolescents, and particularly boys, reported higher levels of conflict with their parents than those in nondeprived and recovery families. Adolescents in deprived families were also rated by their teachers as least socially competent in school. Among recovery families, initially high levels of conflict were reduced as parents became reemployed (Flanagan, 1990; Flanagan & Eccles, 1993). Other research demonstrates that economic pressures within families exert their effects on adolescent behavior through family conflict and the expression of hostility from parents to adolescents (Conger et al., 1994; McLoyd et al., 1994). Continued financial stress is clearly undesirable from the perspective of family and adolescent functioning, and even short-lived financial stresses may take a toll on family life.

# Divorce and Remarriage

Because divorce is now so commonplace, many children and adolescents experience the divorce process and, as a result, live in a single-parent family. Eventually, they may experience the remarriage of one or both parents and may live in a stepfamily. The effects of these changing circumstances on children's lives and the transitions that divorce and remarriage pose for family members are of mounting interest to developmental psychologists and others concerned with optimal human development. Two important questions are What are the effects of divorce on the development of children and adolescents? and How does living in a stepfamily affect child and adolescent development?

## Divorce and Single-Parent Families

As the area of research on the effects of divorce on children has matured, it has become increasingly clear that divorce can have adverse effects on both children and parents (Hetherington, Clingempeel, et al., 1992). With some variations, depending on age and sex, children who have experienced a divorce may regress, withdraw, become aggressive or depressed, exhibit behavior problems, feel responsible for the divorce, blame one or both parents, suffer from a conflict of loyalties, and perform poorly in school and on cognitive tests (Allison & Furstenberg, 1989; Amato & Keith, 1991b; Guidubaldi & Perry, 1985; Hetherington, Cox, & Cox, 1985; Wallerstein, Corbin, & Lewis, 1988). Earlier research had sug-

gested that such problems may disappear after a temporary period of readjustment, perhaps within two years postdivorce, but there is increasing evidence that the initial effects may persist (Amato & Keith, 1991b; Guidubaldi & Perry, 1985; Hetherington & Camara, 1984; Hetherington, Cox, & Cox, 1985). One study found that five years after the parents' separation, one-third of the children appeared resilient, relaxed, and self-reliant; another third appeared to be coping fairly well; and the rest had significant psychological problems and still looked back with intense longing to life before the divorce (Wallerstein, 1985).

Some studies have suggested that boys are more vulnerable to the effects of divorce than girls (Guidubaldi & Perry, 1985; Hetherington, 1989). This conclusion is challenged, however, by a growing body of research demonstrating few sex differences in children's adjustment to divorce (Amato & Keith, 1991b) and by research finding few such differences in adolescence and adulthood (Amato & Keith, 1991a).

The overall effects of divorce on adolescents' functioning are similar to those seen in children. Adolescents whose parents have experienced a divorce may show social, psychological, and cognitive adjustment problems (Forehand et al., 1991; Hetherington, 1993; Hetherington, Clingempeel, et al., 1992; Zimiles & Lee, 1991). Adolescents in single-parent families may be more susceptible to the effects of antisocial peer pressure (Steinberg, 1987b) and may engage in higher rates of deviant behavior (Dornbusch et al., 1985; Hetherington, 1993). They are also more likely to drop out of school (Zimiles & Lee, 1991). Figure 5.7 illustrates the higher levels of serious behavior problems (as reported by their mothers and their fathers) among adolescents who experienced a divorce (Hetherington, 1993). Research suggests that behavior problems among adolescents in single-parent families might result from the parent's lower level of monitoring and control over the child's activities (Dornbusch et al., 1985; Newcomer & Udry, 1987).

As young adults, many people of both sexes—even though they may be getting on successfully with their own lives—still have strong memories of their parents' breakup, along with feelings of sadness, continuing resentment, and a sense of deprivation (Wallerstein, 1985; Wallerstein, Corbin, & Lewis, 1988). One study found that young adults (18 to 22 years old) who had experienced divorce as children were twice as likely as those from intact families to have poor relations with their parents (particularly their fathers), to have dropped out of high school, to have received psychological help, and to show behavior problems (Zill, Morrison, & Coiro, 1993). A number of studies point to poorer psychological adjustment, poorer social relations, a higher likelihood of divorcing, lower educational attainment,

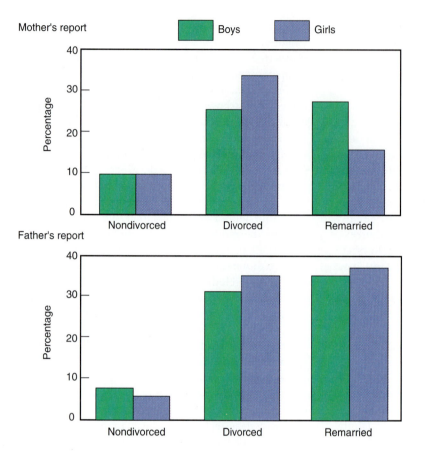

Mother's report

Father's report

Figure 5.7

Fifteen-year-old children showing serious levels of behavior problems. From E. M. Hetherington (1993). An overview of the Virginia Longitudinal Study of Divorce and Remarriage with a focus on early adolescence. *Journal of Family Psychology,* **7,** 39–56. Copyright © 1993 by the American Psychological Association. Reprinted with permission.

and a lower material and occupational quality of life among adults whose parents divorced earlier in their lives (Amato & Keith, 1991a; Booth & Amato, 1994). These findings suggest that there are potentially adverse long-term effects of divorce.

The child's problems in adjusting to divorce are often aggravated by the fact that the parents are preoccupied with their own problems, especially during the first year after the divorce, and have difficulty responding to the child's needs (Hetherington & Camara, 1984). The child often experiences a feeling of being caught in the middle between the two parents, a feeling that is associated with poor adjustment in adolescents (Buchanan, Maccoby, & Dornbusch, 1991).

Divorce is likely to have an immediately disruptive effect on long-established patterns of family life. One study found that task overload, household disorganization, feelings of loneliness, and parenting stress were high among newly divorced mothers, but by two years postdivorce, divorced mothers on the average were less depressed and anxious, drank less, and had fewer health problems than married mothers who were in unhappy, conflicted marriages (Hetherington, 1993).

Where negative effects of divorce occur, they have been attributed primarily to the existence of three con-

ditions: father absence, or the absence of a second parent in the home (typically the father); economic disadvantage, or the declining economic circumstances that accompany the breakup of a household; and interparental conflict, or the conflict that occurs and may continue to occur between divorcing parents. Although all three factors may contribute to the adverse implications of divorce on children, interparental conflict is the strongest predictor of children's adverse postdivorce functioning (Amato & Keith, 1991b; Emery, 1982). Across a number of studies, children whose divorced parents continue to argue and fight perform more poorly on measures of well-being (for example, school achievement, conduct, psychological adjustment, self-concept) than do children whose parents have relatively low levels of conflict, divorced or not. Children whose divorced parents have harmonious relations show significantly better psychological and social adjustment than do children in high-conflict intact homes (Amato & Keith, 1991b). These results suggest that interparental conflict, rather than divorce per se, is a key factor in explaining the adjustment of children of divorce.

Another consideration concerns how children and their parents in divorcing families were doing before the actual divorce. Most divorce studies begin observing chil-

dren *after* the divorce has occurred, and assume that the child's behavior worsened as a result of the divorce. An alternative explanation would be that the child's difficult behavior was present *before* the divorce. One study of families followed a sample of children throughout childhood and adolescence, long before anyone knew which families would divorce. This study revealed behavior difficulties such as low impulse control, aggression, and excessive energy among boys whose parents would subsequently divorce. Presumably, stresses in these families were present early on in the boy's life (Block, Block, & Gjerde, 1986). Similar studies carried out in Great Britain as well as in the United States found similar results. Children whose parents eventually divorced had preexisting behavior problems (Cherlin et al., 1991). In brief, studies that examine children only after a divorce may overestimate negative effects of the divorce.

It is important to note that although the research shows differences among children, adolescents, and adults from divorced and intact families, the differences are not large, and there is considerable overlap between them. That is, many children from divorced families are well-adjusted and some children in intact families—particularly those that are ridden with conflict—do poorly (Barber & Eccles, 1992). As one author remarked, "the fact that a young person comes from a divorced family does not, in itself, tell us a great deal about how he or she is faring on embarking into adulthood" (Zill, Morrison, & Coiro, 1993, p. 100).

Potential *benefits* of divorce have been overlooked as researchers have focused primarily on its costs. This focus on negative effects of divorce is somewhat surprising given that many parents initiate a divorce because they believe that, in the long run, their children's futures will be better, not worse, as a result of the divorce (Galambos & Ehrenberg, in press). The removal of children from a tense and conflicted family situation is but one potentially positive consequence of divorce. In freeing the child from undue family stress, divorce might lead to children's better concentration on their schoolwork, they might receive closer attention from their parents once the initial stress of divorcing is over, and some children of divorce might, as adults, consider their work, spousal, and family choices more carefully and wisely than they would have otherwise.

## Remarriage and Stepfamilies

Just as divorce can be a difficult transition for family members, remarriage may also pose difficulties. This is indicated by the fact that 40 percent of remarriages fail, compared to about one in three first marriages. Children may resent stepparents because they have displaced the original parent or because the stepparent competes with the child for the other parent's love and attention. Research on children (before their entry into adolescence) shows that after divorce mothers and daughters may form close alliances, and on the mother's remarriage the daughter is likely to view the stepfather as an intruder (Hetherington, 1989; Hetherington & Camara, 1984; Peterson & Zill, 1986). Divorced mothers and sons may be involved in a mutual battle of wills and may "have much to gain from the addition of a responsive, authoritative stepfather, who offers support to both the mother and son" (Hetherington, Cox, & Cox, 1985, p. 529). The strains of living in a stepfamily seem to diminish after two years, at least among school-age children (Hetherington, 1989).

The picture of *adolescents'* adjustment to remarriage, however, is more pessimistic. One study found that academic achievement was lower and the school dropout rate was higher among adolescents in remarried families compared to those in intact families (Zimiles & Lee, 1991). Recent research by Mavis Hetherington and her colleagues demonstrated that there was little improvement either in adolescent boys' and girls' adjustment or in relations with their stepfathers in the 26 months following the remarriage of their mothers. Adolescent boys and girls whose mothers remarried showed more seriously high levels of behavior problems than adolescents in nondivorced homes (see Figure 5.7), and this behavior did not improve in the next few years. Stepfather–stepchild relations started off in a polite manner but grew increasingly distant as stepfathers were faced with negative behaviors in their stepchildren. Eventually, stepfathers seemed to give up trying, and became uninvolved with the adolescents (Hetherington, Clingempeel, et al., 1992). Other studies have revealed that relations between stepfathers and adolescent stepdaughters are especially strained, with more conflict and more distance than in stepfather–stepson relationships (Kurdek & Fine, 1993; Vuchinich et al., 1991). For many adolescents, living in a stepfamily is not easy.

Stepparents are also likely to have a difficult time. They may feel insecure about interacting with newly acquired stepchildren (Spanier & Furstenberg, 1982). Where two sets of children live together in a stepfamily, there may be rivalries between them. Remarriage is associated with high sibling conflict (Hetherington & Clingempeel, 1992). Thus, although divorce and remarriage may be better for children's development than remaining in a crisis-ridden family with both original parents present (Hetherington, 1989; Long & Forehand, 1987), the meaning of these transitions for children's and adolescents' development must be considered carefully.

Fundamental to children's healthy development is a climate of love and trust (Erikson, 1968) and authoritative control over children's actions. Such a climate increases the child's chances of becoming a reasonably happy, effective, contributing adult, and of developing a positive self-image and a strong sense of identity (Conger, 1977; Maccoby & Martin, 1983). This kind of climate may be more difficult to foster when there are multiple marital transitions in a family; nevertheless, children can be reared successfully in single-parent and stepfamilies, particularly when the parents are psychologically mature and adequate social support is available. As Mavis Hetherington remarked, "It is the diversity rather than the inevitability of outcomes that is notable in response to divorce and remarriage" (1989, p. 55).

## Abusing Parents

In some cases the stresses of parenting can get out of control, resulting in serious abuse of the child or adolescent. Such abuse is widespread and may be physical, emotional, or sexual in nature. It is difficult to obtain accurate data on rates of incidence because many cases are unreported or unrecognized by authorities, although reporting has clearly improved in recent years (see Figure 5.8). All states now have laws requiring healthcare professionals to report cases of suspected child abuse. As shown in Figure 5.8, in 1992 in the United States, nearly 3,000,000 cases of confirmed or suspected child abuse and neglect were reported, of which about half involved neglect. The actual incidence is probably much higher (CDF, 1994).

Among abusing parents, half the perpetrators of physical abuse are fathers and half are mothers (Martin, 1984). In contrast to popular perceptions, a larger proportion of adolescents than of children under age 12 (particularly girls) are victims of abuse (Garbarino, 1989; Olson & Holmes, 1983). Although child abuse occurs more often among parents who are poorly educated and economically deprived, it occurs with disturbing frequency among parents at all socioeconomic levels.

Much more needs to be learned about the factors that predispose a parent to child abuse. Nevertheless, certain characteristics stand out. Many abusive parents experienced abuse, neglect, parental discord, harsh discipline, or parental loss in their own early years (Cicchetti & Carlson, 1989; Rutter, 1989a). It is important to note that although abusing parents were often victims of abuse themselves, this does not mean that a majority of abused children and adolescents will become abusing parents (Corby, 1993; Zigler & Hall, 1989). Many are able to break the cycle of abuse because of readily available support systems, fewer life stresses, healthier babies who are easier to care for, better psychological understanding, or other favorable circumstances (Kaufman & Zigler, 1987; Zigler & Hall, 1989). Abuse confined to adolescence is less likely to be transmitted between generations than abuse beginning in childhood (Garbarino, 1989; Garbarino & Kelly, 1986; Pelcovitz et al., 1984).

For the most part, abusing parents have not been exposed to models of successful parenting—models that they could apply in rearing their own children. Many abusing parents, including adolescent parents, lack empathy, do not understand the complexity of social relationships, and have extremely unrealistic ideas about the

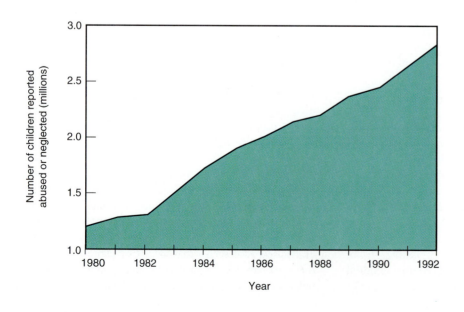

Figure 5.8

Children reported abused or neglected, 1980–1992.
SOURCES: American Association for Protecting Children, National Committee to Prevent Child Abuse, and Children's Defense Fund, 1994.

behavior that can be expected of a child (Belsky & Vondra, 1989; Osofsky, 1990; Pianta, Egeland, & Erikson, 1989). Consequently, when an infant soils its diapers or cries continually, or when a child does not perform a task well, the parent views the child as willfully misbehaving and resorts to punishment, usually without success; this begins a downward spiral in which a deteriorating parent–child relationship is aggravated by further punishment.

If lack of knowledge about child development were the only problem, however, it would be easier to help parents who abuse their children. Such help can often be useful, but the problem usually goes much deeper. Having been deprived of love and care themselves, many abusing parents are hungry for love and acceptance and find it difficult to subordinate their own needs to those of the child (Crittenden & Ainsworth, 1989; Steele, 1987). Moreover, they are often socially isolated, view themselves as bad or unlovable, and lack the ability to make friends or develop broader social support systems (Cicchetti & Carlson, 1989; Mueller & Silverman, 1989). These characteristics can combine with life circumstances to place the parent at risk for abusing the child.

Brandt Steele (1980), a pioneer in the study of the causes and treatment of child abuse, notes that physical abuse usually is not a constant or daily occurrence. Rather, four conditions seem necessary for abuse to occur:

1. A parent who has the predisposition for abuse related to psychological residues of neglect or abuse in his or her own early life.
2. A crisis of some sort placing extra stress on the parent.
3. Lack of sources of help for the parent, either because he or she is unable to reach out or the facilities are not available.
4. A child who is perceived as being in some way unsatisfactory.

## Effects of Abuse

Many abused children, aided by beneficial experiences during development, grow up to be normal adults and nonabusive parents (Corby, 1993; Zigler & Hall, 1989). However, others show long-term adverse effects. For example, they may lack persistence, be easily distracted, have low ego control and low self-esteem, behave aggressively, perform poorly in school, find it difficult to trust others, and experience loneliness (Alexander, Moore, & Alexander, 1991; Briere & Runtz, 1990; Salzinger et al., 1993; Weiss et al., 1992). Abused children "often make great efforts to find a friend among young-

A history of child abuse and neglect is common among adolescent runaways.

sters of their own sex. But these attempts tend to fail because their demands are excessive and are not understood by the friend" (Kempe & Kempe, 1978, p. 10).

In addition, abused children all too often come to believe that the "discipline" they received for "bad behavior" was justified and that such discipline is the right way to bring up recalcitrant children. At the same time, they are likely to develop strong underlying feelings of resentment and anger toward their parents—as much for their lack of care and understanding as for their abuse.

Not surprisingly, a history of child abuse and neglect is common among adolescent runaways and delinquents (Garbarino, Schellenbach, & Sebes, 1986; Janus et al., 1987; Lewis, Mallouh, & Webb, 1989). These findings do not mean that most abused children become delinquent, but they do indicate that a history of prior abuse is common among those who later commit aggressive offenses. Abused adolescents may begin to express the anger that they have felt for so long by engaging in delinquent behavior or by running away. By joining a peer group

with similar problems, the adolescent may experience a feeling of belonging and being wanted. At the same time, the peer group may provide a means of discharging pent-up aggression in group-approved delinquent activities.

## Sexual Abuse

Sexual abuse of children and adolescents is all too common in North America. A recent national survey in Canada found that 18 percent of young women and 10 percent of young men aged 13–16 years reported having experienced sexual abuse (Holmes & Silverman, 1992). The effects of sexual abuse during childhood or adolescence are not uniform, either in kind or in severity. Much depends on the child's age at the time of abuse, the nature of the abusive act, the amount of aggression or physical abuse involved, the relationship between the abuser and the child, and the child's relationships with nonabusing caretakers before, during, and after the episodes of sexual abuse (Browne & Finkelhor, 1986). In general, sexual abuse by a parent, especially if it is accompanied by coercion, physical abuse, or general family disorganization, is likely to be more traumatic and to create more pervasive and lasting problems than abuse by a stranger (Kempe & Kempe, 1984; Phares & Compas, 1992).

Among the longer-term effects that sexual abuse may have are symptoms of post-traumatic stress disorder, including nightmares, sleep disturbances, and poor concentration; feelings of helplessness and inability to control one's own destiny; depression and anxiety; impaired ability to establish trusting relations with others; inability to take pleasure in sexual activity, resulting in total withdrawal from sexual relationships or, in less severe instances, problems of sexual dysfunction; and substance abuse and addiction (Briere & Runtz, 1991; Finkelhor, 1990; Harter, Alexander, & Neimeyer, 1988; Sirles, Smith, & Kusama, 1989). Sexual abuse victims are also more likely than their nonabused counterparts to report thinking about suicide and to have attempted suicide (Briere & Runtz, 1988). Although most research on sexual abuse has been conducted on females, who are more often the targets of sexual abuse, recent research on males suggests that sexual abuse is just as damaging to them (Briere et al., 1988; Finkelhor, 1990).

If it is begun soon enough and continued long enough, individual and group treatment of sexual abuse, including incest, can be successful (Rust & Troupe, 1991) and may even lead to the capacity to enjoy normal, trusting sexual relationships. Without intervention, however, serious long-term consequences may remain.

# Summary

During the past half century, rapid social changes have had profound effects on the nature of the family in North America. Urbanization and mobility, an unstable economy with increasing poverty, the increase in women working outside the home, and the rise in divorce have placed new stresses on families. This stress is compounded by the declining commitment toward government support of families.

Adolescents still must master the important developmental tasks of adolescence. Parents are the single most important external influence on the average adolescent attempting to deal with these tasks.

Two important dimensions of parental behavior are *responsiveness,* which is evidenced by acceptance and warmth, and *demandingness,* which is seen in the control and monitoring of adolescents. Combining these two dimensions results in four parenting patterns that are linked to the adolescent's development in important ways. *Authoritative* parents, who are high on both dimensions, have children who are socially, intellectually, and academically competent. *Authoritarian* parents, who are high on

demandingness but low on responsiveness, are likely to have adolescents who are obedient and conforming, but who also have low self-esteem and negative self-perceptions. The adolescents of *permissive–indulgent* parents (high on responsiveness, low on demandingness) show a mixture of positive and negative characteristics. They tend to be psychologically well-adjusted but engage in some deviant behaviors. The adolescents of *permissive–indifferent* parents (low on both dimensions) show the poorest developmental outcomes. The salience of these patterns is evident across ethnic groups, although authoritativeness has less influence on school performance in Asian- and African-American adolescents.

The parent–adolescent relationship can be characterized in terms of level of conflict. Some conflict appears to be a normal part of most families, but high levels of conflict are harmful. Conflict may increase when there are stresses in the family. The adolescent's developing *autonomy* (which is a sense of self-reliance and self-governance) may be a source of some family conflict. To develop appropriately, autonomy requires

the dual processes of *separation* and *connectedness.* Specifically, parents need to gradually allow adolescents more freedom, but at the same time continue to guide and support them. One of the most marked changes across adolescence is the shift from parents' unilateral authority to more mutual decision-making. Responsible, autonomous behavior is best fostered in authoritative families.

Parent–adolescent interaction is not a one-way street; it is *bidirectional.* Just as parental behavior affects children, the behavior of children affects their parents. Moreover, both children and parents are members of a broader family system, which has characteristics of its own. One of the most important characteristics is the level and kind of communication that occurs. Effective communication helps family members strike a balance between separateness and connectedness. Another important feature in families is the extent to which fathers are involved with their children. Father involvement can open the door to greater warmth and understanding of adolescent children.

Parent–adolescent relations are important in helping the adolescent to form a coherent sense of *identity.* Parents who are fundamentally loving and demanding yet not overprotective will have adolescents who are more likely to establish their identity, to feel competent and self-reliant, and to have the ability to solve problems. This may be especially important for girls, who traditionally have been socialized to be nurturant and not instrumental. Both parents have a role to play in helping their adolescents develop to their fullest potential and achieve the characteristics that will allow them to be flexible in dealing with their environment. Parents of adolescents may have some identity concerns that can influence the parent–adolescent relationship.

One of the ways in which social change has affected family functioning is that two-earner families have become more common than one-earner families. Parents' work influences adolescents' development to the extent that it interferes with or enhances parent–adolescent relations. Working parents can be responsive to and demanding of their adolescents, although parents' stress at work can spill over into strained parent–adolescent relations. Latchkey adolescents have a higher likelihood of behavior problems if their activities are not monitored. Economic (or financial) stress can have a negative impact on family relations.

Another social change has been an increase in divorce. Adolescents whose parents have experienced a divorce may show social, psychological, and cognitive adjustment problems. These difficulties may be the result of parental preoccupation with problems and interparental conflict that continues after the divorce. However, many children from divorced families are well-adjusted and do better than children in conflict-ridden intact families. Researchers have not considered possible benefits of divorce. Remarriage may pose difficulties for adolescents. Research has demonstrated little improvement in adolescent adjustment and in relations with stepfathers in the two years following a remarriage. Children in single- and stepparent families can be reared successfully when parents are psychologically mature and social support is available.

Parenting at its worst is evident in abuse of the adolescent. Physical, emotional, and sexual abuse are all too common, and can have long-term devastating effects on the social, emotional, intellectual, and sexual development of children. Proportionately more adolescents than children are abused. Abusing parents generally have not been exposed to models of successful parenting (they may have been abused themselves) and may have unrealistic ideas about the kind of behavior that can be expected of a child. Moreover, life stresses and social isolation contribute to abuse in the vulnerable parent.

# Review Questions

1. What are the two primary dimensions of parental behavior? How does each of these dimensions affect the development of adolescents?

2. How do authoritative child-rearing practices differ from authoritarian, permissive–indulgent, and permissive–indifferent practices? Which approach is most likely to foster the development of responsible, autonomous behavior? Which is most likely to lead to hostility or feelings of rejection? Why?

3. Describe parent–adolescent conflict as it typically occurs. What family circumstances might contribute to such conflict?

4. Discuss the dual processes of separation and connectedness in the development of age-appropriate autonomy during adolescence.

5. What is meant by the principle of bidirectionality? Give some examples.

6. What characteristics differentiate families scoring high and low on measures of parent–adolescent communication?

7. How might mothers and fathers differ in their roles in the family? How might father involvement affect parent–adolescent relations as well as these roles?

8. Discuss the concept of sex-typing and explain how it might affect the development of autonomy, identity, and self-esteem of males and females. How might parents facilitate the development of instrumentality in their daughters? Why would they want to?

9. What kinds of concerns might working families have about their adolescents' development? What effects do parents' work have on adolescents?

10. Discuss the impact of divorce and remarriage on adolescents. Where there are negative effects of divorce or remarriage, what might account for those effects?

11. Discuss the effects of physical or sexual abuse on the development of children and adolescents. Discuss the characteristics of abusing parents.

## Recommended Readings

Baumrind, D. (1991). Parenting styles and adolescent development. In J. Brooks-Gunn, R. Lerner, & A. C. Petersen (Eds.), *The encyclopedia of adolescence.* New York: Garland.

Frankel, J. (Ed.). (1993). *The employed mother and the family context.* New York: Springer.

Garbarino, J., Schellenbach, C. J., & Sebes, J. M. (1986). *Troubled youth, troubled families: Understanding families at risk for adolescent maltreatment.* New York: Aldine de Gruyter.

Hetherington, E. M., Clingempeel, G. W., Anderson, E. R., Deal, J. E., Hagan, M. S., Hollier, E. A., & Lindner, M. S. (1992). Coping with marital transitions: A family systems perspective. *Monographs of the Society for Research in Child Development, 57*(2–3, Serial no. 227).

Steinberg, L. (1990). Autonomy, conflict, and harmony in the family relationship. In S. S. Feldman & G. R. Elliott (Eds.), *At the threshold: The developing adolescent* (pp. 255–276). Cambridge, MA: Harvard University Press.

Youniss, J., & Smollar, J. (1985). *Adolescent relations with mothers, fathers, and friends.* Chicago: University of Chicago Press.

# Adolescent Sexuality

6

among the many developmental events that characterize puberty and the onset of adolescence, none is more dramatic than the physical and psychological changes associated with sexual maturation. The bodily proportions of boys and girls become increasingly differentiated: Boys develop broader shoulders and show a greater overall gain in muscle development, while girls develop breasts and more rounded hips. Girls experience their first menstruation. Boys experience their first ejaculation. In both sexes the genital organs—penis and scrotum in boys, clitoris, vagina, and labia in girls—increase in size, and the pubic hair develops. All of these physical changes require adjustments by the young person and lead to a changing self-image. As one 16-year-old girl expressed it, "When I was 14 my body started to go crazy" (Bell, 1988).

Although **sexuality**[1] in its broadest sense is a lifelong part of being human (even babies love to be held and may fondle their genitals), the hormonal changes that accompany puberty lead to strong sexual feelings. Not all adolescents react similarly, however, to their burgeoning sexuality. Many adolescents, for instance, may find themselves "thinking more about sex, getting sexually aroused more easily, even at times feeling preoccupied with sex" (Bell, 1988, p. 75) while others are involved in pursuing academic, social, or leisure interests and not particularly aware of sexual feelings. One adolescent may be involved in sexual experimentation while another is not; one may be in love and going steady while another feels that it is much too early for such commitments (Conger, 1980). The timing of puberty is one factor in this variability. Adolescents who are early maturers are more likely than their later-maturing same-age peers to be sexually experienced (Flannery, Rowe, & Gulley, 1993).

---

[1] In contrast to the physical and physiological changes related to sexual maturation or to sexual behaviors, the term *sexuality* refers to the totality of our sexual thoughts, feelings, values, beliefs, actions, and relationships. "In human life, biological forces work in concert with cultural forces—and sex blossoms into sexuality" (Luria, Friedman, & Rose, 1987, p. 5).

The hormonal changes that accompany puberty lead to stronger sexual feelings, although these feelings may be expressed in different ways by different individuals and by the same individual at different times.

Successfully integrating sexuality with other aspects of the young person's sense of self is a major developmental task for both boys and girls. How well this task is handled—the extent to which it becomes a source of joy or despair, challenge and success or failure and defeat—depends on many factors, ranging from the complexities of early parent–child relations to contemporary social standards and values.

## Sex Differences and Similarities in Adolescent Sexuality

Among girls and boys of the current generation, sexual activity is higher than among previous generations. There has been an increase in sexual intercourse such that among teens who turned 18 in the period between 1986 and 1988, 56 percent of women and 73 percent of men had had sexual intercourse, as compared to 35 percent of women and 55 percent of men who turned 18 in the period from 1968 to 1970 (Alan Guttmacher Institute [AGI], 1994). Figure 6.1 illustrates this historical change, and depicts the higher levels of intercourse among males relative to females. Recent national surveys of high school students in grades 9 through 12 indicate little subsequent change overall, at least through 1993 (Centers for Disease Control [CDC], 1995a, 1995b).

For most boys the rapid increase in sexual drive that accompanies puberty is difficult to deny and tends to be genitally oriented. The frequency of erection increases in response to a wide variety of stimuli, sometimes under

awkward circumstances. Sex drive in males reaches a peak during adolescence, as does the frequency of orgasm (primarily through masturbation) (Chilman, 1983; Conger, 1980; Kinsey, Pomeroy, & Martin, 1948).

Among adolescent girls there appears to be a much wider range of individual differences. Some girls experience sexual desire in much the same way as the average boy, but for a majority, sexual feelings tend to be more diffuse, as well as more closely related to the fulfillment of other needs such as self-esteem, reassurance, affection, and love (Bell, 1988; Katchadourian, 1990). For many girls a psychologically intimate relationship with a boy takes precedence over sexual release; consequently, control of sexual impulses may be a less urgent problem.

Although there is a significant increase in sexual interests and behavior among both boys and girls during adolescence, sexual activity in general—and masturbation in particular—is more prevalent among boys than among girls (Katchadourian, 1990). Subjective awareness of specifically sexual pressure also appears to be greater among boys, particularly in early adolescence. The average adolescent boy experiences nocturnal emissions, whereas the average girl does not have nocturnal orgasms during adolescence (Katchadourian, 1985). Among sexually experienced American male and female adolescents ages 13–15 and 16–19, only in the case of 13- to 15-year-old boys did a majority reply affirmatively to the statement, "Sometimes I think I am addicted to sex, the way some people are addicted to drugs" (Sorensen, 1973).

In studies of sexual morality (such as attitudes toward premarital intercourse, the importance of love in a sexual relationship, avoidance of promiscuity, and respect for

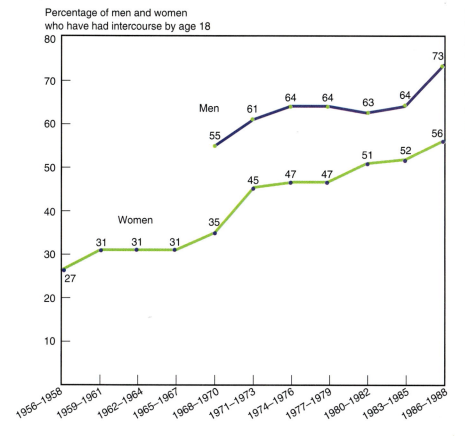

Percentage of men and women
who have had intercourse by age 18

**Figure 6.1**

Historical increase in sexual
intercourse among teens.
Reproduced with the permission
of The Alan Guttmacher Institute
from The Alan Guttmacher
Institute, *Sex and America's
Teenagers,* New York, 1994.

parental or societal wishes), girls consistently display more conservative attitudes than boys. In a national survey in Canada, 41 percent of boys and 59 percent of girls in grade 11 agreed with the statement that "Sex without love is not satisfying." The percentages were nearly identical among college and university students (King et al., 1988). These data clearly show that sex differences in attitudes about sexuality exist, but that there is also much overlap in the attitudes of females and males.

The underlying reasons for sex differences in attitudes are far from clear. A number of theories have been advanced, some primarily physiological and others primarily cultural. Recent changes in adolescent sexual interests, values, and behavior in our society, particularly among girls, as well as findings from other cultures (discussed later in the chapter), provide impressive evidence that cultural influences play a significant role in sexuality (Brooks-Gunn & Furstenberg, 1989; Hotvedt, 1990).

The part played by physical, physiological, and hormonal factors is less evident. One hypothesis is that females are less likely than males to discover sexual responses spontaneously because the girl's sexual organs are less prominent (Chilman, 1983; Katchadourian, 1989). It has also been asserted that there may be basic

physiological differences between males and females in sexual drive and responsiveness, in the capacity of various stimuli to arouse them, or both. Indeed, until the early decades of this century it was simply assumed that normal women did not have strong sexual drives or responses. Scholar Michelle Fine argues that today most of the discussion and policy-making on issues of teen sexuality, sex education, and teen pregnancy actively fails to acknowledge the existence of female sexual desire (Fine, 1988) (see Box 6.1).

Contrary to the assumption of a lack of sexual desire among females, more than two-thirds of girls between the ages of 13 and 19 express the belief that women enjoy sex as much as men (Conger, 1980; Gibbs, 1993; Hunt, 1974). Only one out of every ten adolescent girls believes that women innately have less capacity for sexual pleasure than men. This view receives strong support from William Masters and Virginia Johnson, the first scientists to study human sexual responses comprehensively and objectively. They comment that the female's basic physiological capacity for sexual response surpasses that of males, in that women "have an unlimited orgasm potential, while men . . . are unable to have a rapid series of ejaculations" (Masters, Johnson, & Kolodny, 1992, p. 84).

## 6.1 Pleading for a Discourse of Desire

In a thought-provoking article published in the *Harvard Educational Review*, Michelle Fine (1988) argues that much of the public discussion or discourse on teen sexuality is a denial of female sexual desire. Popular magazines, newspapers, arguments put forth by government officials on sex education and teen pregnancy, and public school sex education courses are among the sources that portray adolescent girls as sexual victims rather than sexual agents. This public discourse equates female sexuality with victimization by depicting males as predators against which females must be protected, by representing sexuality as an activity that will result in pregnancy and sexually transmitted diseases, and by associating sexuality with moral deficiencies.

Although the above issues are of undeniable concern, Fine asserts that this focus and tone in the absence of a "discourse of desire" robs the adolescent girl of the ability to admit to and take charge of her sexuality, to see herself as a decision-maker, and to approach sexuality as a source of joy rather than a source of fear, shame, and guilt. The ultimate irony is that the aim of public discourse, which is to prevent the undesirable consequences of adolescent sexuality, is undermined by taking control away from the very person whose issue it is—the adolescent female. As Fine asserts, "Whether in a classroom, on the street, at work, or at home, the adolescent female's sexuality is negotiated by, for, and despite the young woman herself" (p. 35).

Fine also observes that female sexual pleasure and questions about desire and orgasm are not part of most sex education curricula, and that the topic of passion is but a whisper in the school halls. At the same time, nocturnal emissions, erection, and ejaculation—acceptable evidence of male desire—are part of sex education curricula. In the end, the adolescent girl who recognizes her desire and feels comfortable with it can take action to deal with it responsibly and appropriately (for example, through abstinence, masturbation, or protected intercourse). When adolescent girls have the control they deserve, the negative consequences of sexuality can be avoided.

---

It has also been clearly documented that frequency of orgasm may vary over much wider ranges among girls than among boys (Kinsey et al., 1953).

An even more complex question involves the conditions under which sexual arousal is likely to occur. It has been argued that boys are more easily aroused by a wider variety of external "psychosexual stimuli," such as provocative behavior, erotic art, films, and literature (Katchadourian, 1989; Kinsey et al., 1953). Here, too, the hypothesis appears inadequate. A wide-ranging series of experimental investigations showed that although males are more responsive, the differences between males and females are smaller than is generally supposed (Katchadourian, 1985). Moreover, in some situations some groups of females (those who are younger, more liberal, and more sexually experienced) report greater "sexual excitement" in response to various kinds of sexual stimuli than some groups of males (those who are older, more conservative, more inhibited, and less experienced) (Katchadourian, 1989; Schmidt, 1975).

The fact that significantly more females (particularly younger females) are reporting feelings of sexual arousal today than thirty years ago may be due in large measure to cultural desensitization regarding sexual expression by women (and perhaps also to more opportunities for specific learning of sexual responses). This, in turn, may have lowered women's psychological defenses against sexual arousal and awareness of it. In the past, sexual responsiveness in females was generally less accepted by society and less clearly acknowledged by girls themselves (Brooks-Gunn & Furstenberg, 1989). This situation has changed significantly. However, it should also be recognized that the current, more permissive attitude toward female sexuality remains limited in certain respects. Information about what it means to be sexual and how sexuality is integrated with other aspects of life is lacking (Fine, 1988; Petersen & Boxer, 1982). Moreover, many girls are still brought up to be less accepting and proud of their sexuality than boys are. Although it is less rigid than in the past, the double standard persists:

A teenage boy finds that his sexual adventures are usually tolerated or even encouraged. (Of

course, this is often hard for the boys who aren't interested!) A girl, however, is told she must be the one to say "No!" and to hold off a boy's sex drive. She rarely hears about her own sex drive. So it can be hard for her to let her sexual responses flow freely (Bell, 1988, p. 85).

It is also possible that sexuality in adolescent girls is more closely tied to other considerations, so that the conditions that must be satisfied for arousal to occur or be recognized may be more complex than is generally true for boys. Stimulation that cannot be related to the self as a total person because it is perceived as threatening, conflicts with existing value systems, is impersonal, or is aesthetically offensive may be more likely to "turn off" the average adolescent girl (Conger, 1980; Meikle, Peitchnis, & Pearce, 1985). The fantasies described by both male and female college students during sexual arousal were most likely to involve petting or having intercourse with "someone you love or are fond of" (Miller & Simon, 1980). Fantasies of sexual activity with strangers for whom they had no particular emotional attachment, however, were common among males (79 percent) but not so common among females (22 percent).

However, among females, fantasies of "doing nonsexual things with someone you are fond of or in love with" were about as commonly associated with sexual arousal (74 percent) as fantasies of sexual behavior within a context of affection. As Patricia Miller and William Simon comment, for females,

> The investment of erotic meaning in both explicitly sexual and nonsexual symbols appears to be contingent on the emotional context. The two genders evaluate the meaning of potentially erotic symbols using distinctive sets of criteria. For males, the explicitly sexual is endowed with erotic meaning regardless of the emotional context. For females, the emotional context is endowed with erotic meaning without regard for the presence or absence of explicitly sexual symbols (1980, p. 403).

Finally, the greater sexual assertiveness of adolescent males may be related to the significant increases in androgens that occur among males at puberty. It has been demonstrated that this hormone increases sexual and aggressive behavior in both sexes (Hamburg & Trudeau, 1981; Katchadourian, 1985; Udry, 1988). Testosterone levels have been found to be highly associated with sexual activities in boys independent of the level of pubertal development (which might itself influence sexual behavior) (Udry, 1990). Interestingly, in girls sexual *interests* but not *behavior* are associated with testosterone levels, "sug-

gesting that social factors may play a greater role in their coital behavior" (Brooks-Gunn & Furstenberg, 1989, p. 251; also see Udry, Talbert, & Morris, 1986).

In this respect, girls' sexual behavior may be curtailed by the cultural messages that they receive. A recent study of parent–adolescent communication about sexuality found more discussion between parents (particularly mothers) and daughters than between parents and sons. A significantly larger percentage of daughters than sons discussed with their parents the facts of sex, sociosexual issues such as dating and pregnancy, and morality issues such as whether premarital intercourse is acceptable. The authors of this study concluded that the relative lack of parent communication with sons may in part explain and perpetuate the sexual double standard (Nolin & Petersen, 1992).

A *TIME*/CNN poll also supports the idea that sons and daughters receive different messages from parents. Sixty percent of daughters are told to wait for sex until marriage, but less than half of sons hear the same message. "Kids reflect the double standard: more than two-thirds agree that a boy who has sex sees his reputation enhanced, while a girl who has sex watches hers suffer" (Gibbs, 1993, p. 63).

# Cultural Differences in Sexual Attitudes and Behavior

Learning appears to play a critical role in the development of sexual response patterns. Hence, we find rather wide variations in sexual attitudes and behavior from one culture to another, although there are some cultural generalities, even universals, that reflect commonalities in the human condition (such as incest taboos). Cultural differences appear not only in the amount and type of sexual behavior that is socially accepted but also in the consistency of sexual standards as development proceeds (Barry & Schlegel, 1986; Hotvedt, 1990). Some cultures are restrictive with regard to sexual activity throughout childhood, adolescence, and even to some extent in adulthood. Others are thoroughly permissive at all ages. Still others are highly restrictive during childhood and adolescence and then suddenly become much more permissive about, and even demanding of, sexual activity in adulthood.

There are several examples of cultures that restrict knowledge about and expression of sexuality. Among the Cuna of the coast of Panama, children remained largely ignorant of sexual matters until the last stages of the marriage ceremony. The Ashanti of the west central coast of Africa believed that sexual intercourse with a girl who

had not undergone the puberty ceremony was so harmful to the community that the offense was punishable by death for both partners (Ford & Beach, 1951). In many cultures of the world, the sexual experience of females (and of their male partners) is permanently damaged through the painful and disfiguring practices of clitoridectomy (surgical removal of the clitoris) and infibulation (sewing up), which typically occur at menarche (Hotvedt, 1990).

In contrast, in some societies sexual experience is carefully nurtured from early childhood on. The Chewa of Africa believed that children must have sexual experiences early in life or they will never beget offspring. "Older children build little huts some distance from the village, and there, with the complete approval of their parents, boys and girls play at being husband and wife. Such child matings may extend well into adolescence, with periodic exchanges of partners until marriage occurs" (Ford & Beach, 1951, p. 190). In Mangaia, a small Polynesian island in the South Pacific, the culture endorses sexual pleasure for everyone. Consequently, "less than one out of 100 girls, and even fewer boys—if, indeed, there are any exceptions in either sex—have *not* had substantial sexual experience prior to marriage" (Marshall, 1971, p. 117). Among the Sambia tribe of New Guinea, boys are required to have exclusive and extensive homosexual relations with many other boys beginning from the ages of 7 to 10, and continuing until their marriage, perhaps 10 years later. These activities are carried out to prepare the boy for exclusive heterosexual relations after marriage (Baldwin & Baldwin, 1989).

Until recently, Manus boys of the Admiralty Islands north of New Guinea were in much the same position in sexual matters as American middle-class adolescent boys at the turn of the century (Ausubel, 1954). Whereas the male physiological sex drive was recognized as natural, sexual behavior was strongly tabooed until after marriage. Apparently, the release of sexual tension was achieved primarily through covert homosexual activity and solitary masturbation surrounded by shame. In turn, the Manus girl's position was highly reminiscent of that of a female of the Victorian era. She was taught that sex is not gratifying to women and, in fact, is loathsome, shameful, and repugnant. The difficulties experienced by women in both cultures in adjusting to intercourse after marriage can easily be imagined.

In our own society, despite the "sexual revolution," many children are still taught, consciously or unconsciously, to be anxious about sex and to inhibit and control sexual behavior. Then, when they marry, they are expected to be able to respond without inhibition or anxiety. In effect, many children and adolescents are taught not sexual adaptation, but rather sexual concern.

# Sexual Attitudes and Values of Contemporary Adolescents

Today's adolescents are characterized by somewhat greater openness about sex than their counterparts of earlier generations. This change has manifested itself in a variety of ways, ranging from greater freedom in sexual relations to a desire for more and better sex education, including access to information about birth control.

## Sex Education

School-based sex education is mandated or recommended in 46 states in the United States, and AIDS education is mandated or recommended in all 50 states (Britton, DeMaruo, & Gambrell, 1992/1993). At least three-quarters of adolescents receive sex education in schools, although the quality of such programs varies widely (AGI, 1994; Brooks-Gunn & Furstenberg, 1989). In addition, the age at which formal contraceptive education (in school, clinic, or elsewhere) is first provided has been declining steadily (Brooks-Gunn & Furstenberg, 1989; Dawson, 1986). School sex education programs enjoy widespread public support: 85 percent of parents favor sex education and think it fosters a healthy attitude toward sex (Harris, 1987). Nevertheless, the subject remains highly controversial among members of the militant right and some fundamentalist religious groups and their leaders, although more than two-thirds of all born-again Christians think sex education should be available (Harris, 1987).

Opponents of sex education tend to have traditional views regarding women's roles, the family, and sexuality, and many feel excluded from the social institutions, including school and government, that affect their lives (Richardson & Cranston, 1981). In their view, sex education, even at the high school level, is dangerous and premature for impressionable adolescents and is likely to lead to promiscuity and increased rates of adolescent pregnancy. Some believe that sex education should be carried out only by parents in the privacy of the home (Conger, 1987). Others appear to have reached the awesome conclusion that contemporary adolescents have nothing left to learn about sex—certainly nothing their parents could teach them!

In the light of current statistics on adolescent premarital intercourse, pregnancy, and abortion, as well as the general social climate, it is difficult to see how sex education for adolescents could be viewed as premature. A recent nationwide study found that 48 percent of 15- to 19-year-olds in the United States thought that young

people do not have enough accurate information about sex and reproduction (AGI, 1994). In a way, it appears that adolescents are crying (but only to themselves) about the need for more information about sex and, as we will see, for greater communication with their parents.

Despite the greater openness about sex in contemporary society, many parents do not provide the information their children need (Conger, 1987). As can be seen in Table 6.1, less than a third of teens cite their parents as the most important source of information about sex; friends and school are just as important, with entertainment also serving as a significant source of information (Gibbs, 1993). These figures are strikingly similar to those found in a *Good Housekeeping/CBS This Morning* poll (*Good Housekeeping,* 1993).

Apparently, only a minority of adolescents have experiences like those described by this 16-year-old:

Whenever I have sexual problems or questions I often consult my parents (usually my mother, but sometimes my father too). Our views aren't always the same. Sometimes we feel very different about some things. However, whether we agree or disagree, it's always nice to know that they will always be there and give their opinion if I have a question (Hass, 1979, p. 177).

More often, parents respond with denial, avoidance, teasing, or disapproval. Adolescents might be lectured to instead of listened to; in the words of a 15-year-old boy, his mother "began to preach about what is right and what is wrong. She just didn't understand" (Hass, 1979, p. 176).

Interestingly, adolescents who report that they are able to discuss sex freely and openly with their parents are less likely to be involved in sexual intercourse. Of this group, those who are sexually active are less likely to

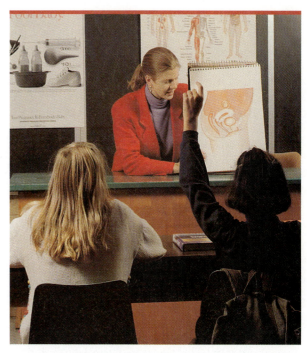

Despite the opposition of a determined and vocal minority, school sex education programs enjoy broad public support: 85 percent of parents favor sex education and think it fosters a healthy attitude toward sex.

become pregnant (Brooks-Gunn & Furstenberg, 1989; Conger, 1987; Sorensen, 1973). Self-reported communication with parents about sexuality is also associated with safer sex practices (attempts to avoid contracting sexually transmitted diseases) (Leland & Barth, 1993). Research has shown that sex education programs are associated with *better* communication with parents about pregnancy and conception (Dawson, 1986; Sex education, 1986).

## Table 6.1 Sources of Adolescent Knowledge About Sex

WHERE HAVE YOU LEARNED THE MOST ABOUT SEX?

| | ADOLESCENT'S AGE | |
| SOURCE | 13–15 YEARS | 16–17 YEARS |
| --- | --- | --- |
| Parents | 30% | 22% |
| Friends | 26 | 37 |
| School | 26 | 15 |
| Entertainment | 15 | 18 |

SOURCE: *TIME*/CNN poll, April 13–14, 1993. © 1993 Time, Inc. Reprinted by permission.

The notion of some adults that adolescents have nothing left to learn about sex also is not supported by the facts. Even today many adolescents think they cannot become pregnant if it is their first intercourse, if they do not have an orgasm, or if they do not want to become pregnant (Meikle, Peitchinis, & Pearce, 1985; Morrison, 1985). In one representative study, less than 40 percent of 15- to 19-year-old adolescent American girls clearly understood the relationship between pregnancy risk and the menstrual cycle; among those who had never had a sex education course, only 27 percent of 15- to 17-year-olds were correct (Hayes, 1987; Kantner & Zelnik, 1973).

There is also no consistent evidence that sex education, including contraceptive information, increases the likelihood that the adolescent will become sexually active. In fact, some school-based programs are associated with a postponement in sexual activity (Zabin, 1992). On the other hand, there is considerable evidence that sexually active adolescents who have had *adequate* sex education (including instruction about how to resist sexual pressures and how to use contraception and prevent disease) are more likely to use effective birth control methods. In addition, teenagers who have had sex education courses are, if anything, less likely to become pregnant (AGI, 1994; Sex education, 1986).

## Sexual Morality

In addition to greater openness and honesty, there is a growing tendency to view decisions about individual sexual behavior as a private rather than a public concern. In 1994 American high school seniors were asked how they felt about a man and woman living together without being married. About one in four said that the couple was experimenting with "a worthwhile alternate life style," and smaller minorities felt either that they were violating a basic principle of human morality or that they were living in a way that was destructive to society. In contrast, slightly over half expressed the view that the couple were "doing their own thing and not affecting anyone else" (Bachman, Johnston, & O'Malley, in preparation).

In part, these trends appear to reflect a decline since the 1960s in the credibility and influence of established social, political, and religious institutions (Conger, 1988; Harris, 1987). But it also appears to reflect greater emphasis on the quality of relationships. What many adolescents appear to be saying is that the morality of sexual behavior can be judged not so much by the nature of the act itself as by its meaning to the people involved.

However, as we have already noted, adolescent girls continue to be more conservative than boys and to place greater emphasis on the nature of the relationship. For example, among American college freshmen in 1994, 56 percent of all males, but 32 percent of females, agreed with the statement, "Sex is okay if people like each other" (Astin et al., 1994). On the other hand, the gap between males and females with respect to approving of sex before marriage is smaller when there is deep involvement. For example, among first-year college students in 1989, 57 percent of men and 45 percent of women endorsed the proposition that people should live together before getting married (Dey, Astin, & Korn, 1991). Only 32 percent of American adolescent girls and 21 percent of boys in another study said that they would be unwilling to live together before marriage (Norman & Harris, 1981). Most

Adolescents who report that they can discuss sex freely with their parents are less likely to be involved in sexual intercourse. Moreover, those who are sexually active are less likely to become pregnant.

adolescents clearly oppose exploitation, pressure, or force in sex; sex solely for the sake of physical enjoyment; and sex between people who are too young to understand what they are getting into (Bibby & Posterski, 1992; Chilman, 1983; Darling, Kallen, & VanDusen, 1984).

Despite a growing emphasis among contemporary adolescents on openness, there is little evidence of an increased preoccupation with sex. Indeed, it may well be that the average adolescent is less preoccupied and concerned with sex than prior generations of young people. Greater acceptance of sex as a natural part of life may well lead to less preoccupation than did anxious concern in an atmosphere of secrecy and suppression. Nor has sex displaced or become synonymous with love in the eyes of most young people. Most adolescents (67–80 percent) disagree with the notion that the most important thing in a love relationship is sex, with older adolescents (both male and female) disagreeing more often than young adolescents (Hass, 1979; Norman & Harris, 1981; Sorensen, 1973). Interestingly, the percentage disagreeing is higher for nonvirgins than for virgins.

Finally, in ranking the relative importance of various goals, adolescents of both sexes stress such goals as having friends, being independent, doing well in school, preparing to accomplish things in life, getting along with parents, being romantically involved with someone, and athletics (Bibby & Posterski, 1992; Hass, 1979; Norman & Harris, 1981). In contrast, "having sex with someone" and "making out" consistently rank at or near the top among goals that are considered *least* important.

# Changing Values and Sexual Behavior

How are the continuing changes in sexual attitudes and values among contemporary adolescents reflected in behavior? The answer depends on what behaviors one is referring to and among which adolescents.

## Masturbation and Petting

Available information indicates that among boys the number who have engaged in masturbation by age 19 has remained fairly stable at around 85–90 percent since their parents' and grandparents' generations (Chilman, 1983; Leitenberg, Detzer, & Srebnik, 1993; Masters, Johnson, & Kolodny, 1992). But it also appears that the number who have done so at younger ages is increasing significantly. In Kinsey's original sample, only 45 percent of males reported masturbating by age 13; in contrast, in later surveys that number had increased to 52–65 percent. Among girls,

there has been an increase in masturbation at all age levels, with incidences in recent years of around 33 percent by age 13 (in contrast to 15 percent in Kinsey's original study) and 60–75 percent by age 20 (compared to 30 percent in Kinsey's study) (Arafat & Cotton, 1974; Chilman, 1983; Hass, 1979; Kinsey, Pomeroy, & Martin, 1948; Kinsey et al., 1953; Masters, Johnson, & Kolodny, 1992).

Even with recent changes, however, girls appear to engage in masturbation during adolescence significantly less often than boys. Moreover, among adolescents who engage in masturbation, girls masturbate less frequently, on the average, though with wider interindividual variability (Chilman, 1983; Katchadourian, 1990; Leitenberg, Detzer, & Srebnik, 1993). One might be tempted to conclude that masturbation would occur most commonly among adolescents who lack other sexual outlets. Interestingly, however, among contemporary adolescents masturbation occurs about three times as frequently among those engaged in sexual intercourse or petting to orgasm as among the sexually inexperienced.

Petting does appear to have increased somewhat in the past few decades, and it tends to occur at slightly earlier ages. The major change, however, has probably been in frequency of petting, intimacy of techniques involved, the frequency with which petting leads to erotic arousal or orgasm, and certainly, frankness about this activity (Conger, 1980; Luria, Friedman, & Rose, 1987). A large survey of adolescents in the southeastern United States in the late 1970s found that among white adolescents, there was a progression in intimacy from "necking" to direct contact with sex organs (breasts, then genitals), and finally, to sexual intercourse. Black adolescents were more inconsistent, with many moving from necking to sexual intercourse without experiencing unclothed petting (Rodgers, 1992).

## Premarital Sexual Intercourse

A topic of great interest to adolescents and their parents, and a source of controversy, is the extent of premarital sexual intercourse among contemporary adolescents. Until recently opinions on this subject were rife, but comprehensive data (except in the case of college students) were scarce. Consequently, as late as the mid-1970s some social observers were proclaiming a "sexual revolution" while others asserted that young people were actually no more sexually active than their parents, but simply more open and honest.

National studies in the United States that have asked about prior or current sexual behaviors have made it clear that the youth revolution of the late 1960s did indeed lead to a transformation not only in sexual atti-

tudes and values but in sexual behavior (Hofferth, 1990; Mott & Haurin, 1988; Sonenstein, Pleck, & Ku, 1989). For example, the National Survey of Family Growth indicates that among women who were teenagers (unmarried and married) in the United States in the 1950s, 8 percent reported having had sexual intercourse by age 16, 27 percent had done so by age 18, and 61 percent experienced intercourse by age 20. By the early 1970s the picture had changed somewhat, with 9 percent of 16-year-olds, 35 percent of 18-year-olds, and 68 percent of 20-year-olds having had intercourse. By 1988, rates of intercourse among all female teenagers had increased dramatically, to 21 percent (16-year-olds), 52 percent (18-year-olds), and 76 percent (20-year-olds) (AGI, 1994).

Twice as many teenage women now engage in *premarital* sexual intercourse as in the 1950s, with the increase most striking among whites (AGI, 1994; CDC, 1995a). In the 1950s there was a significant gap in white and black females' rates of premarital intercourse, with the rate for black women more than double the rate for white women. By 1988 this gap had narrowed considerably—88 percent of black women in their teens and 72 percent of white teenage women had had intercourse before marriage (AGI, 1994).

Changes have been less dramatic for boys, but the absolute incidence of sexual intercourse is higher than among girls, especially at younger ages. Data from a 1988 survey indicated that 30 percent of males who were adolescents in the 1960s had engaged in intercourse by age 16, 55 percent were sexually experienced by age 18, and almost 75 percent had had sex by age 20. The corresponding figures for men who were teens in the first half of the 1980s were 41 percent by age 16, 64 percent by age 18, and 80 percent by age 20 (AGI, 1994).

Although sexual intercourse among teens has become more common, we must recognize that for both females and males, sexual intercourse in *early* adolescence is rare. The majority of adolescents are still virgins at age 16. Of those who are not virgins in early adolescence, a shockingly high number were raped. Seventy-four percent of females who had intercourse before age 14 and 60 percent of those having sex before age 15 reported that they were forced to have sex (AGI, 1994; Moore, Nord, & Peterson, 1989).

Voluntary intercourse increases each year as adolescence progresses, so that by age 19, a majority of teens have had sex (see Figure 6.2) (AGI, 1994). The high incidence of virginity in early to middle adolescence and the gradual increase in sexual intercourse run counter to por-

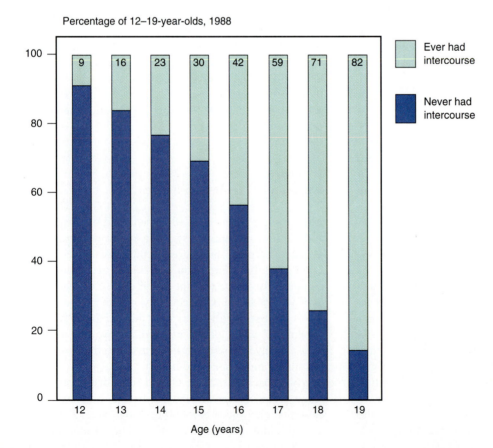

Percentage of 12–19-year-olds, 1988

Age (years)

Ever had intercourse

Never had intercourse

## Figure 6.2

Increased frequency of intercourse in later adolescence. Reproduced with permission of The Alan Guttmacher Institute from The Alan Guttmacher Institute, *Sex and America's Teenagers,* New York, 1994.

trayals in the media of teens overcome by raging hormones and sexual impulses. As one social scientist pointed out, "Even among the minority of 15-year-olds who have had sexual intercourse, most do not have intercourse on a regular basis. Those who have considerable sexual experience only have sex occasionally" (Rodgers, 1992, p. 43). Hormones may be raging, but adolescents are not.

## AIDS and Other STDs

The teen years are a time during which the risk of contracting sexually transmitted diseases (STDs) such as gonorrhea, genital herpes, and AIDS is relatively high. Each year, about a quarter of sexually experienced teens contract an STD (AGI, 1994). Many teenagers engage in risky behaviors such as unprotected intercourse and substance use, and they are more susceptible than adults to peer pressure to engage in these activities. Those who have not yet developed formal operational thought may have difficulty in seeing the connection between today's behavior and tomorrow's health.

Many of the newest cases of HIV infection (the virus that results in AIDS) were contracted in adolescence, and this number is on the rise (Bowler et al., 1992; Rotheram-Borus & Koopman, 1990). Table 6.2 shows that the major source of HIV infection in young people aged 17 and older is unsafe behaviors such as unprotected sex, multiple sexual partners, and sharing needles. Heterosexual transmission is a more common source of HIV infection among females than among males, due to their greater physiological vulnerability (Bowler et al., 1992). The fact that most cases of HIV infection result from high-risk behaviors means that these behaviors are open to change and that adolescents can benefit from educational efforts.

Although there are some encouraging signs, it is still too early to predict the ultimate effects of AIDS information programs on the behaviors of adolescents.

It is too early to predict the ultimate effects of the AIDS information campaign and programs to prevent adolescent pregnancy on the sexual attitudes and behavior of adolescents. From 15 to 39 percent of adolescents report having changed their behavior because of their concern with AIDS (Rimberg & Lewis, 1994). The results of several national surveys of adolescent males are interesting: Although rates of sexual activity have continued to increase, condom use among sexually active 15- to 19-year-olds living in metropolitan areas increased from only 21 percent in 1979 to over 59 percent in 1993 (CDC, 1995a; Sonenstein, Pleck, & Ku, 1989). Moreover, males whose first intercourse occurred in 1987–1988 were more than twice as likely to have used condoms in their most recent intercourse as those whose first inter-

## Table 6.2 Sources of HIV Infection Among Teens and Young Adults

| AGES | TRANSFUSION-RELATED | BEHAVIOR-RELATED | UNKNOWN/OTHER |
|---|---|---|---|
| 13–14 | 91% | 9% | 0% |
| 15–16 | 72 | 24 | 4 |
| 17–19 | 25 | 69 | 6 |
| 20–24 | 2 | 94 | 4 |

SOURCE: S. Bowler, A. R. Sheon, L. J. D'Angelo, & S. H. Vermund (1992). HIV and AIDS among adolescents in the United States: Increasing risk in the 1990s. *Journal of Adolescence, 15*, 345–371. By permission.

## 6.2 The Canada Youth and AIDS Study

AIDS is the top social and health concern among Canadian adolescents. Seventy-seven percent rate the issue of AIDS as very serious, compared to 48 percent of adults (Bibby & Posterski, 1992). In 1987, the Canada Youth and AIDS Study was launched (King et al., 1988). This study involved a nationally representative sample of 38,000 Canadian adolescents between the ages of 11 and 21 who were surveyed to determine what they knew and thought about AIDS, what their sexual behaviors were, and to what extent they were at risk of contracting an STD.

Some of the more interesting results to emerge from this study concerned what adolescents knew about AIDS—and what they did not. The majority (between 67 and 93 percent) of 7th, 9th, and 11th graders had accurate knowledge about how AIDS could be transmitted (through pregnancy, sharing needles, and sexual intercourse). There was misinformation, however, about how one could protect oneself against AIDS. To illustrate, 42 percent of 11th graders did not know that "condoms used with a spermicidal foam or gel give effective protection from the AIDS virus" (true) and 58 percent believed that "vaseline is a good lubricant to use with a condom" (false). Relatively small percentages of adolescents (39 to 54 percent) in grades 7, 9, and 11 realized that "many people who have STDs will not have signs of illness."

Adolescents cannot protect themselves from STDs if they are lacking critical information. The Youth and AIDS Study found that between 70 and 90 percent of adolescents reported that they "need to know a lot more about AIDS." As one 17-year-old stated, "I believe that ongoing publicity about AIDS will gradually help us to be more careful, using condoms and being cautious about our number of partners" (Bibby & Posterski, 1992, p. 49). Ninth graders who had spent four or more hours in school receiving AIDS education were considerably more likely to score high on the AIDS knowledge test (44 percent) than those who had not received such instruction (28 percent). (Given that the Youth and AIDS Survey was conducted in 1987, we might expect adolescents currently to have more accurate information.)

Fortunately, many adults are ready to acknowledge the risks. A 1991 Gallup poll, for example, found that 68 percent of Canadians believed that condoms should be readily available in high schools, a percentage that was as high among Roman Catholics as among Protestants (*The Gallup Report,* 1991). A 1993 Gallup poll in the United States found that 60 percent of adults believe that public schools should have condom distribution programs (Elam, Rose, & Gallup, 1993).

course occurred between 1975 and 1982 (Sonenstein, Pleck, & Ku, 1989).

Condom use at first intercourse among women aged 15–19 more than doubled between 1982 (when 23 percent used condoms) and 1988 (when 48 percent used condoms) (Forrest & Singh, 1990). Substantial numbers of adolescents show a great deal of responsibility by taking measures to prevent unwanted pregnancies and STDs. A quarter of pill users, for example, also use condoms. Although these figures are encouraging, there is less-than-perfect technical use of condoms among many adolescents (and adults); usage is also not reliable from one time to the next. Among women who use condoms for protection, 20 percent did not use one at last intercourse (AGI, 1994). Another important concern is that the lowest rates of con-

dom use are reported by youth who engage in behaviors such as substance use and sex with multiple partners that put them at greater risk of contracting AIDS (AGI, 1994; CDC, 1995b; Ericksen & Trocki, 1994; Sonenstein, Pleck, & Ku, 1989; St. Lawrence et al., 1994).

It appears that the widespread dissemination of information about AIDS since 1987 has begun to have a significant effect on adolescent behavior (Sonenstein et al., 1989). Still, major challenges remain. Some adolescents are harder to reach than others. Homophobic adolescents, for example, are significantly less likely to practice safe sex, believing that AIDS is confined to gay males. Feelings of invulnerability among adolescents must be overcome if significant changes in behavior are to occur (Westerman & Davidson, 1993).

# Diversity of Sexual Attitudes and Behavior

Thus far we have focused on *overall* trends in sexual attitudes and behavior among contemporary adolescents and youth. Such trends have meaning and usefulness in their own right, but they should not deflect our attention from an equally important phenomenon: the diversity of sexual attitudes and behavior in different sectors of the adolescent and youth population. Such factors as age, sex, socioeconomic and educational level, ethnicity, religion, and even geographic area appear to be related to sexual attitudes, values, and behavior. For this reason, the results of almost any survey dealing with adolescent sexuality will inevitably seem exaggerated to some young people and adults, whereas others will view them as understated.

What do we know about some of these variations? First of all, we need to keep in mind that despite the "sexual revolution," many adolescents have not engaged in premarital sexual intercourse. Second, neither virgins nor nonvirgins constitute a homogeneous group. Thus, adolescents who have not had intercourse range from those with virtually no sexual experience to those with a variety of experiences short of intercourse, including petting to orgasm (Luria, Friedman, & Rose, 1987).

## Serial Monogamists and Sexual Adventurers.
As we have already seen, female adolescents and youth continue to be more conservative than their male peers in attitudes, values, and behavior, although sex differences have narrowed. In a pioneering study of 13- to 19-year-olds, Robert Sorensen identified two major subgroups of nonvirgins: **serial monogamists** (the larger group), who generally had a relationship with only one partner over a period of time, and **sexual adventurers** (a much smaller group), who moved freely from one sexual partner to another and felt no obligation to be faithful to any one partner (Sorensen, 1973). Among adolescents who were sexual adventurers, 80 percent were male; in contrast, 64 percent of serial monogamists were female. A more recent survey confirms the high prevalence of monogamy among nonvirgin teenage women. Only 8–11 percent of those who were sexually active in the preceding three months had more than one sexual partner (AGI, 1994).

In Sorenson's study, the monogamists and the adventurers tended to vary significantly in attitudes as well as in behavior. Most monogamists believed that they loved and were loved by their partners, stressed openness and honesty between partners, and denied that sex was the most important thing in a love relationship—although they also expressed greater satisfaction with their sex lives than adventurers did. At the same time, their code emphasized personal freedom without commitment to marriage, although more than half believed that they would or might marry their partner eventually.

Sexual adventurers, in contrast, were primarily interested in variety of experience for its own sake, did not consider love to be a necessary part of sexual relationships, and felt no personal responsibility for their partners, although they did not believe in hurting others. For many adventurers, sex itself was viewed as an avenue to communication; as one young adventurer stated, "Having sex together is a good way for two people to become acquainted."

## Socioeconomic Status, Education, and Religion.
Economically privileged and more highly educated adolescents are less conservative in their sexual attitudes and values (though not in their level of sexual activity) than less-advantaged peers of the same age, although the differences appear to be decreasing (Chilman, 1983; Conger, 1980; Hayes, 1987). Also, it is among economically favored college or college-bound adolescents and youth, especially females, that the greatest *changes* in sexual behavior have occurred. Before the mid-1960s the incidence of premarital intercourse among college seniors was about 55 percent for males and 25 percent for females. In contrast, several more recent investigations of North American college and university students of comparable ages indicate a substantial upward shift for both sexes, but particularly among women (Chilman, 1983; Conger, 1980; Hayes, 1987; King et al., 1988). Still, females who are socioeconomically advantaged and who have a higher level of educational investment have their first intercourse at later ages than the less advantaged (Ohannessian & Crockett, 1993; Wyatt, 1990). For males the incidence of premarital intercourse ranged up to a high of 82 percent; comparable percentages for females ranged up to a high of 76 percent. Whereas the incidence for males appeared to reach a plateau in the early 1970s, the incidence for females continued to increase at least into the early 1980s.

Other factors are also related to sexual attitudes, values, and behavior. Younger adolescents are more conservative about sexual matters than older adolescents (Conger, 1980; Hass, 1979). Politically conservative and religiously oriented youth are more conservative in their sexual attitudes and behavior than liberal or religiously inactive young people (King et al., 1988; Mussen, et al., 1990).

## Ethnicity.
As pointed out earlier, black teens are less likely than are white teens to engage in a predictable pattern of precoital behaviors (necking, petting) leading to

sexual intercourse. Historically, black adolescents, both male and female, have been more active sexually than white or Hispanic adolescents, engaging in sexual intercourse at earlier ages (AGI, 1994; Hofferth, Kahn, & Baldwin, 1987; Rodgers, 1992; Zelnik & Kantner, 1980). Interestingly, however, although the percentage of sexually active black females between the ages of 15 and 19 increased moderately between 1971 and 1979, it *declined* between 1979 and 1982, with the greatest decline occurring among younger adolescents (Hofferth, Kahn, & Baldwin, 1987). In contrast, among white females in the same age group the percentage who were sexually active rose steadily from 1971 to 1982 (Hofferth, Kahn, & Baldwin, 1987). Now, as mentioned earlier, rates of premarital intercourse among whites are almost as high as among blacks. Among 15- to 19-year-old women, 61 percent of blacks, 49 percent of Hispanics, and 52 percent of whites have had intercourse (AGI, 1994; Forrest & Singh, 1990). Although age at first intercourse may be lower among black women than among whites, the frequency of sex and the number of sexual partners also may be lower (Wyatt, 1990).

Black males have been largely overlooked in studies of sexuality, but the data suggest that a large proportion (up to 50 percent) may be sexually experienced by age 14 or 15, and that many become active sexually *before* they have reached puberty (AGI, 1994; Udry, 1990). AIDS is five times more prevalent among black teenage males than among whites. This has been attributed in large measure to the stress, hopelessness, powerlessness, and the inadequate health care and preventive efforts associated with poverty, leading to greater unprotected sex and drug use (Bowler et al., 1992; DiClemente, 1993).

Some ethnic differences in sexual behavior appear to be attributable to a variety of social and economic factors. These factors include current living conditions, the level of education, role modeling, the opportunity structure, social norms within an ethnic group, and family structure and relationships (Jenkins & Westney, 1990; Katchadourian, 1990; Wyatt, 1990). One study suggested that the restricted life options of blacks and Hispanics living in poor, deteriorated neighborhoods put adolescents in a double bind (Sullivan, 1993). They recognized the arguments in favor of waiting to have children, but what would they be waiting for? Poverty and discrimination meant little chance of obtaining an adequate education and improving their economic status. Under these circumstances, if they delayed childbearing until things got better, they might never have children. Another recent study determined that delaying childbirth until age 25 is an economic advantage to white women, but *not* to blacks, possibly because so high a proportion of

black women give birth as unwed mothers and remain single parents (Astone, 1993).

# Influence of Family and Peers

Farida Shah and Melvin Zelnik, population specialists at the Johns Hopkins University, used the data from a comprehensive survey of unmarried 15- to 19-year-old women in the United States to determine the influence of parents and peers on the views of the participants and to find out how that influence was related to premarital sexual behavior and other issues (Shah & Zelnik, 1981; Zelnik & Kantner, 1980). They found that on such issues as going to college and having a career, these young women were influenced more by parents than by friends. On the other hand, with respect to their attitudes toward premarital sex, their views resembled those of their friends much more than those of their parents. In sum, it appears that although parents' views are more influential than those of peers on some issues (such as career plans), peer influence is clearly stronger for the average adolescent on attitudes toward premarital sex; peer views are generally, but not always, more permissive than those of parents; and black adolescents (and to a lesser extent their parents) are more permissive than whites. Other less comprehensive studies have yielded similar results.

In a study of visits to family planning clinics in Maryland, the majority (64 percent) of teenage women who sought contraception were accompanied by someone else (Nathanson & Becker, 1986). In 16 percent of these cases, mothers attended with their daughters (mothers' involvement was higher among black than white women). In 54 percent of the visits, girlfriends came. At the same time, 65 percent of these adolescent women reported that their mothers approved of the visit, and nearly 75 percent felt that it was important to have their mothers' approval. Only 45 percent felt that their girlfriends' approval was important. Clearly, parents' support may be most important for adolescents' contraceptive-seeking behaviors, but where parental support is low, friends may serve this function (Nathanson & Becker, 1986).

A recent study found not only that girlfriends were important in predicting teenage girls' sexual attitudes and behavior, but so were sisters (East, Felice, & Morgan, 1993). Teenage girls who had many sexually active girlfriends or had at least one adolescent childbearing sister were more permissive in their sexual attitudes, had greater intentions of being sexually active in the future, and were more likely to be nonvirgins. Apparently,

friends and sisters provide important reference groups for shaping girls' standards and their actual behavior.

## A "New Morality"

Although the "new morality" of today's adolescents—the greater emphasis on openness, more mutual respect and less exploitation, and a more natural and somewhat better-informed approach to sex—has many positive aspects, it would be a mistake to conclude that the picture is unclouded. Many experienced adolescents, particularly older adolescents and youth, appear to be able to handle their sexual involvement and relationships without undue stress. However, significant minorities report feelings of conflict and guilt, feel exploited or rejected, or discover belatedly that they have gotten in over their heads emotionally (Bell, 1988; Morrison, 1985). Especially after the first experience of intercourse, girls are far more likely to experience negative feelings (Hass, 1979; Norman & Harris, 1981; Sorensen, 1973). Whereas boys are most likely to report being excited, satisfied, and happy, many girls report being afraid, guilty, worried, or embarrassed after their first intercourse.

There are obviously dangers in assuming that sexual involvement is "okay as long as you're in love." Encouraged by such a philosophy among peers, a young person may become more deeply involved emotionally than she or he can handle responsibly at his or her stage of maturity. Some adolescents may also consciously think that their attitudes are more liberal than they actually are, and sexual involvement may lead to unanticipated feelings of guilt, anxiety, or depression.

## Pregnancy and Contraception

There are also some very practical problems associated with adolescent sexuality. Foremost of these are the possibility of pregnancy and the risk of contracting sexually transmitted diseases, including those for which there is currently no cure, such as genital herpes and—most tragically—AIDS (Furstenberg, Brooks-Gunn, & Chase-Landale, 1989; Rotheram-Borus & Koopman, 1991; Task Force on Pediatric AIDS, 1989). There is no doubt that contraceptive use has been increasing among teens in the last two decades. In 1976, 29 percent of sexually active female adolescents consistently ("always") used some form of contraception; this number increased to 48 percent by 1982 (Hayes, 1987; Zelnik & Kantner, 1980). By 1988, 72 percent of 15- to 17-year-olds and 84 percent of 18- to 19-year-olds used a contraceptive on an ongo-

ing basis. Contraceptive use is lower among black and Hispanic women than among whites. Lower contraceptive use is also more evident among poor and low-income women than among women in higher-income homes. At any one time, three-quarters of sexually active adolescent women are at risk of unintended pregnancy, largely because of failure to use contraceptives properly (AGI, 1994). Figure 6.3 illustrates the increase in contraceptive use between 1982 and 1988, which is due largely to a substantial increase in the use of condoms.

Given the imperfect use of contraception, along with current levels of premarital intercourse among adolescents, over one million 15- to 19-year-old girls in the United States (about 12 percent of this age group) become pregnant each year (AGI, 1994). If contraceptive use had not increased in the past two decades, this figure would be even higher. (Most of these pregnancies are conceived out of wedlock.) More than one-third of sexually active adolescent girls become pregnant at some time during their adolescent years (Jones et al., 1987; Trussell, 1988).

We often hear about the "epidemic" of pregnancies among adolescent women, but, in fact, the *pregnancy rate,* which is based on sexually experienced teenage women,

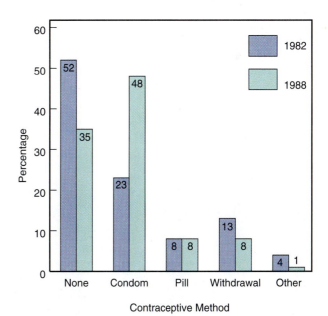

## Figure 6.3

Increase in contraceptive use at first intercourse, 1982–1988, among women aged 15–19 years. Adapted with permission of The Alan Guttmacher Institute from The Alan Guttmacher Institute, *Sex and America's Teenagers,* New York, 1994.

## 6.3 Teenage Pregnancy in Developed Countries

A recent comparison by the Alan Guttmacher Institute has found that the United States leads nearly all developed countries in the incidence of adolescent pregnancy and childbearing (see Figure B6.3). This holds true even for Western industrialized nations with comparable levels of sexual activity. For example, the pregnancy rate in the United States is more than double that in Canada, although the percentages of adolescents aged 15–19 who are sexually active are nearly identical (Bibby & Posterski, 1992).

Opponents of preventive measures such as sex education and access to counseling and contraceptive services for sexually active adolescents have asserted that such measures would further increase already high rates of adolescent pregnancy, abortion, and childbearing. Ironically, comparisons indicate just the opposite. The countries with the most open and straightforward attitudes toward sex, the most effective formal and informal programs of sex education, and the most accessible counseling and contraceptive services for adolescents have the *lowest* rates of teenage pregnancy, abortion, and childbearing (Jones et al., 1987). Sweden is a case in point. Sex education has been compulsory since 1956, and sexuality is discussed whenever it is appropriate in different classes in school, yet Sweden has one of the lowest pregnancy rates in the industrialized world.

has *declined* from 254 per 1,000 women in 1972 to 207 per 1,000 women in 1990. This decline has been attributed to the more effective use of contraception. Adolescent pregnancy is more visible now because, although the pregnancy rate has declined, more adolescents than ever before are sexually active. Thus, we see a higher absolute number of adolescent pregnancies (AGI, 1994).

The consequences of adolescent pregnancies are serious indeed. In 1990, 51 percent of pregnant adolescents gave birth and 35 percent had induced abortions; the remainder miscarried. The birth rate among teens declined from 1972 to 1985, but it has increased since 1986, as more teens opted to have their babies. Now 81 percent of first births among teenagers are out of wedlock, compared to one-third in the early 1960s (AGI, 1994).

Adolescent pregnancies are more likely than pregnancies in adulthood to endanger the physical health of both mother and child. Except in the case of very young adolescents, this risk is due not to maternal age per se,

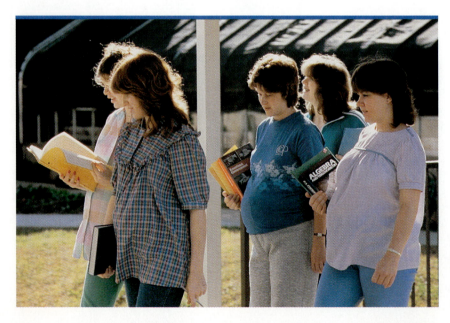

Special programs for pregnant teenagers, such as these in Fort Worth, Texas, help adolescent mothers complete high school and find regular employment.

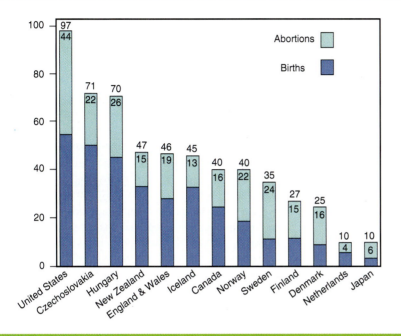

## Figure B6.3

Pregnancies per 1,000 women aged 15–19 and younger, 1988. The United States, compared with many other industrialized countries, has high adolescent pregnancy rates. Reproduced with permission of The Alan Guttmacher Institute from The Alan Guttmacher Institute, *Sex and America's Teenagers,* New York, 1994.

but to social conditions such as poverty that are often associated with early childbearing. In fact, several investigations have shown that adolescents who bear children fare no worse (in terms of maternal and infant health outcomes) than other age groups, once social class and quality of health care are taken into account (Baldwin, 1993; Edelman, 1987; Petersen & Boxer, 1982). Risks can be reduced with adequate prenatal and postnatal care and good nutrition. At present, however, teenage mothers are least likely to receive prenatal care, and their babies are most likely to have low birthweights (Children's Defense Fund [CDF], 1994; Hughes et al., 1989; Seitz & Apfel, 1994) (see Table 6.3). Moreover, the situation is growing worse: By 1991 U.S. infants "were *less* likely than in 1980 to be born to mothers who received early prenatal care and *more* likely to be born of low birthweight" (CDF, 1994, p.10). Low birthweight, in turn, is a major cause of infant mortality as well as neurological defects and childhood illnesses. Among very young teenagers, pregnancy tends to deplete nutritional requirements needed for the girl's own growth, and this places her at higher risk for a variety of illnesses (Edelman, 1987; Hughes et al., 1989).

In addition, teenage mothers—at least 97 percent of whom keep their babies—generally face significant problems in other areas. They are twice as likely as their peers

## Table 6.3 Birth Outcome and Prenatal Care by Age, United States, 1986

| | Under Age 15 | Ages 15–19 | Ages 20–24 | All Women |
|---|---|---|---|---|
| Percentage of babies born at low birthweight (5.5 pounds or less) | 13.8 | 9.3 | 7.0 | 6.8 |
| Percentage of babies born to mothers who received early prenatal care | 36.1 | 53.4 | 70.7 | 75.9 |
| Percentage of babies born to mothers who received late or no prenatal care | 20.8 | 12.5 | 7.4 | 6.9 |

SOURCE: National Center for Health Statistics; Children's Defense Fund, 1989.

# 6.4 Preventing Adolescent Pregnancy

Much can be done to reduce the high rate of adolescent pregnancy, but only if the problem is approached realistically. Sloganeering, scapegoating, and self-righteous moralizing will not solve the problem, and there are no quick fixes or magic bullets waiting to be discovered (Edelman, 1987; Hayes, 1987). The new focus on abstinence education cannot be successful if it denies the very real desires that adolescents feel and if it is not combined with accurate information on what to do if abstinence is not the path chosen by the adolescent. Nevertheless, collective action and willingness to be creative can make a major difference:

1. *Sex education and family life planning.* First, we need age-appropriate family life education, including sex education beginning in the early school years, for all children and adolescents. Adolescents in particular need to be told the facts about sexuality and parenthood; even more important, they need help "in integrating that information into their thinking about themselves and their futures" (Edelman, 1987, p. 58). Family planning clinics have played a significant role in reducing unwanted pregnancies among teens (Kisker, 1990). We need to encourage much greater participation by parents in these efforts.

2. *Access to contraceptive methods.* In addition to more comprehensive, integrated sex education and family life planning, sexually active adolescents need access to contraceptive methods. In many instances these needs can best be met by adolescent clinics, both within and outside the school setting, that provide comprehensive, high-quality, easily accessible health services for adolescents and preadolescents (*Adolescent pregnancy,* 1986; Dryfoos, 1988; Klerman, 1991). Although school-based clinics providing comprehensive health services constitute only a small percentage of all adolescent clinics, and although less than one-third of school clinics

to drop out of school, less likely to gain employment or attain a postsecondary education, and more likely to rely on welfare (Bachrach, Clogg, & Carver, 1993; Furstenberg, Brooks-Gunn, & Chase-Lansdale, 1989; Linares et al., 1991). Many still need mothering themselves and are ill-prepared to take on the psychological, social, and economic responsibilities of motherhood (Osofsky, 1990). Their knowledge of an infant's needs and capabilities is often unrealistic, leading to expectations and demands that their infants cannot meet. Because of their immaturity and the greater stress to which they are subjected, adolescent mothers are more likely to abuse their children. Moreover, a single adolescent mother has less chance of getting married than her peers, and a much greater chance of divorce if she does marry (Furstenberg, Brooks-Gunn, & Chase-Lansdale, 1989).

As a consequence of these many difficulties, children born to adolescent mothers may experience struggles of their own. Evidence shows higher levels of school failure, delinquency and antisocial behavior, sexual activity, and fertility among adolescent children born to teenage mothers (Furstenberg, Brooks-Gunn, & Morgan, 1987). These are not inevitable outcomes of teenage parenthood, but are more likely to occur when there are unstable home environments, parental difficulty in delivering high-quality parenting, and economic hardship (Kandel, Rosenbaum, & Chen, 1994; McLoyd et al., 1994).

This is not to say that all adolescent mothers and children are doomed to failure. In a 17-year study of young and poor black teenage mothers in Baltimore, one-quarter eventually were able, with appropriate health counseling and educational services, to make it into the middle class, though seldom without a struggle. (Furstenberg, Brooks-Gunn, & Morgan, 1987; Furstenberg, Brooks-Gunn, & Chase-Lansdale, 1989). The majority eventually completed high school and a third attained some postsecondary education. Although many were on welfare initially, most did not have to rely on welfare by the time they were in their 30s.

These women also did not have large families: Most completed their childbearing within five years of the first

dispense contraceptives, some of those that do have produced some encouraging results.

At four of the oldest clinics, located in St. Paul, Minnesota, the overall annual rate of first-time pregnancies has been reduced from 80 to 35 per 1000; repeat pregnancies have been reduced to only 1.4 percent, compared to 33 percent nationally (*Adolescent pregnancy*, 1986; Dryfoos, 1988). One of the great advantages of adolescent clinics is that sexuality in all its aspects can be dealt with in the context of overall health care by a staff that is attuned to the special needs and concerns of this age group.

3. *The life options approach.* Better sex education and family-planning services alone will not solve the problem of adolescent pregnancy, particularly for high-risk adolescents. Motivation to avoid pregnancy is also essential. Such motivation can come only when young people feel good about themselves and have a "clear vision of a successful and self-sufficient future" (Edelman, 1987, p. 58). This requires opportunities to build academic and work-related skills, job opportunities,

life-planning assistance, and comprehensive health and mental-health services (Edelman, 1987; Hayes, 1987).

Several new federal initiatives are in place in the United States, with a broad-based approach to increasing adolescents' life skills. Ameri-Corps is a national youth service program that allows youth to earn an education by performing up to two years of community service. Job Corps is a program that focuses attention on job training and education. A project named YouthBuild teaches youth to construct and rehabilitate housing in low-income communities, thereby allowing them to contribute to the strengthening of the community and to gain skills that they can take into the job market (CDF, 1994).

According to Marian Wright Edelman, president of the Children's Defense Fund, "We need investments in young people that will enable them not only to make responsible decisions but to move along a steady path toward self-sufficiency" (*Adolescent pregnancy*, 1986, p. 4).

child. "When asked how well they were doing at the 17-year follow-up, 48 percent of married women with fewer than 3 children who had completed high school replied 'very well'; only 2 percent said 'not so well' or 'not well at all.' In contrast, the percentage for unmarried dropouts with 3 or more children who were doing very well was 29 percent, and 11 percent indicated they were 'not so well or not well at all'" (Furstenberg, Brooks-Gunn, & Chase-Lansdale, 1989, p. 316). In brief, the long-term picture was more optimistic than many people might have expected. At the same time, relative to comparable women who were not early childbearers, these women did suffer significant economic disadvantages. These disadvantages were particularly pronounced among mothers who remained single.

**Reasons for Failure to Use Contraceptives.** In several surveys, the main reasons given by adolescents for failure to use contraceptives were that they (usually mistakenly) thought they could not become pregnant because of time of month, age, or infrequency of inter-

course; or contraceptives were not available when they needed them (Chilman, 1983; Morrison, 1985; Zelnick & Kantner, 1977). The former set of reasons could be remedied with better education, the latter with more adequate service programs (AGI, 1994).

Psychological studies comparing sexually active adolescent girls who do and do not use contraceptives (or use them rarely) have found that those who do not use contraceptives tend to hold fatalistic attitudes: They are more likely to feel unable to control their own lives, have a low sense of personal competence, and take a passive, dependent approach to male–female relationships. They are also more inclined to take risks and to cope with anxiety by attempting to deny possible dangers rather than facing up to them (Chilman, 1983; Dryfoos, 1990).

Some adolescents avoid contraceptive use because they are afraid it will spoil the spontaneity of the relationship or because they think it would indicate that they expected to have intercourse. Because the frank pursuit of sexual relations is still considered to be more

acceptable for boys than for girls (Bell, 1988; Goodchilds & Zellman, 1984), for a significant number of adolescents it is more acceptable for a girl to be swept away by the passion of the moment than to use contraception (Morrison, 1985). Interestingly, girls who frankly accept their sexuality and girls who are able to discuss sexual matters easily with their parents are more likely to use contraceptives than those who deny their sexuality to themselves or others (Brooks-Gunn & Furstenberg, 1989; Chilman, 1986; Conger, 1987; Hayes, 1987).

Consistent contraceptive use is more likely to occur among female adolescents who are older, are in love and involved in an ongoing relationship, have high self-esteem and self-confidence, are making normal progress in school, have positive attitudes toward their parents, and received sex education early and at home, rather than from an acquaintance (Chilman, 1986; Hornick, Doran, & Crawford, 1979; Kelley, 1979; Zelnik & Kantner, 1980).

Among male adolescents, those who are most likely to use contraceptive measures are older, more experienced in dating, and better organized and more responsible in their general approach to life; in addition, their parents are more likely to approve of their sexual activity. Males who are least likely to use contraception tend to be either sexually naïve or permissively reared and exploitive, believing that contraception is the female's responsibility (Chilman, 1983; Goldfarb et al., 1977; Hornick, Doran, & Crawford, 1979; Kelley, 1979).

**Desire for Pregnancy.**   Contrary to popular opinion, only one in fifteen pregnant adolescents intended to get pregnant. This compares with a figure of almost one in two for adult women. Intended pregnancies are higher among poor and low-income adolescents than among higher-income teens, higher among Hispanic teens than among whites and blacks, and higher among married than unmarried teens. About a third of pregnancies among married teens are intended (AGI, 1994).

Among adolescents seeking or not objecting to pregnancy, a common theme is emotional deprivation. In the words of one pregnant 15-year-old, "I guess for once in my life, I wanted to have something I could call my own, that I could love and that would love me." Other related motivations include being accepted as an adult, getting back at one's parents, "holding" a boyfriend, gaining attention from peers, escaping from school, or just looking for a change in an unrewarding existence. One recent study found that ambivalence about wanting to be pregnant was as strongly related to subsequent pregnancy as the clear desire to have a child. Effective and consistent contraception use requires a firm commitment to not getting pregnant (Zabin, Astone, & Emerson, 1993).

# Sexual Behavior and Adolescent Adjustment

## Masturbation

In the United States and many other developed Western countries, masturbation was traditionally condemned, often "as a perversion on a par with homosexual relations" (Ford, 1961, p. 308). Even at the turn of the century, many prominent physicians and teachers, as well as health publications of the U.S. government, warned that masturbation could weaken the individual or cause a variety of diseases and that it might even result in insanity if practiced to excess (Kiell, 1964; Masters, Johnson, & Kolodny, 1992). Despite such warnings, most boys (and a much smaller percentage of girls) continued to engage in this activity, so it is not difficult to imagine the widespread anxiety, conflict, and depression that often ensued, in some cases even resulting in suicide.

Since that time public attitudes and the views of experts on sexual behavior have changed markedly. In a survey of 15- and 16-year-olds conducted in the late 1970s, 76 percent of boys and 70 percent of girls agreed with the statement "it is okay for a boy (girl) my age to masturbate" (Hass, 1979). Among 17- and 18-year-olds, agreement increased to 85 percent for boys and 72 percent for girls. Nevertheless, many adolescents continue to have at least occasional feelings of guilt, anxiety, or depression about masturbation. In the words of one 15-year-old girl,

> When I was really little, my best girlfriend and I would sleep over at each other's house and we'd masturbate together in the same room. We even had our own name for it. We certainly didn't think there was anything wrong with what we were doing: It was just something we did that felt good. But in about fourth grade I found out more about sex and I realized that masturbating was *sexual*. Then, as far as I was concerned, it was definitely not OK to do anymore—especially not with somebody else in the same room. After that I used to feel guilty when I was doing it, like it was kind of humiliating, and I tried to stop myself. Then last year when I heard from a lot of my girlfriends that they do it too, I felt better about it (Bell, 1988, p. 83).

Investigators of sexual behavior among adolescents and adults still find that participants have more difficulty discussing masturbation than any other sexual topic (Luria, Friedman, & Rose, 1987).

In the absence of previously acquired guilt or anxiety, masturbation is enjoyable and serves to reduce tension (Bell, 1988). It also provides a safe and secure opportunity to rehearse responses that will be required in sexual interaction with another and to establish associations between appropriate cues (actual or fantasied) and sexual responses (Katchadourian, 1990; Masters, Johnson, & Kolodny, 1992).

The opportunity to learn techniques of sexual arousal may be particularly valuable for girls. Experts on sexual response have found that orgasmic adequacy among females depends not only on the absence of culturally or parentally invoked patterns of anxiety and conflict but also on the learning and practicing of appropriate techniques, whether through masturbation or with a partner, or both (Kaplan, 1979; Kinsey, Pomeroy, & Martin, 1948; Kinsey et al., 1953; Masters, Johnson, & Kolodny, 1992). Sex therapists have been able to successfully treat orgasmic dysfunction in women largely through training in methods of sexual arousal and anxiety reduction.

## Petting and Premarital Intercourse

Premarital experience in petting to orgasm may perform many of the functions that are ascribed to masturbation. Kinsey found that among females who had never engaged in petting to orgasm before marriage, slightly over one-third did not reach orgasm during the first year of marriage. In contrast, among those "who had reached orgasm in at least some of their premarital petting, only 10 percent had failed to achieve it in the first year of marriage. Similar differences were apparent for some 15 years after marriage" (Kinsey et al., 1953, p. 265).

Similarly, more than 50 percent of females in Kinsey's investigation who had had premarital intercourse that led to orgasm reached orgasm in virtually all their experiences of marital intercourse during the first year of marriage. Among those who had not had any premarital experience of intercourse and had not reached orgasm from any source before marriage, less than one-third "had approached a 100 percent response in the first year of marriage" (Kinsey et al., 1953, p. 329).

These correlations may have depended on selective factors, at least to some extent. Females who had abstained before marriage may have been physiologically less responsive to begin with. However, it also appears likely, in view of the therapeutic experiences of Masters and Johnson and others, that the experiences themselves promoted learning of sexual responsiveness to appropriate stimuli (Masters, Johnson, & Kolodny, 1992).

Petting to orgasm can give young people who are ready for an intimate relationship an opportunity to obtain mutual pleasure and release of tension without having to worry about pregnancy, if they are careful. On the other hand, premarital sexual experiences for which the individual is emotionally unprepared, that arouse guilt and anxiety, or that are traumatic in themselves or lead to unfortunate consequences may inhibit rather than facilitate the young person's capacity for successful response after marriage.

# Homosexuality and Heterosexuality

Many young people fail to distinguish between homosexual *experience* and **homosexuality** (or, more accurately, a primarily homosexual *orientation*). Homosexual experiences or behaviors are not unusual in adolescence. Sexually tinged fantasies or dreams about a member of the same sex, mutual sexual experimentation, or a crush on a teacher or friend might lead adolescents to wonder whether they are homosexual (Bell, 1988). In a society in which many people still have a strong fear of homosexuality and gay males and lesbians are often viewed as immoral or "sick," this concern can lead to considerable anxiety, to the formation of defenses such as asceticism or masochistic self-denial, or even, on occasion, to suicide. Indeed, both male and female homosexual adolescents attempt suicide much more often than their heterosexual peers (*Report,* 1989b). Mental health difficulties (such as depression, conduct problems, substance abuse, difficulties in school, and running away) among homosexual adolescents are often the result of victimization experiences, such as verbal harassment and physical assault. High self-acceptance and family support may offset the potentially negative effects of victimization on the emotional well-being of homosexuals (Hershberger & D'Augelli, 1995; Rotheram-Borus et al., 1995; Savin-Williams, 1994).

There is an important difference between homosexual behaviors and a homosexual orientation. Although many young people have had sexual experiences with the same sex, most of them go on to establish satisfying heterosexual relationships. Among preadolescents, sex play with both same- and opposite-sex peers may involve pleasurable sexual stimulation, but it is usually motivated primarily by curiosity. Among adolescents, a significant number of boys and a much smaller percentage of girls have at least occasional active sexual contacts with others of the same sex (Bell, 1988; Kinsey, Pomeroy, & Martin, 1948). In one national study, 5 percent of boys

age 13–15 and 17 percent of those age 16–19 reported having had some kind of homosexual experience. Among girls, 6 percent of those age 13–15 and a like percentage of those age 16–19 reported having had homosexual experiences (Sorensen, 1973).

A classic and extensive study of homosexual and heterosexual adults by investigators at the Kinsey Institute for Sex Research suggests that having *predominantly or exclusively homosexual feelings* in childhood and adolescence is more closely related to the adoption of a homosexual orientation in adulthood than having had *homosexual experiences* during the developmental years (Bell, Weinberg, & Hammersmith, 1981; Savin-Williams, 1990). For example, among white males 21 percent of heterosexuals had engaged in mutual masturbation with other males before age 19, and a considerably larger number (51 percent) had been involved in some kind of sex play. Eighty-four percent of homosexuals had engaged in mutual masturbation; however, because there are so many fewer gay persons in the population, the total number of heterosexuals having such experience is far greater than the number of homosexuals.

In contrast, when both groups were asked whether their sexual feelings during childhood and adolescence were predominantly homosexual, 59 percent of homosexuals and only 1 percent of heterosexuals replied that they were. It is important to keep in mind the influence that an individual's current situation may have on a retrospective report. However, because these differences are so large, it seems unlikely that they would have resulted primarily from retrospective bias.

Similar results were obtained among white females, although the overall incidence of homosexual activity was far less. Four percent of heterosexuals reported having engaged in mutual masturbation before age 19, compared to 41 percent of homosexuals. As with males, however, the principal characteristic distinguishing those who became homosexual as adults from those who became heterosexual was whether their sexual feelings during childhood and adolescence had been predominantly homosexual (44 percent versus 1 percent). In brief, although homosexual adults are more likely than heterosexuals to have had homosexual experiences in childhood and adolescence, the predominance of homosexual over heterosexual feelings during this developmental period is a considerably better predictor of adult homosexuality.

In the 1970s a U.S. sample of college students was asked to indicate sexual preferences. Ninety-three percent of the males and 91 percent of the females stated that they had an exclusive interest in the opposite sex; an additional 4 percent of the males and 5 percent of the females said that they were interested mostly in the opposite sex

(Chilman, 1983; "Student survey," 1971, 1976). Only 1 percent of the males and 2 percent of the females indicated an exclusive interest in the same sex. The remainder reported equal interest in either sex or an interest mostly in the same sex. These results are consistent with a more recent large-scale national survey in Canada, which found that 1 percent of high school dropouts and of first-year college/university youth reported themselves to be exclusively homosexual (King et al., 1988).

Although most young people (including many who have had some sort of sexual involvement with members of the same sex during childhood and adolescence) develop a heterosexual orientation as adults, a minority do not. Contemporary investigations of adults suggest that about 2–3 percent of males and about 1–2 percent of females are more or less exclusively homosexual after adolescence, although perhaps 10–12 percent of males and about half that number of females have had at least one homosexual experience beyond age 19 (Chilman, 1983; Hunt, 1974; Laumann et al., 1994).

Ritch Savin-Williams (1989), who has conducted studies of homosexuality in adolescence, points out that one's sexual orientation and one's **sexual identity** may not necessarily be congruent. Sexual identity is defined as a personal recognition of one's sexual orientation. (This is distinct from gender identity, which is acceptance of oneself as a biological male or female, as described in Chapter 2). Some adolescents who have a homosexual orientation—who engage mostly in sexual feelings for, fantasies about, or sexual behaviors with the same sex—may label themselves as heterosexuals: Their sexual identity is heterosexual. Other adolescents who have a great deal of heterosexual experience may label themselves as homosexual: They identify with homosexuals. There may be vacillation over time in an adolescent's sexual identity (Remafedi, 1990). Such inconsistencies between sexual orientation and sexual identity, and questions about one's sexual identity, will probably be resolved in adulthood, after the individual has had more experience and more time for self-reflection. Coming to terms with one's sexuality is a long process. For homosexual adolescents, this process also may be a very painful one, given the social stigmatization homosexuality still incurs (Hershberger & D'Augelli, 1995; Savin-Williams, 1990, 1994).

## Nature and Nurture

How can the development of sexual orientation be understood? To what extent is sexual orientation a result of nature (chromosomally or hormonally determined) and of nurture (sex-role training and parent–child relationships)?

In their book *Homosexuality in Perspective,* Masters and Johnson (1979) maintain that homosexuality is a result of learning (nurture)—a view that is also endorsed by Kinsey and others (Baldwin & Baldwin, 1989; Hotvedt, 1990; Kinsey, Pomeroy, & Martin, 1948). In this view, sex drive, especially in humans, is not initially attached inflexibly to any particular object. Consequently, an individual's sexual potential can be channeled in either a homosexual or a heterosexual direction by various learning experiences.

A number of other investigators assert that homosexuality has its roots in hormonal or other biological factors (nature) (LeVay, 1991; Swaab & Hofman, 1990). Even among Kinsey's successors this view finds some support. In a Kinsey Institute study of the development of sexual preference in men and women the investigators conclude that "our findings are not inconsistent with what one would expect if, indeed, there were a biological basis for sexual preference" (Bell, Weinberg, & Hammersmith, 1981, p. 216).

Probably the predominant view held today is that there may be a biological predisposition to sexual orientation, but parental behaviors and social experience interact with that predisposition to foster its development (Green, 1987; Pillard & Weinrich, 1987). John Money, a Johns Hopkins investigator with a long history of research into the determinants of gender identity and sexual orientation, refers to the nature/nurture debate as "obsolete" and argues that "the only scholarly position is to allow that prenatal and postnatal determinants [of sexual orientation] are not mutually exclusive. When nature and nurture interact at critical developmental periods, the residual products may persist immutably" (Money, 1988, p. 50).

## Biological Influences on Sexual Orientation

Much investigation into the biological determinants of sexual orientation is rooted in an understanding of differences between males and females in hormones and their effects on behavior, and in neuroanatomical sex differences in brain structure and function. The dual focus on hormones and the brain derives from the connection between the two: Portions of the brain are responsible for the regulation of hormones, which in turn influence behavior. The basic logic of several decades of research has followed this line of questioning: Are there sex differences in hormonal functioning that affect sexual behavior? Are there sex differences in the brain structures that regulate production of hormones and hormonal functioning? If there are sex differences in the

brain structures and in the hormones that affect sexual behavior, then the roots of homosexuality may lie in variants of these typical sex differences.

**Hormones.**   A number of investigations suggest that prenatal hormonal influences may affect sexual behavior. In several species of animals, male and female sexual behavior is largely controlled by particular brain centers (in the area of the hypothalamus) that mature before or shortly after birth. If androgens (male hormones) are available during the maturation process (as in the case of normal male development), these brain centers become masculinized—the neuroanatomical makeup of the cells shows a pattern that is different from that of females. However, if androgens "are not available during the maturing process, the hypothalamic centers which control sexual behavior mature in a feminine manner and the animal after puberty exhibits essentially female sexual behavior—even in the presence of male hormones" (Brecher, 1971, p. 250). Experimental work demonstrates links between androgens administered prenatally, the structure of the hypothalamus, and later social and sexual behavior in animal species (Money, 1988).

The effect of prenatal levels of hormones on later behaviors in humans is shown in a series of studies in which girls received excess androgens prenatally (either as a result of drugs administered to the mother or because of a genetic abnormality). Relative to a control group of female siblings, these girls exhibited a higher incidence of "masculine" behaviors than their female peers—they showed higher levels of rough-and-tumble play, initiation of fighting, and a preference for boys as playmates. They also appeared less interested in babies and more interested in jobs and careers (Ehrhardt & Baker, 1975; Money, 1988). Such findings suggest that hormonal or other biological factors play a role in fostering personality characteristics and drive patterns that are more typical of one sex than the other.

**The Brain.**   As seen above, it has been known for some time that there are structural sex differences in the brains of animals, particularly in the hypothalamus, which helps to control sexual behavior. In the mid-1980s, a group of researchers from the Netherlands were among the first to document a sex difference in the size of a portion of the hypothalamus known as the suprachiasmatic nucleus (SCN). The SCN in men was larger and contained twice as many cells as in women (Swaab, Fliers, & Partiman, 1985). Perhaps more surprising is that five years later, these researchers found that the SCN differentiated homosexual and heterosexual men. The SCN was nearly twice as large and contained twice as many

cells in homosexuals as in heterosexuals (Swaab & Hofman, 1990). This was the first time that an anatomical difference was found between homosexual and heterosexual men.

The problem with this finding, however, is that the SCN is implicated more in the regulation of Circadian daily rhythms than in sexual behavior. Simon LeVay, a researcher at the Salk Institute for Biological Studies, decided to focus on another portion of the hypothalamus called the INAH 3 (interstitial nuclei of the anterior hypothalamus), which may be more associated than the SCN with sexual behavior, and is different in men and women (LeVay, 1991). LeVay found that the INAH 3 was two times larger in men than in women, and also two times larger in heterosexual men than in homosexual men. The particular significance of this study was that a connection was made between a portion of the brain's anatomy regulating sexuality and sexual orientation in males, thereby suggesting a biological influence on homosexuality.

**Genetic Factors.**  Biological influences are also suggested by recent genetic studies examining the incidence of homosexuality among twins (Bailey & Pillard, 1991; Bailey et al., 1993). Among male homosexuals, the likelihood that both twins would be homosexual was found to be significantly greater for monozygotic (identical) twins (52 percent were also homosexual) than for dizygotic (nonidentical) twins (22 percent). The likelihood is even lower among unrelated adopted brothers (11 percent). Among homosexual females, 48 percent of monozygotic co-twins, 16 percent of dizygotic co-twins, and 6 percent of adopted sisters were also homosexual. Recently, scientists have provided some evidence that there may be a gene involved in men's sexual orientation that is passed from mother to son (Hamer et al., 1993). Located on the X-chromosome, this gene was shared by pairs of brothers, both of whom were homosexual.

# Environmental Influences on Gender Identity and Sexual Orientation

The research that has been conducted to date indicates that environmental factors can play an important role in the development of an individual's gender identity (whether one sees oneself as male or female) and sexual orientation. The most dramatic evidence to support the role of the environment, and particularly of socialization, comes from investigations by John Money and his associates. They studied individuals who were assigned the chromosomally incorrect sex at birth (males

were labeled as females, and females were labeled as males) because of developmental anomalies that made it difficult to correctly distinguish their gender. In one series of cases incorrectly assigned, the young people developed a gender identity and sexual orientation consistent with the assigned sex of rearing and inconsistent with chromosomal sex. Clearly, gender identity and behaviors were determined more by socialization experiences than by chromosomal sex (Money, 1988; Money & Ehrhardt, 1972).

**Parent–Child Relations and Homosexual Orientation.**  Although findings such as those just described indicate that environmental factors can, under some circumstances, play a dominant role in the development of sexual orientation, they do not prove that such factors are responsible in most cases for the development of a primarily homosexual orientation. This can be done only through carefully controlled comparisons of representative groups of homosexuals and heterosexuals. Most such efforts have focused on possible differences in child rearing and parent–child relationships, although peer relationships and other psychological and social functions have also been studied (Bell et al., 1981; Freedman, 1971; Green, 1987).

In one extensive study of the development of sexual preference, the parent–child relationships of heterosexual and homosexual males and females were compared (Bell, Weinberg, & Hammersmith, 1981). There were some marked differences in the parent–child relations of homosexuals and heterosexuals (see Table 6.4). Relative to heterosexual males, the pattern among homosexual males was one of negative feelings for and a distant relationship with their fathers. Homosexual males also felt closer to and identified more with their mothers. Among females, homosexuals felt more negatively about their fathers and their mothers than did heterosexuals. They were also less likely than heterosexual women to identify with their mothers. Similar results were obtained in another study of homosexual and heterosexual women (Siegelman, 1974).

Several considerations need to be kept in mind in attempting to evaluate the results of these and other studies:

1. Although problems in parent–child relationships are generally reported more often in the development of male and female homosexuals than in that of heterosexuals, virtually all studies have found significant numbers of homosexuals who had satisfactory parent–child relationships, as well as significant numbers of nonhomosexuals who had disturbed relations.

# Table 6.4 Sexual Orientation and Parent–Child Relations

|  | Homosexual Males | Heterosexual Males |
|---|---|---|
| Described father positively | 23% | 52% |
| Expressed negative feelings about father | 48 | 29 |
| Saw father as rejecting, hostile, detached | 52 | 37 |
| Felt similar to father | 28 | 66 |
| Felt similar to mother | 72 | 37 |
| Felt close to mother | 47 | 21 |
|  | Homosexual Females | Heterosexual Females |
| Described father positively | 36% | 73% |
| Expressed negative feelings about father | 45 | 23 |
| Had negative relations with mother | 49 | 21 |
| Described mother as bitter, uncommunicative | 48 | 20 |
| Described mother as warm, pleasant, relaxed | 19 | 40 |
| Felt similar to mother | 55 | 85 |
| Wanted to be like mother | 53 | 85 |

SOURCE: A. P. Bell, M. S. Weinberg, & S. K. Hammersmith (1981). *Sexual preference: Its development in men and women.* Bloomington: Indiana University Press. By permission of authors.

2. Associations between perceived parent–child relationships (e.g., mother–son closeness and father–son distance) and the development of a homosexual orientation do not in themselves indicate causality. It may also be that the child's innate characteristics at least partially determine parental reactions and attitudes toward him or her. Given the strong reactions that many people have to homosexuality, it is easy to imagine how any signs of this sexual orientation earlier in childhood or adolescence might lead some parents to react negatively and to alienate their children.

3. Most of the studies conducted to date have been retrospective, making it difficult to determine the accuracy of the individual's recollections and the extent to which they may have been influenced by the sexual orientation they ultimately adopted.

In sum, much remains to be learned about the factors that are likely to lead to the development of a predominately homosexual or heterosexual orientation. At present no definitive conclusions can be reached regarding the role of biological or experiential sets of influences or of interactions among them. Some recent findings indicate that male adolescent homosexuals have a higher-than-average proportion of brothers and a later-than-average birth order in their families (Blanchard et al., 1995). Environmental and biological explanations have been proposed to explain these findings, but both are equally plausible. Just as homosexuals, like heterosexuals, differ enormously from one another as individuals, they may also differ in terms of the roots—biological or environmental—of their homosexual orientation (Bell & Weinberg, 1978). Several studies, for example, suggest that "feminine" males and "masculine" females who are exclusively homosexual may develop a more deep-seated predisposition toward homosexuality early in life than some other homosexuals or bisexuals (Bell, Weinberg, & Hammersmith, 1981; Green, 1987). This appears to be reflected in early gender nonconformity in interests and activities and in more common feelings of "being different" during childhood (Green, 1987). It may also be seen in early emergence of homosexual feelings and lack of heterosexual arousal during childhood and adolescence. The sexual preferences of

## 6.5 A Comment on Being Gay

Over the years I came to realize that I am gay. I did not choose to be. It is simply what I am. I am writing because many people forget that gay people can love, can laugh and, when hurting, can cry.

I have no desire to be part of "a gay movement." That is something I feel puts pressure on people to draw conclusions on what gay or lesbian people "must be like."

I, like many others, go through society unnoticed, working to help in our community, working to make tomorrow better than today.

Whatever label is put on me, in the end I am still a person. Like everyone else, I want to be loved. I want to grow, to learn, to help make life a little better for someone in need.

Being gay is only part of me. Is that so bad?

SOURCE: Letter to the Editor (Name Withheld), *Times-Colonist,* Victoria, BC, August 21, 1994.

bisexuals and some other homosexuals, in contrast, may be "more subject to influence by social and sexual learning" (Bell, Weinberg, & Hammersmith, 1981, p. 201). In this connection, it is interesting to note that people who are more or less exclusively homosexual in their orientation, and have not experienced significant heterosexual arousal, are less likely to find their homosexuality distressing, to seek changes in sexual orientation through therapy, and to accomplish this goal if they do try (Green, 1980).

### Sexual Orientation and Adjustment

Some groups view homosexuality as "deviant" or "sick." On the other hand, members of groups such as the gay liberation movement assert that homosexuality is as normal as heterosexuality. They argue that labeling homosexual behavior as deviant is not only incorrect but a form of discrimination and oppression. They point out that there have been cultures, such as that of the ancient Greeks, in which homosexual behavior was accepted along with heterosexual behavior. They also note that significant numbers of successful artists, scientists, and leaders in all walks of life have been homosexually oriented, and that although some homosexuals may be personally miserable, sexually unsatisfied, and socially ineffective, so are many heterosexuals.

The negative labeling of homosexuals *is* often done pejoratively, for a variety of reasons such as hostility, fear, and as a way of reassuring oneself of one's own normality. As a homosexual-movement leader stated, "calling homosexuality sick is like calling it sinful" (Freedman,

1971, p. 93). In response to such protests, the American Psychiatric Association has removed homosexuality from its diagnostic manual of mental disorders, retaining only a category for people who experience "persistent and marked distress about [their] sexual orientation" (American Psychiatric Association, 1994).

An extensive study of homosexual and heterosexual men and women concluded that homosexual adults who have come to terms with their homosexuality—those who do not regret their sexual orientation and who function effectively sexually and socially—are no more distressed psychologically than heterosexual men and women (Bell, Weinberg, & Hammersmith, 1981; Green, 1980). Clearly, there are many homosexuals who, in terms of overall adjustment and contributions to society, are at least as successful as many heterosexuals.

Nevertheless, a predominantly or exclusively homosexual orientation is likely to present significant problems of adaptation in our society. Despite increased tolerance for differences in sexual preference, large segments of the population, young and old, still consider homosexual behavior wrong or disturbed, even though they may oppose legal regulation of homosexual behavior. In Canada, only 38 percent of teens approve of homosexuality, but 72 percent believe that homosexuals should have the same rights as anyone else (Bibby & Posterski, 1992). Among U.S. college freshmen in 1994, 34 percent stated that they favored prohibition of homosexual behavior. However, this figure represents a 25-year low, and is down sharply from a peak of 53 percent in 1987 at the height of the AIDS scare, suggesting an increased tolerance of homosexuality among students and a better understanding of the nature of HIV infection (Astin et al., 1994; Dey, Astin, & Korn, 1991).

Nevertheless, AIDS, with its high incidence among male homosexuals and intravenous drug users, has not only brought tragedy into the lives of gay people, but also appears to have increased discrimination against homosexuals in employment, social life, and health care. Nowhere is this situation depicted more poignantly than in the film *Philadelphia,* for which Tom Hanks won an Oscar. Hanks plays a character who has to cope not only with the pain of having AIDS and saying good-bye to his loved ones, but must endure and fight unfair and discriminatory treatment by his coworkers and, initially, his own lawyer.

It seems unlikely that a person would be motivated to accept the personal restrictions and social difficulties homosexuals face in the absence of strong attraction to members of the same sex, together with a lack of heterosexual attraction.

As Alan Bell and his colleagues at the Kinsey Institute have observed,

Neither homosexuals nor heterosexuals are what they are by design. Homosexuals, in particular, cannot be dismissed as persons who simply refuse to conform. There is no reason to think it would be any easier for homosexual men or women to reverse their sexual orientation than it would be for heterosexual readers to become predominantly or exclusively homosexual (Bell & Weinberg, 1978, p. 222).

In view of this fact, continued legal and social harassment of homosexuals and attempts to picture them as "perverted" are both cruel and unjustified. In addition, they make it even more difficult for homosexually oriented young people to achieve self-esteem and social adaptation (Hershberger & D'Augelli, 1995; Savin-Williams, 1994).

Today, gay young people have more reliable sources of support than in the past. Social, professional, religious, and political support groups for gay males and lesbians are expanding, as are groups of parents of gays and other interested nongay organizations. More health and mental-health professionals are developing special knowledge and skills (as well as abandoning myths and misconceptions) that will enable them to deal more effectively with the psychological and physical problems of homosexuals. Expert legal and other services are more available, although more are clearly needed.

With further research, we may gain a better understanding of the genesis of sexual orientation. In the meantime, however, it should be possible, given greater self-understanding and understanding of others, for both homosexuals and heterosexuals to enjoy mature, constructive, and rewarding lives.

# Summary

The physical changes associated with sexual maturation require a variety of adjustments by the adolescent and produce changes in his or her self-image. Integrating sexuality with other aspects of the self and relationships with others is a major developmental task for both boys and girls.

Although there is a significant increase in sexual interest and behavior in both sexes during adolescence, sexual activity is more prevalent among boys than among girls, although the size of the difference has narrowed in recent years. Girls are also more likely than boys to stress the importance of love in sexual relationships. A number of theories have been advanced to explain such differences; some are primarily physiological, others primarily cultural.

The role of cultural factors is evidenced both by changes in sexual attitudes and behavior in our own society and by marked variations from one culture to another. Some cultures restrict sexual activity in childhood and adolescence; others are more permissive. Still others are restrictive during some age periods but permissive during others.

Although most adolescents and their parents favor comprehensive sex education, the subject remains highly controversial. In the view of a minority of Americans, sex education is dangerous and premature, even in high school, and is likely to lead to promiscuity. Some believe that sex education should be left to parents. In light of current statistics on premarital intercourse, pregnancy, and abortion, as well as the general social climate, it is difficult to see how sex education for adolescents could be viewed as premature. Moreover, there is no consistent evidence that sex education increases the likelihood that an adolescent will become sexually active. Although parental participation in sex education is clearly desirable, many parents are not providing the knowledge their children need.

Today's adolescents tend to be more open about sex and to view decisions about sexual behavior more as a private concern. Among entering college freshmen,

two-thirds of males, but only one-third of females, agree that "sex is OK if people like each other." However, when there is deep involvement, as in living together before marriage, differences are much smaller.

Changing attitudes and values are reflected in higher rates of sexual activity among adolescents, including masturbation, petting, and premarital intercourse. For example, among American women who were teenagers in the 1950s, 8 percent reported having had premarital sexual intercourse by age 16 and less than one-third by age 18. By 1988, these figures had increased to over 21 percent by age 16 and 50 percent by age 18. It appears that widespread dissemination of information about AIDS since 1987 has led to increasing condom use.

Overall trends in sexual attitudes and behavior do not reveal the diversity that exists in various sections of the population. More females than males are *serial monogamists* and more males are *sexual adventurers,* although sexual adventurers constitute a minority of both sexes. Economically privileged adolescents are more liberal in their sexual attitudes, but not in their level of sexual activity. Sexual permissiveness is higher among politically liberal, less religious, and black youth. Significant cultural differences between nations also exist. The influence of peers on attitudes toward premarital sex may be stronger than that of parents, although teens seem to want parents to talk to them.

Among sexually active female adolescents, about three-quarters use some form of contraception on an ongoing basis. Failure to use contraceptives properly and high levels of premarital intercourse result in about 12 percent of 15- to 19-year-old girls becoming pregnant each year in the United States, a higher rate than is found in any other developed country.

Adolescent pregnancies pose threats to the health of both mother and child, primarily because of poor prenatal care and conditions of poverty. In addition, teenage mothers are more likely to face other problems; many drop out of school, are unemployed, and must depend on welfare. They also are less likely to get married and if they do marry, they are more likely to divorce. With proper support, however, significant numbers of adolescent mothers are able to succeed. Reasons for failure to use contraceptives include incorrect information, unavailability of contraceptives when they are needed, emotional deprivation, low self-esteem and fatalistic attitudes, and persistence of the double-standard. Adolescents who have high self-esteem, are doing well in school, accept their sexuality, and are able to discuss sex with their parents are more likely to use contraceptives. High rates of adolescent pregnancy could be reduced by better sex education and family life planning, greater access to contraceptive methods, and more opportunities to build a successful and self-sufficient future.

Despite dire predictions in the past, neither masturbation nor petting to orgasm poses threats to adolescent adjustment. A significant number of boys and a much smaller percentage of girls have had sexual contacts with members of the same sex, although less than 3 percent go on to establish a basically homosexual orientation in adulthood. Much remains to be learned about the factors that are likely to lead to the development of a predominantly homosexual or heterosexual orientation. There is mounting evidence of biological influences (genetic or hormonal), but a biological predisposition probably interacts with environmental or socialization influences. With additional research, we may gain a better understanding of the genesis of sexual orientation. In the meantime, however, it should be possible, given greater self-understanding and understanding of others, for both homosexuals and heterosexuals to enjoy mature, constructive, and rewarding lives.

# Review Questions

1. How do the sexual attitudes and behavior of adolescent males and females differ? What theories have been proposed to account for those differences?

2. How do the sexual attitudes, values, and behavior of contemporary adolescents differ from those of earlier generations of adolescents?

3. Does sex education increase sexual activity among adolescents? Does it lead to increased pregnancy rates? How do rates of premarital intercourse and pregnancy among adolescents in the United States compare with those found in other developed countries?

4. Has sexual activity among adolescent males and females increased, decreased, or remained steady during the 1970s and 1980s? Discuss trends for younger and older adolescents, males and females, and blacks and whites.

5. Describe the differences between *serial monogamists* and *sexual adventurers.* Which group is better adjusted psychologically?

6. Discuss the relative influence of family and peers on adolescent sexual attitudes and behavior.

7. Discuss current trends in pregnancy and contraceptive use among adolescents. Why do so many adolescent girls and younger women fail to use contraceptive measures? How does pregnancy affect the lives of adolescent mothers and their babies?

8. Discuss what is known about the effects of biological and environmental factors on sexual orientation.

# Recommended Readings

Alan Guttmacher Institute. (1994). *Sex and America's teenagers.* New York: Author.

Bell, R. (1988). *Changing bodies, changing lives: A book for teens on sex and relationships* (Rev. Ed.). New York: Random House.

Brown, S. S., & Eisenberg, L. (1995). *The best intentions: Unintended pregnancy and the well-being of children and families.* Committee on Unintended Pregnancy, Institute of Medicine, National Academy of Sciences. Washington, DC: National Academy Press.

Furstenberg, F. F., Jr., Brooks-Gunn, J. R., & Chase-Lansdale, L. (1989). Teenaged pregnancy and childbearing. *American Psychologist,* **44,** 313–320.

Katchadourian, H. (1990). Sexuality. In S. S. Feldman & G. R. Elliott (Eds.), *At the threshold: The developing adolescent* (pp. 330–351). Cambridge: Harvard University Press.

Michael, R. T., Gagnon, J. H., Laumann, E. O., & Kolata, G. (1994). *Sex in America: A definitive survey.* Boston: Little, Brown.

Patterson, C. J. (Ed.) (1995). Sexual orientation and human development [Special issue]. *Developmental Psychology,* **31**(1).

# Adolescents
# 7
# and Their Peers

# Adolescents

# 8 and Schools

Where relations with parents are troubled, understanding and supportive peers may help a boy or girl to gain a clearer self-concept, a feeling of personal worth, and renewed hope for the future.

autonomy, self-confidence, and personal values may be severely tried.

During adolescence, more than at any other time in life, the young person needs to be able to share emotions, doubts, and dreams (Parker & Gottman, 1989; Savin-Williams & Berndt, 1990). Adolescence is typically a time of sociability, but it can also be a time of loneliness (Marcoen, Goosens, & Coes, 1987; Moore & Schultz, 1983; Parkhurst & Asher, 1992). Consequently, being accepted by peers generally, and especially having one or more close friends, can make a great difference in the young person's life.

Finally, the role of the peer group in helping an individual define his or her own identity becomes particularly important during adolescence because at no other stage of development is one's sense of identity so fluid. No longer a child, but not yet fully accepted as an adult, the adolescent must prepare to meet society's demands for social independence, new kinds of rela-

tionships, vocational competence, a responsible role as a citizen, and, in many cases, marriage and parenthood.

For all these reasons, adolescents need the guidance, support, and communion of their peers. No matter how understanding parents and other adults may be, their role is limited by the fact that they are already adults, whereas the adolescent and his or her peers are struggling to achieve adult status. Young people often do not know how they are going to accomplish this task. But they know that previous generations of adolescents have done so, and they reason that if they can stick with their peers—who, after all, are in the same boat—they too will succeed.

## Conformity

Because of the heightened importance of the peer group during adolescence, the motivation to conform to the values, customs, and fads of the peer culture increases during this period. Although evidence of a need for such conformity is clearly observable in middle childhood, and although there are wide individual differences in the strength of this need at all ages, most studies indicate that there is a rather rapid rise in need for conformity during the preadolescent and early-adolescent years, followed by a gradual but steady decline from middle through late adolescence (Berndt, 1979; Mussen et al., 1990; Steinberg & Silverberg, 1986). Although the need for conformity may vary, depending on such factors as sex, socioeconomic background, relationships with adults, school environment, and personality, variations are likely to occur in the extent of conformity or the exact age at which it peaks, rather than in the overall developmental pattern (Clasen & Brown, 1985; Coleman, 1980; Cooper & Ayers-Lopez, 1985; Steinberg & Silverberg, 1986). Even among those who are lower in conformity relative to their peers, there is likely to be an increase in conformity in early adolescence followed by a decrease.

Studies have found that young people with low status among peers are more conforming than those with high status; that boys and girls differ little in need for conformity, except when group norms favor misconduct (in which case boys are more susceptible); and that children and adolescents with favorable attitudes toward adults are less subject to peer pressure than those with negative attitudes toward adults (Berndt, 1979; Brown, Clasen, & Eicher, 1986; Steinberg & Silverberg, 1986). Adolescents with high self-esteem and strong feelings of competence are less conforming than their peers (Cooper & Ayers-Lopez, 1985; Gavazzi, Anderson, & Sabatelli, 1993).

Recent findings regarding adolescent conformity are generally similar to those obtained some years ago. In short, whereas the *manifestations* of peer group conformity change rapidly in our society, there can be little

doubt that most adolescents, particularly younger ones, have a strong need to conform to peer group norms and pressures, and that this need is reflected in behavior (Berndt, 1979; Brown, 1990; Clasen & Brown, 1985).

Of course, adolescents may deny or fail to recognize what an outside observer may perceive as excessive conformity to peer pressure. What looks like conformity to the observer may seem to the young person to be a bold exercise in individuality. One adolescent girl, for example, was very proud of the fact that she was not like most of the students at her prep school—especially in terms of fashion. She did not seem to realize, however, that her style of dress—oversized, black, secondhand clothing—was the only acceptable fashion among counterculture adolescents living in her city. The explanation of this paradox lies in the different perspectives of the observer and the adolescent: An adolescent may perceive his or her behavior as highly individual because it differs markedly from that of parents and other adults, or even a segment of peers; in contrast, the observer's attention is likely to focus on the similarities between the adolescent's behavior and peers of the same age.

Needless to say, conformity is not an exclusively adolescent phenomenon. Parallels exist in the conforming behavior of adults, who may also fail to recognize it. Self-conscious liberal or conservative adults may see themselves as paragons of rugged individualism because their attitudes, beliefs, and behaviors differ from those of a majority of their fellow citizens. What they fail to recognize is that they are conforming to the myths, customs, fads, and philosophical clichés of their own cultural subgroup.

Having left the world of childhood forever without yet being admitted to the world of adults, adolescents are virtually forced to create at least a semblance of an interim culture of their own. Obviously, it is important that this culture, whatever form it may take, be clearly recognizable as different from that of adults. Once adults recover from their initial dismay and adopt some adolescent fashions and tastes as their own (as has happened with dress, hairstyles, music, and even language), adolescents need to create new fads to preserve their separateness.

Parents are often mystified, and in some cases threatened, by the shifting trappings of adolescent peer culture—from fashions in clothes and music to special and rapidly changing vocabularies. They may wonder why adolescents need to behave in such a "bizarre" manner. Yet that is one of the main reasons for the existence of adolescent fads: They establish a clear line of demarcation from adults. In one school, adolescent girls took to public spitting so much that a local newspaper reporter, who was astonished by this behavior, wrote an article on it.

Rather than viewing such incidents with abhorrence and fear, parents and other adults might actually take some comfort from these outward indicators of the "differentness" of adolescents. By achieving a group identity of their own in these relatively superficial ways, adolescents may partially satisfy the need to be different from their parents in more fundamental matters. Although, as we shall see, adolescent values and behavior are different from those of adults, there is also a fundamental and often overlooked continuity in many of the values and beliefs of parents and their children (Conger, 1991b; Cooper & Ayers-Lopez, 1985).

## Parental and Peer Influences—A False Dichotomy?

We should not be misled by superficial differences between parents and adolescents, however conspicuous they may be. Although it is commonly asserted that parental and peer-group values are incompatible and that an inevitable consequence of heightened dependence on peers during adolescence is a sharp decline in parental influence, this is not true for most adolescents.

In the first place, there is usually a considerable overlap between the values of parents and peers because of commonalities in their social, economic, ethnic, religious, educational, and even geographic backgrounds. For example, boys from an Irish-American, Catholic, blue-collar neighborhood in a large city are more likely to share the values of their parents and peers than to share those of boys (or parents) from an upper-middle-class WASP background in the same city (Conger, 1975, 1991c; Lerner & Knapp, 1975; Youniss & Smollar, 1989).

Another factor that limits potential conflicts between parental and peer influences is the uncertainty of some parents about the behavior they should expect from adolescents. Parents may feel that social change has occurred so rapidly that they lack the experience to teach their children how to deal with today's world. This was particularly true in the late 1960s and early 1970s, but it is still true of a significant number of parents in the 1990s.

Such a view can easily become a self-fulfilling prophecy. While bemoaning the adolescent's conformity to the peer group, parents may be encouraging the child to turn to the peer group for guidance. Moreover, many parents, particularly upper- and middle-class parents, place great emphasis on popularity and success, thereby strengthening the adolescent's motivation to conform to peer expectations.

Another important consideration that is often overlooked is that neither the influence of parents nor that of peers extends to all areas of adolescent decision-making and behavior (Berndt, 1979; Clasen & Brown, 1985;

Wilks, 1986). The weight given to parental or peer opinion depends to a significant degree on the adolescent's appraisal of its relative usefulness in a specific situation. For example, the influence of peers (especially same-sex peers) is more likely to dominate in such matters as tastes in music and entertainment, fashions in clothing and language, patterns of interaction with same- and opposite-sex peers, and the like. Parental influence is more likely to dominate in such areas as educational plans and aspirations, moral and social values, and understanding of the adult world (Conger, 1971, 1991c; Kandel, 1985; Sebald & White, 1980; Wilks, 1986).

Similarly, adolescents are likely to turn to other significant adults, such as grandparents and teachers, for advice in areas in which "expert" knowledge of the adult world is viewed as relevant (Steinberg, 1985; Wilks, 1986; Young & Ferguson, 1979). One must also recognize that when the peer group assumes an unusually dominant role in the lives of adolescents, it is due as much to lack of attention and concern at home as it is to the attractiveness of the peer group (Bronfenbrenner, 1970; Devereux, 1970; Galambos & Silbereisen, 1987).

Parents of strongly peer-oriented adolescents are likely to show passive neglect (i.e., a relative lack of concern and affection) rather than active punitiveness. They appear to neither support nor control their children to any significant degree, hence leaving them to seek approval and affection elsewhere (Condry & Siman, 1974; Conger & Petersen, 1984). In contrast, the parents of adolescents with lower peer involvement are more active: more nurturant, more demanding, and more consistent, providing more companionship and discipline.

In one study, parental influence was found to be greatest when there was a high level of parent–adolescent affect as measured by parental interest and understanding, willingness to be helpful, amount of shared family activity, and so on (Larson, 1972a, 1972b). In another, the amount of weekend time adolescents spent with their families counteracted the influence of delinquent friends on adolescent delinquent activities. Among adolescents with delinquent friends, those who reported more weekend family time committed significantly fewer offenses (Warr, 1993).

As psychologist Laurence Steinberg (1985) points out, investigations that are designed to force adolescents to choose between parental and peer influence do not allow them to demonstrate autonomy with respect to both. However, investigations that have measured the extent of adolescents' conformity to parents *and* to peers separately have found that, on average, conformity to parents tends to decline during preadolescence and early adolescence while conformity to peers rises (Berndt, 1979; Steinberg & Silverberg, 1986). Not until middle and late adolescence do increases in overall autonomy

occur, for only then does conformity both to parents *and* to peers decline for a majority of young people—most dramatically with respect to peer pressure to engage in antisocial behavior (see Figure 7.1).

However, at all ages *some* adolescents demonstrate a relatively high degree of autonomy with respect to both parents and peers (Devereux, 1970; Steinberg & Silverberg, 1986). Figure 7.2 shows the percentage of adolescent males and females in grades 5–9 in one study who were autonomous (high in both parent and peer autonomy), nonautonomous (low in both parent and peer autonomy), parent-oriented (low in parent autonomy but high in peer autonomy), and peer-oriented (high in parent autonomy but low in peer autonomy). As can be seen, even in the early years of adolescence a significant minority of adolescents in this study (more girls than boys) demonstrated a relatively high degree of autonomy (Steinberg & Silverberg, 1986).

Finally, we tend to overlook the fact that the need for rigid conformity to either parents or peers varies

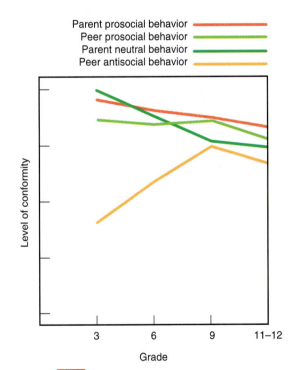

**Figure 7.1**

Changes in conformity to the different types of behaviors of peers and parents during adolescence. SOURCE: T. J. Berndt (1979). Developmental changes in conformity to peers and parents. *Developmental Psychology*, **15**, 606–616. Copyright © 1979 by the American Psychological Association. Reprinted with permission.

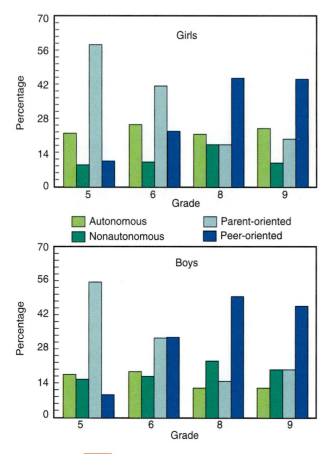

**Figure** `7.2`

Proportions of autonomous, nonautonomous, parent-oriented, and peer-oriented adolescents across four grade levels. From L. Steinberg & S. B. Silverberg (1986). The vicissitudes of autonomy in early adolescence. *Child Development, 57,* 841–851. By permission.

enormously from one adolescent to another (Berndt, 1979; Conger, 1979; Steinberg & Silverberg, 1986). More self-confident, autonomous adolescents may be able to profit from the views and learning experiences provided by both parents and peers without being strongly dependent on either. Nor are they unduly troubled by differences between the views of parents and peers (Cooper & Ayers-Lopez, 1985; Hartup, 1983). Ironically, an adolescent who has gained confidence in his or her own self-image, and is relatively individualistic and unconcerned about popularity, may find that peers flock to him or her as a tower of strength.

## Sources of Difficulty

There are four conditions in which serious difficulties are most likely to arise and parents are most likely to find

themselves feeling helpless. Briefly, they are as follows:

1. There is a very strong, homogeneous peer group, with patterns of behavior and attitudes that differ markedly from those of the adolescent's parents. This might be especially evident among adolescents whose parents were born into another culture.

2. The parents lack interest in and understanding of the adolescent and are unwilling to be helpful, and few family activities are shared.

3. The parents' own values and behaviors are inconsistent, uninformed, unrealistic, maladaptive, or obviously hypocritical.

4. The adolescent lacks either the self-confidence or the independence training to act autonomously without undue concern (Conger, 1977).

In most cases in which young people have forsaken or renounced family values for those of deviant peer groups, one or more of these conditions is likely to be present.

As indicated earlier, the parents' task may be easier in the traditional small-town culture, which is characterized by extended kinship and neighborly ties and by continual interaction between parents and other adults, peers, the schools, and other social institutions. Under such circumstances fundamental values and customs are more firmly held and widely shared among adults and adolescents.

The parents' task may be much more difficult in other settings, such as a large city, in which both the nuclear family and the peer group may be relatively isolated from interaction or even communication with other individuals and groups in the community. We see examples of this situation in inner-city neighborhoods that have high unemployment rates, deteriorated buildings, families in poverty, and schools with few resources. Peer groups may be involved in drug use, sexual activities, delinquent behavior, and, increasingly, gang-related violence. In this setting, parents may be confronted with seemingly insurmountable problems as the peer group exerts strong pressure for conformity.

It is worth noting that negative effects of peer conformity can be seen among adolescents in affluent settings as well. Some suburbs or malls in relatively safe Canadian cities have experienced "swarming" incidents, in which crowds of adolescents terrorize one or two people whom they corner and subsequently assault or rob. One suburban mall experienced a near-riot as a crowd of adolescents suddenly began breaking windows in stores and stealing.

The more discrepant or deviant the peer-group setting, the more important it is for parents to attempt to take the authoritative approach to child rearing (described in Chapter 5) and to carefully monitor the adolescents'

friends and activities. Equally crucial are efforts to communicate with, understand, and interact actively with the adolescent. Both the permissive parent, who provides neither guidance nor a strong model of basic standards and values, and the authoritarian parent, who neither understands nor feels any need to understand the views and problems of the adolescent, are likely to lose whatever influence they might have had and to leave the adolescent vulnerable to deviant peer-group influences.

## The Changing Nature of Adolescent Peer Groups

Although we have spoken of the adolescent peer group or peer culture as if each were a single entity, this is not actually the case. In reality, the adolescent interacts in different ways with a number of overlapping peer groups that vary in size and in the degree of intimacy among their members. In addition, the nature of these groups and the functions they serve change with age. During middle childhood and preadolescence peer relations tend to center on neighborhood play groups (Brown, 1990; Hartup, 1983; Mussen et al., 1990). From an early age (by age 3), boys and girls seem to segregate themselves into same-sex play groups, which are characterized by different patterns of behavior. Boys in same-sex peer groups, for instance, show dominance-related behavior such as interruptions, noncompliance to peer demands, threats, name-calling, and boasts. Girls in same-sex peer groups tend to be polite, agree with other girls, give others a chance to speak, and acknowledge their points. Psychologist Eleanor Maccoby (1990) argues that childhood peer groups "constitute powerful socialization environments in which children acquire distinctive interaction skills that are adapted to same-sex partners" (p. 516). These interaction skills are then used in mixed-sex interactions that take place more frequently in adolescence.

Largely informal at first, play groups become more highly structured with increasing age (from about age 10 on). Aspects of formal organization, such as special membership requirements and elaborate rituals for conducting meetings, appear. Even so, the members may change frequently and the group itself may not last long. The predominance of same-sex groups during this period is perpetuated by the presence of differences in interests and activities that are more easily served by such groups (Huston, 1983; Mussen et al., 1990).

Throughout the middle-childhood and preadolescent years, boys are more likely than girls to participate in gangs. However, girls tend to have more intimate interpersonal relationships than boys even at these ages, perhaps as a natural outgrowth of the considerate behavior

learned earlier in all-girls groups (Hartup, 1983; Maccoby, 1990; Youniss & Smollar, 1985). The peer relations of both boys and girls during the middle-childhood years tend to be limited to neighborhood acquaintances and schoolmates (who tend to come from the same or adjoining neighborhoods). However, as the young person enters junior high school and spends less and less time at home, the range of peer relations broadens to include a much wider circle of casual acquaintances (Csikszentmihalyi & Larson, 1984).

In general, the adolescent's peer relations fall into three broad categories: the **crowd** or "set," the **clique,** and individual friendships. A pioneering study of adolescent peer groups in an urban setting found two basic types of groups: relatively large crowds and much smaller cliques (Dunphy, 1963, 1980). The most inclusive and least personal of these categories is the crowd. In a sense, a crowd is a "forced group" made up of individuals who share interests, likes, social ideals, fashions of dress, and behaviors. The members may meet or interact on the basis of shared activities, not because of mutual attraction (Brown, 1989; Coleman, 1980; Dunphy, 1972). The crowd is essentially an association of cliques; clique membership appears to be a prerequisite for crowd membership (Coleman, 1980). No subject in the study just mentioned was found to belong to a crowd without also belonging to one of its component cliques. On the other hand, an individual might well be a member of a clique without also belonging to the crowd. Girls' cliques tend to be smaller, more restricted in age range, and, as mentioned earlier, more intimate than those of boys (Brown, 1989; Hartup & Overhauser, 1991; Savin-Williams, 1980a, 1980b).

Cliques and crowds perform different functions for their members. The smaller clique encourages far more intimacy and group cohesion than the larger crowd. In fact, that cohesion is made possible by the limited mem-

Girls' cliques tend to be smaller, more restricted in age range, and more intimate than those of boys.

bership of cliques. The similarity in size between the family and the clique may facilitate the transfer of allegiance to the clique and allows it to provide an alternative center of security. Clique interactions consist largely of talking, especially on the telephone. An analysis of the content of these conversations showed that the clique performs an important practical function in the preparation of activities, the dissemination of information about them, and subsequent evaluation.

The crowd, on the other hand, provides for larger and more organized social activities such as parties, which are a setting for interaction between the sexes. The crowd "acts as a reservoir of acceptable associates who can be drawn on to the extent required by any social activity. Thus cliques and crowds are not only different in size; they are also different in function" (Dunphy, 1963, p. 235) (see Box 7.1).

## Stages of Peer-Group Development

As adolescence proceeds, structural changes in the nature of peer groups take place; these, in turn, are related to the changes that occur in the course of adolescent development, particularly the development of heterosexual relationships (Blyth, Hill, & Thiel, 1982; Brown, 1990; Csikszentmihalyi & Larson, 1984; Dunphy, 1980). As the young person enters adolescence, same-sex cliques predominate, but these single-sex cliques gradually begin to interact with cliques of the opposite sex, leading to the formation of the adolescent crowd (Hallinan, 1981; Hartup, 1983). At least initially, such heterosexual interactions are tentative and are usually undertaken in the group setting, where the individual is supported by the presence of his or her same-sex friends.

Only in the next stage of peer group development do we see the formation of genuinely heterosexual cliques, in which heterosexual interactions between individuals are begun (usually by higher-status clique leaders). However, adolescents who belong to these emerging heterosexual groups maintain their membership in the same-sex clique. Throughout adolescence (through grade 12), males and females rate their same-sex friendships as more supportive (for example, intimate and affectionate) than their opposite-sex friendships. By late adolescence, on the other hand, romantic partners begin to rival same-sex friendships in terms of their supportive functions (Furman & Buhrmester, 1992; Lempers & Clark-Lempers, 1993).

In the stage of adolescent group development following the formation of heterosexual cliques, the situation shifts, and we see the emergence of the fully developed adolescent crowd made up of a number of heterosexual cliques in close association. Participation in these mixed-sex peer groups seems to be a key factor in the development of romantic relationships (Connolly & Konarski, 1994). Finally, in late adolescence couples and loosely associated groups of couples are often seen; same-sex friendships continue but become more stable and less intense (see Figure 7.3). The importance of the crowd begins to diminish as the need for conformity to peers lessens and the perceived need to establish an individual identity grows (Coleman, 1980; Csikszentmihalyi & Larson, 1984; Dunphy, 1963, 1980).

Although adolescents currently tend to enter these stages at somewhat younger ages, the sequence of stages seems to have persisted, despite individual variations and occasional regressions. One of the principal functions served by the crowd is to make possible the transition from the same-sex cliques of early adolescence to the heterosexual cliques of later adolescence. At the same

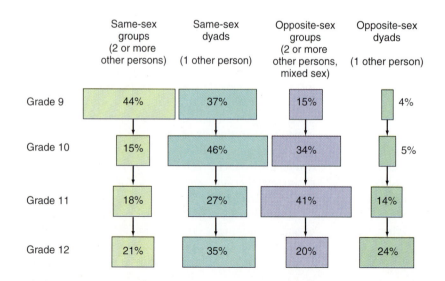

**Figure 7.3**

The shift from same-sex to opposite-sex friends during high school years. The diagram shows the percentage of time with friends that students in each grade spent with different types of friends.
SOURCE: M. Csikszentmihalyi & R. Larson (1984). *Being adolescent: Conflict and growth in the teenage years.* Copyright © by Basic Books, Inc. Reprinted by permission of Basic Books, a division of HarperCollins Publishers, Inc.

# 7.1 Who's In, Who's Out? Who's a Brain, and Who's Not?

All of us have experienced the peer crowd phenomenon. Peer crowds make up an important part of the adolescent experience, and they are ever-present in American and Canadian secondary schools. Such crowds are so clearly observable that they go by different labels such as "brains," "nerds," or "toughs," labels that attest to the existence of multiple peer cultures and that describe the stereotypic characteristics—behavioral, personality, and appearance—of the crowd's members. Such crowds are reputation-based in the sense that assignment to a crowd is based on *peer* judgments about who has the characteristics to belong (Brown, 1990).

Given that a crowd represents a relatively large group, not all members of the crowd necessarily spend time together. What is important is that they are perceived by others to share similar characteristics, such as socioeconomic status, behaviors and interests, or ethnicity. Not only are perceived similarities the basis for membership in the crowd, those similarities may be reinforced further when the crowd provides the adolescent with standards for how to look, what attitudes to hold, and how to behave (Brown, 1990; Durbin et al., 1993).

Although it has often been assumed that peer influences take control over the adolescent's behavior as parental influences wane, parents in fact remain important. They influence the adolescent's behaviors, and these behaviors, in turn, influence with whom or what crowd the adolescent associ-

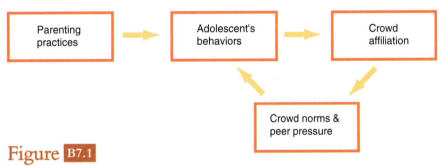

## Figure B7.1

Conceptual model of the connections among parenting behaviors, peer group influences, and adolescent behavior. From B. B. Brown, N. Mounts, S. D. Lamborn, & L. Steinberg (1993). Parenting practices and peer group affiliation in adolescence. *Child Development,* **64,** 467–482. By permission.

time, associations with same-sex individuals and groups continue in somewhat muted form throughout adolescence and into adult life. Such associations may be seen in small circles of friends, individual friendships, fraternities and sororities, clubs, or interest groups.

Socioeconomic status plays a significant role in determining crowd and clique membership. There is usually little cutting across class lines, particularly in the case of girls, whose cliques tend generally to be closer, more exclusive, more impregnable to outsiders, and somewhat more enduring (Coleman, 1980). There is somewhat more democracy and flexibility in male cliques, in which athletic skills and overall sociability have a leveling influence.

Other influences may also play a role in crowd or clique formation. Among these are shared interests and hobbies; social and athletic skills; academic goals; personal and sexual maturity; traditionalism versus rebellion in cultural values; participation in or avoidance of drug use, sexual experimentation, or delinquent behavior; degree of academic involvement; personality characteristics; ethnic group membership; and residential proximity (Berndt, 1982; Coleman, 1980; Hartup, 1983).

Cliques may exhibit considerable intolerance or contempt for nonmembers who are different in various ways. Individuals—particularly girls—who are personally secure and emotionally mature are most likely to be

ates. The crowd then helps to shape adolescent behaviors through peer pressure to follow the crowd's norms (Brown, et al., 1993). The process by which parents may have an influence on adolescent crowd affiliation is depicted in Figure B7.1.

What is the research evidence that describes parental influences on adolescents' crowd affiliation? In a study of over 3700 adolescents by Bradford Brown and his colleagues, adolescents were assigned to six crowds by peer raters (Brown et al., 1993). These six crowds (populars, jocks, brains, druggies, normals, and outcasts) differed according to the adolescent member's pattern of grades in school, drug use, and

self-reliance (see Table B7.1). This study found that parents influenced adolescent crowd membership through the effect they had on adolescents' grades, drug use, and self-reliance. Specifically, parents who encouraged achievement had adolescents with higher grades and higher self-reliance, parents who monitored their adolescents' activities carefully had adolescents with lower drug use and higher self-reliance, and joint decision-making between parents and adolescents was associated with higher grades, lower drug use, and higher self-reliance. Through these parent-influenced behaviors, parents were able to affect the adolescent's fit with a particular crowd.

## Table B7.1 Some Distinguishing Characteristics of Adolescents in Six Peer Crowds

| CROWD | GRADES | DRUG USE | SELF-RELIANCE |
| --- | --- | --- | --- |
| Populars | High | High | High |
| Jocks[a] | Moderate | — | — |
| Brains | High | Low | — |
| Normals | Moderate | Low | — |
| Druggies | Low | High | — |
| Outcasts | Low | Low | Low |

NOTE: —indicates that this variable was unrelated to membership in the crowd.

[a]Athletic ability was not measured.

SOURCE: B. B. Brown, N. Mounts, S. D. Lamborn, & L. Steinberg (1993). Parenting practices and peer group affiliation in adolescence. *Child Development, 64,* 467–482. Adapted by permission.

able to reach out and establish relationships with members of other cliques. In general, older students are also more likely to cross clique boundaries.

There are also some people who, either through choice or as a result of rejection by peers, belong neither to cliques nor to crowds. Although adolescents today seem to have somewhat more tolerance for difference than was true in some earlier generations, the fact remains that many adolescents—preoccupied with themselves, uncertain of their own worth, and eager to gain security and status through acceptance by the in-group—can be remarkably indifferent or even cruel toward those who do not fit in. As we shall see, for many isolated

young people the adolescent years can be a lonely and difficult time.

## Friendships and Identity Development

Friendships hold a special place among the peer relationships of adolescents. Compared to more general interactions with peers, friendships typically are more intimate, involve more intense feelings, are more honest and open, and are less concerned with social acceptance

(Berndt, 1992; Hartup & Overhauser, 1991; Konopka, 1985; Youniss & Smollar, 1985). Consequently, close friends often can contribute to an adolescent's development in ways that the broader peer group cannot. "The particular advantage of the adolescent friendship is that it offers a climate for growth and self-knowledge that the family is not equipped to offer, and that very few persons can provide for themselves" (Konopka, 1976, p. 174). At the same time, because it plays such a vital role in adolescence, friendship gains an importance and intensity that are lacking in earlier and later stages of development. The **intimacy** that is characteristic of adolescent close friendships is important to the interpersonal adequacy and socioemotional adjustment of girls and boys. In one study, adolescents with more intimate friendships were less hostile, were less anxious and depressed, had higher self-esteem, and were more sociable than adolescents in less intimate friendships (Buhrmester, 1990).

The young person who is attempting to adjust to a changing self (psychologically and physiologically) and to meet rapidly changing societal demands may experience doubts, anxieties, and resentments. In most situations these reactions must be concealed. To admit them to any but one's closest friends is to open the door to the possibility of misunderstanding, lack of acceptance, scorn, or rejection. In a meaningful friendship, however, such defensiveness is not required.

In one intensive study, middle-class adolescents of both sexes selected their "close friend" as the person they were most likely to "talk openly" with and share "true feelings" with. Moreover, the relationship was viewed as reciprocal: Close friends "are not afraid to talk about [their] doubts and fears," they "depend on each other for advice," and even when they disagree, they listen to each other's reasons (Youniss & Smollar, 1985, p. 103). In the words of one adolescent girl, "A friend is someone who I can talk to, who'll understand, and don't turn you down and say they don't want to listen and they don't want to hear what you're saying" (Konopka, 1976, p. 85).

In view of the sensitivity of adolescents to the dangers associated with revealing their inner feelings, it is not surprising to find that they emphasize the need for security in a true friendship: They want a friend to be loyal, trustworthy, and a reliable source of support in any emotional crisis (Berndt, 1992; Cooper & Ayers-Lopez, 1985; Hartup & Overhauser, 1991; Youniss & Smollar, 1985). Untrustworthy behavior is cited by adolescents as the primary cause of serious conflict between close friends (see Table 7.1). As one 14-year-old girl from an urban ghetto stated, "A friend don't talk behind your back. If they are a true friend they help you get out of trouble and they will always be right behind you and they help you get through stuff. And they never snitch on you. That's what a friend is" (Konopka, 1976, p. 85).

At their best, friendships help young people to learn to deal with their own feelings and those of others.

Under favorable circumstances, adolescents may reveal a talent for friendship that is not shared by younger children or most adults. A major distinction between the adolescent and the child or adult is that the adolescent often enters friendships with a considerable degree of flexibility and readiness for change. Younger children may not be happy with themselves as they are, but they tend to accept the situation as a fact of life. However, with the beginning of adolescence and formal-operational thinking, young people become more aware of themselves as having a social persona that can be changed by conscious intent (Douvan & Adelson, 1966; Tesch, 1983; Youniss & Smollar, 1985). Close friends can often help each other identify and change behaviors that may turn off others, develop new tastes and social skills, and learn to express ideas effectively.

Along with openness to change, adolescents show greater openness to inner states of experience. They have not yet defined the boundaries of the self or made the commitment to a particular way of life that, though resulting in a sharper definition of the self, also tends to

# Table 7.1 Number of Adolescents Describing Issue as Causing the Most Serious Conflict in a Close Friendship

| ISSUE | FEMALES | MALES |
|---|---|---|
| 1. *Untrustworthy acts* (doesn't keep secrets, talks behind back, gets other into trouble, breaks promises, lies, takes a job away, takes opposite-sex friend away, goes out with other's opposite-sex friend) | 59 | 43 |
| 2. *Lack of sufficient attention* (leaves other out, ignores other, doesn't come to party, doesn't call, spends time with others, doesn't include in plans, wants to be with opposite-sex friend, ignores when opposite-sex friend is around) | 28 | 13 |
| 3. *Disrespectful acts* (is snotty, is rude, calls names, puts down, makes fun of, is bossy, uses other, hits, argues with, fights with, breaks something of others, steals something from other) | 17 | 39 |
| 4. *Unacceptable behaviors* (talks too much, is too moody, drinks too much, has a bad temper, is conceited, lies, quits school, is stubborn, is spoiled, brags, acts stupid, smokes pot) | 18 | 14 |

SOURCE: J. Youniss and J. Smollar (1985). *Adolescent relations with mothers, fathers, and friends.* Chicago: University of Chicago Press. By permission.

limit the individual's openness to other possibilities. As a result, they often exhibit "a psychic flexibility, or vulnerability to conflict, [and] an affective lability which together give adolescent intimacies so much of their characteristic flavor" (Douvan & Adelson, 1966, p. 180).

At their best, friendships may help young people learn to deal with their own feelings and those of others. They can serve as a kind of therapy by allowing freer expression of suppressed anger or anxiety and by providing evidence that others share many of the same doubts, hopes, fears, and feelings. As one 16-year-old girl expressed it, "My best friend means a lot to me. We can talk about a lot of things I could never talk about with my parents or other kids—like hassles we're getting or problems we're worried about, and like ideals and things. It really helps to know you're not the only one that has things that bother them" (Conger, 1979, p. 70).

Similar thoughts are expressed by a 13-year-old boy:

A best friend to me is someone you can have fun with and you can also be serious with about personal things, about girls, what you're going to do with your life or whatever. My best friend, Jeff, and I can talk about things. His parents are divorced too, and he understands when I feel bummed out about the fights between my mom and dad. A best friend is someone who's not going to make fun of you just because you

do something stupid or put you down if you make a mistake. If you're afraid of something or someone, they'll give you confidence (Bell, 1988, p. 64).

Finally, close friendships may play a crucial role in helping young people develop a sense of their own identity. By sharing their experiences, plans, hopes and fears—in short, by explaining themselves to each other—adolescent friends are also learning to understand themselves. There is an implicit awareness that self-definition and a coherent view of external reality cannot be achieved solely by reflection, that without the corrective functions of an external voice, one "risks self-delusion or egoism" (Youniss & Smollar, 1985, p. 167). In the words of one adolescent, "You can't always decide what you want to do yourself. You need a second opinion" (Youniss & Smollar, 1985, pp. 164–165). There is also an awareness that mutual understanding is a reciprocal process: "You have to give a friend advice when he has a problem because a lot of times when a person is involved in a problem, he can't see it too well" (Youniss & Smollar, 1985, p. 164). Moreover, when a friend who "really understands" the adolescent still likes and values him or her, the young person's confidence and self-esteem are bolstered (Berndt, 1992; Osterrieth, 1969; Parker & Gottman, 1989). In sum, under favorable circumstances friendships may help the adolescent both to

define his or her own identity and to have confidence and pride in it.

Unfortunately, the circumstances of adolescent friendship are not always so favorable. By virtue of their very intensity, these friendships are more easily imperiled than those of most adults, which are likely to involve more modest demands (and yield more modest returns). Even the more stable and rewarding adolescent friendships are likely to blow hot and cold in response to the rise and fall of feelings in oneself and others. Just as closeness is a feature of relationships with friends, so too is conflict, although in most cases the conflict does not disrupt the relationship and in fact is perceived by adolescents as improving it (Laursen, 1993). This may be because adolescents do not have as much conflict with peers as they do with parents or siblings, and conflict with peers is more likely to be resolved through negotiation and compromise. Adolescent girls seem especially likely to use these resolution strategies so that disagreement is minimized (Laursen, 1996).

## Similarity in Friendship Pairs

Close friendships are most likely to develop between adolescents with similar demographic characteristics (age, school grade, sex, socioeconomic status, and ethnic background) (Bukowski et al., 1993; Epstein, 1989; Hartup & Overhauser, 1991; Urberg, 1992). The percentage of a person's close friends who are members of the opposite sex increases with age, but even in late adolescence same-sex friendships predominate, particularly in the case of "best friends" (Blyth, Hill, & Thiel, 1982; Fischer, 1981; Kandel, 1978b; Lempers & Clark-Lempers, 1993). Same-race friendships also predominate in adolescence, but blacks are more likely than whites to report having cross-race friendships (Clark & Ayers, 1992; DuBois & Hirsch, 1990).

Similarities in the *behaviors* and *attitudes* of best friends can be observed. Best friends are more similar than acquaintances in intelligence, educational and career aspirations, sociability, cooperative activities, school behavior and grades, conformity to adult expectations, amount of participation in peer-group activities, and use of drugs and alcohol. Some evidence suggests, however, that black adolescent best friends are less similar to each other than are white best friends on dimensions such as drug use, sexual activity, verbal achievement, and some personality characteristics (such as dominance) (Billy & Udry, 1985; Clark & Ayers, 1992; Tolson & Urberg, 1993).

Although similarities in the personality and behavior of adolescent friends are generally more evident than differences, this is not always the case (Epstein, 1989). Indeed, parents sometimes find it difficult to understand

their adolescent children's choices of friends. What, they may ask, does their Sally, who has always been so neat, quiet, and studious, see in noisy, extroverted Barbara, who seems more interested in being constantly on the go than in her schoolwork, or indeed in any serious activity? When such an attraction of opposites occurs, it is usually because the young person finds in the friend something that is felt to be desirable but is lacking in the self. Extroverted Barbara may be helping Sally become less inhibited and self-conscious and learn to get along more easily with peers. Barbara, in turn, may find in Sally someone who can help her understand some of her own previously hidden feelings—someone who is really willing to listen (Storr, 1975).

The fact that in many instances friends tend to be similar in behavior, values, and interests could have two sources. These sources of friendship similarity have been cast as hypotheses known as the selection and socialization hypotheses. The *selection hypothesis* predicts that individuals who share personally relevant similarities are attracted to each other and will select each other as friends on the basis of those similarities. Alternatively, the *socialization* hypothesis states that the friendship itself produces greater similarities among individuals, socializing them to become more similar; increasing similarity is the result of the friendship. It seems likely that both processes are involved. In a longitudinal investigation of high school students in New York State, Denise Kandel and her colleagues were able to study individuals before they became friends, during the course of their friendship, and in some cases after their friendship had broken up (Kandel, 1978a, 1978b, 1985; Kandel & Andrews, 1987). They found that both hypotheses were supported. Adolescents tended to choose as friends others who were similar to them in such characteristics as use of legal and illegal drugs, academic interests (educational aspirations, grades, willingness to cut classes, and school program), and participation in peer activities. However, the researchers also found that friends tended to resolve imbalances in such characteristics by becoming more like each other. In instances in which this did not happen, friendships were more likely to be dissolved. Other investigators also have found that these two sets of influences play a part in the formation and maintenance of adolescent cliques (Cohen, 1972; Epstein, 1989; Tuma & Hallinan, 1977).

## Variations in Friendship Patterns

**Age.** The function, quality, and content of friendship patterns vary with age, sex, and ethnicity. Before puberty, friendships tend to be more superficial than they will be later (Dorval et al., 1987; Mussen et al., 1990; Parker &

Gottman, 1989). The young person wants a friend who is readily available, is fun to be with, and can share interests, activities, and possessions. It is expected that friends will cooperate with and help each other, and there is growing emphasis on equality in relations between friends. What tends to be lacking is "the sense that friendship can be emotionally relevant" (Douvan & Adelson, 1966, p. 186). As the young person moves through adolescence, however, there is increasing emphasis on mutual understanding, empathy, emotional investment, and eventually a sense of shared identity, in which "I and you" become "we" (Selman, 1980; Youniss, 1980; Youniss & Smollar, 1985).

By middle adolescence the personality of the friend and his or her response to the self become the central themes of the friendship. During this period the opportunity for shared thoughts and feelings may help ease the transition toward sexual relations and a newly defined sex-role identity (Dorval et al., 1987; Douvan & Adelson, 1966). This is the age when emphasis on a friend's loyalty, trustworthiness, and respect for confidences reaches its peak and when the emotional intensity and vulnerability of friendships are likely to be at their height.

In contrast, by late adolescence the passionate quality of friendship tends to recede and to be replaced by a more equable autonomous interdependence, in which friends can still be close, yet at the same time grant each other autonomy and independence (Selman, 1981). In the words of one older adolescent, "If you are really close friends and trust each other, you can't hold on to everything. You gotta let go once in a while. Give each other a chance to breathe" (Selman & Selman, 1979, p. 74). Although having someone to share confidences with is still important, there is a greater, more objective emphasis on the friend's personality and talents—on what he or she can bring to the relationship in the way of interest and stimulation—and a greater degree of tolerance for, and even appreciation of, individual differences. As the adolescent begins to define herself or himself, to find a basis for his or her identity, and to develop fairly secure psychological defenses, dependence on identification with close friends is reduced. In addition, more meaningful heterosexual relationships have begun to develop, further diluting the exclusiveness of the adolescent's reliance on same-sex friends.

**Sex.** Adolescent friendship patterns also vary by sex. Girls' friendships typically are more numerous, deeper, and more interdependent than those of boys; moreover, in their friendships girls reveal more empathy, a greater need for nurturance, and the desire for and ability to sustain intimate relationships (Connolly & Konarski, 1994; DuBois & Hirsch, 1993; Lempers & Clark-Lempers, 1993; Miller, 1990; Youniss & Smollar 1985). Boys, in contrast, tend to place relatively more emphasis on having a congenial companion with whom one shares an interest in sports, hobbies, or other activities. Of course, shared activity may be one route through which boys achieve closeness to their friends (Camarena, Sarigiani, & Petersen, 1990).

In one study of middle and late adolescence (Fischer, 1981), two major aspects of friendships were identified: a friendship factor (voluntary involvement in mutual activities with a unique other) and intimacy (closeness, ease of communication, attachment and affection, and lack of egocentrism). On the basis of these two dimensions, male and female adolescents were divided into four categories: relatively uninvolved (below the median on both friendship and intimacy), friendly (above the median on friendship, below the median on intimacy), intimate (the reverse of friendly), and integrated (above the median on both intimacy and friendship). The investigators found that male high school students were most likely to be classified as either relatively uninvolved or friendly in their relationship styles, whereas female college students were most likely to be classified as integrated or intimate (see Table 7.2). Interestingly, when the gender of the subject and his or her friend was taken into account, female–male friend-

# Table 7.2 Males and Females with Different Friendship Styles, Percentages

| STYLE OF CLOSE RELATIONSHIP | MALE | | FEMALE | |
| --- | --- | --- | --- | --- |
| | HIGH SCHOOL | COLLEGE | HIGH SCHOOL | COLLEGE |
| Uninvolved | 39% | 28% | 31% | 17% |
| Friendly | 24 | 23 | 26 | 11 |
| Intimate | 15 | 23 | 15 | 30 |
| Integrated | 22 | 26 | 28 | 42 |

SOURCE: J. L. Fischer (1981). Transitions in relationship style from adolescence to young adulthood. *Journal of Youth and Adolescence,* **10,** 11–23. New York: Plenum Publishing Corporation. By permission.

ships showed the highest incidence of integrated relationships, followed in order by male–female, female–female, and male–male friendships (see Table 7.3). On the basis of these findings, it appears possible that "late adolescent females socialize the males for heterosexual relationships on the basis of their practice in intimacy with their girlfriends" (Fischer, 1981, p. 21). Similar arguments have been made by others, suggesting that many adolescent males must learn to develop strategies for maintaining closeness in friendships and romantic relationships (Laursen, in press; Youniss & Smollar, 1985).

The differences in emphasis between girls' and boys' friendships are not surprising because throughout adolescent and adult life, women have traditionally tended to maintain a stronger interpersonal orientation in adjusting to life. Adolescent and adult females are more likely than males to be strongly motivated by the need for love and nurturance and they may be generally less reluctant to appeal to others for support and nurturance. Adolescent and adult males, on the other hand, are more likely than females to be motivated by a need for autonomy and to rely on oneself or on a group of peers (the gang or the clique) in dealing with competitive demands (Huston, 1983; Newman, 1975a, 1975b; Savin-Williams, 1980a). Adolescent boys tend to be more competitive and more hesitant about expressing support or warmth in all-male discussion groups than do girls in female groups; as the study just described might suggest, boys are somewhat freer in talking about personal feelings in mixed-sex groups than in same-sex groups (Ariès, 1974; Newman, 1975a, 1975b; Youniss & Smollar, 1985). Apparently, despite recent social changes, group discussions centering on interpersonal intimacy are somewhat more threatening to males than to females.

It is important to note that there are still significant differences *within* each sex in friendship patterns (Cooper & Grotevant, 1987; Fischer, 1981; Sharabany, Gershoni, & Hoffman, 1981). Some men are more interpersonally oriented, concerned with intimacy, and willing to express emotion than others. By the same token, some women are more concerned with autonomy and meeting the competitive demands of society, and less concerned with intimacy and self-disclosing communication.

Such individual variations may be strongly influenced by prior experiences and patterns of interaction within the family (Cooper & Grotevant, 1987; Huston, 1983; Sroufe & Fleeson, 1986). Thus, parental encouragement of individuality and "separateness" (see Chapter 5) appears to play an important part in fostering the development of autonomy and independence in girls, probably because society encourages these traits more in boys (Hauser et al., 1987; Huston, 1983). Conversely, high levels of parental warmth, support, and connectedness, particularly in a boy's relationship with his father, appear to be important in encouraging boys to develop close friendships with peers (Baumrind, 1979; Cooper & Grotevant, 1987; Grotevant & Cooper, 1988; Huston, 1983).

**Ethnicity.** As noted earlier, the friendship patterns of black and white adolescents may be different in some respects. Compared to blacks, whites report having fewer cross-race friendships, and resemble their friends more (Clark & Ayers, 1992; DuBois & Hirsch, 1990). This research points out the limitation placed on our knowledge about adolescent peer relations attributable to the almost exclusive historical focus on white, middle-class adolescents. The extent to which the bulk of the research can be applied to other segments of the North American population is questionable, and awaits further research.

Some insight into this gap in knowledge was pointed out in a large interview study of the friendship and

## Table 7.3 Friendship Pairs Characterized by Relationship Style, Percentages

| STYLE OF RELATIONSHIP | GENDER OF ADOLESCENT–GENDER OF FRIEND | | | |
| --- | --- | --- | --- | --- |
| | FEMALE–MALE | MALE–FEMALE | FEMALE–FEMALE | MALE–MALE |
| Uninvolved | 15% | 12% | 28% | 46% |
| Friendly | 22 | 27 | 16 | 22 |
| Intimate | 15 | 24 | 28 | 17 |
| Integrated | 48 | 36 | 29 | 15 |

SOURCE: J. L. Fischer (1981). Transitions in relationship style from adolescence to young adulthood. *Journal of Youth and Adolescence,* **10,** 11–23. New York: Plenum Publishing Corporation. By permission.

family relations of black and white adolescents (Giordano, Cernkovich, & DeMaris, 1993). The authors of this study found evidence against the common assumption that black adolescents are more peer-oriented because their family relations are less supportive—an assumption called the compensation argument. In fact, this study found that blacks were less peer-oriented and were less intimate with and felt less pressured by peers than did whites. Blacks also saw similarity with friends as less important than did whites. Their relations with their families were more intimate and they perceived more parental control than did white adolescents.

The authors of this study suggested that the model portraying increasing autonomy from parents and increasing dependence on peers in adolescence is more characteristic of white than black adolescents. Black adolescents' strong reliance on the family may be important in shielding them from the difficult social and economic pressures they face. This is not to say that the peer relations of black and white adolescents are different in all respects. Consistent with other research, regardless of race, girls reported higher levels of intimacy in their friendships than did boys (Giordano, Cernkovich, & DeMaris, 1993).

## Peer Acceptance, Neglect, and Rejection

As we have implied, an adolescent's personality characteristics, cognitive skills, and social behaviors affect his or her chances of being accepted by peers. Whether the adolescent is well-liked by many peers (popular) or accepted by most (the average adolescent), his or her personal characteristics seem to be associated with peer acceptance. In general, adolescents who are accepted by their peers are perceived as liking other people and as being tolerant, flexible, and sympathetic. They are portrayed as lively, cheerful, and good-natured, possessing a sense of humor, low in anxiety and having a reasonable level of self-esteem, acting naturally and self-confidently without being conceited, and possessing initiative, enthusiasm, and drive. Adolescents who are viewed favorably tend to make others feel accepted and involved, to promote constructive interaction between peers, and to plan and initiate interesting or enjoyable group activities. They are adept at interpersonal understanding, know how to communicate effectively, are knowledgeable about peer group norms and values, and are able to infer and vicariously experience their peers' moods and feelings (Allen, Weissberg, & Hawkins, 1989; Coleman, 1980; East et al., 1992; Parkhurst & Asher, 1992; Vernberg et al., 1994).

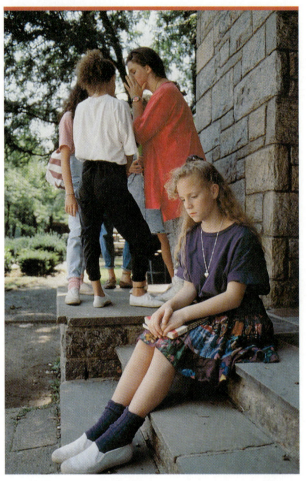

Few adolescents are immune to social neglect or rejection. Most are dependent for feelings of self-worth on the approval of their peers.

Adolescents who do not have these characteristics are likely to be neglected (neither liked nor disliked by peers). For instance, the adolescent who is ill-at-ease and lacking in self-confidence and who tends to react to discomfiture with timidity, nervousness, or withdrawal is more likely to be neglected than accepted or rejected. In contrast, adolescents who are rejected by their peers (actively disliked) are most likely to be aggressive, self-centered and inconsiderate, conceited, and demanding of attention. An inability or unwillingness to perceive and meet the needs of others, sarcasm, tactlessness, and little contribution to the success of group efforts add to the probability of being rejected (Asher & Renshaw, 1981; Kupersmidt & Coie, 1990; Morison & Masten, 1991).

There are, of course, many other factors that may affect an adolescent's chances of being accepted by peers. These include intelligence and ability, physical attractiveness, special talents, socioeconomic status, and ethnic-

## 7.2 Peer Relations and Subsequent Adjustment

In view of the importance of peer relations in our society, it should not be surprising to find that relationships with peers in childhood and adolescence are significantly related to subsequent adjustment during adolescence and adulthood. A review of research on this subject found that more than thirty studies revealed positive correlations between rejection in childhood and problems later in life (Parker & Asher, 1987). Poor peer relations are predictors of adult neurotic and psychotic disturbances as well as conduct disorders, delinquency, disturbances in sexual behaviors, and school maladjustment (Cowen et al., 1973; Elliott, Huizinga, & Ageton, 1985; Hartup & Overhauser, 1991; Kupersmidt & Coie, 1990; Morison & Masten, 1991; Rutter & Giller, 1984). For example, in a comprehensive longitudinal study of schoolchildren in a large metropolitan area, differences between future delinquents and nondelinquents (who were matched, or similar to, the future delinquents on age, social class, IQ, school attended, residence area, and ethnicity) emerged as early as the period from kindergarten to the third grade. Future delinquents showed "more difficulty in getting along with peers, both in individual one-to-one contacts and in group situations, and they were less willing or able to treat others courteously, tactfully, and fairly. In return, they were less well liked and accepted by their peers" (Conger & Miller, 1966, p. 68).

Such studies show that there is reason to believe that poor peer relations figure prominently in the development of a variety of emotional and social maladjustments (Hartup & Overhauser, 1991; Rutter & Giller, 1984). The precise role peer relations play, however, is not clear. Poor peer relations could be just as much a *result* of an adolescent's maladjusted behavior as a *cause*. To illustrate, recent studies have indicated that aggressiveness in childhood may be more highly linked than is peer rejection to problems such as delinquency in adolescence. In this case, early aggressiveness is a primary factor in explaining both peer rejection and later problems in adjustment (Kupersmidt & Coie, 1990; Morison & Masten, 1991; Parkhurst & Asher, 1992). Even if peer rejection is a result of the child's maladaptive behaviors, it undoubtedly combines with these behaviors to make an unfavorable situation even worse.

---

group membership. Athletic ability among boys (Cavior & Dokecki, 1973; Hartup, 1983) and social skills among girls contribute significantly to an individual's status in most adolescent peer groups (Coleman, 1980). Some characteristics, such as physical size, athletic ability, and physical assertiveness, are more strongly related to group status among younger adolescents than among older ones; conversely, intelligence, creativity, and social skills play a relatively larger role among older adolescents.

Although not enough studies have distinguished between the consequences of peer neglect versus rejection, it appears as though peer rejection in childhood is consistently and significantly associated with psychosocial adjustment difficulties later on (see Box 7.2) (Conger, 1977; Hartup & Overhauser, 1991; Parker & Asher, 1987; Price & Dodge, 1989; Savin-Williams & Berndt, 1990). The consequences of peer neglect remain to be seen. Although a few individualists, confident of their own goals and interests and having a strong sense of ego identity, may neither need nor seek the approbation of peers, most adolescents, judging their own worth largely in terms of others' reactions to them, are dependent on the approval and acclaim of prestigious peers.

Unfortunately, an adolescent who is not accepted by peers is likely to be caught in a vicious cycle. Perhaps emotionally troubled, self-preoccupied, and insecure, he or she is likely to meet with rejection or indifference. In turn, an awareness of this lack of acceptance, coupled with lack of opportunities to participate in and learn from peer-group activities, further undermines the adolescent's self-confidence and increases his or her sense of social isolation, leading to further inappropriate behavior with peers. Intervention programs designed specifically to train adolescents in social skills such as perspective-taking and the appropriate communication of feelings can have significant effects on adolescents' socially adaptive behaviors (Chalmers & Townsend, 1990; Murphy & Schneider, 1994).

Other things being equal, social acceptance by peers is desirable, particularly if it is based on mutual helpful-

ness and shared interests. However, many parents—particularly upper- and middle-class parents—place undue emphasis on the pursuit of popularity. Greater emphasis on the importance of being oneself and remaining faithful to individual values and goals, and less on the importance of popularity and superficial appearances—of fitting in at all costs—would be more beneficial to the child in the long run.

But as we have already noted, it would be unrealistic to expect the average adolescent—unsure of his or her own identity and unclear about the demands made by a rapidly changing society—to be immune to the favor of peers. Most adolescents, at one time or another, feel that they do not belong, and the pain, however temporary, can be very real; parents' insistence on popularity can only compound the young person's difficulties.

# Relations With Other-Sex Peers

Before the middle years of adolescence, peer relationships—especially close friendships—tend to be restricted largely to members of the same sex. This preference for same-sex friendships reflects a greater liking for the same sex, rather than an active dislike of the other sex (Bukowski et al., 1993). To some extent, this pattern is culturally imposed and hence is subject to variation and modification. For example, among preadolescents in some coeducational boarding schools, cross-sex friendships are more common than is generally the case. To a large extent, however, preference for same-sex friends reflects the needs of young people themselves. Before the years in which sex drive increases, the young person is more likely to find others with similar concerns, interests, talents, and skills among same-sex peers. One study found that enjoyment of activities involving gross motor skills was higher among boys than girls, and that this was a significant basis for boys' same-sex preferences. Girls who enjoyed gross motor activities, however, were more likely to prefer boys as friends (Bukowski et al., 1993). Learning culturally sanctioned behaviors (other than those that are specifically heterosexual) may be more easily accomplished in company with others engaged in similar efforts. During a period of rapid physical and psychological change, finding out about one's changing self and discovering (often with considerable relief) that one is not so different or peculiar may be facilitated by communication with same-sex peers.

Moreover, the awakening of sexual impulses and related physiological and psychological changes is likely to provoke at least a temporary period of self-consciousness and anxiety about sex in general and about opposite-sex peers. The sex antagonisms that are common in the preadolescent years appear to be at least partly defensive, as though the young person were saying, "I must be a real boy (or girl) because I'm certainly not like those strange people of the opposite sex." Partly, too, such antagonisms appear to facilitate avoidance of premature heterosexual relationships, with which the adolescent is unprepared to cope.

At this stage of development, when family ties and preoccupations with the self are still strong, seeking to achieve a sense of identity through identification with others of the same sex (through friendship or crushes) appears to be a precondition for later cross-sex friendships, infatuations, and, eventually, mature love (Blos, 1971a, 1971b, 1979a; Feinstein & Ardon, 1973).

As maturation continues, boys and girls begin to pay more attention to one another. Earlier sex antagonisms and crushes begin to wane and heterosexual interests increase. Nevertheless, in their early stages heterosexual relationships reflect many preadolescent characteristics (Conger, 1979). Self-preoccupation remains strong, deep emotional involvement with opposite-sex peers is rare, and heterosexual interactions usually have a superficial, gamelike quality (Kolaric & Galambos, 1995). During this period heterosexual group activities are common and may offer the security of having familiar same-sex peers present. Such activities provide graduated opportunities to learn ways of relating to other-sex peers and ensuring that one will not be alone on a date with an other-sex peer before one is ready to begin dating.

Gradually, however, experiences in heterosexual cliques promote increasing confidence in one's ability to relate to individual peers of the opposite sex. At the same time, greater maturity—reduced self-preoccupation, a clearer sense of self, and increased concern for others—increases the likelihood that such relationships will be more mature and involve not only sexual attraction but feelings of mutual trust and confidence, a genuine sharing of interests, and a serious involvement in the well-being of the other person.

## Going Out (Dating)

In our society dating (or "going out," as it is currently known) is the traditional vehicle for the development of individual heterosexual relationships. Although dating clearly provides a ritualized structure for engaging in heterosexual interactions, it may also promote superficiality and, at times, dishonesty and competitiveness in relations between the sexes. Because dating is ubiquitous in North America, we often take it for granted, neglecting the fact that dating tends to occur earlier and to play a more dominant role in adolescent peer relations here than in

# 7.3 Peer Relations Gone Wrong
## HARASSMENT, ABUSE, AND DATE RAPE

Although peer relations can be a source of happiness, learning, and self-esteem among adolescents, they can also take an abusive turn, causing pain, confusion, and emotional difficulties that may last well into adulthood. Relative to child or spouse abuse, peer abuse has received relatively little notice, even though it is very common (Conger, 1991c). Peer abuse may be verbal or physical in nature, and it may range from derogatory remarks, name-calling, and other forms of verbal harassment to physical assault and date rape. Although the media have recently focused much attention on the violence and abuse perpetrated by and between adolescent gang members, peer abuse is a widespread phenomenon that probably takes place in every school and schoolyard in North America.

What is the extent of abuse among peers? We

are aware of only one study to date that has examined this issue. Using autobiographical statements written by two groups of university students (one group in 1974 and the other in 1989), sociologist Anne-Marie Ambert (1994) found that peer abuse was recalled more often than was parental abuse. Nearly 27 percent of the autobiographical statements written in 1989 described negative peer treatment in adolescence that had detrimental lasting consequences for the abused students. The comparable figure for parental abuse was about 9 percent. Moreover, the figure for peer abuse in 1989 seems to have increased since 1974, when it was 17 percent. Ambert estimates that about 20 percent of children will be abused by their peers at some time during their young lives.

The devastating effects of such abuse can be seen in the following account by a female student:

many other countries. Although there are regional, ethnic, and socioeconomic variations, most girls and boys in the United States begin dating by the age of 15, with sizeable percentages having had their first date at ages 13 or 14 (Dornbusch et al., 1981; McCabe, 1984; Thornton, 1990). In a 1992 national survey of U.S. high school seniors, nearly half of the males and just over half of the females indicated that they went out on a date at least once a week. A minority (about one in seven) indicated that they never went out (see Table 7.4).

Under favorable conditions dating serves a number of functions in addition to recreation. It aids in the development of social and interpersonal skills in relations with members of the other sex, it provides opportunities to meet other-sex peers within a social framework that allows for terminating unwanted relationships (and finding new ones) with minimal loss of face, it offers a means for finding and testing identity, and it provides occasions for sexual experimentation and discovery within mutually acceptable limits (Bell, 1988; Hansen, Christopher, & Nangle, 1992; Thornton, 1990). Perhaps most important as far as future marriage is concerned, dating may permit the development of genuine trust, love, and mutual concern between romantic partners.

Whether dating encourages depth and maturity in interpersonal relationships is more open to question.

Particularly in the earlier years of adolescence, there seems to be less emphasis on the development of warm, spontaneous, meaningful interactions between two individuals and more emphasis on the development of the so-called dating personality. Many aspects of the "good" date (superficial social and conversational skills; charm; a bright, interested manner, regardless of one's true feelings; and sexual attractiveness) seem irrelevant if not inimical to the development of deeper, more honest and complex emotional relationships, particularly if dating is begun too early. As noted earlier, overly eager pursuit of popularity can sometimes work against the development of a richer personal identity and inner resourcefulness.

## Current Dating Patterns

Although dating is considerably less formal and structured today than it was in earlier generations, the characteristics adolescents look for in a prospective date, the doubts and anxieties they share, and the "rules of the dating game" are not nearly as new and different as one might expect (Bell, 1988). Young people are still concerned with such issues as "Does he like me?" "If I ask her to go out with me, will she turn me down?" "Will

The boys of my elementary school were rude, disgusting and held no respect for any of the girls. They felt that whenever they wanted to, they could grab you wherever they want[ed]. In addition to this they also loved to fabricate stories about the girls and what they were able to do to them. . . . I was faced with dealing with these idiots and their actions and attitudes never allowed me to get close to a guy that I'd liked for years (Ambert, 1994, p. 123).

One male student recalled:

The other boys used to pick on me, hide my coat, steal my lunches and would never include me in their games. They'd laugh at me openly and the girls started avoiding me too because it wasn't cool being seen with the most unpopular boy. . . . You can't imagine how many times my mother had to keep me home because I'd start throwing up (Ambert, 1994, p. 125).

Forms of sexual coercion (such as date rape) are among the most painful incidents that adolescents can experience at the hands of their peers. A recent U.S. study of adolescent girls in grades 7, 9, and 11 found that 21 percent reported having experienced sexual coercion, including unwanted touching and rape, in the past year (see Figure B7.3) (Small & Kerns, 1993). (This is comparable to figures reported in Canada by Holmes & Silverman, 1992). Boyfriends, friends, and first dates were most often the perpetrators of this abuse (see Table B7.3).

Although such abuse can have serious longterm effects, including a loss of self-esteem, it is often ignored—by parents, teachers, and even counselors—in the mistaken belief that adolescent relationships are transitory and not serious (Conger, 1991b). However, an increasing number of schools in the United States are responding by instituting guidelines against harassment among students, whether it takes place in the classroom or on the playground.

*box continues*

he call?" "Will I know what to say and how to act if I go out with her?" "What about making out?"

For a young person who is shy, socially inexperienced, or fearful of rejection, asking someone out is not easy. In the words of one 16-year-old boy,

The way you think about yourself really has a lot to do with how you act. Like you might stop

yourself from going up to someone you might want to meet because you think, Oh, I'm not attractive enough or I don't have a good enough personality. You think you won't make a good impression so you're afraid to make an effort. For me, it was always that I was afraid I'd be rejected or—even worse than that—ignored. But what I've learned is that you may have something

## Table 7.4 Frequency of Dating Among U.S. High School Seniors, 1994

|  | MALES | FEMALES |
|---|---|---|
| Never | 17.2% | 16.7% |
| Once a month or less | 20.0 | 18.9 |
| Two or three times a month | 17.7 | 14.8 |
| Once a week | 16.4 | 15.3 |
| Two or three times a week | 18.9 | 21.3 |
| Over three times a week | 9.7 | 13.1 |

SOURCE: J. G. Bachman, L. D. Johnston, & P. M. O'Malley. (In preparation.) *Monitoring the future: Questionnaire responses from the nation's high school seniors, 1994.* Ann Arbor: Institute for Social Research, University of Michigan. By permission.

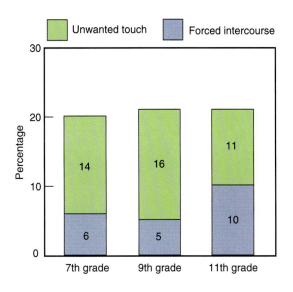

Legend: Unwanted touch | Forced intercourse

| | 7th grade | 9th grade | 11th grade |
|---|---|---|---|
| Unwanted touch | 14 | 16 | 11 |
| Forced intercourse | 6 | 5 | 10 |

## Figure B7.3

Incidence of sexual coercion in the past year among 7th-, 9th-, and 11th-grade females

SOURCE: S. A. Small & D. Kerns (1993). Unwanted sexual activity among peers during early and middle adolescence: Incidence and risk factors. *Journal of Marriage and the Family,* **55,** 941–952. Copyright © 1993 by the National Council on Family Relations, 3989 Central Ave. NE, Suite 550, Minneapolis, MN 55421. Reprinted by permission.

In the United States and Canada, dating tends to occur earlier and to play a more dominant role in adolescent peer relations than in many other countries.

inside you that the other person would like very much. You have to give yourself a chance because if you put yourself down too quick you never get anywhere (Bell, 1988, p. 67).

Despite the so-called sexual revolution and the women's movement, many traditional stereotypes about dating appear to be alive and well. Thus, most girls are reluctant to ask a boy out first, although in national surveys most boys say they would welcome it (Bell, 1988; Gaylin, 1978, 1979). According to one 17-year-old boy, "I think it's great when a girl calls up a guy to ask him out. A lot of guys are shy, like I was shy for a long time. It was hell for me to ask a girl out. And a lot of the girls I know are much less shy than I am, so it makes me feel wonderful when one of them asks me out" (Bell, 1988, p. 69). Nevertheless, the average adolescent still feels constrained by traditional sex role expectations:

I think boys have it really hard. Once you get to be a teenager, suddenly everybody expects you to start calling up girls and going out with them. But, hey, I think it takes a lot of courage to call a girl up and ask her out. You know, you

## Table B7.3 Relationship of Perpetrator to Victim

| | TYPE OF CONTACT | |
| RELATIONSHIP | UNWANTED TOUCH | FORCED INTERCOURSE |
| --- | --- | --- |
| Boyfriend | 25% | 41% |
| First date | 20 | 15 |
| Dated more than once | 8 | 5 |
| Friend | 25 | 16 |
| Acquaintance | 13 | 15 |
| Stranger | 3 | 4 |
| Other | 5 | 4 |

SOURCE: S. A. Small & D. Kerns (1993). Unwanted sexual activity among peers during early and middle adolescence: Incidence and risk factors. *Journal of Marriage and the Family*, **55**, 941–952. Copyright © 1993 by the National Council on Family Relations, 3989 Central Ave. NE, Suite 550, Minneapolis, MN 55421. Reprinted by permission.

always worry that she'll say no. . . . It's not so easy for me to just pick up the phone and act cool. I get nervous (Bell, 1988, p. 68).

Nor is the situation easier for the girl who has been taught to wait to be asked:

Sitting around waiting for the phone to ring is a big part of my life—you know, wondering if some boy's going to call and ask you out for the weekend. Like on Monday night I'll sit there and say to myself, Well, the phone's going to ring by the time I count to twenty-five. Then if it doesn't ring I count to a new number. It makes me so nervous I can't concentrate on anything else and I'm always yelling at everybody else in the family to get off the phone if they're using it (Bell, 1988, p. 68).

Although nearly 40 percent of boys and nearly 50 percent of girls still think the boy should pay all the expenses of a date, the picture is changing. Today, especially among older adolescents and youth, there is a more egalitarian approach to the costs of going out.

Many contemporary adolescents, like their peers of an earlier day, are concerned about what kinds of sexual activity are or are not appropriate at various stages of the dating process, and about how to initiate or respond to sex-related behavior. Although sexual standards are generally more liberal than they were in earlier decades, most adolescents still expect the boy to take the lead in "making out." Nearly two out of three adolescent girls say that they prefer to have the boy take the lead, even though less than one boy in four says that he would be turned off by the girl taking the lead (Bell, 1988; Lindsay, 1985).

**Preferred Characteristics.** In one national survey in the United States, girls between the ages of 16 and 21 were asked what qualities in boys turned them on or off (Gaylin, 1979). Rated as most important (90 percent or more) were good personality, kindness, good manners, and a sense of humor; these were followed by compassion, good looks, and charm (over 70 percent). The following were the most frequently cited turn-offs: heavy drinking, inability to communicate feelings, profanity, and drug use (all over 70 percent), followed by indecisiveness, "super-jock," and "don't kiss goodnight" (40 percent or more). Apparently, these young women wanted boys to be somewhat androg-

ynous: sensitive and compassionate but also reasonably assertive and decisive.

In a similar survey of boys in the same age range, a number of interesting findings emerged. Three-quarters of the boys said that the first thing that attracts them to a girl is her looks—whether she has an attractive figure and a pretty face. However, when asked what they considered most important in a girl, or what would lead them to want to continue dating her, personality and a sense of humor ranked first, followed by beauty, intelligence, and personal warmth (Gaylin, 1978).

In other surveys, desirable qualities that were often mentioned by members of both sexes included good looks, kindness and honesty, responsible and dependable behavior, intelligence, friendliness, confidence without conceitedness, conversational skill, a sense of humor, and a pleasant personality ("fun to be with") (Hass, 1979; Lloyd, 1985; Roscoe, Diana, & Brooks, 1987). Older adolescents were more likely to rate "shares same interests" and "has set goals for the future" as important personal characteristics in choosing a dating partner. Conversely, younger adolescents gave greater weight to characteristics associated with popularity and social prestige, such as "dresses fashionably," "approved of by parents," "well-liked by many people," "gets along well with others," and "does not take drugs" (Roscoe, Diana, & Brooks, 1987).

**Steady Relationships.** About 20 percent of adolescent girls and boys have "gone steady" by the age of 15. Adolescents who begin dating earlier move to steady relationships sooner than later-dating or nondating peers. Having a steady relationship brings the adolescent one step closer to sexual intimacy. Involvement in steady relationships is linked with greater sexual experience, as well as to more permissive sexual attitudes (Thornton, 1990). The adolescent who begins going steady at too early an age is likely to miss a number of important developmental experiences. For one thing, same-sex friends are often replaced by the new romantic partner; in the process the young person may give up the important benefits of like-sex friendships discussed in the preceding section (Shulman, 1993). The young adolescent heavily involved in a romantic relationship may miss opportunities for social support from a same-sex friend during times of stress as well as the possibility of achieving a deeper understanding of himself or herself that may result from identification with a same-sex friend.

Moreover, when adolescents begin going steady while they are still emotionally and socially immature, the relationship itself is likely to have these qualities. Progress toward becoming mature, self-reliant persons in their own right may be jeopardized. They may use their relationship as a way of avoiding other developmental tasks. They also miss out on valuable opportunities to know, understand, and enjoy a wide variety of acquaintances of both sexes.

Girls who begin dating early (ages 11–14) are at a developmental disadvantage. Relative to their later-dating peers, they demonstrate lower self-esteem, immaturity, superficiality, and limited interests and friendships with other girls (Douvan & Adelson, 1966; Simmons et al., 1979). Early dating, combined with early pubertal development and entrance into a junior high school, puts girls at a significant risk for low self-esteem. Boys, on the other hand, seem to suffer no ill effects of dating early (Simmons et al., 1979).

**Stages in Dating Behavior.** Dating behavior generally proceeds through a progression of four steps (Padgham & Blyth, 1991). First, adolescents place themselves in situations where the other sex is likely to be found, such as at a mall. Second, adolescents participate in social gatherings that encourage interactions with the other sex, such as parties or dances. Third, group dating takes place in which mixed-sex groups of adolescents participate in social activities together, such as going to the movies. Finally, adolescents become involved in traditional dating activities, involving a couple (Padgham & Blyth, 1991).

In early adolescence dating functions largely as a source of recreation and enjoyment, a means of achieving or maintaining status with peers, and a way of developing social and interpersonal skills; younger adolescents are often self-conscious and somewhat anxious in their relationships with other-sex peers (Bell, 1988; Roscoe, Diana, & Brooks, 1987; Schofield, 1981). Only in late adolescence, with the advent of greater cognitive and emotional maturity, are genuinely intimate relationships likely to develop—relationships characterized by sensitivity and mutual understanding, freedom to reveal thoughts and feelings, emotional involvement, and trust and commitment (Laursen, 1996; Roscoe, Diana, & Brooks, 1987; Sharabany, Gershoni, & Hoffman, 1981).

Among girls, the capacity for intimacy in same-sex relationships is stronger than among boys. In both sexes, intimacy with the other sex increases across adolescence, with girls typically reporting higher intimacy in girl–boy relationships than do boys (see Figure 7.4) (Blyth, Hill, & Thiel, 1982; Laursen, 1996; Sharabany, Gershoni, & Hoffman, 1981). Adolescent girls are more likely than boys to report that they pursue boy–girl relationships to satisfy needs for intimacy (McCabe & Collins, 1979; Roscoe, Diana, & Brooks, 1987). Even in late adolescence, however, most dating relationships tend to be rather stereotyped and superficial and do not involve a

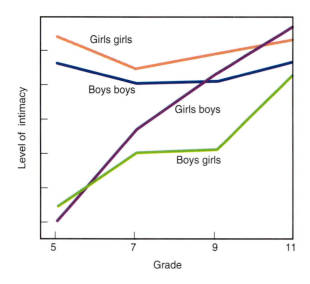

# Figure 7.4

Age differences in reported intimacy in same- and opposite-sex relationships. SOURCE: R. Sharabany, R. Gershoni, & J. Hoffman (1981). Girlfriend, boyfriend: Age and sex differences in intimate friendship. *Developmental Psychology,* **17,** 800–808. Copyright © 1981 by the American Psychological Association. Reprinted with permission.

high degree of intimacy (Kacerguis & Adams, 1980; Steinberg, 1985).

**Adolescent Love.** When American adolescents were asked whether they had ever been in love, 56 percent replied that they had, 39 percent that they had not, and 5 percent that they were not sure (Gallup, 1979). Boys between the ages of 12 and 15 were least likely to say that they had been in love (47 percent); girls between the ages of 16 and 18 were most likely to say that they had been in love. Among those who said that they had been in love at some point, slightly over half (52 percent) said that they were currently in love. Girls were more likely than boys to say that they were currently in love (61 percent versus 42 percent), with older girls having the highest frequency (69 percent) and younger boys the lowest (38 percent).

In some cases adolescent romances evolve gradually into stable, committed, long-term relationships; more often they involve an "intense emotional experience that lasts a while and then changes" (Bell, 1988, p. 70). Nevertheless, during the relationship the feelings can be just as vital, and the capacity for joy or despair just as great, as in adult love affairs. To be in love with someone who does not reciprocate is painful; it is "even more painful when you are still in love with someone who's no longer in love with you" (Bell, 1988, p. 71). For adults to dismiss adolescent "puppy love" as not serious (or even as amusing) indicates a lack of sensitivity as well as a short memory. Breaking up with a boyfriend or girlfriend can lead to genuine depression; one 17-year-old girl described her feelings as follows: "I just feel like my life's over, like there's never going to be anything to smile about again" (Bell, 1988, p. 71). Fortunately, in most cases the hurt gradually fades, but having a close friend to talk

to can be very helpful at such a time.

On the other hand, adolescents sometimes seek to maintain a relationship simply for the security involved, thereby limiting their own continued development: "It's comforting to know that you'll always have a date for the weekend and that someone cares about you and is choosing to spend time with you. But fear—fear of being alone, fear of going out with new people, fear of hurting the other person's feelings, fear of being rejected—is not a healthy basis for a relationship" (Bell, 1988, p. 72).

In brief, it appears that the young person who is best prepared for the responsibilities of adult life and for the emotional demands of marriage is one who is able to try out a variety of social and personal roles during adolescence. This involves establishing and maintaining relationships both with other-sex peers and with close friends of the same sex in the early years of adolescence and, in the later years of adolescence, having opportunities to develop meaningful, trusting, and mutually supportive relationships with a romantic partner.

# Adolescents and Marriage

In our society the role requirements associated with marriage are complex and often difficult to fulfill. They appear to be becoming more so as societal rewards for marriage have diminished and traditional role relationships have become less clearly defined and more controversial, particularly among more advantaged youth (Astin, et al., 1994; Bachman, Johnston, & O'Malley, in preparation; Dey, Astin, & Korn, 1991). Among American high school seniors in 1994, only about one-third agreed that "most people will have fuller and happier lives if they

choose legal marriage, rather than staying single, or just living with someone"—an idea that was virtually an article of faith in their parents' generation (see Table 7.5). Similarly, a *New York Times/CBS News* Poll conducted in 1994 on a U.S. national sample of 1055 teens aged 13 to 17 found that two-thirds would still be happy if they did not get married, but there was a striking sex difference. Substantially more girls (73 percent) than boys (61 percent) would not miss married life (Lewin, 1994).

Nevertheless, more than three-fourths of contemporary U.S. adolescents and youth plan to marry (85 percent of youth in Canada), and less than 5 percent think they are not likely to marry, with the remainder uncertain (Bachman, Johnston, & O,Malley, in preparation; Bibby & Posterski, 1992; Lewin, 1994). The responsibility of marriage, fear of the loss of freedom, and, among girls especially, interference with career plans and dissatisfaction with women's overall larger share of the domestic burden are some of the reasons adolescents have against marriage (Lewin, 1994; Norman & Harris, 1981). Although the importance attached to being married and raising a family declined dramatically between the late 1960s and the mid-1970s, it increased steadily in the 1980s and early 1990s.

For example, among all first-year female college students in the United States, the percentage citing "raising a family" as an essential or very important value declined from 77.8 percent in 1970 to only 56.8 percent in 1976; by 1994 it had risen to 71.7 percent. The corresponding figures for males were 63.5 percent in 1970, declining to 53.3 percent in 1974, and rising to 69.3 percent in 1994 (Astin et al., 1994). As may be seen, although significantly more women than men considered raising a family very important or essential in 1970, by 1994 this difference had almost vanished.

This similarity between the sexes in the desire to raise a family is also seen among younger teens aged 13 to 17. Nearly half of males (47 percent) and females (49 percent) said that they would miss it if they "don't have children" (Lewin, 1994).

Both the greater decline among women in the first half of the 1970s and the smaller subsequent increase probably reflect the increased importance of careers in women's value systems during the past 25 years (Astin et al., 1994). The percentage of women who desire administrative responsibility more than doubled during this period, and there were large increases in the number who wish to succeed in their own businesses, to be authorities in their fields, or to be well-off financially.

**Adolescent Marriages.**   The burdens of marriage are likely to be greatest for adolescents, who may still be struggling to complete their education, establish themselves in a vocation, or complete the process of identity formation. Typically, married adolescents are also economically insecure or dependent on parents for financial assistance, situations that may create additional problems.

Young married couples are under greater pressure than their single peers to meet complicated cultural demands, both in social relationships with others and in the increasingly complex and changing world of work. Along with the rapid increase in two-job families in recent years has come the need to balance these jobs with household work and child rearing; the result may be increased stress on the family.

In any marriage both husband and wife have to learn to cope with new restrictions on personal freedom, adjust their personal wishes and habits to those of their partner, and shift much of their emotional concern from themselves to their spouse and children. This can

Table **7.5** Agreement That Marriage is Important for Happiness, U.S. High School Seniors, 1994

|  | MALES | FEMALES |
| --- | --- | --- |
| Disagree | 18% | 28% |
| Mostly disagree | 12 | 14 |
| Neither | 31 | 27 |
| Mostly agree | 15 | 13 |
| Agree | 19 | 19 |

SOURCE: J. F. Bachman, L. D. Johnston, & P. M. O'Malley (in preparation). *Monitoring the future: Questionnaire responses from the nation's high school seniors, 1994.* Ann Arbor: Institute for Social Research, University of Michigan. By permission.

## 7.4 Girls' and Boys' Work–Family Expectations

### WHERE WILL THE TWAIN MEET?

The 1994 *New York Times/CBS News* Poll of teens aged 13 to 17 found that 86 percent of girls expected to work after marriage and only 7 percent expected to stay at home (the rest did not know). Had this poll taken place two or three decades ago, these expectations most certainly would have been different, with the majority of girls expecting to stay home. In view of the large proportion of women now in the labor force, these girls' responses are not so surprising. What was surprising was the gap between the girls' expectations and the expectations boys had for their future marriages. Fifty-eight percent of boys expected that their wives would work after marriage and 19 percent expected that their wives would stay home, with the rest unsure. As a group, many more boys than girls had visions of a traditional marriage, with the husband bringing home the income and the wife staying home to raise children and do the housework. As one boy said, "I'd rather my wife stayed home. Why? So I wouldn't have to do the cleaning" (Lewin, 1994, p. C10).

The debate over who does the housework and who brings home the bacon may very well end up a part of these young women's and men's future lives. After all, research shows that even among young couples with an egalitarian view of marriage, in which the husband makes an effort to share household tasks and child care, the burden of these responsibilities is still likely to fall most heavily on the wife, whether she is employed or not. This inequitable division of labor often becomes a source of marital conflict and dissatisfaction (Hochschild, 1989).

Follow-up interviews with some of the participants confirmed the girls' strong desire for a career and their recognition that household work is typically not equally distributed between husbands and wives. As one girl stated, "I think a career is the most important thing, then children, then marriage. I've always wanted to succeed in a work field, maybe something like being a marine biologist. I know I will work. If I get married, I would want it to be with someone who did as much of the housework as me" (Lewin, 1994, p. C10). Another girl stated, "Men will have to change, to keep up with women. If men don't involve themselves with things around the house women won't marry them. They'll wait and find someone who will" (Lewin, 1994, p. C10). This view did not mesh with the views of those boys who desired a 1950s-style marriage. As one boy said, "I think girls should do the cooking and cleaning because they're better at it, and boys should do the yard work and the planting. I know a lot of girls think it's real sexist to say they belong in the kitchen, and they think we should kick in on cleaning, but I think they're wrong. It's not a boy's job" (Lewin, 1994, p. C10).

The girls and boys in this sample agreed on one thing: the desirability of having one parent at home to take care of children. Both sexes believed that this would be better for children in the long run (Lewin, 1994). It would appear from the results of this poll that the next generation of marriages is no less likely than the present generation to experience difficulties in combining work and family life.

be particularly difficult for young people who are still preoccupied with the formation of their own identity. In the words of a young woman who married while still in high school,

Sometimes I wish I would have never married, had my baby and gotten older. I'm doing fine, I guess. I've never known any years that passed me by so very fast. I went straight from having

to be in the house when the lights went on to having to be in when the child cried or the husband called.

I don't know what's going on with me. Dick treats me good and we never really fight. He's always there when I need him but he's never there when I don't. Please try to tell me what's wrong. I still love him very much (Lindsay, 1985, p. 46).

# 7.5 Age Trends in Marriages Among Youth

In the past two decades there has been a steady increase in age at first marriage among both males and females (from 20.6 years for women and 22.5 years for men in 1970 to 23.7 years for women and 25.5 years for men in 1988, the last year for which data were available) (U.S. Bureau of the Census, 1994). For most young people, these figures reflect postponement of marriage, and not, as some have suggested, abandonment of marriage as an institution (after all, the vast majority of adolescents will eventually marry).

What accounts for the delay? One factor that clearly plays a role is the greater social and personal acceptability of sexual relationships between unmarried youth and young adults, especially those who are going steady or engaged. Many more young couples are living together or involved in fairly stable premarital relationships than ever before (Glick, 1984; U.S. Bureau of the Census, 1989). Increased rates of high school and college attendance also appear to contribute to the reduction in rates of adolescent marriage (Schulenberg & Ebata, 1994).

In addition, growing concern with material values and "making it," combined with the increased difficulty of achieving financial stability and such goals as home ownership in the face of in-creased costs, are leading many young people to postpone the responsibilities of marriage until they feel more secure.

Moreover, for many young people, especially young women, there is less pressure from peers to rush into marriage and parenthood and increased concern with achieving financial and social independence and becoming well-established in a career—that is, developing a social and vocational identity—before taking on the commitments of marriage and family life.

Finally, the rise in divorce rates and the amount of marital conflict observed by young people, not only among members of their parents' generation but among married peers who are struggling with their new responsibilities, may cause more young people to want to be sure of their decision before committing themselves to marriage.

Paradoxically, however, recent changes in the lifestyles and values of young people may portend greater marital stability within the next decade. Insofar as low income, low education, and early age at marriage increase the probability of eventual divorce, current trends away from these conditions are consistent with a favorable prognosis for future marital stability (Glick, 1984; Norton & Moorman, 1986).

In addition, our society's emphasis on marriage as a continuing romantic affair may attach unrealistic expectations to what is already a difficult emotional interaction. Considerable personal maturity and integration into other adult roles enhance a couple's chances of achieving a successful marriage. Adolescents themselves tend to agree with this statement; in one national survey, more than eight out of ten young people expressed the belief that a person should be over 20 before marrying (Lindsay, 1985) (see Box 7.5).

Adolescent marriages are often complicated by the fact that they are likely to have resulted from pregnancy. In the early 1960s, 26 percent of teen mothers (aged 15–17 years) who conceived out-of-wedlock married before the birth; in the late 1980s, this figure was 11 percent (AGI, 1994). Although most babies born to teen mothers are now born out-of-wedlock, premarital preg-nancy may lead some young people to marry someone they otherwise would not have chosen. Even when the choice is one they would ultimately have made, however, they have less time to become adjusted to each other and to the demands of marriage before undertaking the responsibilities of parenthood. A majority of young people would prefer to wait at least two years after marriage before having children, and actually do so (Bachman, Johnston, & O'Malley, in preparation; U.S. Bureau of the Census, 1994).

When we add to these considerations the facts that young married people are statistically more likely than people marrying at later ages to have lower intelligence test scores, lower school grades, and lower educational levels, to drop out of school, and to be employed at unskilled and semiskilled jobs, it is not surprising to find that adolescent marriages are two to three times more

likely to break up than those of couples who marry in their twenties (Astone & Upchurch, 1994; Edelman, 1987; Hayes, 1987). The younger the adolescent partners are when they marry, the greater the likelihood of divorce or legal separation. In 1985 one-third of women who had married before age 20 were divorced; the proportion declined steadily with increasing age at first marriage, reaching a low of 12 percent among women who first married at 30 or older (Norton & Moorman, 1986).

Premaritally pregnant adolescent girls are even more likely to suffer marital breakups (Furstenberg, Brooks-Gunn, & Morgan, 1987; Hayes, 1987). One Baltimore study found that three out of five premaritally pregnant mothers age 17 or younger were separated or divorced within six years of the marriage. One-fifth of the marriages were dissolved within 12 months, two and one-half times the proportion of broken marriages among classmates of the adolescent mothers who were not pregnant premaritally (Furstenberg, Brooks-Gunn, & Morgan, 1987). Even at the end of three years, the premaritally pregnant teenage brides were nearly twice as likely to have separated as their classmates. Teenage mothers who married the father before the child's delivery were more likely to stay married than those who did not marry until after the birth.

Nevertheless, significant numbers of adolescent marriages are successful. What makes the difference between those that end in divorce and the larger number that succeed despite the difficulties involved? Several factors appear to differentiate successful young marriages from those that end in failure, including higher educational levels among both partners, delayed pregnancy, previous dating experience with other potential partners, economic independence, parents who are supportive of the marriage, and interpersonal competence of the partners (Burchinal, 1965). Obviously, the larger the number of positive factors operating in a particular adolescent marriage, the greater its chances of survival; conversely, the larger the number of negative factors, the greater the likelihood of additional problems arising from the marriage (Burchinal, 1965; Lindsay, 1985).

The formidable obstacles faced by many young marriages, their demonstrably higher divorce rates, and the less-easily-documented identity foreclosure (an identity formed without the benefit of having explored alternatives) that may sometimes result offer considerable justification for not encouraging adolescent marriages. At the same time, it is important to realize that no matter what the circumstances and no matter how ill advised it may seem, adolescent marriage is not a crime.

Some schools have taken proactive approaches to make students aware of the realistic problems and demands of marriage. Marriage and family courses, for instance, might ask students to "marry" for a term, during which they learn to face such problems as working out a budget, obtaining housing, providing child care, facing random crises, and even obtaining a divorce. Schools may offer special services to pregnant teenagers and adolescent parents so that they can continue their education. In the United States, public schools are prohibited from barring pregnant students from attending classes. Some offer child care and career planning services, and may offer courses teaching infant care and parenting. Such approaches are geared toward facilitating better adjustment through a difficult transition and to increasing adolescents' chances for a better future.

# Summary

Peers play an important role in the psychological and social development of most children and adolescents. Relationships with peers during the adolescent years serve as prototypes for adult relationships in social relations, work, and interactions with members of the opposite sex. Adolescents are also more dependent on peer relations than younger children because ties to parents become looser as the young person gains greater independence. More than two out of three adolescents believe that a close friend understands them better than their parents do.

Adolescence may provide opportunities for repairing psychological damage incurred earlier. However, relations with peers during this vulnerable stage of development may also be harmful. The young person may be put down, laughed at, rejected, or pressured into behaviors he or she may regret.

Because of the heightened importance of the peer group during adolescence, motivation for conformity to the values, customs, and fads of peer culture increases during the preadolescent and early adolescent years, followed by a gradual but steady decline from middle through late adolescence. The need to conform may also vary with sex, socioeconomic status, relationships with parents, and personality factors.

Although it is commonly asserted that parental and peer-group values are incompatible and that an inevitable result of heightened dependence on the peer

group is a sharp decline in parental influence, this is not generally true. For one thing, there is usually considerable overlap between the attitudes of an adolescent's parents and those of his or her peers. Also, neither the influence of parents nor that of peers is all-encompassing. Peers are likely to be more influential in such matters as fashions in music, dress, language, and patterns of peer interaction. Parental influence is likely to be predominate in educational plans and underlying moral and social values. Recent studies have shown that, on average, during preadolescence and early adolescence conformity to parents tends to decline while conformity to peers rises. Not until middle and late adolescence do increases in overall autonomy occur, for only then does conformity both to parents and to peers decline. Even at an early age, however, some adolescents show a higher degree of overall autonomy than their peers.

During middle childhood and preadolescence, peer relations tend to center on neighborhood play groups and same-sex gangs. The adolescent's peer relations fall into three broad categories: the broader crowd or set, the smaller, more intimate clique, and individual friendships. As adolescence proceeds, the nature of peer groups changes, as do the functions they serve. Gradually cliques of one sex begin to interact with cliques of the other sex, leading to the formation of the adolescent crowd. Only in the next stage do we see the formation of genuinely heterosexual cliques, in which heterosexual interactions between individuals are initiated. Finally, in late adolescence couples and loosely associated groups of couples are formed. Same-sex friendships are maintained but become more stable and less intense.

Among the peer relationships of adolescents, friendships hold a special place: They are typically more intimate, involve more intense feelings, and are more open and honest than the friendships of earlier and later stages of life. Close friends can contribute to an adolescent's development in ways in which the broader peer group cannot. Adolescents of both sexes name close friends as the people with whom they are most likely to talk openly and share true feelings. Thus, it is not surprising to find that the main requirements for a friend are to be loyal and trustworthy and to provide support when it is needed. At their best, friendships may help young people learn to deal with their own feelings and those of others; they may also contribute to identity formation.

Friendships are most likely to develop between adolescents who are similar in terms of background, personality characteristics, and interests. However, sometimes an attraction of opposites occurs, in which an adolescent finds in a friend qualities that are felt to be desirable but are lacking in the self. Adolescent friendship patterns also vary with age, sex, and ethnicity. Friendships become more intimate and empathic in middle adolescence and more autonomously interdependent in late adolescence. Girls' friendships are typically deeper and more interdependent than those of boys. Black adolescents have more cross-race friendships and are less similar to their friends than are white adolescents.

An adolescent's personality characteristics, cognitive skills, and social behaviors affect his or her chances of being accepted by peers. Adolescents who are viewed favorably tend to make others feel accepted and involved, promote constructive interaction between peers, or plan and initiate interesting or enjoyable group activities. In contrast, a young person who is self-centered and inconsiderate and reacts to discomfiture with overaggressiveness, conceit, or demands for attention is likely to meet with active dislike and rejection.

Under favorable conditions going out, or dating, may serve a number of useful functions; among other things, it provides opportunities to meet members of the other sex and develop social and interpersonal skills. On the other hand, many of the characteristics of the so-called good date (e.g., superficial conversational skills and a bright, interested manner) appear to be irrelevant to the development of more genuine emotional relationships. Despite recent social changes, many traditional stereotypes (and many traditional anxieties) about dating appear to be alive and well.

Adolescents who begin going steady too early may not achieve some of the continuing benefits of like-sex friendships and may also limit their chances of developing into mature, self-reliant individuals. The young person who is best prepared for social and vocational responsibilities in adult life, and also for the emotional demands of marriage, has been able to try out a variety of social and personal roles during adolescence. This involves establishing and maintaining relationships both with other-sex peers and with close friends of the same sex in the early years of adolescence and, in the later years, opportunities to develop a meaningful, trusting, and mutually supportive relationship with an other-sex peer.

Adolescent marriages are two to three times more likely to fail than those of couples in their twenties because of a variety of social, psychological, and economic stresses (including, in some instances, premarital pregnancy). Nevertheless, a significant number of adolescent marriages can succeed if the young people receive appropriate parental and social support, including a chance to complete their education.

# Review Questions

1. Discuss the role played by peers in helping or hindering the adolescent's psychological and social development.

2. What is the developmental pattern in conformity during the adolescent years? What function does conformity serve? Give examples of conformity.

3. Are parental and peer influences on adolescent values and behavior necessarily in opposition? In which areas are the influences of parents likely to be stronger? In which are the influences of peers likely to be stronger?

4. Describe the structural changes in the nature of peer groups that occur as adolescence proceeds. Distinguish between a clique and a crowd.

5. How do close friendships help young people develop a sense of identity? How do friendship patterns vary with age, sex, and ethnicity?

6. What personality characteristics and behaviors are likely to lead to peer acceptance, neglect, or rejection? In what ways does peer acceptance, or lack thereof, influence subsequent adjustment?

7. What is the nature of other-sex relations in adolescence? Describe the nature and role of dating in early, middle, and late adolescence.

8. What qualities differentiate successful adolescent marriages from those that fail?

# Recommended Readings

Bell, R. (1988). *Changing bodies, changing lives* (rev. ed.). New York: Random House.

Brown, B. B. (1990). Peer groups and peer cultures. In S. S. Feldman & G. R. Elliott (Eds.), *At the threshold: The developing adolescent* (pp. 171–196). Cambridge, MA: Harvard University Press.

Bukowski, W. M., Newcomb, A. F., & Hartup, W. W. (Eds). (1996). *The company they keep: Friendship during childhood and adolescence.* New York: Cambridge University Press.

Konopka, G. (1985). *Young girls: A portrait of adolescence.* New York: Harrington Park Press.

Savin-Williams, R. C., & Berndt, T. J. (1990). Friendship and peer relations. In S. S. Feldman & G. R. Elliott (Eds.), *At the threshold: The developing adolescent* (pp. 277–307). Cambridge, MA: Harvard University Press.

Youniss, J., & Smollar, J. (1985). *Adolescent relations with mothers, fathers, and friends.* Chicago: University of Chicago Press.

P eers play a crucial role in the psychological and social development of most adolescents, especially in age-segregated, technologically advanced societies, in which entry into the adult world of work and family responsibility is increasingly delayed. Of course, peer influences do not begin in adolescence. From early childhood on, the peer group provides opportunities to learn how to interact with others, control social behavior, develop age-relevant skills and interests, and share problems and feelings (Berndt, 1992; Bukowski, Newcomb, & Hartup, 1996; Hartup & Overhauser, 1991; Savin-Williams & Berndt, 1990). But the role of peers is especially critical during adolescence. Relations with both same- and opposite-sex peers during the adolescent years come closer to serving as prototypes for adult relationships in social relations, work, and interactions with members of the opposite sex. The young man or woman who has not learned how to establish satisfactory relationships with peers by the time he or she reaches adulthood is likely to face serious obstacles in the years ahead.

Adolescents also become more dependent on peer relations than younger children as their ties to parents become looser and they gain greater independence. In addition, their relations with family members may be charged with conflicting emotions. Especially in the early years of adolescence, dependent yearnings exist alongside independent strivings, hostility is mixed with love, and conflicts occur over cultural values and social behavior. Consequently, many areas of the adolescent's inner life and outward behavior cannot readily be shared with parents.

Studies show that more than two out of three adolescents believe that a close friend understands them better than their parents do, that they are more "themselves" with that friend, and that they can learn more at this time in their life from that friend than from their parents (Bibby & Posterski, 1992; Youniss & Smollar, 1985). Parents, having grown distant from the emotional ups and downs of their own adolescence, may have difficulty understanding their adolescent children's problems, even though they make an effort to do so and are truly interested in the welfare of their children.

As we saw in Chapter 5, in some cases parental warmth and understanding may be lacking, as in the case of a 16-year-old girl who said of her relationship with her father, "I get along, but, I mean, we're really not that close. Like he's got his business and I've got my school work. He just doesn't seem interested in what I do" (Konopka, 1976, p. 69). In other cases there may be parental hostility, neglect, or exploitation. In such circumstances interested and competent peers may provide not only a means of escaping from a difficult family situation but a source of understanding and support as well. They may also serve as role models for achieving mutually rewarding interactions with others (Conger, 1979, 1991c; Hartup & Overhauser, 1991). As Peter Blos (1979a), Anna Freud (1958), and others have observed, adolescence may sometimes provide the last major opportunity for repairing psychological damage incurred during early and middle childhood and developing new and more rewarding relationships both with oneself and with others.

A mature, warm, interested, and, above all, nonexploitive adolescent peer may play a crucial role in helping a boy or girl gain a clearer self-concept, a feeling of personal worth, and renewed hope for the future. For example, consider the adolescent girl who is in a hostile, critical, and rejecting family—one in which the girl often hears from parents and siblings such comments as "You're stupid" or "There you go eating again." Warmth and support provided by a close relationship with another girl may well offset some of the negative consequences of this derogatory behavior. Or consider the adolescent boy who put all his effort into studying for an exam, only to obtain a poor grade, resulting in anger from his parents. The support of another boy who says, "It's okay. It's just one grade. You can try again," might be crucial in boosting this boy's mood and self-esteem. Where parent–adolescent relations are troubled, supportive peer relations may contribute to the adolescent's positive psychosocial adjustment (Gavazzi, Anderson, & Sabatelli, 1993).

Of course, there is another side to the coin. Relations with peers during this vulnerable stage of development may also be harmful. For example, the boy or girl who is put down, laughed at, or rejected in his or her initial efforts to establish sexual relationships or to join a high school clique may acquire anxious, avoidant responses that are difficult to extinguish. Moreover, adolescents may be pressured by peers into suspending their own better judgment and engaging in behaviors that they may later regret. Such behaviors can range from relatively minor improprieties to more serious, sometimes tragic incidents such as the destruction of school property, participation in hazing activities or initiation rites (for example, drinking such excessive amounts of alcohol that death occurs), or attacks on members of other social or ethnic groups. In such situations the adolescent's

t oday the school is the one major social institution other than the family with which nearly everyone is involved during the critical years of childhood and adolescence. Although this may seem entirely normal, in fact it is a relatively recent development. When North America was primarily an agrarian society, the level of educational skills required for economic survival was generally lower and the need for young people to help with farm work and other tasks was greater. In the United States in 1890, for instance, less than 7 percent of all 14- to 17-year-olds were enrolled in school; by 1900, this figure had risen, but only to 11.4 percent (U.S. Department of Education, 1980). The primary institutional settings in which most young people grew up were the home and the workplace. There were fewer occupations from which to choose, and children typically followed in their parents' footsteps.

As society became more complex, the influence of other social institutions, including the family, the workplace, and the church, on young people's development was reduced. Responsibility for the development not only of academic skills but also of other vital capabilities—including the ability to manage one's own affairs and life plans effectively—increasingly shifted to the schools. How well the schools are meeting these varied responsibilities, and whether they can reasonably be expected to accomplish such a diverse mission, are crucial questions in today's rapidly changing world.

## The Quality of Education in the United States

Let us begin by asking how well American schools (public comprehensive schools) are meeting their traditional responsibility for developing basic academic skills. A number of widely publicized reports issued in the 1980s concluded that they were not performing this task well enough (Carnegie Council, 1989; Congressional Budget Office [CBO], 1987). In 1983 the report

of the National Commission on Excellence in Education, *A Nation at Risk,* stated that "the educational foundations of our society are presently being eroded by a rising tide of mediocrity that threatens our very future as a nation and a people. What was unimaginable a generation ago has begun to occur—others are matching and surpassing our educational attainments" (National Commission on Excellence, 1983, p. 5). In 1986 another influential report, *A Nation Prepared: Teachers for the 21st Century,* demanded "an improved supply of young people with the knowledge . . . and skills to make the nation once again fully competitive" (Task Force on Teaching, 1986, p. 2).

These reports and others pointed to a series of studies indicating that youth in the United States were performing poorly on a wide variety of measures of academic performance, both in relation to the youth of other industrialized countries and, in some cases, to earlier generations of youth (Boyer, 1983; CBO, 1987; National Commission on Excellence, 1983). On most standardized tests, U.S. high school students scored lower in the 1970s than they had when Sputnik, the Russian satellite, was launched in the late 1950s, spurring a renewed concern for excellence in the United States. Among 17-year-olds who were still enrolled in school in the 1970s, only 50–60 percent (depending on the year of assessment) were able to solve simple problems involving percentages (e.g., "A hockey team won 5 of its 20 games. What percentage of the games did it win?") (National Assessment of Educational Progress, 1979). An intensive nationwide investigation conducted by the National Assessment of Educational Progress (1981, 1986) found evidence of a continuing decline in reading and writing skills between 1970 and 1980 among both 13- and 17-year-olds.

## Recent Trends

Has academic performance improved in the years since the 1983 report, *A Nation at Risk?* In some respects it has, but not nearly enough to meet the increasing need for informed citizens and productive workers who can compete effectively in the world of the late 1990s and beyond (see Chapter 9).

In an effort to accelerate educational improvement, the President of the United States and the nation's governors in 1989 adopted an ambitious set of six educational goals (expanded to eight by Congress in 1994) that should be achieved by the year 2000 (*America 2000,* 1991; National Educational Goals Panel, 1994). These goals range from ensuring that all children start school intel-

lectually and physically ready to learn to establishing better teacher preparation, increased parental participation, and freedom of schools from drugs and violence. Goal 5 states that "By the year 2000, the United States will be first in the world in mathematics and science achievement." Based on progress to date, this will not be easy. Let us look at the record.

**Science.**   Although the science achievement scores of 17-year-olds improved in the decade between 1982 and 1992 after more than a decade of steady decline, 1992 scores remained below those of 1969 (see Figure 8.1). According to the National Assessment of Educational Progress (Mullis et al., 1994), less than half of the nation's 17-year-olds display some detailed scientific knowledge and an ability to evaluate the appropriateness of scientific procedures, and only 10 percent are able to integrate specialized scientific information. Less than 10 percent have the knowledge needed to undertake college-level science courses (Mullis & Jenkins, 1988; Mullis et al., 1994; *National excellence,* 1993).

These findings are reinforced by the results of a recent international science assessment, which found that United States students are among the lowest achievers in all of the participating countries (International Association, 1988; *National excellence,* 1993). For example, in one recent comprehensive study, 13-year-olds in the United States ranked thirteenth in science achievement among fifteen participating countries (Lapointe, Mead, & Askew, 1992). Perhaps most discouraging, the further U.S. students progress in school, the greater the discrepancy between their performance and that of students in other countries (*National excellence,* 1993; Stevenson & Stigler, 1992; Stevenson, Lee, & Stigler, 1986).

**Mathematics.**   The 1992 National Assessment of Educational Progress found only slightly more encouraging results in mathematics performance (Mullis et al., 1994). Despite a decrease between 1973 and 1982, the mathematics scores of 17-year-olds in 1992 slightly exceeded those obtained in 1973 (see Figure 8.1). Moreover, among 13-year-olds and, especially, 9-year-olds, 1992 scores exceeded earlier scores by wider margins than among 17-year-olds, suggesting that the future picture for 17-year-olds may continue to improve. At present, most 17-year-old students (97 percent) are able to carry out the four basic functions of addition, subtraction, multiplication, and division, and to apply them in simple situations such as making change (Mullis et al., 1994). Less than 60 percent show an understanding of number systems (computing with

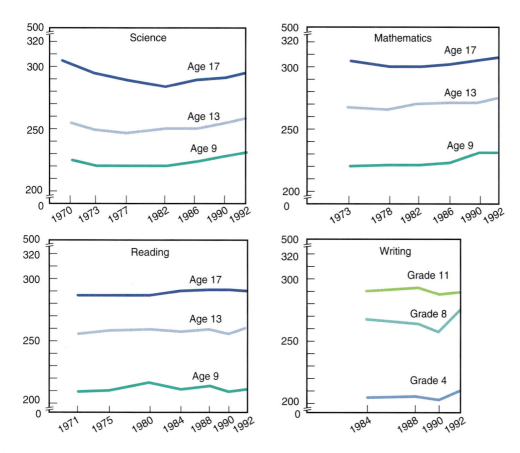

# Figure 8.1

National trends in average achievement in science, mathematics, reading, and writing.

SOURCE: National Assessment of Educational Progress (NAEP) (1994). Science, Mathematics, Reading, and Writing Trend Assessments, 1992.

decimals and percents) and an ability to solve simple linear equations.

Only 7 percent are capable of complex problem-solving and algebra, which involve applying a wide range of reasoning skills to multistep problems. Students in this group can solve routine problems involving fractions and percents, recognize properties of basic geometric figures, and work with exponents and square roots. Despite improvements during the past decade in lower-order skills, there has been virtually no change in the percentage of students able to function at these more advanced levels. Consequently, increasing numbers of entering college students require remedial courses in mathematics, and many businesses are forced to devote a disproportionate amount of their resources to training in basic skills (*Hudson Institute,* 1987; Mullis et al., 1991, 1994).

As in the case of science achievement, international comparisons highlight the seriousness of this situation. In

a 1992 study of mathematical performance among 13-year-olds in fifteen countries, United States students ranked next to last (Lapointe, Mead, & Askew, 1992). Despite impressive exceptions, when the mathematics performance of the top 1 percent of United States high school students (those taking advanced placement courses) was compared with those of their counterparts in thirteen other countries, U.S. students ranked thirteenth in algebra and twelfth in geometry and calculus (*National excellence,* 1993) (see Box 8.1).

High school students in the United States still study only about one-half to one-third as much science and mathematics as their counterparts in Japan, Germany, and other developed countries, including the Soviet Union, and consequently they know far less about these subjects (Carnegie Council, 1989; Fiske, 1987a). A National Science Teachers Association survey found that 7000 of the nation's high schools offer no courses in physics, 4000

## CHAPTER EIGHT

# 8.1 Perfect Performance for a United States Math Team

Although U.S. high school students generally score well below their counterparts in other developed countries on standardized tests of achievement, talented students can achieve academic excellence with the help of good public schools and strong parental support. The six students shown here with the imposing bronze statue of Alfred Einstein in front of the National Academy of Sciences in Washington were chosen to represent the United States in the 1994 International Mathematics Olympiad in Hong Kong. They were selected because of their top scores in a national mathematics competition, the American High School Math Exam, and a number of follow-up tests.

To the astonishment of the judges, the entire team achieved perfect scores on a 9-hour test of advanced algebra, geometry, and numbers theory—the first time this has occurred in the competition's thirty-five-year history. Their flawless performance swept them to victory over teams from sixty-eight countries.

Team member Jeremy Bem is the son of psychologist Sandra Bem, an authority on sex-role identity. No United States team at the competition has ever included girls, although adolescent

girls commonly participate on other countries' teams, and two girls obtained perfect scores on this year's test. "America is just behind other countries in getting girls to perform at the highest level," said Professor Bem, who teaches women's studies at Cornell University (*The New York Times*, 1994, July 20, p. A16).

offer no courses in chemistry, and 2000 offer no courses in biology (Fiske, 1987b).

**Reading and Writing.** In reading, the performance of 17-year-olds in the United States improved modestly between 1971 and 1984, but has leveled off since then (see Figure 8.1). In writing skills, 11th graders showed no improvement between 1984 and 1992, although significant gains did occur among 8th graders and 4th graders between 1990 and 1992 (see Figure 8.1).

Currently, however, only a little over one-third of 11th graders are able to write reasonably complete and informative responses on tasks such as filling out a job application. Only 2 percent are capable of effective, coherent writing. In sum, far too few of today's high school graduates are prepared to meet the needs of an

increasingly complex society for young people who can understand, analyze, and communicate relatively complicated information (Applebee, Langer, & Mullis, 1986; Mullis et al., 1994; *National excellence*, 1993). According to the chair of the Xerox Corporation, one out of three major corporations already must provide new workers with basic reading, writing, and arithmetic courses, at a cost of $25 billion a year (Kearns, 1987, cited in Dossey et al., 1988, p. 8; *National excellence*, 1993).

**A Common Culture?** Finally, if we believe that an informed citizenry should share a common culture and some knowledge of its history and the forces that have shaped it, the picture is at best ambiguous. A U.S. national assessment of 11th-grade students' knowledge of history and literature was conducted in 1986 (Ravitch &

Finn, 1987). The results can be interpreted as indicating that "the glass is half full or half empty." Although the questions dealt with "fundamental material that students of this age might reasonably be expected to know" (Ravitch & Finn, 1987, p. 7), only 54 percent of the history questions and 52 percent of the literature questions were answered correctly (see Box 8.2). It does not appear likely that this situation has changed markedly since 1986, although about 10 percent more 17-year-olds in 1992 than in 1984 reported reading biographies, science books, poems, plays, and books about other places (Mullis et al., 1994).

## Possible Reasons for These Trends

The reasons for the declines in academic performance during the 1960s and 1970s, and for subsequent limited improvements, are not completely clear (CBO, 1987; *Everybody counts,* 1989; Lapointe, Mead, & Askew, 1992; National Educational Goals Panel, 1994; *National excellence,* 1993; Shea, 1994).

Among the factors that have been cited as contributing to declining test scores and performance are the following:

- A decline in academic standards (e.g., watered-down curricular requirements, less homework, grade inflation, easier textbooks, lower teacher expectations and too few teachers prepared to teach the subjects their students need).
- Increased alcohol and drug use, school violence, and delinquency; and higher prevalence of separation, divorce, and single parenthood.
- Less mental stimulation in the home and other nonschool settings, including many thousands of hours spent watching television at the expense of reading.
- Changes in the socioeconomic mix of students attending school, particularly at the upper secondary school and college levels.
- Increases in the percentage of all students who choose to take tests such as the Scholastic Aptitude Test, thereby diluting the scores of the highest-scoring students. Beginning in the mid-1970s, the share of high school graduates taking the SAT grew sharply, from 31 percent in 1976 to 33 percent in 1980 and 41 percent in 1995 (College Board, 1995; College Entrance Examination Board [CEEB], 1988, 1994; CBO, 1987; Shea, 1994, 1995b). Until recently, this was associated with a stagnation in average SAT scores (see Figure 8.2).

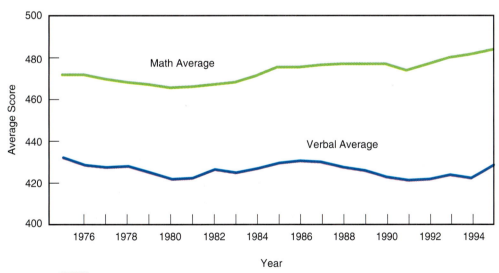

## Figure 8.2

Average SAT scores for college-bound seniors, 1975–1995.

SOURCE: The College Board (1995). *National Report: College-Bound Seniors.* New York: The College Board. By permission.

## 8.2 What do Adolescents Know?

In 1986 Diane Ravitch and Chester E. Finn, Jr., in collaboration with the National Assessment of Educational Progress, conducted a national survey of 8000 11th-graders' core knowledge in the areas of history and literature. As noted in the text, only 54 percent of the history questions and 52 percent of the literature questions were answered correctly. Among the survey's findings were the following:

In history, four out of five students knew that the Bill of Rights guarantees free speech and religion. Sixty to 80 percent identified Lincoln as the author of the Emancipation Proclamation, knew the meaning of the term *Holocaust,* and knew that the United States had been provoked into entering World War I by German submarine attacks on American ships. On the other hand, less than one-third knew in what twenty-year period Lincoln was president or in what half-century the Civil War occurred. Closer to the present, only four in ten knew that the controversy surrounding Senator Joseph P. McCarthy focused on investigations of people whom he suspected of engaging in Communist activities. Perhaps most surprising, only 22 percent of girls and 23 percent of boys recognized Betty Friedan and Gloria Steinem as leaders of the women's movement in the 1970s (Ravitch & Finn, 1987).

In literature, two-thirds or more of the adolescents surveyed were familiar with *Robinson Crusoe,* *The Adventures of Huckleberry Finn, Uncle Tom's Cabin,* and *Romeo and Juliet.* But only 20–25 percent could associate De Tocqueville, Dostoyevsky, Joseph Conrad, Ibsen, William James, or Thomas Hardy with their principal works. Less than 40 percent were familiar with the best-known works of Steinbeck, Orwell, and Hemingway (Ravitch & Finn, 1987).

Adolescents' knowledge of geography is also surprisingly incomplete. In a 1989 Gallup Organization survey conducted in 10 countries, participants were asked to identify unnamed places on a world map (such as Vietnam). Americans aged 18–24 scored in last place, well below the Soviet Union, Canada, and Mexico (see Figure B8.2). Nearly one in four Americans (across all ages) could not identify the Pacific Ocean. The United States was the only nation in which youth performed below the level of adults aged 55 years and older (Grosvenor, 1989).

Thomas Jefferson was convinced that history "by apprising [people] of the past will enable them to judge of the future" (quoted in Ravitch & Finn, 1987, p. vii). It may be argued that literature and geography are just as important. If the above statistics are any indication of the preparedness of youth for the continuing demands of personal growth and responsible citizenship, we, adolescents, and schools have a long way to go.

---

Conversely, factors that are cited as contributing to recent limited gains include the following:

- A narrowing of the "gender gap" in all ethnic groups, reflecting the fact that girls are taking more academically challenging courses in high school. Although girls continue to have lower verbal scores (421 vs. 425) and mathematics scores (460 vs. 501) than boys, since 1987 girls have gained six points on boys in each part of the SAT (College Board, 1995; CEEB, 1994; Shea, 1995).
- Larger percentage increases in the scores obtained by minorities, including African Americans, Mexican Americans, Puerto Ricans, and Asian Americans in the past decade and a half, although (with the excep-

tion of Asian-American scores in mathematics), absolute scores remain lower than those of whites (College Board, 1995) (see Figure 8.3).
- Long-term positive effects of Head Start and other childhood education programs and, in some instances, more rigorous academic demands and improved student attitudes and motivation (CBO, 1987; Putka, 1988; Shea, 1994).

### Schooling for What?

Although much remains to be learned about the educational effects, positive or negative, of these and other

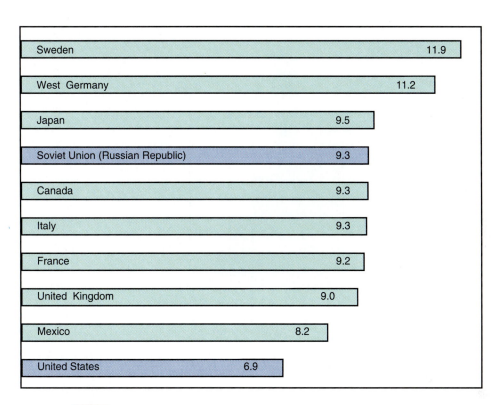

## Figure B8.2

Average number of correct responses to sixteen questions.

From G. M. Grosvenor (1989). Our year in review: Superpowers not so super in geography. *National Geographic,* **176,** 816–821. Courtesy, National Geographic Society, 1989.

factors, one thing seems clear: No single factor in itself is adequate to explain recent trends. But whatever the ultimate findings regarding the academic performance of American students and the variables contributing to them, there is widespread agreement that the school experience of many young people leaves much to be desired. This is so not only for the poor, who are generally at the greatest disadvantage, but for more advantaged students as well.

Many public schools, including many middle-class schools, tend to concentrate on what Charles Silberman (1970) called education for docility. They place excessive emphasis on order, discipline, and conformity at the expense of self-expression, intellectual curiosity, creativity, and the development of a humane, sensitive individual (Carnegie Council, 1989; *Everybody counts,* 1989; Lapointe, Mead, & Askew, 1992; *National excellence,* 1993). Because adolescents are viewed as harder to control than younger children, junior high schools tend to be even more authoritarian than elementary schools. This is particularly ironic because it is during the junior high school years that cognitive changes open up the possibility of new intellectual and cultural horizons for the developing young person. Yet as Seymour Sarason (1983) noted a decade ago in *Schooling in America,* too many schools are still "uninteresting places," at least partly because schooling has been viewed traditionally as something to be imposed on children rather than as a joint venture in intellectual exploration.

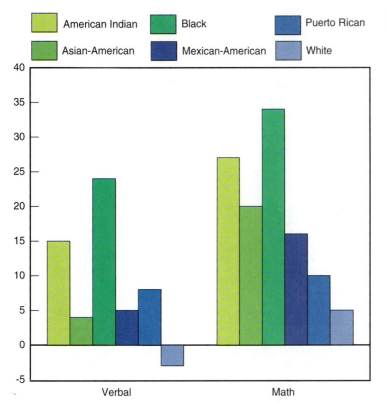

American Indian | Black | Puerto Rican
Asian-American | Mexican-American | White

**Figure 8.3**

Average point increases in SAT scores, 1976–1995.

SOURCE: The College Board (1995). *National Report: College-Bound Seniors.* New York: The College Board. By permission.

Obviously, not all schools fit this rather dismal picture. A growing number (though still too few) are developing competency-based curricula and innovative learning programs designed to meet the needs of students—including gifted students—from a variety of backgrounds. They are attempting to combine the development of core knowledge and skills with exciting and creative experiences in the arts, sciences, and humanities, and are challenging students to work at the peak of their capacities, to think for themselves, and, perhaps most important, to learn how to learn (Carnegie Council, 1989; *Everybody counts,* 1989; Sarason, 1983). Gifted students, especially, need greater flexibility to go at their own pace (Boyer, 1983; *National excellence,* 1993). Only a minority of schools currently "provide their most talented students with advanced learning opportunities, mentors, extracurricular activities based on students' special interests, or other opportunities for developing their potential" (*National excellence,* 1993, p. 21).

One of the mistakes some critics make is to assume that improving basic skills requires conformity, docility, and the elimination of creative activities such as art, music, and theater. Comparative studies of Japanese and American secondary education indicate that the one area in which American students have an edge over their Japanese peers is creativity and the ability to think for themselves (Tharp, 1987). As the results of some innovative programs are demonstrating, creativity and high academic standards are not incompatible.

## Education for Inequality

Even more troubling than inadequacies in the average school is the disparity among schools in numerous important characteristics, ranging from physical facilities, equipment, and curricular strength to teacher and pupil composition (Boyer, 1983; Schorr, 1988). Before the rapid increases in urbanization and geographic mobility that have occurred in recent decades, a majority of young people lived in smaller cities and towns and on farms, where the quality of education was more evenly distributed geographically and socioeconomically (if not always racially). Students from varying socioeconomic backgrounds were more likely to attend the same or similar high schools, to interact socially and academically, and to receive similar educational experiences. This is no longer the case: The differences between a wealthy suburban high school and its counterpart in the inner city are so great as to make broad statements about what is wrong with contemporary American education misleading and even, in some cases, irrelevant.

Many schools in wealthy suburban areas are well-equipped with libraries, computers, and modern physical facilities. In contrast, as many as one-third of U.S. schools are in physical disrepair and are seriously deficient in textbooks, support services, and even basic supplies and equipment.

A 1995 report to Congress by the General Accounting Office found that as many as one-third of United States schools are in such poor repair that the students attending them are being housed in unsuitable or unsafe conditions. Conditions putting children at risk include asbestos and flaking lead paint, rotting roof beams, broken plumbing, bad lighting, and inadequate heating and ventilation. Many of these schools are also seriously deficient in textbooks, libraries and computers, and basic supplies and equipment. They are far more likely than schools in affluent areas to have inexperienced or poorly trained teachers and a lack of support services and staff. Moreover, many inner-city students are exposed daily to drug pushers, gangs, and threats of physical violence, or, in some cases, to the danger of being shot on their way to or from school, or at school. Later in this chapter we will consider the needs and experiences of adolescents from disadvantaged backgrounds and what can be done to improve their opportunities.

## Do Schools Make a Difference?

In the 1970s a number of large-scale studies concluded that schools make no difference, or only a minimal difference, in the subsequent educational and occupational attainments of students (Averch et al., 1974; Bachman & O'Malley, 1978; Coleman et al., 1966; Jencks et al.,

1972). Instead, these studies asserted, what makes a difference are the home environment, the abilities the child is born with, and other personal characteristics (such as motivation and curiosity) that the child brings to school in the first place.

As we shall see, there can be little argument that factors other than the school itself play an important role both in the educational stimulation of children and adolescents and in their subsequent educational and vocational attainments. Socioeconomic status, home and community background, and parents' educational level and involvement are as clearly related to educational and vocational aspirations and accomplishments as the student's ability (Entwisle, 1990; Mullis & Jenkins, 1988; Useem, 1991). After these variables are taken into account, it is difficult to identify school attributes that make a difference (Entwisle, 1990). This does not mean, however, that schools may not play a crucial role.

One reason that a number of studies have found little effect of schools may be in the similarities among many public elementary and secondary schools (Good & Weinstein, 1986). The content and approaches to teaching (such as teacher-dominated instruction, little group work, similar grading methods, the division of schooling into subjects and periods) and even the basic structural features of schools (such as course offerings, laboratories, libraries, and classrooms) are often very similar from one school to another (Bachman & O'Malley, 1978, p. 51), making it more difficult to find measures that differentiate schools enough to produce varied student outcomes.

## School Processes

Another possible explanation, however, has to do with the *kinds* of school variables used in these studies. Most have assessed dimensions of schools such as average socioeconomic status, school size, teacher–student ratios, and physical facilities. Because these dimensions are so broad in characterizing the school climate, the extent to which they are related to student behavior is limited. However, when the potential effects of **school process** variables— what goes on *in* schools—have been examined, differences in educational outcomes have been found (Rutter et al., 1979). In a large-scale study of twelve schools in inner London, child psychiatrist Michael Rutter and his colleagues measured characteristics of pupils and their families at the time of entry into secondary school so as to separate preexisting characteristics from the effects of secondary schooling. These preexisting characteristics included verbal reasoning skill, parental occupation, and teachers' ratings of student behavior. Outcome measures included behavior in school, regularity of attendance, the proportion of students who stayed in school beyond the required age, success on public examinations, and delinquency rates.

Several specific school processes turned out to be quite important predictors of student outcomes. They included homework assignments, teachers' expectations, total teaching time spent on lessons, percentage of teacher time spent in interaction with the class, provision of rewards and incentives (coupled with less emphasis on punishment), provision of a pleasant and comfortable environment, provision of opportunities for responsibility in school life, and continuity of teachers and staff. As the authors point out, all of these factors may be under the control of school staff.

A key aspect of Rutter's study is its focus on *processes,* or the ways in which various factors may directly influence students. It was also the first study to provide information on the relative importance of different types of variables. More recent studies by other investigators have provided further evidence of the importance of a variety of school processes (Entwisle & Hallinan, 1991; Wigfield & Eccles, 1995). Assigning students to particular ability-based learning groups, or tracks, is one such process (see Box 8.3).

## Attributes of the School Environment

**School Size.** In the latter half of this century, the number of students enrolled in public high schools (school size) rose dramatically, both as a function of increasing urbanization and the philosophy that larger schools would offer more to students (Entwisle, 1990; Minuchin & Shapiro, 1983). But is bigness really better?

Studies by Roger Barker, Paul Gump, and others found that because of more opportunities and greater encouragement, students in smaller high schools were more likely than those in large high schools to participate in a variety of school activities and to hold positions of responsibility in school organizations (Barker & Gump, 1964; Boyer, 1983; Wicker, 1968). As a result, students in small schools were more likely than those in large schools to report that involvement in school activities had helped them develop skills or abilities, gain more confidence in themselves, prove themselves, feel needed, gain a sense of accomplishment, and learn how to work closely with others (Simmons & Blyth, 1987; Wicker, 1968).

These results are consistent with findings that in all instances performers (students who were actively and responsibly involved in an activity) reported more gains than nonperformers (students who were only marginally involved or were spectators) in both large and small schools. Because small schools have a larger percentage of performers participating in a larger number of activities (Gump, 1966), it could be predicted that they would show more gains.

Probably partly because of their greater participation in school activities and their greater sense of being needed and being important to the success of those activities, marginal students in small schools were less likely to drop out of school than marginal students in large schools (despite comparable IQs, grades, and home backgrounds).

Finally, studies show that compared with large schools, small schools are more orderly and coherent, they tend to have lower crime rates, and students are less likely to be victimized by peers (Blyth, Hill, & Smyth, 1981; Boyer, 1983; Garbarino, 1980). From the teacher's perspective, smallness might be more desirable as well, given that in small schools there is more face-to-face interaction among teachers and the administration (Bidwell & Quiroz, 1991).

The principal advantage of large schools is the greater variety of courses they offer. However, it takes a lot of added size to yield a little added variety (Gump, 1966). In the matter of school size, as in so many other areas of contemporary society, it appears that the slogan "bigger is better" is questionable. A possible answer for schools that are already too big may be to organize themselves into smaller units—"schools-within-a-school"—in order to "establish a more cohesive, more supportive social setting for all students" (Boyer, 1983, p. 235).

## 8.3 School Tracking

### WHO DOES IT BENEFIT?

Tracking, which places students into instructional groups based on ability, is a common practice in secondary schools. Most often, students are assigned to English and math tracks, but tracking may also occur in other subject areas, and it may be used to funnel students into college- or work-bound paths of instruction (Hallinan, 1994). The argument behind tracking is that it increases teaching effectiveness and facilitates learning by allowing teachers to direct their instruction toward the students' levels and needs (Hallinan, 1991).

Why, then, has tracking created a controversy in the educational literature? First, tracking creates inequalities in educational opportunities. Students in higher-level tracks may be assigned to the best teachers and may experience the best instruction, they obtain a larger share of the school's resources, and they experience higher standards (and incentives) for achievement (Hallinan, 1991; Rosenbaum, 1991). As a consequence, students in lower-level tracks may experience a loss of motivation and self-esteem, whereas students in the higher-level tracks become more academically motivated (Oakes, 1985). (In at least one school in the 1970s, the lower-level track was labeled "below-average," and all students in the school knew it). Second, assignment to tracks may be influenced by the backgrounds of the students, including socioeconomic status, race, and gender. One study found that students from lower-income families were more likely to be placed in lower-level tracks (Hallinan, 1991); such placements might then exaggerate the gap in learning opportunities between these students and their more fortunate peers.

Students in more advanced or college-bound tracks (usually those who are assessed as being of medium- to high-ability) make the strongest achievement gains, they evaluate their own intelligence and academic abilities more positively, and they associate more with academically oriented peers, as compared to their counterparts in no track at all (Fuligni, Eccles, & Barber, 1995; Hallinan, 1994; Rosenbaum, 1991). Low-ability students, on the other hand, are better off in terms of long-term achievement when they are placed in a more challenging track or no track at all rather than in a low-ability track (Fuligni, Eccles, & Barber, 1995). As it is usually done, then, tracking may benefit the most able students while it costs the least able. To be sure, there is a great deal of variability across schools in the type and number of tracks, the methods by which students are assigned to tracks, the quality of instruction within tracks, and the degree of student flexibility in switching tracks. These differences act to increase or decrease the inequities created by tracking (Rosenbaum, 1991). The challenge to schools is to track their own progress, carefully evaluating assignments to tracks and student experiences and outcomes. This is the only way to maximize the benefits of tracking for all students.

Currently, a student body of 500–1000 is seen to be most desirable (Entwisle, 1990).

## School Transitions

The transition from elementary to junior high school is an important event in the lives of most younger adolescents. Instead of having one main teacher and a relatively small, stable set of classmates, new seventh graders are catapulted into a large bureaucratic maze "with teachers, classrooms, and often classmates constantly changing over the course of the day" (Simmons & Blyth, 1987; Simmons et al., 1987). Many are likely to feel anonymous—that they know nobody and are known by nobody (Blyth, Simmons, & Carlton-Ford, 1983). To complicate matters, the educational transition to secondary school is likely to coincide with other major changes in the young person's life, including the onset of puberty and changing social expectations (Carnegie Council, 1989; Conger, 1979; Fenzel, Blyth & Simmons, 1991; Simmons et al., 1987).

The school transition experience could be affected by the size of the schools adolescents are leaving and entering. In one study conducted in Australia, adolescents *about to move* from a small to a large school (small–large) had higher expectations for positive experiences with schoolwork and older kids than did those moving from a large elementary school to a large secondary school (large–large) (Cotterell, 1992). After the actual transition, however, those who moved from a small school were significantly more anxious and enjoyed school less than did those who moved to a large school from a large school. Students moving from a medium-size elementary to a medium-size secondary school (medium–medium) fell between the other two groups (see Figure 8.4).

In another study, adolescents making the transition to junior high school were compared with peers who remained in elementary and middle school through the 9th grade. Girls in transitional groups were found to suffer a decrease in self-esteem and boys' grade point averages decreased. Both girls and boys engaged in fewer extracurricular activities compared with nontransitional students (Simmons et al., 1979). Other studies have found an initial decline in grades (Berndt & Hawkins,

1985; Hirsch & Rapkin, 1987) and, at least initially, a decline in self-esteem that rebounds by the end of grade 7 (Wigfield & Eccles, 1994).

Although there is agreement that school transitions in early adolescence are often associated with a reduction in the perceived quality of junior high school life, as well as a decrease in commitment to school and a deterioration in the social climate of the classroom (Berndt & Hawkins, 1985; Hirsch & Rapkin, 1987; Wigfield & Eccles, 1994), adolescents still have more positive than negative comments to make about their new schools after the transition (Berndt & Mekos, 1995). One study suggested, however, that a less supportive school climate, declines in extracurricular participation, and decreases in school involvement may be especially pronounced and long-lasting in urban schools attended by poor youth (Seidman et al., 1994).

How stressful or difficult the junior high transition is depends largely on how many other potential stresses the young person is encountering and on the extent to which he or she finds social support in the school setting (from peers and teachers) and in the home (Berndt & Hawkins, 1985; Lord, Eccles, & McCarthy, 1994; Simmons et al., 1987). In a well-designed study of students in the Milwaukee public schools, Roberta Simmons and her colleagues demonstrated that the more other life transitions (early individual dating, moving to a new neighborhood, and major family disruptions such as death or divorce) coincide with the transition to junior high school, the greater the adverse effect (Simmons et al., 1987). For example, among 7th-grade girls, self-esteem, grade point average, and participation in extracurricular activities were all lowest for those who were facing the greatest number of life transitions (see Figure 8.5). Similar results were obtained for boys, except in the area of self-esteem, where no significant relationship was found.

In discussing their results, the investigators call attention to the adolescent's need for an "arena of comfort:"

If the child is comfortable in some environments, life arenas, and role relationships, then discomfort in another arena should be able to be tolerated and mastered. Children appear less able to cope if at the same time they are uncomfortable with their bodies because of physical changes, with family because of changes in family constellation, with home because of a move, with school because of great discontinuity in the nature of the school environment, and with peers because of the emergence of opposite-sex relationships and the disruption of prior peer

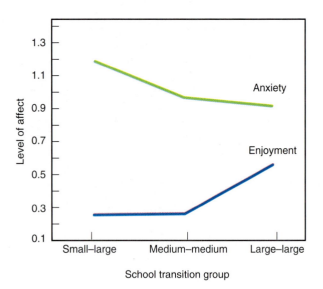

**Figure** 8.4

Higher anxiety and lower enjoyment among adolescents who moved from small to large schools.
From J. L. Cotterell (1992). School size as a factor in adolescents' adjustment to the transition to secondary school. *Journal of Early Adolescence,* **12,** 28–45, Copyright © 1992 by Sage. Adapted by permission of Sage Publications, Inc.

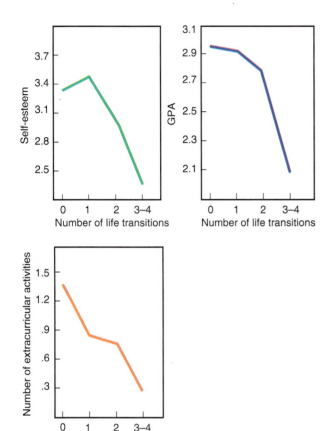

**Figure** 8.5

Girls' self-esteem, GPA, and extracurricular activities decline as life transitions increase. From R. G. Simmons, R. Burgeson, S. Carlton-Ford, & D. A. Blyth (1987). The impact of cumulative change in early adolescence. *Child Development,* **58,** 1220–1234. By permission.

networks. There needs to be some arena of life or some set of role relationships with which the individual can feel relaxed and comfortable, to which he or she can withdraw and become reinvigorated (Simmons et al., 1987, pp. 1231–1232).

A number of authorities on adolescence have argued that 7th grade may be too early for a major shift in the school environment. They believe that for many young people this change may occur too close in time to other major life changes (Lipsitz, 1977; Simmons et al., 1987). They point out that "many youngsters are forced to cope simultaneously with dramatic changes in biology, social definition, and organizational context" (Simmons et al., 1987, p. 1221).

An increasingly popular way of avoiding this problem is the middle school (grades 5–7, 5–8, or 6–8). Whereas junior high schools are likely to be modeled after high schools, with a primary focus on subject matter, middle schools tend to focus more on the specific developmental needs of young adolescents (Eichorn, 1980). Middle schools may have an additional advantage: their relative isolation from the influence of older students. The results are likely to include a decrease in feelings of anonymity, less concern with being picked on or beaten up, increased participation in school activities, decreased substance abuse, an increase in dating (but less sexual intercourse), less premature sophistication, and an increase in self-esteem (Blyth, Hill, & Smyth, 1981).

## The Principal

Good principals with clear goals have often been cited as a key factor in creating effective schools (Dryfoos, 1990; Schorr, 1988). A strong principal, one who acts as an educational leader, appears to be especially important in schools where the majority of students are socially and economically disadvantaged. In many schools it is the principal who sets the tone, maintains school values, and reinforces school practices with respect to everything from academic expectations to support services and codes of behavior.

Although the principal bears a great deal of responsibility, he or she is also subject to the will of the school board, parents, and teachers and their unions—a position that often results in diminished authority (McAndrew, 1981; Schorr, 1988). A study of 1600 principals found that fully one-quarter intended to quit in the near future (Boyer, 1983). Many complained of being caught in a bureaucratic web:

> Far too many of our school systems are top-heavy with administration; they are administered to within an inch of their lives. School leadership is crippled by layer upon layer of administration. And, while control is rooted in the need for accountability, the reality is that it makes change in many schools all but impossible (Boyer, 1983, p. 224).

Principals who lack vision and are incapable of educational leadership—who view themselves as "middle managers"—are unlikely to satisfy their varied, and

sometimes conflicting, constituencies. But even principals who possess the necessary interpersonal skills, energy, commitment, and academic vision will have limited success unless they are given essential resources and sufficient freedom and flexibility in using them (Boyer, 1983). However, when an inspired principal has the resources required for educational leadership, the results can be astonishingly successful, even against seemingly overwhelming odds.

## Teachers

Teachers play a highly influential role in schools because they have the most direct contact with students. The kinds of teachers encountered by an adolescent determine in great measure whether the school experience will foster the young person's overall development or simply increase his or her problems and frustrations. The right teachers may help young people overcome handicaps and make the most of their talents and interests, whereas teachers who are ill-suited for working with young people may create serious difficulties. This is especially true in the case of teachers working with economically disadvantaged, ethnically diverse young people.

Teachers, as well as schools themselves, have come in for increasingly harsh criticism in recent years (Boyer, 1983; *National excellence,* 1993; Tifft, 1988). Although there are many skilled and intellectually challenging teachers, there are also significant numbers who lack minimal competency, even in basic communication skills (*Everybody counts,* 1989; National Commission on Excellence, 1983; Tifft, 1988). Despite a modest renewal over the last decade in young people's interest in pursuing teaching careers (Astin et al., 1988; Astin, Korn, & Riggs, 1994), the SAT scores of high school seniors planning to major in education are below those of students generally and well below those planning to major in fields such as English, health, and the physical and social sciences (Evangelauf, 1988).

**Obstacles to Learning.** It should be recognized that in many instances in which teachers appear to be failing to meet the needs of students, the source of the difficulty may lie elsewhere. Overly large classes, impossible workloads, rigid curricula and administrative regulations, poorly prepared or poorly motivated students, problems in the larger community, shortages of teaching materials, and lack of agreement among various constituencies as to the proper goals of education—all of these factors may frustrate the efforts of even the most sensitive, imaginative, and dedicated teacher. Moreover, in a growing number of instances, particularly in large metropolitan areas, violence and vandalism have been making the jobs of teachers and administrators increasingly difficult (Boyer, 1983; Tifft, 1988; U.S. Department of Justice, 1995).

As is often true of social institutions, a specific component of the system—such as teachers—is seldom the sole cause of a problem. Many experts feel that the solution must be sought in the priorities of society itself (*National excellence,* 1993). As one prominent educator has put it, "By and large, society gets what it deserves out of its school system. It gets what it expects. If you don't value things, you don't get them" (*Time,* 1980, p. 63).

**Effective Teachers.** Despite the problems confronting teachers, many are able to teach effectively. Students like and respond to some kinds of teachers better than others. There are also individual differences in the kinds of teachers to whom different kinds of students respond favorably. Table 8.1 summarizes teacher characteristics that are likely to improve the student's chances for learning.

## Table 8.1 Summary of Teacher Characteristics That Promote Learning

- Intellectually competent and well-trained (meets competence requirements, including effective communication)
- Emotionally supportive (warm and sympathetic to students)
- Firm but fair (has high but realistic expectations)
- Organized teaching style (well-planned with regular homework assignments and frequent evaluation)
- Has enthusiasm for material (comfortable with and excited about material)
- Unbiased approach to and treatment of all students (expectations and behaviors not influenced by gender, racial, or other stereotypes)

Jaime Escalante, the Los Angeles high school teacher portrayed in *Stand and Deliver,* teaching a calculus class. As a result of his enthusiasm, confidence, and insistence on high standards, hundreds of his students were able to overcome social or economic handicaps and master the Advanced Placement calculus examination.

In general, adolescents prefer and respond more favorably to teachers who are warm, enthusiastic, sympathetic, adaptable, and responsive to their concerns—in short, to those who provide an emotionally supportive environment (Norman & Harris, 1981; Ryan, Stiller, & Lynch, 1994). The emotional climate of the classroom affects not only the student preferences for particular teachers but also their achievement. Classrooms that produce high achievement gains are most often described as pleasant and convivial (Brophy, 1986; Gamoran & Nystrand, 1991; Ryan, Stiller, & Lynch 1994). Conversely, studies have consistently found negative relationships between student achievement and measures of teacher criticism, threat, ridicule, or punishment of students. Often such negative indicators of emotional climate are associated with poor classroom management skills (Brophy, 1986).

Students also want teachers who are firm yet fair and impartial. Not least, they want their teachers to be effective *as teachers:* able to plan and organize, to explain things clearly, and to be knowledgeable and enthusiastic about their subjects (Brophy, 1986; Norman & Harris, 1981). They want them to have a teaching style that actively involves students in the learning process (Mullis & Jenkins, 1988; Rutter et al., 1979). Effective teachers make regular homework assignments, provide frequent evaluations of the students' work, and manage to cover the curriculum in a flexible manner (Entwisle, 1990).

There is mounting evidence that teachers' expectations for students exert a powerful influence on student behavior, by shaping behavior in line with these expectations (Minuchin & Shapiro, 1983; Mussen et al., 1990;

Parsons, Kaczala, & Meece, 1982). The most effective teachers have expectations based on the student's actual ability and potential rather than on **stereotypes.** Several studies have shown that teachers are likely to have relatively low expectations for academic achievement among disadvantaged minority children and adolescents (Mullis & Jenkins, 1988; Panel on High-Risk Youth, 1993). However, when teachers believe that these young people can achieve, and when they convey their expectations to their students and adapt their teaching to meet the students' needs, performance often improves dramatically (Hirschorn, 1988).

In several studies, education majors and student teachers were more likely than others (e.g., psychology majors, Teacher Corps interns) to have a high regard for pupils who were described as rigid, conforming, and orderly, and a lower opinion of those who were described as independent, active, and assertive (Minuchin & Shapiro, 1983). To the extent that this respect for conformity shapes subsequent teacher–student interactions and teacher expectations for achievement, the nonconforming students may be at a disadvantage.

Boys and girls are also likely to be treated differently, with girls generally receiving less criticism than boys, less praise, and fewer high-level questions (Fine, 1981; Matyas & Kahle, 1986; Parsons, Kaczala, & Meece, 1982). Girls who are in classrooms where they are treated differently from boys have lower expectations for their own achievement. In addition, textbooks may imply that the most notable accomplishments in science are those of white males. Parents, peers, and the media may reinforce the idea that only certain roles are appropriate for female

or minority students (Mullis & Jenkins, 1988). Such stereotyping is a major deterrent to the participation of female and minority students in math and science courses and related activities (Mullis & Jenkins, 1988; Tocci & Engelhard, 1991).

To reverse such differential treatment and the differential outcomes it produces, teachers, parents, and other influential adults need to become "aware of the more subtle behaviors that communicate low expectations to particular students" (Mullis & Jenkins 1988, p. 9). In addition, effective teachers take care to expose students to a variety of appropriate sex, racial, and ethnic role models in books, films, and videotapes and in person.

Although the above characteristics may distinguish effective teachers from ineffective ones, it would be a mistake to conclude that the successful teacher fits some bland stereotype. Most readers will agree that the teachers who influenced them most were unique human beings. It is also clear that there are group and individual differences among pupils in the kinds of teachers to whom they respond most favorably or most negatively.

## Person–Environment Fit

Developmental psychologist Jacquelynne Eccles and her colleagues have described the importance for school success of a good **person–environment fit**— an appropriate match between the student (person) and the school (environment) (Eccles et al., 1993). The student who is most likely to succeed will be in a school environment that is attuned to the developmental needs of the student. Effective teachers have a role to play, as they "provide the optimal level of structure for children's current levels of maturity while providing a sufficiently challenging environment to pull the children along a developmental path toward higher levels of cognitive and social maturity" (Eccles et al., 1993, p. 92).

The concept of person–environment fit explains why the effectiveness of different teaching methods may vary from one student to another (Brophy, 1986; Snow, 1986). Students who feel secure and confident, for example, have different needs in the classroom than those who are anxious or alienated (Brophy, 1986). Students who are low in manifest anxiety perform better in more informal, student-centered classes (in which active student participation is encouraged at all times); students who are high in manifest anxiety perform better in more formal, structured, teacher-centered classes (Dowaliby & Schumer, 1971).

Similarly, socioeconomically advantaged students are more likely to be self-confident, eager to participate, and responsive to challenge: "They want respect and require feedback but usually do not need frequent encouragement or praise. They thrive in an atmosphere that is academically stimulating and somewhat demanding" (Brophy, 1986, p. 1073). In contrast, students from less-advantaged backgrounds are more likely to require warmth and support, encouragement for their efforts, and praise for their successes, as well as good instruction (Brophy, 1986).

The importance of person–environment fit is shown in research examining students and their math teachers as students made the somewhat stressful transition from elementary school to junior high school. Those who moved from a less supportive elementary teaching environment (in math) to a more supportive junior high teaching environment (in math) *increased* the value they attached to mathematics. Those who went from a high-support teacher to a low-support teacher became less positive about the value of math. The lowest-achieving students were particularly hard-hit by the move from high to low support (Eccles et al., 1993). Similar results were observed when math teachers' self-efficacy (confidence in teaching) was considered. Students' expectations for and evaluations of their math performance were dramatically lowered if they moved from a high-efficacy math teacher to a low-efficacy math teacher. The decline was especially evident among low-achieving students (Eccles et al., 1993). Consistent with previous research, low-achieving students may need the most supportive teaching environment if they are to avoid entering a downward spiral that ultimately may lead to school dropout.

Studies such as these demonstrate that different teachers and teaching methods may well have very different effects on different kinds of children and adolescents. They also serve as a needed corrective to the tendency of both students and teachers to assume that a technique that seems to work for them individually (or for their school) would automatically be better for others as well.

# Family Influences on Educational Aspirations and Achievement

The family environment is probably the most important predictor of the adolescent's success in school. This environment can be characterized along a number of

dimensions, including broad features such as the family's socioeconomic status (typically based on parental education, income, and occupational prestige) as well as specific qualities of the parents (for example, their values with respect to education) and their parenting practices (their role in facilitating the acquisition of an education). Table 8.2 summarizes important features of the family that together seem to promote achievement in adolescents.

## Socioeconomic Status

Socioeconomic status (SES) is significantly related to the level and nature of students' educational aspirations and to their actual educational attainment. Compared to lower-middle- and lower-class youth, upper-middle- and upper-class youth have traditionally aspired to higher levels of educational attainment, are less likely to drop out of high school, and obtain higher school grades and higher scores on standard tests in reading, writing, science, and mathematics. The disparities are especially marked when comparing youth from affluent, highly educated homes with those from severely economically disadvantaged backgrounds. These differences tend to be clearly established by age 9 and change little thereafter (Bachman, O'Malley, & Johnston, 1978; Johnson, 1975; Mullis & Jenkins, 1988; National Assessment, 1986).

Some of the reasons for these persistent disparities are fairly clear; others are more subtle. A poor young person is more likely to face serious economic problems in continuing his or her education. Government and private assistance is grossly inadequate to meet the needs of many students and is becoming more so (Conger, 1988; Schorr,

1988). Moreover, disadvantaged adolescents are more likely to have had poor academic preparation throughout their schooling. As noted earlier, their schools are physically inferior and poorly equipped, with inadequate curricula and severe shortages of trained teachers and auxiliary personnel.

Because of poor nutrition and inadequate health care, many more children at the lowest socioeconomic levels have serious health problems that may interfere with their ability to do academic work (Bryant et al., 1978; Children's Defense Fund, 1994; Schorr, 1988). Moreover, many thousands of children still go to school hungry, a condition that interferes with alertness and attention to studies. Other, more subtle, factors also operate to limit the educational aspirations and accomplishments of poor and working-class youth, including broad, class-related customs and values and the influence of parents and peers.

Parents at different socioeconomic levels vary in their views of schooling for their children. Middle- and upper-class parents are more likely to value schooling for the sake of the education—both academic and social— it provides. Working-class or poor parents, in contrast, have traditionally looked on school as necessary for vocational success because of the skills gained and credentials earned. However, most parents have reinforced the value of school to some degree because they have expected the school to do something for their children (Mussen, Conger, Kagan, & Huston, 1984).

Why do young people and adults from higher socioeconomic backgrounds have more positive attitudes about the value of schooling? For one thing, most school programs have actually been more relevant to the needs, customs, and expectations of people in these classes. Indeed, one of their principal functions has traditionally

## Table 8.2 Summary of Family Characteristics That Facilitate Achievement

- Higher socioeconomic status (highly educated parents)

- Positive parental attitudes (believe education, competence, and achievement to be important for later success)

- Parental involvement in children's education (help with homework, guide adolescent's decision-making, and talk to children about school experience, without being controlling, negative, or punitive)

- Access to resources (parents provide books, newspapers, magazines, exposure to art, music, and culture)

- Authoritative parenting (show praise and approval in a context of clear expectations for appropriate behavior)

- Match between parent expectations and student abilities (parents' expectations are in line with adolescent's abilities and needs, and parents do not exert excessive pressure on adolescent to succeed)

been to prepare succeeding generations of young people for admission to a society that is dominated by the middle class. As psychologist Boyd McCandless commented, "schools succeed relatively well with upper- and middle-class youngsters. After all, schools are built for them, staffed by middle-class people, and modeled after middle-class people" (1970, p. 295). School success is also more important for maintaining class membership in the higher socioeconomic classes than in the lower classes, and, increasingly, students seem to be realizing this. In 1994, making more money was seen as a very important goal by over 70 percent of U.S. college and university freshmen, a slight decline from an all-time high set in 1993 (see Figure 8.6) (Astin, Korn, & Riggs, 1993; Astin et al., 1994).

Better-educated, more affluent parents are more likely than less-educated parents to "manage" their children's education: They encourage their children to work hard in school, they tend to take an active interest in their children's schoolwork, and they are more involved in decision-making processes such as which courses the child should take (Davies & Kandel, 1981; Dossey et al., 1988; National Assessment, 1986; Useem, 1991). Eleventh-graders whose parents are college graduates are almost twice as likely as those whose parents did not graduate from college to report that their parents talk to them about what they are learning (Mullis & Jenkins, 1988). Parents with higher levels of education are also more likely to provide access to books, magazines, newspapers, and reference materials at home, to discuss ideas with their children, to help them with school projects, and to take them to museums and cultural events. Not too surprisingly, parental interest and involvement in schoolwork and greater exposure to reading and reference materials in the home are positively associated with proficiency in reading, mathematics, and science (Dossey et al., 1988; Mullis & Jenkins, 1988; Mullis et al., 1994; National Assessment, 1986).

The effects of social-class differences and attitudes on student achievement may cut across racial, ethnic, and other minority groups. For example, among middle- and upper-class African Americans, the concern of parents for their child's scholastic success and, consequently, their approval of his or her successful efforts are, if anything, stronger than among middle-class whites.

Perhaps most important of all, there are wide individual differences in orientation to education in all socioeconomic, ethnic, racial, and other subgroups. Educators certainly believe that when parents are truly interested in their children and motivated to help them succeed academically, and when relevant educational opportunities exist in the community, the effects of parental influences may override the otherwise limiting effects of lower socioeconomic status or the negative influences of peers. One study found that parents' educational aspirations for their children were equaled only by the young person's academic ability as predictors of adolescents' educational aspirations. Interestingly, the parents' actual aspirations were higher than their adolescent children's *perceptions* of those aspira-

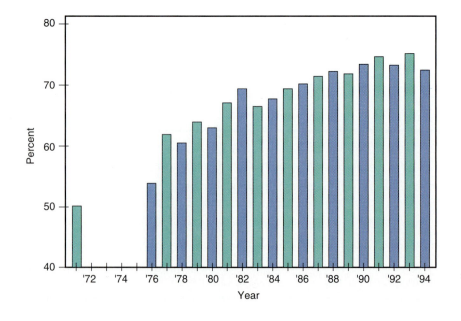

**Figure** 8.6

Freshmen believing making more money is a very important reason to attend college. From A. W. Astin, W. S. Korn, & E. R. Riggs (1994). *The American freshman: National norms for fall 1994.* Los Angeles: Higher Education Research Institute, Graduate School of Education UCLA. By permission.

tions. "These findings are important, for they document that the interpersonal influences of parents are exerted in subtle ways, and not necessarily with the awareness of the adolescent being influenced" (Davies & Kandel, 1981, p. 376).

## Parenting Behaviors and School Success

One of the most important factors in predicting adolescents' school success is the expectations parents have for their children's educational attainment (Hess & Holloway, 1984). For example, one study showed that parents' expectations are strongly related to the child's attitudes about and performance in mathematics (Parsons, Adler, & Kaczala, 1982). Despite the fact that before the study the boys and girls had performed equally well in mathematics courses and on their most recent standardized test, parents reported sex differences in the abilities of their children. Parents of daughters were more likely than parents of sons to report that their children had to work hard at mathematics and science. In addition, parents of sons were more likely than parents of daughters to feel that mathematics and science are important. The belief that success for girls is due to effort rather than ability, together with the lesser importance placed on these subjects for girls than for boys, is likely to decrease girls' motivation to continue in these courses. A recent study confirmed that in early adolescence, boys more than girls saw themselves as competent in math despite the fact that girls liked math as much as did boys and rated its importance equally (Wigfield & Eccles, 1994).

What kinds of parents have academically motivated, achieving children? Such parents are likely to place a high value on autonomy and independence and on mastery, competence, and achievement in general. They tend to be democratic and to interact actively with their children. They also exhibit curiosity and respect for knowledge while gently encouraging their children's academic work (Dornbusch et al., 1987; Ginsburg & Bronstein, 1993; Hess & Halloway, 1984; Paulson, 1994; Steinberg, Elmen, & Mounts, 1989). The parents of children with low aspirations and achievement do not share these values or characteristics even if they are similar to the parents of achieving children in socioeconomic status and intelligence.

Taken together, these positive parental attributes are generally characteristic of authoritative parents—those who are responsive (warm) yet demanding (have clear expectations). In a study of nearly 8000 high school students in the San Francisco Bay area, authoritative parenting was most closely associated with good grades, whereas authoritarian and permissive parenting were associated with poorer school performance (Dornbusch et al., 1987). Generally, the parents of underachieving children and adolescents have been found to be more domineering, more restrictive, more likely to engage in severe and arbitrary punishment, and more likely either

Parents of academically motivated, achieving students tend to be authoritative—warm and caring, but with clear expectations for age-appropriate, responsible behavior. These parents encourage their children's academic performance and exhibit intellectual curiosity and respect for knowledge.

# 8.4 Single-Sex Schooling

## ADDRESSING A PROBLEM

One of the most vivid examples of sex differences in educational aspirations and attainments exists in the area of math and science. Compared to boys, girls in secondary school and beyond have less interest in math and science, more often drop out of or elect not to take math and science courses, and avoid educational and career paths that require these courses (Kavrell & Petersen, 1984). Much of this difference has been attributed, not to the abilities of girls (who perform comparably to boys when they have equivalent backgrounds and academic experiences), but to teacher and parent expectations for girls' lower achievement and interest in math and science (Parsons, Kaczala, & Meece, 1982; Parsons, Adler, & Kaczala, 1982). Additionally, boys are given greater time, attention, and encouragement in the classroom (Mullis & Jenkins, 1988). What this amounts to is a serious disadvantage for girls.

How can this problem be solved? One study provides tantalizing evidence that one possible solution to this problem may be to enroll girls in all-girls schools. Using data from the large-scale *High School and Beyond* study, educational psychologists Valerie Lee and Anthony Bryk compared the experiences of over 1800 girls and boys enrolled in similarly constituted coeducational and single-sex private Catholic schools as they moved from grade 10 through grade 12. They investigated a wide variety of student outcomes including academic and social attitudes, school-related behaviors, course enrollment, academic achievement, educational aspirations, self-concept, and sex-role attitudes. After carefully adjusting for family background and school variables, the results were consistently in favor of girls who attended all-

to be overly protective of their children or to pressure them excessively for achievement (DeBaryshe, Patterson, & Capaldi, 1993; Ginsburg & Bronstein, 1993; Rosenthal & Feldman, 1991; Steinberg, Elmen, & Mounts, 1989). Granting young people autonomy in family decision-making too early is also associated with poorer school performance (Dornbusch et al., 1990). Joint decision-making, involving both parents and children, is more effective than decision-making by either youth alone or parents alone during the formative years of adolescence.

A potential factor in the extent to which parents influence their adolescent children is the response of the adolescent to each parent. A strong and positive parent–child relationship is surely important. On the other hand, an adolescent may find it difficult or impossible to identify with either parent. Under these circumstances the parent's potential influence is reduced. Indeed, in the search for a workable identity the young person may even attempt, consciously or unconsciously, to be as *unlike* the parent as possible, and consequently may reject the parent's academically oriented values.

## Peer Influences on School-Related Behavior and Aspirations

Adolescents have a strong need for acceptance by peers. Depending on the values of the peer group in general and of close friends in particular, the young person's educational aspirations may be either strengthened or reduced. The educational aspirations of most adolescents are consonant with those of their peers (Berndt, 1982; Davies & Kandel, 1981; Steinberg et al., 1992). Moreover, degree of agreement with peer values is directly related to intimacy of peer relations.

One extensive study of high school students used three indicators of intensity of friendship: whether the friendship choice was reciprocated, how often the adolescent saw the friend out of school, and whether the best school friend was also the best friend outside of school (Kandel & Lesser, 1969). This study found that friends whose choices were reciprocated were in somewhat greater agreement about educational goals than friends whose choices were not reciprocated. There was

girl schools. Relative to girls in coeducational schools, girls in single-sex schools did more homework, associated more with academically oriented peers, expressed more interest in math and English, took more math courses, made more gains in reading and science achievement across the two-year period, had higher educational aspirations, rated their schools and teachers more positively, and became increasingly more egalitarian in their sex-role attitudes from grade 10 to grade 12. Boys in single-sex schools also experienced advantages relative to their coeducational counterparts (for example, they enrolled in more math and science courses and had higher achievement scores in some areas), but the differences were weaker, and on most variables (educational aspirations, self-concept, and gains in achievement), there were no school differences at all (Lee & Bryk, 1986).

If single-sex schooling is one answer for parents who wish to maximize their daughters' learning opportunities, this goal will be difficult to accomplish, given that the number of single-sex schools in the United States has been on the decline since the 1960s (Entwisle, 1990). Although it is not likely that single-sex schools will become widely available in the near future, there are some promising variants on this theme. Some coeducational schools are experimenting with all-girls' classes. At Marin Academy in San Rafael, California, for instance, girls were enrolled in all-girls' biology and geometry classes. Anecdotal evidence indicates that the girls improved their grades. Similar experiments are taking place elsewhere at coeducational high schools in the United States (Massey, 1993). While the debate continues among educators about the advantages of single-sex schooling, public schools in the United States may have their hands tied. Civil rights legislation does not allow public schools to segregate students based on gender (Massey, 1993).

also greater agreement among friends who were seen often out of school, compared to those who were seen only rarely. Concordance on educational plans was highest among reciprocated best friends who were best friends both in and out of school.

A subsequent study by the same investigators showed that similarity in educational aspirations among peers may not be the *result* of peer influence or socialization (Davies & Kandel, 1981). Rather, adolescents' educational aspirations (and other attitudes and behavior, such as drug use) can lead them to *select* similar friends. Only subsequently does interaction with the friend strengthen or reduce the young person's existing aspirations or beliefs. Because of these processes (selecting similar friends and then becoming more alike), educational aspirations are widely shared in peer groups. This is very evident in studies examining the educational aspirations and values of different ethnic groups (see Box 8.5).

It is often assumed that with educational aspirations, as with most other values, irreconcilable differences are likely to arise between parents and peers, and that in any such confrontation peer values will win out over those of parents. As we have seen, however, there is usually considerable overlap between the values of parents and those of peers because adolescents select friends who share values with which they were raised. Where there are clashes between the values of parents and peers, they may arise from the consequences of economic impoverishment and racial discrimination, or from breakdowns in communication between parents and adolescents.

Adolescents who are good friends both in and out of school tend to have similar educational aspirations.

# 8.5 Ethnic Differences in Parental and Peer Influences on School Success

Comparisons consistently find that when it comes to success in school, Asian Americans score highest, outperforming whites; African-American and Hispanic students attain the lowest grades and are most likely to drop out of school (Steinberg, Dornbusch, & Brown, 1992). Much discussion about the source of these differences places emphasis on ethnic variability in parenting practices and, to some extent, the influences of peers.

With respect to the strong performance of Asian students in general, Japanese and Chinese parents (in their native countries) have higher expectations for achievement, are more involved in their children's education, and emphasize more the value of hard work than do American parents; these parenting practices are correlated positively with academic achievement (Stevenson & Lee, 1990). In contrast,

studies in the United States have found that parents of Asian-American students were *less* involved in their children's education than were white parents, yet the Asian-American students still outperformed the white students (Rosenthal & Feldman, 1991; Steinberg et al., 1992). In addition to less involvement, the Asian-American parents were significantly less likely than white parents to be authoritative, a parenting style that in white samples is associated generally with high achievement (Steinberg et al., 1992). What is it about Asian-American students that leads them to academic success without the strong involvement of authoritative parents?

One possibility is that authoritative, involved parents may not be so important (for academic achievement) in a family context in which parents focus on instilling a strong work ethic and the belief

## Personality Characteristics, Intelligence, and School Achievement

A number of adolescent characteristics, including but not limited to intelligence, are associated with school achievement. These characteristics are summarized in Table 8.3. One important characteristic—intellectual level—is clearly related to school success, with **correlations** between intelligence and measures of academic achievement generally ranging from about .50 to .70 or .75 (Snow & Yalow, 1988). The results of one investigation are typical (Kavrell & Petersen, 1984); the correlations between IQ scores and achievement test scores for a longitudinal sample of boys and girls in the 6th and 8th grades are shown in Table 8.4. Although the correlations are quite similar for boys and girls in the 6th grade, by the 8th grade IQ is less related to achievement for boys than for girls.

Although boys and girls generally have similar IQ test scores, there are sex differences in scores on achievement tests; boys tend to score higher than girls on math-

ematics and some science tests, whereas girls tend to score higher than boys on verbal and language tests (Dossey et al., 1988; Mullis & Jenkins, 1988; Mullis et al., 1994). Girls often earn higher grades overall than boys until college (Kavrell & Petersen, 1984; Maccoby & Jacklin, 1974). This may be explained at least partly by girls' greater conformity and boys' more active and disruptive behavior in the classroom (Fine, 1981).

As these findings suggest, intelligence is not the only determinant of school achievement; indeed, among some students it may be far less important than many other factors, such as motivation, interest, work habits, and personality characteristics such as persistence (Guerin et al., 1994; Lao, 1980; Rosenthal & Feldman, 1991; Snow, 1986). In one investigation of 475 high school seniors, students were divided into three subgroups: those whose academic performance (in English, science, mathematics, and social science) exceeded what would have been anticipated statistically on the basis of their IQs (**overachievers**), those whose performance was about what would have been anticipated (**normal achievers**), and those whose performance fell below

that there is a payoff to academic success. This strong work ethic is reinforced further by association primarily with other Asian-American youth who share the same values. High achievement, then, is the ultimate outcome of immersion in a culture (parent and peer) that supports the value of academic effort (Steinberg et al., 1992). Contrary to media reports that the pressure for academic success among Asian students results in psychological distress, one study found more stress among U.S. high school students than among students in Japan or Taiwan (Crystal et al., 1994).

Why are African-American students so disadvantaged with respect to academic achievement? It is not for a lack of seeing the value of education: The majority of African-American adolescents believe that education is important (Ford, 1992). It appears that these students realize that, given limited economic opportunities and the existence of racial discrimination, the probability of job success is not high (Taylor et al., 1994). The result is that African-American students put less effort into their schoolwork

than do other groups of students (Ford, 1992). Also, the African-American peer group may be skeptical about the chance that education can lead to a better life for them, and do not value academic striving. This may make it difficult for African Americans to devote time to their studies, even if they want to, for academic success may challenge their very belongingness to the peer group. Academic mediocrity, or at worst, failure, is one potentially serious cost of maintaining friendships (Steinberg et al., 1992).

For African-American students in this context, no matter how hard their parents might cherish the thought of academic success and employ authoritative parenting practices, the peer culture may have the stronger impact. African-American parents are more authoritative than Asian-American parents and they see academic achievement as a route to a better future for their children, but this apparently is not enough to overcome the negative effects of living in a society that seems to offer so little (Steinberg et al., 1992).

expected levels (**underachievers**). When these three groups were compared, a number of significant differences emerged.

Overachievers demonstrated significantly better work habits, greater interest in schoolwork generally, and more persistence in carrying out assignments, and they tended to be more grade-conscious. They also emerged as more responsible, conscientious, and likely to plan than normal achievers, although they were similar to them in many other respects. Underachievers differed markedly from normal achievers and overachievers. They appeared to have more difficulty in self-regulation and were more impulsive, uninhibited, pleasure-seeking, and interested in immediate rewards. They also seemed to have greater difficulty in interpersonal relationships with peers and appeared to be less cooperative, more selfish, less dependable, less sociable, and "less diligent in their efforts to attain socially acceptable goals" (Gawronski & Mathis, 1965, p. 153). They enjoyed both school and home less than normal achievers, manifested more defensive and resentful behavior, and were more likely to become disorganized, particularly under pressure.

Despite these characteristics, underachievers were less likely than either overachievers or normal achievers to report not having enough time for their studies. Finally, they displayed greater pessimism about their future opportunities.

Obviously, these findings represent only general trends, and there are many exceptions. For example, whereas many high-achieving students are well-adjusted, self-confident, and mature, significant numbers have feelings of inadequacy and unworthiness, are overly worried about the impressions they make on others, are concerned about loss of parental love if they do not measure up to expectations, and are overly dependent and conforming (Conger & Petersen, 1984). For such young people, overachieving may be a way of compensating for self-doubts and warding off potential rejection by parents and others. By the same token, some students who are classified as underachieving in the usual academic sense—and history provides some distinguished examples, such as Darwin, Churchill, and Einstein—may merely be marching to the beat of a different drummer. It is also clear that the fact of achievement or underachievement can influence the

# Table 8.3 Summary of Personal Characteristics That Facilitate Achievement

- Intellectual ability (ability to reason and to solve problems)
- Positive self-value (optimism, self-confidence, self-acceptance, and high self-esteem)
- Acceptance of authority (conformity to expectations of teachers and parents, eagerness to please them)
- Positive interpersonal relations (interest in, and responsiveness to, the feelings of others)
- Little conflict over independence versus dependence (freedom to make choices and initiate activities and to lead, although within a generally conforming context)
- An academic orientation (orderly study habits, high motivation for academic achievement, and interest in academic values and subject matter)
- Realistic goal orientation (a drive to organize and plan, basic seriousness of purpose, ability to delay short-term pleasures for longer-term goals, industry, efficiency, and energy)
- Better control over anxiety (direction of inner tensions into organized task-related activities) (Schuerger & Kuna, 1987)

developmental course of self-esteem and academic self-concept (Kifer, 1975). Therefore, achievement can be as much a *cause* of psychological characteristics as a *result* of such characteristics.

## Dropping out of School

Approximately 11 percent of United States students ages 16–19 drop out of high school before graduation—a decline of 25 percent in the past two decades (U.S. Bureau of the Census, 1994). In view of this continuing decline, why do we hear so much concern expressed about "the dropout problem"? A key reason is that overall statistics mask wide regional, socioeconomic, and ethnic differences.

As Figure 8.7 indicates, dropout rates in some states are more than twice as high as those in other states (U.S. Bureau of the Census, 1994). The dropout rate is highest among young people living in ethnically segregated urban and rural slums; 25 percent of all poor urban high schools have dropout rates of 50 percent or higher (Braddock & McPartland, 1992). In contrast, less than 1 percent of all other high schools have such extremely high dropout rates (Panel on High-Risk Youth, 1993). In 18- to 24-year-olds, the dropout rate among Hispanic students (33.9 percent)

# Table 8.4 Correlations for Boys and Girls Between Group Intelligence Test Scores and Standardized Achievement Test Scores

| Achievement Test Score | Sixth Grade | | Eighth Grade | |
|---|---|---|---|---|
| | Boys | Girls | Boys | Girls |
| Reading | .72 | .77 | .58 | .75 |
| Mathematics | .70 | .79 | .52 | .72 |
| Total achievement[a] | .82 | .75 | .59 | .78 |

[a]Based on other areas besides those listed.

Source: S. M. Kavrell & A. C. Petersen (1984). Patterns of achievement in early adolescence. In M. L. Maehr & M. W. Steinkamp (Eds.), *Women and science.* Greenwich, CT: JAI Press. By permission.

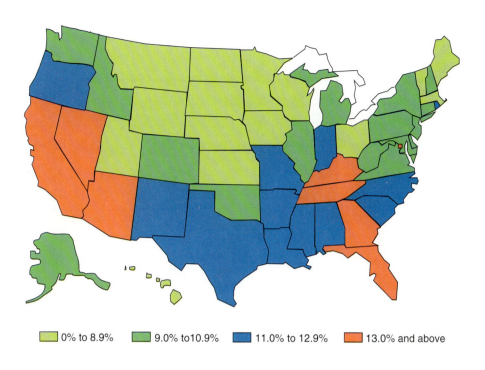

0% to 8.9%  9.0% to10.9%  11.0% to 12.9%  13.0% and above

## Figure 8.7

High school dropout rates, 1990.

SOURCE: U.S. Bureau of the Census, 1994; *Chronicle of Higher Education Almanac,* September 1, 1994.

is nearly three times that of whites (12.2 percent) and twice that of blacks (16.3) (U.S. Bureau of the Census, 1994). Among Native Americans, the situation is particularly troubling; fewer than 10 percent graduate from high school (LaFromboise & Low, 1989).

Dropping out is more common among the poor in general than among the affluent (Dryfoos, 1990; Goertz, Ekstrom, & Rock, 1991). At the highest socioeconomic level, dropping out is extremely rare; at the bottom of the socioeconomic ladder, as many as one in two young people may drop out of high school (Bachman, O'Malley, & Johnston, 1978; Panel on High-Risk Youth, 1993; Sebald, 1984).

In an era when the number of unskilled jobs is declining steadily while the number of jobs requiring high levels of education and technical skills is rising rapidly, the employment prospects for most dropouts are increasingly bleak (see Chapter 9). Dropouts are almost twice as likely to be unemployed as high school graduates (U.S. Bureau of the Census, 1994). Even if they find a job, it is likely to be menial work with the lowest pay and few chances of advancement (*America 2000,* 1991; *The forgotten half,* 1988; U.S. Department of Labor, 1994).

## Why Do Young People Drop Out?

A wide variety of factors—educational, socioeconomic, cultural, and personal—play a role in adolescents' decisions to drop out of school (Dryfoos, 1990; Goertz, Ekstrom, & Rock, 1991; Panel on High-Risk Youth, 1993). Although dropout rates are highest among poor youth, financial difficulties and home responsibilities are not the principal reasons for dropping out of high school. Most males cite school-related reasons, including dislike of school, poor performance, and suspension or expulsion (see Table 8.5). Among females, the most commonly cited reasons are pregnancy and marriage (Rumberger, 1983; Upchurch, 1993).

School difficulties, both academic and social, play a prominent role in the histories of most dropouts. The typical dropout, despite an average IQ, is two years behind in reading and arithmetic by the time he or she reaches the 7th grade; moreover, dropouts are likely to have failed one or more school years. Although dropouts tend to fall further behind in academic skills during the course of their school experience, future dropouts and graduates differ significantly even in the early school years

# Table 8.5 Primary Reason High School Students Drop Out, Ages 14 to 21, by Race and Sex

| REASON FOR LEAVING SCHOOL | FEMALE | | | | MALE | | | | OVERALL |
|---|---|---|---|---|---|---|---|---|---|
| | BLACK | HISPANIC | WHITE | TOTAL | BLACK | HISPANIC | WHITE | TOTAL | TOTAL |
| School Related | 29% | 21% | 36% | 32% | 56% | 36% | 55% | 53% | 44% |
| Poor performance | 5 | 4 | 5 | 5 | 9 | 4 | 9 | 9 | 7 |
| Disliked school | 18 | 15 | 27 | 24 | 29 | 26 | 36 | 33 | 29 |
| Expelled or suspended | 5 | 1 | 2 | 2 | 18 | 6 | 9 | 10 | 7 |
| School too dangerous | 1 | 1 | 2 | 1 | 0 | 0 | 1 | 1 | 1 |
| Economic | 15 | 24 | 14 | 15 | 23 | 38 | 22 | 24 | 20 |
| Desired to work | 4 | 7 | 5 | 5 | 12 | 16 | 15 | 14 | 10 |
| Financial difficulties | 3 | 9 | 3 | 4 | 7 | 9 | 3 | 5 | 4 |
| Home responsibilities | 8 | 8 | 6 | 6 | 4 | 13 | 4 | 5 | 6 |
| Personal | 45 | 30 | 31 | 33 | 0 | 3 | 3 | 2 | 17 |
| Pregnancy | 41 | 15 | 14 | 19 | 0 | 0 | 0 | 0 | 9 |
| Marriage | 4 | 15 | 17 | 14 | 0 | 3 | 3 | 2 | 8 |
| Other | 11 | 25 | 19 | 20 | 21 | 23 | 20 | 21 | 19 |
| Total percent | 100 | 100 | 100 | 100 | 100 | 100 | 100 | 100 | 100 |

SOURCE: *National Longitudinal Survey of Youth Labor Market Experience.* In R. W. Rumberger (1983, Summer). Dropping out of high school: The influence of race, sex, and family background. *American Educational Research Journal,* **201,** 199–200. Copyright © 1983 by the American Educational Research Association. Reprinted by permission of the publisher.

(Brooks-Gunn, Guo, & Furstenberg, 1993; Dryfoos, 1990; Holmes, 1989; Mensch & Kandel, 1988; Panel on High-Risk Youth, 1993). One study found that future high school dropouts could be identified by the end of 3rd grade with 75 percent accuracy, using such factors as school grades, scores on intelligence and achievement tests, family characteristics, and socioeconomic status (Lloyd, 1978).

Family income and parents' educational levels are also strong predictors of dropping out. Children whose parents are well-educated and who are exposed to a variety of cultural resources at home are more likely to remain in school and graduate (Bianchi, 1982; Commission on Chapter 1, 1992). As noted earlier, however, the negative effects of low income and low parental educational level may be significantly offset by strong parental guidance and support.

Peers may also increase the likelihood of an adolescent's dropping out. Dropouts are more likely to have friends who have low expectations for school, cut classes, engage in "acting out" behavior, and become dropouts themselves (Dryfoos, 1990).

The quality of the school plays an important role in influencing whether a young person will drop out. Students have higher dropout rates in segregated schools with low teacher–pupil ratios, large schools with large classes, and schools where students do not have a sense of belonging and feel powerless in student–teacher relationships (Dryfoos, 1990). In one study, 70 percent of dropouts said they might have stayed in school "if teachers paid more attention to students" and "if we were not treated as inmates" (Dryfoos, 1990; Wells, 1983).

## Psychological Characteristics of Dropouts

Overall, dropouts are more likely than graduates to be emotionally troubled, to lack confidence in their own worth, to have low self-esteem, to lack a clearly defined self-image and sense of identity, and to lack structured values and goals. Dropouts report higher rates of drug use and delinquency before dropping out; they also have higher rates of depression (Bachman, O'Malley, &

Johnston, 1978; Dryfoos, 1991; Ekstrom et al., 1986; Mensch & Kandel, 1988). As mentioned earlier, pregnancy and early childbearing play prominent roles in adolescent girls' dropping out.

Dropouts are more likely than their peers who stay in school to have hostile, angry feelings and to resent authority in any form. Influenced more by frustrations from which they are trying to escape than by longer-term goals toward which they are striving, these adolescents tend to live for the moment: responding impulsively, planning little, showing little sustained, goal-directed activity, and seeking immediate gratification (Cervantes, 1965; Dryfoos, 1993).

In an important national study in the United States, over 2000 young men were studied longitudinally until one year after most had graduated from high school (Bachman, Green, & Wirtanen, 1972). It was found that many of the problems that dropouts are likely to encounter after leaving high school—unemployment, personality problems, low aspirations, and low self-esteem—are as likely to reflect the kinds of problems that led to dropping out in the first place as they are to result from the act of dropping out itself. For example, after dropping out, the self-esteem of dropouts increased from the low levels present before leaving school. The greatest challenge is not to keep a young person in a school situation that is unrewarding or irrelevant, but to ameliorate the conditions that lead to dropping out, beginning as early as possible in the child's life.

# New Directions for Schools

The available evidence indicates that the U. S. educational system is failing to meet the needs either of society or of young people themselves. As a whole, youth are not being well enough prepared to compete effectively in an increasingly global economy or to assume their responsibilities as informed citizens (*America 2000,* 1991; Carnegie Council, 1989; Mullis et al., 1994; National Educational Goals Panel, 1994). As we have seen, calls for educational reform have yielded some gains in recent years, but much more remains to be done.

If reform efforts have produced limited gains for students generally, they have had even less impact on the increasing number of poor and minority children growing up in urban and rural ghettos. Terrell H. Bell, who commissioned *A Nation at Risk* when he was Secretary

of Education in the Reagan administration, commented: "The school reform movement has had no significant impact on the 30 percent of our students who are low income minority students. We are still not effectively educating them" (quoted in Schorr, 1988, p. 220). Indeed, although improvements are being made in a number of economically advantaged schools, urban schools with economically disadvantaged, largely minority students are getting worse (Boyer, 1983; Levin, 1985; Schorr, 1988). As Lisbeth Schorr noted in her compelling book, *Within Our Reach: Breaking the Cycle of Disadvantage,* "The failure of our education system to provide all American youngsters with basic skills exacts a high price, whether measured in personal, moral, or economic terms" (Schorr & Schorr, 1988, p. 221).

## Recommendations for Educational Reform

Recommendations for reform have focused largely on three issues: what needs to be taught, how it should be taught, and the kinds of support that are needed if educational efforts are to succeed.

**What Should Be Taught?**    Many schools fail to provide sufficiently advanced courses (or sometimes any courses) in important curricular areas. This is perhaps most apparent in the sciences and mathematics, but it is often true in other areas as well, including foreign languages, history, geography, literature, and the arts.

In his report on secondary education in America, Ernest Boyer, president of the Carnegie Foundation for the Advancement of Teaching, proposed a core high school curriculum that includes two-year sequences in mathematics and in the biological and social sciences and at least two years of foreign-language study, as well as coursework in literature, history, civics, and the arts. Few schools provide such comprehensive curricular opportunities and in many of those that do, few students participate fully (Fiske, 1987a, 1987b; Mullis et al., 1994). For example, in 1988 only about 6 percent of all U. S. high school students took advanced courses in biology, compared with 45 percent of the students in Finland and 28 percent of the students in English-speaking Canada (International Association, 1988, cited in Mullis & Jenkins, 1988, p. 10). Although the number of students taking courses in mathematics, biology, chemistry and physics increased moderately in the past decade (see Table 8.6), the percentages taking advanced courses has remained low. For example, in 1992 only 10

percent of 17-year-old students had studied precalculus and calculus, and only 14 percent had studied physics (Mullis et al., 1994).

**How Should Students Be Taught?**   The effectiveness of what is taught depends on how it is taught. One reason that school is often "an uninteresting place" (Sarason, 1983) is teachers' heavy reliance on lecturing *to* students, with minimal give-and-take between teacher and student. Teachers also tend to convey "facts" rather than stimulating questions and to encourage the regurgitation of rote answers—often on multiple-choice tests—as a measure of what a student has learned. Through this process, students tend to be cast in the role of passive recipients of knowledge.

Such a one-sided approach flies in the face of what we know about both the nature of children and adolescents and the nature of intellectual accomplishment. Children are naturally curious; adolescents, with their greater cognitive development, are increasingly capable of raising questions, producing hypotheses, considering possible answers (solutions), and testing each against the available evidence (Carnegie Council, 1989; Keating, 1988; see Chapter 4). Teachers can and should involve students in hands-on activities that allow them to use and develop further these cognitive capabilities, in an *active* learning process. This will benefit them not only as they pursue scientific endeavors but as they attempt to understand and integrate knowledge in other areas as well.

In *The Reading Report Card,* which assessed the status of reading in U. S. schools, the authors encouraged students' active participation in the learning process: "Improvements in higher-level reading skills cannot come about simply by an emphasis on reading instruction in isolation from the other work students do in

## Table 8.6 Trends in Science Course Taking at Age 17, 1986 to 1992

| | TOTAL | MALE | FEMALE |
|---|---|---|---|
| **General science** | | | |
| 1992 | 84% | 86% | 83% |
| 1990 | 82 | 84 | 81 |
| 1986 | 83 | 84 | 82 |
| **Biology** | | | |
| 1992 | 92 | 91 | 93 |
| 1990 | 89 | 87 | 91 |
| 1986 | 88 | 87 | 88 |
| **Chemistry** | | | |
| 1992 | 49 | 47 | 51 |
| 1990 | 45 | 45 | 45 |
| 1986 | 40 | 42 | 39 |
| **Physics** | | | |
| 1992 | 14 | 15 | 12 |
| 1990 | 14 | 16 | 13 |
| 1986 | 11 | 14 | 8 |

SOURCE: National Assessment of Educational Progress (NAEP), 1992 Science Trend Assessment. Cited in V. S. Mullis et al. (1994). *NAEP 1992 trends in academic progress* (p. 65). Washington, DC: U.S. Government Printing Office.

school. To foster higher-level literacy skills is to place a new and special emphasis on thoughtful, critical elaboration of ideas and understandings drawn from the material students read and from what they already know" (National Assessment of Educational Progress, 1986, p. 8).

**The Context of Teaching.** Teaching and learning do not take place in a vacuum. If curricula are to be upgraded and if more innovative, student-oriented approaches to teaching are to succeed, the support of school boards, principals, and parents is essential (Boyer, 1983; National Educational Goals Panel, 1994; Schorr, 1988). As we have already noted, school boards need to give principals greater administrative flexibility, and principals in turn need to give teachers greater freedom to teach in creative ways that are responsive to the needs and potential of their students. Parents need to be encouraged to participate as active partners in the education of their children wherever possible, understanding, supporting, and, when necessary, questioning the efforts of teachers and administrators (Rich, 1985; Schorr, 1988).

## The High-Risk Student

New approaches to learning are also required for students who, by virtue of poverty, minority status, or both, have the greatest need for appropriate education but are least likely to receive it. As noted earlier, most proposed reforms "have relatively little to offer educationally disadvantaged students" (Levin, cited in Schorr, 1988, p. 221), many of whom are growing up in socially disorganized inner-city ghettos. Some, particularly in inner-city environments, may be homeless, a condition that leads to low attendance, frequent absences, and perhaps a failure to even register in school (Roberts, 1987).

When one considers the problems disadvantaged young people face in meeting traditional academic, social, and vocational demands, it seems reasonable that they should be given more assistance in school than better-prepared, more advantaged middle-class youth. Yet the reverse is typically the case. It would be a mistake, however, to conclude that what disadvantaged children and adolescents need is simply more of the traditional educational programs provided for the average middle- and upper-class young person. Certainly, like all children, they need decent physical surroundings and educational facilities and dedicated, skillful teachers. But they also need new and imaginative approaches to psychological development in general and educational

development in particular. They need curricula and programs geared to their specific talents, needs, and problems (academic and social) and skilled academic, vocational, and personal guidance.

Despite the difficulties involved, educational programs that are successful—not only in developing essential academic, social, and vocational skills but also in fostering self-pride and a sense of meaningful and rewarding cultural identity—are being instituted in many communities. An equally important, though little acknowledged, fact is that these programs can make learning and living joyful and exciting (Boyer, 1983; Dryfoos, 1990; Schorr, 1988).

One such program is the *Yale Child Study Center–New Haven School System Intervention*. This intervention began in 1968 with two New Haven, Connecticut, elementary schools "that were at the bottom in achievement, attendance, and behavior" (Comer, 1992, p. 28). The schools were attended by African-American children from poor families faced with economic and social stress. The philosophy behind the intervention was not to punish or control the misbehaviors, fighting, and disrespect for teachers that were rampant in these schools—behaviors that were understood to be the result of their chaotic environment—but to address the developmental needs of the students. To accomplish this, a governance and management team consisting of parents, teachers, administrators, and nonprofessional support staff was formed to identify problems and possible solutions, all with the goal of creating a sense of community out of an atmosphere of alienation and despair. Through the active coordination among team members, the social climate of the school gradually became supportive of students, accompanied eventually by the maintenance of order and control. A social skills curriculum was also developed. By 1984, the two "bottom" schools were among the top five (out of thirty-three) in the city. Because of the success of this program, these same principles are being followed in over 165 schools across the United States. Many are showing significant gains (from 40 to 60 percentile points) on standardized achievement tests (Comer, 1992).

Innovative schools such as these demonstrate that it is possible to reach even seriously disadvantaged students. But unless the number of such schools is expanded significantly, and soon, many more millions of adolescents will enter adulthood unprepared to lead reasonably happy, self-sufficient, and productive lives (Carnegie Council, 1989; Dryfoos, 1990; *The forgotten half,* 1988).

# Summary

In the United States the school is the one major social institution, other than the family, to which everyone is exposed during the critical years of childhood and adolescence. As society has become more complex, the importance of the school has grown while that of other social institutions has diminished. However, schools are not meeting their traditional responsibility for developing basic academic skills. American youth perform poorly in science, mathematics, reading, and writing compared with young people in other industrialized countries and, in some cases, earlier generations of American youth. A variety of reasons for this situation have been cited, ranging from declining academic standards to increased substance use, school violence, less mental stimulation in the home, and changes in the socioeconomic mix of students attending school. Although some progress has been made in the past few years, particularly among African- and Mexican-American students, much remains to be done.

Some theorists have asserted that schools make little or no difference in the subsequent educational and occupational attainments of students. However, more recent research indicates that some aspects of school do indeed make a difference. These include school size, the timing of school transitions, teachers' expectations, amount of teacher time spent in interaction with the class, opportunities for responsibility in school life, and the competence of teachers.

Small schools may be more desirable than large schools. Students in small schools are involved in more activities and are given more responsibility than students in large schools, resulting in greater involvement in school activities, gains in self-confidence and a sense of accomplishment, and opportunities to work closely with others.

The transition from elementary to junior high school is a major one for adolescents and coincides with other important life changes and stresses, including puberty and new social expectations. An increasingly popular—and promising—means of reducing the number of pressures that the young person must cope with during this age period is the middle school.

Good principals with clear goals are a key factor in creating effective schools. To be successful they need sufficient resources and more freedom and flexibility in using them. Teachers also play a vital role because they have the most direct contact with students. Recently, teachers have come under increasing criticism. However, it should be recognized that much of the responsibility for failure to meet the needs of students lies elsewhere. Among the factors that interfere with teacher effectiveness are overly large classes, rigid curricula, poorly prepared or poorly motivated students, shortages of materials, violence, and vandalism.

Nevertheless, many teachers are effective; such teachers are perceived as warm, enthusiastic, knowledgeable, well-prepared, and firm, but also fair and impartial. The emotional climate of the classroom is also important. Specific characteristics of students or teachers, including class, race, or gender stereotypes, may enhance or inhibit student–teacher interactions. The effectiveness of different teaching methods may also vary from one student to another; some students profit more from formally structured teaching, whereas others benefit from greater independence and initiative. Students with a better person–environment fit—those who are in a school environment that matches the developmental needs of the student—are more likely to be successful than students for whom the school provides a poor fit.

Socioeconomic status is significantly related to educational aspirations and attainment. Middle- and upper-class youth score higher, on average, than their working-class peers and much higher than seriously disadvantaged youth, for a variety of reasons. Nevertheless, there are wide individual differences within all socioeconomic, ethnic, and other subgroups in aspirations and accomplishments. When parents are motivated to help their children succeed academically, and when relevant educational opportunities are available, the effects of parental influence may override the otherwise limiting effects of lower socioeconomic status and negative peer influence. In general, children of warm, academically motivated, authoritative parents who spend time with their children do better than children with authoritarian or permissive parents.

Depending on the values of the peer group, especially close friends, adolescents' educational aspirations may be either strengthened or reduced. The educational values of parents and peers often overlap; when they do not, parental influence is likely to be greater if parent–child interactions are positive.

Intelligence, motivation, interests, work habits, and personality characteristics are all related to school achievement. Overachievers, for example, have greater interest, better work habits, and more persistence, and are more self-confident, responsible, and conscientious. Underachievers have more difficulty controlling their impulses, are more anxious and less cooperative, and are more pleasure-seeking and interested in immediate rewards.

Approximately one in ten students drops out of school before graduation—a significant problem in an era when the number of jobs for unskilled workers is declining while the number of jobs that require a high level of educational ability and technical skills is increasing. Dropout rates are highest in ethnically segregated inner cities and rural slums. The reasons given for dropping out

include dislike of school, poor academic performance, and pregnancy. Compared with students who graduate, dropouts are more likely to be emotionally troubled, to be less self-confident, to have lower self-esteem, to be more resentful of authority, and to have less-structured values and goals. They also exhibit higher rates of delinquency and drug use. In most cases these difficulties are among the factors that lead to dropping out, rather than being consequences of failure to finish high school.

If schools are to meet the needs of contemporary adolescents, curricula must be upgraded and more innovative student-oriented approaches to teaching are needed. In addition, the combined support of school boards, principals, teachers, parents, and the community is essential if such changes are to be effective. This is particularly critical in the case of disadvantaged students, who have the greatest need for appropriate education but are least likely to receive it.

# Review Questions

1. How well are schools in the United States meeting their responsibility for the development of basic academic skills? How does the performance of students in the United States compare with that of students in other industrialized countries? Discuss possible reasons for these trends.

2. Some theorists assert that schools make little or no difference in students' subsequent educational and occupational attainments. Others disagree. How can these differences be explained?

3. How does school affect students' self-confidence, development of skills and abilities, and participation in school activities? What are the effects of school size and school transitions on young people?

4. What personal and professional attributes do students look for in teachers? What teacher characteristics are most likely to evoke negative and positive responses from students?

5. Discuss the relationship between socioeconomic status and the educational aspirations and attainment of adolescents and youth.

6. What kinds of parents are most likely to have academically motivated, achieving children?

7. What personal characteristics contribute to achievement in youth?

8. What socioeconomic, cultural, school, and personal factors are related to dropping out of school?

9. What reforms in the American educational system are needed if schools are to meet the needs of society and of young people themselves, including economically disadvantaged children and adolescents?

# Recommended Readings

Carnegie Council on Adolescent Development, Task Force on Education of Young Adolescents. (1989). *Turning points: Preparing American youth for the 21st century.* Washington, DC: Carnegie Council on Adolescent Development (11 Dupont Circle NW, Washington, DC 20036).

Dryfoos, J. (1990). *Adolescents at risk: Prevalence and prevention.* New York: Oxford University Press.

Entwisle, D. R. (1990). Schools and the adolescent. In S. S. Feldman & G. R. Elliott (Eds.), *At the threshold: The developing adolescent* (pp. 197–224). Cambridge, MA: Harvard University Press.

Entwisle, D. R., & Hallinan, M. T. (Eds.). (1991). School characteristics and student outcomes [Special issue]. *Journal of Research on Adolescence, 1*(3).

Freedman, S. G. (1990). *Small victories: The real world of a teacher, her students & their high school.* New York: Harper & Row.

Steinberg, L., Dornbusch, S. M., & Brown, B. B. (1992). Ethnic differences in adolescent achievement: An ecological perspective. *American Psychologist, 47,* 723–729.

Wigfield, A., & Eccles, J. S. (Eds.). (1995). Middle grades schooling and early adolescent development, part 2: Interventions, practices, beliefs, and contexts [Special issue]. *Journal of Early Adolescence, 15*(1).

# Adolescents, Work,

# 9 and Careers

Choosing and preparing for a career is one of the major developmental tasks of adolescence. Some theorists assert that adolescence can end only with practical experience in the working world. Before then the career goals of adolescents tend to have a highly theoretical quality. When they go to work, however, young people begin to learn whether they can resolve the inevitable conflicts between their ideals, values, and goals on the one hand and the sometimes harsh realities of adult life on the other. In the process, they begin to reassess the adult world, as well as their own assets and limitations.

Opportunities for constructive and appropriate work experience can give adolescents a sense of purpose and responsibility and a feeling that they are participating meaningfully in society. Such opportunities also may reduce communication barriers between adults and young people, give young people a chance to learn about career possibilities, develop their interests, and test their developing skills and talents against the demands of the so-called real world.

Such opportunities have become increasingly more difficult to come by, however, for two reasons. First, in this century, the role of student has replaced the role of worker. Before 1925, most teenagers entered the work force by age 15; only the most affluent young people were likely to continue their education without interruption (Kett, 1977; Greenberger & Steinberg, 1986). Now, about 89 percent of young people complete high school, with 60 percent of them moving into postsecondary institutions (Schulenberg & Ebata, 1994; U.S. Bureau of the Census, 1994). This means that work experience has taken a backseat to educational experience as a valuable way of advancing into a selected occupation. A second reason that many adolescents do not have constructive work opportunities is that many of the rapidly paced, lower-level service-oriented jobs that are available to them are stressful, do little to teach basic work skills, and place them in contact mostly with peers rather than adults (Greenberger & Steinberg, 1986). As we shall see later in this chapter, the costs of part-time work often outweigh the benefits. Other countries, such as Germany and Denmark, do much better in providing

valuable work experiences to adolescents through the implementation of apprenticeship programs (Hamilton, 1994).

A limited number of programs in North America are providing high school (and college or university) students with well-planned exposure to the kinds of work involved in careers in health, industry and business, the arts, and local government and social-service agencies. Programs that combine academic work with monitored work experience have a record of solid achievement, and merit more attention than they have thus far received (Dryfoos, 1990; *The forgotten half,* 1988). Some students work with research scientists in their laboratories or with business executives; tutor younger students who are having problems in school; provide services to children, the elderly, or the handicapped; or work in business-funded training programs, such as renovating buildings in the community (Bacas, 1986; Greenberger & Steinberg, 1986; Hamilton, 1994).

## Career Choice and Social Change

In earlier periods, the problem of choosing a career was considerably simpler than it is today. More traditional societies in earlier periods typically offered fewer occupations, and adolescents were likely to be familiar with most of them through observation or apprenticeship. In earlier periods in our own society, particularly in rural areas and small towns, young people were far more likely to have observed parents or other adults pursuing the occupations they themselves were considering, and to have opportunities for early apprenticeships, whether informal and occasional (e.g., summer or after-school work) or formal and sustained.

Ellen Greenberger and Laurence Steinberg note that "three occupations historically have provided continuity in young people's passage from adolescent to adult employment: the skilled trades and crafts, factory work, and farm work" (1986, p. 50). In each of these occupational groups adolescent jobs have clear adult counterparts. In the past 50 years, however, adolescent work in these fields has diminished significantly and has been largely replaced by employment in service and sales jobs. These trends are expected to continue as we enter the next century (see Figure 9.1). Moreover, for most adolescents many of these newer jobs have little continuity with their eventual adult employment, even in the same field. For example, "wrapping hamburgers at the local fast-food franchise is less likely to lead to a management position in the food service industry than is a master's degree in business administration" (Greenberger & Steinberg, 1986, p. 50).

Today many adolescents may have difficulty in learning about the many different kinds of jobs available. There is no easy way to know which jobs they would be able to do successfully and would enjoy doing. They are not aware of the training required for a specific job or of the demand for workers in various occupations. This problem is becoming increasingly prevalent as our society

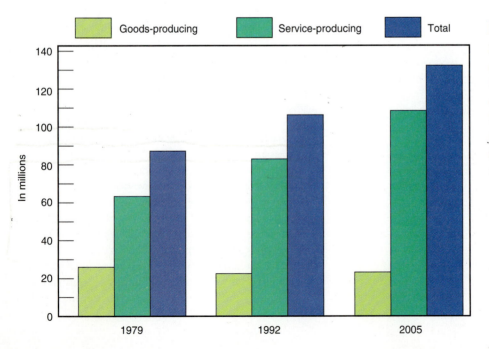

**Figure 9.1**

Nonfarm wage and salary employment, 1979–2005. SOURCE: U.S. Department of Labor, Bureau of Labor Statistics (1994). *Tomorrow's jobs,* Bulletin 2450–1. Washington, DC: U.S. Government Printing Office.

grows more complex, more specialized, and more technologically oriented. The most recent *Dictionary of Occupational Titles* lists more than 20,000 different occupations and it is probably safe to say that many of them are unfamiliar not only to contemporary adolescents and their parents, but to most vocational counselors as well (U.S. Department of Labor, 1991, 1993). Furthermore, the kinds of skills required by employers are changing rapidly as new technologies are developed. As a result of increasing automation, there are ever fewer opportunities for unskilled or semiskilled workers; prior education and training are becoming increasingly necessary for admission to the world of work (Schorr, 1988).

## Adolescents at Work

Part-time employment among high school students is far more common in the United States than in other industrialized countries. About three-quarters of U.S. high school seniors work for pay during the school year (Bachman & Schulenberg, 1993). In Canada, about 42 percent of full-time students have part-time jobs (Posterski & Bibby, 1988). Higher rates of part-time work in the United States are due partly to the greater ease of fitting work in after school (school days are generally shorter and business hours longer in the United States) and partly to the fact that opportunities for part-time employment are more readily available in the United States than in other countries. Much greater after-school demands are placed on students in other countries. Many European and Japanese students, for example, are assigned four to five hours of homework nightly (L. Steinberg, 1985). In contrast, American students, on average, spend about an hour a day on homework (Csikszentmihalyi & Larson, 1984).

Many people believe that adolescents who work will gain some benefits, such as a greater understanding of money matters, increased work orientation, and more self-reliance. It is doubtful, however, whether the kinds of jobs that are most often available to adolescents attending school, such as working at fast-food outlets, washing cars, and packing groceries, can accomplish these objectives. Some studies have found some such benefits; others have not. On the other hand, the research has been consistent in indicating that adolescent jobs do little to encourage higher educational and career aspirations and planning for future employment. For some young people, especially those who work long hours and are poorer students to begin with, such employment may interfere significantly with school performance (Bachman & Schulenberg, 1993; Greenberger & Steinberg, 1986; Steinberg & Dornbusch, 1991).

If the goals set for American education in recent

Part-time employment for high school students is far more common in the United States than in other industrialized countries.

reports are to be achieved, the question of how much time young people can afford to spend in academically unproductive part-time employment may need to be readdressed. Of course, some students may need substantial part-time employment in order to help support themselves or their families. A majority of students, however, spend none of their income on family living expenses or future educational needs (Greenberger & Steinberg, 1986; Mortimer et al., 1990). Moreover, long hours, poor or hazardous working conditions, and a high degree of stress may interfere with a young person's health (see Box 9.1).

Under some conditions, work experience may help an adolescent interact more effectively with others, including employers. However, in many of the jobs available to adolescents, opportunities to learn from or model oneself after a successful adult mentor are rather limited (Greenberger & Steinberg, 1986; Hamilton, 1994; Markward, 1992). In some shoddy or unchallenging work settings, adolescents may become more cynical

# 9.1 Part-Time Work

## HOW MUCH IS TOO MUCH?

A large scale study of 15- to 18-year-olds found no positive relations between part-time employment and adolescents' self-reliance or work orientation, contrary to the popular view that work teaches adolescents the importance of personal responsibility and a strong work ethic (Steinberg & Dornbusch, 1991). Replicating earlier research, this study found that as the number of hours of part-time work increased (particularly beyond 10 hours per week), adolescents experienced poorer grades, more distress, and higher rates of substance use and delinquency (see Figure B9.1a).

These findings were similar across different ethnic groups, with the exception of one finding: Work hours were not related to the grades of African-American or Hispanic-American students. Why does part-time work sometimes have negative consequences? Possibly because as adolescents spend more time working, they spend less time on homework, they are more fatigued in school, and their parents have a harder time monitoring their activities (Steinberg & Dornbusch, 1991).

Other research has found similar associations between working more than 10 or 15 hours a week and adolescents' psychological and behavioral adjustment. Additionally, longer work hours are associated with poor sleep, eating, and exercise habits (Bachman & Schulenberg, 1993; Marsh, 1991) (see Figure B9.1b). The association between longer work hours and behavior problems, however, could be attributable to troubled adolescents *selecting* themselves into jobs with longer work hours. A study of over 70,000 high school seniors found that students' difficulties in school were evident *before* they chose to take a job and work longer hours. In other words, adolescents who have a history of school difficulties may steer themselves into working long hours in the first place (Bachman & Schulenberg, 1993). Working may then amplify these problems (Steinberg, Fegley, & Dornbusch, 1993).

How much work is too much? Given this picture, adolescents have little to gain from working more than a few hours a week; working more than 20 hours a week is cause for real concern (Steinberg & Dornbusch, 1991). Moreover, although having had part-time jobs during adolescence may have a positive effect on the adult employability of high school dropouts (Greenberger & Steinberg, 1986; Stevenson, 1978), it is postsecondary education, rather than early work experience, that has become increasingly necessary for maintaining a good standard of living (Schulenberg & Ebata, 1994).

about the intrinsic rewards of work and more accepting of questionable business practices (Steinberg et al., 1981; Stephenson, 1979).

Studies of the quality of work point to the ways in which job conditions can affect adolescents' psychological health and well-being. For instance, a recent study by Jeylan Mortimer and her colleagues (1992) examined how specific features of adolescents' part-time jobs were related to their mental health and behavioral adjustment. Among boys, more stress at work (feeling overloaded and pressured for time) was related to symptoms of depression and feelings of inadequacy, and lower feelings of control over their lives. On the other hand, jobs that were seen as teaching skills to adolescents (such as learning to take responsibility and to manage money) were linked to stronger feelings of control, psychological well-being, and self-esteem, and lower alcohol use. For girls, the most significant predictor of mental health and behavioral adjustment was the extent to which work interfered with school. When interference with school was high, girls felt more depressed and less in control of their lives, experienced lower psychological well-being, and had poorer self-esteem. Compatibility between school and work, however, was linked to girls' better mental health (Mortimer et al., 1992). Another study indicated that adolescents' higher skill use (being able to use existing skills or to learn new ones) on the job was linked to lower substance use, higher life satisfaction and future hope, and lower interference between the job and family life (Schulenberg & Bachman, 1993). In addition, long work hours were not associated with higher substance use when the adolescent was using important skills on the job. The pattern of results from these studies suggests that part-time work can confer psycholog-

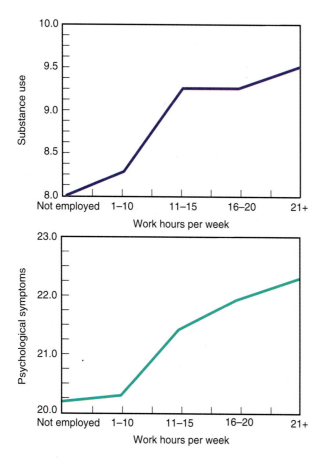

## Figure B9.1A

Hours of work per week and adolescent substance use (cigarette, alcohol, marijuana, and other drugs) and psychological symptoms (anxiety, depression, and tension). From L. Steinberg & S. M. Dornbusch (1991). Negative correlates of part-time employment during adolescence: Replication and elaboration. *Developmental Psychology, 27,* 304–315. Copyright © 1991 by the American Psychological Association. Reprinted with permission.

*box continues*

ical benefits on adolescents when conditions are good, but it can also take away from psychological well-being when the job is stressful or unproductive, or when it makes it difficult to complete educational or other important tasks.

## Psychological Significance of Work

In our society the choice of a particular line of work may help crystallize and reinforce an adolescent's self-concept (Super, 1967, 1980). For most people, young and old alike, vocational identity is an important part of their overall identity (Erikson, 1968; Marcia, 1980; Wallace-Broscious, Serafica, & Osipow, 1994). Consequently, it is

not surprising that having a job that society values—and doing it well—enhances self-esteem and aids in the development of an increasingly secure, stable sense of identity. Conversely, being given the message that one is not needed and that meaningful employment is not available fosters self-doubt, resentment, and loss of self-esteem, and increases the likelihood of identity confusion.

A very important aspect of most people's working lives is the fact that working gives them something to do and a sense of purpose in life. In 1994 American high school seniors were asked, "If you were to get enough money to live as comfortably as you'd like for the rest of your life, would you want to work?" Seventy percent stated that they would want to work, with girls outnumbering boys (78 percent versus 64 percent) (Bachman, Johnston, & O'Malley, in preparation).

Psychological benefits of working are shown in

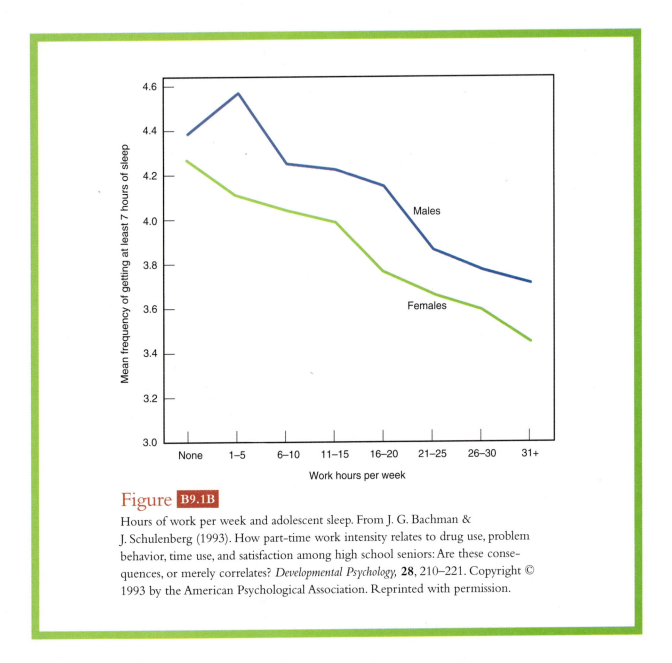

# Figure B9.1B

Hours of work per week and adolescent sleep. From J. G. Bachman & J. Schulenberg (1993). How part-time work intensity relates to drug use, problem behavior, time use, and satisfaction among high school seniors: Are these consequences, or merely correlates? *Developmental Psychology, 28,* 210–221. Copyright © 1993 by the American Psychological Association. Reprinted with permission.

research indicating that women who are employed outside the home are more likely to indicate overall satisfaction with their lives than those who are employed full-time as homemakers. Among both white- and blue-collar working women, employment may enhance feelings of self-worth and provide a sense of challenge (L. W. Hoffman, 1989; Sears & Galambos, 1993). At the same time, work that is unrewarding, frustrating, or extremely stressful, or that leads to failure, can have a negative effect on an individual's self-concept and create stresses in other areas (Conger, 1984; Kessler & McRae, 1982; Sears & Galambos, 1992). For example, when either mothers or fathers experience excessive strain resulting from the hassle of juggling the two roles of worker and parent, the effects may be disruptive, both for children and for parents—and for the family as a whole (Galambos et al., 1995; L. W. Hoffman, 1989).

The importance of work to one's psychological well-being can also be seen in studies demonstrating what happens when the opportunity to work is withdrawn. Unemployment, or job loss, results in significant psychological distress for the unemployed worker. Job loss is accompanied by increases in anxiety, depression, psychosomatic complaints, and negative and hostile moods—symptoms that begin to disappear once em-

High school students helping third graders. Jobs that require taking responsibility and using existing skills or learning new ones increase feelings of competence, control, and self-esteem.

ployment is reestablished. The absence of work also interferes with spousal and family relations, as spouses of unemployed workers suffer psychological distress, and the marital relationship becomes less supportive and more conflicted (Bolger et al., 1995; Flanagan, 1990; Liem & Liem, 1990).

## Development of Career Goals

As the time approaches when young people must support themselves, they are likely to spend more time thinking about career goals. They also become gradually more realistic about those goals. According to pioneering vocational theorists Eli Ginzberg (1972) and

Donald Super (1967, 1980), the following progression characterizes the development of occupational goals:

- *Childhood and pre-adolescence.* Occupational goals tend to reflect fantasy more than reality; children are likely to select occupations that seem active and exciting, such as cowboy or cowgirl, actor, baseball player, astronaut, firefighter, airline pilot or flight attendant, and explorer. When asked what she would like to be when grown up, one preschooler announced that she would like to be Tinkerbell.
- *Early to middle adolescence.* With the advent of more mature cognitive ability, young people tentatively begin to balance their interests against actual job opportunities and their own capabilities (Santilli & Furth, 1987). At about age 15 or 16, adolescents enter a period of exploration: They become increasingly aware of the need to make career decisions, and they are likely to seek out relevant occupational information. In a process known as crystallization, the young person searches for a workable match between his or her self-concept and the actual demands and opportunities of various careers (Osipow, 1986; Super, 1967, 1980). With adolescents' growing concern for articulating their values and beliefs, they are likely to look for occupations that allow for the expression of these values (Ginzberg, 1972), such as interest in service to others (Fuhrman, 1986).
- *Late adolescence.* Between the ages of 18 and 21, career choices tend to become increasingly specific (Super, 1967). Decisions made during this period can have important consequences for the young person's career. For example, a general interest in a career in business evolves into specific consideration of being a corporate lawyer. The individual identifies the specific education and training required for such a career and implements his or her educational plans and job experiences accordingly during the transition into adulthood.
- *Adulthood.* Younger adults are likely to settle on an occupation that represents a realistic reconciliation between what they would like to do and what they think they might actually be able to do. In the period of stabilization, adults (from ages 25 to 35) establish themselves in their career. This is followed by the period of consolidation (after age 35), in which they seek advancement into higher-status positions (Super, 1967, 1980).

Empirical studies support the concept of a steady but gradual maturation in vocational thinking during the adolescent years (Borow, 1966; Jepsen, 1984; Osipow,

1986), but most developmental theorists now believe that there is not a fixed cutoff point for settling into a career: Occupational choice is a lifelong decision-making process. This is demonstrated in the increasing numbers of mature students returning to universities to reshape their careers and in the interest many women show in obtaining an education or a job after their families are grown.

Approached from a life-span perspective, career development can be viewed in terms of the individual continually attempting to find the optimal fit between his or her career goals and the changing realities of the world of work. As circumstances, job experience, and characteristics of the person change over the years, new choices may be made, and new opportunities may be pursued, though sometimes not without some financial, social, or personal costs.

As we noted in Chapter 2, difficulty in choosing a career can be viewed in part as a problem in the development of a clear sense of identity. Certainty about the career one should follow is linked with the achievement of an overall sense of identity, whereas career indecision is likely to be found among adolescents who have not developed a coherent identity (Vondracek et al., 1995). In a society as complex as ours, in which the actual requirements of most jobs and their availability in the labor market are not matters of common knowledge, young people clearly need help in making career decisions. However, the availability of knowledgeable, skilled assistance is extremely limited. Consequently, the young person's career interests usually develop in a rather unsystematic fashion, guided by such influences as parental desires, relationships with parents, suggestions by school counselors, contact with people in various occupations, and the kinds of jobs friends are choosing.

## Personality Characteristics and Career Interests

An adolescent's personality characteristics, interests, and needs also help to shape vocational preferences. Vocational counselors use inventories (questionnaires) to guide the career decision-making process by identifying the individual's pattern of personality characteristics and personal interests. This pattern can then be compared with the patterns of successful individuals in various careers to find the best match. Vocational theorist John Holland has argued that a higher congruence or match between one's own personality and that of others in one's vocation is associated positively with eventual satisfaction, achievement, and stability in the job (Holland, 1985).

Holland's (1985) theory proposes six vocational interest types: realistic, investigative, artistic, social, enterprising, and conventional. Early studies showed that adolescent boys with vocational interests in artistic fields were more likely than boys with other interests to perceive themselves as introspective, intuitive, disorderly, imaginative, original, sensitive, unconventional, enthusiastic, rebellious, and impractical (Holland, 1963a, 1963b). Boys with investigative interests were more likely to perceive themselves as analytical, imaginative, curious, reserved, and scholarly. Those with entrepreneurial or enterprising interests (e.g., sales manager) were more likely to perceive themselves as aggressive, striving, dominant, conventional, energetic, extroverted, industrious, practical, persuasive, and not particularly interested in artistic, idealistic, scholarly, or scientific pursuits.

More recent studies indicate that young women and men with social and enterprising interests have extroverted personalities. Investigative and artistic interests are found among those who score high on openness. Finally, those with conventional interests are likely to be higher on self-control (Gottfredson, Jones, & Holland, 1993).

Although vocational interest inventories are widely used to fit personality and interest patterns to career choices, some theorists argue that such inventories are of limited usefulness to the people who need them most: those who are most indecisive about what career to follow (Schwartz, 1992). This problem may stem in part from a gap between the stereotyped image of what an occupation involves and occupational reality. For example, some interest inventories assume that dentistry is an occupation most suitable for those with investigative interests but, in fact, studies have pointed out that dentistry might best serve those with realistic more than investigative interests (Schwartz, 1992).

An adolescent's own stereotypes may limit his or her career possibilities. Many adolescents have a fantasy or a stereotyped picture of what an engineer, army officer, veterinarian, actor, or nurse is like and what he or she does—a fantasy that contains some of the gratifications sought by the young person and usually has at least some relationship to reality. To illustrate, the most common attributes assigned to engineers by high school seniors of superior ability were found to be (in order of frequency): practical, builders, useful, intelligent, inventive, important, interesting, and hard-working (Holland, 1963a). Teachers, in contrast, were seen as underpaid, dedicated, indispensable to society, patient, and helpful. Accountants were seen as dull, precise, mathematically inclined, boring, methodical, and unimaginative, but also as necessary. Such stereotypes obviously can be misleading, and the chances of a student's selecting an occupa-

tion that is consonant with his or her own needs will be greatly enhanced by actual knowledge about a variety of careers. Unfortunately, such knowledge is all too limited and often influenced by stereotyped thinking, even among vocational counselors.

# Subcultural Influences on Career Choice

**Socioeconomic Status.**     Status attainment research, which examines the factors associated with adolescents' educational and occupational aspirations and achievements, identifies family socioeconomic status (SES) as a significant influence on career choice. Youth from higher-SES families aspire to higher-prestige careers more often than do their counterparts in lower-SES families. Females from such backgrounds are more likely to choose nontraditional, high-prestige occupations (Hannah & Kahn, 1989; Holms & Esses, 1988; Wilson, Peterson, & Wilson, 1993).

Why does family SES matter? For one thing, it helps to determine the kinds of occupations to which the young person is exposed and which he or she is likely to consider. In addition, it plays an important role in determining the social acceptability (i.e., reward value) of particular occupations. Certain types of occupations are considered appropriate to members of a particular family economic background, whereas others may be seen as inappropriate. The person who deviates from these expectations is likely to evoke the disapproval of family and peers, particularly if the chosen occupation is associated with lower prestige.

The very young child from a high-SES background may be indulged or even encouraged when he or she mentions the desire to become an ice cream vendor or a truck driver. During adolescence, however, when vocational choice takes on practical implications, the child's parents are not likely to find such notions amusing. Choices of lower-status occupations run counter to the parents' ideas about appropriate behavior for a member of their family, and consequently are likely to be discouraged.

Many otherwise tolerant and reasonably flexible middle- and upper-middle-class parents would react severely to an adolescent daughter's announcement that she intends to be a cashier in a grocery store, or a son's statement that he intends to drive a cab, in order to devote as much time as possible to painting or writing poetry. Parents may fear that such choices will lead to social disapproval both of their child and of themselves. Moreover, when the economic rewards of the selected

occupation are meager, parents may fear that the child will not be able to live in the same kind of neighborhood as they do, or to afford the same social, recreational, and educational advantages.

For adolescents from lower-SES backgrounds, aspirations toward higher-status occupations may lead to social disapproval (particularly if they are flaunted) because such aspirations may be viewed as incongruent with the adolescent's social background, threatening to others in the adolescent's social milieu, or simply as unattainable dreams. In this case, however, the disapproval is likely to be less strong and, in the adolescent's view, may be more than outweighed by the prospect of higher rewards. A longitudinal study that followed low-income rural Appalachian adolescent females into young adulthood found that their eventual occupational attainment was largely dependent on the father's education (one measure of SES). Female adolescents with better-educated fathers were expected by their parents to do better educationally and occupationally; these higher expectations, in turn, were translated into higher occupational attainments in adulthood. The converse was true for females whose fathers were more poorly educated and whose parents had lower educational and occupational aspirations for them (Wilson, Peterson, & Wilson, 1993).

Many adolescents may be somewhat unrealistic about the occupational goals they can attain. Nevertheless, young people possess some awareness of the practical obstacles that may modify their aspirations, and these, in turn, are certainly affected by socioeconomic status. Although some adolescents can improve their status with the encouragement and help of their parents (Wilson, Peterson, & Wilson, 1993), a working-class girl whose parents are unable or unwilling to help her go to college is less likely to aspire to be an engineer than one whose parents encourage such a vocational choice and are in a financial position to help her. Similarly, a boy whose parents expect him to go to work after the 9th grade is not likely to spend much time contemplating the idea of becoming a dentist.

**The Growing Underclass.**     The career outlooks of both middle- and working-class students are quite different from those of a growing **underclass**—people who have been, and see themselves as, excluded from participation in the system (Dryfoos, 1990; Lemann, 1986; Panel on High-Risk Youth, 1993). As discussed later in this chapter, desperately poor, predominantly minority young people growing up in the heart of a socially disorganized inner city who see that the great majority of their peers are out of work, with virtually no prospect of future employment, are likely to have no sustainable

vocational hopes, or, more rarely, to have highly unrealistic aspirations (Children's Defense Fund [CDF], 1995; Edelman, 1987; Freeman, 1986).

## Gender

Just as the social and economic environment can limit adolescents' occupational aspirations, so too can gender. Despite women's increased participation in the labor force, the influence of the women's movement, and decreased sex-role stereotyping, the career choices of many teens of both sexes still reflect relatively traditional, sex-related occupational aspirations, such as secretary or teacher for females and skilled worker for males (*America's youth,* 1988; Schulenberg, Goldstein, & Vondracek, 1991). However, at least as many female as male high school seniors now aspire to managerial and professional occupations such as office manager, lawyer, physician, dentist, and college professor (Bachman, Johnston, & O'Malley, in preparation).

Such gender differences and similarities in occupational aspirations are also seen after high school. On entering college, more young women than men are planning to enter such occupations as clinical psychologist, nurse, elementary schoolteacher, and physical or occupational therapist (see Table 9.1). Conversely, more young men are planning to enter such occupations as engineer, business owner, computer programmer, and the skilled trades (Astin et al., 1994).

Although there are still dramatic sex differences in some fields (in particular, engineering and nursing), the gap has been closing in other fields in which males traditionally dominated. In 1994, for example, slightly more

## Table 9.1 Sex Differences in Probable Occupations of First-Year College and University Students, 1994

| PROBABLE OCCUPATION | MEN | WOMEN |
|---|---|---|
| Accountant or actuary | 3.1% | 4.4% |
| Architect or urban planner | 3.4 | 1.0 |
| Business executive | 8.2 | 5.7 |
| Business owner or proprietor | 4.0 | 1.3 |
| Clinical psychologist | 0.7 | 2.6 |
| Computer programmer or analyst | 4.0 | 1.5 |
| Engineer | 12.5 | 2.5 |
| Law enforcement officer | 2.9 | 0.6 |
| Lawyer or judge | 3.9 | 4.6 |
| Military officer or enlistee | 1.3 | 0.3 |
| Nurse | 1.1 | 8.8 |
| Physician | 5.3 | 5.6 |
| Social, welfare, or recreation worker | 0.5 | 2.6 |
| Therapist (physical, occupational, speech) | 2.6 | 5.5 |
| Teacher (elementary) | 1.7 | 8.4 |
| Teacher (secondary) | 3.8 | 3.6 |
| Writer or journalist | 1.7 | 2.3 |
| Skilled trades person | 2.9 | 0.3 |

SOURCE: A. W. Astin, W. S. Korn, L. J. Sax, & K. M. Mahoney (1994). *The American freshman: National norms for fall 1994.* Los Angeles: Higher Education Research Institute Graduate School of Education, University of California. By permission.

female than male first-year college and university students reported that their probable occupation would be physician. The percentage of females interested in being a lawyer or judge also surpassed the percentage of interested males (see Table 9.1). Data on educational aspirations support the perception that the gap between males and females is narrowing, at least in some fields. Twenty-eight percent of U.S. women who were in their first year of college in 1994, for instance, aspired to an advanced degree (a doctoral, medical, or law degree) compared to 26 percent of men. This represents a dramatic change in the years since 1968, when fewer than 10 percent of first-year college women aspired to an advanced degree (see Figure 9.2) (Astin et al., 1994).

One source of sex differences in occupational choices may be the differences in the occupational values men and women hold. Women often place a high value on helping people through their occupations, whereas men traditionally have been more concerned with the extrinsic aspects of work, such as attaining money, status, and security (Lueptow, 1992). Data on high school seniors in the 1976 through 1994 graduating classes indicate consistent sex differences in adolescents' views of the importance of helping others in a job (see Figure 9.3). Although there is a consistent sex difference in the importance of earning a good deal of money, with more

More adolescent girls than boys are currently choosing jobs traditionally filled by members of the opposite sex, partly as a result of changing occupational values, but also because of the greater number and variety of traditionally male jobs in our society.

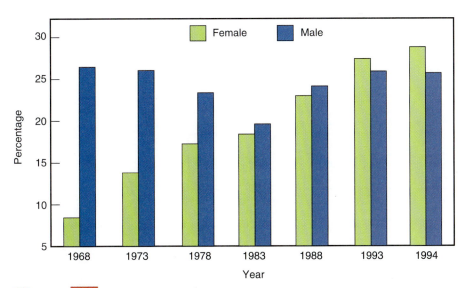

## Figure 9.2

Aspirations toward advanced degrees (doctorate, medicine, law) of male and female entering college and university students, 1968–1994. From A. W. Astin, W. S. Korn, & E. R. Riggs (1993). *The American freshman: National norms for fall 1993;* and A. W. Astin, W. S. Korn, L. J. Sax, & K. M. Mahoney (1994). *The American Freshman: National norms for fall 1994.* Los Angeles: Higher Education Research Institute Graduate School of Education, University of California. Adapted by permission.

males having this goal, there was a dramatic rise in the late 1970s and 1980s in the importance of money to females, thereby narrowing the gap between females and males (Schulenberg et al., 1995). This increasing emphasis on extrinsic rewards among females might be partly responsible for the inroads they are making into some previously male-dominated fields. In the 1990s, however, the gap has widened; initially, the importance of this goal declined among both sexes, but then leveled off among males, and not among females (see Figure 9.4).

The trend toward females' interest in formerly male-dominated occupations may be due not only to changing occupational values, but also to the greater number and variety of traditionally male jobs in our society and to many girls' newfound freedom from inhibitions about aspiring to male-dominated occupations. Most mothers of adolescent girls are now in the workplace, modeling work as a natural part of life. Some of these mothers hold jobs not traditional for females. Both black and white girls whose mothers have non-traditional jobs are more likely to choose such occupations than are girls with mothers in female-dominated jobs (Etaugh, 1993; McLoyd, 1993).

## Parental Influences on Career Choice

Parents play a significant role in a young person's vocational choice. In general, if parents set high educational and occupational goals and reward good schoolwork, their children have high levels of aspiration. Working-class adolescents are more likely to choose advanced education and occupational mobility if their parents urge them to do so (L. W. Hoffman, 1989). A major reason for the superior academic success of many Asian students, including children of recent immigrants, lies in the great importance their families attach to education and hard work, together with the high credibility of parental

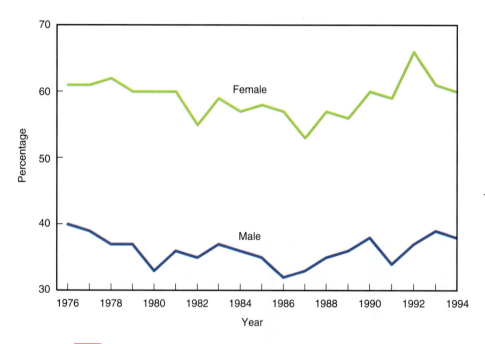

## Figure 9.3

Sex differences in percentages of adolescents who indicated it is very important to have a job in which they can help others. From J. Schulenberg, J. G. Bachman, L. D. Johnston, & P. M. O'Malley (1995). American adolescents' views on family and work: Historical trends from 1976–1992. In P. Noack, M. Hofer, & J. Youniss (Eds.), *Psychological responses to social change* (pp. 37–64). New York: Walter de Gruyter; J. G. Bachman, L. D. Johnston, & P. M. O'Malley. (In preparation.) *Monitoring the future, 1993–1994.* Ann Arbor: Institute for Social Research, The University of Michigan. By permission.

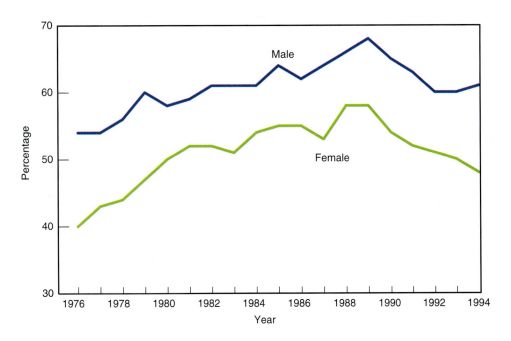

**Figure** 9.4

Sex differences in percentages of adolescents who indicated it is very important to have a job in which they can earn a good deal of money. From J. Schulenberg, J. G. Bachman, L. D. Johnston, & P. M. O'Malley (1995). American adolescents' views on family and work: Historical trends from 1976–1992. In P. Noack, M. Hofer, & J. Youniss (Eds.), *Psychological responses to social change* (pp. 37–64). New York: Walter de Gruyter; J. G. Bachman, L. D. Johnston, & P. M. O'Malley. (In preparation.) *Monitoring the future, 1993–1994.* Ann Arbor: Institute for Social Research, University of Michigan. By permission.

values in the eyes of their children (Brand, 1987). As we will see, parents' occupations and the way parents view their work also can significantly influence the career choices of their children.

## Father's Occupation

Perhaps the clearest indication of the effect of a father's occupation on adolescent career choices is in the consistent findings that the number of sons following in their father's footsteps greatly exceeds what one would expect by chance, even if socioeconomic influences are taken into account (Barling, 1991; Mortimer, 1974, 1976; Mortimer, Lorence, & Kumka, 1986). For example, sons of physicians, lawyers, and scientists are far more likely to enter these occupations than are other young men of similar socioeconomic status.

These findings can probably be explained partly in terms of such obvious factors as greater opportunity to

become familiar with one's father's occupation, greater access to that occupation, and at least in some cases (such as physicians), strong parental motivation—and sometimes pressure—for the son to enter the occupation. However, recent research suggests that more subtle factors also play a part; one such factor is the communication of values from parent to child (Mortimer, 1976; Mortimer, Lorence, & Kumka, 1986).

Several theorists believe that "through one's job one develops notions of what qualities and values are important for success, and these ideas are embodied in child-rearing patterns" (L. W. Hoffman, 1986, p. 184). For example, fathers in middle-class white-collar occupations that involve the manipulation of ideas, symbols, and interpersonal relations, and that require considerable flexibility, thought, and judgment place a high value on self-direction and independence (Kohn & Schooler, 1978, 1982). Accordingly, they emphasize achievement, independence, and self-reliance in child-rearing. In contrast, lower-class or blue-collar fathers whose occupa-

## 9.2 Family Values and Career Goals

Most adolescent girls and boys expect to combine a career with raising children, but because of different gender-related pressures and the low level of institutional support for employed parents, the burdens associated with this contemporary lifestyle fall more often on the shoulders of women. Wives in general perform more than their share of the household chores and child care, and more often leave the labor force or work part-time (Camarena, Stemmler, & Petersen, 1994). This pattern contributes to women's lower levels of pay, occupational prestige, and slower advances through the career hierarchy relative to men.

Although most adolescent girls intend to combine work with family, many will give up career opportunities, at least in young adulthood. One longitudinal study conducted in Sweden found that most young women (at age 26) could be characterized as having either a homemaking orientation (having children) *or* a career orientation (following a postsecondary educational path); very few actually integrated the two (Gustafson, Stattin, & Magnusson, 1992). The career-oriented young adult women were significantly more likely than their homemaking counterparts to have had higher educational motivation as adolescents (at age 15). They were also less likely to have associated with older peers and working peers, and to have had a boyfriend during adolescence. This study suggests that for many young women, work and family are incompatible, and the path that women take in early adulthood begins to take shape in adolescence.

Other studies have suggested that adolescent boys expect continuity in their work and family

lives (having both are not incompatible) or they do not question their future ability to combine both worlds. Adolescent girls are more likely to anticipate the conflicts that will arise, particularly in late adolescence, and to incorporate such concerns into the identity development process (Archer, 1985, 1989; Camarena, Stemmler, & Peterson, 1994; Holms & Esses, 1988).

What factors contribute to a strong career orientation among young women? High-status occupational expectations are more likely to be found among women with less-traditional sex-role attitudes, and less (but not an absent) emphasis on children and marriage. Young women who plan to enter nontraditional careers typically score higher on measures of academic ability (particularly in the physical and biological sciences and in mathematics) and have higher grades. They are also likely to be more independent and assertive and more concerned with exhibiting competence. Their mothers are more likely to work outside the home and to have a positive orientation toward working (Etaugh, 1993; Galambos, Peterson, & Lenerz, 1988; L.W. Hoffman, 1989; Holms & Esses, 1988; Marini, 1978).

In contrast, the young women who plan to become full-time homemakers are likely to strongly endorse traditional values with respect to the occupational and domestic roles of men and women. They also have more traditional perceptions of male and female behavior generally and lower educational aspirations, and they are strongly committed to marrying and having children.

tions are more standardized, less complex, more closely supervised, and more likely to require the manipulation of physical objects than of ideas or interpersonal relationships are more likely to value obedience and conformity in their child-rearing practices.

Although other factors clearly play a role in determining the values and practices emphasized by parents, there are indications that on-the-job experiences also make an important contribution (L.W. Hoffman, 1989). In one study, workers in a plant that actively engaged

workers in management decision-making were asked about some of the effects of their experiences (Crouter, 1984). Many described how their personal experiences on the job had led them to use similar methods with their children:

I have a 16-year-old son and I use some of the things we do at work with him instead of yelling. We listen better here, we let people tell their side.

I say things to my 8-year-old daughter that I know are a result of the way we do things at work. I ask her, "What do you think about that?" or "How would you handle this problem?"

In terms of dealing with my family, I'm more willing to get their opinions. We hold "team meetings" at home to make decisions (Crouter, 1984, pp. 81–82).

In an interesting series of studies, Mortimer (1974, 1976; Mortimer, Lorence, & Kumka, 1986) investigated the hypothesis that value differences between business and professional occupations and work activities are transmitted from fathers to sons and influence their sons' subsequent occupational choices. Professional occupations were seen as placing greater emphasis on intrinsic work satisfactions such as autonomy, expert knowledge, and opportunities for service; business occupations, in turn, were found to place more emphasis on such extrinsic rewards as high income and advancement. This investigator examined the occupational choices of college students whose fathers were professionals (such as physicians, scientists, lawyers, and teachers), high-prestige businessmen, or lower-prestige businessmen. In addition, the degree of closeness between father and son was measured. A number of interesting findings emerged. As predicted, sons of professionals were more likely than sons of businessmen to choose a profession; the latter were more likely to choose business. However, sons were far more likely to choose a vocation similar to that of the father when the father's job had high prestige and the son had a close relationship with his father. For example, among the sons of high-prestige businessmen, those who were close to their fathers were almost twice as likely to choose a career in business as those who were not close to their fathers. When the prestige of the father's job was low, even sons who felt close to their fathers apparently were motivated to look elsewhere to find their life's work.

**Fathers as Role Models.**  The kinds of role models—both positive and negative—that parents provide affect not only career choice but also overall vocational adjustment. In addition, the relevance of parental models may vary considerably with age. Both of these possibilities were investigated in a longitudinal study of male adolescents that assessed them during the 9th grade (average age 15) and again when they had been out of high school for 7 years (age 25) (Bell, 1969).

Using interviews, the investigators attempted to determine the adolescent's primary role models in various "life spheres" (i.e., educational, occupational, and personal), as well as the position occupied by the model on a dimension ranging from highly positive to negative. Vocational adjustment was measured by a variety of criteria, including fulfillment of original occupational goal, job stability, reasons for changing jobs, occupational level, job competence and success, job satisfaction, and the like. The following interesting findings emerged:

- The most commonly mentioned role model, both in 9th grade and in young adulthood, was the father. However, with age the importance of the father decreased and that of other figures, including peers, teachers, adult relatives, employers, and other adults, increased.
- Of all the role models adolescents possessed when they were in the 9th grade (such as father, mother, siblings, and adult relatives), only the father's role-modeling was related to the sons' vocational adjustment and behaviors 10 years later.
- In general, boys who at age 15 had fathers as strong and positive role models tended to achieve higher levels of vocational adjustment than those for whom fathers were either weak or nonexistent role models or negative models.
- Sons of negative role models were less likely to have achieved vocational success than were sons of weak or nonexistent role models.
- The kinds of relationships obtained between father-modeling at age 15 and vocational adjustment at 25 are no longer found when father-modeling at age 25 and vocational adjustment at 25 are examined. At age 25 *moderate* use of the father as a positive role model is significantly more often associated with successful vocational adjustment than either strong positive modeling or negative modeling.

The researchers concluded that a father who is a strong and positive role model may be an important source of self-definition in adolescence, but that this importance wanes somewhat in young adulthood as reliance on the father decreases and other individuals emerge as sources of influence (Bell, 1969, p. 34).

Although this research points to ways in which fathers transmit occupational values to their sons, fathers' employment generally has been called a "neglected influence on children" (Barling, 1991, p. 181). We still know relatively little about how fathers' jobs influence their children, and this is particularly true for fathers and their daughters. The availability of studies of the influences of mothers' employment on children, however, is a different story.

## Mother's Occupation

Studies of fathers' influence on adolescents' career goals have tended to focus on the idea that the father's occupation affects the child because the traits required for success in that occupation are valued and passed on to the child (L. W. Hoffman, 1984). In studies of the mother's influence, the focus has been primarily on her employment status per se (whether she is employed or not) (Bronfenbrenner & Crouter, 1982; Frankel, 1993; Greenberger & Goldberg, 1989; Hoffman, 1989). Until recently, it was assumed that maternal employment outside the home was likely to have an adverse effect on the general development of children and adolescents. However, a mounting body of research suggests that this is not the case. There is little evidence that maternal investment in work occurs at the expense of appropriate child rearing (Greenberger & Goldberg, 1989; Lerner & Galambos, 1991). Working does not produce poor parenting, just as staying home does not guarantee good parenting.

The picture that recent research paints is that many employed mothers spend no less time with their children than do nonemployed mothers, but the activities that they engage in may be somewhat different. One study showed that young adolescents (ages 10 to 13) with full-time employed mothers spent as much time with their mothers as adolescents who had part-time employed or nonemployed mothers (Richards & Duckett, 1994). The time that was shared was simply more likely to take place in the evenings than in the afternoons. What adolescents and mothers did together also differed by mothers' employment status. Mothers employed full-time spent more time on homework and less time in general leisure with their adolescents. Mothers employed part-time engaged in more shared sports activities with their adolescents. This study also found that adolescents in two-earner families spent more time alone with their fathers (Richards & Duckett, 1994).

Engaging in mother–child activities may be the key to effectively combining family and work. One study found that full-time employed mothers who compensated for longer work hours by *frequently* sharing mother–child activities had children who did well socially and academically. Full-time employed mothers who infrequently shared activities with their children had children with poorer social and academic outcomes (Moorehouse, 1991).

**Attitudes Toward Sex Roles, Family, and Work.** A number of studies have indicated that the views of girls and young women (and, in most cases, males) regarding the appropriate roles for women and men were influenced by their mothers' employment status. In the middle-childhood and adolescent years, girls and boys whose mothers worked outside the home were more likely than those with nonemployed mothers to view both men and women as typically engaging in a wider variety of adult activities, including those that have traditionally been stereotyped as masculine or feminine. They were also more likely to say that they approved of maternal employment (Gold & Andres, 1978a, 1978b; Hartley, 1960; L. W. Hoffman, 1989; Marantz & Mansfield, 1977; Stephan & Corder, 1985).

Girls and young women whose mothers are employed outside the home also are more likely to view work as something they will want to do if and when they become mothers (Galambos, Peterson, & Lenerz, 1988; Huston, 1983). A study of high school students compared males and females in dual-career families (both parents working in high-prestige occupations) to those in traditional single-career families (father working in a high-prestige occupation). Females from a dual-career background were more likely to expect to combine work and motherhood, desired fewer children, and expected their future husbands to help more with child care. Males from dual-career families also were more likely than males from single-career families to expect that their future wives would combine work and motherhood. Both female and male adolescents in dual-career families had less traditional sex-role attitudes (Stephan & Corder, 1985). In a study of the sex-role perceptions of college students, one team of investigators found that young women and young men with employed mothers perceived smaller male–female differences compared with children of nonemployed mothers on such generally sex-stereotyped attributes as competence and warmth-expressiveness, with females being more affected by maternal employment than males (Vogel et al., 1970).

The sex-role attitudes and occupational aspirations of children and adolescents are influenced not simply by the fact of maternal employment as such but by the mother's attitude toward employment, her degree of satisfaction and accomplishment in her work, and her ability to successfully combine the roles of worker, mother, and wife (Galambos, Petersen, & Lenerz, 1988; Gottfried, Gottfried, & Bathurst, 1988; Guidubaldi & Nastasi, 1987; L. W. Hoffman, 1989). One study found that whether a young woman expresses positive attitudes toward employment combined with homemaking depends on "whether her mother endorses it and, if the mother works, upon how successfully she has integrated her two roles. Mothers who worked but had also experienced negative personal consequences because of their careers had daughters who evaluated women's competence highly but were unfavorable to the dual role pattern" (Baruch, 1972, p. 37). The daughter's attitudes were also influenced by whether her father expressed acceptance of his wife's career orientation.

A variety of investigations have found that "highly achieving women and women who aspire to careers, particularly to less conventionally feminine careers, are more likely to be the daughters of educated women and the daughters of employed women. The high-achieving woman has a high-achieving daughter" (L. W. Hoffman, 1973, p. 213). Lois Hoffman (1989) suggests several reasons for this. First, the mother provides a model of achievement for her daughter. Second, such mothers are more likely to encourage independence in their daughters; this is particularly important because many girls are handicapped by overprotection and encouragement of dependency. Daughters of working mothers tend to be more autonomous, active, self-reliant, and achievement-oriented. They also are somewhat more likely to view their mothers as people whom they admire and want to be like (Almquist & Angrist, 1971; Gold & Andres, 1978a; Hock, 1978; L. W. Hoffman, 1989; Stephan & Corder, 1985). Some of the apparently positive consequences of mothers' employment for girls may have to do with the greater responsibility they are given. Adolescent daughters in dual-earner families spend significantly more time doing household chores than daughters in single-earner families (Benin & Edwards, 1990). Finally, optimum conditions include a good relationship with the father, who encourages the girl's independence and achievement while accepting her as a female (Hoffman, 1989).

**Employed Mothers and Their Sons.** Although encouragement of independence by employed mothers is likely to have positive effects on daughters, it is not clear whether it is an advantage or a disadvantage to sons. Sons traditionally have received more independence training than daughters, and although this seems to be an advantage in families with nonemployed mothers, it may be too much in those in which the mother is employed (L. W. Hoffman, 1989). Among middle-class boys, in contrast to girls, maternal employment is associated with somewhat lower IQ scores, lower school performance, and, possibly, a greater incidence of aggressive behavior and adjustment problems (Gold & Andres, 1978b; L. W. Hoffman, 1980, 1986; Montemayor, 1984; Montemayor & Clayton, 1983).

Some theorists have suggested that the sons of working mothers, perhaps because of their greater independence, may be more likely to become involved in peer groups that undermine adult socialization (Bronfenbrenner & Crouter, 1982; Montemayor, 1984). Conversely, sons of full-time homemakers were more inhibited and conforming in early adolescence, but they also performed better in school (Moore, 1975). It may be that employed mothers place too much pressure for independence on their adolescent sons, whereas mothers who are full-time homemakers unwittingly encourage con-

formity and place too little emphasis on independence training (L. W. Hoffman, 1989).

Investigators have also found that employed mothers (and their husbands) have more positive views of their daughters than of their sons, whereas the reverse is true for nonworking mothers (Bronfenbrenner, Alvarez, & Henderson, 1984). Whereas employed mothers tend to view their daughters as self-reliant and helpful, they are more likely to complain about their sons' noncompliance and aggressiveness. In turn, adolescent sons (but not daughters) report more frequent, longer, and more intense conflicts with employed mothers than with nonemployed mothers (Montemayor, 1984). It may be that employed mothers are less tolerant than nonemployed mothers of the greater aggressiveness and rebellious tendencies of adolescent boys. It is also possible that the lack of supervision and greater peer group involvement of sons of employed mothers tends to foster increased conflicts with parental values and expectations (Bronfenbrenner & Crouter, 1982; Montemayor, 1984). Considerably more research will be needed before firm conclusions can be reached on this subject.

In brief, full-time involvement of mothers in careers that they enjoy and do well in appears to have positive effects on the educational and vocational aspirations of adolescent girls. However, the picture is not as clear or as positive in the case of middle-class sons of employed mothers.

# Current Trends in Career Values

The vocational values and attitudes of young people today differ in a number of important respects from those of their counterparts in earlier generations (Conger, 1981, 1988, 1991a). Reflecting the youth culture of the time, young people (particularly college students) in the late 1960s became more concerned than their predecessors with finding work that provided opportunities for individuality, self-expression, and personal growth. Moreover, the number who felt that this could not be done within the existing economic system reached an all-time high (Yankelovich, 1974). Some sought alternative occupations as a means of self-expression (art, music, or skilled crafts), as a way of achieving a new lifestyle (through communal living), or to promote social change (by working as counselors of runaway children or organizers of the poor in ghettos). However, most planned to and eventually did enter relatively traditional careers, although they remained far more critical of business values and practices than their predecessors a decade earlier.

In the intervening years there have been profound changes in social values, rapid and often unpredictable shifts in patterns of occupational demand, and, perhaps most significant, stagnant or declining earnings (in constant, inflation-adjusted dollars) and a dramatic rise in the cost of goods and services. In contrast to the situation in earlier periods, even a reasonably well-paying job no longer guarantees access to a home of one's own, a college education for one's children, or financial security during retirement.

Consequently, it is hardly surprising that the percentage of strongly career-minded college students has increased steadily in recent years while the number of students who view their college experience as a period of self-discovery and change has declined considerably (Astin et al., 1994; Yankelovich, 1981). Between 1969 and 1994 the percentage of first-year college students in the United States who cited being very well-off financially as an essential or very important objective increased from slightly less than half to more than three out of four (76 percent of males and 72 percent of females). Among high school seniors, too, there has been a parallel but less dramatic increase in the number for whom the chance to earn a good deal of money was

rated as very important in a job, although the trend shifted downward in the early 1990s (see Figure 9.4) (Schulenberg et al., 1995).

In accordance with these changing concerns and values, the percentages of college students enrolling in the arts and humanities and the sciences declined steadily during the 1970s and much of the 1980s. Interest in the arts and humanities seems to have recovered slightly in the early 1990s, however. But interest in the biological and physical sciences has continued to decline, and interest in mathematics and statistics has declined by 85 percent, to a mere 0.6 percent of entering college students in 1994—nowhere near the level necessary to sustain an increasingly technological society (Astin et al., 1994).

Perhaps reflecting the trend toward the valuing of financial security, the percentages of first-year college and university students enrolling in such fields as business and preprofessional programs increased in the 1970s and 1980s (Astin et al., 1994; Dey, Astin, & Korn, 1991). Since the late 1980s, however, interest in a business major has declined sharply (from a peak of 27.3 percent in 1987 to only 15.9 percent in 1994), while interest in preprofessional programs and in all allied health fields continued to rise significantly (see Figure 9.5).

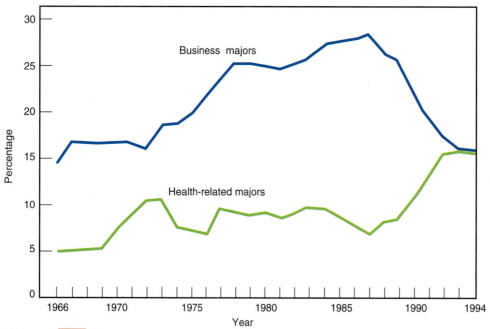

## Figure 9.5

Changing interest in business and health-related majors of entering college and university students, 1966–1994. Adapted from A. W. Astin, W. S. Korn, & E. R. Riggs (1993). *The American freshman: National norms for fall 1993*; A. W. Astin, W. S. Korn, L. J. Sax, & K. M. Mahoney (1994). *The American freshman: National norms for fall 1994*. Los Angeles: Higher Education Research Institute, Graduate School of Education, University of California. Adapted by permission.

How can we explain the sharp drop in interest in business? It may be that the business scandals of the 1980s—insider trading, corporate crime, stock frauds, and the savings and loan debacle—made careers in business seem less attractive. Perhaps the increased competition and the job dislocations of corporate downsizing in the 1990s led more students to look elsewhere, as evidenced by rising interest in allied health fields, such as physical therapy, and in graduate professional programs, such as medicine and clinical psychology, all of which reached recent highs (Astin et al., 1994; Dey, Astin, & Korn, 1991).

The kinds of changes we have been discussing have been particularly evident among entering women students. For example, although interest in such traditional fields as teaching and nursing has risen slightly in the last few years, it remains well below the levels of 30 years ago (Astin et al., 1994; Dey, Astin, & Korn, 1991). In contrast, interest in fields such as medicine, law, and engineering has expanded exponentially in the same period (often by as much as 500 percent).

Do the kinds of changes in the vocational interests of today's entering college students mean, as some social critics have suggested, that contemporary adolescents and youth are engaged in a return to pre-1960s vocational values and goals? The answer is clearly no. A study of college students in the late 1950s found them to be "models of the status quo," with few real commitments and a rather uncritical acceptance of the values and practices of social institutions generally, including those of government and big business (Goldsen et al., 1960; Wolensky, 1977).

In contrast, today's adolescents and youth, although they are generally more willing to adjust to the demands of the workplace and more ready to accept compromise than their predecessors, are far less willing than the youth of the 1950s to suppress their individuality and need for self-expression. Nor are they as ready or willing to accept a sharp dichotomy between their private lives and their work, and they do not see a great need to do so. Although they acknowledge an interest in economic security and "getting ahead," they are also concerned that their work be personally rewarding (Conger, 1981, 1988). When 1994 college-bound American high school seniors were asked what things they rated very important in a job, the three most frequent responses were having "interesting things to do" (85 percent), "using skills and ability" (71 percent), and "not having to pretend to be the type of person you are not" (72 percent). Only 28 percent stressed "high status, prestige," but over 61 percent wanted "good chances for advancement" and 66 percent considered a "predictable, secure future" very important (Bachman, Johnston, & O'Malley, in preparation).

Nor do today's youth share the unquestioning faith in big business (and other social institutions) that charac-

terized their counterparts in the 1950s, although their views were somewhat more favorable in the 1990s than they were at the beginning of the 1980s. For example, in 1994 less than one-third believed that corporations are doing a good or very good job for the country (Bachman, Johnston, & O'Malley, in preparation). Only 28 percent thought that corporations should have less influence on people's lives (down from 55 percent in 1980). In brief, today's young people want to combine challenging work, self-expression, and time for family, friends, and outside interests with at least a moderately high income, economic security, and the chance to get ahead.

# Career Prospects in a Changing World

What, then, are the prospects for today's adolescents and young adults, in terms of the numbers and kinds of jobs that are likely to be available? Between 1960 and 1980 the number of youth of working age increased by nearly 50 percent. Together with the dramatic increase in the participation of women in the labor force during the same period (from 38 percent to 52 percent), this produced a surge in available workers that could not easily be absorbed by the labor market (Fullerton, 1986; Smith, 1979). Teenage unemployment rates increased accordingly, reaching a high of over 20 percent for all teenagers by 1980.

Since 1980, however, the number of young people has been declining steadily, and it will continue to do so into the next century (U.S. Department of Labor, 1994a). As a consequence, young people between the ages of 16 and 24, who made up nearly one-quarter of the total workforce in 1980, accounted for only 19 percent of all workers in 1987; this figure is projected to drop further, to 16 percent, by 2005 before rising again (U.S. Bureau of the Census, 1994; U.S. Department of Labor, 1994a, 1994b). Whereas the postwar baby-boom generation faced a growing shortage of jobs, the employers of the "baby-bust" generation have encountered a growing shortage of entry-level workers.

At present, the problem for employers is most acute in retail and service businesses such as fast-food restaurants, gasoline stations, department and convenience stores, and sectors of the lodging and recreation industries, which have traditionally relied heavily on younger workers. But many employers who look to graduates of colleges and skilled training programs will increasingly feel the impact as this shrinking population group moves through the economy behind the baby-boom generation (who are now in the 35–50 age bracket).

These population trends appear to augur well for the vocational prospects of the generation of young peo-

ple who are now coming of age. However, a number of cautions are necessary. In the past 25 years automation and rapid technological change (especially in the development and application of computer technology), the consolidation of small businesses and farms into larger ones, and increased urbanization have produced significant shifts in employment patterns. Even for qualified workers, there will be significant variations in the kinds of skills that are in demand at any one time, together with marked regional variations in overall employment rates, as the economy continues to shift away from the production of goods to the provision of services (U.S. Department of Labor, 1994a, 1994b).

The number of jobs available to unskilled industrial workers and farm workers declined during the 1970s through the early 1990s; meanwhile, the number of jobs for professional and technical workers, and for workers engaged in service occupations and clerical and sales positions, rose significantly (Hudson Institute, 1987; Personick, 1986; U.S. Department of Labor, 1994b). These trends are expected to continue well into the next century. In particular, occupations involving trade and services will con-

tinue to employ many more people than those involving the production of manufactured goods (see Figure 9.1). Moreover, among service jobs, the fastest-growing and better-paying will require increasingly higher educational skills as our technologically oriented, information-based society becomes ever more complex. When jobs in the U.S. economy were ranked according to the skills they required, it was found that the fastest-growing require much more mathematical, language, and reasoning capabilities than current jobs generally, whereas jobs that require less are the slowest growing.

It is clear from these trends that poorly educated youth with few skills will find themselves increasingly penalized in the years ahead (see Figure 9.6). For example, among 16- to 21-year-olds who were seeking work and not in college in 1993, more than twice as many dropouts as high school graduates were unemployed (24 percent versus 15 percent) (U.S. Bureau of the Census, 1994).

Even more critical, however, is the fact that large segments of poor and minority youth have become increasingly isolated not only from participation in the economy but from the mainstream of American society.

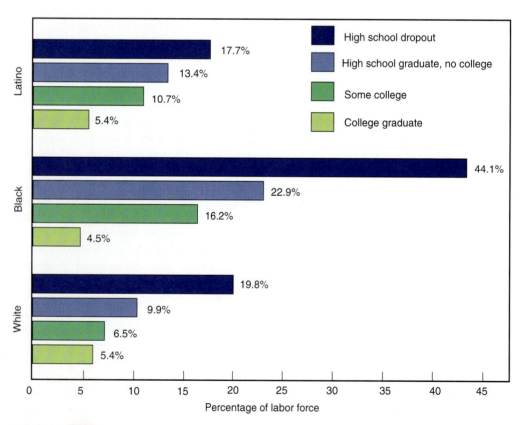

## Figure 9.6

Unemployment rates of youth not enrolled in school, by race/ethnic origin, and educational attainment.

SOURCE: U.S. Department of Labor, Bureau of Labor Statistics and Children's Defense Fund, 1995.

Although the current economic recovery and the shrinking youth population have contributed to a decline since the early '80s in the unemployment rate among black youth, in late 1993 it was still over 40 percent for males and over 37 percent for females, much higher than the rates for white teenagers (slightly less than 18 percent for males and 15 percent for females). Among Hispanics, the comparable rates were 26 percent for both males and females (U.S. Bureau of the Census, 1994). In some inner-city areas the teenage minority unemployment rate still runs as high as 70 percent or more. What is particularly troubling is that the discrepancy between whites and blacks has increased steadily in the past four decades; in 1954, the teenage unemployment rate for blacks exceeded that for whites by only 4.5 percent (16.5 percent versus 12 percent). Our society is in real danger of creating a permanent underclass of poor minority youth (Freeman, 1986; Panel on High-Risk Youth, 1993; U.S. Department of Labor, 1994b).

**Prisoners of the City.** Why have young blacks fared so badly in the labor market, even during periods of prosperity? One reason for high unemployment among young blacks is that they tend to be concentrated in the inner-city areas of larger, and often poorer, cities. As a result, they are likely to be exposed to inadequate and inappropriate educational facilities and to a climate of social disorganization (CDF, 1995; Panel on High-Risk Youth, 1993). In many of these areas conditions have deteriorated steadily since the 1950s and early 1960s as people who were able to move away did so. Those who left included community leaders who had played an important role in creating and maintaining stability in social institutions such as schools, churches, businesses, theaters, social clubs, and political organizations (Lemann, 1986; Panel on High-Risk Youth, 1993).

As neighborhoods have eroded, crime, unemployment, inadequate education, high dropout rates, drug use (especially use of crack cocaine), and gang violence have all escalated. Not surprisingly, young people growing up in such an environment are less likely to view conventional employment as a workable alternative to crime or welfare dependency; even when this is not the case, many inner-city teenagers lack the minimum skills in reading, arithmetic, and interpersonal interaction necessary to master even entry-level jobs (Freeman, 1986; Panel on High-Risk Youth, 1993).

At the same time, new job opportunities keep moving farther away from the inner-city areas where they are needed. For many inner-city youth, the only realistic chance of breaking out of the cycle of poverty and depression lies in specifically targeted, adequately funded educational and training programs and accessible initial employment opportunities (CDF, 1995; *The forgotten half,* 1988; Panel on High-Risk Youth, 1993; Schorr, 1988; Simons, Finlay, & Yang, 1991).

Unfortunately, government policies and practices have been moving in the opposite direction in the past decade, a trend accelerated by the elimination of many job and training programs for youth by the new congressional majority in 1995. Although a few private employers have attempted to deal with some of these problems (by hiring unqualified inner-city young people and training them for entry-level jobs), a great deal more needs to be done, both by government and by the private sector.

One reason that so many young blacks have fared badly in the labor market is that they tend to be concentrated in inner-city areas of larger, and often poorer, cities with inadequate schools, a climate of social disorganization, and few job opportunities.

It is doubtful that job-related activities alone can be effective on a broad scale unless some effort is also made to address social conditions that have created many of the problems (CDF, 1995). In the words of Neil Short-house, director of Exodus, a business-backed job-train-ing program for disadvantaged youth in Atlanta, "These kids are imprisoned in social and educational bondage, and they're not going to get free unless we help them" (Bacas, 1986, p. 20).

## Women in the Work Force: New Opportunities and Old Realities

**Women and Work: The Revolution.** One of the most dramatic and significant changes in North American society since the end of World War II has been the precipitous rise in the number of women entering the job market. Women are entering the labor market in numbers that far outstrip all earlier projections, and there is no sign of a letup in the current decade. Approximately 60 percent of all women between the ages of 16 and 64 (compared to 75 percent of men) cur-rently work outside the home for pay, and their ranks are increasing at the rate of over a million per year (U.S. Bureau of the Census, 1995; U.S. Department of Labor, 1994b). As we saw in Chapter 5, the largest increases in labor-force participation rates in the last decade were among women with children under age 6. More young women are working before marriage, delaying marriage, and returning to work after the birth of children.

The reasons for these profound social changes are both economic and social. They include a sharply de-clining birthrate, increased employment opportunities, higher salaries for women, and changing social and sex roles (Wessel, 1986). The shrinking dollar and the decline in real income during the 1980s (Panel on High-Risk Youth, 1993) were also in part responsible for women entering the labor force as two incomes became—and continue to be—an economic necessity for many families. Many mothers were also thrust into the labor force as they became divorced or pregnant outside of marriage; the number of single-parent house-holds almost doubled between 1970 and 1990, with most of these headed by mothers (Panel on High-Risk Youth, 1993).

Combining work with motherhood, however, is extremely demanding. It is not surprising that although the majority of working mothers are currently employed full-time, most of those with younger children would prefer to work part-time, to have more flexible hours,

or to work from their homes if it were economically fea-sible (Kantrowitz, 1986; Taylor, 1986). In a continuing national survey, the attitudes of high school seniors toward various hypothetical working arrangements were investigated. In 1992, 73 percent of males and 83 per-cent of females indicated that if they were married with no children it would be desirable or acceptable for both husband and wife to work full-time. This represents a dramatic change from 1976, when the figures were 48 percent (males) and 66 percent (females) (Schulenberg et al., 1995).

The picture changed significantly when the pres-ence of preschool children was considered. In 1992, slightly less than one-third of male and female high school seniors believed that full-time employment for both husband and wife was desirable or acceptable if there were preschool children. These figures represent-ed an all-time high, and contrasted sharply with the 1976 senior class, in which 12 percent of males and 13 percent of females found such arrangements desirable or acceptable (Schulenberg et al., 1995).

**Career Prospects.** It is estimated that women will account for three-fifths of the growth of the labor force between 1993 and 2005 (U.S. Bureau of the Census, 1995; U.S. Department of Labor, 1994). What are the career prospects for women entering the labor force? If one looks only at current statistics for women as a whole, one may conclude that the prospects are not very good. Full-time earnings for women are still only about 70 per-cent of those for men. Moreover, the great majority of working women still hold jobs in the fields in which women have traditionally been employed, such as secre-tary, typist, or word processor; registered nurse, licensed practical nurse, or nurse's aide; bookkeeper, office clerk, or record processor; sales clerk (retail trade) or cashier; waiter or food-service worker; health care worker or technician; and private household worker (U.S. Bureau of the Census, 1995; U.S. Department of Labor, 1994). It is also the case that at the highest levels of corporate America, women still encounter a glass ceiling; in 1995, less than 5 percent of the top executives of the Fortune 500 companies were women (Reich, 1995).

Nevertheless, the opportunities for women with appropriate education or training are expanding signifi-cantly. For example, since the early 1970s the percentages of female lawyers and judges, physicians, economists, accountants and auditors, bank officials, financial man-agers, scientists, engineers, computer systems analysts, sales managers, electricians and carpenters, telephone installers and line workers, firefighters, police officers, and detec-tives more than doubled, and in some instances increased

The myth of Supermom, who juggles a demanding job, children, and household responsibilities smoothly and skillfully without stress or fatigue, had pretty well faded by the mid-1990s.

sixfold (U.S. Department of Labor, 1983, 1994a; U.S. Bureau of the Census, 1978, 1994). Between 1972 and 1993 there were dramatic rises in the percentage of female lawyers and judges (from 3.8 to 22.8 percent), physicians (from 10.1 to 20.5 percent), accountants and auditors (from 21.7 to 45.7 percent), and sales managers in retail trade (from 15.6 to 31.8 percent) (U.S. Bureau of the Census, 1978, 1994).

The age at which women begin working and the continuity of their work experience play important roles in career development. Advancement in a career is, in part, a function of continuity and experience on the job. Significant interruptions are likely to result in a loss of relative position in the competition. But reconciling the demands of work and family life can be difficult, particularly when children are small and when the job is one that demands great flexibility and long hours, as is the case for many corporate executives (Kantrowitz, 1986; Taylor, 1986).

Several studies have shown that significantly more women MBAs than men who are parents leave jobs in corporate management 10 years after graduation from business school. They do so in order to assume less all-consuming jobs or to start businesses of their own, either full- or part-time, that involve more flexible hours (Cowan, 1989; Taylor, 1986). Even in less-demanding jobs, however, juggling job, children, and household responsibilities is not easy. The myth of Supermom, who handles all of these demands smoothly and skillfully without stress or fatigue, had pretty well faded by the mid-1990s.

If women are to succeed in combining these multiple responsibilities, greater support is needed, not only from other family members but from society as a whole. The United States does less than many European countries to accommodate working parents through family support systems such as paid leaves, child allowances, subsidized day care, and free health services (*Workforce 2000,* 1987). More companies are instituting programs such as temporary part-time or at-home work after a child is born, more flexible hours, job sharing, unpaid child-care leaves, and company-operated day care facilities. Nevertheless, in the words of former labor secretary William Brock, "It's just incredible that we have seen the feminization of the work force with no more adaptation than we have had. It is a problem of sufficient magnitude that everybody is going to have to play a role: families, individuals, businesses, local government, state government" (Kantrowitz, 1986, p. 47).

## College Graduates: Demand and Supply in the 1990s

Although throughout the 1990s there will be more job opportunities for youth with more skills and education, this does not mean that graduation from a college or university will guarantee a high-level job, even with smaller numbers of young people coming into the job market. A major reason for this is the unprecedented rise in the number of college graduates, which increased more than 2.5 times between 1960 and 1994. The num-

ber of professional, technical, and managerial occupations did not expand rapidly enough to absorb this increase; about one in five college graduates is likely to take a job that does not usually require a degree (U.S. Department of Labor, 1986a, 1986b, 1988, 1994b; U.S. Bureau of the Census, 1989, 1994).

The oversupply of college graduates is likely to continue through the 1990s. Not all occupations that require a college degree will be overcrowded, however. For example, there will be good opportunities for systems analysts, engineers, computer scientists, physical therapists, psychologists, nurses, and elementary- and secondary-school teachers (see Figure 9.7). There are many other occupations where the numbers required are less, but the need will still be great; as we saw in Chapter 8, there is an urgent and growing need for individuals with high levels of mathematical skills, yet ever fewer students are taking degrees in mathematics (Mullis et al., 1994). Moreover, in all occupations, crowded or not, people who are knowledgeable, and have superior skills in language, mathematics, and reasoning ability are more likely than their less well-prepared peers to succeed.

Overall, earnings continue to be consistently higher and unemployment rates lower for university graduates (U.S. Department of Labor, 1994b). A college degree is still needed for most high-paying and high-status jobs.

One of the problems of a high-technology society competing in a global economy is that it demands highly specialized, often nontransferable skills, but it also generates rapid shifts in technology and in the economy that may make those skills obsolete in a relatively short period of time. The problem of preparing young people for the vocational demands of tomorrow is not a simple one. If anything, it is likely to become more difficult in the future as our society grows more complex, more specialized, more technologically oriented, and more subject to the effects of forces beyond our immediate control. Nevertheless, it is a problem that can be solved if society is willing to increase its commitment to the well-being of the nation's youth. From this perspective, current efforts to reduce the nation's budget deficit by eliminating or drastically cutting educational, training, and other support programs for children and youth appears penny wise and pound foolish.

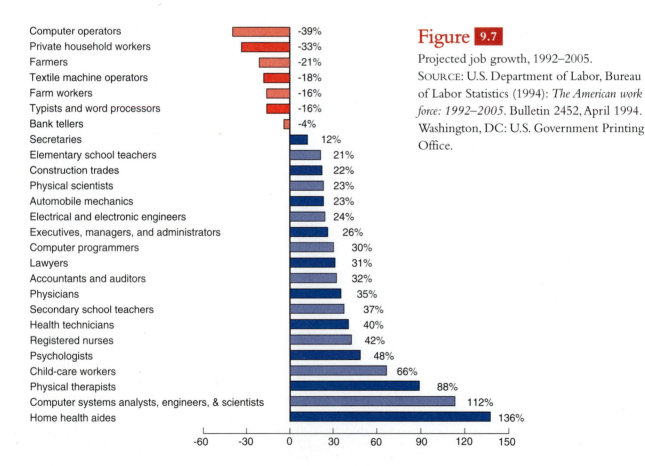

**Figure** 9.7

Projected job growth, 1992–2005.
SOURCE: U.S. Department of Labor, Bureau of Labor Statistics (1994): *The American work force: 1992–2005.* Bulletin 2452, April 1994. Washington, DC: U.S. Government Printing Office.

# Summary

Deciding on and preparing for a vocation is one of the major developmental tasks of adolescence. Constructive work experience can give adolescents a sense of purpose and a feeling that they are participating in society. However, many of the jobs that are most commonly available to adolescents, such as working at a fast-food outlet, do little to encourage educational and vocational planning. In some instances they may also interfere with schoolwork.

Having a job that society values enhances self-esteem and contributes to a person's sense of identity. Conversely, getting the message that one is not needed and that meaningful employment is not available fosters self-doubt and resentment.

In earlier times choosing a vocation was much simpler than it is in today's complex, rapidly changing society. In the past 50 years there has been a marked shift from the "old workplace" (craftshop, factory, farm) to the "new workplace" (service and sales business). As a result of automation there is less and less opportunity for unskilled and semiskilled workers.

Before adolescence a child's occupational goals are likely to reflect fantasy more than reality. With the advent of more mature cognitive ability, young people begin to balance their interests against actual job opportunities and their own capabilities. In the late teens, career choices tend to become increasingly crystallized and specific, as well as more stable. In contemporary society, however, career development can be a lifelong process, with some people shifting occupations in their adult years.

Personality characteristics, interests, and needs are related to vocational interests. For example, young women and men with interests in social and enterprising (e.g., business) vocations tend to have extroverted personalities. Those with investigative (e.g., scientific) and artistic interests are more likely than others to score high on openness. Those with conventional interests (e.g., bank tellers, file clerks) are more likely to score high on control.

Socioeconomic status and gender play a role in the development of career goals. Adolescents from lower-SES families are less likely to aspire to high-prestige occupations. Those in the growing underclass of poor families living in the inner cities, with few prospects of meaningful future employment, are likely to have no sustainable vocational hopes.

Although the career choices of many young people still reflect traditional sex-related aspirations, many more young women are planning to enter traditionally male fields such as law and medicine. Young women with high-status occupational expectations are likely to have less-traditional sex-role attitudes. In contrast, the minority of young women who plan to be full-time homemakers tend to endorse traditional sex roles. Occupying a middle ground are adolescents who plan to stay home while their children are young but work before having children and after their children are in school.

Parents play a significant role in vocational choice. If they set high educational and occupational goals, their children are likely to have high aspirations. Fathers are likely to have the strongest influence on the career choices and vocational values of their sons when there is a close relationship with the father and when the father's job has high prestige. Adolescents of both sexes whose mothers are employed are less likely to have stereotyped views regarding appropriate sex and vocational roles for women.

Employed mothers are more likely than nonemployed mothers to encourage independence in their children, and, indeed, their daughters are likely to be more autonomous, self-reliant, and achievement-oriented. Whether encouragement of independence by employed mothers has a similarly positive effect on sons is more open to question. Among middle-class boys maternal employment is associated with lower school performance and, possibly, a greater incidence of aggressive behavior and adjustment problems.

The percentage of strongly career-oriented college students has increased steadily in recent years, whereas the number who view college as a period of self-discovery has declined. Among both high school and college students, "getting ahead" and making money have become increasingly important goals; accordingly, the percentages of students enrolling in the arts and humanities declined steadily through the 1980s (but with a slight recovery in the early 1990s) whereas the numbers enrolling in preprofessional programs have increased. Interest in business rose through the 1980s but has declined dramatically in recent years. Although contemporary youth are willing to work hard, they are not willing to suppress their individuality and need for self-expression. Today's young people want to combine challenging work, self-expression, and time for family, friends, and outside interests with at least a moderately high income, economic security, and the chance to get ahead.

The reduced number of young people who will be entering the job market in the 1990s generally augurs well for their vocational prospects. However, poorly educated youth with few skills will find themselves increasingly penalized in the years ahead. The situation is most critical for poor and minority youth living in inner cities, who have become increasingly isolated from the mainstream of North American society. In some such areas unemployment rates still run as high as 70 percent or more.

One of the most significant changes in North American society since World War II has been the rapid increase in the number of women entering the job market. A majority of married women with children under 6 are now employed outside the home. Although a majority of women continue to enter traditional occupations, opportunities for appropriately educated and trained women are expanding. The percentages of female lawyers and judges, economists, financial managers, computer systems analysts, and scientists more than doubled since the 1970s. Nevertheless, reconciling the demands of work and family can be difficult, and much greater support is needed from society in the form of paid leaves, subsidized day care, more flexible hours, and the like.

Although in the 1990s more jobs will be available for youth with more skills and education, a college degree will not guarantee a high-level job. Whereas the number of college graduates increased by 2.5 times in recent decades, the number of professional, technical, and managerial positions did not expand rapidly enough to absorb the increase. Even so, unemployment rates will remain consistently lower for college graduates. A college degree is still needed for most high-paying and high-status jobs.

# Review Questions

1. Some authorities maintain that work experience during adolescence promotes personal growth and aids in the transition to the adult world; others disagree. Can these opposing views be reconciled? Discuss.

2. Describe the development of vocational interests and goals from childhood through adolescence.

3. Are personality characteristics, interests, and psychological needs related to vocational interests? If so, how?

4. In what ways do socioeconomic status and gender influence vocational goals in adolescence, and why?

5. In what ways do fathers and mothers influence the vocational attitudes and goals of female and male adolescents?

6. How have the vocational values and goals of male and female adolescents and youth changed in the past three decades?

7. What effects has the women's movement had on the participation of women in the workforce?

8. What are the vocational prospects for male and female adolescents and youth in the 1990s, and how do they differ by ethnicity? Discuss the specific problems faced by many poor inner-city youth. How important is graduation from college?

# Recommended Readings

Fox, M. F., & Hesse-Biber, S. (1984). *Women at work.* Mountain View, CA: Mayfield.

Frankel, J. (Ed.). (1993). *The employed mother and the family context.* New York: Springer.

Greenberger, E., & Steinberg, L. (1986). *When teenagers work: The psychological and social costs of adolescent employment.* New York: Basic Books.

Hoffman, L. W. (1989). Effects of maternal employment in the two-parent family. *American Psychologist, **44,** 283–292.

Osipow, S. H. (1986). Career issues through the life span. In M. Pallak & R. O. Perloff, *Psychology and work: Productivity, change, and employment* (pp. 141–168). Washington, DC: American Psychological Association.

Schulenberg, J., Bachman, J. G., Johnston, L. D., & O'Malley, P. M. (1995). American adolescents' views on family and work: Historical trends from 1976–1992. In P. Noack, M. Hofer, & J. Youniss (Eds.), *Psychological responses to social change: Human development in changing environments* (pp. 37–64). Berlin: Walter de Gruyter.

# Moral Development
# and Values

## 10

S eldom is a person as likely to be concerned about moral values and standards as during adolescence. This should not be surprising. In the first place, rapid cognitive development tends to make adolescents more aware of moral questions and values and better able to deal with them in a relatively sophisticated way. In addition, the social expectations and demands confronting young people, and the experiences they are undergoing, change at an accelerated rate during these years; this is especially so during periods such as the present, when society itself is changing rapidly (Conger, 1988, 1993). As a consequence, the developing adolescent is likely to be exposed to a multiplicity of shifting, sometimes conflicting values and standards of behavior.

The task of choosing among these values and standards is often complicated by a discrepancy between adolescents' increased capacity for comprehending moral issues and their limited experience in dealing with moral issues and their consequences in everyday life. Nevertheless, choices that involve morality must be made. For some adolescents, having moral convictions and acting on them plays a central role in the development of a strong identity: Even in the early years of adolescence, they are actively defining themselves in part by their morality (e.g., "I am honest and kind"). Other young people may take more time to acquire an identity in which moral judgments and behaviors play a central role. Finally, a minority of adolescents may never really consider moral values to be a central and enduring part of themselves (Colby & Damon, 1992; Damon & Hart, 1992; Davidson & Youniss, 1991, 1995). In considering what morality is, psychologists William Damon and Daniel Hart argue that "In some ways, morality represents the abnegation of one's self-interest in favor of the welfare of others. In other ways, morality clearly represents the best way to achieve one's enlightened self-interest" (1992, pp. 444–445).

Although there is little debate about the importance of moral issues and values to adolescents, there is considerable controversy about the nature of **moral development,** its maturational course, and the factors influencing it. Three basic approaches have been taken toward understanding moral development: cognitive, affective, and

social (Youniss, 1981). The cognitive view of moral development, as developed by Jean Piaget and Lawrence Kohlberg, focuses on moral reasoning and considers cognitive development to be the necessary stimulus for changes in moral development, with changes occurring in predictable stages paralleling the stages of cognitive development. The affective perspective, as developed by psychologists such as Carol Gilligan, views morality in more personal terms, stressing the importance of feelings such as empathy, sympathy, compassion, and guilt, all of which are thought to be strongly influenced by socialization. The social perspective views morality as linked primarily to peer experiences and the related sense of community. At the core of morality, whether its roots are more cognitive or more social, is the development of a conscience: an *internalized* set of moral standards and prohibitions. As we shall see, parents play an important part in the socialization process that produces a conscience; so do peers and the larger community.

Morality is a complex phenomenon. A fully developed individual morality has been described as involving four elements (Carroll & Rest, 1982; Rest, 1986):

- Recognition of, and sensitivity to, a given social situation, leading to an awareness that a moral problem exists
- Moral judgment, in order to determine what ought to be done in a given situation
- Values and influences that affect one's plan of action consistent with moral ideals, but that consider non-moral values and goals that the situation may activate, as well as the influence of situational pressures
- Execution and implementation of moral action, involving behavior consistent with one's goals despite distractions, impediments, and incidental adjustment

As an illustration of these four elements, imagine that one day, Dave, an office worker, is wrongly accused of stealing some valuable materials from the private office of the vice-president. Dave knows that his job is on the line, and he has some reason to suspect that a manager, Sheila, actually has the stolen materials in her locked private office in the workplace. Late in the day, as Dave passes by Sheila's office, he observes that the custodian has left the door slightly ajar. Does he go in and look through Sheila's belongings?

With respect to the four elements of morality, Dave first recognizes that he is faced with a moral dilemma: It is wrong to enter Sheila's private office but it is also wrong if he loses his job unfairly. Second, Dave judges the situation: He should not search Sheila's office if he is to behave in a moral manner. Third, Dave considers that if he searched Sheila's office and found the stolen materials he could appropriately point the finger at her.

Despite the temptation, Dave plans instead to suggest his suspicions about Sheila to the vice-president. Taking action, Dave walks past Sheila's office, and discusses his suspicions with the vice-president the next day. How many people would take this action, having recognized the moral dilemma and having judged it in the same manner that Dave did?

Although common sense tells us that moral actions are rooted in moral thinking or judgments, research has documented that there can be a disjunction between moral judgment and behavior. Sometimes people behave in ways that they know they should not (Damon & Hart, 1992). When people are asked to name models or exemplars of morality (such as Mother Theresa), they often justify their choices in terms of the consistency of words and action, choosing people who not only make thoughtful moral judgments, but act accordingly (Walker et al., 1995).

Too often there has been a tendency to view morality in terms of a single component. For example, some have argued that morality involves the ability to think adequately about a moral situation. Others have construed morality as primarily involving values. Still others have argued that it has to do mainly with what people do, rather than what they think or believe.

It seems clear, however, that morality involves all of these components. A person may fail to act morally because of lack of sensitivity to the needs of others, because of limited cognitive capacities, because of constraints in the situation (such as threats from others), because of some limitation that prevents him or her from carrying out the appropriate behavior (such as not knowing how to swim and, hence, not rescuing someone who is drowning), or because the rewards of not behaving morally are simply too great to be passed up (e.g., "the store won't miss that extra $20 that was unintentionally given to me").

## Piaget's Cognitive Perspective on Moral Development

Jean Piaget's conceptualization of moral development was the starting point for much research in this area. Piaget (1948) argued that the organizing principles of the child's world, though different from those of the adult's world, have a coherent structure of their own. This view contrasted sharply with the dominant view of the time, in which moral development was viewed primarily as a process of socialization whereby the moral standards of the adult world were taught to children and eventually internalized by them (Durkheim, 1961). Although Piaget did not dispute the importance of socialization, he

maintained that the organization of moral thought in younger children is quite distinct from that found in older children and adults. According to Piaget, younger children base their moral judgments largely on the consequences of their actions, whereas older children are more likely to take intentions into account.

One method Piaget used in his investigations of morality was to present children with a pair of hypothetical stories. One such story depicted a boy who knocked over fifteen cups while coming to dinner; the other story depicted a boy who broke one cup while attempting to sneak some jam out of a cupboard. Younger children were more likely to consider the first boy naughtier because he broke fifteen cups whereas the second boy broke only one. Older children consistently viewed the second boy as naughtier because he was trying to sneak some jam.

Though generally supporting Piaget's position, more research showed that the situation is more complex than Piaget thought (Karniol, 1978; Rest, 1983). In the example cited earlier, Piaget confounded *consequences* (the number of broken cups) with *intentions* (trying to sneak jam versus an accident). However, when children are presented with stories in which intent can be separated from outcome, even 6-year-olds are able to use intentions as a basis for their moral judgments (Feldman et al., 1976; Schultz, Wright, & Schleifer, 1986).

# Kohlberg's Cognitive–Developmental Perspective on Moral Development

Piaget's work was extended and refined by Lawrence Kohlberg, a psychologist at Harvard, and his associates (Colby et al., 1980; Kohlberg, 1979, 1987; Kohlberg, Boyd, & Levine, 1990). They expanded Piaget's method by presenting a more complicated set of moral dilemmas that involve twelve basic moral concepts, values, or issues. Participants are asked to describe what the actor in the moral dilemma ought to do, and to justify that course of action. For example, in order to gain information about a person's conceptualization of "the basis of moral worth of human life," he or she is asked such questions as whether a druggist should give a life-saving drug to a dying woman when her husband cannot pay for it, and whether it is better to save the life of one important person or the lives of a large number of unimportant people.

On the basis of the responses obtained, the investigators concluded that children and adolescents tend to progress through six stages of moral thought, which are divided into three major levels: **preconventional, conventional,** and **postconventional,** or autonomous (Kohlberg & Gilligan, 1971).

## Level 1: Preconventional Reasoning

**Stage 1: Punishment–Obedience.** During the preschool years the child is governed mostly by whatever he or she wants to do at a particular moment. With the advent of concrete-operational thinking, however, the child may enter the first of two preconventional stages of moral development. During this stage the child is responsive to cultural labels of "good" and "bad" but interprets these labels largely in terms of their tangible consequences (for example, whether a particular behavior is followed by punishment). Behaviors that are punished are perceived as bad and to be avoided, and there is likely to be an "unquestioning deference to superior power" (Kohlberg & Gilligan, 1971, p. 1067). The child in this stage refrains from writing on the walls with a crayon not because she sees that property would be damaged, but because Mom has threatened to send her to bed if she does it.

**Stage 2: Instrumental Hedonism.** During the second preconventional stage some progress is made beyond the punishment–obedience orientation. At this juncture the child is more likely to conform in order to obtain rewards, have favors returned, and the like. "Human relations are viewed in terms like those of the market place. Elements of fairness, reciprocity, and equal sharing are present, but they are always interpreted in a physical, pragmatic way. Reciprocity is a matter of 'you scratch my back and I'll scratch yours,' not of loyalty, gratitude, or justice" (Kohlberg & Gilligan, 1971, p. 1067). For example, when asked, "Should Joe tell on his older brother to his father?" (for going someplace he was not supposed to go), one boy replied, "I think he should keep quiet. He might want to go someplace like that, and if he squeals on Alex [the older brother], Alex might squeal on him" (Kohlberg, 1969, p. 243).

In our society, by the time the average child reaches adolescence his or her thinking about moral issues has already shifted away from Stage 1, in which the child is governed by literal obedience to rules and authority with the aim of avoiding punishment. A majority of children have also begun to shift away from Stage 2, which is characterized by a rather simply conceived doctrine of reciprocity: acting to meet one's own needs and letting others do the same, and doing what is "fair" or what constitutes an equal exchange.

# Level 2: Conventional Reasoning

**Stage 3: Good Boy–Good Girl.** During adolescence, conventional moral thinking tends to be dominant. In conventional morality a focus on societal needs and values takes precedence over individual interests. Initially this is likely to involve a strong emphasis on being "a good person in your own eyes and those of others" (Kohlberg, 1976, p. 34), which means having good motives and showing concern about others. Typically, there is considerable emphasis on conformity to stereotypical images of majority or "natural" behavior. Reflecting increased cognitive development, the intentions behind behavior, not simply the behavior itself, take on greater importance; one seeks approval by "being good." This kind of reasoning is evident in the argument offered by some people that homosexuality is unacceptable because the majority of the population is heterosexual.

**Stage 4: Authority Maintenance.** This approach is subsequently expanded to include an orientation toward authority, fixed rules, and the maintenance of the social order. Right behavior consists of doing one's duty, showing respect for authority, and maintaining the given social order for its own sake. At this stage, a social perspective takes precedence; there is concern not only with conformity to one's social order, but also with maintaining, supporting, and justifying this order (Kohlberg & Gilligan, 1971, p. 1067). From the perspective of someone in this stage, rules or laws should not be bent. For example, even though stealing a drug for a penniless dying woman would save her life, stealing cannot be condoned because it is against the law. Contrary to earlier assumptions, it appears that many adolescents (and adults) may not advance beyond this level (Kohlberg, 1987; Rest, 1986; Turiel, Edwards, & Kohlberg, 1978).

# Level 3: Postconventional Reasoning

**Stage 5: Social Contract.** Some do advance to what Kohlberg called postconventional or principled thinking. At this level, particular societal arrangements are seen as deriving from a broader moral perspective, which the rational, moral individual has to develop for herself or himself; Kohlberg calls this a "prior-to-society" perspective (Colby et al., 1980; Kohlberg, 1976). Reflecting the acquisition of formal-operational think-

ing, this level is characterized by a "major thrust toward abstract moral principles which are universally applicable, and not tied to any particular social group" (Kohlberg & Gilligan, 1971, pp. 1066–1067). The person who grapples with the issue of euthanasia, considering and recognizing the various conflicting perspectives, and arrives at an answer that reflects "the greatest good for the greatest number" would be reasoning at this stage of moral thought.

**Stage 6: Universal Principle.** In the most advanced, and least likely to be achieved, stage of formal principled thinking, there is an effort to formulate abstract ethical principles that appeal to logical comprehensiveness, universality, and consistency. These principles include equal rights for all humans and respect for the dignity of human beings as individual persons. The adolescent may no longer be able to adopt without question the social or political beliefs of his or her parents (Elkind, 1968, 1984). Principled thinking is shown in the response of an adolescent boy, age 16, who was asked whether a husband should steal an expensive black-market drug from an exploitive druggist to save his wife's life. The response was, "By the law of society he was wrong but by the law of nature or of God the druggist was wrong and the husband was justified. Human life is above financial gain. Regardless of who was dying, if it was a total stranger, man has a duty to save him from dying" (Kohlberg, 1969, p. 244).

# Transitions Through Kohlberg's Stages

Placement of individuals into Kohlberg's stages originally relied on a method of scoring so complicated and requiring so much training that other methods of assessment were developed. One of these, called the Defining Issues Test (DIT), was developed by James Rest, a psychologist at the University of Minnesota. It is based on the same theoretical perspective as Kohlberg's method, but it uses a multiple-choice format that allows for more objective scoring (Rest, 1986). In addition to the format differences, the DIT is a recognition task that involves identifying the way of thinking most like the research participant's, whereas Kohlberg's test is a production task that requires participants to generate a line of reasoning on their own. Different methods may yield similar, but not always identical, results.

The six-stage model of moral judgment has been validated in both cross-sectional and longitudinal studies using different methods, although individuals are

rarely found in the sixth stage (Colby & Kohlberg, 1987; Colby et al., 1980; Galotti, Kozberg, & Farmer, 1991; Holstein, 1976; Rest, 1986). Change from one stage of moral development to another appears to be gradual and slow, with considerable overlap between stages (Carroll & Rest, 1982; Walker, 1989). Although some longitudinal studies indicate that about 7 percent of the participants actually move downward in moral level at some juncture, most of the movement is upward. In a 20-year longitudinal study of males, Kohlberg and his colleagues found a gradual change from stage to stage, with all participants showing the same sequence of stages and no one skipping a stage (Colby et al., 1980). Similar results have been found in societies as diverse as Mexico, Turkey, Britain, Canada, and New Zealand. However, development tends to be slower and more limited in more traditional, lower-income, and rural areas (Colby et al., 1980; Edwards, 1980; Turiel, Edwards, & Kohlberg, 1978).

## Influences on Moral Reasoning

One influence on moral reasoning is the individual's cognitive abilities. A number of studies have shown that a certain level of cognitive development is necessary for a given level of moral reasoning. At the same time, the level of cognitive development is not sufficient to guarantee moral reasoning at a corresponding level (Rowe & Marcia, 1980; Walker, 1980).

Piaget suggested that moral development was influenced by cognitive disequilibrium—awareness that there are multiple and conflicting perspectives on a problem—and by experiences of cooperation with peers (Piaget, 1970). Kohlberg emphasized the importance of social experiences, particularly opportunities for role playing, in which the individual is able to take the viewpoint of another person, as in the case of shared confidences among friends in childhood and adolescence (Kohlberg, 1969; Rest, 1986). Others have stressed the importance of breadth and diversity in life experiences, including the diversity that can be present in school and family settings (Lam et al., 1993; Power, Higgins, & Kohlberg, 1989; Spickelmier, 1983).

There is support for each of these assertions. Moral judgment is strongly correlated with level of formal education. Higher levels of education and higher degrees of involvement in educational activities generally increase opportunities to be exposed to diverse and sometimes conflicting views (cognitive disequilibrium) and to peer influences (Barnett & Volker, 1985;

Colby et al., 1983; Rest, 1986). Research has found that cognitive disequilibrium is associated with transitions to higher stages of moral reasoning (Walker & Taylor, 1991b). In peer discussions, for example, cognitively immature people whose arguments are critiqued and challenged by their more cognitively advanced peers subsequently advance to higher levels of moral reasoning (Berkowitz, Oser, & Althof, 1987). For most people, it is not specific moral experiences (such as moral education programs or being confronted with moral crises) that foster moral development, "but rather becoming more aware of the social world in general and one's place in it" (Rest, 1986, p. 177; also see Carroll & Rest, 1982). Exposure to stimulating and challenging social and cultural environments and meeting new and different kinds of people appear to foster a higher level of moral development (Mischel & Mischel, 1976; Rest, 1986).

In the family setting, exposure to higher levels of moral reasoning in a supportive (but not critical) context is linked with more advanced moral reasoning. One study found that children and adolescents who made the highest gains in moral reasoning over a two-year period had parents who engaged in a supportive style of interaction when discussing real-life moral dilemmas with children (Walker & Taylor, 1991a). This supportive style of interaction was characterized by asking for the child's opinion, paraphrasing the child's statements, and checking to be sure that the parent understood the child's perspective. The effect of this interactional style on moral development was enhanced in families where the parents were considerably more advanced in terms of moral reasoning than were the children. On the other hand, children of parents who directly criticized their children's perspective or who simply provided their opinions (i.e., lectured their children) made fewer overall gains. This study and others (Speicher, 1992, 1994) point to the importance of the family context in influencing moral development.

Influences on moral reasoning also may include the individual's personal characteristics. Although research on the influences of personality on moral reasoning is rare, one study found that adolescents with more mature defense mechanisms, such as being able to allow for objective evaluations in an emotion-laden situation, have more advanced levels of moral reasoning (Hart & Chmiel, 1992). One authority on moral reasoning asserts that:

The people who develop in moral judgment are those who love to learn, who seek new challenges, who enjoy intellectually stimulating

environments, who are reflective, who make plans and set goals, who take risks, who see themselves in the larger social contexts of history and institutions and broad cultural trends, who take responsibility for themselves and their environs (Rest, 1986, p. 57).

# Gilligan's Care Perspective on Moral Development

For Carol Gilligan, a psychologist at Harvard, the conceptions of moral development adopted by Piaget and Kohlberg reflect a similar orientation in which the primary emphasis is on morality as a sense of *justice* based on abstract, rational principles (Gilligan, 1977, 1982; Gilligan & Attanucci, 1988). In her view, this conception of moral development unduly favors males because Kohlberg's theory was based solely on research he conducted with males, and the socialization of males places greater emphasis on justice-based morality. In contrast, Gilligan maintained, women are brought up to view morality in more personal terms, as a matter of *caring* and showing compassion for others, especially for those with whom one is intimately connected. Consequently, when women are assessed by justice-oriented (Kohlbergian) measures, their level of moral development appears to be less mature than that of men.

But do boys and girls actually differ in level of moral reasoning? Although there is some research to support Gilligan's position (Holstein, 1976; Kohlberg & Kramer, 1969), the vast majority of recent studies show no difference in the stages of moral development reached by males and females (Damon & Hart, 1992; Friedman, Robinson, & Friedman, 1987; Gibbs, Arnold, & Burkhart, 1984; Rest, 1986; Thoma, 1984; Walker, 1984, 1989, 1991). How, then, can we evaluate Gilligan's assertions?

One possibility is that although females and males may not differ on abstract tests of their moral reasoning skills, they may still differ in their responses to the events of daily living. On average, women may be more intimately involved with and concerned about the welfare of people they know about; men may be more concerned with the establishment of laws and broad social policies. A focus on the real-life dilemmas of individuals, rather than on their responses to (Kohlbergian) hypothetical dilemmas, could bring out such a sex difference. Studies that asked participants to discuss their own real-life dilemmas, however, have been inconsistent in their support for the idea that women focus more on

interpersonal dilemmas and men focus more on impersonal dilemmas (Skoe & Diessner, 1994; Walker, de Vries, & Trevethan, 1987; Walker et al., 1995).

In the long run, Gilligan's principal contribution may be not so much an explication of sex differences as a broadened conception of morality. Effective morality needs to include both justice and rights *and* care, compassion, and responsibility for others (Damon & Hart, 1992; Gilligan & Attanucci, 1988; Smetana, Killen, & Turiel, 1991; Walker, 1991; Walker et al., 1995). Indeed, although Kohlberg continued to view justice as central to morality, he maintained that the development of justice and the development of caring and compassion are interrelated. He noted that the Golden Rule of the New Testament encompassed both orientations: "Do unto others as you would have them do unto you" and "Love thy neighbor as thyself" (Kohlberg, Levine, & Hewer, 1983) (see Box 10.1).

# Changing Societal Demands and Adolescents' Moral Development

Changing societal demands during adolescence are likely to increase preoccupation with moral values. The younger child lives in a world that is relatively more homogeneous, more immediate, and more limited than that of the adolescent. As a result, there are fewer occasions for making moral choices. Living according to a fairly circumscribed set of rules established for the most part by parents, the child and his or her peers learn to satisfy their needs within this context. Granted, the child must establish internal controls as a necessary part of socialization, and controls are related to the problem of values. But establishing controls is not synonymous with learning to make value decisions, often under ambiguous circumstances.

In contrast, adolescents *must* make choices. Not only are they changing, but the immediate social world, and their relations with it, are changing too. As they progress through adolescence, young people are confronted with an increasingly diverse world in which the opportunities and the necessity for choice are multiplied. They find, for example, that there are many ways to live their lives and that they must make choices. How will they earn a living? What sort of person do they eventually want to marry (if, in fact, they want to marry at all)?

Such choices cannot be made independently from personal values, although, of course, many other factors are also involved. An adolescent who is strongly con-

## 10.1 Adolescents' Moral Reasoning about Sexually Transmitted Diseases

How do adolescents score when it comes to reasoning about a moral issue that is close to their hearts, health, and emotional well-being? Adolescents' reasoning about sexually transmitted diseases (STDs) is such an issue, one that is especially timely because of adolescents' involvement in sexual activity and the risks that such activity can pose (such as HIV infection). A group of researchers from the University of Wisconsin presented to adolescents four hypothetical dilemmas involving the potential transmission of an STD, and asked them to describe what the protagonist in the situation should do (Jadack, Hyde, Moore, & Keller, 1995). For example, participants were asked to tell whether the protagonist should proceed to intercourse in a new, caring relationship where a condom is not available. Another situation asked whether the protagonist should tell a potential sexual partner in a caring relationship about the presence of HIV. These dilemmas were presented to two age groups of college students (18 and 22 years of age).

Participants' responses were coded into Kohlberg's moral stages. The results showed that the older students reasoned at a significantly higher level than did the younger ones. The 18-year-olds reasoned, on average, at a stage 2 or 3 level (late preconventional and early conventional). The 22-year-olds reasoned primarily in stages 3 and 4 (conventional). There were no gender differences in stage of reasoning. The responses were also coded with respect to Gilligan's moral orientations (justice and care perspectives). This study found no age or gender differences in moral orientation. Younger and older students and women and men used justice and care perspectives similarly in their responses to the moral issue of sexually transmitted diseases. This study adds to the research suggesting that women and men do not approach moral dilemmas differently.

The authors concluded that programs to promote safer sex practices among 18-year-olds will continue to do well by focusing on the use of condoms to protect against personal risk—a strategy that is congruent with the individualistic orientation (concern for self) of adolescents at this age. Programs aimed at older students, however, can promote safer sex by focusing not only on personal risk but on the rights of and responsibilities to others, a strategy that is congruent with the conventional level of moral reasoning.

---

vinced of the importance of helping others may make a different career choice than one who places a high value on material success. If he or she believes more in freedom and autonomy than in security, different choices may be made. If young people believe that honesty is the best policy, they may be less likely to enter certain occupations than if they believe that there's a sucker born every minute and that an individual's main responsibility is to survive in a social jungle.

As we have seen, the time perspective of adolescents, in contrast to that of children, becomes greatly extended (particularly into the future); this, too, increases the urgency of developing a set of values (Erikson, 1968, 1983). The adolescent who is beginning to think about an entire lifetime is much more in need of a set of guiding moral principles to lend order, consistency, and meaning to life than a child whose chief concern at a given moment may be whether he or she will be going to an amusement park or to the dentist the next day.

Moreover, the adolescent is confronted with a wider range of conflicting pressures for the adoption or modification of personal values than is the younger child. The peer group may be urging one set of values and the parents another. The adolescent may be motivated to conform to the values of peers in order to gain acceptance or to avoid rejection. Increasingly, other influences enter the arena of moral choice, including teachers, books, television, and representatives of conflicting groups in society.

Adolescents are confronted far more often than younger children with the need for making moral decisions. Here volunteer members of an urban Clean Green Team are restoring a mural by painting over graffiti.

Such conflicting pressures have always been part of adolescence, but they appear to have increased significantly during recent decades as society has been confronted with more issues on which consensus is difficult to attain. This has made it more difficult for young people to progress from a parent-knows-best sort of preadolescent moral thought to the beginning of postconventional thought, with its emphasis on social consensus (Turiel, 1983). It appears to have increased the danger that some adolescents will fall into an extreme and chronic kind of **moral relativism** (not having absolute principles to guide actions) at this critical juncture in their development. There is also the danger, on the other hand, that adolescents will adopt a very rigid moral stance, as is seen among some cults that are popular with a small percentage of adolescents.

## Intrapsychic Conflict, Moral Values, and Moral Development

To complicate matters further, the adolescent may need to wrestle with moral value judgments not simply for their own sake but also as a way of coping with personal problems (Conger & Petersen, 1984; Freud, 1966, 1969; Mussen et al., 1990). For example, preoccupation with the moral issues of war and peace, or the nature of aggression, may reveal a rational concern with these matters for their own sake. But they may also reflect concern with being able to handle aggressive feelings, a

concern that is related to greater size and strength as well as to increased expectations of assertion and dominance, particularly for boys.

Similarly, the involvement of adolescents in cults or restrictive religious groups may be a way of resolving moral dilemmas by letting the group dictate the adolescent's values and behavior. Differences with parents over moral or political values and beliefs may reflect the adolescent's efforts to establish an independent identity or to express a deep resentment toward parental hostility or indifference.

The increased preoccupation with moral values and beliefs that characterizes many adolescents is likely to have its roots in expanded cognitive development, increased (and often contradictory) societal demands, and intimate (sometimes unconscious) intrapsychic concerns and conflicts.

## Moral Relativism, Identity, and Social Change

During adolescence the young person may progress from conventional moral reasoning—with its rather simplistic, absolute concepts of what is right and true and its dependence on socially accepted stereotypes and respect for authority—to principled moral reasoning. The ability to make this progression depends on the development of the capacity for formal-operational thought, which includes the ability to think hypothetically (that is, to consider a variety of possible solutions rather than simply looking for the "right" answer).

The ability to think hypothetically, so obvious in intellectual problem solving, extends equally to moral problems. In some ways it is a two-edged sword. On the one hand, it can help free the young person from rigid, arbitrary, stereotyped thinking and promote flexibility and adaptability in the search for internally consistent and principled values. On the other hand, it can be overwhelming. Freed from conventional morality, the adolescent may find himself or herself adrift in a sea of possible alternatives and may conclude that there is no way of choosing among them—that one set of beliefs or values is no better or worse than another.

The danger of this transitional period in cognitive and moral development is one of what Kohlberg calls extreme relativism. It is well-illustrated in the following statement by one of Kohlberg's research participants, an upper-middle-class high school student:

> I don't think anybody should be swayed by the dictates of society. It's probably very much up to the individual all the time and there's no general principle except when the views of society seem to conflict with your views and your opportunities at the moment and it seems that the views of society don't really have any basis as being right and in that case, most people, I think, would tend to say forget it and I'll do what I want (Kohlberg & Gilligan, 1971, p. 1074).

There have been conflicting perspectives on such moral relativism, with cognitive developmentalists, such as Kohlberg, arguing that moral relativism is most likely to be found among children. In their view, moral relativism indicates less developmentally advanced thinking. Universalistic thinking (the converse of moral relativism) has been seen as an advanced form of reasoning, one that is present most often in adults (Wainryb, 1993). However, others have argued that initially, children are relativistic, but they move to more universalistic thinking in adolescence, followed in the late adolescent and early adulthood years by an abandonment of absolute moral principles in favor of relativistic thinking based on the context of the moral dilemma (Murphy & Gilligan, 1980; Wainryb, 1993).

A recent study designed to examine moral relativism across different age groups demonstrated that early (6th grade), middle (10th grade), and late adolescents (college students) used *both* relativistic and nonrelativistic reasoning. Adolescents of all ages not only had universal moral principles (such as seeing corporal punishment of children as unacceptable), but they also took into account specific situations and contexts in making moral judgments (for example, corporal punishment might be acceptable if a culture believes that the only way to rid children of evil spirits is to spank them) (Wainryb, 1993). These results challenge assumptions that relativistic thinking is specific to any particular age or stage of development.

## Socialization Techniques and Moral Development

Thus far the primary emphasis has been on factors that sensitize adolescents to questions related to moral values and influence the degree of sophistication with which they conceptualize moral problems. But there is another side to the issue of moral development: the extent to which, and the manner in which, cognitive understanding is reflected in behavior. It is clear that a person may be able to conceptualize moral issues with considerable sophistication and to formulate the proper moral course to take, but may not always act in accordance with that formulation. Moral reasoning is consistently but only weakly related to moral action (Blasi, 1984; Thoma, Rest, & Davison, 1991; Walker et al., 1995).

In one study (Tapp & Levine, 1972), participants were first asked, "Why should people follow rules?" and were then asked, "Why do *you* follow rules?" In responding to the latter question, most middle-school children and adolescents showed a shift toward earlier, more "primitive" levels of moral development, although they were cognitively capable of understanding loftier reasons and subscribed to them. For example, although only 3 percent of older adolescents said that people *should* follow rules to avoid negative consequences, 25 percent said that they personally *would* do so.

Similarly, in another study adolescents were asked to respond to one of two kinds of stories: one in which they were asked to take the perspective of a fictitious other or one in which they were to respond as they would themselves (Weiss, 1982). Those responding from the self-involved perspective demonstrated increased concern about punishment and consequences as well as less mature moral reasoning than those responding from the fictitious-other perspective.

Some adolescents show a reasonable degree of adherence to personal moral principles, even under duress, whereas others yield rather quickly to temptation or group pressure. Still others appear to be guided almost solely by the possibility of external sanctions

rather than by internalized standards. In short, knowledge alone, even sophisticated knowledge of moral standards, does not guarantee an effective conscience (M. L. Hoffman, 1975).

Whether people will do what they know to be right depends on the extent to which morality is central to their self-concept and sense of identity. For a person whose moral convictions are an important part of his or her self, to violate those convictions is to betray one's identity (Blasi, 1980, 1984). "The resulting feeling of guilt is a direct effect of perceiving one's inconsistency, one's lack of intactness and wholeness, one's lack of integrity" (Moshman, Glover, & Bruning, 1987, p. 555).

## Factors Affecting the Development of Conscience

The development of conscience begins long before adolescence. Indeed, even during the preschool years the child begins to develop a set of standards for acceptable behavior, generally acts in accordance with those standards, and feels guilty if he or she violates them (Mussen et al., 1990).

How does conscience develop? In Freud's view, conscience is a product of identification with parents. The young child's behavior is determined largely by external rewards and sanctions. Gradually, however, the child begins to internalize moral standards and prohibitions in the same way that he or she adopts other parental attributes. The adoption of parental standards makes the child feel similar to his or her parents and, therefore, to identify more strongly with them. Children who have internalized moral standards will punish themselves, or feel anxious or guilty, whenever they do (or think) something for which they believe their parents might punish them (Freud, 1964; Kochanska, 1993, 1994; Whiting & Child, 1953).

Many researchers have investigated and elaborated on various elements (such as cognitive aspects, modeling, and social learning) that are implicit in Freud's basic formulation. It has been found, for example, that the kind of model a parent provides and the kind of discipline he or she uses will influence the extent and nature of the child's developing conscience (Grusec & Goodnow, 1994; Hart, 1988; M. L. Hoffman, 1983). In general, as we shall see, parents who appeal to positive, growth-enhancing motives in the child through their disciplinary techniques appear to foster positive identification and genuine moral maturity to a greater extent than those who appeal to negative motivations

such as fear of losing the parent's love or fear of parental aggression (Grusec & Goodnow, 1994; M. L. Hoffman, 1980). The child's temperament plays a role, too, as characteristics such as arousability, anxiety, fearfulness, and impulsivity may influence not only how the child reacts to parental discipline and attempts to instill standards, but also in how the child evaluates moral dilemmas (Kochanska, 1993).

## Effects of Child-Rearing Practices

Martin Hoffman, a psychologist at New York University, distinguishes between two basic parental disciplinary patterns that affect moral orientation. They are termed **power-assertive** and non-power-assertive (M. L. Hoffman, 1980, 1983, 1994). Non-power-assertive discipline can be divided into two main subtypes: **love withdrawal** and **induction** (in which the parent provides

Inductive discipline, combined with affection, is most likely to result in advanced moral development.

explanations or reasons for requiring certain behaviors from the child).

A parent who uses power-assertive techniques does not rely on the child's inner resources (such as guilt, shame, dependency, love, and respect) to influence the child's behavior, nor does the parent give the child information necessary for the development of such resources. Instead, the parent seeks to accomplish this end by punishing the child physically or materially or by relying on fear of punishment. Power assertion tends to be related to "a moral orientation based on fear of external detection and punishment" (M. L. Hoffman, 1980, p. 322). The child or adolescent is less likely to act on the basis of internalized moral norms and more likely to continue to be influenced by external sanctions. Not surprisingly, a pattern of power assertion is often found among the parents of some kinds of delinquents (see Chapter 12).

Parents who use love withdrawal give psychological but not physical expression to their anger or disapproval of the child for engaging in some undesirable behavior. They may ignore the child, refuse to speak to him or her, express dislike, or threaten abandonment. As Hoffman observes, "Like power assertion, love withdrawal has a highly punitive quality. Although it poses no immediate physical or material threat to the child, it may be more devastating emotionally than power assertion because it poses the ultimate threat of abandonment or separation" (M. L. Hoffman, 1970, p. 285). Love withdrawal is not consistently related to the child's development of internalized moral standards, although the child is more likely than children of power-assertive parents to confess to violations and to accept blame. Moreover, love withdrawal disrupts communication (and, hence, learning opportunities) between child and parent, and fails to make use of the child's capacity for empathy. There is some evidence that love withdrawal may contribute to inhibition of anger (M. L. Hoffman, 1980).

Induction involves using techniques in which the parent gives explanations or reasons for requiring certain behaviors of the child, such as pointing out the practical realities of a situation or explaining how inappropriate behavior may be harmful to the child or others. Unlike either of the other two approaches, induction is also likely to include appeals to the child's pride and his or her desire for maturity or to be "grown up." Inductive techniques, in addition to promoting positive identification, "help foster the image of the parent as a rational, nonarbitrary authority. They provide the child with cognitive resources needed to control his own behavior" (M. L. Hoffman, 1970, p. 331). Not surprisingly, inductive discipline, combined with affection, has been found to be most likely to result in advanced moral development, as evidenced by an internal moral orientation and self-induced guilt about violations of internal standards (M. L. Hoffman, 1980).

Few parents use one type of discipline exclusively. For example, even a parent who endorses the use of inductive techniques is likely at times to resort to power assertion (e.g., "Stop that, right this minute!" "Go to your room!") or to express strong disapproval (e.g., "How could you do an irresponsible thing like that?" "You can't treat your sister like that. It's hurtful and wrong and I won't have it!"). As Hoffman points out, such disciplinary techniques may be necessary to get children to stop what they are doing and pay attention. "Having attended, children will often be influenced cognitively by the information contained in the inductive component and thus experience a reduced sense of opposition between their desires and external demands" (M. L. Hoffman, 1980, p. 324).

Mature moral development involves not only avoidance of prohibitions but also motivation toward positive, altruistic, helpful, or prosocial behavior—behavior that is voluntary and intended to benefit another (Boehnke et al., 1989; Eisenberg, 1990; Eisenberg-Berg & Mussen, 1989). A longitudinal study of children followed from age 4 through 14 found that several forms of higher-level prosocial reasoning emerged in late childhood or adolescence while lower level reasoning declined. Adolescents who reasoned at higher levels also showed more helping behavior, empathy, sympathy, and perspective-taking (Eisenberg et al., 1991).

Much recent research on moral development has focused on factors leading to prosocial motivation and behavior. To behave morally, people need to be secure in their own personal values and standards, resistant to deviant pressures, and concerned with the welfare of others as well as their own. Parents who serve as models for altruistic behavior, who encourage positive identification through unconditional love, and who employ inductive disciplinary techniques are most likely to produce children who go on to become truly inner-directed, concerned, and morally mature (Eisenberg, 1990; Grusec & Goodnow, 1994; M. L. Hoffman, 1980; Leahy, 1981; Mussen et al., 1990) (see Box 10.2).

# The Development of Political Ideas

Research on **political socialization** was a hot topic of study in the 1960s and 1970s, when political activism among adolescents had reached a high point. This research focused on how adolescents learn and feel about their government, political leaders, laws, and policies, as well as how they learn about being a good cit-

## 10.2 Doing Good in Bad Times
### PARENTAL MODELS AND ALTRUISTIC BEHAVIOR

The personal histories of unusually altruistic adults provide impressive evidence of the contribution of parental modeling and identification to the development of prosocial behavior. Non-Jews who risked their lives trying to rescue Jews from the Nazis during World War II characteristically identified strongly with parents who held strong moral convictions and acted in accordance with those convictions (London, 1970). When asked why they risked their lives to save Jews in World War II, thirty-six gentiles in fourteen countries in a recent film on the subject ("Tzedek: The Righteous") gave such simple and direct answers as "Because it was the right thing to do," "Because I would have been ashamed if I had not done so," "Because I am a Christian," and "What would I have told my children?" (Halter, 1995; Riding, 1995).

One study of altruism examined volunteers at a crisis counseling center who underwent rigorous training and worked very hard, at a great sacrifice of time and effort. Those who had warm, positive relationships with altruistic parents during childhood completed their commitment to this prosocial work even if they found the training difficult and unrewarding. However, those who had poor early relationships with nonaltruistic parents sustained their crisis work only if they found the training situation personally rewarding (Clary & Miller, 1986).

---

izen. Since then little research on political socialization has taken place (Torney-Purta, 1990). Much of what we know about the development of political ideas derives from research conducted in the 1960s and 1970s.

### Age Differences in Political Thinking

Joseph Adelson (1975, 1986, 1991), a social scientist who conducted classic research on political socialization, describes five characteristics of political thinking in older adolescents:

- *Abstractness:* Older adolescents are able to engage in abstract political thought.
- *Time:* Older adolescents are able to consider the past and future, in addition to the present.
- *Change:* The older adolescent accepts that laws, social forms, and government can, and perhaps should, change.
- *Relative costs and benefits:* Older adolescents recognize that political decisions involve competing interests and the need for compromise.
- *Principles:* Older adolescents have developed an increasing knowledge of political principles, such as democracy.

Evidence for these characteristics is drawn from an ingenious series of investigations conducted by Adelson and colleagues in the United States, West Germany, and England. To avoid conventional stereotypes and differing degrees of factual information, and to make the results from different countries more comparable, they avoided questions about existing political systems and presented participants with the premise, "Imagine that a thousand people venture to an island in the Pacific to form a new society; once there they must compose a political order, devise a legal system, and in general confront the myriad problems of government" (Adelson, 1971, p. 1014). They then explored adolescents' thinking on a variety of relevant issues (such as the purpose of government, law, and political parties). Proposed laws were suggested and problems of public policy explored.

The results of the study showed that there is a significant developmental shift in the direction of greater abstractness of thought. For example, when asked the purpose of laws, one 12-year-old replied, "If we had no laws, people could go around killing people." In contrast, a 16-year-old replied, "To ensure safety and enforce the government" (Adelson, 1971, p. 1015).

Lacking the capacity to formulate abstract concepts such as law, society, equal representation, individual rights, and the like, the younger adolescent's political thought tended to be personalized. When asked about

the law, young adolescents mentioned "the mayor, or the President, or the congressman, and much of the time none of these but rather a shadowy though ubiquitous set of personages known as 'they' or 'them.' ('They do it, like in schools, so that people don't get hurt')" (Adelson, 1971, pp. 1015–1016).

The older adolescents' ability to use abstract thought was well-illustrated by a question in which the participants were told that 20 percent of the people on the island were farmers and that they were concerned that laws might be passed contrary to their interests. The participants were asked what might be done about this situation. The youngest adolescents could usually do little more than assert that people wouldn't want to hurt farmers or that the farmers should fight or move to another part of the island—if they were able to produce an answer at all. Slightly older adolescents made suggestions such as "The farmers should talk to the rest of the people and make their problems understood."

By mid-adolescence, however, many participants were able to suggest such solutions as forming a union to press for their collective rights or electing legislators to defend their interests. Older adolescents were also able to take an extended time perspective (i.e., to look ahead to future as well as present consequences of various political alternatives) and to take motivation into account as a significant factor in social and political behavior.

Adelson's research also showed that authoritarianism was characteristic of younger adolescents' political thinking. For example, "On questions of crime and punishment, they were able—without seeming to bat an eyelash—to propose the most sanguinary means of achieving peace and harmony across the land," willing to mete out arbitrary punishments so that criminals would "learn their lesson" (Adelson, 1982, p. 9).

This view of society gradually gives way to an entirely different view of the purpose of law. Generally, by the time adolescents are 15 or 16 years old, and certainly by age 18, the emphasis on arbitrary punishment has diminished markedly. The idea that laws are a code guiding human conduct becomes more prevalent in the later years of adolescence.

Two other motifs also signaled the end of the early-adolescent view of laws. One was the tendency to see laws as benevolent rather than restrictive, as designed to help people. Another motif linked law to the larger notion of community and saw laws as providing a means for achieving interpersonal harmony, either among competing social groups or in the nation or state as a whole. These changes, which range from a purely restrictive to a benevolent or normative view of law, appear to be as predictable as the cognitive shift from the concrete to the abstract (see Box 10.3).

# Links to Cognitive and Moral Reasoning

The young person's cognitive reasoning abilities may play a role in the development of political thought (Adelson, 1982; Santolupo & Pratt, 1994). As cognitive reasoning abilities mature in general, with adolescents' reasoning becoming more abstract and considerate of multiple perspectives, this should be reflected in their political thinking. Research has found, however, only modest connections between general reasoning abilities (for example, as measured by Piagetian tasks) and political reasoning (Torney-Purta, 1990).

The lack of a strong connection may be because people use different reasoning strategies depending on the particular issue they are addressing (Torney-Purta, 1990). Adolescents' judgments about what a person should do in a specific situation, for instance, depends on the nature of the situation. Some issues may be defined as moral ones that involve the welfare or rights of others. Spanking children involves potential harm to people and may violate the rights of children and, as such, constitutes a moral issue. Other issues are defined as social conventional, regulated by social codes. Social conventional issues include expected modes of behavior or dress in a particular context such as a workplace or school. Yet other issues are personal, having consequences that apply primarily to the self. Whether to eat high-fat foods, for instance, is a personal issue (Smetana, 1988b; Turiel, Hildebrandt, & Wainryb, 1991). There is much research showing that children's and adolescents' cognitive reasoning varies depending on whether the issue is a moral, social conventional, or personal one (Turiel, Hildebrandt, & Wainryb, 1991). Given the specificity with which people approach different issues, it is not surprising that the connection between general reasoning abilities and reasoning about political issues specifically would not be a strong one.

Some research has hypothesized a link between general (Kohlbergian) moral reasoning abilities and political reasoning. In a study of the moral reasoning of college students and their political choices in the 1988 United States presidential election (Thoma, 1993), conventional reasoners (e.g., those in Kohlberg's Stages 3 and 4) were most likely to choose the conservative candidate—a choice that is congruent with a law-and-order orientation. Preconventional reasoners (those in Kohlberg's Stages 1 and 2) were slightly more likely than the

# 10.3 Are Adolescents more Tolerant than Children?

One goal of a democratic society is for its members to be tolerant of others who disagree with them and to allow the expression of personal beliefs. Tolerance, then, is an important aspect of children's political socialization in North America (Sigelman & Toebben, 1992). There have been two general approaches to research on tolerance. The political *tolerance* approach has examined adolescents' willingness to grant democratic rights to extremist groups. For example, to what extent do adolescents agree that Nazis should be able to speak about their opinions in public? The *belief-discrepancy* approach examines adolescents' evaluations of peers who disagree with them (who have beliefs discrepant from their own) (Enright et al., 1984; Sigelman & Toebben, 1992). This approach asks: To what extent are peers with different beliefs judged to be good or bad, smart or foolish, and so on?

In one study, political tolerance and belief-discrepancy judgments were assessed in a sample of 2nd, 5th, and 8th graders (Sigelman & Toebben, 1992). The goal was to determine whether there were age differences in political tolerance and belief-discrepancy judgments. To accomplish this goal, the participants were presented with four distasteful proposals made by hypothetical individuals (the proposers). These proposals were to take all pets away from owners, prohibit talking at school except during lunch, require public oral exams of all students, and require students to clean the city for free in their leisure time. Participants were then asked how tolerant they would be of speeches made by

conventional reasoners to choose the liberal candidate (Michael Dukakis), possibly because they would be receptive to politicians who would do the most for them personally. Postconventional reasoners (those in Kohlberg's Stages 5 and 6) were most likely to choose the liberal candidate (Michael Dukakis), a choice that may reflect their concern with carrying out principles of justice in the context of social change. This study demonstrates some support for a link between general moral reasoning and political choice.

## Changing Religious Beliefs

In most religions adolescence is marked by some kind of ritual that recognizes that an important developmental transition is taking place. Thus, it is during adolescence that many Christian youth formally enter into church membership through confirmation ceremonies. Similarly, Jewish youth become adult members of their congregations through Bat or Bar Mitzvah ceremonies.

To some extent the religious beliefs of adolescents also reflect their level of cognitive development (Elkind, 1978; Mussen et al., 1990; Nelsen, Potvin, & Shields,

1977). The young person's religious beliefs are likely to become more abstract and less literal between the ages of 12 and 18 (Elkind, 1978; Farel, 1982; Fowler, 1981). For example, God comes to be seen more as an abstract power and less as a fatherly human being. Religious views also become more tolerant and less dogmatic. Interestingly, a recent study found that when moral beliefs were put into conflict with the dictates of religion (adolescents and adults were asked what they should do when their moral judgment tells them to do something that is against their religion), the majority of respondents (77 percent) believed that morality should take precedence over religious beliefs; a minority (11 percent) believed that it was more important to adhere to religious beliefs (Walker et al., 1995).

There appears to be some decline in the stated importance of religion—at least formal religion—during adolescence, although more than nine out of ten adolescents continue to believe in God (*America's youth,* 1988). Significantly more young people of high school age than of college age believe that religion is important to them, and more high school than college students attend church regularly (Bachman, Johnston, & O'Malley, in preparation; Potvin, Hoge, & Nelsen, 1976; Yankelovich, 1981).

the proposers. They were also asked to assess how good and smart the proposers were, and whether they would want to interact with the proposers.

With respect to political tolerance, the results showed that participants were more likely with age to endorse the right to free speech among proposers whose ideas were most distasteful, with adolescents (8th graders) most tolerant and young children (2nd graders) least tolerant. With respect to belief-discrepancy judgments, younger children (2nd graders) judged the proponents of disagreeable ideas more negatively on goodness and intelligence than did older children (5th and 8th graders). There were no age differences, however, on willingness to interact socially with proponents of distasteful ideas, although the participants did not want to interact with proponents of the "no pets" proposal—the proposal that participants found most disagreeable.

In characterizing the changes that occur with age the authors concluded:

> It was as if second graders were saying, "Unless I like your ideas, I'll think less of you, I won't want to be around you, and I won't want you to express yourself." By adolescence, however, responses to dissenting others had become more differentiated so that, for example, support for free speech was uncorrelated with the perceived acceptability of a person's idea and judgments of the person's worth and desirability as a social partner. (Sigelman & Toebben, 1992, p. 555–556)

The above results point to important developmental changes that occur across childhood and adolescence in political tolerance, with adolescents showing more tolerance than younger children.

## Cultural Changes

Cultural as well as age changes in religious values appear to be at work. Although most young people still express a general belief in God or a universal spirit, since the 1960s there has been a steady decline in the importance of religion in young people's lives. In 1980, 32 percent of American high school seniors stated that religion was very important in their lives; by 1994 this figure had declined to 29.6 percent (Bachman, Johnston, & O'Malley, 1981, in preparation). The decline was greatest among the part of the population in which religious concerns formerly were highest, namely, young people who are not attending and not planning to attend college. Although more noncollege than college-bound youth continue to consider religion very important, the magnitude of the difference has decreased dramatically. As with other values, during the past two decades there has apparently been a rather rapid diffusion of religious values from a minority of economically and socially privileged youth to the majority of their working-class peers.

At least part of this relative decline of interest in religion is clearly related to changing values among young people and a perception on the part of many that religion—at least formal, institutionalized religion—is failing

to reflect these changes (*America's youth,* 1988; Mussen et al., 1990; Walker et al., 1995). For example, rightly or wrongly, approximately half of all adolescents believe that churches are not doing their best to understand young people's ideas about sex. Contemporary adolescents are more likely to state that God has understanding attitudes about sex than to attribute such attitudes to institutionalized religion.

A number of young people, particularly in the women's movement, also feel that the Catholic church and some Protestant denominations are not according full status and recognition to women. A majority of Catholic youth disagree with their church's positions on birth control, annulment and divorce, and the right of priests to marry.

At the same time, an increased interest in more fundamentalist religious traditions can be seen in a significant number of young people. Nearly half of all Protestant teenagers and 22 percent of their Catholic peers report having had a "born-again" experience—a turning point in their lives involving personal commitment to Christ (Gallup, 1978; Norback, 1980). These figures are similar to those obtained among adults.

**Sects and Cults.** It is estimated that there are currently 5000 sects or cults in the United States, and that

In most religions, adolescence is marked by some kind of ritual that recognizes that an important developmental transition is taking place. Jewish youth become adult members of their congregations through Bat or Bar Mitzvah ceremonies.

in the last 20 years, about 20 million Americans have been involved in such cults (Singer, 1992). Although past media attention has focused on religious cults such as Children of God, there are many different types of cults, including but not limited to political, psychological, Satanic, women's separatist, and flying saucer cults. Cults range in size from a few members to large international organizations with perhaps millions of members. Moreover, there are differences among cults in the activities they sponsor, ranging from actions that demonstrate concern for others to the killing and maiming of innocent victims (Singer, 1992).

Many cults require the surrender of individual autonomy and complete conformity in both behavior and belief to the dictates of leaders. Often, coercive control is used to attract and retain cult members. Cult expert Margaret Singer argues that "almost anyone, at a vulnerable period in his or her life, is a potential cult recruit" (1992, p. 700). Periods of transition, experiences of loss, feelings of loneliness, or difficulties with parents are examples of situations that can make people vulnerable to cult recruitment (Conger & Petersen, 1984; Singer, 1992). Initially, the cult provides a seemingly safe place where cult members feel respected and loved.

One study found that delinquent youths who were involved in Satanism were more highly attached to their peers and less attached to parents and school than were delinquent youths who were not involved in Satanic activities (Damphousse & Crouch, 1992). Another study found that young adults who defected from cults were more likely than continuing members to have parents

who disapproved of cult activities and to have experienced smooth parent–adolescent relations (Wright & Piper, 1986). Nevertheless, about two-thirds of young adults in cults have no obvious family or personal difficulties (Singer, 1992).

## Current Trends in Adolescent Values

As with so many other aspects of adolescent development, the greatest danger in discussing trends in adolescent values is overgeneralization. In the 1960s and early 1970s, much was made of a so-called revolution in the values of young people. It was believed that adolescents were developing a set of values, beliefs, and lifestyles so different from that of their more traditional elders that a profound generation gap had developed. The values of the average adolescent did change in a number of important respects during these turbulent years, as many youths became disillusioned with what they perceived to be an unjust society (Conger, 1988), but the extent of the changes was far more limited than popular stereotypes suggested. Indeed, in many ways the values, attitudes, and beliefs of the majority of adolescents remained surprisingly conventional.

Today we are in danger of falling into another trap of overgeneralization. Many contemporary commentators may be misinterpreting the meaning of recent trends showing adolescents' greater concern for materialism and

financial security, a sharp decline in political activism, and diminishing interest in the welfare of others. In the minds of some critics, these trends are the harbingers of an across-the-board return to the "traditional" attitudes, values, and beliefs of an earlier, supposedly simpler, era—a perception that is echoed in a number of respects by some proponents of the recent so-called conservative revolution in government in the United States. But this is not the case, if for no other reason than that the world of the 1990s, in which young people are coming to maturity, is vastly different from the world of the 1950s and early 1960s, which some now view with such nostalgia.

To explore contemporary adolescent values we turn first to what we know about college students—those who tend to be trendsetters for shifts in values.

## College Students and College-Bound Youth

In many respects, contemporary adolescents and youth have needs and values that are far from new. They want self-esteem; feelings of competence; respect from parents, peers, and society; recognition for their accomplishments; growing independence; some close friendships; someone to love; and some idea of where they are headed and what they are going to do with their lives. However, the ways in which these needs and values are expressed, and the importance they are given, may vary with social, economic, and political change. Indeed, what sometimes seem to be dramatic changes in

values may actually represent newly aroused concerns brought on by social changes. At any rate, it would be difficult to make progress toward understanding recent changes in expressed attitudes and values without reference to changing social and economic conditions.

**Social and Economic Values.** For most of the past two decades there has been a steady increase in young people's concern for personal well-being, together with a decrease in their concern for the welfare of others—particularly the disadvantaged—and of society itself (Astin et al., 1994; Bachman & Johnston, 1980; Bachman, Johnston, & O'Malley, in preparation; Conger, 1981, 1988). As we noted earlier, during these years the percentage of strongly career-minded college students rose sharply (at least partly as a function of changing economic conditions), while the percentage of students who viewed their college experience as a period of self-discovery and change decreased markedly. For example, being very well-off financially was cited as a very important objective by only 39 percent of entering college students in the United States in 1970; by 1980 that figure had increased to 63 percent, and in 1987 it reached an all-time high of just over 75 percent; since then it has declined slightly (see Figure 10.1). In contrast, developing a meaningful philosophy of life declined as a very important objective, from 82.9 percent in 1967 to 50.4 percent in 1980, before reaching a record low of 31.9 percent in 1987. Gaining recognition from peers, having administrative responsibility, and being an authority in one's field all grew

Teenage students debating in a Texas legislative workshop. Older adolescents are more likely to see laws as providing a means for achieving harmony among individuals, social groups, and nations with competing interests.

in importance in the past two decades, and again, all of these objectives also peaked in 1987 before undergoing moderate declines (Astin et al., 1994; Dey, Astin, & Korn, 1991). Among high school seniors, parallel but less dramatic increases occurred in the proportion who rated the chance to earn a good deal of money and to have a predictable, secure future as very important in a job (see Chapter 9).

Along with increasing concern with personal well-being and material success, the past 25 years saw a marked decline in social and political activism. The limited activist movements that have emerged recently have tended to emphasize issues that are directly related to immediate personal concerns (such as student financial aid) or are broadly shared (such as environmental pollution) (Astin et al., 1994). In 1994, only a little over one-quarter of college-bound high school seniors considered making a contribution to society a very important value, and only 15 percent considered working to correct social and economic inequities a very important

value (Bachman et al., in preparation). Among students entering college in 1986 and 1987, record lows were reached for interest in participating in community action programs, participating in programs to clean up the environment, and promoting racial understanding; interest in these issues turned up briefly during the rest of the decade, but has since resumed its decline (Astin, Korn, & Riggs, 1993; Astin et al., 1994; Dey, Astin, & Korn, 1991). Even at a more personal level, the number of college students who considered helping others in difficulty to be a very important objective declined among males from 58 percent at the end of the 1960s to a low of 48 percent in 1986, before rising slightly to 51.1 percent in 1994. Among females, there was a more modest decline—from 75 percent in 1969 to 65.5 percent in 1986, and a subsequent rise to 70.6 percent in 1994.

However, it is in political activism that the most dramatic changes have occurred: Among entering college students in 1994, keeping up with political affairs was

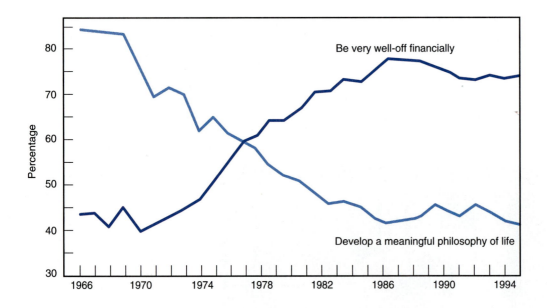

## Figure 10.1

Changing life goals of first-year students, 1966–1995. From E. L. Dey, A. W. Astin, & W. S. Korn (1991). *The American freshman: Twenty-five-year trends;* A. W. Astin et al. (1994) and Sax et al. (1995). *The American freshman: National norms for fall 1994, 1995.* Los Angeles: Higher Education Research Institute Graduate School of Education, UCLA. By permission.

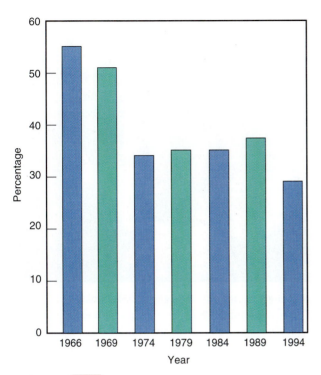

## Figure 10.2

Percentage of freshmen agreeing that keeping up to date with political affairs is a very important goal in life. From A. W. Astin, W. S. Korn, L. J. Sax, & K. M. Mahoney (1994). *The American freshman: National norms for fall 1994.* Los Angeles: Higher Education Research Institute Graduate School of Education, UCLA. By permission.

(The number of students viewing themselves as either far left or far right remained relatively flat over the years—never exceeding 3.1 percent on the left or 1.6 on the right). Those placing themselves in "the middle-of-the-road" increased from a low of 45.4 percent in 1970 to a high of 60.3 percent in 1983 (mostly at the expense of the liberals), before declining to 52.6 percent in 1994—still a majority (see Figure 10.3).

What does the dramatic shift in political and social values during the past 25 years mean? Does it indicate a retreat from the so-called new values that rose to prominence in the 1960s and early 1970s along with a return to an acceptance of the "traditional" values and institutional authority of an earlier, supposedly simpler, era? The available evidence clearly indicates otherwise.

Despite a resurgence in positive attitudes toward societal institutions during the first half of the 1980s,

cited as very important by only 31.9 percent—a 29-year low (see Figure 10.2). Moreover, despite widely publicized efforts such as MTV's 1992 "Choose or Lose" campaign to register young voters, there has been a steady decline in voter turnout among 18- to 24-year-olds since 1972, when 20-year-olds were given the vote, according to Curtis Gans, director of the Committee for the Study of the American Electorate (Shea, 1995a).

The relative shift in emphasis from social to personal concerns was accompanied by an initial decline in political liberalism and an increase in the proportion of young people who view themselves as "middle of the road." In 1970, one-third of all students described themselves as liberals; in 1981 less than one in five did so, although this figure increased to one in four by 1994 (Astin et al., 1994; Dey, Astin, & Korn, 1991). During the same period, the number of students describing themselves as conservative or far right rose gradually from a low of 14.5 percent in 1973 to 22.4 percent in 1994.

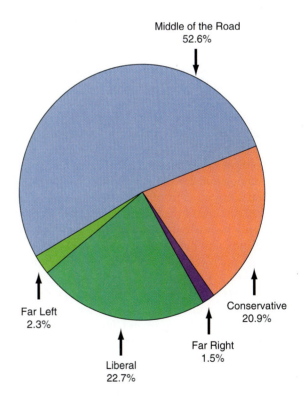

## Figure 10.3

Political views of first-year college students. From A. W. Astin, W. S. Korn, L. J. Sax, & K. M. Mahoney (1994). *The American freshman: National norms for fall 1994.* Los Angeles: Higher Education Research Institute Graduate School of Education, UCLA. By permission.

today's young people (and adults as well) remain more, not less, skeptical about the infallibility and even the morality of major institutions and their values—including big business, big labor unions, Congress, the executive branch of government, the courts, the schools, law enforcement agencies, and so on—than they were in the late 1960s. For example, only about one in five college-bound high school seniors currently think that Congress, the executive branch of government, and the courts have been doing a good job on the whole (Bachman et al., in preparation). Big business, labor unions, the public schools, the churches, and law enforcement agencies do not fare much better. The military and the news media are viewed favorably by more than one in three seniors, but only colleges and universities are judged favorably by a substantial majority (72 percent) (Bachman et al., in preparation).

Similarly, among students entering college a strong majority agree that government is not protecting the consumer, controlling pollution, or doing enough to control guns, that a national health care plan is still needed, and that the wealthy should pay more taxes. Interestingly, however, less than a quarter think that taxes generally should be raised in order to reduce the federal deficit (Astin et al., 1994).

**Personal and Moral Values.** In personal and moral values, today's young people show little resemblance to those of earlier eras. The so-called sexual revolution among middle- and upper-class adolescents and youth was a major aspect of the "new morality" of the late 1960s, and one of the most enduring (see Chapter 6). Not only has there not been a return to "traditional" sexual morality, but previous trends have accelerated, at least until recently. For example, in 1971 about 28 percent of all 15- to 19-year-old girls had engaged in premarital intercourse (Hayes, 1987). But by 1988 the rate had increased to 60 percent, although it appears to have leveled off since then (Alan Guttmacher Institute, 1994; Centers for Disease Control, 1995a, 1995b; London et al., 1989).

The trend toward considering sexual behavior more a matter of personal decision than a subject for socially imposed moral codes intensified during the past 25 years. In 1994, American high school seniors were asked their reactions to a man and woman who live together without being married; slightly over half stated that such people were doing their own thing and not affecting anyone else. As noted earlier, beginning in the latter half of the 1980s and continuing into the 1990s, a slight majority of college-bound high school seniors and first-

A significant minority of young people think that for such values as self-fulfillment and self-expression to be psychologically growth-enhancing, they must be accompanied by a concern for the welfare of others and of society itself.

year college students endorsed the proposition that living together before getting married was a good idea (Bachman et al., in preparation; Dey, Astin, & Korn, 1991). At the same time, only 43 percent of 1994 entering college students agreed that sex is OK if people like each other, compared to a high of 52 percent in 1987. In addition, the proportion of students who believe that it is important to have laws prohibiting homosexual relationships declined to an all-time low of one-third in 1994, compared to a high of a little over half in 1987 (Astin et al., 1994).

As we shall see in detail in the following chapter, perceptions of the harmfulness of drugs and disapproval of drug use, which had been rising among junior high, high school, and college students for more than a decade, began to decline in 1991 (Johnston, O'Malley, & Bachman, 1995a, 1995b). This trend was accompanied by a corresponding increase in the use of many drugs. Among first-year college students, the percentage agreeing that marijuana should be legalized, which had fallen precipitously from a high of over 50 percent in 1977 to a low of a little under 17 percent in 1989, has risen every year since, to 33 percent in 1994 (see Figure 10.4).

In some other respects, however, adolescents were less permissive in their personal and moral values in the mid-1990s than they were just a few years earlier. Thus, support for abolishing capital punishment declined to an all-time low of 20.1 percent in 1994 (down from 57.6 percent in 1971) (see Figure 10.5).

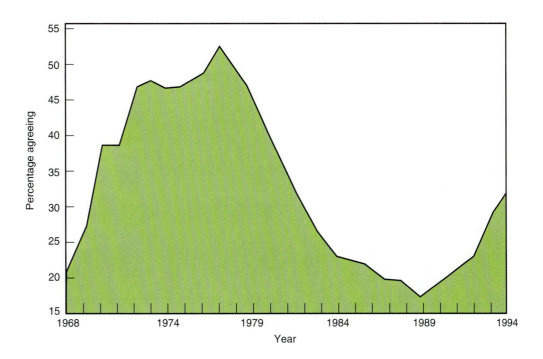

**Figure** `10.4`

Percentage of college freshmen agreeing that marijuana should be legalized.
From A. W. Astin, W. S. Korn, L. J. Sax, & K. M. Mahoney (1994). *The
American freshman: National norms for fall 1994.* Los Angeles: Higher Education
Research Institute Graduate School of Education, UCLA. By permission.

Moreover, agreement that there is too much concern in the courts for the rights of criminals reached an all-time high of 73 percent, compared to 50 percent in 1973 (Astin et al., 1994).

The great majority of adolescents and youth still look forward to getting married and having children, although having children is increasingly seen as a matter of individual choice, not as a duty to society (Astin et al., 1994; Bachman, Johnston, & O'Malley, in preparation; Yankelovich, 1981). Between 1975 and 1994 the percentage of students entering college who considered raising a family to be a very important objective rose from 57 percent to 72 percent for females (following a dramatic decline from 78 percent in 1969, at the height of the "youth revolution"). For males, it increased from 53 percent to 69 percent (after falling from 67 percent in 1969), so that males and females currently have similar views (Astin et al., 1994; Dey, Astin, & Korn, 1991).

More broadly, two important values that were legacies of the sixties—fulfilling oneself as a person and having opportunities for self-expression—have remained strong. Support for freedom, self-determination, and equality for women—an issue that, contrary to popular perceptions, was only beginning to emerge among young people in the 1960s—became increasingly widespread in the 1970s and early 1980s, although even today much still remains to be done (Conger, 1981, 1988). Discrimination on the basis of age (which affects both the young and the old) is also under siege politically, culturally, and legally. For many of today's young people, self-realization—physical, psychological, or material—continues to be a major goal.

In our view, the appropriate question to raise is not whether today's adolescents and youth are engaged, as some have argued, in an across-the-board retreat from the inherited values of the sixties. Rather, it is whether the extension and expansion of such values as self-fulfillment and self-expression can be psychologically growth-enhancing without a corresponding sense of commitment to the welfare of others and of society itself. Significant minorities of today's young people clearly think it cannot, and they are expressing concern and becoming actively involved with such problems as homelessness, child abuse,

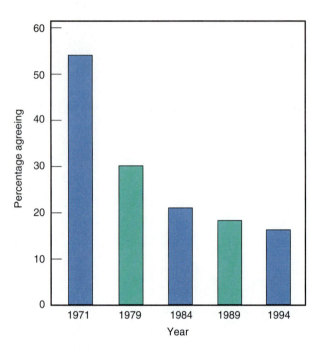

# Figure 10.5

Percentage of college freshmen agreeing that capital punishment should be abolished. From A. W. Astin, W. S. Korn, L. J. Sax, & K. M. Mahoney (1994). *The American freshman: National norms for fall 1994.* Los Angeles: Higher Education Research Institute Graduate School of Education, UCLA. By permission.

increased hunger and malnutrition, and inadequate educational, health, and social services for poor children and adolescents. But their numbers continue to shrink, as does support from government and society (Edelman, 1995). Whether the tide will turn again as we prepare to enter the next century remains to be seen.

# The Blue-Collar Revolution

As we noted earlier, a major error made by many social observers in the late 1960s was a tendency to ascribe to the majority of young people the values and behaviors of a relatively small minority of social activists and advocates of alternative lifestyles. Even on college campuses, the views of the great majority of students remained more traditional than those of this avant-garde minority.

In turn, the views of noncollege working-class youth remained markedly more conservative than those

of college youth in many areas, ranging from attitudes toward sexual freedom, use of drugs, and conformity in dress to views on the Vietnam War, business and government, minority rights, and law and order (Conger, 1981; Yankelovich, 1969, 1974, 1981).

Interestingly, however, a significant change occurred during the 1970s. By the mid-1970s the values of noncollege adolescents and youth were similar to an almost uncanny degree to those of college youth of the late 1960s in many areas, including sexual morality, religion, patriotism, politics, work, family, and attitudes toward business and government (Yankelovich, 1974). In short, there was a rapid transmission of values from a minority of college youth to young people in general.

These trends continued through the 1980s and into the 1990s. In most areas differences between the values of college students or college-bound young people today and those of their noncollege peers remain considerably smaller than was the case in the 1960s. For example, high school seniors, whether or not they plan to attend a four-year college, share generally similar views on race relations, drug use, the role of women in the workforce, living together before marriage, and the importance of marriage and family life (Bachman, Johnston, & O'Malley, in preparation). However, the noncollege youth (especially male) still tends to hold somewhat more traditional views about appropriate family roles for men and women. Thirty-seven percent of the noncollege group, but only 24 percent of the college-bound, agreed with the statement that "It is usually better for everyone involved if the man is the achiever outside the home and the woman takes care of the home and family"; 60 percent of the college-bound and 45 percent of noncollege seniors disagreed, while the remainder were neutral. Members of the noncollege group also express less interest or concern about what's going on in government or about social problems of the nation and the world and about how they might be solved, although interest in these subjects among both groups continued to decline during the 1980s and 1990s (Bachman, Johnston, & O'Malley, 1990, in preparation).

Of particular interest is the fact that college and noncollege youth show increasingly similar vocational values. Overwhelming majorities of both groups say that it is very important to have a job that is interesting, makes the best use of one's skills and abilities, and provides opportunities to learn new skills.

The diffusion of many of the values of college students to noncollege youth poses a growing problem. Noncollege youth are less likely than more highly educated youth to find work that satisfies their needs for personal fulfillment, creativity, and self-expression. Only about

one-quarter of employed noncollege youth state that their current job allows much opportunity "to do the things that I do best" or that it serves as "a good stepping stone toward the kind of work I would like to do in the future," and less than one-third feel that it gives them a good chance to develop their skills and abilities (Bachman et al., in preparation). As we noted in Chapter 9, a major challenge of our era is to find work for young people that offers some opportunity for self-fulfillment and personal growth, as well as adequate pay and economic security. For minority youth, particularly in the nation's inner cities, the problem is reaching epidemic proportions. The task will not be easy, and it will require a far greater societal commitment to the welfare of youth than has been evident to date.

# Summary

At no point earlier in life is a person as likely to be concerned about moral values and standards as during adolescence. This is due partly to the multiplicity of shifting, sometimes conflicting values and standards to which the adolescent is exposed, and partly to the adolescent's increasingly sophisticated ability to comprehend moral issues.

Some theorists have argued that morality involves the ability to reason clearly about a moral situation. Others have construed morality as primarily involving values. Still others have argued that morality is mainly a matter of what people do, rather than what they think or believe. It seems clear, however, that morality involves all of these components.

Jean Piaget's conceptualization of moral development stimulated much subsequent work on this topic. Piaget asserted that the organization of moral thought is quite different in younger children than in older children and adults, largely because children are at earlier stages of cognitive development. Lawrence Kohlberg extended Piaget's conceptualization by positing three major levels of moral development: preconventional, conventional, and postconventional, each of which is divided into two stages.

During adolescence conventional moral thinking tends to become dominant: Right behavior is seen as doing one's duty, showing respect for authority, and maintaining the existing social order. Contrary to earlier assumptions, many adolescents may not progress beyond this level. However, some do advance to postconventional levels. Postconventionality reflects the acquisition of formal-operational thinking and is characterized by a major thrust toward abstract moral principles that are universally applicable, not tied to any particular social group.

Cognitive disequilibrium (awareness that there are multiple and conflicting perspectives on a problem) may foster transitions to the next higher stage of moral development. Experiences in educational, peer, and family settings promote advances in moral reasoning if these experiences produce cognitive disequilibrium.

Carol Gilligan has observed that Piaget's and Kohlberg's conceptions of moral development emphasize justice, based on abstract moral principles (a justice orientation), rather than seeing morality as a matter of caring and compassion (a care orientation). In an effort to redress this perceived imbalance, Gilligan argued that females approach moral dilemmas in terms of principles of care whereas males more often approach moral issues from a justice perspective. Research does not support sex differences in moral orientation: Both sexes use care and justice perspectives. Effective morality needs to include both justice and rights *and* care, compassion, and responsibility for others.

Preoccupation with moral values is fostered by the changing and varied societal demands confronting adolescents. In contrast to younger children, adolescents face an increasingly diverse world in which opportunities for choice are multiplied. Moreover, these choices cannot be made independently from personal values: An adolescent who is strongly concerned with helping others may make a different career choice than an adolescent who places a high value on material success. Intrapsychic conflicts may also play a part. In the face of varied and conflicting pressures—from parents, peers, teachers, and society—some adolescents may be in danger either of falling into an essentially directionless moral relativism or of adopting the rigid kind of moral stance seen in some cults.

Intellectual understanding of moral values does not guarantee that people will always act in accordance with them. Whether people will do what they know to be right depends on the extent to which morality is central to their self-concept and sense of identity. The development of strong internalized moral values is fostered by parents who use *inductive* techniques to enforce restrictions. Such techniques include explanations of the reasons for the parents' actions and appeals to the child's pride and growing matu-

rity. In contrast, neither *power-assertive* disciplinary techniques (based largely on fear of punishment) nor *love withdrawal* (based ultimately on fear of abandonment or separation) encourage moral or emotional maturity.

With increasing age, political thinking becomes more abstract, less authoritarian, more concerned with motivation, and more aware of the need to reconcile competing interests. Similarly, the religious beliefs of adolescents become more abstract and less literal between the ages of 12 and 18. These changes occur in part because of developmental advances in general cognitive abilities. Still, depending on the particular issue, adolescents may or may not reason at the highest level they are capable of.

Since the early 1960s there has been a decline in the number of young people who view religion as a very important value; at the same time, however, there seems to be an increased interest in fundamentalist religious traditions among a significant minority.

Although today's adolescents and youth share many of the needs and values of earlier generations, they show greater concern for their own well-being and material success (including being very well-off financially) and diminished concern for the welfare of others—particularly the less advantaged—and of society itself. (Fewer than one in four of today's high school seniors consider making a contribution to society or working to correct social and economic inequities to be very important values.) In contrast, emphasis on fulfilling oneself as a person and having opportunities for self-expression remains strong, as does support for self-determination and equality between the sexes. These values are now likely to be seen among working-class or blue-collar youth, as well as among college youth.

# Review Questions

1. Why are young people particularly likely to be concerned with moral values and standards during the adolescent years?

2. Describe Piaget's approach to moral development and the role cognitive disequilibrium plays in promoting advances in moral reasoning.

3. Describe Kohlberg's six stages of moral development.

4. What kinds of experiences in the school, family, and peer settings promote advances in moral reasoning?

5. What are Carol Gilligan's objections to Piaget's and Kohlberg's conceptions of moral development? What alternatives does she propose? Can these two approaches be reconciled?

6. Martin Hoffman has identified three parental disciplinary patterns that affect moral reasoning: *power assertion, love withdrawal,* and *induction.* Define each. Which pattern is most likely to result in advanced moral development, and why?

7. What are the hallmarks of the development of political thinking in adolescence? What is the relation between political thinking on the one hand and cognitive and moral reasoning on the other?

8. What kinds of personal needs and values do contemporary adolescents and youth share with earlier generations of young people?

9. In what ways have the personal, social, political, and economic values of American adolescents and youth changed since the late 1960s?

# Recommended Readings

Conger, J. J. (1988). Hostages to fortune: Youth, values, and the public interest. *American Psychologist, **43,*** 291–300.

Gilligan, C. (1982). *In a different voice: Psychological theory and women's development.* Cambridge, MA: Harvard University Press.

Grusec, J. E., & Goodnow, J. J. (1994). Impact of parental discipline methods on the child's internalization of values: A reconceptualization of current points of view. *Developmental Psychology, **30,*** 4–19.

Killen, M., & Hart, D. (Eds.). (1995). *Morality in everyday life: Developmental perspectives.* New York: Cambridge University Press.

Kurtines, W. M., & Gewirtz, J. L. (Eds.). (1995). *Moral development: An introduction.* Boston: Allyn & Bacon.

Torney-Purta, J. (1990). Youth in relation to social institutions. In S. S. Feldman & G. R. Elliott (Eds.), *At the threshold: The developing adolescent* (pp. 457–477). Cambridge: Harvard University Press.

# Adolescents at Risk I: Drugs and Behavior

## 11

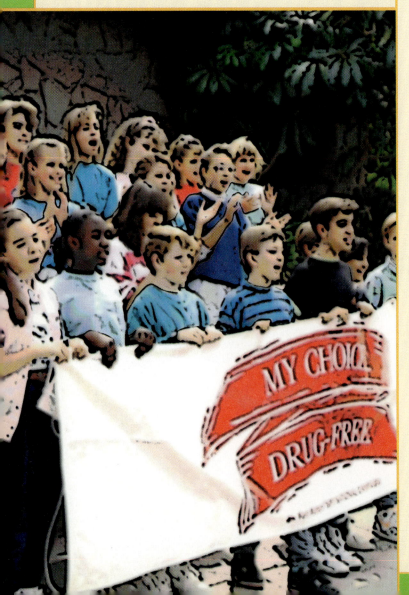

s we learned in earlier chapters, adolescence is a period of many accelerated changes on the road to adulthood: biological, cognitive, psychological, and social changes within the young person, and changes in the adolescent's world and the demands placed on her or him by parents and by a society that is itself in rapid transition (Conger, 1991a). Under favorable circumstances, the outcome of these changes may be a well-functioning adult—one who can get along and find satisfaction in the social world; operate effectively in school and, ultimately, in the workplace; establish intimate and loving relationships; and, in most cases, nurture and raise competent and healthy children.

These developmental changes may also expose the young person to increased risks to health and well-being. Adolescence can be a period of increased vulnerability because, although increasing maturity opens the door to developing new kinds of relationships outside the family and to entering new kinds of settings such as the workplace, going through the door into a wider world exposes the adolescent to more risks than are usually encountered in childhood.

Take as an example the adolescent's increasing fondness for spending time with peers. As we have seen, peer involvement can provide a safe place where intimacy is explored, where social perspective-taking is expressed, and where alternative identities are tried on; increased peer interaction can facilitate the adolescent's progress toward social, cognitive, and emotional maturity. But it can also provide a climate in which inhibitions are freed and the adolescent and his or her friends become more likely to engage in behaviors that may pose a risk to their health and well-being. Drinking and then driving, committing acts of vandalism, and engaging in unprotected sexual intercourse are examples of behaviors that emerge out of the adolescent's newfound autonomy and desire to participate in the peer culture. Such behaviors may have serious consequences, or they may not, depending on a host of factors, including how often risks are taken, the seriousness of the adolescent's actions, and, sometimes, blind luck. The consequences of adolescents' risk-taking behaviors include drug **addiction,** pregnancy, trouble

with the law, dropping out of school, and sometimes death (nowhere more visible than when reckless driving results in multiple teen deaths).

However, not all problems that adolescents experience are necessarily the result of risk-taking. The stresses of adolescence generally, or of living in a particular environment or family situation, may lead to psychological disturbances such as depression or anorexia nervosa. Emotional disorders may first appear in adolescence or be accentuated in adolescence if they were already present in childhood (Conger, 1991b). These problems deserve discussion, too, as we explore the nature of adolescent development.

Whereas the first ten chapters in this text covered the course of normal adolescent development, the final three chapters, including this one, focus on problems of adolescent development. We begin in this chapter by considering an overarching perspective on **problem behaviors** in adolescence, followed by a discussion of one of the most prevalent of these behaviors: substance use and abuse. Chapter 12 focuses on adolescent alienation, crime, and delinquency. Chapter 13 discusses psychological disorders in adolescence.

# What is Adolescent Problem Behavior?

In recent years, the concept of problem behavior has been increasingly used as a way of grouping together many adolescent activities that have the potential to create problems or difficulties for the adolescent or for others. Problem behavior may be defined as "behavior that departs from familial or social standards, that poses some risk to the individual or to society" (Maggs & Galambos, 1993, p. 79). As such, it includes explicitly illegal acts such as shoplifting and status (underage) offenses such as drinking. Some researchers also consider problem behavior to include seemingly less serious actions such as disobeying the rules of parents or school authorities (for example, missing curfew or cutting class). Examples of commonly studied problem behaviors are cigarette, alcohol, and marijuana use, sexual intercourse without contraception, delinquent behaviors, and aggressive acts. All problem behaviors have in common the violation of expected modes of behavior and the possibility, or risk of, negative consequences (Maggs & Galambos, 1993). Problem behavior among adolescents receives a lot of media and scientific attention because of its potential social, economic, and psychological costs (Bell & Bell, 1993; Ketterlinus & Lamb, 1994; Millstein, Petersen, & Nightingale, 1993; Patterson, DeBaryshe, & Ramsey, 1989).

The reason for grouping together a number of adolescent risk behaviors under the rubric of problem behavior is not merely convenience. Many adolescents who engage in one risk behavior (such as binge drinking) also engage in others (such as unprotected sexual intercourse) (Ensminger, 1990; Farrell, Danish, & Howard, 1992). Adolescents who engage in multiple risk behaviors may be said to evidence a problem behavior syndrome (Jessor, 1992; Jessor & Jessor, 1977). Although it is currently recognized that multiple problem behaviors may be present in the same adolescent, most research has examined one behavior at a time. Many earlier studies, for example, focused only on early sexual intercourse, drug use, or antisocial behavior, with few studies actually considering combinations of such behaviors. There are some notable exceptions, however (see Box 11.1).

# The Course of Problem Behavior

Adolescence, more than any other stage in the life span, is likely to involve experimentation, exploration, and risk-taking. Consequently, it is not surprising that we observe the emergence of problem behaviors, such as sexual intercourse and substance use, during this stage (Hurrelmann, 1990). Two broad trends characterize the nature of problem behavior in adolescence. First, some problem behavior is *normative* in adolescence. A majority of adolescents, for example, will at least experiment with smoking and drinking (Baumrind, 1987; Johnston, O'Malley, & Bachman, 1995a, 1995b; Shedler & Block, 1990). Second, problem behaviors *increase* in adolescence, although the developmental course a problem behavior follows (when it reaches its height, for example) is unique to the specific behavior (Arnett, 1992). Delinquency, for instance, rises and falls in adolescence, but alcohol use and sexual intercourse continue to increase into adulthood (Petersen, Richmond, & Leffert, 1993).

Given that the majority of adolescents will engage at one time or another in one or more problem behaviors, how do we know when the behavior is a genuine problem, one that is likely to pose significant threats to the adolescent's health and well-being? There are several clues. First, problem behavior is most likely to turn out to be a real problem when it begins early. Young people who begin engaging in delinquent acts at the age of 9 or 10, for instance, are more likely than those with a later onset to be headed for trouble, and they are more likely to engage in other problem behaviors as well. Second, continued engagement in problem behavior, rather than experimentation, is likely to signal future difficulties. Parents of a 16-year-old adolescent whose only brush with the law was getting caught shoplifting once at the age of 12 can

probably chalk it up to experience. Third, the adolescent may already be in significant trouble when he or she becomes immersed in a problem-behavior lifestyle to the exclusion of a constructive, positive lifestyle. A problem-behavior lifestyle may be indicated by continuing engagement in multiple or very serious problem behaviors and a set of close friends who engage in the same activities (Elliott, Huizinga, & Menard, 1989; Jessor & Jessor, 1977; Petersen et al., 1993; Shedler & Block, 1990).

The nature and course of adolescent problem behavior differ across a number of variables, including sex of the adolescent, geographic location, and socioeconomic status. Girls, for instance, are less often engaged in problem behaviors than are boys and are likely to terminate their involvement in such behaviors sooner than do boys (Ensminger, 1990; Petersen et al., 1993). Urban youth are more likely than rural youth to cease alcohol and marijuana use but less likely to cease engaging in serious delinquency. More middle- than low-income adolescents stop engaging in serious delinquent behavior (Petersen et al., 1993). Such differences will be explored later as we discuss problem behaviors, such as alcohol and drug use, more specifically.

## Why Do Adolescents Engage in Problem Behavior?

Why do adolescents engage in activities that may harm their health or other people? Increasingly, researchers recognize that problem behavior presents a paradox: At the same time that it may incur costs to the adolescent it may also present opportunities. In other words, adolescent problem behavior *may* be as constructive for adolescent development as it is potentially destructive. Consider the adolescent boy who one night drinks with abandon, overcomes his shyness, and finally is able to make some progress with the sought-after girl who formerly ignored him. Consider the adolescent girl who drives her parents' car recklessly, thereby achieving status in the eyes of her peers, who previously thought that she was a goody-goody. The point is that problem behavior can result in positive as well as negative consequences for the adolescent.

Many functionally positive consequences of problem behavior have been outlined. These include being accepted by peers, having fun and experiencing thrills, doing things adults are allowed to do, letting off steam (a way of relaxing), and finding a way to spend leisure time (Arnett, 1992; Beyth-Marom et al., 1993; Silbereisen & Noack, 1988). One study found that the extent to which adolescent boys and girls reported engaging in four different problem behaviors was a function of how much fun and how risky the behaviors were believed to be: The most fun and least risky behaviors, such as dis-

obedience to parents and school misconduct, were reported more often than behaviors that were less fun and more risky, such as substance use and antisocial behavior. Moreover, actual engagement in problem behaviors was associated with increased levels of perceived acceptance by peers, a clear benefit of engaging in problem behavior. Over time, however, problem behavior was associated with decreases in self-image, illustrating the personal costs that can be incurred (Maggs, Almeida, & Galambos, 1995).

Some problem behaviors may serve to boost the adolescent's self-esteem. Adolescents who begin using drugs, for instance, may do so because they have been rejected by a peer group that espouses traditional or conventional standards (such as achievement in school and having money to spend on clothing). These rejected young people may experience enhanced feelings of self-worth when a "deviant" peer group that endorses nonconventional attitudes and behaviors, such as drug use, provides warmth and acceptance (Newcomb & Bentler, 1988). In a study of late adolescents in the first weeks of their transition to college, intentions to drink alcohol and actual alcohol use (including binge drinking) were highest among those who felt accepted by their peers, perceived themselves more negatively, and rated drinking as a lot of fun with little risk (Maggs, in press). These studies point to the importance of understanding the widely varying sources of problem behavior—the psychological and social motivations behind it—and the perceived and actual consequences of engaging in it.

In order to do this, we need to consider the adolescent's decision-making processes. What are adolescents thinking when they conduct themselves in a way that could be risky? Are they thinking of the consequences and weighing the potential benefits and costs? Psychologists Lita Furby and Ruth Beyth-Marom (1992) argue that

> What little evidence there is . . . suggests that to at least some small extent teens choose to engage in behaviors which are more likely to bring consequences they perceive as positive and less likely to bring consequences they perceive as negative. Thus, the existing evidence does not support the contention that adolescents are prone to "irrational" risky behavior (i.e., behavior which they see as more likely to diminish their well-being than to improve it). (1992, pp. 3–4)

Recent evidence supports this conclusion (Lavery et al., 1993; Maggs, in press; Maggs et al., 1995) and suggests that adolescents' abilities to evaluate the positive and negative consequences of risk behaviors are not signifi-

# 11.1 Multiple Serious Problem Behaviors Among Inner-City Adolescents

Although multiple problem behaviors often occur, it is not always the case that adolescents who engage in one type of problem behavior engage in another. What proportion of adolescents engage in multiple problem behaviors and how do their backgrounds and experiences differ from those of adolescents who engage in no problem behaviors or a single problem behavior? Sociologist Margaret Ensminger sought the answers to these questions by using data from the Woodlawn study, a longitudinal study that followed a group of 705 poor, inner-city, black adolescents from first grade until they were 16 or 17 years old. The co-occurrence of *serious* involvement (occurring on numerous occasions) in three problem behaviors in adolescence was assessed: sexual intercourse, substance use (use of beer, marijuana, or hard liquor), and physical assault (such as beating up someone or using a weapon) (Ensminger, 1990).

As shown in Table B11.1, 57.4 percent of females exhibited no serious problem behaviors, 23.4 percent engaged in one (sex or substance use), 16.6 percent reported serious engagement in two problem behaviors, and 2.6 percent had been involved in all three. The males in the sample were more generally involved than females in problem behaviors, but 21.9 percent had not engaged seriously in any of the three problem behaviors. About 29 percent of the males had engaged seriously in one problem behav-

ior (primarily sex), nearly 30 percent had engaged in two (primarily sex combined with substance use), and 19.1 percent had engaged in all three. Although a substantial proportion of adolescents engaged in multiple (more than one) serious problem behaviors, involvement in a single problem behavior only (particularly frequent sex) was not rare.

On what family and school characteristics did the no-problem, sex-only, and multiproblem adolescents differ? Compared to no-problem females, the sex-only females were more likely to have been born to teenage mothers, to have mothers who did not graduate from high school, and to have lax rules at home about curfew. These family features may play a role in encouraging girls' involvement in sexual activity, but do not necessarily encourage other problem behaviors. Multiproblem females, compared to no-problem females, were less strongly attached to school, had more truancy, and had lax household rules about curfew. Multiproblem females also had weaker bonds to school than did sex-only females. These results suggest that for females, noninvolvement in school and a lack of close supervision by parents were important risk factors in the development of multiple problem behaviors.

The no-problem and sex-only males did not differ on any of the school and family characteristics. The multiproblem males, however, were more aggressive in first grade, had a history of truancy,

cantly different from those of adults (Beyth-Marom et al., 1993; Quadrel, Fischhoff, & Davis, 1993). From the perspective of the adolescent, then, problem behavior can be the result of rational thinking.

An adolescent who is considering sexual intercourse, for instance, might engage in the following thinking process (Furby & Beyth-Marom, 1992):

1. *Identify possible actions* (I can engage in sex or not).
2. *Consider the positive and negative consequences of those actions* (Sex would make me feel good, but I don't want a baby).
3. *Evaluate the desirability of each consequence* (Sex is becoming really important, but getting pregnant is the last thing I want).
4. *Assess the likelihood of each consequence* (I bet I'll enjoy sex, but I probably won't get pregnant, particularly if I use contraception).
5. *Weigh the likelihood of positive and negative consequences to choose among possible alternatives* (The odds are in my favor if I use contraception. I'm going to do it).

A different adolescent might assess as higher the odds of getting pregnant and might arrive at a different decision.

## Table B11.1 Co-Occurrence of Three Serious Problem Behaviors Among Adolescent Girls and Boys

| NUMBER OF SERIOUS PROBLEM BEHAVIORS | FEMALES | MALES |
|---|---|---|
| None | 57.4% | 21.9% |
| One | | |
|   Sex | 15.5 | 26.6 |
|   Substance use | 7.9 | 2.8 |
|   Total | 23.4% | 29.4% |
| Two | | |
|   Sex/substance use | 14.0 | 27.0 |
|   Substance use/assault | 2.6 | 2.5 |
|   Total | 16.6% | 29.5% |
| Three | | |
|   Sex/substance use/assault | 2.6 | 19.1 |

SOURCE: M. E. Ensminger (1990). Sexual activity and problem behaviors among black, urban adolescents. *Child Development,* **61**, 2032–2046. By permission.

and had weaker curfew rules at home. The multi-problem males were also more likely to have been born to an adolescent mother than were the no-problem males. These results point out that some of the seeds of multiple problem behaviors in adolescence may be sown in childhood, with early aggressive behavior, birth to a teen mother, and a lack of close supervision comprising important risk factors (Ensminger, 1990).

Overall, this study points to the necessity for differentiating among adolescents who engage seriously in multiple problem behaviors and those who engage in none or a single problem behavior. Relative to adolescents who limit their problem behavior, adolescents who engage in multiple problem behaviors may well have a more disadvantaged or unstable history, and the potential costs to these adolescents and to society may well be greater.

Few studies have actually considered such decision-making processes.

**Antecedents of Problem Behaviors.** Although the adolescent's engagement in problem behavior at any one time may be the result of a decision-making process wherein immediate results or consequences are all-important, some antecedents seem to predispose adolescents to engaging in problem behaviors. Broadly speaking, factors that increase the likelihood of adolescents' involvement in problem behavior include coming from a disorganized or unstable family, poor

parental monitoring of adolescents, living in a high-risk, inner-city neighborhood, having more than normal conflict with parents, hanging out with peers who engage in deviant activities, experiencing failure in school, having personal characteristics that include a higher propensity to take risks, and having low self-esteem that may be boosted by engaging in problem behavior (Arnett, 1992; Barber, 1992; Baumrind, 1987; Dishion et al., 1991; Ensminger, 1990; Maggs & Galambos, 1993; McCord, 1990; Newcomb & Bentler, 1988; Vuchinich, Bank, & Patterson, 1992). All of these antecedents may be considered factors that place the

adolescent at risk for engaging in serious problem behaviors. These risk factors may combine to make adolescents vulnerable psychologically to the allure of behaviors that provide good feelings or increase peer acceptance (such as the use of drugs). These factors may also make adolescents vulnerable physically because they may locate them in a social context that exposes them to neighborhoods, people, or schools that foster a problem behavior lifestyle without providing the benefit of a strong guiding hand in the other direction.

We turn now to a discussion of adolescents and drugs. Drug use is one of the most common and recognized problem behaviors in adolescence; as such, it deserves attention as we move forward in our understanding of adolescents at risk.

## Adolescents and Drugs: The Nature of the Problem

Society has been developing into a drug culture for many years—one that is not restricted just to youth. For example, one-quarter to one-third of all prescriptions currently written in the United States are for amphetamines (pep or diet pills) or tranquilizers and antidepressants, such as Valium and Prozac.

Television and radio bombard viewers with insistent messages that relief for almost anything—anxiety, depression, restlessness, or other ailments—is just a swallow away. In the words of one 13-year-old, "We're not supposed to take drugs, but TV is full of commercials showing people running for a pill because something is bugging them." Moreover, adult use of a number of drugs has increased as members of the baby-boom generation and their immediate successors have aged, replacing older adults who were frequent users of alcohol and tobacco but infrequent users of many other drugs, such as marijuana, cocaine, and hallucinogens (Johnston, O'Malley, & Bachman, 1995a, 1995b; National Household Survey on Drug Abuse [NHSDA], 1994, 1995).

### Two Worlds of Drugs

We need to recognize that "the drug problem" is not, in reality, a single problem. In terms of root causes, severity of the problem, or prospects for change, the drug problem among economically favored, well-educated youth and young adults is not the same as the drug problem among impoverished, poorly educated young peo-

ple growing up in the socially disorganized, crime-ridden sections of large cities.

### Adolescent Drug Use

Although far too many adolescents become high-risk drug users, the majority do not (see Figure 11.1). Although use of marijuana, alcohol, and tobacco is still widespread among U.S. high school students and about one-quarter have tried amphetamines (stimulants), use of other substances on the youth drug scene has never exceeded one person in five in the United States (Johnston, O'Malley, & Bachman, 1995a, 1995b, 1996; NHSDA, 1994, 1995). Moreover, from 1981 through 1992 adolescent use of most drugs declined steadily (see Tables 11.1 and 11.2).

Crack use and dealing, and the large numbers of other crimes associated with these activities, have become a major threat to survival among children and adolescents in America's inner cities.

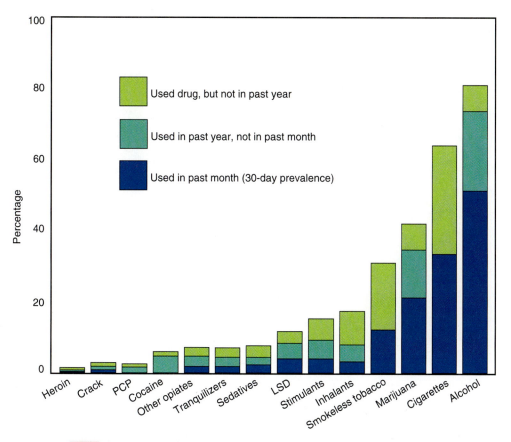

**Figure 11.1**

Prevalence and recency of use of specific drugs for 12th graders, 1995. Adapted from L. D. Johnston, P. M. O'Malley, & J. G. Bachman (1996). *National survey results on drug use from the monitoring the future study, 1975–1995. Vol. 1, Secondary school students.* Washington, DC: National Institute on Drug Abuse. Adapted with permission.

However, these encouraging trends ended in 1992, after which adolescent drug use has been rising. The increase has been especially evident in the case of marijuana: Among high school seniors, annual use increased by more than half between 1992 and 1995 (from 22 percent to 35 percent); among 10th graders it nearly doubled (from 15 percent to 29 percent). Among 8th graders use rose two-and-one-half times between 1991 and 1995 (from 6 percent in 1991 to 16 percent in 1995) (Johnston, 1995a). Although the upward trend has been most marked in the case of marijuana, gradual increases have also occurred among other drugs, including LSD and other hallucinogens, inhalants, stimulants, barbiturates, and, in 1994, cocaine and crack (see Tables 11.1 and 11.2).

Although adolescent drug use still remains well below levels reached in the late 1970s and early 1980s, Lloyd Johnston, an expert in drug use among adolescents

and young adults, notes that over a third of all eighth-graders have used some illicit drug, including inhalants, while over 40 percent of all tenth-graders, and nearly 50 percent of all twelfth-graders have done so (Johnston, 1994, 1995a). Furthermore, it is a problem which is getting worse at a fairly rapid pace (Johnston, 1994, 1995a).

Johnston and his colleagues (Johnston, 1994, 1995a; Johnston, O'Malley, & Bachman, 1995a) are particularly concerned because adolescents' perceptions of the risks associated with drug use, which rose steadily in the seventies and eighties, are now declining, as are the percentages of young people expressing disapproval of drugs. As they have demonstrated through their longitudinal research on adolescent drug use over the past two decades, changing attitudes are important predictors of subsequent use.

We cannot lose sight of the fact that rates of illicit drug use are significantly higher among school dropouts,

# Table 11.1 Percentage of Twelfth Graders Who Used Specific Types of Drugs in Last Thirty Days, 1975–1995

| | CLASS OF 1975 | CLASS OF 1976 | CLASS OF 1977 | CLASS OF 1978 | CLASS OF 1979 | CLASS OF 1980 | CLASS OF 1981 | CLASS OF 1982 | CLASS OF 1983 | CLASS OF 1984 | CLASS OF 1985 |
|---|---|---|---|---|---|---|---|---|---|---|---|
| Any illicit drug | 30.7 | 34.2 | 37.6 | 38.9 | 38.9 | 37.2 | 36.9 | 32.5 | 30.5 | 29.2 | 29.7 |
| Any illicit drug other than marijuana | 15.4 | 13.9 | 15.2 | 15.1 | 16.8 | 18.4 | 21.7 | 17.0 | 15.4 | 15.1 | 14.9 |
| Marijuana/hashish | 27.1 | 32.2 | 35.4 | 37.1 | 36.5 | 33.7 | 31.6 | 28.5 | 27.0 | 25.2 | 25.7 |
| Inhalants | — | 0.9 | 1.3 | 1.5 | 1.7 | 1.4 | 1.5 | 1.5 | 1.7 | 1.9 | 2.2 |
| Hallucinogens | 4.7 | 3.4 | 4.1 | 3.9 | 4.0 | 3.7 | 3.7 | 3.4 | 2.8 | 2.6 | 2.5 |
| Cocaine | 1.9 | 2.0 | 2.9 | 3.9 | 5.7 | 5.2 | 5.8 | 5.0 | 4.9 | 5.8 | 6.7 |
| Crack | — | — | — | — | — | — | — | — | — | — | — |
| Other cocaine | — | — | — | — | — | — | — | — | — | — | — |
| Heroin | 0.4 | 0.2 | 0.3 | 0.3 | 0.2 | 0.2 | 0.2 | 0.2 | 0.2 | 0.3 | 0.3 |
| Other opiates | 2.1 | 2.0 | 2.8 | 2.1 | 2.4 | 2.4 | 2.1 | 1.8 | 1.8 | 1.8 | 2.3 |
| Stimulants | 3.5 | 7.7 | 8.8 | 8.7 | 9.9 | 12.1 | 15.8 | 10.7 | 8.9 | 8.3 | 6.8 |
| Crystal meth. (ice) | — | — | — | — | — | — | — | — | — | — | — |
| Sedatives | 5.4 | 4.5 | 5.1 | 4.2 | 4.4 | 4.8 | 4.6 | 3.4 | 3.0 | 2.3 | 2.4 |
| Barbiturates | 4.7 | 3.9 | 4.3 | 3.2 | 3.2 | 2.9 | 2.6 | 2.0 | 2.1 | 1.7 | 2.0 |
| Methaqualone | 2.1 | 1.6 | 2.3 | 1.9 | 2.3 | 3.3 | 3.1 | 2.4 | 1.8 | 1.1 | 1.0 |
| Tranquilizers | 4.1 | 4.0 | 4.6 | 3.4 | 3.7 | 3.1 | 2.7 | 2.4 | 2.5 | 2.1 | 2.1 |
| Alcohol | 68.2 | 68.3 | 71.2 | 72.1 | 71.8 | 72.0 | 70.7 | 69.7 | 69.4 | 67.2 | 65.9 |
| Been drunk | — | — | — | — | — | — | — | — | — | — | — |
| Cigarettes | 36.7 | 38.8 | 38.4 | 36.7 | 34.4 | 30.5 | 29.4 | 30.0 | 30.3 | 29.3 | 30.1 |
| Smokeless tobacco | — | — | — | — | — | — | — | — | — | — | — |
| Steroids | — | — | — | — | — | — | — | — | — | — | — |

*(continued)*

although accurate figures are more difficult to obtain (Johnston, 1994; Mensch & Kandel, 1988; NHSDA, 1994, 1995). This is especially true in the case of out-of-work young people living in deteriorated, crime-ridden neighborhoods in large metropolitan areas. In such surroundings, participation in drug dealing—particularly in crack cocaine—may appear to provide the easiest, and by far the most lucrative, if dangerous, way out of poverty (Feigelman, Stanton, & Ricardo, 1993; Johnson & Muffler, 1992). For other young people, vulnerability to drug use is greatly increased by easy accessibility, peer influence, and a pervasive sense of despair.

The greatest concern of those who work with young people is the young person who turns repeated-

ly to drugs in order to cope with insecurity, stress, tension, low self-esteem, feelings of rejection or alienation, conflicts with parents, or problems of daily living. One of the important developmental tasks of adolescence is to learn how to cope with stress, conflict, and frustration; other tasks include the development of cognitive, social, and vocational skills and the establishment of rewarding interpersonal relationships with peers and adults. Failure to master these essential developmental demands during adolescence because of repeated escapes into the world of drugs leaves the young person ill-prepared to meet the demands of responsible adulthood (Baumrind & Moselle, 1985; Kandel et al., 1986; Newcomb & Bentler, 1988).

Unfortunately, a significant number of vulnerable

# Table 11.1 Percentage of Twelfth Graders Who Used Specific Types of Drugs in Last Thirty Days, 1975–1995 (cont.)

| | CLASS OF 1986 | CLASS OF 1987 | CLASS OF 1988 | CLASS OF 1989 | CLASS OF 1990 | CLASS OF 1991 | CLASS OF 1992 | CLASS OF 1993 | CLASS OF 1994 | CLASS OF 1995 | '94–'95 CHANGE |
|---|---|---|---|---|---|---|---|---|---|---|---|
| Any illicit drug | 27.1 | 24.7 | 21.3 | 19.7 | 17.2 | 16.4 | 14.4 | 18.3 | 21.9 | 23.8 | +1.9 |
| Any illicit drug other than marijuana | 13.2 | 11.6 | 10.0 | 9.1 | 8.0 | 7.1 | 6.3 | 7.9 | 8.8 | 10.0 | +1.2 |
| Marijuana/hashish | 23.4 | 21.0 | 18.0 | 16.7 | 14.0 | 13.8 | 11.9 | 15.5 | 19.0 | 21.2 | +2.2 |
| Inhalants | 2.5 | 2.8 | 2.6 | 2.3 | 2.7 | 2.4 | 2.3 | 2.5 | 2.7 | 3.2 | +0.5 |
| Hallucinogens | 2.5 | 2.5 | 2.2 | 2.2 | 2.2 | 2.2 | 2.1 | 2.7 | 3.1 | 4.4 | +1.3 |
| Cocaine | 6.2 | 4.3 | 3.4 | 2.8 | 1.9 | 1.4 | 1.3 | 1.3 | 1.5 | 1.8 | +0.3 |
| Crack | — | 1.3 | 1.6 | 1.4 | 0.7 | 0.7 | 0.6 | 0.7 | 0.8 | 1.0 | +0.2 |
| Other cocaine | — | 4.1 | 3.2 | 1.9 | 1.7 | 1.2 | 1.0 | 1.2 | 1.3 | 1.3 | 0.0 |
| Heroin | 0.2 | 0.2 | 0.2 | 0.3 | 0.2 | 0.2 | 0.3 | 0.2 | 0.3 | 0.6 | +0.3 |
| Other opiates | 2.0 | 1.8 | 1.6 | 1.6 | 1.5 | 1.1 | 1.2 | 1.3 | 1.5 | 1.8 | +0.3 |
| Stimulants | 5.5 | 5.2 | 4.6 | 4.2 | 1.7 | 3.2 | 2.8 | 3.7 | 4.0 | 4.0 | 0.0 |
| Crystal meth. (ice) | — | — | — | — | 0.6 | 0.6 | 0.5 | 0.6 | 0.7 | 1.1 | +0.4 |
| Sedatives | 2.2 | 1.7 | 1.4 | 1.6 | 1.4 | 1.5 | 1.2 | 1.3 | 1.8 | 2.3 | +0.5 |
| Barbiturates | 1.8 | 1.4 | 1.2 | 1.4 | 1.3 | 1.4 | 1.1 | 1.3 | 1.7 | 2.2 | +0.5 |
| Methaqualone | 0.8 | 0.6 | 0.5 | 0.6 | 0.2 | 0.2 | 0.4 | 0.1 | 0.4 | 0.4 | 0.0 |
| Tranquilizers | 2.1 | 2.0 | 1.5 | 1.3 | 1.2 | 1.4 | 1.0 | 1.2 | 1.4 | 1.8 | +0.4 |
| Alcohol | 65.3 | 66.4 | 63.9 | 60.0 | 57.1 | 54.0 | 51.3 | 48.6† | 51.1 | 51.3 | +1.2 |
| Been drunk | — | — | — | — | — | 31.6 | 29.9 | 28.9 | 30.8 | 33.2 | +2.4 |
| Cigarettes | 29.6 | 29.4 | 28.7 | 28.6 | 29.4 | 28.3 | 27.8 | 29.9 | 31.2 | 33.5 | +2.3 |
| Smokeless tobacco | — | 11.5 | 11.3 | 10.3 | — | — | 11.4 | 10.7 | 11.1 | 12.2 | +1.1 |
| Steroids | — | — | — | 0.8 | 1.0 | 0.8 | 0.6 | 0.7 | 0.9 | 0.7 | −0.2 |

NOTES: —indicates data not available. Sample size ranged from 9400 to 17,800.

†In 1993, question was changed slightly to indicate that a "drink" meant "more than a few sips."

SOURCE: Adapted from L. D. Johnston, P. M. O'Malley, & J. G. Bachman (1996). *National survey results on drug use from the monitoring the future study, 1975–1995. Vol. 1, Secondary school students.* Washington, DC: National Institute on Drug Abuse. Reprinted with permission.

adolescents are finding that drug use becomes a psychological crutch that is increasingly difficult to renounce. In addition, a highly addictive drug such as crack produces such an intense high and such a powerful subsequent crash that it may lead to compulsive repetitive behavior, even among first-time users.

Our principal aim in this chapter is to examine the reasons that adolescents take drugs. But first it is necessary to examine the range of drugs available to young people, and their effects.

## Alcohol

Some years ago clinicians and others who work with young people often heard parents make comments such as, "I'm becoming concerned that Johnny (or Susie) may be drinking a bit too much. But at least it's better than drugs." What these parents failed to realize, of course, is that alcohol is just as much a **psychoactive drug** as, for example, marijuana, and its dangers have been far more clearly

# Table 11.2 Percentage of Twelfth Graders Reporting Daily Use of Specific Types of Drugs, 1975–1995

| | CLASS OF 1975 | CLASS OF 1976 | CLASS OF 1977 | CLASS OF 1978 | CLASS OF 1979 | CLASS OF 1980 | CLASS OF 1981 | CLASS OF 1982 | CLASS OF 1983 | CLASS OF 1984 | CLASS OF 1985 |
|---|---|---|---|---|---|---|---|---|---|---|---|
| Marijuana/hashish | 6.0 | 8.2 | 9.1 | 10.7 | 10.3 | 9.1 | 7.0 | 6.3 | 5.5 | 5.0 | 4.9 |
| Inhalants | — | ★ | ★ | 0.1 | ★ | 0.1 | 0.1 | 0.1 | 0.1 | 0.1 | 0.2 |
| Hallucinogens | 0.1 | 0.1 | 0.1 | 0.1 | 0.1 | 0.1 | 0.1 | 0.1 | 0.1 | 0.1 | 0.1 |
| Cocaine | 0.1 | 0.1 | 0.1 | 0.1 | 0.2 | 0.2 | 0.3 | 0.2 | 0.2 | 0.2 | 0.4 |
| Crack | — | — | — | — | — | — | — | — | — | — | — |
| Other cocaine | — | — | — | — | — | — | — | — | — | — | — |
| Heroin | 0.1 | ★ | ★ | ★ | ★ | ★ | ★ | ★ | 0.1 | ★ | ★ |
| Other opiates | 0.1 | 0.1 | 0.2 | 0.1 | ★ | 0.1 | 0.1 | 0.1 | 0.1 | 0.1 | 0.1 |
| Stimulants | 0.5 | 0.4 | 0.5 | 0.5 | 0.6 | 0.7 | 1.2 | 0.7 | 0.8 | 0.6 | 0.4 |
| Crystal meth. (ice) | — | — | — | — | — | — | — | — | — | — | — |
| Sedatives | 0.3 | 0.2 | 0.2 | 0.2 | 0.1 | 0.2 | 0.2 | 0.2 | 0.2 | 0.1 | 0.1 |
| Barbiturates | 0.1 | 0.1 | 0.2 | 0.1 | ★ | 0.1 | 0.1 | 0.1 | 0.1 | ★ | 0.1 |
| Methaqualone | ★ | ★ | ★ | ★ | ★ | 0.1 | 0.1 | 0.1 | ★ | ★ | ★ |
| Tranquilizers | 0.1 | 0.2 | 0.3 | 0.1 | 0.1 | 0.1 | 0.1 | 0.1 | 0.1 | 0.1 | ★ |
| Alcohol | | | | | | | | | | | |
| Daily | 5.7 | 5.6 | 6.1 | 5.7 | 6.9 | 6.0 | 6.0 | 5.7 | 5.5 | 4.8 | 5.0 |
| Been drunk daily | — | — | — | — | — | — | — | — | — | — | — |
| 5+ drinks in a row/ last 2 weeks | 36.8 | 37.1 | 39.4 | 40.3 | 41.2 | 41.2 | 41.4 | 40.5 | 40.8 | 38.7 | 36.7 |
| Cigarettes | | | | | | | | | | | |
| Daily | 26.9 | 28.8 | 28.8 | 27.5 | 25.4 | 21.3 | 20.3 | 21.1 | 21.2 | 18.7 | 19.5 |
| Half-pack or more per day | 17.9 | 19.2 | 19.4 | 18.8 | 16.5 | 14.3 | 13.5 | 14.2 | 13.8 | 12.3 | 12.5 |
| Steroids | — | — | — | — | — | — | — | — | — | — | — |

*(continued)*

established. Moreover, use of alcohol provides no assurance that other drugs will not be used; indeed, prior and concomitant use of alcohol (and tobacco) is more common among marijuana and other drug users than among nonusers (Esbensen & Elliott, 1994; Kandel, 1991; Kandel & Faust, 1975; Yamaguchi & Kandel, 1984a, 1984b).

What many such parents appeared to be saying was that alcohol use was a more familiar and more socially acceptable phenomenon. However, as public awareness of the severity of alcohol problems among adolescents increased, parental attitudes began to change. In recent polls adults have expressed as great (or greater) concern with alcohol use among adolescents as with marijuana use.

On many college and university campuses, administrators, faculty, and students cite excessive use of alcohol as a major problem and a number have instituted programs to try to deal with it more effectively (Gose, 1995; Maggs, in press; Shea, 1994). Indeed, the prevalence of occasions of heavy or binge drinking (five or more drinks in a row in the past two weeks) is higher among college students than among nonstudents in their

## Table 11.2 Percentage of Twelfth Graders Reporting Daily Use of Specific Types of Drugs, 1975–1995 (cont.)

| | CLASS OF 1986 | CLASS OF 1987 | CLASS OF 1988 | CLASS OF 1989 | CLASS OF 1990 | CLASS OF 1991 | CLASS OF 1992 | CLASS OF 1993 | CLASS OF 1994 | CLASS OF 1995 | '94–'95 CHANGE |
|---|---|---|---|---|---|---|---|---|---|---|---|
| Marijuana/hashish | 4.0 | 3.3 | 2.7 | 2.9 | 2.2 | 2.0 | 1.9 | 2.4 | 3.6 | 4.6 | +1.0 |
| Inhalants | 0.2 | 0.1 | 0.2 | 0.2 | 0.3 | 0.2 | 0.1 | 0.1 | 0.1 | 0.1 | +0.1 |
| Hallucinogens | 0.1 | 0.1 | ★ | 0.1 | 0.1 | 0.1 | 0.1 | 0.1 | 0.1 | 0.1 | 0.0 |
| Cocaine | 0.4 | 0.3 | 0.2 | 0.3 | 0.1 | 0.1 | 0.1 | 0.1 | 0.1 | 0.2 | +0.1 |
| Crack | — | 0.1 | 0.1 | 0.2 | 0.1 | 0.1 | 0.1 | 0.1 | 0.1 | 0.1 | 0.0 |
| Other cocaine | — | 0.2 | 0.2 | 0.1 | 0.1 | 0.1 | ★ | 0.1 | 0.1 | 0.1 | +0.1 |
| Heroin | ★ | ★ | ★ | 0.1 | ★ | ★ | ★ | ★ | ★ | 0.1 | 0.0 |
| Other opiates | 0.1 | 0.1 | 0.1 | 0.2 | 0.1 | 0.1 | ★ | ★ | 0.1 | 0.1 | 0.0 |
| Stimulants | 0.3 | 0.3 | 0.3 | 0.3 | 0.2 | 0.2 | 0.2 | 0.2 | 0.2 | 0.3 | +0.1 |
| Crystal meth. (ice) | — | — | — | — | 0.1 | 0.1 | 0.1 | 0.1 | ★ | 0.1 | 0.0 |
| Sedatives | 0.1 | 0.1 | 0.1 | 0.1 | 0.1 | 0.1 | 0.1 | 0.1 | ★ | 0.1 | +0.1 |
| Barbiturates | 0.1 | 0.1 | ★ | 0.1 | 0.1 | 0.1 | ★ | 0.1 | ★ | 0.1 | +0.1 |
| Methaqualone | ★ | ★ | 0.1 | ★ | ★ | ★ | 0.1 | 0.0 | 0.1 | 0.1 | 0.0 |
| Tranquilizers | ★ | 0.1 | ★ | 0.1 | 0.1 | 0.1 | ★ | ★ | 0.1 | ★ | 0.0 |
| Alcohol | | | | | | | | | | | |
| Daily | 4.8 | 4.8 | 4.2 | 4.2 | 3.7 | 3.6 | 3.4 | 3.4† | 2.9 | 3.5 | +0.6 |
| Been drunk daily | — | — | — | — | — | 0.9 | 0.8 | 0.9 | 1.2 | 1.3 | +0.1 |
| 5+ drinks in a row/ last 2 weeks | 36.8 | 37.5 | 34.7 | 33.0 | 32.2 | 29.8 | 27.9 | 27.5 | 28.2 | 29.8 | +1.6 |
| Cigarettes | | | | | | | | | | | |
| Daily | 18.7 | 18.7 | 18.1 | 18.9 | 19.1 | 18.5 | 17.2 | 19.0 | 19.7 | 21.6 | +2.2 |
| Half-pack or more per day | 11.4 | 11.4 | 10.6 | 11.2 | 11.3 | 10.7 | 10.0 | 10.9 | 11.2 | 12.4 | +1.2 |
| Steroids | — | — | — | 0.1 | 0.2 | 0.1 | 0.1 | 0.1 | 0.4 | 0.2 | −0.2 |

NOTES: —indicates data not available. Sample size ranged from 9400 to 17,800. ★ indicates less than .05 percent.

†In 1993, question was changed slightly to indicate that a "drink" meant "more than a few sips."

SOURCE: Adapted from L. D. Johnston, P. M. O'Malley, & J. G. Bachman (1996). *National survey results on drug use from the monitoring the future study, 1975–1995. Vol. 1, Secondary school students.* Washington, DC: National Institute on Drug Abuse. Reprinted with permission.

age group (Johnston, O'Malley, & Bachman, 1995b). A recent study found that 40 percent of U.S. college students had indulged in binge drinking within the past two weeks; more men (50 percent) than women (39 percent) were binge drinkers. A smaller follow-up study of 13 colleges where at least half of the students were binge drinkers found that in this atmosphere 41 percent of freshmen engaged in binge drinking for the first time during their first semester, although only 6 percent had planned to do so (Gose, 1995).

Another area of significant concern is drunken driving. Between 45 and 60 percent of all fatal crashes are alcohol-related (*Alcohol and health,* 1994). Most states have increased, or are planning to increase, their legal drinking age to 21. Between 1982 and 1989, the percent of motor vehicle accidents among drivers under 18 declined from

On many college campuses, excessive use of alcohol has become a major problem and a number of programs have been initiated to deal with it more effectively. Although most students do not become problem drinkers, the prevalence of heavy drinking is higher among college students than among nonstudents in their age group.

19 to 10 percent, largely because of changes in minimum driving age (*Alcohol and health,* 1994).

## Adolescent Use of Alcohol

How widespread is the use of alcohol among adolescents? The great majority of young people have at least tried alcoholic beverages by the end of adolescence (Johnston, O'Malley, & Bachman, 1995a; NHSDA, 1994, 1995). Among high school seniors in the United States in 1994, four out of five acknowledged having used alcohol at some time—a higher overall incidence than for any other psychoactive drug, including marijuana (Johnston, O'Malley, & Bachman, 1995a).

Frequency of alcohol use has been found to vary with such factors as age, sex, education, ethnic background, and region of the country (*Alcohol and health,* 1994; Freedman & Humphrey, 1985; Jessor, 1984b; Johnston, O'Malley, & Bachman, 1995a, 1995b). For example, although differences are decreasing, among 12th graders in 1994, 55 percent of boys and 47 percent of girls had used alcohol in the past month. Thirty percent of male seniors but only 21 percent of females reported incidents of heavy drinking (five or more drinks in a row in the past two weeks).

Students who do not plan to complete four years of college are no more likely to become drinkers than those who do, but they tend to drink more heavily, as do school dropouts (Johnston, O'Malley, & Bachman, 1995a; Mensch & Kandel, 1988). Students living in the

Northeast and North Central states drink the most; those in the West and South drink the least. Black youth drink far less than whites and Hispanics (Johnston, O'Malley, & Bachman, 1995a, 1995b).

Overall alcohol use among adolescents decreased significantly between 1981 and 1993, but has since stabilized: In 1995, 51 percent of all high school seniors had used alcohol in the last month, down from a high of 72 percent in 1980 (see Table 11.1).

It should be emphasized that the majority of adolescents who drink are temperate in their use of alcohol and are likely to remain so. What is of far greater concern to clinicians and others who work with young people is the relatively small but important minority who continue to drink frequently and heavily: Three and one half percent of 1995 high school seniors reported daily use of alcohol in the past month (down from 6 percent in 1980), and nearly 30 percent reported heavy drinking (more than five drinks in a row) in the past two weeks (see Table 11.2). Over fourteen percent of 8th graders and 24 percent of 10th graders had engaged in heavy drinking in the same period (Johnston, 1995a; Johnston, O'Malley, & Bachman, 1996).

In summary, it appears clear that most adolescents are not problem drinkers and are unlikely to become so; nevertheless, the fact that more than 14 percent of 8th graders have already engaged in heavy drinking can hardly be viewed as reassuring. Moreover, these nationwide findings are restricted to young people who are still in school. The incidence of problem drinking is known to be much higher among school dropouts.

## Characteristics of Student Drinkers

In general, adolescent abstainers are more likely than either moderate or heavy drinkers to be conservative, controlled, responsible, studious, cautious, religious, and interested in solitary pursuits. They are less likely to be adventurous, outgoing, socially assertive, impulsive, socially and sexually active, subject to mood swings, critical of society, and tolerant of socially deviant behavior (Braucht, 1984; Cloninger, Sigvardsson, & Bohman, 1988; Donovan & Jessor, 1978; Donovan, Jessor, & Jessor, 1983; Jessor, Donovan, & Widmer, 1980; Rachal et al., 1984). Abstainers are more likely to come from close-knit families with conservative, religious, hard-working, nondrinking parents who place a high value on education (Barnes, 1984; Braucht, 1984; Harberg et al., 1990; Jessor, 1984b; Jessor & Jessor, 1973; Rachal et al., 1984).

In contrast, young people who are heavy or problem drinkers are more likely than either abstainers or moderate drinkers to place a high value on independence; to engage heavily in social activities such as dances, parties, and dating; to be impulsive and engage in socially disapproved or deviant behavior (such as cutting classes, cheating on examinations, driving too fast, and using other drugs); and to be dominant and outgoing (Braucht, 1984; Crowley & Riggs, 1995; Donovan & Jessor, 1978; Jessor & Jessor, 1977; Martin et al., 1993).

Compared to abstainers or moderate drinkers, heavy drinkers are more likely to experience feelings of exuberance and excitement. However, they are also more likely to be pessimistic, bored, impulsive, distrustful, and irresponsible, and to have low self-esteem (Clark & Midanik, 1984; Rachal et al., 1984; Yanish & Battle, 1985). Among college students, many heavy drinkers, especially females, reported more frequent feelings of an inability to get going, of boredom, and of vague uneasiness. Furthermore, "significantly greater proportions of female heavy drinkers reported feeling lonely or remote from people, angry at some minor frustration, depressed or unhappy, and restless" (Moos, Moos, & Kulik, 1976, p. 357).

At all levels from junior high school to college, problem or heavy drinkers report more difficulties in relations with their parents. They are also less likely to value academic achievement; they expect less academic success and do, in fact, obtain lower grades (Braucht, 1980, 1984; Kandel, Kessler, & Margulies, 1978; Reeves, 1984). At the college level, they exhibit higher rates of academic failure and dropping out. Finally, heavy drinkers are more likely to have parents who drink heavily—in a disproportionate number of cases—as well as

friends and best friends who also drink (Hawkins, Catalano, & Miller, 1992; Kandel, 1985; Schuckit, 1995).

## Effects of Alcohol

Despite the popular notion that alcohol is a stimulant, it has a depressant effect on the central nervous system. Even in small doses, alcohol impairs perception and time estimation and reduces reasoning, learning ability, and memory. Consequently, it is not surprising that alcohol plays a major role in half of all fatalities in automobile accidents.

In higher dosages alcohol impairs basic brain functions, resulting in abnormality of gross bodily functions and mental faculties and ultimately in coma. In extreme instances—as in "chugalug" drinking contests—alcohol intake may even cause death (although usually the individual passes out before consuming enough alcohol to suspend the brain functions that regulate breathing and heart action). In addition to its direct effects on the central nervous system, alcohol may adversely affect kidney, cardiovascular, brain, and, most prominently, liver functioning (*Alcohol and health,* 1994; Frances & Miller, 1991). In combination with smoking, excessive use of alcohol appears to be related to the development of certain cancers.

Heavy drinking during pregnancy can adversely affect fetal development. It is currently estimated that full-blown **fetal alcohol syndrome** (characterized by retarded growth, physical abnormalities, and intellectual defects) may result from maternal consumption of 3 ounces of absolute alcohol per day (about six drinks). Smaller doses (perhaps as little as an ounce a day) increase the likelihood of low birthweight, developmental delays, physical difficulties (such as in breathing and sucking difficulty), and spontaneous abortion (*Alcohol and health,* 1994; Blume, 1992). Because no safe level of alcohol consumption has been established, it is generally recommended that women refrain from drinking during pregnancy.

# Tobacco

Cigarette smoking among adolescents appears to have reached a peak in 1977, after which it declined until 1992 (Johnston, 1995a, 1995b; Johnston, O'Malley, & Bachman, 1995a, 1996; NHSDA, 1994, 1995). Since that time there has been a significant rise, despite a rising tide of adverse publicity and restrictive legislation in the past decade. Among high school seniors, those smoking in the last month increased from 28.3 percent in 1991 to

33.5 percent in 1995 (See Table 11.1). Among 8th and 10th graders, smoking rates have also *increased* significantly in the last several years. Perhaps most troubling, only 50 percent of 8th graders and 57 percent of 10th graders now view smoking regularly as a high-risk behavior (Johnston, 1995b).

Although one-fourth fewer seniors engaged in daily use of cigarettes in 1995 (21.6 percent) than in 1976 (28.8 percent), this overall decline masks differing patterns for girls and boys: In 1976, for the first time, girls exceeded boys in daily use of cigarettes, a trend that continued until 1991. Since then, however, male smoking rates have again exceeded rates for females, but only very slightly (Johnston, 1995b; Johnston, O'Malley, & Bachman, 1995a, 1995b). Also noteworthy is the fact that seniors who do not plan to complete four years of college are far more likely (43.5 percent versus 29.9 percent) to smoke than those who plan to complete college (Johnston, 1995b). Among young people who do not graduate from high school, smoking rates are even higher for both boys and girls (Johnston, O'Malley, & Bachman, 1995a; Kandel, Raveis, & Kandel, 1984).

## Why Do Adolescents Smoke?

It has been clearly established that smoking substantially increases the risk of heart disease, lung cancer, chronic bronchitis, emphysema, and other ailments, and that it decreases longevity (Centers for Disease Control [CDC], 1989, 1994; Lynch & Bonnie, 1994) Moreover, smoking by pregnant women lowers their infants' birthweight and resistance to illness. It also increases the chances of spontaneous abortion, premature birth, and long-term problems in the physical and intellectual development of their children (CDC, 1994). In the words of former U.S. Surgeon General Julius Richmond, "Smoking is the largest preventable cause of death in America" (*Smoking and health,* 1979, p. ii). Though often overlooked, or downplayed in importance, the rapid rise in recent years in the use of smokeless tobacco by adolescents also presents serious health hazards and fosters addiction (see Box 11.2).

Why do adolescents begin and continue smoking? Clearly it is not simply because of ignorance of the associated health hazards. More than three-fourths of young people ages 12 to 17 believe that it is better not to start smoking than to have to quit and that smoking is habit-forming; four out of five believe that it can cause lung cancer and heart disease (Evans et al., 1979; Lynch & Bonnie, 1994). Two-thirds of high school seniors believe

Despite a rising tide of adverse publicity, since the mid-1980s there has been little further reduction in adolescent smoking, except among black youth.

that regular smoking entails great personal risk, although the number is declining (Johnston, O'Malley, & Bachman, 1995a). However, fewer than half of eighth-graders currently think that there is "great risk in smoking a pack-or-more a day"—a time when many teenagers start smoking (Johnston, 1995b).

In asking why adolescents smoke, despite the personal dangers, it is necessary to consider *initiation* of smoking separately from *continuation* of the habit. Once established, dependence on cigarettes can be very difficult to overcome, both physiologically and psychologically. Largely because of its nicotine content, tobacco is physiologically addictive, and cessation of smoking can produce symptoms of withdrawal that are comparable in many ways to those of withdrawal from narcotics (Institute of Medicine, 1980; Lynch & Bonnie, 1994). Psychological dependence is fostered by continued use of tobacco in specific circumstances, such as when one is anxious or bored, trying to concentrate, or attempting to deal with a difficult social situation, or in association with alcohol or coffee. Surveys of teenage smokers and ex-smokers found that about three-fourths had tried to quit, but at least 40 percent had failed (Allen et al., 1993; Lynch & Bonnie, 1994). Thus, it is relatively easy to understand why adolescents continue to smoke.

But what factors encourage initiation of use? Although we still have much to learn, a number of factors increase the likelihood of smoking. One is parental influence. Except in the instance of African-Americans, who generally view smoking negatively (see Box 11.3),

# 11.2 Do Real Men Really Chew Tobacco?

Although it has received less attention, the mounting use of chewing tobacco and other forms of smokeless tobacco (SLT), such as snuff, by adolescents is a serious public health problem (Johnston, O'Malley, & Bachman, 1995a; Lynch & Bonnie, 1994). In 1993, nearly one-third of 12th graders and nearly 20 percent of 8th graders—had at least tried smokeless tobacco; 10.7 percent of 12th graders and 6.6 percent of 8th graders had used it in the last 30 days (Johnston, O'Malley, & Bachman, 1995).

A major obstacle in efforts to combat the SLT problem is the widespread perception that it is safe. Fewer than four in ten high school seniors believe that SLT use is a high-risk behavior, and more than four out of five think it is much safer than cigarettes (Johnston et al., 1994; Lynch & Bonnie, 1994). Acceptance by parents of their children's chewing or "dipping" contributes to the perception that SLT is safe.

In fact, smokeless tobacco is highly addictive, and efforts to quit result in signs of symptoms of nicotine deprivation similar to those seen among cigarette smokers attempting abstinence (Boyd & Glove, 1989; Lynch & Bonnie, 1994). SLT also presents many of the same health hazards as smoking, such as increased risk of heart disease, as well as causing oral lesions, which may become malignant.

Because use of smokeless tobacco by adolescents is a relatively recent phenomenon, systematic prevention efforts are still being developed. Most are school-based, although a few programs have been implemented in nonschool settings, such as 4-H clubs, Little League baseball clubs, and Native American community centers (Lynch & Bonnie, 1994; Severson et al., 1991). The most successful efforts to date have been addressed to middle-school boys (rather than those in high school), and combine learning about the physical consequences of SLT use with a social influence program aimed at developing refusal skills (Severson et al., 1991; Sussman et al., 1995).

Chewing tobacco and snuff are widely used by sports stars, encouraging young people to emulate them; indeed, several look-alike gum products (such as "Big League Chew") have been promoted. Attempts have been made recently to decrease the visibility of sports heroes chewing (a study of 1987 World Series TV broadcasts had documented 24 minutes of viewing time of baseball players chewing) (Jones, 1987). Nevertheless, significant exposure still remains.

in families where both parents smoke, both boys and girls are significantly more likely to become smokers than in families where neither parent smokes (CDC, 1994; Evans, 1984; Hamburg, Elliott, & Parron, 1982; Lynch & Bonnie, 1994).

More important, however, are parents' attitudes and reactions to smoking (Johnston, 1995b; Lynch & Bonnie, 1994). When parents set clear standards disapproving of tobacco use, young people are far less likely to take up smoking, regardless of whether their parents smoke (Cimoski, 1994; Cimoski & Sheridan, 1994; Hunter et al., 1987; Lynch & Bonnie, 1994). In one study of 10,000 adolescents, parental opposition to smoking was found to be a more important predictor of adolescents' initiation to smoking than parents' smoking behavior (Swan, Creeser, & Murray, 1990). Thus, as a recent report by the Institute of Medicine points out,

even parents who smoke can be effective if they consistently reinforce a standard of no tobacco use for their children, accompanied by "an explanation of the regrettable addictiveness of nicotine, which is controlling their own tobacco use. It is the *lack* of a parent's concern for his or her child that seems to increase the risk of tobacco use, whereas general parental support appears to decrease risk" (Lynch & Bonnie, 1994, p. 84).

Among younger adolescents in particular, peer pressure and conformity to group norms exert a strong influence on smoking behavior (Evans, 1984a, 1984b; Evans, Smith, & Raines, 1985; Furby & Beyth-Marom, 1992). Other factors that may play a role in encouraging smoking include nonparental adult models, such as teachers or sports figures, and advertising, which portrays smoking as sophisticated, sexy, and masculine (Lynch & Bonnie, 1994).

# 11.3 What Do Black Adolescents Know That Whites Don't?

One of the most interesting and encouraging trends in tobacco use has been the continued decline in smoking among black adolescents (Johnston, O'Malley, & Bachman, 1995a). After dramatic declines in the 1970s, daily smoking rates among white and Hispanic adolescents leveled off in the mid-1980s. In contrast, smoking by black adolescents continued a steady decline, reaching a level of only 4.4 percent in 1994. Hispanics, who smoked less than blacks in the 1970s, now smoke more than blacks, though still significantly less than whites. Moreover, white adolescents were the only group whose daily smoking rate increased recently (Johnston, O'Malley, & Bachman, 1995a).

What accounts for black adolescents' rejection of smoking? According to epidemiologist Sherry Mills, the answer lies not in higher cigarette prices or in a shift to other drugs. (Black adolescents have also reduced their use of alcohol, marijuana, and other drugs) (Johnston, O'Malley, & Bachman, 1995a). Rather, it stems from a change in attitudes and social norms. In focus group discussions with black and white adolescents across the country, she found that a number of factors were at work,

including family and community pressures. Black parents are more insistent in telling their children not to smoke; there also is a widespread belief in black communities that cigarette makers are targeting blacks, which has led to anger and resentment and a determination not to become victims.

Moreover, black adolescents have changed their idea of a good time. In a recent interview, Mills stated, "Whereas black kids will go to a party to dance and mingle, white kids definitely will go—and this is their self-reporting—to drink beer and smoke cigarettes. Black kids just don't see that as fun" (Hiltes, 1995, p. B7).

According to Michael Eriksen of the Centers for Disease Control and Prevention in Atlanta, "Blacks seem to be turning off the message from cigarette companies that smoking is cool. For blacks, it no longer provides that function. You hear black teens saying "smoking's a white thing" (Hiltes, 1995, p. B7).

An important national challenge is to find ways of convincing white—and to a somewhat lesser extent, Hispanic—youth of what blacks already appear to know: "Smoking isn't cool; it just kills."

**Individual Characteristics.** Attempts to find personality characteristics that may predispose a young person to become a smoker have had only limited success. Compared with young people who do not smoke, those who become smokers are slightly more likely to be extroverted, tense, and anxious, and inclined to take risks and be rebellious. They are also somewhat more likely to believe that their fate is determined by external events and chance rather than by their own efforts, and to have lower academic expectations (Evans et al., 1978; Gerber & Newman, 1989; Lynch & Bonnie, 1994). Other variables include low self-esteem, poor social skills, social anxiety, and depression (Hamburg, Elliott, & Parron, 1982; Hirschman, Leventhal, & Glynn, 1984; Lynch & Bonnie, 1994).

**Sex Differences.** A variety of explanations have been offered for the rise in smoking among girls during the 1970s, a time when smoking was declining among boys. Perhaps girls felt that they were less likely to devel-

op diseases associated with smoking, such as lung cancer and heart disease, because the incidence of these diseases was significantly lower in women at the time (CDC, 1989, 1994; Molotsky, 1986; U.S. Bureau of the Census, 1995). More recently, however, there has been an alarming increase in smoking-related diseases among women as rates of smoking among women have increased (CDC, 1994). The incidence of lung cancer in women, for example, has shown more than a fivefold increase since the early 1960s, and among women with comparable smoking experiences, it is rapidly approaching the levels found in men. In the words of former Surgeon General Julius Richmond, "It is becoming clear that women who smoke like men die like men who smoke" (*Smoking and health,* 1979, p. 1).

Another possibility is that changing sex roles and greater similarity between the sexes is involved. Smoking was once considered more socially acceptable for men than for women, particularly in public; clearly, this is no

longer the case. As the manufacturer of one brand of cigarettes targeted toward younger women proclaimed, "You've come a long way, baby!" It would be ironic to find that the women's movement has "freed" adolescent girls to develop the same future disabilities as their male peers. At any rate, as we have seen, females are not only smoking almost as much as males, but appear to be smoking earlier and more heavily (Lynch & Bonnie, 1994; *Women and smoking,* 1980).

## Prevention

In view of the difficulties involved in giving up smoking, prevention appears to offer the brightest prospect for significantly decreasing tobacco use. Although many traditional approaches to prevention (such as lectures on the health risks linked to smoking) have proved relatively ineffective, some newer approaches seem promising (CDC, 1994; Lavin, Shapiro, & Weill, 1992; Lynch & Bonnie, 1994).

Because schools are so directly involved in the daily lives of children and adolescents, school-based prevention programs, reinforced by community support, offer the greatest promise in preventing smoking initiation. The most effective programs appear to to be those "that identify the social influences prompting youth to smoke and that teach skills to resist such influences," whether from peers, the media, or adults (Lynch & Bonnie, 1994, p. 154; also see McAlister et al., 1980; Rooney, 1992). Generally, these efforts have been directed toward adolescents, beginning in about the 7th grade; if a person succeeds in avoiding smoking during the adolescent years, his or her chances of smoking in adulthood are significantly reduced (Conger, 1991b; Evans, Raines, & Getz, 1992; Lynch & Bonnie, 1994; Matarazzo, 1984).

The effectiveness of such programs can be strengthened by supplementing them with community-wide programs involving parental participation, mass-media campaigns focused on smoking prevention or cessation, environmental regulations, and changes in the social climate of the community with respect to smoking (Lynch & Bonnie, 1994).

## Marijuana

After tobacco and alcohol, marijuana is the drug most often used by young people. The active chemical ingredients in marijuana—primarily tetrahydrocannabinols, or THC—are the principal cause of the so-called marijuana high.

An increasing concern of public health officials is that most marijuana is far more potent now than it was dur-

ing the 1960s and early 1970s; in some highly developed varieties, levels of THC are thirteen times more potent (Kerr, 1986). These officials are concerned that parents who were able to smoke a joint and then drive a car or go to class when they were students may not realize that at current dose levels, driving is far more dangerous and impairment of short-term memory is far more disruptive.

Marijuana use among adolescents declined significantly between 1978 (when it reached an all-time high) and 1992. For example, among high school seniors, marijuana use within the past 30 days (30-day use or prevalence) decreased from 37.1 percent in 1978 to 11.9 percent in 1992 (see Table 11.1). Since 1992, however, marijuana use has risen significantly: Among 12th graders, the 30-day prevalence rose 78 percent between 1992 and 1995 (from 11.9 to 21.2 percent). Among 8th and 10th graders, 30-day use began to increase in 1991, a year earlier than for 12th graders, rising among eighth-graders from 3.2 percent in 1991 to 9.1 percent in 1995. Among 10th graders, it more than doubled, from 8.1 percent to 17.2 percent in the same period (Johnston, 1995a). In addition, among seniors, active *daily* use of marijuana rose from 1.9 percent in 1992 to 4.6 percent in 1995 (Johnston, 1994, 1995a; Johnston et al., 1995a).

The recent increase in marijuana use has been accompanied by a decline in disapproval and perceived risk (see Figure 11.2), which suggests that further increases are likely.

As in the case of alcohol, marijuana use among high school students is more common among males and among those who do not plan to go on to four years of college. Geographically, use is still most common in the West and Northeast and least common in the South; it also is most common in large metropolitan areas and least common in rural areas (Johnston, O'Malley, & Bachman, 1995a; NHSDA, 1994). College students' overall marijuana use is about average, or similar to that of high school seniors and to that of their noncollege peers; daily use is actually lower (Johnston, O'Malley, & Bachman, 1995b; NHSDA, 1994).

Among both adults and young people, the largest percentage of marijuana users are experimenters or occasional users, and the smallest percentage are heavy users. However, as will become evident, it is this minority of chronic users who are most likely to have significant drug problems.

## Subjective Effects of Marijuana

Most social users and clinical observers agree that the subjective effects of marijuana are extremely dependent on

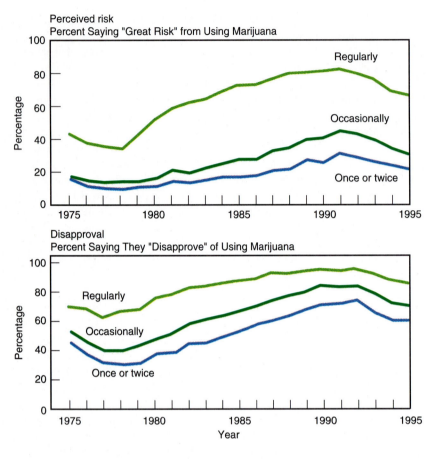

**Figure** `11.2`

Trends in perceived harmfulness and disapproval of marijuana use for twelfth graders. Adapted from L. D. Johnston, P. M. O'Malley, & J. G. Bachman (1996). Adapted from *National survey results on drug use from the monitoring the future study, 1975–1995. Vol. 1, Secondary school students.* Washington, DC: National Institute on Drug Abuse. Reprinted with permission.

both the strength of the dosage and the user's expectations and psychological and physical characteristics, both transient and enduring. An already depressed, seriously anxious, or paranoid person may become more so after using marijuana. One who is more emotionally stable and is looking forward to a pleasant, relaxing experience with good friends may indeed have such an experience.

At very mild dosage levels, the most common responses are alterations in mood, especially feeling happy, silly, and relaxed. At higher levels, colors seem brighter and hearing keener, the body feels lighter, and alterations in time perception are often reported. At still higher levels, these subjective effects are more pronounced and a majority of users report changes in body image, illusions, delusions, and hallucinations—toxic reactions that occur with excessive dosages of many chemicals that affect the nervous system (Committee, 1982; Grinspoon & Bakalar, 1992).

## Adverse Effects of Marijuana: Fact or Fiction?

Despite assertions to the contrary, marijuana is not a narcotic and is not physiologically addictive; nor is marijuana

use likely for most users to lead to the use of hard drugs such as heroin (Committee, 1982; Grinspoon & Bakalar, 1992; Hollister, 1986; Kandel, 1991; Kandel & Faust, 1975). At low dosage levels and on simple or familiar tasks, cognitive and psychomotor impairment is usually minimal, but clearly impaired performance is observable on complex or unfamiliar tasks at higher dosage levels (Grinspoon & Bakalar, 1992; Jaffe, 1990; Schuckit, 1995).

Even at relatively low dosage levels, however, such perceptual and psychomotor functions as signal or cue detection (such as the ability to perceive a brief flash of light) and tracking (the ability to follow a moving stimulus) are significantly and consistently impaired; evidence of such impairment may last from 4 to 8 hours beyond the feeling of intoxication (Carroll, 1985). Such impairments present a very real danger for drivers, pilots, or users of machinery (Yesavage et al., 1985).

At larger doses, marijuana may produce changes in body image, subjective sensations, and a feeling of loss of bodily boundaries or fusion with surroundings (Carroll, 1985; Committee, 1982; Jaffe, 1990). Many users may view this as pleasurable, but in those with conscious or unconscious fear of loss of control or those whose contact with reality is tenuous, this experience may produce extensive psychological distress, including

anxiety reactions and panic attacks, and, in some instances, psychotic episodes, although these are usually short-lived (Frances & Miller, 1991). Flashbacks, which involve the spontaneous recurrence of feelings previously experienced in the intoxicated state, may occur and be a source of anxiety, requiring reassurance that they are usually time-limited (Frances & Miller, 1991; Schuckit, 1995).

Although marijuana is not physiologically addictive, psychological dependence on the drug can become a serious problem for a minority of young people—probably not more than 5 to 10 percent—who are heavy users. However, for them marijuana can present real dangers that are comparable in severity to those faced by chronic alcoholics. It can also result in serious pulmonary problems (Frances & Miller, 1991; Hollister, 1986; Schuckit, 1995). Moreover, if an adolescent is using marijuana chronically to escape from stress, his or her psychological growth is likely to be impaired because he or she is not learning how to deal with frustration and with daily problems (Newcomb & Bentler, 1988).

Because marijuana can reduce performance on cognitive tasks and impair longer-term memory, the minority of students who come to school stoned or become stoned during the school day are endangering their academic performance. Consistent users eventually appear to suffer academically. Whether prolonged heavy use of marijuana actually damages the brain's long-term capacity to function is not known; chronic marijuana smokers may show electroencephalographic (brain wave) changes that persist for several months, but their significance is not clear (Committee, 1982; Grinspoon & Bakalar, 1992; Schuckit, 1995). Whether chronic heavy use can produce genetic or prenatal damage to unborn children is still a matter of scientific debate; what does appear likely is that smoking by pregnant mothers can produce problems with the baby's oxygen intake, leading to decreased growth and possibly to altered behavior and learning in the neonate (Robins & Mus, 1993; Schuckit, 1995).

There is considerable controversy about whether chronic heavy marijuana use produces "burnout" (Grinspoon & Bakalar, 1992; Schuckit, 1995). Some professionals who work with young people, as well as parents, have reported that such prolonged use may cause the user to become mentally blunted, dulled, and mildly confused, with a diminished attention span, as well as passive and lacking in goal-directed activity (what has been called the amotivational syndrome) (Baumrind, Moselle, & Martin, 1985; Jaffe, 1990; Newcomb & Bentler, 1988). Although there is little doubt that such effects are seen in a minority of "potheads," it is difficult to establish causality. Did chronic marijuana use lead to

the personality changes, or did the personality changes accelerate marijuana use? To complicate matters further, heavy marijuana use is almost always accompanied by multiple use of other drugs (Kandel, 1980, 1991; Single, Kandel, & Faust, 1974).

At present, the most reasonable conclusion appears to be that the final chapter on marijuana use has yet to be written (Committee, 1982; Grinspoon & Bakalar, 1992). It may be that many fears of physical or physiological damage will prove groundless. But long experience with drugs and chemicals of all sorts that were once considered harmless—ranging from aspirin to thalidomide, from DDT to food additives and estrogenic compounds such as stilbestrol—cannot help but dictate caution, particularly in the case of women who are or might be pregnant (Carroll, 1985; Hollister, 1986; Petersen, 1980).

## Personal Characteristics of Marijuana Users

A variety of investigations have attempted to determine whether marijuana users and nonusers differ in their personal characteristics. Although there are many differences among individuals in any category of marijuana users, a number of fairly consistent findings emerge if we differentiate among categories of users.

**Early Users, Late Users, and Nonusers.** One might expect that young people who begin using marijuana early in adolescence, when it is less common and less sanctioned, would differ significantly from late users as well as from nonusers. In a large-scale longitudinal study of over 12,000 students in grades 4 through 12 in the greater Boston area, this proved to be the case (Smith & Fogg, 1978). Both in peer ratings and on personality test responses, the greatest differences were found between nonusers and early users (before the 9th grade), with late users (10th grade or later) falling between the two extremes. Nonusers were described as most orderly, curious, hardworking, self-confident, determined, persistent, tenderhearted, achievement-oriented, and obedient, and as most likely to feel valued and accepted and in control of their lives. In contrast, early users were most likely to be perceived as impulsive, dependent, not responsible or considerate, unable to be trusted consistently, immature in their interests, emotional, talkative, sociable, and pessimistic.

**Extent of Marijuana Use.** Even more salient is the extent of marijuana use. The occasional experimenter

and the chronic "pothead" are using marijuana in very different ways and may be expected to differ significantly in personality and behavior as well. Experimenters (those who have tried marijuana a few times and either given it up completely or engaged in subsequent use only very infrequently) appear to be basically similar to nonusers, especially in peer groups in which marijuana use is not a rarity. Experimenters may be slightly more open to experience, less conventional and concerned with rules, more interested in creative pursuits, less reserved, less authoritarian, more adventuresome, and more interested in novel experiences (Jessor, 1979; Kandel, 1980; Kovach & Glickman, 1986; Shedler & Block, 1990). In general, however, experimenters tend to be motivated primarily by curiosity or the desire to share a social experience and are as "disciplined, optimistic, self-confident, . . . responsible, goal-oriented as nonusers" (Robins, 1979, p. 44; also see Grinspoon & Bakalar, 1992).

As a group, moderate or intermittent users are less conventional, more adventuresome, more independent, less authoritarian, more impulsive, more sensation-seeking, less inclined to delay gratification, more concerned with self-expression, and generally more open to experience than either experimenters or nonusers (Jessor, 1979; Kandel, 1980; Shedler & Block, 1990). They are also more likely to be uncertain of their future identity, somewhat more anxious, more rebellious, and more critical of existing social institutions. Studies of high school and college students indicate that moderate users are more likely to hold anti-establishment views regarding politics, religion, and restraints on personal freedom. They are also likely to be less religious and more tolerant of deviant behavior generally (Cohen, Brook, & Kandel, 1991; Jessor, 1979; Jessor & Jessor, 1977; Kandel, 1980; Slappy, 1985).

The clearest differences from nonusers or experimenters, however, exist among heavy users (Grinspoon & Bakalar, 1992). It is among the latter group that fairly consistent indications of significant psychological and social disturbance are observed. Significantly, but perhaps not surprisingly, it is in this group that multiple drug use is more common and most extensive (see Figure 11.3). In a number of studies, heavy marijuana use has been found to be associated with poor social and work adjustment, increased hostility, greater difficulty in mastering new problems, and the desire for a psychotomimetic (psychosis-like) experience in marijuana use, rather than simple tension reduction or pleasurable stimulation (Grinspoon & Bakalar, 1992; Victor, Grossman, & Eiseman, 1973).

Heavy users score significantly higher (in the direction of pathology) than control subjects on psychological tests, and they tend to be anxious, restless, depressed, insecure, irresponsible, immature, or incapable of sustained intimate relationships with others (Carroll, 1985; Jaffe, 1990; *Marihuana and health,* 1980). They also tend to be undependable, unproductive, lacking in high aspirations, opportunistic, and self-indulgent, and to have difficulty in getting things done (Shedler & Block, 1990).

Very heavy users tend to lose interest in activities other than drug use, and they may exhibit extreme lethargy and inappropriate social behavior. They are likely to feel that they have nothing to look forward to, and turn to drugs for immediate, if temporary, gratification (Grinspoon & Bakalar, 1992; Shedler & Block, 1990). It should be noted, however, that in North American society heavy marijuana use is typically associated with multiple use of other drugs. Therefore, one cannot infer that psychological disturbance in this group is a direct result of heavy marijuana use. Moreover, studies of multiple drug users suggest that heavy drug use is primarily a result of psychological and social disturbances rather than their cause, although once such drug use has begun, a vicious cycle may become established.

# Other Drugs

Although young people still are more likely to use marijuana than other drugs (except for alcohol and tobacco), smaller percentages of youth have used other drugs as well. Those drugs include cocaine, pills (barbiturates, tranquilizers, and amphetamines), hallucinogens (morning glory seeds, mescaline, LSD, and PCP), and hard narcotics (heroin). In addition, some adolescents have used inhalants, sniffing glue and other volatile hydrocarbons ranging from gasoline and paint thinner to dry-cleaning fluid.

Despite significant declines since 1992, especially among younger adolescents, a substantial majority of young people in 1995 still disapproved of even experimenting with the more serious illicit drugs. A majority also disapproved of *regular* use of all nonprescription drugs, including marijuana, alcohol, and cigarettes; friends were perceived as having similar views (Johnston, 1995a; Johnston, O'Malley, & Bachman, 1996).

## Cocaine

Once confined largely to ghetto residents, cocaine use increased rapidly during the 1970s, especially among middle-class youth and affluent young adults who could

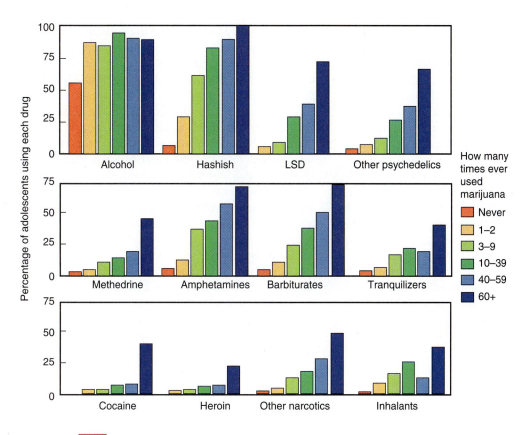

## Figure 11.3

The use of other drugs as related to marijuana use. Adapted from E. Single, D. Kandel, & R. Faust (1974). Patterns of multiple drug use in high school. *Journal of Health and Social Behavior*, **15**, 344–357. By permission.

afford its mounting costs (Johnston, O'Malley, & Bachman, 1990). Between 1975 and 1985 the proportion of high school seniors who reported having at least tried cocaine increased from 9 percent to 17 percent; the number who reported having used it during the past month increased from 1.9 percent to 6.7 percent (see Table 11.1).

Among young adults, the numbers were substantially larger; indeed, cocaine is unique among illicit drugs in that use is higher among young adults aged 18 to 34 than among older or younger age groups in the population as a whole (Johnston, O'Malley, & Bachman, 1995a, 1995b; NHSDA, 1994, 1995). By 1986, nearly one-third of young adults aged 19 to 28 who were high school graduates had at least tried cocaine (Johnston, O'Malley, & Bachman, 1995b).

Ironically, as cocaine use broadened to include ever-larger segments of society, what had become a drug of the privileged and affluent in the 1960s returned to the urban ghettos in the mid-1980s in a particularly lethal form: crack or rock.

Since 1986, use of cocaine among high school seniors, college students, and other young adults has dropped markedly, despite greater availability (Johnston, O'Malley, & Bachman, 1995a, 1995b; NHSDA, 1994, 1995; National Institute on Drug Abuse, 1989). Among high school seniors, the percentage who said they had at least tried cocaine dropped from a high of over 17 percent in 1985 to 6.0 percent in 1995 (Johnston, 1995a); the number reporting use in the past month declined from a high of 6.7 percent in 1985 to 1.8 percent in 1995 (see Table 11.1). Similarly, among young adults, lifetime use declined from 32 to 17 percent between 1986 and 1993; use in the past month declined from 8.2 to 1.4 percent during the same period.

As might have been predicted (see page 314), the decline in users was accompanied by a rise in the perceived danger of cocaine use (Johnston, O'Malley, & Bachman, 1995a, 1995b). Among seniors, the percentage who said there is great risk associated with even *experimenting* with cocaine rose from 34 percent to almost 60

percent between 1986 and 1991 (see Figure 11.4); the percentage who saw great risk associated with occasional use rose from 54 percent to almost 77 percent during the same period before leveling off.

However, perceived risk fell slightly between 1991 and 1995. Whether this trend will continue and lead to increased use remains to be determined (Johnston, 1995a). Similar trends were observed among young adults, although they tended to view occasional use as slightly less dangerous, and regular use as *more* dangerous, than the seniors (Johnston, O'Malley, & Bachman, 1995b). Disapproval of cocaine use also increased among both age groups, reaching a level of over 90 percent for regular use (Johnston, O'Malley, & Bachman, 1995a, 1995b).

Among high school seniors, reported use of crack cocaine within the past year—never high—declined from 4 percent in 1986 to 1.9 percent in 1994, though rising slightly to 2.1 in 1995; similar declines occurred among college students and other young adults (Johnston, O'Malley, & Bachman, 1995a, 1995b;

NHSDA, 1994, 1995). Despite these generally encouraging trends, in 1993 more than 1.3 million persons in the United States used cocaine, and over one-third of a million used crack, monthly or more often (NHSDA, 1994, 1995).

Cocaine is a powerful stimulant to the central nervous system, producing a general activation or excitement that is similar in many respects to the effects of amphetamines (Gold, 1992; Gold, Miller, & Jonas, 1992). Heart rate and blood pressure increase. In high doses, cocaine may cause heart rate to suddenly decrease or become irregular and may depress respiration, sometimes resulting in delirium, convulsions, and cardiovascular collapse.

Although further work is necessary, animal research at the National Institute of Mental Health suggests that extended use of cocaine may have a "kindling" effect that makes the brain more sensitive to the drug (Bales, 1986; Schuckit, 1995). It appears that the brain becomes more susceptible to lethal convulsions from repeated cocaine use than from a single large dose (which can also

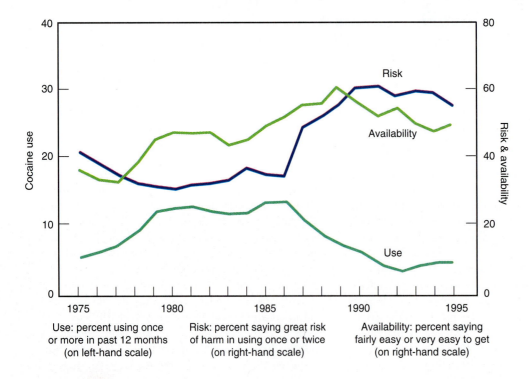

Use: percent using once or more in past 12 months (on left-hand scale)

Risk: percent saying great risk of harm in using once or twice (on right-hand scale)

Availability: percent saying fairly easy or very easy to get (on right-hand scale)

## Figure 11.4

Cocaine: Trends in perceived availability, perceived risk of trying, and prevalence of use in past year for twelfth graders. Adapted from L. D. Johnston, P. M. O'Malley, & J. G. Bachman (1996). *National survey results on drug use from the monitoring the future study, 1975–1995. Vol. 1, Secondary school students.* Washington, DC: National Institute on Drug Abuse. Reprinted with permission.

cause fatal seizures). Consequently, it is possible that what was previously a normal dose for a particular user could become a fatal dose.

The most striking immediate effect of a moderate dose of cocaine is a state of intense euphoria (sometimes decribed as analogous to an orgasm). Other changes include giddiness, boisterousness, and feelings of enhanced mental and physical abilities. After a few minutes, the euphoria becomes milder and mixed with anxiety or apprehension, a state that can last for an hour or more. This is followed by a more protracted period of anxiety, depression, and irritability that lasts for hours (Gold, Miller, & Jonas, 1992). It appears that cocaine triggers the simultaneous release of a number of chemical transmitters in the brain (chiefly dopamine, serotonin, and epinephrine), leading to euphoria in the experienced user. But cocaine also blocks the return of these neurotransmitters to the brain for reuse, leading to depression, irritability, and a craving for further stimulation (Crowley, 1987; Gold, Miller, & Jones, 1992; Jaffe, 1990).

Repeated high dosages of cocaine increasingly diminish the euphoria and lead to marked anxiety, loss of judgment and control of one's thoughts, paranoid delusions, and both visual and (more commonly) tactile hallucinations, such as bugs crawling on one's skin. Increasing hostility, impulsiveness, social withdrawal, and general deterioration of behavior may also result (Crowley, 1987; Gold, 1992; Grabowski, 1984; Washton & Gold, 1984). Prolonged use can inflame or destroy nasal tissue or cause perforation of the septum separating the nostrils, although this occurs less often than was previously thought.

**Crack or Rock.** **Crack** is an inexpensive, extremely potent, and highly addictive form of cocaine (Gold, 1992; Gold, Miller, & Jonas, 1992; Schuckit, 1995). Since it arrived on the drug scene in the mid–1980s, use of the drug has spread rapidly, becoming a major public health and crime problem, initially in the inner cities of large metropolitan areas such as New York and Los Angeles, but increasingly in other parts of the United States as well (Johnson & Muffler, 1992; Kolata, 1989; Lamar, 1986; Wilkerson, 1995).

Crack is made by mixing ordinary cocaine with baking soda and water; the resulting solution is then heated, dried, and broken into tiny chunks or rocks. Unlike regular cocaine, which has traditionally been sniffed or "snorted," crack is smoked: The resulting intoxication is far more rapid and the euphoria is much more intense. Correspondingly, however, the duration of the high is much shorter than it is from sniffing (8 to 10

seconds, compared to 1 to 2 minutes) and the subsequent anxiety, depression, irritability, and craving for another "hit" are also much greater (Gold, 1992).

The likelihood of addiction depends largely on the method of administration (Gold, 1992; Gold & Vereby, 1984). Some experts estimate that an addiction to regular cocaine typically develops after 3 to 4 years, whereas crack users are usually hooked after only 6 to 8 weeks, sometimes sooner.

Crack dealing by gangs, and the violence that often erupts from turf wars, together with crimes committed by youthful victims to support their addiction, have played a major role in the recent rise in youth crime, particularly violent crime (see Chapter 12).

The rising number of crack-addicted mothers poses a great threat to their children, both because of neurobiological damage during prenatal development and because of the inability or lack of desire of many of these mothers to care for their children (Brody, 1988; Gold, 1992). Women who use cocaine during pregnancy have high rates of spontaneous abortion and infant mortality (Chasnoff et al., 1985; Gold, 1992). Of those who survive, many suffer from nervous system irritability (the "jittery baby" syndrome), low birthweight, birth defects, and neurobiological and behavioral impairments (Chasnoff et al., 1985; Finnegan & Kandall, 1992; Gold, 1992). They are also five to ten times more likely than the babies of mothers not using drugs to fall victim to infant death syndrome (SIDS) (Chasnoff, 1987; Gold, 1992; Johnson & Muffler, 1992; Ward, Schuetz, & Seymore, 1986).

## Pills

The problems posed by pills—barbiturates, tranquilizers, and amphetamines—vary, although all of these substances are overused both by adolescents and by adults. In this section we discuss the effects of each of these substances and the problems associated with them.

**Sedatives.** Barbiturates ("downers," "yellows," "phennies," "reds"), or sleeping pills, account for over 3000 accidental or intentional deaths a year in this country alone, but habituation and addiction are far more common problems. Barbiturate intoxication is characterized by intellectual impairment, self-neglect, slurred speech, tremor, defective judgment, drowsiness, mood swings, bizarre behavior, and **ataxia** (difficulty in coordinating muscular movements) (Frances & Miller, 1991; Wesson, Smith, & Seymore, 1992). Contrary to popular opinion, withdrawal symptoms are more serious for barbiturate

Women who use cocaine during pregnancy have high rates of spontaneous abortion and infant mortality. Of infants who survive, many suffer from nervous system irritability (the "jittery baby" syndrome), low birthweight, birth defects, and neurobiological and behavioral impairment.

addiction than for heroin; if withdrawal is abrupt, they may include nausea, high fever, delirium, hallucinations, convulsions, stupor, and sometimes fatal coma.

Because they are nonspecific general depressants, they do not provide a true high, and after a brief period of relaxation in which tension may seem to disappear, they provide only physical and mental lassitude. In 1995, only 4.7 percent of high school seniors reported using barbiturates in the previous 12 months, although this represented an almost two-thirds increase from 2.9 percent in 1992 (Johnston, 1995a; Johnston, O'Malley, & Bachman, 1996).

Methaqualone, usually known on the street as Quaalude (one of its commercial names) or ludes, is a nonbarbiturate sedative hypnotic (Schuckit, 1995; Wesson, Smith, & Seymore, 1992). As a "downer," methaqualone "appears to have an inordinate capacity to produce a dissociative 'high' and ultimately a compelling addiction. Users describe a loss of physical and mental self" (Pascarelli, 1973, p. 103). As one adolescent stated, "It's like being hit with four joints at once." The drug also has a reputation among some young people as an aphro-

disiac and has been referred to as "the love drug" (Winick, 1992).

Overdoses may result in coma, heart failure, convulsions, and death. Fortunately, use of this drug has declined sharply in recent years: In 1995, less than 1 percent of high school seniors reported having used methaqualone in the past year, compared to a peak of 7.6 percent in 1981 (Johnston, 1995a; Johnston, O'Malley, & Bachman, 1989, 1995a, 1996). Among college students and other young adults, the decline was even greater (1995b).

**Amphetamines (Stimulants).** The amphetamines ("bennies," "dex," "meth," "ice," "speed," "pep pills") belong to a class of drugs known as sympathomimetics, which produce effects resembling those resulting from stimulation of the sympathetic nervous system (King & Ellinwood, 1992). In various forms, such as Benzedrine, and the more potent Dexedrine (dextroamphetamine) and Methedrine (methamphetamine), they may be used to suppress appetite, restore energy, or elevate mood.

Withdrawal from amphetamines can produce depression, lassitude, drowsiness, increased appetite, and intense or frightening dreams. It can also be extremely dangerous. Overdoses may result in convulsions, coma, and cerebral hemorrhage; as the hippies of the late 1960s succinctly stated, "Speed kills." In contrast to the majority of central nervous system stimulants, amphetamines may produce a high degree of tolerance (i.e., rapid physiological adaptation) that affects various systems selectively. Although increased dosage levels may be necessary to maintain feelings of energy and well-being, the same dosage level may result in marked increases in nervousness and insomnia. An alternating vicious cycle between amphetamines and barbiturates ("runs and crashes") often characterizes heavy users. Continued heavy usage may produce impairment of judgment and intellectual function, aggressive or violent behavior, lack of coordination, and hallucinations, as well as extreme irritability and suspicious or paranoid feelings (Carroll, 1986; Crowley & Rhine, 1985; King & Ellinwood, 1992; Noble, 1978).

In 1995 only a little over 4 percent of college students, but over 9 percent of senior high school students, reported use of amphetamines in the past year. Less than 2 percent of college students and only 4 percent of high school seniors reported having used them in the past 30 days—up, however, from an all-time low of 1.7 percent in 1990 (Johnston, 1995a; Johnston, O'Malley, & Bachman, 1995a, 1995b). At present, there appears to be a resurgence in street sales of methamphetamine ("ice"), especially among chronic users of cocaine and other drugs. This trend is at least partly due to the relative ease and low cost of manufacturing this drug.

# LSD and Other Hallucinogens

The hallucinogens (i.e., drugs that can produce hallucinations or distortions of reality in one or more sensory systems) vary in strength from mild (marijuana and nutmeg) to moderate (psilocybin, mescaline, and peyote) to highly potent (LSD-25). LSD in its pure form is an odorless, tasteless white crystalline powder that is readily soluble in water and highly potent. It was originally derived from a fungus growing on wheat and rye.

Youthful experimentation with LSD and other hallucinogens increased rapidly in the late 1960s, appeared to reach a plateau in the early 1970s, and then declined steadily until 1991, when it began to rise again (Abelson et al., 1977; Johnston, 1995a; Johnston, O'Malley, & Bachman, 1995a, 1995b; NHSDA, 1994, 1995). Among high school seniors, LSD use within the past year, which had fallen from 7.2 percent in 1975 to 5.2 percent in 1991, rose again to 8.4 percent in 1995 (Johnston, O'Malley, & Bachman, 1995a).

Not surprisingly, this recent increase was accompanied by a significant decline from over 84 percent in 1991 to 78 percent in 1995 in the number of seniors viewing regular use of LSD as harmful. Whereas many former users in the seventies and eighties discontinued use of LSD because of fear of physical damage or psychological harm or because they had upsetting experiences with the drug, it may be that a new generation of young people is less aware of the drug's possible consequences (Johnston, 1995a; Johnston, O'Malley, & Bachman, 1995a).

For some people at some times, LSD may be predominately a positive experience, producing a sense of timelessness, vivid panoramic hallucinations, and heightening or blocking of sensory experiences. For other people, or at other times, however, an LSD trip may produce bizarre and frightening images, a sense of isolation and depersonalization, acute panic, and paranoia. LSD use also carries with it danger of subsequent unanticipated flashbacks, and in psychologically unstable people it sometimes precipitates acute psychosis (Ungerleider & Pechnick, 1992; Wikler, 1970).

Possible long-term physiological or psychological effects of LSD, including brain damage or genetic or prenatal damage to one's offspring, have not been established (Carroll, 1985; Ungerleider & Pechnick, 1992)

Other naturally occurring drugs, such as mescaline (from the mescal bud of the peyote cactus), psilocybin (from the Mexican mushroom of the same name), and morning glory seeds, also act as hallucinogens, as do a seemingly endless number of synthetic hallucinogens (such as DMT, MDA, STP, and DOB) that have appeared over the years (Carroll, 1985; Ungerleider &

Pechnick, 1992). Some are similar to mescaline or peyote in their effects at the dosage levels in which they are usually consumed; others are far more dangerous and more similar to LSD.

**PCP (Phencyclidine).** Also known as angel dust, crystal, or DOA (dead on arrival), PCP is a street drug that was originally developed as an experimental anesthetic. However, its use was stopped when some patients developed psychoses after receiving it (Zukin & Zukin, 1992). One of its principal dangers is the variability of its effects, which may range from a pleasant, dreamlike state to extreme confusion, paranoia, psychotic states, and violent, assaultive behavior. PCP may also lead to loss of orientation in space, muscle rigidity, lack of coordination, and inability to sense imminent danger (Carroll, 1985; Crowley & Rhine, 1985; Zukin & Zukin, 1992). Significant numbers of homicides, suicides, and accidental deaths have been related to PCP use. In large doses PCP has also been known to produce coma and death when combined with other drugs. There are some indications that long-term use may produce memory loss and an inability to concentrate, and withdrawal may lead to depression.

PCP use declined in the past two decades (National Institute on Drug Abuse, 1989; NHSDA, 1994, 1995). Among high school seniors in the United States, annual use of PCP dropped from 7 percent in 1979 to 1.8 percent in 1995).

# Inhalants

Inhalants fall into three broad categories (Carroll, 1985). Sniffing of commercial solvents, such as glue and other volatile hydrocarbons (gasoline, cleaning fluid, and paint thinner), is largely confined to younger adolescents and children, some as young as 8 or 9. Although such substances may sometimes produce a sense of euphoria and dizziness, they may also cause severe headache and vomiting. In addition, many of them can cause permanent damage to the kidneys, brain, and liver; acute poisoning can cause death (Sharp & Rosenberg, 1992).

Aerosols are particles suspended in gas, as in hair sprays. They include amyl nitrite capsules, which are used in treating some heart patients and produce a flushing sensation and light-headedness through dilation of the arteries, and butyl nitrite, a room deodorizer that produces a short high (Carroll, 1985). Anesthetics, such as chloroform, ether, and nitrous oxide (laughing gas), may produce the euphoria of intoxication but pose the dangers of confused behavior or a potentially lethal overdose.

Use of inhalants has been rising intermittently since the early 1980s, with a nearly 25 percent increase occur-

ring between 1991 and 1995. What is particularly disturbing is that use is highest among younger students, with annual use among 8th graders increasing from 9 percent in 1991 to 12.8 percent in 1995 (Johnston, 1995a; Johnston, O'Malley, & Bachman, 1996). In fact, until the large rise in marijuana use in 1994, "inhalants constituted the most widely used class of drugs among eighth graders" (Johnston, 1994, p. 3).

## Heroin

Until the 1960s the use of heroin and other hard narcotics was confined largely to the most depressed sectors of our society. In fact, heroin has been described as the drug of despair—a drug that is used not to "turn on" to one's surroundings or to expand one's consciousness, but rather to shut out physical pain, mental anguish, and a sense of emptiness. The drug produces a brief euphoria and release of tension that is characterized externally by apathy, listlessness, and inertia.

Heroin traditionally had little appeal for adolescents or adults outside the ghetto. But beginning in the second half of the 1960s, experimentation with heroin spread to middle-class suburban schools, and by 1972 approximately 6 percent of all young people between the ages of 12 and 17 acknowledged having at least tried heroin (Josephson & Carroll, 1974; Single, Kandel, & Faust, 1974). Fortunately, this figure has gone down over the years; in 1993, less than 0.5 percent of all 12- to 17-year olds had ever used heroin (NHSDA, 1994, 1995). Among high school seniors, the number who had ever used heroin dropped from 2.2 percent in 1975 to 0.9 percent, before rising to 1.6 percent in 1995 (of whom two-thirds had used it in the past year) (Johnston, 1994, 1995a; Johnston, O'Malley, & Bachman, 1995a, 1996).

When dissolved in water and injected into a vein (a method called **mainlining**), heroin may produce an acute episode of nausea and vomiting ("a good sick") and heightened feelings of physical warmth, peacefulness, and increased self-esteem and confidence; some users have described the initial feelings as similar to a prolonged orgasm (Committee, 1982; Crowley & Rhine, 1985; Jaffe, 1992).

The potential danger of addiction to heroin is very real, despite the fact that, contrary to public opinion, not all users become addicts (Jaffe, 1992; Robins, 1979). Tolerance for the drug develops quickly, and ever-larger doses may be needed to maintain its effects and avoid withdrawal symptoms. Heroin acts as a strong depressant, and large doses may slow respiration to as little as two or three breaths a minute, thereby starving the brain of oxygen and leading to deep sleep, coma, shock, and even death. Other complications may include pneumonia or

edema (i.e., waterlogging) of the lungs (Carroll, 1985; Jaffe, 1990, 1992).

Use of dirty needles, which is common among intravenous users of heroin and other drugs, is one of the causes of the spread of AIDS (acquired immunodeficiency syndrome), a fatal viral disease that destroys the ability of the immune system to ward off disease, as well as directly attacking the brain and possibly other organs. The overwhelming majority of cases of AIDS are transmitted through sexual relations and through the use of dirty needles (Turner, Miller, & Moses, 1989). Currently, as a result of improved screening, only a relatively small number of cases result from blood transfusions or through transmission from mother to infant, at least in the United States, although the number of such transmissions is rising.

**Psychological Characteristics.** Heroin-dependent people have been variously described as immature, resentful of authority, passive-aggressive, emotionally

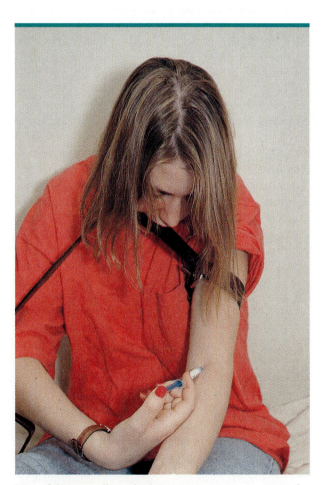

Use of dirty needles, which is common among users of heroin and other drugs, is a major cause of the spread of AIDS.

labile, sexually inadequate, anxious, and socially isolated. They are also likely to have a low tolerance for frustration and a need for immediate gratification, as well as low self-esteem and a tendency to manipulate others (characteristics that are often associated with antisocial personality disorder) (Crowley & Rhine, 1985). It is sobering to find that the median age of initial heroin experience in some urban ghettos is about 14 for males and 15 or 16 for females (Bernstein & Shkuda, 1974; Schuckit, 1995). Moreover, young people are usually introduced to the drug by peers rather than by adult pushers.

## Patterns of Multiple Drug Use

Thus far we have discussed the use of each of a variety of drugs separately. However, there is increasing evidence of multiple drug use among adolescents (Donovan & Jessor, 1983; Esbenson & Elliott, 1994; Kandel, 1980; Kandel, Kessler, & Margulies, 1978; Keyes & Block, 1984; Welte & Barnes, 1985; Yamaguchi & Kandel, 1984a, 1984b). In general, users of one drug are more likely to use another drug that is similar with respect to its legal status and pharmacological properties than they are to use a dissimilar drug. In one extensive study (see Figure 11.3), the correlation between marijuana use and use of hashish was .78 and that between heroin use and cocaine use was .48. In contrast, the correlation between use of beer or wine and use of heroin was only .05. Heavy use of any drug markedly increases the likelihood of use of any other drug, legal or illegal (Kandel & Faust, 1975; Single, Kandel, & Faust, 1974; Yamaguchi & Kandel, 1984a, 1984b).

Young people who have used marijuana only once or twice are unlikely to use any other drugs, with the exception of alcohol. However, as marijuana use increases, the likelihood of using other drugs increases rapidly (Johnson & Muffler, 1992; Kandel, Murphy, & Karus, 1985). In the 1970s among heavy marijuana users (sixty or more times) 84 percent also reported use of pills (methedrine, amphetamines, barbiturates, or tranquilizers), 78 percent used LSD or other psychedelics, and 62 percent used cocaine, heroin, or narcotics other than heroin (Single, Kandel, & Faust, 1974). Other investigators have obtained similar results (Johnston, 1973; Josephson, 1974; Yamaguchi & Kandel, 1984a, 1984b).

Young people who become involved in the use of a variety of drugs appear to follow a chronological progression. Most users of heroin or other hard drugs have previously used marijuana. This fact was interpreted for many years by federal authorities and others as indicating

that marijuana use leads to use of heroin. Two points need to be made in this regard, however: Few adolescent marijuana users (9 percent or less) have ever tried heroin, and prior use of marijuana among heroin users does not establish a causal relationship. It seems more likely that a person who is predisposed to heroin use, for whatever reasons, will also be predisposed to trying other drugs.

Nevertheless, it is interesting to note that when multiple use occurs there is a statistically significant pattern (Donovan & Jessor, 1983; Kandel & Faust, 1975; Yamaguchi & Kandel, 1984a, 1984b). Beer and wine are most likely to be tried first, tobacco and hard liquor second, and marijuana third, followed in chronological order by pills, psychedelics, tranquilizers, methamphetamine, cocaine, and heroin. If one were to accept the "first fatal step" theory that was formerly asserted by narcotics authorities, it would appear that cigarettes and alcohol would lead the way to, or at least share the limelight with, marijuana. However, for reasons more political and social than scientific, this was not the case historically, despite the fact that use of marijuana rarely takes place without prior use of liquor or tobacco.

## Why Do Adolescents Take Drugs?

The reasons that adolescents take drugs vary widely, as does the seriousness of their drug use. There is a world of difference between the curious young adolescent who tries marijuana at a party and the lonely, despairing young person who becomes hooked on heroin as "an escape to nowhere" (in the words of a 14-year-old ex-addict), or the crack-dependent young mother who abandons her newborn infant or stops caring for her other children—a problem whose frequency has escalated in recent years (Finnegan & Kandall, 1992).

One reason adolescents may try a drug is simply because it is there. As noted at the beginning of the chapter, our entire society has, to a large extent, become a drug culture. We take drugs to relax, to restore energy, to sleep, to relieve anxiety and depression, to relieve boredom, and for many other purposes. It is no surprise that many adolescents, like adults, conclude that they can find "better living through chemistry."

Moreover, all kinds of drugs are readily available to young people. Almost nine out of ten high school seniors in the United States recently reported that they could easily obtain marijuana, and half said they could easily obtain cocaine (Johnston, O'Malley, & Bachman, 1995a). Other drugs, ranging from amphetamines to tranquilizers and LSD, are readily available. In the inner cities of some metropolitan areas, drugs are virtually

endemic. Unlike the average young person of 50 years ago, for whom opportunities for illicit drug use were limited to alcohol and tobacco, today's adolescent may choose from a cornucopia of drugs, both those sold in pharmacies and those available only on the street.

Adolescents characteristically are curious about their expanding world and far more inclined than most adults to take risks. They do so partly to prove their boldness ("not being chicken") and sense of adventure, and partly because they do not believe that anything disastrous can really happen to them. Thus, many adolescents may experiment with drugs merely because of curiosity, a sense of adventure, and opportunity (Hawkins, Catalano, & Miller, 1992; Johnston & O'Malley, 1986).

## Parental Influences

Parents influence drug use through their own attitudes, values, and behavior and through the kinds of relationships they have with their children. Parents who believe strongly that drug use is harmful, socially unacceptable, or morally wrong, and who convey these attitudes to their children, are less likely to have children who engage in drug use (Andrews et al., 1993; Brook et al., 1990; Jessor, 1984b; Kandel, 1980). Parental use of tranquilizers, amphetamines, or barbiturates, as well as alcohol and tobacco, is positively correlated with use of marijuana and other illegal drugs by their children (Hawkins, Catalano, & Miller, 1992; Kandel, 1991; Kandel, Kessler, & Margulies, 1978).

Moreover, parental influences tend to be substance-specific; that is, parental use of a specific substance is most strikingly related to adolescent initiation of the same substance, whether it is alcohol, tobacco, marijuana, or some other substance (Andrews et al., 1993; Glynn, 1981; Kandel & Andrews, 1987; Lau, Quandrel, & Hartman, 1990).

Some young people try drugs as a way of rebelling against the constraints imposed by adults, particularly parents. At one time or another all adolescents need ways of asserting independence from their parents. Whether this takes the form of serious drug use appears to depend to a large extent on the kind of relationship the adolescent has with his or her parents (Baumrind, 1991a; Newcomb & Bentler, 1988; Stice & Barrera, 1995). For a child of democratic, authoritative, loving parents (especially those with relatively traditional values) who give their children age-appropriate opportunities to test their wings while still exerting age-appropriate controls, the risk of serious drug use is generally low (Barnes, 1984; Baumrind, 1991a, 1991b; Jessor, 1984a, 1984b; Kandel & Andrews, 1987; Kovach & Glickman, 1986).

For a child whose parents have not been loving and are neglectful, overly permissive, or authoritarian and

hostile, the risk of drug abuse is much greater. One angry adolescent said of his parents, "They're always telling me what to do, like I don't have any mind of my own. And like my father is sitting around having his third martini before supper, and telling me like he's some big expert, and I'm an idiot, about how marijuana will destroy my brain. Well, the hell with him!" (Conger, 1979, p. 82). Another adolescent seemed to be trying to get some response—any response—from her parents as a sign that they cared: "I've been on drugs since I was 12. My parents think I'm rebelling about something, but they don't know what. It's them. Not that they're strict. It's just that they're not really there and you feel you have to jump up and down and scream before they really notice."

## Peer Pressure

Peers play a major part in adolescent drug use (Brook et al., 1990; Elliott, Huizinga, & Ageton, 1985; Farrell & Danish, 1993; Hawkins, Catalano, & Miller, 1992). Indeed, one of the best predictors of whether an adolescent will use a drug, and how heavily, is use of that drug by friends, especially the young person's best friend (Jessor, 1979; Kandel, 1980, 1991; Kovach & Glickman, 1986; Yamaguchi & Kandel, 1984a, 1984b).

For example, in a comprehensive study of drug use among public secondary school students in New York State, Denise Kandel and her associates (1973, 1974, 1980; Kandel et al., 1986) found that involvement with other drug-using adolescents is a more important correlate of adolescent marijuana use than parental use of psychoactive drugs, including alcohol. For example, among participants whose best school friends had never used marijuana, only 15 percent reported using the drug themselves; in contrast, among subjects whose best school friends reported using marijuana sixty times or more, reports of use increased to 79 percent. However, parental use of these drugs (especially alcohol) also played a role, though a more modest one. The highest rates of marijuana usage were found among adolescents whose parents *and* best school friends were drug users (see Table 11.3).

In Kandel's view, findings on the relative influence of parents and peers on adolescent drug use fit a "cultural deviance" model of behavior: The family can potentially lead the young person toward some form of socially disapproved behavior (drug use or delinquency) either because the family engages in the behavior itself and the young person imitates that behavior, or because the family creates a negative climate in the home and the young person seeks to escape from it. Although either or both of these factors may characterize the family, the young person usually will not engage in deviant behavior unless such

## Table 11.3 Adolescent Marijuana Use by Best School Friend Marijuana Use and Parental Psychoactive Drugs Use

| PARENTAL DRUG USE | PERCENTAGE OF ADOLESCENTS WHO HAVE USED MARIJUANA | |
| --- | --- | --- |
| | BEST FRIEND NEVER USED | BEST FRIEND USED |
| Parent never used: | 13 | 56 |
| Parent used: | 17 | 67 |

NOTE: Use patterns for each group are self-reported.

SOURCE: D. Kandel (1974). Inter- and intragenerational influences on adolescent marijuana use. *Journal of Social Issues, 30*, 107–135. Adapted by permission of the Society for the Psychological Study of Social Issues.

behavior is present in the immediate peer culture. "Peer behavior is the crucial determining factor in adolescent drug use; parental behavior becomes important when such behavior exists in the peer group" (Kandel, 1974, p. 126). In addition, adolescents already involved with drugs, for whatever reasons, are likely to *select* as friends peers who are similarly involved (Farrel & Danish, 1993).

Because peers play such an important role in adolescent life, any evidence of changes in adolescent attitudes toward drugs is significant. Unfortunately, as we have seen, adolescent attitudes toward drug use have become less negative in the last several years, after nearly two decades of a steady rise in the percentage of young people disapproving of drug use and perceiving a high degree of risk in regular use (Johnston, 1995a; Johnston, O'Malley, & Bachman, 1995a, 1996). These shifts in attitudes closely parallel changes in the actual rates of use of most drugs.

At the same time, we should not forget that there are young people for whom drug use is a private response to stress, feelings of social isolation, rejection, low self-esteem, anxiety, depression, or alienation and hence is not directly related to peer group values and behavior (Conger, 1979; Hawkins, Catalano, & Miller, 1992; Kovach & Glickman, 1986).

### Escape from the Pressures of Life

Another reason adolescents give for using drugs is to escape from tension and the pressures of life, or from boredom (Conger et al., 1991; Johnston & O'Malley, 1986; Simons et al., 1991). When high school seniors were asked their reasons for using drugs, infrequent users tended to stress social or recreational reasons reflecting positive affect, such as "to have a good time with my friends" or "to feel good or get high." Heavy users (particularly daily users), while also acknowledging social or recreational reasons, were far more likely to cite reasons that involved coping with negative affect and stress, such as "to get away from my problems," "to deal with anger and frustration," "to relax and relieve tension," or "to get through the day" (Johnston & O'Malley, 1986). As noted earlier, persistent use of drugs is likely to compromise the young person's ability to meet the demands of adulthood.

### Emotional Disturbance

For other young people, particularly heavy users of multiple drugs, reliance on drugs may reflect emotional disturbance and inability to cope with the demands of living or to find a meaningful personal identity. In some such cases we need to look to significant disturbances in family relationships during the course of development for clues to the young person's difficulties (Brehm & Khantzian, 1992; Glynn, 1981; Hawkins, Catalano, & Miller, 1992). Among adolescents in residential treatment centers and halfway houses for alcohol and drug users, common themes are feelings of parental rejection or indifference, lack of acceptance by peers, emotional isolation, and low self-esteem con-

## 11.4 What Can Parents Do?

In an era when the availability and use of drugs is widespread, even the most enlightened, sensible parents cannot guarantee that their children will not become involved in some experimentation with drugs. However, there are a number of steps parents can take to minimize the likelihood of adolescent drug use or to limit its seriousness. In particular, they can seek to keep open the lines of communication between themselves and their children, to be fair, and to encourage their children to participate in family decision-making, while still retaining ultimate responsibility and expecting adherence to reasonable standards of behavior (Baumrind, 1991a; Bell & Wildflower, 1983; Conger, 1991a). In brief, parents should strive to be authoritative (responsive yet demanding) in their relations with their adolescents (see Chapter 5).

Parents of drug-abusing adolescents are far more inclined than parents of nondrug-abusing adolescents to engage in scapegoating: blaming family problems and difficulties in decision-making on the adolescent (Gantman, 1978). Moreover, parents of drug-abusing adolescents are far less likely to consult with the young person about his or her views; instead, they simply tell the adolescent what to do. In addition, in the families of normal, nondrug-abusing adolescents all members were free to express themselves openly and there was greater clarity of communication and more equal participation by all family members.

Parents can also encourage their children long before the onset of adolescence to become more independent and to take increasing responsibility for their own actions. Obviously, such learning experiences should be geared to the age of the child and should be expanded only as the child becomes more mature. Parents who think that they can continue—sometimes indefinitely—to run the lives of their

cealed behind a defense of appearing "cool" (Conger & Petersen, 1984).

In some cases a genetic predisposition may contribute to an adolescent's vulnerability to the use of alcohol or other drugs. As we have seen, children and adolescents whose parents have a history of alcohol abuse are somewhat more likely than other children to become problem drinkers themselves, even if they were separated from their parents at an early age. Although convincing evidence of genetic influences is lacking in the case of other drugs, such as cocaine, genetic factors may play a part in the development of some personality characteristics that are more often found in adolescents and adults who become heavy drug users (Anthenelli & Schuckit, 1992; Schuckit, 1995). Such people tend to be impulsive, sensation seeking, restless, and emotionally labile (Kagan, Reznick, & Snidman, 1988a, 1988b; Plomin, 1986; Scarr & Kidd, 1983). In this way, genetic influences *might act indirectly* to increase a person's likelihood of trying drugs or continuing to use them. In addition, excessive alcohol or drug use can *sometimes* be symptomatic of an underlying emotional disturbance (such as severe depression) in which genetic influences may play a part (Klerman, 1988a, 1988b; Puig-Antich, 1986; Vandenberg, Singer, & Pauls, 1986).

Some young people who have been using alcohol or drugs steadily since preadolescence acknowledge that they have never known any other way to cope with anxiety, boredom, depression, fear of failure, or lack of purpose. An important aim of one treatment program, in addition to helping young people learn to deal with their problems and establish genuine friendships with peers, was simply to teach them something many did not know how to do: to have fun without using drugs!

## Societal Rejection

In some cases of adolescent drug abuse, an indifferent society must share much of the blame. Many disadvantaged adolescents face the future without hope. Confronted with economic, social, and racial discrimination, with impossible living conditions, often with untreated physical ills, and with disorganization in their

adolescent children and to protect them from any adverse consequences of their actions are not preparing them to cope with exposure to drugs or with life itself.

In addition, parents need to remember that they are role models and that children take their cues from what parents do as well as from what they say. If parents present models of stable, responsible, problem-solving behavior, their children are likely to behave in those ways (see pages 133–134). With respect to drug use, we have already seen that drug-using parents are more likely to have drug-using children, even though the actual drugs may differ. If parents use drugs rarely, and only for responsible, well-defined purposes, their adolescents are much more likely to do the same than if the parents are constantly running from one drug to another to help them sleep, stay awake, relax, or cope with anxiety or pressure.

It is important for young people to know that their parents have basic values and that they are making a real effort to live by them. Whether the young person disagrees with some of those values is far less important than the knowledge that the values exist. In the end, this knowledge provides young people with a sense of trust and security, encourages them to think through their own basic values, and promotes respect for parents and willingness to listen to their views.

Finally, parents must show adolescents that they really care about them, not just in the abstract but in concrete, demonstrated ways: by sharing family activities and by knowing about and taking an interest in their children's schoolwork, hobbies, friends, social life, goals, and dreams. None of these parental efforts can guarantee that a young person will not experiment with drugs, but they can do much to lessen its likelihood and to minimize its seriousness should it occur.

social environment and in their families, they may give up the search for meaning and identity and seek escape in drugs.

In sum, unless our society becomes willing to match the rhetoric of the "war on drugs" with a far greater commitment to action—not only in law enforcement efforts but in education, treatment, and, above all, prevention—hundreds of thousands of children will be permanently lost to society and to any hope of a productive, rewarding existence.

## Summary

Although there are significant generational differences in patterns of drug use, our society has been developing into a drug culture for many years. It is also important to recognize that the "drug problem" is actually twofold. The problem among economically favored, well-educated adolescents, youth, and young adults is not the same as the problem among impoverished, poorly educated young people growing up in economically depressed, socially disorganized, crime-ridden sections of large cities. The drug problems in these two groups differ significantly in terms of root causes, severity, and prospects for change.

Overall drug use by young people declined significantly between the late seventies and the early nineties; since then, however, it has been rising. At the same time, perceptions of the harmfulness of drugs and disapproval of their use have been declining, except for cocaine, suggesting that use may continue rising in the future.

The problem is far worse, however, for young people living in deteriorated crime-ridden neighborhoods in large metropolitan areas. For many of them, drug dealing may appear to be the easiest, most lucrative escape from poverty. For others, vulnerability to drug use is increased by easy accessibility, peer influence, and a pervasive sense of hopelessness and despair.

Despite the widespread public concern about other drugs, alcohol is by far the most widely used and abused drug (distantly followed by cigarettes and marijuana). Although overall alcohol use decreased significantly in the eighties and early nineties, it has since stabilized. In 1995, over 14 percent of 8th graders and 24 percent of 10th graders had engaged in heavy drinking within a 2-week period. Heavy drinking during pregnancy can result in fetal alcohol syndrome; even smaller doses increase the likelihood of low birthweight and developmental delays.

Cigarette smoking among adolescents reached a peak in 1977, after which it declined markedly until the mid-eighties. Since then, however, there has been little overall change; indeed, among 8th and 10th graders smoking rates have *increased* in the last several years. Because smoking is the largest preventable cause of death, there is an urgent need for further reduction in rates of smoking. Adolescents who smoke are aware of the dangers, but the addictive properties of nicotine make it difficult to quit. Prevention therefore appears to offer the greatest promise.

Marijuana use among adolescents declined between 1978, when it reached an all-time high, and 1992. Since then, however, use has risen rapidly. For example, the number of high school seniors using marijuana during the past month increased from 11.9 to 19 percent between 1992 and 1994; among 8th graders use more than doubled between between 1991 and 1994.

Other drugs, including cocaine, barbiturates, tranquilizers, amphetamines, hallucinogens, inhalants, and narcotics (such as heroin), were used far less often than alcohol, tobacco, and marijuana, and use of those drugs generally declined during the late 1970s and the 1980s. An exception was use of cocaine, which reached a peak among adolescents and young adults in the mid-1980s before declining sharply, primarily because of increased awareness of the dangers associated with it. During the 1990s, however, use of these other drugs began rising again, although the turnaround has been less dramatic than in the case of marijuana.

One of the most frightening aspects of drug abuse is the number of young women using cocaine, alcohol, amphetamines, and other drugs during pregnancy, often causing neurobiological impairment in their infants. The rapid spread of crack, a cheap, extremely potent, highly addictive form of cocaine, has created major problems for drug treatment centers and law enforcement officers, especially in large metropolitan areas, but increasingly throughout the country.

Adolescents take drugs for a wide range of reasons, and the seriousness of their drug use also varies widely. One reason that adolescents may try a drug is simply its easy availability. Adolescents are curious about their expanding world and more inclined than adults to take risks. Other important reasons include parental influences, peer pressure, desire to escape from the pressures of life, emotional disturbance, and societal rejection.

Unless our society becomes more willing to match the rhetoric of the "war on drugs" with a far greater commitment to effective action, hundreds of thousands of children will be permanently lost to society and to any hope of a productive, rewarding existence.

# Review Questions

1. What are the "two worlds of drugs" and how do they differ?

2. Did overall drug use among high school students increase, decrease, or remain steady during the 1980s and during the 1990s? Why?

3. Which three drugs are most commonly used by adolescents? Which illicit drug is used more commonly by young adults than by adolescents?

4. What have been the effects of the rise in the use of crack, especially among young people in inner cities? Why has crack use spread so rapidly? How does crack differ from regular cocaine?

5. How do adolescents who are heavy drinkers, moderate drinkers, or abstainers differ from one another in personality characteristics and behavior?

6. What causes fetal alcohol syndrome and what are its effects?

7. Do long-term trends in smoking behavior differ among white, black, and Hispanic adolescents and between males and females? If so, how and why?

8. How do the personality characteristics of early marijuana users, late users, and nonusers differ?

9. Name five reasons why adolescents take drugs. Discuss each briefly.

# Recommended Readings

Baumrind, D. (1991). The influence of parenting style on adolescent competence and substance abuse. *Journal of Early Adolescence, 11,* 56–95.

Hawkins, J. D., Catalano, R. F., & Miller, J. Y. (1992). Risk and protective factors for alcohol and other drug problems in adolescence and early adulthood: Implications for substance abuse prevention. *Psychological Bulletin,* **112,** 64–105.

Johnston, L. D., O'Malley, P. M., & Bachman, J. D. (1996). *National survey results on drug use from the monitoring the future study, 1975–1995. Volume 1, Secondary school students.* Washington, DC: U.S. Government Printing Office.

Kandel, D. B. (1985). On processes of peer influences in adolescent drug use: A developmental perspective. *Advances in Alcohol and Substance Abuse,* **4,** 139–163.

Lowinson, J. H., Ruiz, P., Millman, R. B., & Langrod, J. G. (Eds.). (1992). *Substance abuse: A comprehensive textbook* (2nd ed.). Baltimore: Williams & Wilkins.

Lynch, B. S., & Bonnie, R. J. (1994). *Growing up tobacco free: Preventing nicotine addiction in children and youths.* Washington, DC: National Academy Press.

Shedler, J., & Block, J. (1990). Adolescent drug use and psychological health: A longitudinal inquiry. *American Psychologist,* **45,** 612–629.

# Adolescents at Risk II:

# 12 Alienation and Delinquency

despite their skepticism about many of the policies, practices, and values of government and other social institutions, most young people do not appear to be deeply troubled about their own lives. Most feel pretty happy, are satisfied with their lives as a whole, have a positive attitude toward themselves, and feel that they will be successful in life (Bachman, Johnston, & O'Malley, in preparation). When asked whether they thought their lives would be better in five years, 86 percent of American high school seniors said that they would (Bachman, Johnston, & O'Malley, in preparation). Although many young people wish they had more good friends (not just acquaintances) and would like more opportunities for self-expression and self-fulfillment, the majority expect to be able to find a rewarding life for themselves within the existing social order (Astin et al., 1994; Bachman, Johnston, & O'Malley, in preparation; Dey, Astin, & Korn, 1991). For some, a pragmatic emphasis on achieving a rewarding lifestyle is not accompanied by a corresponding concern about the well-being of society in general, and the poor and otherwise disadvantaged in particular (Astin et al., 1994; Bachman, Johnston, & O'Malley, in preparation; Conger, 1988, 1991a).

There are significant minorities of young people who do not share optimistic feelings about their futures, who are deeply dissatisfied with either themselves or society, or both. These include young people who, for one reason or another, are alienated from society and its values, emotionally isolated, dependent on drugs, or delinquent. It also includes the growing number of young people who have attempted suicide, are runaways or "throwaways," or suffer from serious psychological disturbances (Conger, 1988, 1991b).

Alienated youth include over 10 percent of high school seniors who feel that their lives are not very useful, that life often seems meaningless, that they have few friends they can spend time with or turn to for help, and that there is little sense in planning for the future because plans hardly ever work out anyway (Bachman, Johnston, & O'Malley, in preparation). Similarly, over 21 percent

Significant minorities of young people are deeply dissatisfied either with themselves and their lives or with society and its values, or both.

shows and in active efforts to defeat incumbent politicians and reduce the role of government. More often, however, both young people and adults have responded with political apathy and diminished social concern (see pages 282–289).

Nevertheless, there are still young people—and adults—who feel sufficiently disturbed by current social policies to engage actively in efforts to change them. For some, the primary issue is women's rights; for others, it is opposition to destruction of the environment or violence on television and in the movies and assault weapons on the streets. For still others, it is the rights of the have-nots—children, minority adolescents, the homeless, the elderly, victims of AIDS, the handicapped, or the mentally ill (Conger, 1988, 1991b; Children's Defense Fund [CDF], 1995; Moynihan, 1986).

Although today's young activists differ in their views on the nature of society's ills and the appropriate responses to them, they are united in the belief that the American dream is being tarnished. And they are not happy about it.

## The Roots of Alienation

In the late 1960s, it became fashionable to refer to young people who did not fit in as being alienated (Conger, 1976). Through such labeling we gained the illusion that we were saying something significant about them. But as Kenneth Keniston noted at the time, all we were really doing was implying that something was wrong and suggesting the loss or absence of a previously desirable relationship (Keniston, 1960). Unless we can go on to specify what relationships the individual has lost—what he or she is alienated from—we have accomplished little. Moreover, it is important to know whether the **alienation** has been imposed on the individual largely by external forces, as in the case of the disenfranchised poor and some minority groups, or whether it is largely chosen by the individual, as in the case of some disaffected middle- and upper-class youth.

Viewed in this manner, it becomes clear that alienation among groups of young people may differ in important ways. Some aspects of alienation are relatively widespread in a particular culture; others tend to be limited to smaller subgroups. As a result of the decline in clearly defined religious faith in the past century, many adolescents and adults feel alienated from what previously appeared to be a meaningful and orderly universe with a personal God at its center. This feeling of "existential outcastness," of a lack of meaning in the

of college-bound high school seniors (and almost 37 percent of those who do not plan to attend a four-year college) agree or mostly agree that "Every time I try to get ahead, something or somebody stops me" (Bachman, Johnston, & O'Malley in preparation).

Despite popular perceptions to the contrary, distrust of government and other major social institutions among both youth and adults is greater now than it was during the turbulent sixties and early seventies. Among high school seniors, for example, confidence in the executive, legislative, and judicial branches of government, big business and labor, the media, and the schools has steadily declined in the past two decades (Bachman & Johnston, 1979; Bachman, Johnston, & O'Malley, in preparation; Conger, 1988; Harris, 1987). Adults, too, have become increasingly disenchanted with traditional sources of authority, as represented by the medical profession, religious leaders, large corporations, schools, and government (Hull, 1995). Sixty-three percent of those in their twenties (the so-called twenty-somethings) and 71 percent of those in their forties (the "baby-boom" generation) said they are "dissatisfied with the way things are going in the United States" (Roper Center, 1994). In recent polls, a majority of Americans expressed the belief that "what I think doesn't count" and that "the people running the country don't care about you and me."

In part, sentiments such as these appear to have fueled the kind of discontent and distrust of government and the establishment expressed recently on call-in radio talk

universe as a whole, can be painful indeed, and can result in feelings of deprivation and outrage. This is especially likely to be true of adolescents because of their sensitivity, their need for absolute values, and their relative lack of repressive defenses (Conger, 1976; Seeman, 1975).

Many adolescents also share what Keniston has called "developmental estrangement": a sense of alienation or loss that comes with the abandonment of ties to one's childhood self and, indeed, the whole world of childhood—an egocentric world that, as many of us can recall, seemed to have been created specifically for us—with us at its center. How difficult this sense of estrangement is to deal with depends in great measure both on the particular kinds of childhood experiences the person has had and on what he or she finds to take their place. The other side of the coin of childhood dependence is autonomy, and for the young person who can find new emotional ties and new challenges and rewards, the loss of the world of childhood is much less painful.

In a period of rapid social change such as our own, there is likely to be another keenly felt alienation: an acute sense of historical loss. "Most social innovations replace customs, outlooks, or technologies that are in that measure left behind; and those who are most firmly attached to what has been replaced inevitably mourn their loss" (Keniston, 1960, p. 461). The persistent American myth of the small town and the currently popular nostalgia revival bear at least superficial witness to contemporary feelings of historical loss.

Alienation may also take the form of a sense of estrangement from what is vaguely felt to be one's real self, as Karen Horney, Eric Fromm, and others noted many years ago (Fromm, 1955; Horney, 1950; Seeman, 1975). Whether as a result of unfortunate developmental experiences or because of the demands of society, some young people feel that they have somehow lost touch with the inner core of their being and that much of what they do is empty, flat, and devoid of meaning. Such feelings characterize some instances of adolescent depression (see Chapter 13).

Young people may show all of these and other forms of alienation to varying degrees. In the 1960s the most prominent form of alienation involved explicit rejection of traditional societal values and practices. Although they were often alienated in other ways as well, significant numbers of young people became disillusioned with the goals, values, and practices of American society. They reacted against what they perceived as the ultimate futility of an obsessive preoccupation with materialistic rewards and social status, as well as the shallowness and hypocrisy of many of society's values and practices.

## A "New" Alienation

The intensity and extent of this sort of alienation among privileged youth decreased dramatically in recent years, only to be replaced by a newer form of alienation, at least among a significant number of youth and young adults. This "new" alienation is more subtle and elusive than the highly public, intense, and strongly articulated alienation and dissent of the 1960s. It is characterized by feelings of loneliness; desire for (but difficulty achieving) intimacy; a sense of rootlessness, uncertainty and concern about what the future holds; and loss of a sense of community and common purpose in contemporary society (Bachman, Johnston, & O'Malley, in preparation; Conger, 1988; Hull, 1995; Yankelovich, 1981, 1995).

In part, this newer alienation can be traced to new economic and political realities. Although corporate profits and stock prices recently reached all-time highs, and the income of those at the top of the economic ladder followed suit, many of these gains came as a result of corporate downsizing, stagnant wages, excessive (and exhausting) overtime, and replacement of full-time workers by part-time or temporary workers (Church, 1994). Adjusted for inflation, middle-class incomes have actually lost ground in the last 20 years, while those of the lowest 20 percent of the population have been decimated. Currently, the bottom one-fifth of the U.S. population receives less than one percent of the nation's total income and benefits; in contrast, the top one-fifth receives over 50 percent (U.S. Bureau of the Census, 1995; U.S. Department of Labor, 1994).

In addition, there is widespread concern with increasingly senseless crime and violence, a sense of deteriorating moral values, deep divisions about what those values should be, lack of an overarching sense of national purpose and direction, and a loss of confidence in the power of political leaders and our social institutions to resolve these problems. This lack of confidence is only heightened by the apparent inability of the United States and other world leaders to prevent new forms of genocide, whether in Bosnia, Somalia, Rwanda, or currently, in other troubled areas of the world.

Some young people and adults, including a growing number of politicians, have responded to this multiplicity of issues with an increasingly narrow focus on their own welfare, often at the expense of the relatively powerless have-nots in our society, including children and the poor. As we noted earlier, efforts to realize oneself can be valuable and productive. But without a corresponding commitment to others and their well-being, self-realization is ultimately meaningless. Psychologically, as well as economically, there is no free lunch. Today's adults have

done far too little to help young people understand that "self-realization is not synonymous with self-indulgence, that concern for others is a necessary ingredient of concern for self, and that there can be no freedom without responsibility" (Conger, 1981, p. 1484).

As we have seen throughout this book, achieving a sense of identity is a crucial developmental task of adolescence. But as Erik Erikson has emphasized, maturity also requires the development of a capacity for intimacy—a true sharing of oneself with another that involves caring, trust, and sustained commitment, come rain or come shine. This is especially true in love, but it is also true in friendship; a fair-weather friend is just that. However, large numbers of Americans, young and old, recognize that although they have many acquaintances, they have few close friends, and they are likely to experience this as a significant void in their lives (Bachman, Johnston, & O'Malley, in preparation; Conger, 1991a; Yankelovich, 1981).

**A Sense of Community.** Can these trends be reversed? We are beginning to see widespread efforts to develop a greater sense of community as an antidote to the political, economic, psychological, and social isolation that afflicts contemporary life. In addition to traditional clubs and societies based on cultural interests, sports, hobbies, and ethnic or religious affiliations, there are now a multitude of mutual-support groups whose diversity almost defies description. They range from groups for children of alcoholics, families of mentally ill or physically disabled children, and single parents to AIDS victims, Vietnam-era nurses, survivors of natural disasters, and neighbors banding together to fight crime, drugs, and environmental blight. How successful such groups will be in combating the "new" alienation remains to be seen.

## Alienation Among Minorities and the Poor

As we noted earlier, there can be important differences in the sources of alienation and the ways in which it is expressed. Among minorities and the poor—and especially among people who are members of both of these categories—alienation is often imposed from without. Quite simply, these young people are prevented from sharing in the affluent society they see around them, both in the real world and on television. The vast majority of adolescents in these disadvantaged groups (i.e., blacks, Hispanics of Mexican-American or Puerto Rican origin, Appalachian whites, and Native Americans) are born into a culture of poverty, whether they grow up in urban ghettos, in rural slums, or on reservations. Even at birth the odds are against them: The infant mortality rate among Americans living below the poverty level is far higher than among those living above it (CDF, 1995; Panel on High-Risk Youth, 1993; U.S. Bureau of the Census, 1995). Among blacks alone, the infant mortality rate is nearly twice the rate for whites, and the disparity is widening (CDF, 1995).

As we noted in earlier chapters, in their developing years poor and minority youth, especially in the nation's inner cities, are often exposed to hunger and malnutrition, inadequate or nonexistent health care, run-down housing that often lacks adequate plumbing, and harassment both by police and other authorities and by petty criminals, drug dealers, youth gangs, slum landlords, and exploitative merchants. Their parents (often a mother with no husband present) are often so poorly educated, so worn down, or so powerless that they can do little to help their children cope with an increasingly complex society (although some do manage to survive—and to help their children to survive—what would seem to most middle- and upper-class adults to be insurmountable obstacles).

Poorly prepared intellectually, psychologically, and socially, disadvantaged children are likely to enter overcrowded, rundown schools. Under these conditions they may fail to make normal school progress and may drop out of school as soon as they can. Few jobs are available at their skill level, and they may find themselves discriminated against even in jobs for which they are qualified.

Currently, 14 percent of white youth (aged 16–19) in the job market and almost three times that number of black youth are unemployed, not counting those who have given up and are no longer actively seeking work (U.S. Department of Labor, 1995). As we saw earlier, for those living in the socially and economically impoverished ghettos in large cities, unemployment may exceed 70 percent. For such young people, the idea of the American dream can become a nightmare.

### Alienation, Identity, and Self-Esteem

Still worse, under such circumstances, young people not only may become alienated from the dominant American culture; in some cases they may also be cut off from the possibility of developing a clearly defined, self-confident personal and cultural identity. Although the ascendance of racial and ethnic pride in recent decades, particularly among young people, played an important part in stem-

ming the development of a negative sense of identity and increasing self-esteem, one wonders how long truly disenfranchised youth can persevere in the face of pervasive societal rejection.

This situation has recently been aggravated by massive federal cutbacks in social, vocational, health, educational, and other programs that are desperately needed by the poor and the near-poor, at a time when tax benefits for the wealthy have been increased substantially. Among the programs scheduled for reduction or elimination a number are of particular concern for young people. They include youth training and employment programs, nutritional programs for pregnant women and infants, food stamps, Medicaid, Head Start, child abuse and runaway centers and services, family planning services and counseling for adolescents, and educational and training programs for disabled children and youth, as well as basic health, mental health, and rehabilitative services (CDF, 1995).

## Adolescent Runaways

The issue of adolescent runaways is a significant problem. Each year in North America about 2 million young people run away from home. Of these, perhaps half return after a few days or weeks. Most of the rest become, for all intents and purposes, homeless (Janus et al., 1987; McCarthy & Hagan, 1992; Rotheram-Borus, Rosario, & Koopman, 1991). Although those who return home after a brief interval are more likely than nonrunaways to have adjustment problems and difficulties in family relationships, those who do not return are of greatest concern to youth workers. These adolescents are in jeopardy for a variety of reasons: They are more likely to come from dysfunctional homes; to have significant adjustment problems; to be victims of exploitation, neglect, or even death on the streets; and to be at risk for HIV infection (Adams, 1992; Garbarino, Schellenbach, & Sebes, 1986; Rotheram-Borus et al., 1991). Today's runaways typically are poor, lack support and acceptance, and are powerless and vulnerable to exploitation (McCarthy & Hagan, 1992).

Studies of the families of "serious" runaways typically reveal chronic patterns of family conflict and lack of communication. Often, however, there are even worse problems in these children's homes. They may include parental alcoholism, family violence, physical and sexual abuse (including incest), chronic neglect, and outright rejection (Adams, 1992; Janus et al., 1987; McCarthy, 1994; Rotheram-Borus, Rosario, & Koopman, 1991). In a study of homeless runaways in Toronto, for example, 73 percent reported having been beaten and 51 percent

reported sexual abuse (Janus et al., 1987). Clearly, many "runaways" could more aptly be described as "throwaways," even when parental mistreatment has not included actual ejection of the young person from the home (see Box 12.1).

In some cases running away from home may be a healthy response to an impossible situation (Schulman & Kende, 1988; Silbert & Pines, 1980). Too often, however, the young person already carries the psychological scars of prior mistreatment. These may include low self-esteem, mistrust, lack of social competence, suicidal impulses, emotional isolation, fear of sex, feelings of going crazy, and psychological problems such as depression (Brennan, Huizinga, & Elliott, 1978; Janus et al., 1987; Rotheram-Borus, 1993). Runaways who have been subjected to extremely stressful events, such as rape and assault, may show symptoms of post-traumatic stress dis-

Lacking money, food, or shelter, adolescent runaways who flock to major cities are often ready candidates for exploitation or violence. Their need for human services—health care, shelter, protection, and counseling—is often desperate.

# 12.1 Runaway or Throwaway?
## ONE RUNAWAY'S RESPONSE TO ABUSE

Marie is a 16-year-old black female, 5 feet, 5 inches tall and weighing 110 pounds; with black, curly hair and a pretty, if overly made-up face. At the beginning of the interview, Marie appeared shy and nervous. She rarely raised her eyes; she spoke in a quiet, somewhat mumbled voice, and she twisted two fingers of her left hand with her right hand.

Marie first ran away from home at age 15 and has run away twice. She last left home about a month before our interview and has been on her own for the last week.

The earliest that Marie remembers being physically abused is at age 6. She says that both her mother and her father beat her at that time. When asked to recall that specific first instance, Marie is unable to do so and says that she thinks she was beaten because she did not do her chores. She recalls that her brother was being hit with a stick and dragged down stairs, and she remembers knowing she was hurt. Marie explains that she has trouble remembering things, as there were so many incidents that she cannot separate them. She was beaten every day that she can remember until she ran away from home.

When questioned about whether she had ever been sexually abused, Marie initially said she had not. However, during the discussions of her relationship with her father, it becomes apparent that her father molested her frequently, often during the physical beatings. Marie remembers his "always pinching my buttocks and touching my breasts." She says that her grandmother once told her that her father had raped his sister and that Marie should try to stay away from him.

When Marie was 15 years old, she told her friends that she could not stand it any more and that she was leaving. Without saying anything to her parents, she left for a babysitting job, called a girlfriend, and after getting permission from her girlfriend's parents, took a bus to her friend's home. She says that being physically abused was the most important reason for running away.

Her girlfriend's parents called the Children's Aid Society, and Marie told them about the abuse. She said that they didn't believe her and that they brought her back home. Her parents were angry with her when she returned home because "I left and because they said I made up stories."

The parental physical abuse continued during her final year at home, and when she could stand it no longer, Marie ran again to the same girlfriend's home. Her father and mother, when contacted by her girlfriend's parents, were angry. Sometime in the next few weeks her mother told her father that Marie was sleeping with a boy at the girlfriend's home. The father became enraged, went to the friend's home, and beat Marie. He "grabbed me by the breasts and threw me into a chair and then a wall." Marie ran away from her friend's home and traveled from her province to Toronto. Marie had arrived at the shelter the day before the interview.

Marie reports suffering from headaches, dizzy spells, and sleep problems (nightmares) during childhood and at present. She has always felt lonely and has always been afraid of adult men and women. She admits to shyness, nervousness, self-mutilation, and suicidal feelings.

order similar to those found among combat veterans. These symptoms include denial of the traumatic event or obsessive preoccupation with it, unpredictable flashbacks, fears both of social involvement and of being alone, crying spells, suicidal thoughts, sleep problems, and self-deprecating feelings (Janus et al., 1987). In a sample of adolescent runaways in New York City, more than one-third had attempted suicide, with 44 percent of these having made an attempt in the month before the study (Rotheram-Borus, 1993).

Ironically, "the personal maladjustment, family conflict, and parental mistreatment that often precipitate running away also make the adolescent especially vulnerable to the risks that running away itself produces" (Garbarino, Schellenbach, & Sebes, 1986, p. 45). Lacking money, food, or shelter, adolescent runaways who flock

to major cities are ready candidates for exploitation (Mussen, Conger, Kagan, & Huston, 1990; Weisberg, 1985). Thousands of adolescent runaways have become involved in heterosexual and homosexual prostitution and in the production of pornographic films and magazines, especially in large metropolitan areas such as Los Angeles and New York (Rotheram-Borus, Rosario, & Koopman, 1991; Weisberg, 1985). The average age at which adolescent girls enter prostitution is 14, and the great majority are under 16 (Weisberg, 1985). In addition, many runaways are robbed, physically assaulted, underfed, or lured into drug use and small-time pushing. Their need for adequate human services—health care, shelter, protection, and counseling—is often desperate (Janus et al., 1987). Each year more than 5000 young people are buried in unmarked graves because nobody has identified or claimed them.

Temporary shelters make a valiant effort to protect and assist young runaways, but they are typically understaffed and underfunded, and they are forced to turn away many young people (Janus et al., 1987; Scott, 1980; Weisberg, 1985). It is estimated that no more than one in twelve of the runaway and homeless youth who have actually been identified and counted are currently receiving shelter, and no more than one in three are receiving services of any kind. When the large number of such youth who escape the attention of youth workers or police is taken into account, the figures become even more alarming (Janus et al., 1987). There is an urgent need for society to assume far greater responsibility for abused and exploited children and adolescents.

# Adolescent Delinquency

Despite the attention it has received in recent years, adolescent **delinquency** is not a new phenomenon. Three hundred years ago the great English educator John Locke deplored delinquency in much the same way that we do today. Six thousand years ago an Egyptian priest carved on a stone, "Our earth is degenerate. . . . Children no longer obey their parents" (Johnson, 1959, p. 840). Nevertheless, current rates of delinquency are reason for serious concern, especially in the United States, where murders of children and adolescents by other young people using guns have reached unprecedented levels in recent years (Elliott, 1994b; U.S. Bureau of the Census, 1995; U.S. Department of Justice, 1994).

Delinquency is basically a legal concept that is defined in different ways in different times and places. In our society the term **juvenile delinquent** is generally applied to persons under 18 years of age who exhibit behavior that is punishable by law. It is important to recognize that what we call delinquency includes not only serious offenses such as burglary, aggravated assault, robbery, murder, and rape, but also status offenses—acts such as curfew violation, truancy, running away, sexual activity, or "incorrigibility" that would not constitute violation of the law if they were committed by an adult (Binder, 1988; U.S. Bureau of the Census, 1995).

## Incidence of Delinquency

We know a good deal about the incidence of recorded delinquency through various governmental and other compilations; actual rates, though difficult to pinpoint, are significantly higher (Elliott, 1994b). After rising rapidly in the 1960s and 1970s, the delinquency rate reached a peak in 1980 and then declined slightly for two years, after which it resumed its upward climb, reaching a record level of over 51 per thousand by 1991, the last year for which figures are available (U.S. Bureau of the Census, 1989, 1994).

Although delinquency is most common in adolescence, reaching a peak between the ages of 15 and 17, closer examination reveals that in many cases delinquent behaviors actually began during middle childhood (Elliott, 1994b; Elliott et al., 1983; Farrington, 1987; Gold & Petronio, 1980; Rutter & Giller, 1984).

## Sex Differences in Delinquency

There are clear sex differences in the incidence of recorded delinquency. Boys exceed girls in juvenile arrests, particularly for serious offenses, although the male/female ratio has declined in the last half-century both in the United States and in England (Farrington, 1987; U.S. Bureau of the Census, 1995). In the past decade alone, the overall arrest rate for boys in the United States increased 19 percent, while the rate for girls increased 33 percent (U.S. Department of Justice, 1994). Boys exceed girls in arrests for homicide by 16 to 1, and for burglary and robbery by approximately 10 to 1. In contrast, ratios are lowest for nonviolent offenses such as theft and shoplifting (less than 3 to 1). Girls also tend to become involved in delinquency at later ages than boys; the male/female ratio is highest in early adolescence (Elliott et al., 1983; Farrington, 1987; McGarrel & Flanagan, 1985).

In attempting to explain these findings, some investigators have linked the higher prevalence of more serious offenses among males to biologically based differences in aggressiveness and physical strength (Maccoby & Jacklin, 1974; Wilson & Herrnstein, 1985). Not

all offenses are linked to aggression or physical strength, however. Another possible explanation for the relationship between delinquency and gender is that boys and girls are socialized differently (Farrington, 1987). Despite recent social changes, delinquent behavior, especially active or aggressive behavior, is still more strenuously discouraged among girls than among boys, not only by parents but by society and even by their peers (Farrington, 1987; Rutter & Giller, 1984). On the other hand, adolescent girls may be drawn into delinquency by family conditions. Much sexual delinquency among adolescent girls involves rebellion against parents, a search for substitute sources of affection, or in some cases both (Weiner, 1982).

As David Farrington, an expert on delinquency research, points out, gender differences in sex roles, social habits, and opportunities may all play a part in accounting for male/female ratios for various offenses (Farrington, 1987). For example, boys are more likely to hang around together on the street at night, a situation that is linked to burglary and violence (Elliott, Huizinga, & Ageton, 1985). Girls, on the other hand, are more likely to spend time shopping, which may help explain why shoplifting is the most common offense among adolescent girls. The rapid rise in white-collar crime among women in recent years has been linked to increased employment of women in jobs that present opportunities for theft, fraud, or embezzlement. It is still too early to predict what overall effect changing sex roles will ultimately have on the patterns and extent of crime and delinquency.

## Social Class, Ethnicity, and Delinquency

Reported delinquency rates are significantly higher among adolescents and youth from lower-income families, particularly those living in urban ghettos (Elliott et al., 1983; Gold, 1987; Huizinga & Elliott, 1987; Panel on High-Risk Youth, 1993; Rutter & Giller, 1984). Some limited surveys based on self-reports have shown considerably smaller social-class differences than do official delinquency statistics (Elliott et al., 1983; Gold, 1987; Rutter & Giller, 1984). However, both in the United States and in England self-report studies, as well as official delinquency records, reveal significant social-class differences when large, representative samples are used, when urban areas are included, when the focus includes the more serious offenses, and when truly lower-class, socioeconomically disadvantaged adolescents and youth are differentiated from their working-class and middle-

class peers (Burchard & Burchard, 1986; Elliott & Ageton, 1980; Elliott et al., 1983; Farrington, 1987; Rutter & Giller, 1984). One representative national survey of adolescents and youth age 11 and 12 found that lower-class youth were two or more times as likely as middle-class youth to become involved in serious and violent offenses (Elliott et al., 1983). Moreover, the higher the level of delinquency (number of offenses per person), the greater the social-class differences (Elliott & Ageton, 1980; Elliott et al., 1983).

Nevertheless, a sizable and growing number of both minor and more serious offenses are committed by middle-class delinquents (Braithwaite, 1981; Gold & Petronio, 1980; Quay, 1987b; Reiss & Roth, 1993; Wilkerson, 1994). Consequently, theories of delinquency, although they cannot ignore relationships between poverty or social deprivation and delinquency, cannot be based solely on these relationships. It should also be noted that the majority of low-income young people, even those living in urban ghettos, do not become seriously delinquent (Gold, 1987). As we shall see, in many cases strong parental guidance and supervision appear to play a major role in the young person's resistance to destructive social forces (Patterson, DeBarsyshe, & Ramsey, 1989; Rutter & Giller, 1984; Snyder & Patterson, 1987).

Delinquency rates (both recorded and self-reported) also vary with ethnic-group membership. The rates for blacks and Hispanics are higher than those for whites, particularly for more serious offenses, and the rates for Asian Americans are lower (CDF, 1995; Farrington, 1987; U.S. Bureau of the Census, 1994; U.S. Department of Justice, 1994; Visher & Roth, 1986). In attempting to account for these differences, it has been hypothesized that ethnicity per se is not an important causal factor, but that blacks and whites differ in known precursors of delinquency, such as low income, inadequate education, poor parental control and supervision (often in single-parent families), discrimination, and having to live in a socially disorganized environment (Farrington, 1986, 1987; Lehmann, 1991; Panel on High-Risk Youth, 1993).

For example, one English study found that black–white differences in reported delinquency did not hold independently of differences in social class or school attainment (Ouston, 1984). In contrast, the relatively low delinquency rate of Asians in the United States and England has been attributed to a close-knit family system with strong family controls on the activities of children and adolescents (Farrington, 1987; Gold, 1987; Mawby, McCulloch, & Batta, 1979). Further research on ethnic differences is needed, but it appears

likely that both family influences and social and economic conditions play an important role.

**Discrimination.** In cases in which official statistics show large social-class or ethnic differences in delinquency, one or more of the following factors may be present: differences in actual rates of delinquent behavior, discrimination against lower-status youth by juvenile authorities and society generally, greater surveillance by police or citizens in high-crime areas, and greater difficulty in finding nonlegal (e.g., parental) solutions to the problems posed by delinquent behavior (Braithwaite, 1981; Farrington, 1987; Federle & Chesney-Lind, 1992; Gold, 1987; Panel on High-Risk Youth, 1993). Not all social-class differences in the way delinquency is treated are a result of discrimination, especially in the case of more serious offenses. In some instances, the intent is to protect the young person himself or herself. For example, a lower-class youth may be remanded to the custody of the court because of adverse family conditions (such as alcoholic, irresponsible, or delinquent parents) whereas an upper-class youth who has committed a similar offense may be remanded to his or her parents' custody without formal charges.

# Serious Crimes and Violence

In the past decade, the incidence of more serious offenses among young people has been rising faster than that of delinquency in general (CDF, 1995; Elliott, 1994a, 1994b; U.S. Department of Justice, 1994). As Figure 12.1 shows, the prevalence of serious crimes is highest between the ages of 15 and 19. Moreover, because the numbers of adolescents in that age group began expanding in 1993, and will continue to do so well into the next century, the number of young people committing serious crimes will continue to rise even if the rate per capita remains the same, which does not appear likely under current circumstances (see Figure 12.2).

The largest—and most disturbing—increases in crime rates in recent years, however, have been in the number of the nation's children and adolescents murdered each year, and in the number of adolescent males arrested for murder (CDF, 1995; U.S. Bureau of the Census, 1995; U.S. Department of Justice, 1994). Firearm deaths among young black males more than

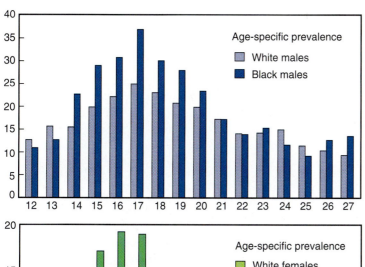

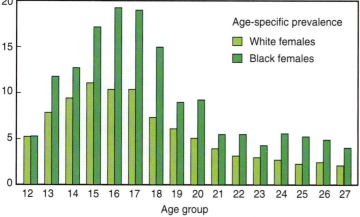

**Figure** 12.1

Prevalence of serious violence among males and females, ages 12–27. From D. S. Elliott (1994). Serious violent offenders: Onset, developmental course, and termination. *Criminology, 32,* 1–21. Based on National Youth Survey Data. By permission of the American Society of Criminology.

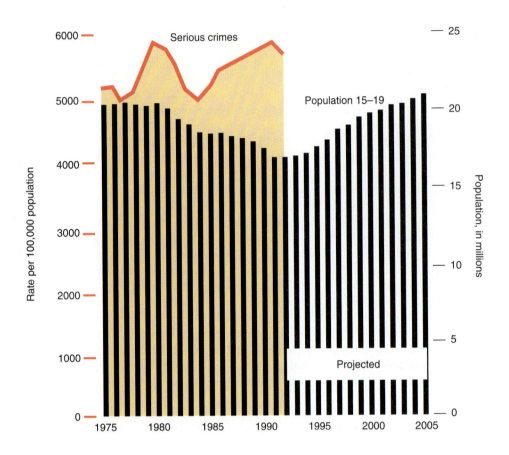

## Figure 12.2

Serious crimes★ per 100,000, and population projections in millions, for youth ages 15–19, 1975–2005. Adapted from U.S. Department of Justice, *Uniform crime reports,* annual; U.S. Bureau of the Census, *Statistical abstract of the United States, 1994.*
★Serious crimes include homicide, manslaughter, rape, robbery, aggravated assault, burglary, larceny, motor vehicle theft, and arson.

tripled between 1985 and 1993 (see Figure 12.3); homicide is now the leading cause of death among black youth (Panel on High-Risk Youth, 1993). The number of adolescents arrested for murder increased 168 percent between 1984 and 1993, according to FBI data (CDF, 1995); among 17-year-olds, annual homicide arrest rates recently exceeded 52 per 100,000 (U.S. Department of Justice, 1995). What particularly alarms government officials and scholars of adolescence, as well as members of the public, is that the "reasons" for so much of the violence appear senseless: arguments over a girlfriend, a "disrespectful" manner, wanting a pair of Nikes, or desiring an expensive team jacket (Herbert, 1994; Dugger, 1994; Elliott, 1994b). A Harris poll recently found that one in eight youths carry a weapon for protection (Applebome, 1996).

Both victimization and homicide rates, as well as rates of delinquency in general, are significantly lower among females than among males, although, as we shall see, differences have narrowed in the last half century, both in the United States and in England (Elliott, 1994; Farrington, 1987; U.S. Bureau of the Census, 1995). Why have adolescent homicide rates increased so much faster than the rates for other serious offenses? One critically important reason is that violent acts today are more likely to lead to serious injury or death: "And this dramatic increase in the lethality of adolescent violence is explained almost entirely by the increased use of hand guns in these violent exchanges" (Elliott, 1994b, p. 2).

But how can we account for the development of the underlying violence itself, and why do many of these young people have so little respect for human life? In

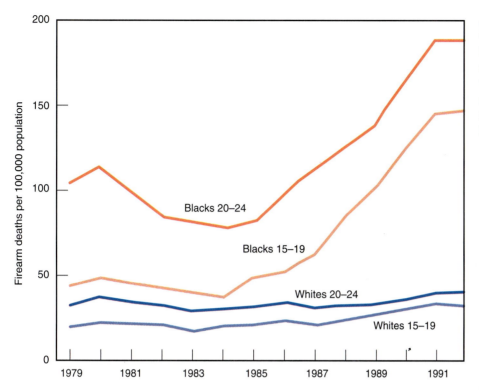

**Figure 12.3**

Firearm deaths among young males by age and race, 1979–1992. SOURCE: U.S. Department of Health and Human Services, National Center for Health Statistics.

addressing this question, Delbert Elliott (1994a, 1994b), a leading authority on youth delinquency and violence and director of the Center for the Study and Prevention of Violence, maintains that most violent behavior is learned behavior. He notes that most young people have learned other effective ways of achieving their goals; in addition, commitment to the conventional norms of social behavior that characterize their friends and family inhibits the use of violent behavior. Unfortunately, however,

> for too many youth, violence is either the only or the most effective way to achieve status, respect, and other basic social and personal needs. There is little prosocial modeling of alternative ways of dealing with conflict. Like money and knowledge, violence is a form of power, and for some youth, it is the only form of power available. When such limited alternatives are combined with a weak commitment to moral norms (internal controls) and little monitoring or supervision of behavior (external controls), violent behavior becomes rational. (Elliott, 1994b, p. 3).

If these perceptions are to change, not only for today's youth but for the rising numbers of young people following in their footsteps, there must be major changes in the principal sources of these perceptions and the violent behavior to which they lead. In Elliott's (1994b) view, these include the family context, the neighborhood context, the school and peer context, and the impact of alcohol, illicit drugs, and firearms. As will become apparent, each of these factors plays a major role not only in the development of youth violence, but in delinquency generally.

## The Family: Parent–Child Relationships and Delinquency

The influence of families on the development of delinquent behavior cannot be viewed in isolation. As we shall see, other social factors, including the kinds of communities young people grow up in, the kinds of schools they attend, the peers they associate with, and the kinds of social pressures they encounter, all play an important role—whether directly through their influence on adolescents themselves or indirectly because of their impact on the efforts of parents to engage in responsible and successful child-rearing.

Nevertheless, in most instances families remain the primary setting for child-rearing, and it is in the family that many of the child's earliest formative experiences

take place (Elliott, 1994b; Panel on High-Risk Youth, 1993). A representative national study of the family backgrounds of 10th-grade boys found that the single most predictive indicator of actual (not simply recorded) adolescent delinquency is the boy's relationship with his parents: "We . . . find a strong inverse association between family relations and delinquency: The better a boy reports getting along with his parents, the less delinquency" (Bachman, 1970, p. 171). This general finding has been replicated in a number of less extensive, but more intensive, studies of the home backgrounds and family influences of delinquents and nondelinquents (Kroupa, 1988; Patterson, DeBarsyshe, & Ramsey, 1989; Rutter & Giller, 1984; Sampson & Lamb, 1994). With remarkable consistency, these investigations indicate that the early disciplinary techniques to which delinquents have been subjected are likely to be lax, erratic, or overly strict. Moreover, they tend to involve physical punishment rather than reasoning with the child about misconduct and responding consistently and appropriately to both antisocial and prosocial behaviors (Loeber & Dishion, 1983; Olweus, 1980; Patterson, DeBarsyshe, & Ramsey, 1989; Sampson & Lamb, 1994).

Recent research indicates that the extent and adequacy of parental supervision may be a particularly critical factor (Galambos & Maggs, 1991; Steinberg, 1986). In a study conducted in England, the family variable that was most strongly associated with delinquency was weak parental supervision, as indicated by characteristics such as not requiring children to say where they were going and when they would return home, allowing children to roam the streets, and not knowing where a child was much of the time (Wilson, 1980).

Similarly, in their work with families of aggressive and delinquent children at the Oregon Social Learning Center, Gerald Patterson and his colleagues have found four aspects of family interaction to be associated with delinquency: lack of "house rules" (so that there is neither a predictable routine for meals or chores nor a clear set of expectations about what children may and may not do); lack of parental monitoring of their children's behavior (so that the parents do not know what a child is doing or how he or she is feeling, and tend not to respond to deviant behavior because they have not themselves seen it); lack of effective contingencies (so that parents are inconsistent in their responses to unacceptable behavior, tending to shout and nag but not to follow through and not to respond with an adequate distinction between praise for positive activities and punishment for negative or antisocial activities); and lack of ways of dealing with family crises or problems (so that conflicts lead to tension and dispute but are not resolved)

(Patterson, 1982; Patterson et al., 1989; Snyder & Patterson, 1987).

The parent–child relationships of delinquents are far more likely than those of nondelinquents to be characterized by lack of communication, understanding, or identification (Canter, 1982; Rutter & Giller, 1984; Wadsworth, 1979; West & Farrington, 1977). They are also far more likely to be characterized by mutual hostility, lack of cohesiveness, and parental rejection, indifference, dissension, or apathy (Olweus, 1980; Simons, Robertson, & Downs, 1989; Snyder & Patterson, 1987). Parents of delinquents are more likely to have minimal aspirations for their children, to avoid engaging in leisure activities as a family, to be hostile or indifferent toward school, and to have a variety of personal and emotional problems of their own (Canter, 1982; Hirschi, 1969; Rutter & Giller, 1984; West & Farrington, 1973). Parents who have a criminal record—especially one extending into the child-rearing years—are especially likely to have delinquent offspring (Osborn & West, 1979; Robins, West, & Herjanic, 1975; Snyder & Patterson, 1987).

Fathers of delinquents are more likely to be rated by independent observers as cruel, neglecting, and inclined to ridicule their children (particularly sons) and less likely to be rated as warm, affectionate, or passive. In turn, their delinquent children, especially sons, are likely to have few close ties to their fathers and to consider them wholly unacceptable as models. Mothers of delinquents are more likely to be rated as careless or inadequate in supervising their children and as hostile or indifferent; they are less likely to be rated as loving (Canter, 1982; Kroupa, 1988; Snyder & Patterson, 1987). Female delinquents, especially recidivists (i.e., repeat offenders), more often acknowledge hostility toward their mothers and report that their mothers spent less time with them (Duncan, 1971). In contrast, democratic, authoritative child-rearing practices can help to increase a young person's resistance to delinquent pressures. Such parents are able "to foster a child's skills, to model and encourage normative values, and to provide a caring environment" (Snyder & Patterson, 1987, p. 225).

## Violent Youth and Family Influences

In discussing the causes of violent behavior, Delbert Elliott emphasizes many of the findings cited above, such as weak family bonding, ineffective monitoring and supervision, and parental neglect. In accord with his contention that violent behavior is learned behavior, he

also cites exposure to and reinforcement for violence in the home (which may involve witnessing violence or being subjected to physical abuse or both) and the acquisition of expectations, attitudes, beliefs, and emotional responses that support or tolerate the use of violence (Elliott, 1994b) (see Box 12.2).

**Television.** In many homes, television is the de facto babysitter, with little or no monitoring or supervision of content (Elliott, 1994b; Reiss & Roth, 1993; *Violence and youth,* 1993). Although exposure to actual violence and physical abuse on the part of family members has stronger modeling effects, heavy exposure to violence on television is also causally linked to later violence. One longitudinal study of boys found a clear relationship between exposure to television violence at age eight and antisocial acts, including violent criminal acts and spouse abuse, 22 years later (*Violence and youth,* 1993). "When there is strong family bonding, effective teaching of moral values and norms, and effective monitoring of behavior, the effect of exposure to violence on TV is probably negligible; without this protection, its effect can be quite strong" (Elliott, 1994b, p. 3). What is learned is not only how to do violence, but increased fear of becoming a victim of violence, a desensitization to violence, and rationalizations for disengaging one's moral obligations to others (Elliott, 1994b; *Violence and youth,* 1993).

Even if violence is not modeled in the home, "the absence of effective social bonds and controls, together with a failure of parents to teach (and children to internalize) conventional norms and values, puts children at risk of later violence" (Elliott, 1994b, p. 3). Indeed, Elliott argues that parental neglect may have an even stronger effect than physical abuse on later violence, because it appears to be more damaging to the subsequent course of youth development and involves three times as many youth (Elliott, 1994b).

It appears that one reason for the apparent emotional indifference of many young people to killing is that they have never, even as infants and young children, experienced the warm, caring relations with others, including parents, that foster empathy and mutual trust. Finally, in several studies of delinquency a broken home has been found to be significantly associated with a higher incidence of delinquent behavior (Dryfoos, 1990; Rutter & Giller, 1984; Snyder & Patterson, 1987). However, it has also been shown that the likelihood of adolescent delinquency is far higher in nonbroken homes characterized by mutual hostility, indifference or apathy, and a lack of cohesiveness than in broken homes (usually with only the mother present) characterized by cohesiveness and mutual affection and support (Adams, Milner, & Schrepf, 1984; Panel on High-Risk Youth, 1993; Rutter & Giller, 1984). It may be that conflict and discord are more critical variables than parental absence or divorce, although clearly the latter events are likely to be stressful in their own right (Hetherington & Camara, 1984; Snyder & Patterson, 1987; Wallerstein, 1985).

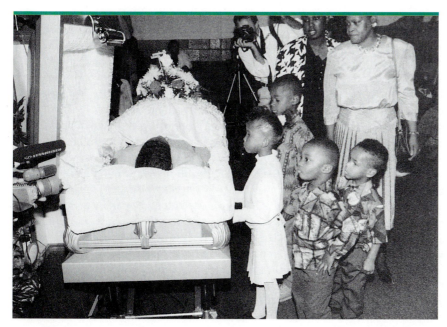

Children viewing the body of Robert S., an 11-year-old Chicago boy. Bounced from one group home or detention center to another, Robert killed a 14-year-old at the urging of older members of his street gang and was, in turn, killed by them—probably out of fear of exposure. "I brought my grandson here to see what can happen in gangs," said one woman. "That's a *boy* in there and I'm scared for mine."

## 12.2 Two Boys and a Gun
### THE FACE OF VIOLENCE

Ten-year-old Jacob Gonzales and his accomplice, 14-year-old Damien Dorris, were waiting near a Detroit automated teller machine for someone to rob. Mrs. Alvarez, pregnant and the mother of three, was hurrying to get cash for a birthday party. When she refused to hand over her $80, Damien fatally shot her in the head with a .22-caliber pistol. Jacob looked at the woman, then he backed away. The boys thought the bullet might explode. They ran off to divide the proceeds. Jacob's take was $20. He bought a chili dog and some Batman toys. Both boys were arrested the next morning.

Violence among the young is growing at a time when a generation of children born to teenage mothers is coming of age in neighborhoods already weakened by the addictive power of crack and the destructive force of the drug dealers. In many ways, this is the story of Jacob and Damien,

each born to a woman on welfare who first gave birth at the age of 14.

Just about all that Jacob Gonzales has known in his short life is violence. His home on the southwest side of Detroit was a crack house. His father used to beat his mother. Jacob saw his sister shot in the face when he was 4 or 5. His father was shot to death in a bar fight about the same time. He can rattle off the names and calibers of guns as if they were baseball players and batting averages.

He has seen family friends pull guns on one another and knows the subtleties of detecting a pistol. "You can tell when somebody's carrying a gun," Jacob said. "They hold their side and limp a little."

He was 9 when he took his first drag of marijuana. An older sister gave it to him. His mother, Bonnie, who was raped in the seventh grade, is a welfare recipient with eight children; Jacob is her

## Neighborhoods: Breeding Grounds for Crime?

Adolescents and their families do not exist in a vacuum. They live in neighborhoods, and it is in neighborhoods that most of their social interactions take place (Dryfoos, 1990; Elliott, 1994b). Some neighborhoods, particularly in the inner cities of large metropolitan areas, appear to breed crime: They provide ample opportunities for learning delinquent, often violent behavior through daily exposure to gangs, guns, and drug dealing. In many such areas, most children and adolescents have had friends killed, and many have witnessed street killings or drive-by shootings; in some instances, peers have been killed in the corridors or playgrounds of their schools (Wilkerson, 1994). All too often, gang members and drug dealers provide positive social and financial rewards for serious criminal or violent behavior (Elliott, 1994b). Under such circumstances, trying to raise children to stay out of trouble and to become competent, caring, emotionally mature adults can be difficult and at times disheartening.

The problem that parents face is likely to be compounded by the lack of any effective social or cultural organization in these neighborhoods, and by the absence of even informal support systems of friends and neighbors. As we noted earlier, neighborhoods with high concentrations of poverty are much more stratified, ethnically and racially, and have much higher proportions of unmarried mothers, single-parent families, and unemployed young men (Jargowsky & Bane, 1990; Panel on High-Risk Youth, 1993). Few have the energy or opportunity to be supportive to neighbors when their own needs are not being met. In addition, high levels of transience increase the difficulty of establishing common values and norms of behavior, informal support networks, and effective social controls. "Illegitimate enterprises and gangs emerge in these neighborhoods, in part because the neighborhood has no effective means of resisting such activity, and in part as a means of providing some stable organization for youth and some economy for the neighborhood" (Elliott, 1994b, p. 3).

Not all poor neighborhoods are disorganized, however. Recently, residents of a number of poor, crime-rid-

youngest. Court records show that Mrs. Gonzales drank heavily, used crack and once even sold her children's clothes for drug money. She failed to show up at Jacob's first court hearings on the armed-robbery charge. She was drunk when she finally came to testify, said Michael Batchelor, the boy's lawyer, who added, "You could smell it." Her testimony was of little help, Mr. Batchelor said. She did not even know her son's birthday.

"Jake is a product of his environment," Mr. Batchelor said. "He comes from a dysfunctional family. The older neighborhood boys were his heroes. They sold drugs. They had guns. They were his role models. He wanted to be like them."

His heroes were troubled and neglected themselves. Damien Dorris, the 14-year-old who killed Mrs. Alvarez, was abandoned by his father, beaten by his mother and was essentially rearing himself. He had dropped out of school after the seventh grade and lived with an older teen-age brother. The brother

was a drug dealer, the police said, and Damien picked up the trade. . . . By last summer, he told the police, he had grown bored with drug dealing and was trying to get out. But he had to find a way to pay his $430 debt to his drug suppliers. He told court officials he had been given 24 hours to come up with the money or be killed. But Jacob carried out his role because, he said, he was hungry, he wanted some money and it was something exciting to do. . . .

Damien pleaded guilty to second-degree murder. Jacob, whose detention garb had to be rolled up at the ankles and wrists and secured at the waist to keep from falling off, pleaded guilty to armed robbery. Both boys were sentenced to the maximum term, to remain in state custody until they are 21.

SOURCE: Isabel Wilkerson (1994). Excerpted from "2 Boys, a debt, a gun, a victim: The face of violence. Second report in a periodic series, When Trouble Starts Young." *The New York Times,* May 16, p. 1. Copyright © 1994 by The New York Times Company. Reprinted by permission.

den neighborhoods have banded together successfully to revitalize their neighborhoods, combat drugs and violence, and restore city services. Interestingly, in most instances the determination of a single energetic, courageous, and frustrated individual has provided the spark to ignite the process of taking back the neighborhood.

Serious delinquent behaviors, including impulsive, seemingly senseless violent crimes, are not confined to the inner cities of large metropolitan areas (Eckholm, 1993; U.S. Department of Justice, 1994). As gangs, guns, and drugs have spread to the suburbs and to smaller cities across the United States, gang- and drug-related offenses, including homicide, have risen rapidly. Even where gangs and drugs have not been involved, however, the incidence of senseless, violent acts has been increasing. In a recent case, a small group of middle-class youth from one suburban school, for no clear reason, tracked down, attacked, and (whether intentionally or not) killed a young man from a neighboring town. Nevertheless, absolute rates of crime and delinquency remain highest in concentrated poverty areas in the nation's inner-cities (Panel on High-Risk Youth, 1993; U.S. Department of Justice, 1994).

# Schools and Peers

Schools play an important part in adolescent delinquency, both in their own right and because—together with the neighborhood—they constitute a primary setting for peer interaction. Doing poorly in school is strongly related to the incidence of delinquency. Adolescent delinquents have a long record of academic difficulties (Dryfoos, 1990; Lorion, Tolan, & Wahler, 1987; Panel on High-Risk Youth, 1993). They are likely to have entered school poorly prepared for academic work, and their difficulties only mounted during the elementary school years. By adolescence, most have fallen several years behind their peers in grade level, and many drop out of school as early as they can. Academic aspirations are usually low to begin with, and repeated experiences of failure have in all likelihood reduced them even further (Panel on High-Risk Youth, 1993). For many delinquents and future delinquents, their school experience becomes irrelevant at best and a source of frustration, resentment, and alienation at worst. Once a young person drops out of school, his or her chances of engaging in serious delinquent behav-

ior increase significantly (Dryfoos, 1990; Panel on High-Risk Youth, 1993).

All too often, schools themselves compound the problem. Many high-risk adolescents come from low-income families living in poor or "underclass" neighborhoods (see Chapter 8). Consequently, they are likely to enter poorly equipped, understaffed, often unsafe schools that do little to encourage students or to give them a sense of belonging or a feeling that the school genuinely cares about them and their development. More affluent schools provide superior facilities and equipment, such as libraries and computers, better-qualified teachers and higher teacher/student ratios, more support services, and a school atmosphere less disrupted by disciplinary problems and more conducive to learning. Their curricular level is higher, as are expectations for student performance. Not surprisingly, 25 percent of all inner-city schools have dropout rates of 50 percent or higher—a rate higher than that of 99 percent of all other high schools (Braddock & McPartland, 1992; Panel on High-Risk Youth, 1993).

In addition to its direct effects, the school provides a major locus for peer-group interactions. In Elliott's (1994b) view, much of the violence at school that emerges during the junior high and high school years is related to competition for, and confrontations about, status:

> Ability tracking also contributes to a collective adaptation to school failure and peer rejection by grouping academically poor students and those who are aggressive troublemakers together in the same classes. Delinquent peer groups tend to emerge out of these classes and individual feelings of anger, rejection, and alienation are mutually reinforced in these groups (Elliott, 1994b, p. 4).

Involvement with a delinquent peer group plays a major role in instigating serious violent behavior, as well as delinquency in general (Elliott, 1994b; Elliott, Huizinga, & Ageton, 1985; Farrington, 1986; Patterson, DeBarsyshe, & Ramsey, 1989; Rutter & Giller, 1984). One extensive longitudinal study showed that male and female adolescents who had close ties ("bonding") to delinquent peers and weak bonds to prosocial, nondelinquent peers engaged in delinquent activity with increasing frequency over a 3-year period, whereas those who had only weak or no ties to either group did not (Elliott, Huizinga, & Ageton, 1985). For those with strong bonds to both delinquent and prosocial peers, the relationship with prosocial peers appeared to offset, but

not negate, the influence of delinquent peers. The authors conclude that bonding with delinquent peers plays a vital role in the development of delinquency.

## Peer Influence and Gangs

Traditionally, lower-class youth in urban ghettos have been more likely than youth in more affluent neighborhoods to join delinquent gangs. Although these groups were likely to encourage delinquency, the better-organized and less-violent gangs often helped meet needs that are common to all youth—the need for a sense of personal worth, a meaningful social life and acceptance by peers, and protection from rival gang members or abusive parents (Elliott, Huizinga, & Ageton, 1985; Gold, 1987; Huff, 1992). To some extent this is still true today: Gangs may still perform such positive functions, especially in socially disorganized neighborhoods, and not all gangs are involved in more serious or violent crimes and drug dealing (Elliott, 1994b; Hinojosa, 1995). However, in the 1990s youth gangs in the United States have become much more violent, especially in the ghettos and barrios of America's largest cities, but increasingly in smaller cities and towns as well (Huff, 1992). Los Angeles alone has been averaging nearly 500 gang-related deaths a year; moreover, about half of the victims are not gang members, but innocent bystanders, including many children.

Another significant development in recent years has been "gang migration": Earlier gangs were largely local and concerned with issues such as defending their turf, as in the classic *West Side Story*. Although such local groups still exist, they are increasingly being replaced by "supergangs," such as the Crips and Bloods, which are heavily involved in drug dealing (Huff, 1992).

Although originally Los Angeles gangs, both have now extended their reach to nearly all fifty states in the United States and beyond. Much of this expansion has been financially driven and due primarily to the less-intense competition and less-sophisticated law enforcement, as well as greater profit potential from drug sales in the nation's smaller cities and towns. More recently, the ranks of gangs such as the Crips and Bloods have been augmented by newer arrivals, including Jamaican posses (notorious for their viciousness), Chinese, and Vietnamese gangs (Chin, 1990; Huff, 1992).

Many gangs are organized along ethnic, national, and geographic lines. In Los Angeles county alone, there are hundreds of gangs: Honduran, Salvadoran, Nicaraguan, Guatemalan—even Tonganese and Samoan

## 12.3 The Girls in the Gang

Despite the women's movement and the efforts of female gang members to subscribe to such goals as independence, equality, and sisterhood, traditional male dominance remains alive and well in today's youth gangs. In her remarkable account of the life of girls in three representative New York gangs, *The Girls in the Gang,* social psychologist Anne Campbell comments:

> While some writers have argued for the existence of a set of focal concerns specific to lower-class male life, this should not be parodied into a simplistic belief that gang members are isolated from society at large or hermetically sealed in an alien set of norms. As much as anyone, they are exposed through the media to the images of a life lived with limitless luxury, in which everyone is beautiful and relationships are passionate, stormy, superficial, and ultimately selfish. They subscribe to this as the natural order. There is no counterculture in the gang, only the rehearsal in microcosm of an American belief in consumerism, in the equation of money with power, in competition and success, and in a hierarchy through which the initiate may climb to power and one day become president. All are proud to be American, some have fought for their country, and most would do so enthusiastically if the need arose.
>
> In understanding the fundamentally conservative structure and values of the gang, the position of girls becomes more explicable. Females must accept the range of roles within the gang that might be available to them in society at large. The traditional structure of the nuclear family is firmly duplicated in the gang. In straight society the central, pivotal figure is the male. His status in the world of societal and material success is the critical factor, while the woman supports, nurtures, and sustains him. The gang parodies this state of affairs without even the economic infrastructure to sustain it, for the male rarely works and often it is the female who receives a more stable income through welfare. Nevertheless, the males constitute the true gang. . . .
>
> Nor are the double standards of morality forgotten by gang members. Hell's Angels distinguish promiscuous "sheep" from wifely "old ladies." Girls who sleep around within the gang are disparaged by the males and disciplined by the females. The Sex Girls [part of The Sex Boys and Girls (as in *Essex Street*), a black and Hispanic New York City gang] discuss the girls of rival gangs as only interested in indiscriminate sex with the boys. At the same time, the sexual adventures of the boys are considered an unremarkable aspect of the male character. The perpetuation of such values keeps the girls very firmly in their place.

SOURCE: From *The Girls in the Gang,* by Anne Campbell, pp. 242–243. © 1984 by Anne Campbell. Published by Basil Blackwell Ltd., Oxford and New York. By permission.

(Barich, 1986; Huff, 1992; Schwartz, 1992). Even in the affluent suburbs, there are gangs of white teenagers who, despite their comfortable environment, take to the streets.

As we noted earlier, violent acts today are far more lethal. Disputes that used to be settled by fists or relatively primitive weapons, such as homemade zip guns, are now resolved—too often, permanently—by semiautomatic assault weapons. Since 1985, the firearm-related homicide rate has increased by more than 150 percent, and three-fourths of all homicides of young black males result from firearms (CDF, 1994, 1995; Elliott, 1994b; U.S. Department of Justice, 1994).

Ronald Huff (1992), director of the Criminal Justice Research Center at the Ohio State University, argues that youth gangs are a symptom of more fundamental, underlying socioeconomic problems, which require long-term strategies for prevention and control. Unless these are addressed, no amount of short-term quick fixes will succeed in reducing the rising toll of violent crime,

death, and despair that are poisoning our society and our relations with each other.

Of course, even in high-delinquency areas many adolescents do not become delinquent. Conversely, many adolescents who are not economically deprived, who come from well-established middle-class homes, and whose parents are neither culturally displaced nor members of struggling minority groups, do become delinquent. Indeed, although the absolute rate of delinquency remains lower among middle-class suburban youth, the greatest increases in delinquency rates in recent years have occurred in this group.

# Personality and Delinquency

Why does one child from a particular neighborhood, school, social class, and ethnic background become delinquent whereas another, apparently subject to the same environmental influences, does not? In approaching this problem investigators typically use a research design in which delinquents and nondelinquents from the same kind of background are compared with respect to personality characteristics and parent–child relations at various ages. What have been the findings?

## Intelligence

On average, delinquents score about eight points lower than nondelinquents on tests of intelligence (Hirschi & Hindelang, 1977; Quay, 1987a). When only recidivists (repeaters) are included, the difference rises to as much as twelve points (Rutter & Giller, 1984). In both instances delinquents consistently score more poorly in verbal skills than in performance skills (Grace & Sweeney, 1986; Hubble & Groff, 1982; Quay, 1987a).

There is also a somewhat higher incidence of mental retardation among delinquents than in the population at large. Nevertheless, most delinquents are not retarded, and low intelligence itself does not appear to have a direct impact on delinquency in a majority of cases. It should be noted that the relationship between IQ and delinquency is not simply a reflection of social-class status or ethnic-group membership. Several studies have found significant correlations between IQ and delinquency even after controlling for the effects of these variables (Binder, 1988; Hirschi & Hindelang, 1977; Quay, 1987a; Rutter & Giller, 1984).

What accounts for the relationship between delinquency and IQ? One hypothesis has been that lower IQ—particularly verbal IQ—leads to poorer school performance, "which leads to a negative attitude toward school, which in turn leads to delinquency" (Quay, 1987a, p. 104). Partial support for this hypothesis is provided by studies showing that improving academic performance may significantly reduce disciplinary problems in the classroom. Researchers have also found a higher incidence of reading disability among delinquent students (Binder, 1988). It should also be noted that delinquency rates tend to fall after young people leave school (Bachman, O'Malley, & Johnson, 1978; Rutter & Giller, 1984).

## Conduct Disorders

Clearly, school difficulties are not the whole story. For one thing, antisocial behavior, as well as more general behavioral disturbances, may precede school failure (Moffitt, 1990; Patterson, DeBarsyshe, & Ramsey, 1989; Richman & Lindgren, 1981; Richman, Stevenson, & Graham, 1982). Moreover, it is possible that cognitive deficits and conduct disorders may "to some extent share a common etiology—either in terms of socio-familial variables or temperamental characteristics" (Rutter & Giller, 1984, p. 167; Quay, 1987a; Taylor, 1994). Several studies of children adopted shortly after birth have found that delinquency and adult criminality are related to such behavior in the adoptee's biological parents but not in their adoptive parents, suggesting that genetic factors may play a role in creating a predisposition for delinquent behavior (Earls, 1994; Robins, 1978; Rutter & Giller, 1984; Trasler, 1987). However, family and peer relationships, together with other psychological influences, appear to play a far more critical role.

## Personality Development

Personality differences between delinquents and nondelinquents emerge early and vary in the course of development.

**Delinquent Boys.** In an extensive study spanning the period from kindergarten through the 9th grade, investigators found that by the end of the 3rd grade, boys who later became delinquents were viewed by their teachers as more poorly adapted than individually matched nondelinquent classmates. They were less considerate and fair in dealing with others, less friendly, less responsible, more impulsive, and more antagonistic to authority. In return, they were less well-liked and accepted by their peers (Conger & Miller, 1966).

In school they were much more easily distracted, day-dreamed more, and had greater difficulty maintaining attention and sticking to the task at hand. They were less likely to display any special ability or interest. Not surprisingly, these social and academic problems appeared to reflect underlying emotional problems, and in the opinion of their teachers future delinquents more often came from disturbed home environments and were overly aggressive.

Although this general picture continued into the 4th to 6th grades, some additional differences and changes in emphasis emerged. Thus, in the middle-school years inconsistent academic performance by future delinquents became increasingly evident. These children were more likely to be viewed as underachieving and showed poorer work habits. They demonstrated less leadership ability and had a narrower range of general interests, although they were becoming more and more attention-seeking. On the other hand, future delinquents and nondelinquents showed similar levels of resentment toward and rejection of school authority, "possibly because problems with authority are generally more common at this age than among school beginners" (Conger & Miller, 1966, p. 186).

In the 9th grade delinquents continued to display significantly less respect and consideration for the rights of others than did nondelinquents. Not surprisingly, they were much less cooperative in observing school rules and regulations and meeting their responsibilities as members of a social group. Moreover, at this age delinquents showed much more antagonism toward authority compared with nondelinquent peers than was true in the 4th through 6th grades. Apparently in the years between middle childhood and adolescence the attitudes of the nondelinquents toward authority improved considerably whereas among delinquents they continued to deteriorate.

Peer relations remained significantly poorer among the delinquents during adolescence. The delinquents were less friendly and pleasant toward classmates and, in return, were less well-liked and accepted by their peers. In their academic activities the delinquents continued "to have greater difficulty than their nondelinquent matches. Their work habits were still significantly poorer; they were more careless in their work, appeared more often to be working below their capabilities, and needed much more supervision from teachers. Attendance was more often a problem among these youths" (Conger & Miller, 1966, p. 187). The delinquents were more distractible; they manifested much less capacity for sustained attention, daydreamed more, and tended to give up more easily when challenged academically.

In general, the delinquents were rated as less well-adjusted, more lacking in self-confidence and self-respect, less cheerful and happy, less able to get along with members of their own and the opposite sex, and more attention-seeking. Again, teachers were much more likely to mention spontaneously a "disturbed home environment" as a significant problem for delinquents. These impressions of poorer adjustment among the delinquents seemed to find support in the reports of the boys themselves, as indicated by the results of psychological testing at the end of junior high school. In the various group tests, the delinquents emerged as clearly less well-adjusted.

**Delinquent Girls.** Somewhat similar results were obtained for girls, with significant differences between future delinquents and nondelinquents becoming evident as early as the period from kindergarten to the 3rd grade (Conger, 1973). Future delinquents were significantly less well-adjusted socially, emotionally, and academically than their nondelinquent matches. They were less poised and more emotionally unstable; less likely to be cheerful, happy, or friendly; and less likely to have a sense of humor. They had more difficulty relating to same- and opposite-sex peers and were less likely to show respect and consideration for the rights of others; in return, they were less well-liked and accepted by others.

The delinquent girls also displayed significantly more antagonism toward adult authority of any kind, including the school, and were much less cooperative in observing rules and regulations. At the same time, they appeared to have greater difficulty in learning to think for themselves, developing a clear set of values of their own, and setting realistic goals. They showed less creative ability and fewer special abilities or interests. Their work habits were significantly poorer than those of their nondelinquent peers.

Many of these differences are similar to those found in boys. However, there are some variations in emphasis. The largest differences between delinquent and nondelinquent girls were found in the areas of emotional adjustment and conformity; among boys, the largest differences occurred in the areas of conformity, creative ability, self-reliance, and relations with peers.

# Social Class, Delinquency, and Emotional Disturbance

Thus far we have considered overall differences between delinquents and nondelinquents. However, a number of theorists have argued that there may be social-class dif-

ferences in the characteristics that differentiate delinquents from nondelinquents (Conger & Miller, 1966; Rutter & Giller, 1984; Quay, 1987b). For example, some investigators have postulated that a middle- or upper-class youth who becomes involved in delinquency is much more likely to be emotionally disturbed than not, whereas the opposite is true in the case of lower-class children (Johnson, 1959; Kvaraceus, 1945; Quay, 1987b). The basic assumption is that delinquency is much less likely to involve norm-violating behavior in lower-class groups and hence is less likely to be a sign of individual emotional disturbance.

There is little question that many lower-class adolescents—particularly those living in urban ghettos—are subjected to greater cultural pressure toward delinquency than their more privileged peers. But does this mean that lower-class delinquents as a group have fewer emotional problems than middle- and upper-class delinquents? In a seminal study of a large group of delinquents, A. J. Reiss encountered a type of lower-class delinquent youth (the integrated delinquent) who tended to come from a stable family and who did not appear to be particularly troubled emotionally (Reiss, 1952). The integrated delinquent came from a high-delinquency area and simply tended to adopt the asocial values of the delinquent group with whom he interacted. However, Reiss also found another type of lower-class delinquent who would not usually be described as emotionally normal. This type, the defective-superego delinquent, was likely to come from a lower-class background and typically grew up in a very unstable family marked by divorce, desertion, alcoholism, or consistent lack of nurturance. He showed very little guilt about his asocial behavior, lacked a well-defined conscience, and had no clearly established goals. He felt a great deal of resentment toward the social environment and expressed his anger through delinquent acts. In many respects he resembled what is now described in the American Psychiatric Association's *Diagnostic and Statistical Manual* (DSM-IV) as undersocialized, aggressive conduct disorder (see Chapter 13).

Other investigators (Arbuthnot, Gordon, & Jurkovic, 1987; Binder, 1988; Rutter & Giller, 1984) have noted signs of poor emotional adjustment and impaired self-concept across a rather wide range of socioeconomic levels of delinquency. One extensive longitudinal study found that both lower- and middle-class delinquents were more poorly adjusted than either socioeconomically deprived or nondeprived nondelinquents (Conger & Miller, 1966). On some traits, at some ages, and at some IQ levels, deprived delin-

quents scored more poorly than nondeprived delinquents, whereas in some other instances the reverse was true. In general, however, socioeconomically deprived delinquents tended to score more like nondeprived delinquents than like nondelinquents, either deprived or nondeprived.

It would appear to be more meaningful, and probably more accurate, to emphasize the greater accomplishment—emotionally, socially, and academically—of the deprived youth who nevertheless manages to avoid delinquency than to assert that the nondeprived delinquent is much more likely to be emotionally disturbed than the deprived delinquent or that the latter is generally "normal" (i.e., similar to nondelinquents in degree of emotional stability).

## Adolescent Delinquency and Adult Criminality

Does delinquency during childhood and adolescence lead to criminal behavior in adulthood? The answer appears to be that it depends on how early delinquent behavior begins, the seriousness of the offenses, how often they are repeated, and the extent to which delinquent behavior is part of a generally antisocial lifestyle (Farrington, 1983; Loeber & Stouthamer-Loeber, 1986; Robins & Price, 1991). Although it is uncommon for individuals to become seriously criminal for the first time in adulthood, it is also true that most adolescents who have been involved in occasional instances of delinquent behavior—even when they have had to appear in juvenile court—do not progress to criminal careers in adulthood. A number of studies have found the following indicators to be associated with a greater likelihood that delinquent or criminal activities will continue into adulthood (Farrington et al., 1986; Osborn & West, 1980; Patterson, DeBarsyshe, & Ramsey, 1989; Rutter & Giller, 1984):

- Early age of onset of delinquent behavior
- Rearrests
- Serious rather than minor offenses committed
- Involvement in a delinquent peer group
- Parental criminal activity

In short, most adolescents' delinquent behavior has only a modest relationship to antisocial behavior in adulthood; in contrast, "a record of extremely delinquent behavior in adolescence is singularly predictive of adult pathology" (Gold & Petronio, 1980, p. 517).

# Prevention and Treatment of Delinquency

Although a variety of approaches have been used in efforts to prevent or treat delinquency, the results have not been particularly encouraging. Counseling and psychotherapy, cognitive therapy, institutional treatment in "therapeutic communities," family casework, contact with traditional street-corner youth workers, foster-home placement, intensive community-based treatments, recreational programs, educational and vocational programs, youth service bureaus, and combinations of these and other approaches (such as health care and legal aid) have not been very successful (Dryfoos, 1990; Gordon & Arbuthnot, 1987; Krisberg, 1992; Lipsey, 1992; Lorion, Tolan, & Wahler, 1987; Panel on High-Risk Youth, 1993; Quay, 1987c).

However, most approaches—even those using a combination of possible solutions—have concentrated largely on young people who are already experiencing serious problems, and for the most part they have been a matter of too little, too late. Moreover, when the data are examined more closely it becomes clear that the intervention techniques used are often of poor quality or inconsistently applied (Dryfoos, 1990; Panel on High-Risk Youth, 1993; Sechrest & Rosenblatt, 1987). For example, the effectiveness of a group counseling program cannot be said to have been tested adequately when the counselors are poorly trained and poorly

motivated and when the counseling itself is superficial and haphazardly arranged. In other instances studies are so poorly designed that it is impossible to reach valid conclusions about the meaning of the findings, even when they are favorable.

**Correctional Institutions.**   On the other hand, there is considerable evidence that imprisonment in traditional correctional institutions makes matters worse by subjecting the young person to traumatic and embittering experiences, often including sexual and physical abuse, while providing little or no psychological, educational, or vocational help. Such institutions have been described as finishing schools for future criminal behavior (Feld, 1992; Kaufman, 1979; Panel on High-Risk Youth, 1993; Prescott, 1981). Not surprisingly, reconviction rates among previously institutionalized youth generally run between 60 and 70 percent (Rutter & Giller, 1984).

Although there are clearly instances in which institutionalization may be the only practical alternative, particularly for violent or "professional" offenders, in many cases suspended sentences, official and unofficial probation, and formal police warnings are at least as effective in terms of recidivism rates. Indeed, several studies indicated that for first offenders, such noncustodial alternatives resulted in somewhat lower reconviction rates (Dixson & Wright, 1975; Rutter & Giller, 1984; Soler, 1992).

Nevertheless, in many states where juvenile courts have considerable discretion in dealing with juvenile

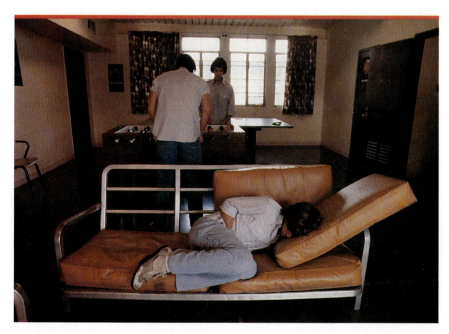

In many states where juvenile courts are free from adult constitutional due-process requirements, adolescents who have committed only status offenses are often institutionalized.

offenders, without the strict rule of law and constitutional due process required in adult jurisdictions, adolescents who have committed only status offenses are often institutionalized (Feld, 1992; Schwartz, 1992). A national study of 722 institutions conducted by the Law Enforcement Assistance Administration (LEAA) found that two-thirds of the girls and one-third of the boys had been confined solely because of status offenses (behaviors not punishable among adults). Many girls are institutionalized only for sexual activity (Federle & Chesney-Lind, 1992; Wooden, 1976). Moreover, conditions in large numbers of supposedly more humane and rehabilitation-oriented juvenile facilities are often as, or more, punitive than those in many adult facilities, with fewer legal safeguards against physical, sexual, and psychological abuse (Feld, 1992; Orlando & Crippen, 1992). "Rehabilitative euphemisms, such as 'providing a structured environment,' cannot disguise the punitive reality of juvenile confinement. . . . Evaluation research provides scant support for the effectiveness of such 'rehabilitative' programs" (Feld, 1992, p. 76).

In contrast, because of the organizational chaos, underfunding, and understaffing of the court system for juveniles in large metropolitan areas such as New York City, adolescents and youth who have committed repeated violent offenses often serve little or no time in correctional institutions (Kaufman, 1979; Schwartz, 1992). Such incongruities in the system of juvenile justice—or injustice—led the Juvenile Justice Standards Project of the American Bar Association and others to conclude, after a decade of research, that juvenile courts, like all other courts, should be bound by the rule of law (Feld, 1992; Kaufman, 1979; Schwartz, 1992). Acts that would be crimes if they were committed by adults should be handled in a similar fashion. In the view of Irving R. Kaufman, chief judge of the U.S. Court of Appeals in New York, "Children whose actions do not amount to adult crimes should be dealt with outside the judicial system" (1979, p. 58).

## Promising Approaches to Prevention and Treatment

Although many programs aimed at prevention and treatment fail in the long run to reduce delinquency, a number of recent approaches have provided some encouragement (Dryfoos, 1990; Elliott, 1994b).

**Early Childhood Interventions.** In one such effort in Michigan (the Perry Preschool Program), a two-year preschool enrichment program supplemented

by weekly home visits from program staff had significantly better long-term outcomes than a matched control group: By age 19, the program group had significantly fewer arrests than the controls—22 percent versus 38 percent—and fewer became chronic offenders (Berrueta-Clement et al., 1986). Analyses indicated that the preschool program improved later school classroom behavior and academic performance, which in turn led to lower dropout rates and less subsequent delinquency.

**Family Interventions.** As we have already seen, an important contributor to adolescent delinquency is lack of adequate parental guidance and support. In one carefully designed series of investigations, Gerald Patterson and his colleagues at the Oregon Social Learning Center used a behaviorally oriented parental training program (Patterson, 1982; Patterson, DeBarsyshe, & Ramsey, 1989; Snyder & Patterson, 1987). The basic assumptions underlying behavioral approaches "are that behavior may be modified by its consequences" (Rutter & Giller, 1984, p. 276). In accordance with the principles of operant learning or behavior modification, appropriate behavior is systematically rewarded and inappropriate, negative behavior results either in lack of reward or in unpleasant consequences such as a temporary loss of some privileges. However, intervention must be planned "on the basis of a detailed functional analysis of how the individual's behavior is affected by the environment in actuality (rather than on the basis of theoretical assumptions)" (Rutter & Giller, 1984, p. 276). In these investigations, parents were helped to use positive, noncoercive methods of control, to interact more positively as a family, to monitor their children's activities better, and to deal more decisively with deviant behavior. They were shown how to negotiate behavioral contracts with their children and to help them develop improved social problem-solving skills. Detailed observations were made of parental behavior, child behavior, and parent–child interactions in the home. Although these carefully worked out procedures were found to be remarkably effective in the treatment of overly aggressive children, they appeared to have few lasting effects on delinquents (Dryfoos, 1990; Patterson, 1982).

Another study of young people who had been referred by the courts primarily for status offenses (such as truancy, running away, and ungovernable behavior) yielded more encouraging findings. In this study, the relative effectiveness of three treatment programs were compared: a behavioral approach aimed at improving family communication (and including behavioral contracts), family therapy discussions without behavioral

techniques, and a no-treatment group. Over a 6- to 18-month follow-up period, overall recidivism rates for the three groups were 26 percent, 57 percent, and 50 percent, respectively; when only actual criminal offenses were considered, the comparable figures were 17 percent, 21 percent, and 27 percent (Alexander & Parsons, 1973).

**School-Based Interventions.** School-based intervention programs have ranged from highly specific (programs aimed at improving problem-solving or social skills) to school-wide efforts to improve school organization and classroom management (Dryfoos, 1990). One interesting demonstration program involving some 200 schools used a school team approach (Dryfoos, 1990; Grant & Cappel, 1983). Teams consisting of six to eight members, including parents, students, school staff, and community residents, were trained to deal as a group to formulate plans for dealing with problem behavior. The policies adopted included a time-out room for disruptive students (rather than suspension), visits to the homes of problem students, and increased use of monitors and advisors for individual students. School crime and disruptive behaviors decreased, especially among middle-school students— primarily as a result of better parent–teacher relations and improved handling of disciplinary and security problems (Grant & Cappel, 1983).

**Community-Based Multicomponent Interventions.** As Joy Dryfoos (1990) notes, many young people at high risk for delinquent behavior are so alienated from school that interventions must be placed in community or neighborhood settings if they are to have any chance of succeeding (Dryfoos, 1990). One promising program, called Targeted Outreach, has been implemented by the Boys Clubs of America in more than 200 local clubs across the nation (Boys Clubs, 1986, 1987). The program, which concentrates on recruiting and mainstreaming high-risk adolescents aged 12 to 18, uses an individual case management approach with links to a wide variety of relevant community agencies, including the juvenile justice and school systems. Individual counseling and mutually agreed-on behavior contracts are combined with a variety of recreational and other club activities, such as "Smart Moves," a prevention curriculum involving group counseling sessions to foster intelligent decision-making regarding sex and drugs. To date, 39 percent of the young people involved in the program have shown a significant improvement in academic performance and 93 percent of those who have completed the program

have not become involved further with the juvenile justice system (Boys Clubs, 1986; Dryfoos, 1990).

Another carefully researched program, the Adolescent Diversion Program, focuses on young people who have already committed delinquent acts but who have not yet been formally adjudicated by the juvenile court (Davidson & Redner, 1988; Dryfoos, 1990; Panel on High-Risk Youth, 1993). The program is designed to develop empowerment skills in young people and their families by building on their existing strengths. The instrument of change is a trained family worker (university student or community volunteer) who spends 3 hours a week for 4 to 5 months with each individual, identifying desired behavioral changes in the young person and community resources that will be needed, working out behavioral contracts for change with the young person, and serving as an advocate with the schools, the juvenile justice system, and other institutions. Results of the program have been very positive: Program participants have had significantly lower recidivism rates than similar delinquents not in the program.

Denver Partners, another program involving high-risk young people who have already had contact with the juvenile justice system or have been identified as high-risk has also reported encouraging results. Trained adult volunteers are individually matched with young people in an effort to find workable solutions to the young person's problems. Support is provided by the staff of the program through counseling and guidance, training in needed life skills, social and recreational activities, and linkages with a wide variety of community resources, including social service agencies, the juvenile justice system, the schools, and mental health workers, as well as a Health Corps of dentists, pediatricians, and family physicians, as needed (Feldman, 1988).

As these brief examples suggest, relatively few clearly successful prevention and treatment models have been identified to date (Dryfoos, 1990; Garmezy & Masten, 1994; Panel on High-Risk Youth, 1993). In part, this can be attributed to the intractability of the problem in many instances; in part, however, it appears to be due to the limited scope of most programs. The roots of delinquent or criminal behavior are often deep and pervasive. They range, as we have seen, from negative patterns of family interaction beginning early in life to growing up in socially disorganized, economically deteriorated neighborhoods lacking either formal or informal social support systems, and with inadequate, often unsafe schools. Day in and day out, children and adolescents are exposed to violence, drugs and drug dealing, and peer and gang pressures. More fundamentally, the roots of much serious delinquency include poverty, joblessness, societal

indifference, lack of constructive activities in the present, and a pervasive hopelessness about the future (Panel on High-Risk Youth, 1993; Wilkerson, 1994).

In view of the deep-rooted, multifaceted nature of the problem, especially in the case of serious offenses, it is not surprising that the most promising delinquency programs are those that cast a wide net. Joy Dryfoos (1990), an expert on high-risk adolescent behavior, notes that if delinquency prevention programs are to be maximally effective, they should have broader goals than simply trying to prevent delinquency, while failing to address other aspects of the child's or adolescent's life. They also must begin early in the child's development; they must include multiple components within the family, the schools, and the community; and they must be sustained (Dryfoos, 1990).

Above all, if troubled young people are to find a way through the many obstacles that confront them and into a productive future, they need sustained adult support—if feasible from parents, but if parents are unable or unwilling, then from other adult mentors who can serve as counselors and advocates and who demonstrate that they care about young people (Garmezy, 1987; Garmezy & Masten, 1994; Panel on High-Risk Youth, 1993). Unfortunately, such programs require funding, which in the present political climate is increasingly being shifted from prevention and treatment or rehabilitation to punishment and the building of ever more prisons. In the words of Dr. Barry Krisberg, president of the National Council on Crime and Delinquency,

> We're fighting the wrong enemy. We're blaming the kids. We should be fighting the gun lobby, the people pushing drugs and alcohol to kids and violence on television. We seem to think that with a little tinkering we can solve the structural displacement of an entire class of people (Wilkerson, 1994, p. C11).

As Attorney General Janet Reno recently told a convention of juvenile court officials, "Unless we are willing to invest in children early on, we will never be able to build enough prisons ever to begin to cope with the problem 13, 15, 18 years from now" (Wilkerson, 1994. p. C11).

In the final analysis, delinquency is a symptom of serious underlying problems—social, psychological, economic, educational, vocational, physical, and even philosophical. Patchwork approaches—attempts to salvage particular groups of children or adolescents—appear destined to have limited success as long as society does little to ameliorate the societal conditions that are, as we have seen, the breeding ground of delinquency.

# Summary

Despite their disenchantment with some of the policies and practices of government and other social institutions, most adolescents are optimistic and feel that their lives are going reasonably well. However, there remain significant minorities of young people who feel deeply dissatisfied with either themselves or society or both. Such alienation among youth has differed in important ways over time. With the decline in clearly identified religious faith in the past century, some youth have a feeling of "existential outcastness." Many adolescents also share a sense of developmental estrangement—the feeling of alienation or loss that comes with the abandonment of ties to one's childhood self without finding a rewarding replacement. In a period of rapid social change another kind of alienation may emerge: a sense of historical loss, as evidenced by nostalgia for the past. Alienation may also take the form of estrangement from what is vaguely felt to be one's real self; many young people feel that they have somehow lost touch with the inner core of their being and that much of what they do is devoid of meaning.

In the 1960s many middle- and upper-class adolescents and youth became disillusioned with the goals, values, and practices of American society, which they believed was shallow, hypocritical, and overly preoccupied with material rewards and social status. In recent years, a newer, more subtle form of alienation appears to have taken root among a significant number of youth and young adults. It is characterized by feelings of loneliness, desire for (but difficulty achieving) intimacy, feelings of rootlessness, uncertainty about what the future holds, and loss of a sense of community and common purpose in contemporary society. Much of the alienation among minorities and the poor is imposed from outside by an affluent society from which they have been largely excluded economically, socially, and politically.

Each year about two million young people in North America move away from home, many permanently. Studies of the families of serious runaways typically reveal chronic patterns of family conflict; in many instances, however, the problems are much worse and may include family violence, neglect, and physical and sexual abuse. Adolescent runaways, particularly in large cities, are at risk for robbery, assault, prostitution, drug use and small-time pushing, and disease, including AIDS. They urgently need help, but existing facilities are unable to meet their needs adequately.

The adolescent delinquency rate reached a peak in 1980 and then declined slightly for 2 years, after which it climbed again, reaching a record level of 51 per thousand in 1991. The incidence of serious offenses has risen more rapidly than that of delinquency in general. Although the male/female ratio has declined, boys still exceed girls in juvenile arrests, particularly for more serious offenses. Delinquency rates are also higher among lower-income youth, including those who are members of minority groups, particularly in urban ghettos. Nevertheless, a growing number of offenses are committed by middle-class youth living in the suburbs, especially those characterized by a high degree of social and geographic mobility and without stable community ties.

The largest increases in crime rates in recent years have been in the numbers of children and adolescents murdered each year. Firearm deaths among black males have more than tripled in the past decade, and homicide is now the leading cause of death among black males. Moreover, many of these crimes appear to be senseless or random. A major reason for the rapid increase in homicides is that violent acts today are more lethal, due to the proliferation of guns in our society.

For many youth, the use of violence may be seen as the most effective way to achieve status and respect and other personal and social needs. This cannot be changed without major changes in the family, in the neighborhoods where young people grow up, in the schools, and in peer groups, including gangs. The single best predictor of adolescent delinquency is the young person's relations with his or her parents. The disciplinary techniques to which delinquents were subjected in childhood are likely to have been lax, erratic, or overly strict, and to involve physical punishment rather than reasoning with the child about misconduct and responding consistently and appropriately to both antisocial and prosocial behaviors. The parent–child relationships of delinquents are far more likely than those of nondelinquents to be characterized by mutual hostility, lack of family cohesiveness, and parental rejection, indifference, dissension, or apathy.

Witnessing violence in the home and being abused oneself, together with weak family bonding and a lack of parental supervision and controls, are the most influential precursors of violent behavior in youth. Repeated exposure to television violence also plays a part, especially among already vulnerable youth.

Some neighborhoods, particularly in the socially and economically deprived inner cities of large metropolitan areas, are a breeding ground for crime: Lacking either formal or informal support systems, they provide ample opportunity for learning delinquent, often violent behavior through daily exposure to gangs, drugs, and guns.

Schools can also contribute to delinquency, both by failing to meet the needs of economically deprived, often high-risk youth, and by providing a locus for negative peer interactions, including exposure to gangs. Peers play an important role in instigating and maintaining delinquent behavior.

In earlier periods, many gangs—although they encouraged delinquency—often helped meet needs that are common to all youth: a sense of personal worth, a social life, and acceptance by peers. Contemporary gangs are far more violent and socially destructive, particularly in large cities, often terrorizing entire neighborhoods. Another recent development has been "gang migration": the spread of "supergangs" such as the Crips and the Bloods across the nation, propelled largely by the great profit potential of drug dealing.

The average delinquent scores about eight points lower than nondelinquents on IQ tests, although low intelligence does not appear to have a direct impact on delinquency in most cases. Genetic and other biological factors may also play a role in creating a predisposition to delinquency.

Personality factors are also involved. Even in the early school years, future delinquents appear to be more poorly adjusted, less considerate, less friendly, less responsible, more impulsive, and more antagonistic to authority than nondelinquents.

Many lower-class youth—particularly those living in urban ghettos—are subjected to greater cultural pressures toward delinquency than middle- and upper-class youth. But this does not mean that lower-class delinquents as a group are more free from emotional problems than middle- and upper-class delinquents. What does appear evident is that the economically deprived lower-class youth who manages to avoid delinquency is accomplishing more than is a nondeprived youth.

Although a variety of approaches have been used in efforts to prevent or treat delinquency, the results have not been particularly encouraging. Those that appear to be most promising have broader goals than simply trying to prevent delinquency while failing to address other aspects of the child's or adolescent's life. They also begin early in the child's life, they include multiple components within the family, the schools, and the community, and they are sustained over time. Above all, they include active and continuing adult support.

Patchwork approaches—attempts to salvage particular groups of children or adolescents—appear to be destined to have limited success as long as society relies principally on punishment after the fact and does little to ameliorate the underlying societal conditions that are the breeding ground of most delinquency.

# Review Questions

1. Discuss the different forms youthful alienation may take. What is meant by a "new" alienation?

2. How widespread is the problem of adolescent runaways? What are the findings of studies of the families of serious runaways? What dangers are runaways likely to encounter?

3. Boys are arrested more often than girls by a ratio of 15 to 1 for crimes such as burglary and robbery, but by a ratio of less than 3 to 1 for offenses such as theft and shoplifting. Girls also tend to become involved in delinquency at later ages than boys. What theories have been advanced to account for these differences?

4. Current high rates of delinquency appear to be related, at least in part, to changes in our society over the past quarter-century. What are some of these changes, and why may they have led to increases in delinquency?

5. What factors account for the rapid recent increase in violent behavior, including aggravated assault and homicide? Why have homicide rates risen at a faster rate than other delinquent or criminal offenses? Who have been the primary victims?

6. How have urban youth gangs and their role in the lives of their members changed in recent years?

7. Research indicates that the personality characteristics and social behavior of children who become delinquents during adolescence are likely to differ from those of their nondelinquent peers during the middle-childhood years. Describe the differences.

8. In what ways do the home backgrounds and parent–child relationships of male and female delinquents differ from those of nondelinquents? What parental behaviors are especially likely to lead to youth violence?

9. Some theorists have argued that lower-class children who become involved in delinquency are less likely to be emotionally disturbed than middle- and upper-class children. Discuss the rationale for this assertion and whether or not it represents an oversimplification.

10. How successful have been efforts to prevent or treat delinquency? What approaches currently appear to offer the greatest promise for the treatment of delinquency? What social changes are needed if delinquency rates are to be reduced significantly?

# Recommended Readings

American Psychological Association. (1993). *Violence and youth*. Washington, DC: American Psychological Association.

Dryfoos, J. (1990). *Adolescents at risk: Prevalence and prevention*. New York: Oxford University Press.

Hinojosa, M. (1995). *Crews: Gang members talk to Maria Hinojosa*. New York: Harcourt Brace

Janus, M.-D., McCormack, A., Burgess, A. W., & Hartman, C. (1987). *Adolescent runaways: Causes and consequences*. Lexington, MA: Lexington Books.

Kotlowitz, A. (1992). *There are no children here*. New York: Bantam Books (paperback).

National Research Council. (1993). *Losing generations: Adolescents in high-risk settings*. Washington, DC: National Academy Press.

Quay, H. C. (1987). *Handbook of juvenile delinquency*. New York: Wiley.

Schwartz, I. M. (Ed.). (1992). *Juvenile justice and public policy*. New York: Lexington Books.

# Adolescents at Risk III: 13 Disorders in Development

anxiety, frustration, and conflict are part of the human condition, and every young person will encounter some psychological problems in the course of his or her development. Moreover, there is evidence that psychological problems are more common at certain ages than at others. Studies of community populations (assessing nearly all adolescents in a particular geographic setting) find that adolescence, particularly the years from age 15 to 19, is a critical period for the development of such disorders as depression and alcohol and drug abuse (Burke et al., 1990; Reinherz et al., 1993). Epidemiological studies, which document the incidence of physical and psychological disorders, indicate that during any one year 10–15 percent of adolescents in the United States and England are suffering from recognizable disorders (Committee, 1989).

Adolescence represents a transitional stage during which accelerations in physical and cognitive development, as well as rapid changes in parental expectations and general social demands, require new adjustments. In early adolescence, all of these changes are at work simultaneously. Consequently, by its very nature adolescence in our society involves at least some disruption in whatever psychological equilibrium may have been established previously. There is no doubt that all of adolescence involves important challenges to the individual, requiring change and often stimulating growth.

In some instances, however, the number of changes required in adolescence, particularly if too many of them occur at once, may be overwhelming. For some vulnerable young people any additional stress may be too much. The extent of the disruption experienced by a majority of adolescents, and the difficulties encountered in reestablishing a new, more mature equilibrium, have often been exaggerated (see Chapter 1); nevertheless, psychological disturbances do occur in a significant number of young people.

Our aim in this final chapter is to consider the origins, symptoms, and prognosis of some of the more prominent psychological disturbances encountered in adolescence. As will become apparent, although the roots of these disturbances can usually be found in earlier peri-

ods of development, in many cases they are manifested or become worse during adolescence (Ebata, Petersen, & Conger, 1990; Graham & Rutter, 1985; Reinherz et al., 1993). For example, eating disorders such as anorexia nervosa, bulimia, and some kinds of obesity; certain kinds of depression; suicide or suicide attempts; some forms of delinquency; and schizophrenia all are more likely to emerge during adolescence than in earlier periods. In most instances the emergence or worsening of these disturbances appears to be linked in one way or another to the physical, physiological, sexual, and cognitive changes that take place during adolescence (Cicchetti, 1990; Conger, 1991b). In this chapter we also review a number of therapeutic approaches currently used with adolescents, as well as some of the special problems associated with the treatment of adolescents.

## The Nature of Symptoms

Some of the manifestations of psychological problems in adolescence are relatively easily understood. The adolescent whose efforts to establish mutually rewarding relationships with same- or opposite-sex peers have consistently met with rejection or ridicule may become painfully anxious and uncertain in the presence of peers and may tend to withdraw into lonely isolation. The young person who has been subjected to an endless series of injustices or rejection on the part of parents and, at the same time, has had only harsh or inconsistent discipline may become angry and destructive, as do some delinquents. It is not difficult to appreciate the transient depression of a young person who has recently lost a parent, sibling, or close friend, or the acute anxiety and bad dreams of an adolescent who has just been through a terrifying real-life experience. As seen in Chapter 2, the adolescent's coping abilities play a crucial role in helping the adolescent adapt to stressful experiences. Psychological disturbances may result when the personal, financial, or emotional resources that are available to the adolescent do not match the resources that are required to deal adequately with the stress.

Some symptoms may not be so easily understood in terms of stresses that the adolescent is facing: the victim of anorexia nervosa, wasting away while worrying about being fat; a suicide attempt that, on the surface, may seem to have been precipitated by a relatively minor disappointment; and acute anxiety, or even panic, that seems to have no identifiable source. The original source of such symptoms may be anxiety about something—separation or loss of love, angry or hostile feelings, sexual impulses, feelings of inadequacy, or concern about having no separate identity of one's own (Conger, 1979). Proponents of the psychoanalytic perspective believe

Adolescents whose efforts to establish rewarding relationships with peers have resulted in rejection or ridicule may withdraw into lonely isolation.

that such anxiety may involve guilt, in that the young person's impulses are unacceptable to his or her conscience—that is, to the internal standards he or she has developed about what is right and wrong. To deal with these unacceptable impulses, the young person may erect psychological defenses that guard against the expression of these impulses, and that consequently ward off anxiety and guilt (see Table 2.1 in Chapter 2). When the adolescent's coping strategies and defense mechanisms are ineffective or only partially effective, generalized anxiety, either acute or chronic, may result.

## Anxiety

**Anxiety** states are characterized by apprehension, fearfulness, and tension and are often accompanied by symptoms such as muscle tension, sometimes leading to shaking, perspiring, headaches, or stomachaches. Unlike both normal fears of realistically dangerous situations and

phobias that are intense and unrealistic, anxiety states may occur under any circumstances and are not restricted to specific situations or objects (Bernstein & Borchardt, 1991; Livingston, 1991). Symptoms of anxiety are among the more common complaints in childhood and adolescence (Last & Perrin, 1993; March, 1995). Every adolescent will inevitably experience some anxiety in the course of development. It is only when the anxiety is excessively strong and disabling or appears to be chronic that it makes sense to speak of anxiety reaction as a clinically significant disturbance or disorder.

The most recent diagnostic manual of the American Psychiatric Association (1994) describes two major categories of **anxiety disorders** that may be seen in childhood or adolescence: **separation anxiety,** in which the predominant disturbance is excessive anxiety on separation from major attachment figures or from home or other familiar surroundings (e.g., when leaving home to go away to school); and **generalized anxiety** (formerly called overanxious disorder when it appeared in children or adolescents), in which the sources of anxiety are generalized and diffuse and lead to unrealistic worry about future events, preoccupation with the appropriateness of one's past behavior, overconcern about one's competence, and restlessness and irritability. In some cases, people may exhibit symptoms of both of these disorders as well as of other anxiety-based conditions, such as phobias (Bernstein & Borchardt, 1991). Recent studies of community samples have found that at any time, about 6 to 18 percent of children and adolescents may be experiencing symptoms of anxiety that are diagnosable as separation anxiety, generalized anxiety, panic disorder, or phobia (Costello & Angold, 1995).

## Acute Anxiety

An adolescent with an acute anxiety reaction feels a sudden fearfulness, as if something bad were about to happen. He or she may become agitated and restless, startle easily, and complain of physical symptoms such as dizziness or headache, sometimes accompanied by nausea and vomiting. The young person may appear distracted and have a limited attention span. Sleep disturbances are common: They include difficulty falling asleep and limited, restless sleep with much tossing and turning, perhaps accompanied by nightmares (Livingston, 1991).

The adolescent suffering from an acute anxiety reaction may be puzzled or alarmed by it or may attribute it to isolated external circumstances or incidents (Barlow, 1988). On more careful examination, however, it usually becomes clear that more extensive and fundamental factors are involved, such as disturbed parent–child relations, concern about the demands of growing up, or per-

vasive fears and guilt regarding sexuality or aggressive impulses, even though the adolescent may not be consciously aware of their role in the disturbance.

For example, an adolescent girl experienced an acute anxiety reaction following a minor automobile accident from which she escaped unhurt (Senn & Solnit, 1968). In the following weeks she suffered from nightmares, complained of being unable to breathe, and became fearful of going anywhere. Obviously, her response was disproportionate to the seriousness of the accident. On further exploration it was learned that the girl's parents were on the verge of divorce and family tensions were high. Moreover, it turned out that the girl had recently been upset by menarche, for which she had been poorly prepared. She had also been apprehended in sexual play with a neighbor boy a few weeks before, and her mother was accusing her of masturbation because she spent long periods in the bathroom—an accusation that she tearfully denied. She had in fact engaged in masturbation, both alone and with her sisters, but largely because of her mother's reaction she felt guilty about it. Reassurance about the normality of her sexual behavior and an opportunity to talk about her difficulties with her mother and her concern for the future of the family resulted in rapid alleviation of the acute anxiety symptoms, although longer-term therapy with both mother and daughter was required to deal with the underlying problems.

**Panic Disorder.** In some instances acute anxiety may be so intense that it produces almost unbearable panic and terror (Bernstein & Borchardt, 1991; Nemiah, 1988). The sufferer is likely to be overwhelmed by a strange sense of dread, a feeling that he or she is about to be engulfed by catastrophe. Such attacks are usually brief (often lasting only minutes) but are likely to recur. Panic attacks often occur completely unexpectedly, thereby increasing the victim's fear of a subsequent attack (Black, 1995).

Although **panic disorder** has been observed in children, it usually does not occur before late adolescence (Black, 1995). Strong separation anxiety in childhood may predispose a person to this disorder. It also appears that familial influences, including a genetic predisposition, may heighten vulnerability to panic disorder (American Psychiatric Association, 1994). In some instances psychotherapy is effective in treating this disorder; in other cases relaxation techniques, including meditation, are helpful. Recent research also indicates that several antidepressant drugs may help control panic attacks (Klein, 1994). Often a combination of these approaches may be effective in dealing both with the immediate effects of this disorder and with its underlying causes (Barlow, 1988; Bernstein & Borchardt, 1991).

## Chronic Anxiety

Most of what has been said about acute anxiety also applies to chronic anxiety. Indeed, chronic anxiety often results from acute anxiety that has not been resolved (Mussen et al., 1990; Nemiah, 1988). An important difference between the anxiety reactions of adolescents and adults is that in adolescents the link between the anxiety reaction and its causative and precipitating factors is usually clearer and more direct. Consequently, attempts at intervention have more chance of success with adolescents (Conger, 1979; Hersov, 1985a). It is essential to begin intervention while the relevance of these causal factors is still apparent and can be dealt with, and before chronic anxiety and the individual's response to it (such as psychological withdrawal, impairment of schoolwork, or continuing physical symptoms such as pains, diarrhea, shortness of breath, and fatigue) become a way of life.

# Fears and Phobias

People of all ages experience fears, but the frequency and nature of fears may be related to age. For example, younger children (in the preschool or early childhood years) are more likely than older children and adolescents to manifest unrealistic fears such as fear of the dark, strangers, animals, and imaginary creatures such as ghosts. Fears in middle childhood (ages 8–10) are more realistic, tending toward bodily injury (e.g., from fire) rather than toward imaginary creatures (Campbell, 1986; Klein, 1994). One study found that fears were more common among 7- to 10-year-olds than among 11- to 13- and 14- to 16-year-olds (Ollendick, King, & Frary, 1989). Fears that are common to middle childhood and adolescence include not being able to breathe, being hit by a car, being bombed, falling from high places, burglars, fires, earthquakes, death, poor grades, and snakes (King et al., 1989). Generally, the frequency of fears is higher among girls than among boys (Bernstein & Borchardt, 1991).

Although young people sometimes carry over a childhood fear unchanged into adolescence, other fears are likely to emerge, either for the first time or in a new form. Many fears arising in adolescence are related to the changing demands of this period. The adolescent may have fears related to growing up, meeting new groups of peers, advancing in school, contracting diseases, or starting a job. More advanced cognitive development enables the adolescent to grasp potentially fearful events, such as death, more fully.

Fears may be realistic or unrealistic. An adolescent boy with a recurring illness that has endangered his life may fear death. A girl who has been repeatedly rejected by people close to her may fear further rejection. A young person who has been in an airplane crash may develop a fear of flying. Such fears are not difficult to understand, and within limits they may even be adaptive if the feared person, object, or event is in fact dangerous or threatening.

Unrealistic fears, though less common in adolescence, nevertheless do occur. For example, an adolescent may develop an unrealistic fear of traveling or even of leaving the house, or, conversely, may develop a fear of being in confined spaces (Horowitz, 1988).

## Phobias

An intense fear that the individual consciously recognizes as unrealistic is called a **phobia.** When the person is unable to avoid or escape the phobic situation, he or she may become extremely apprehensive and experience faintness, fatigue, palpitations, perspiration, nausea, tremor, and even panic (American Psychiatric Association, 1994).

How can phobias be explained? The behavioral approach views phobias as learned or acquired. For example, one 8-year-old developed a severe phobia to bathrooms because of her experience of seeing spiders in the family's outhouse at home. The association of spiders with toileting behaviors produced the phobia (Livingston, 1991). Faulty cognitions may be involved as well. The child or adolescent who thinks in catastrophic, irrational, or negative terms may be more likely to develop or maintain a phobia (Silverman & Ginsburg, 1995).

The psychodynamic approach attributes the development of a phobia to fear of some person, object, or event that is too painful and anxiety-producing to be given conscious recognition (Silverman & Ginsburg, 1995). The fear has been displaced onto some other, less unacceptable object or situation, usually one that is in some way symbolic of the original fear. For example, fear of attack by ghosts or giants may symbolize unconscious fears of parental punishment. One adolescent's intense fear of automobiles represented a displaced fear of his father (Chapman, 1974).

A variety of techniques, sometimes in combination, have been used to treat phobias (Silverman & Ginsburg, 1995). The use of behavioral modification strategies may be appropriate; for example, modeling (the person observes others handling the feared situation) and reinforcement may enable the person to come closer to the feared situation. Cognitive techniques that teach the child or adolescent self-control and rational thinking when faced with the feared situation may be effective. Finally, antidepressant drugs sometimes may be helpful as an adjunct in quelling the anxiety, even panic, produced by being in a phobic situation (Barlow, 1988; Silverman & Ginsburg, 1995).

# School Refusal

**School refusal** is a fear, which may approach panic, of leaving home and going to school. Children and adolescents who exhibit school refusal are not a homogenous group in terms of the underlying reasons for their fear (Berg, 1991; Silverman & Ginsburg, 1995; Wenar, 1994). Children may refuse to go to school because they fear a specific feature in the school setting (such as a particular teacher) or a certain social situation such as speaking in class, in which case the underlying concern is a true school phobia. Young people who remain overly dependent and are uncertain about their sexual identity, or who fear sexual relationships, may become acutely anxious in school when peers begin to organize their social life around dating, parties, and other sexual relationships and preferences. Ridicule or failure in school also might be the source of a school phobia.

Other children may fear separation from a parent, in which case the problem is not a school phobia but a separation anxiety disorder (Silverman & Ginsburg, 1995; Wenar, 1994). Children and adolescents whose school refusal stems from separation anxiety are often excessively dependent. In such young people school refusal may be precipitated by a move to a new home, absence of the parents on a vacation, or illness of family members. In a minority of children and adolescents, school refusal is accompanied by a depressed mood and even, in some instances, by serious depressive disorder (Hersov 1985b; Kearney, 1993; Weiner, 1992). Consequently, the possibility of significant depression should not be overlooked in the assessment of school refusal.

Many parents, particularly mothers, of children who refuse to attend school because of separation anxiety are threatened by the possibility of their children's independence from them. Often this stems from unresolved problems of dependency on their own parents, which may be reflected in an inverted dependency of parent on child (Hersov, 1985b; Weiner, 1992). Moreover, these parents themselves are likely to see the school as a cold, forbidding place and go to great lengths to protect their children not only from school but also from other painful facts of existence. The child or adolescent, in turn, perceives—at least unconsciously—the parent's underlying desire to maintain the dependent relationship and responds accordingly. The young person is likely to fear separation from the parent because of both dependency and hostility.

Although there are no gender differences in rates of overall school refusal, more boys than girls have true school phobias and more girls than boys seem to have separation anxiety disorders that result in school refusal. When school refusal is the manifestation of a separation anxiety disorder, the onset is more likely to occur prepubertally; the onset of true school phobias is more likely to occur in middle adolescence (Last & Strauss, 1990; Wenar, 1994). School refusal should not be confused with the occasional mild reluctance to go to school that can be seen in normal children and adolescents, or with realistic fears of going to school (such as fear of the class bully or of abusive treatment by a teacher). In such cases the young person is only too aware of the true source of his or her apprehension and of its realistic nature.

School refusal also has little in common with typical truancy (Berg, 1991; Hersov, 1985b). The truant adolescent usually dislikes or does poorly in school, skips classes on an irregular basis as the fancy takes him or her, and spends truant time in pleasurable activities away from home without parental knowledge or consent (Heath, 1983; Hersov, 1985b). Children and adolescents who suffer from school refusal, in contrast, stay home with their parents' consent, if not approval, earn average or better grades, and claim to like school, to have high achievement standards, and to value academic pursuits (Berg, 1991; Berg et al., 1975; Hersov, 1985b; Weiner, 1992).

Forcing a child or adolescent with genuine, intense school refusal to go back into the dreaded situation without appropriate treatment will only aggravate the phobia. Understanding the source of school refusal, whether it is a specific phobia or a separation anxiety disorder, is important for making decisions about treatment (Silverman & Ginsburg, 1995). Prompt therapy to determine and deal with the real source of the youngster's anxiety is essential and in most cases must involve not only the child or adolescent but the parents as well. Behavioral and cognitive therapies (involving child and parents) have been efficacious in treating school refusal (Bernstein & Borchardt, 1991).

# Depression

Depressive disorders cover a wide spectrum, from mild, temporary states of sadness, often in response to a life event, to severely disturbed conditions that may involve cognitive as well as mood disturbances (Committee, 1989; Compas, Ey, & Grant, 1993; Harrington, 1994). Until recently, it was widely assumed that children and younger adolescents rarely exhibited **depression.** Clinical and research studies have demonstrated clearly, however, that this is not the case. Both major and minor forms of depression have been found during childhood, puberty, and adolescence (Kovacs, 1989; Petersen et al., 1993). In addition, rates of depression among youth appear to have increased since World War II (Harrington, 1994; Klerman & Weissman, 1989).

# Manifestations of Depression

Three categories of adolescent depression have been identified and investigated (Compas, Ey, & Grant, 1993; Petersen et al., 1993). The first category is depressed mood, which is indicated by adolescents' reports of feeling sad, blue, or unhappy. Studies of nonclinical samples indicate that 15–40 percent of adolescents experienced depressed mood in the previous 6 months (Compas, Ey, & Grant, 1993). Because depressed mood is so common, it cannot be interpreted automatically as indicative of a psychological disturbance that should be dealt with clinically, but it could be a sign.

Some, but not all, adolescents who experience depressed mood will eventually evidence a depressive syndrome (the second category of depression), which is a particular configuration of behaviors and emotions that together form a pattern of depression. For example, one confirmed syndrome is when the adolescent shows a set of behaviors and emotions that reflect both anxiety and depression (the anxious/depressed syndrome). About 5–6 percent of adolescents score in the clinical range on measures of this syndrome, indicating that their depression is severe enough to warrant concern (Achenbach, 1991; Compas, Ey, & Grant, 1993).

The third category of adolescent depression is clinical depression. Clinical depression is diagnosed through the presence, duration, and severity of a set of symptoms such as depressed mood that lasts at least two weeks, changes in weight, changes in sleep and activity patterns, loss of energy, feelings of worthlessness, and recurrent thoughts of suicide or death. When these symptoms are severe, the adolescent may be diagnosed with one of the more common types of clinical depression: **major depressive disorder** (American Psychiatric Association, 1994; Compas, Ey, & Grant, 1993). The person with clinical depression is viewed as seriously distressed. About 1–3 percent of adolescents are diagnosable at any point in time as clinically depressed. Psychologist Bruce Compas believes that such adolescents will have moved through a sequence initiated by depressed mood, eventually evidenced in a depressive syndrome, and, finally, clinical depression (Compas, Ey, & Grant, 1993).

With respect to age differences in prevalence, clinical depression appears to be less common in childhood and early adolescence than in later adolescence (Fleming & Offord, 1990; Rutter, 1986; Weller & Weller, 1991). However, depression may be manifested in different ways at different ages, depending on the person's level of cognitive, psychological, social, and biological development (Ebata, Petersen, & Conger, 1990; Harrington, 1994; Shaw, 1988). In early adolescence young people are unlikely to express their feelings openly and tend to deny negative and self-critical attitudes. They are less likely to exhibit the gloom, hopelessness, and self-deprecation that are seen in adult depressives, although these symptoms may occur (Committee, 1989; Conger, 1991b; Shaw, 1988).

Adolescents, particularly younger adolescents, may manifest feelings of depression through boredom, restlessness, or inability to be alone, coupled with a constant search for new activities (Achenbach & Edelbrock, 1981; Kovacs, 1989; Nicholi, 1988). Obviously, these characteristics are found in many adolescents at one time or another, but when they become dominant and persistent the possibility of depression should be explored. Escape from feelings of depression and loneliness may also be attempted through frequent and excessive use of alcohol and drugs or through promiscuous sexual activity. Some adolescent delinquents use the defense mechanism of denial and acting-out behavior as a way of coping with and avoiding depressed feelings (Nicholi, 1988; Weiner, 1992).

A depressed adolescent may also reveal his or her feelings through bodily complaints such as waking up tired and fatigued or exhibiting hypochondriacal symptoms and excessive preoccupations with physical conditions (Klerman, 1988a). Difficulty in concentrating and failing school performance are often signs of a depressed state in young people (Kovacs, 1989; Turner & Shaffer, 1992). One study of college dropouts concluded that depression was the most common and most significant causal factor in the decision to drop out of college, either temporarily or permanently (Nicholi, 1988).

Two themes are commonly encountered in some instances of adolescent depression where psychological factors appear particularly relevant (Conger, 1991b). One is expressed as a sense of emptiness and loss, as though the childhood self has been abandoned and no growing adult self has yet replaced it, engendering a high level of anxiety (Josselyn, 1971; Nicholi, 1988). This kind of depression resembles a state of mourning, in which the lost loved one is experienced as a part of the self.

The other theme, and one more difficult to resolve, involves a feeling of having tried hard to solve problems and achieve personally meaningful goals, but without success (Seligman & Peterson, 1986). The final straw in this type of depression is often the loss of a meaningful relationship, whether with a parent, friend, boyfriend, or girlfriend. Telling such an adolescent to "snap out of it," as well-meaning adults often do, is likely to be ineffective because the adolescent feels he or she has no solutions left to try. The young person who has reached this stage of hopelessness is probably most in danger of suicide (Curran, 1987).

## Influences on Depression

As noted above, depressive symptoms are more common in older than younger adolescents. In a large study of the population of the Isle of Wight in England, Michael Rutter and his colleagues found that only one in nine 10- to 11-year-olds reported moodiness, misery, depression, or feelings of self-deprecation, compared to nearly 40 percent of 14- to 15-year-olds (Rutter, 1980, 1989b; Rutter, Tizard, & Whitmore, 1981). Early pubertal maturation, however, may also play a role. For example, when 14- to 15-year-old boys were subdivided into prepubertal, pubescent, and postpubertal categories, very few of the prepubertal boys showed depressive feelings, whereas about one-third of the post-pubertal boys did (Rutter, 1980, 1986) (see Figure 13.1). As the investigators note, "Whether this surprisingly strong association with puberty was a function of endocrine changes, psychological responses to sexual maturation, or indeed some other influence remains unknown" (Rutter, Izard, & Read, 1986, p. 11). Studies of adolescent girls also have found that those who attain menarche early are more likely to suffer depressed feelings than those who are "on time" or are late maturers (Petersen, Sarigiani, & Kennedy, 1991; Rierdan & Koff, 1985a, 1991).

The family also seems to play an important role in the development of depressive symptoms among adolescents. Higher levels of family cohesion (togetherness and warmth) and family social support are associated with lower levels of depressive symptoms in nonclinical (selected from a school or community setting) and clinical (selected from a clinical setting such as a hospital or mental health clinic) samples of adolescents (Cumsille & Epstein, 1994; Petersen, Sarigiani, & Kennedy, 1991).

There is evidence that genetic factors influence the development of major depressive disorder (American Psychiatric Association, 1994; Harrington, 1994; Klerman, 1988a; Weissman et al., 1984b). In one study of monozygotic (identical) twins reared apart, it was found that if one twin had major depression, the chances were greater than 40 percent that the other twin also suffered from the disorder. Among dizygotic (nonidentical) twins, the comparable figure was 29 percent (Winokur, 1975).

There are also people who develop depressive disorders without a history of disturbance in the family. In this connection it is worth noting that stress alone has been found to produce measurable changes in the levels of certain chemicals in the brain (such as norepinephrine) similar to those found in patients with depressive illness (Fawcett, 1975; Weller & Weller, 1991).

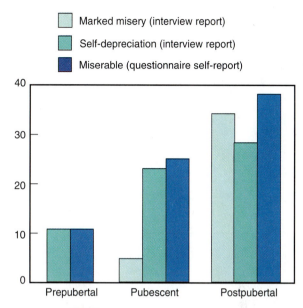

### Figure 13.1

Boys' depressive feelings and stage of puberty. From M. Rutter, C. E. Izard, & P. B. Read (Eds.) (1986). *Depression in young people.* New York: Guilford Press. By permission.

## Sex Differences in Depression

During adolescence more girls than boys become depressed (see Figure 13.2). This sex difference appears to emerge after age 13 and is maintained throughout adulthood, with adult women evidencing depression at two to three times the rate of adult men (Ge et al., 1994; Klerman & Weissman, 1989; Nolen-Hoeksema & Girgus, 1994). One of the most challenging contemporary research questions is: Why more girls? (Conger, 1991b; Petersen, Sarigiani, & Kennedy, 1991).

Three alternative explanations have been offered for the emergence of sex differences in depression in adolescence (Nolen-Hoeksema & Girgus, 1994). These explanations assert that adolescent girls are more likely to manifest depression for the following reasons:

- They experience more stresses than do boys *beginning in adolescence,* and this higher prevalence of stresses leads to their higher rates of depression.
- There are different risk factors leading to depression in girls and boys (such as social difficulties for girls and athletic incompetence for boys) and early adolescence exposes girls to more of their risk factors.
- Girls are exposed to more risk factors for depression *before adolescence* (such as concern for others and low

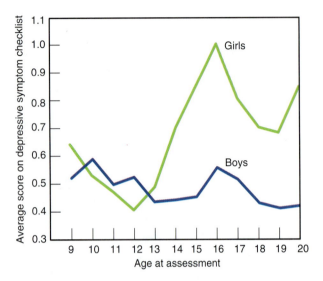

## Figure 13.2

The gender difference in depressive symptoms after age 13. From X. Ge, F. O. Lorenz, R. D. Conger, G. H. Elder, Jr., & R. L. Simons (1994). Trajectories of stressful life events and depressive symptoms during adolescence. *Developmental Psychology, 30,* 467–483. Copyright © 1994 by the American Psychological Association. Adapted with permission.

assertiveness), and this early risk combines with new challenges of adolescence (such as puberty and dating) to produce depression.

With respect to the first explanation, adolescent girls do seem to be exposed to more stressors, such as early puberty, sexual abuse, difficulties with family members, and negative life events (Ge et al., 1994; Gore, Aseltine, & Colten, 1993; Nolen-Hoeksema & Girgus, 1994). Girls generally experience greater discontinuity than boys in the transition to adolescence, and they encounter more mixed messages about sexuality, appropriate sex roles, and social and vocational aspirations (Conger, 1991b). Girls are known also to be more dissatisfied with their bodies in adolescence (Petersen, Sarigiani, & Kennedy, 1991). However, there is not yet clear and convincing evidence connecting this differential prevalence of stressors in adolescent girls and boys to the gender difference in depression (Nolen-Hoeksema & Girgus, 1994), although one study of adolescents clearly linked stressful events in girls' lives to increases in their depressive symptoms (Ge et al., 1994). The validity of this first explanation for the sex difference in depression is an open question awaiting further research.

The second explanation seems to be countered by the available evidence; generally, the risk factors for the development of depression in girls are similar to the risk factors for boys (Nolen-Hoeksema & Girgus, 1994). When they exist, difficulties in social relationships (with peers or parents), ruminative coping (i.e., dwelling on or brooding about personal problems), body dissatisfaction, feelings of helplessness, and low school achievement are all correlated with increased depressive symptoms in both sexes (Nolen-Hoeksema & Girgus, 1994; Reinherz et al., 1990; Windle, 1992). Although girls may have more experience with some of these risk factors than do boys, these risk factors appear to create as much distress for boys as for girls.

The third explanation for sex differences in adolescent depression may offer the most promise (Nolen-Hoeksema & Girgus, 1994). Risk factors such as having a cooperative rather than aggressive interpersonal style or using a ruminative coping style are more prevalent in girls *before* adolescence; these early risk factors probably combine with the typically greater challenges of adolescence for girls to produce substantial differences in

Mother and daughter talking about feelings. After puberty, depression is more common among girls than among boys.

# 13.1 Is Youthful Depression Becoming More Common?

Gerald Klerman and Myrna Weissman, experts on the epidemiology, or incidence, of depression, note that the age of onset of major depressive disorders is occurring earlier, and overall incidence is greater, among today's adolescents and younger adults. As can be seen in Figure B13.1, people born between 1957 and 1963 are at greater risk than people in older age cohorts (Klerman & Weissman, 1989; Weissman et al., 1984a).

Klerman and Weissman believe that these findings suggest that environmental as well as genetic factors can play a significant role in the onset of major depressive disorders (Klerman, 1988b; Klerman & Weissman, 1989). But what kinds of factors? Though not ruling out the possible role of other environmental factors such as nutrition, viruses, or chemical agents in the air or water, these experts consider a more likely explanation to be the particular stresses to which recent generations of adolescents have been subjected. In support of this contention, they cite parallel increases in youthful suicide and homicides, alcohol and drug abuse, and other health problems.

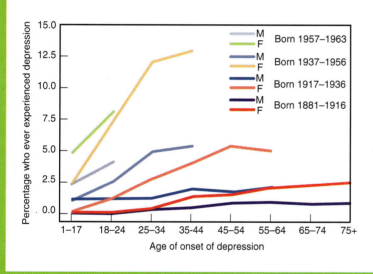

## Figure B13.1

The affective disorders—age at first onset of major depression: Results from the ECA study. From M. M. Weissman et al. (1984). The epidemiology of depression: An update on sex differences in rates. *Journal of Affective Disorders*, **7**, 179–188. Adapted by permission.

depression in adolescence (Nolen-Hoeksema & Girgus, 1994; Petersen et al., 1993). More research is needed, however, to provide evidence for this explanation.

## Bipolar Disorder

Although they are relatively rare, reports of **bipolar (manic–depressive) disorder** among adolescents, particularly older adolescents, have become more common (Committee, 1989; Kashani & Eppright, 1991; Kovacs, 1989). This disorder is characterized by periods of excessive euphoria, grandiosity, hyperactivity, and poor judgment (i.e., mania), alternating with periods of normality and periods of severe depression, loss of energy, and feelings of worthlessness.

Of the major mental disorders, bipolar disorder appears to have the strongest genetic component. If one identical twin has bipolar disorder, the chances are nearly two out of three (65 percent) that the other twin will also suffer from this disorder (Klerman, 1988a; Plomin, 1986). In the case of nonidentical twins, the chances of the other twin also developing bipolar disorder are less than one in sixteen (14 percent).

Although sample sizes are still inadequate, studies of identical twins reared apart show a high incidence of bipolar disorder among the twins of people suffering from this disorder. The incidence is not as high as it is for identical-twin siblings reared with the patient, however, indicating that environmental influences also may play a part. Investigators have attempted to identify specific genetic mechanisms involved in bipolar disorder

(Detera-Wadleigh et al., 1987; Egeland et al., 1987), but results have generally proved disappointing (Kelsoe et al., 1989; Robertson, 1989). Recently, however, a gene that appears to be linked to susceptibility to bipolar disorder has been located in a portion of chromosome 18 (Berretini et al., 1994; Marzuk & Barchas, 1995), but further research is needed.

As in the case of schizophrenia, even an identical twin of a person with bipolar disorder does not necessarily develop the disorder. Despite an apparently strong genetic influence, psychological stress or its absence may play an important role (Goldstein, 1987). Recent studies suggest that the quality of family interactions may affect the onset and likelihood of relapse in depressive disorders (Goldstein, 1987; Radke-Yarrow & Sherman, 1990).

## Suicide

Suicide is rare in children and almost as rare among young adolescents (Shaffer & Piacentini, 1994). Beginning at about age 15, however, the reported suicide rate increases rapidly. In general, suicide rates are lower among blacks and females than among white males. In 1991, among white males it reached a level of 19.1 per 100,000 for ages 15–19 and 12.2 per 100,000 among black males ages 15–19. The rate for white females ages 15–19 was significantly lower (4.2 per 100,000), and the rate for black females ages 15–19 was so low that a reliable estimate could not be supplied (see Figures 13.3 and 13.4). In white and nonwhite 15- to 19-year-old males, suicide rates quadrupled between 1950 and 1991. In the same time period, the comparable rate among white females tripled; the increase in nonwhite females was barely perceptible (Holinger et al., 1994; U.S. Bureau of the Census, 1994). Recent statistics in Canada indicate that the overall suicide rate (13.5 per 100,000) among 15- to 19-year-old adolescents quadrupled between 1962 and 1991, with Canada having an overall rate (both sexes and all races combined) of 13.5 suicides per 100,000 in 1991—higher than the overall rate of 11.0 in the United States (Nemeth, 1994; U.S. Bureau of the Census, 1994).

Females are more likely than males to use passive methods of suicide, such as ingestion of drugs, and less likely to use active methods, such as shooting or hanging.

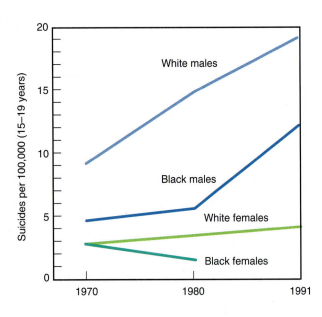

## Figure 13.3

Adolescent suicide rates by sex and race, 15- to 19-year-olds, 1970–1991. Note: No 1991 figure is supplied for black females because the base rate was too low to provide a reliable estimate. SOURCE: U.S. Bureau of the Census. *Statistical abstract of the United States,* 1989, 1994. Washington, DC: U.S. Government Printing Office, 1989, 1994.

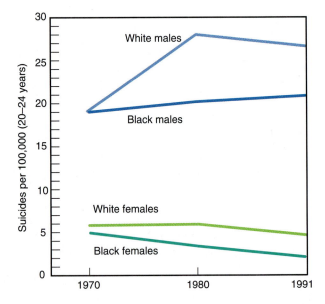

## Figure 13.4

Adolescent suicide rates by sex and race, 20- to 24-year-olds, 1970–1991. SOURCE: U.S. Bureau of the Census. *Statistical abstract of the United States,* 1989, 1994. Washington, DC: U.S. Government Printing Office, 1989, 1994.

The reported suicide rate increases rapidly after age 15. Although suicide may be precipitated by a particular event such as the breakup of a romance, school failure, or the loss of a parent or friend, the young person's reaction to the event generally turns out to be the culmination of a long series of mounting difficulties.

Among both sexes, firearms and explosives account for the greatest number of *completed* suicides, whereas drugs account for the greatest number of *attempted* suicides. Although male adolescents outnumber females in completed suicides, attempted suicides are far more common among females (Holinger et al., 1994; Worden, 1989).

In a national survey, almost four of every ten 8th- and 10th-grade girls (42 percent) and one-fourth of the boys report having seriously thought about committing suicide at some time in their lives; 18 percent of the girls and 11 percent of boys report that they have actually tried to commit suicide (National Adolescent Student Health Survey, 1988). Although percentages are higher, similar sex differences have been found among college students who have considered suicide at some time (Bolger et al., 1989).

**Reasons for Adolescent Suicide Attempts.** In considering adolescent suicide attempts, it is important to distinguish between immediate precipitating factors and longer-term predisposing factors. Precipitating events may include life events or stresses such as the breakup or threatened breakup of a romance, pregnancy (real or imagined), worries about homosexual feelings, school failure, conflicts with parents, rejection by a friend, being apprehended in a forbidden or delinquent act, loss of a parent or other loved person, suicide of a friend or relative, and fear of serious illness or imminent mental breakdown (Bolger et al., 1989; Curran, 1987; Miller, Chiles, & Barnes, 1982; Shaffer & Piacentini, 1994). On closer examination, however, it becomes clear

that the adolescent's reaction to such events is generally the culmination of a series of mounting difficulties, not usually a single event or experience (Pfeffer, 1991).

Often, adolescents who attempt suicide have a long history of escalating family instability and discord (Jacobs, 1971; Pfeffer, 1989, 1991). They have reached a point at which they feel unable to communicate with their parents or turn to them for support. Early parental loss is also more common among suicidal adolescents (Bolger et al., 1989; Curran, 1987). Typically, suicidal adolescents have fewer close friends, but their relationships with them are much more intense: "Their relationships become supercharged with a degree of desperation and need that is often not shared by their friends and lovers" (Curran, 1987, p. 30).

An important longer-term predisposing factor is psychological disturbance. Recent studies have shown that at least 90 percent of adolescents who have completed suicide would have met the criteria for a psychiatric disorder (Setterberg, 1992; Shaffer, 1988). This suggests that many suicides could be prevented if such disorders were recognized and treated (Holinger et al., 1994) (see Box 13.2).

**Treatment.** Treatment of potentially suicidal adolescents or those who have made suicide attempts must be prompt. Many communities now have hotlines that people who are considering suicide or feeling desperate can call for help. More extended treatment should deal both with the immediate events and life circumstances that are troubling the young person and with long-standing

## 13.2 Prediction of Suicide Risk

There is a dangerous myth, not only among the general public but also among some clinicians, that a person who talks about committing suicide will not do so. The tragic fact, however, is that many people who have threatened suicide and been ignored—or dismissed as attention-seekers—have subsequently taken their own lives. Moreover, in talking about suicide adolescents are conveying a message that something is wrong and that they need help, even though they may not yet be seriously intent on suicide as the only remaining solution to their problems.

Talk of suicide should always be taken seriously (*Report,* 1989b; Rotheram, 1987; Setterberg, 1992). Predicting suicide risk is not easy, but there are a number of warning signals that can alert the careful observer to the possibility of suicide. Those signals include the following:

1. A persistently depressed or despairing mood (or frantic activity alternating with intolerable boredom and listlessness)
2. Eating and sleeping disturbances
3. Declining school performance
4. Gradual social withdrawal and increasing isolation from others
5. Breakdown in communication with parents or other important people in the young person's life
6. A history of suicide attempts or involvement in accidents
7. Seemingly reckless, self-destructive, and uncharacteristic behavior, such as serious drug or alcohol use, reckless driving, sexual acting out, delinquency, or running away
8. Statements such as "I wish I were dead" or "What is there to live for?"
9. Inquiries about the lethal properties of drugs, poisons, or weapons
10. Unusually stressful events in the young person's life, such as school failure, breakup of a love affair, or loss of a loved one
11. Having a close friend or family member who attempted or committed suicide
12. Presence of a psychological disturbance, such as a mood, personality, or psychotic disorder, especially when combined with thoughts about suicide

---

problems, conflicts, and psychological disturbances (Curran, 1987; *Report,* 1989a; Setterberg, 1992). Schools must deal carefully with the suicide of one of their students, given that psychological contagion can lead to further suicides (Shaffer & Piacentini, 1994). "Large group activities designed to process the event may be counterproductive. Help or counseling should be readily available, but forums for mass identification with the victim should be avoided" (Setterberg, 1992, p. 867).

In some instances involving depressive disorders, it may be helpful to combine medication with psychotherapy, although use of drugs with children and adolescents should not be undertaken lightly, given the propensity of suicidal adolescents to overdose on drugs and the lethality of antidepressant overdosage (Committee, 1989; Ryan et al., 1987; Setterberg, 1992). In addition, further research on the effects of various drugs in this age group is clearly needed; some antidepressant drugs, such as imipramine, appear to be less effective with adolescents than with children or older adults (Ryan et al., 1987).

## Eating Disorders

At no other stage in development is the person as likely to be preoccupied with physical appearance as during adolescence. Adolescents may be concerned about their ultimate height, the adequacy of their sexual development, or their general physical attractiveness. Among female adolescents, however, weight is likely to be the primary concern (Attie & Brooks-Gunn, 1989; Leon et al., 1993; Lucas, 1991; Richards et al., 1990). This is hardly surprising. For one thing, puberty normally results in a significantly higher ratio of fat to lean tissue and a lower resting metabolic rate in women than in men (see Chapter 3). Before puberty, girls have 10–15 percent more fat than boys; after puberty, they have almost twice as much fat as boys (Marino & King, 1980).

In addition, there is greater cultural pressure on women to be thin (Russell, 1985). Ironically, this pressure is greatest in affluent societies, especially during adolescence and young adulthood (Pate et al., 1992).

Even mild degrees of overweight are likely to be viewed as unattractive and a sign of self-indulgence.

Many adolescents go through brief periods in which their weight deviates upward or downward from generally accepted norms. However, once growth has stabilized, most adolescents correct their weight through regulation of their diet. A minority, however, will not or cannot do so. In some cases sustained overeating may lead to serious **obesity.** In other cases, pathologically prolonged and extreme dieting may lead to serious, sometimes life-threatening degrees of weight loss. The latter condition, known as **anorexia nervosa,** is most likely to occur during adolescence and is far more common among girls than among boys. Another eating disorder that affects girls primarily is **bulimia,** which involves abnormal eating behavior without abnormal weight loss or gain. In some cases bulimia may be linked to a history of anorexia nervosa; in other instances it may be associated with obesity (Russell, 1985; Steinhauser, 1994). Each of these conditions, and some of the psychological and psychophysiological factors that may be involved, will be discussed briefly.

## Obesity

Childhood obesity has become a significant public health problem in the United States, as it has increased steadily since the 1960s. The prevalence of adolescent obesity has increased as well, with a quarter or more of adolescents aged 15 to 19 years classifiable as overweight. The largest increases in obesity have been seen among Native-American and Hispanic groups, particularly females (Harlan, 1993).

It is important to recognize that serious obesity is a complex and far from uniform condition (Barinaga, 1995; Halaas et al., 1995; Pelleymounter et al., 1995). Biological, psychological, and social factors may all play a role. Obesity in developed countries is far more common at lower socioeconomic levels than at upper levels (Stunkard, 1985). Recent studies using identical twins have shown that hereditary factors can predispose a person to obesity (Bouchard & Pérusse, 1993; Stunkard et al., 1990). Obesity may result from disturbances in metabolic functioning or endocrine imbalance and variations in the number and size of cells in the adipose tissues (Ravussin et al., 1988; Striegel-Moore, Silberstein, & Rodin, 1986; Stunkard, 1985). Recent research indicates that many people may become obese because their bodies burn calories too slowly as they have a low metabolic rate, not because they eat too much; moreover, low metabolic rates may be inherited (Ravussin et al., 1988; Roberts, 1993).

In some instances, psychological and social problems appear to play a role in obesity, and if those problems can be corrected or ameliorated the person may be able to reach and maintain a reasonable weight level. This is particularly likely in the case of excessive weight gains that begin in adolescence (Bruch, 1974; Woolston, 1991).

**Psychological Factors.** It is necessary to distinguish between psychological characteristics that may predispose the adolescent to obesity (psychological causes) and those that emerge because of societal reactions to the condition (psychological consequences). Because most studies of obesity have not followed adolescents over time, our ability to separate causes from consequences is limited. Moreover, all studies considered together have not been consistent in finding associations between obesity and psychological distress or personality characteristics (Friedman & Brownell, 1995).

Nevertheless, it appears that some obese adolescents react to social discrimination and criticism with at least partial acceptance of it as valid. As a consequence, they tend to be preoccupied with being fat and to become passive or timidly withdrawn, eager to please, and tolerant of abuse (Friedman & Brownell, 1995; Stunkard, 1985). In brief, sometimes an obese adolescent accepts the negative evaluation of others "and settles down to live with it" (Bruch, 1974, p. 277). Those who reach adolescence with low self-esteem and a sense of helplessness (often fostered by parental criticism or rejection) are much less resistant to social criticism than those who have gained self-esteem, competence in a variety of skills, and a sense of autonomy.

The psychological and social factors that may predispose an adolescent to obesity are not uniform. In some cases parents may overfeed their children as a way of showing love or, conversely, of expressing unconscious hostility. The child or adolescent may overeat as a way of avoiding pressures of social interactions, athletic activities, or sexual relationships in which he or she feels inadequate. Some may overeat to fill a feeling of emptiness or loneliness. Others may do so to give themselves a feeling of "bigness" as a form of compensation for feeling psychologically small or insignificant. Clinical and experimental investigations indicate that obese young people are less likely than their nonobese peers to feel that they are self-directed, separate individuals with the capacity to identify and control their biological urges and to define and present their needs in ways that yield appropriate rewards (Bruch, 1979; Graham, 1985).

Obese adolescents often cannot discriminate accurately among bodily urges. When exposed to food in a controlled experimental situation, normal students ate considerably less when their stomachs were full than when their stomachs were empty. In contrast, obese students ate as much (and in some instances more) when their stomachs were full as when they were empty.

Whereas normal people regulate their eating according to physiological cues of hunger, obese people do not (Schacter, 1971).

Investigators have recently identified a gene that plays a critical role in controlling obesity in one strain of obese mice (Barinaga, 1995; Halaas et al., 1995; Pelleymounter et al., 1995). When this gene is normal, it causes fat cells to manufacture a hormone called leptin; as fat increases, so does the production of leptin. When too much leptin reaches the brain, metabolism speeds up and the brain signals the body to stop eating and become more active, thus resulting in weight loss. When this gene is defective, as in the case of the strain of obese mice, it cannot produce this fat-regulating hormone. However, when the missing leptin is injected in these obese mice, they apparently "get the message," and their weight rapidly returns to normal.

In obese humans, however, elevated levels of liptin do not produce a similar effect, suggesting resistance to liptin. Why this occurs, and how it might be overcome, are important questions for further research. In any case, however, there will still be a need to exercise and maintain a healthy diet.

**Treatment of Obesity.** Approaches to treating obesity have focused on changing the person's eating patterns and responses to cues that previously provoked eating behavior, and ameliorating underlying psychological problems while promoting personal growth and a sense of identity, autonomy, and control of one's own body. Often these approaches are combined, and parents are enlisted to aid in weight-reduction efforts. Even when continued overeating has psychological roots, the eating itself is likely to become overlearned as a response to a variety of familiar cues, and substantial relearning through behavioral approaches is required (Williams & Kimm, 1993). At the same time, it is important to recognize that for people with low metabolic rates, or for whom a heavier weight than others appears to be biologically normal, it will be a lifelong struggle to lose weight and keep it off. However, the results of future biological research may well make the task easier (Barinaga, 1995; Halaas et al., 1995; Pelleymounter et al., 1995).

## Anorexia Nervosa

**Anorexia nervosa** is characterized by pathologically prolonged and extreme dieting, which may lead to serious, sometimes life-threatening degrees of weight loss. The condition is particularly puzzling because anorectics have such a distorted body image that they may continue to complain of being too fat even when severely emaciated. Severe undereating and consequent malnutrition and serious weight loss may accompany other disorders such as depression and obsessive–compulsive behavior, as well as a variety of undiagnosed organic disorders (American Psychiatric Association, 1994). However, the clinical picture in genuine (primary) anorexia nervosa is remarkably similar from one patient to another. The disorder is most likely to begin during adolescence, with peak rates of onset at ages 14 to 18 years (Coupey, 1992; Halmic et al., 1979), although cases appear as early as age 8 (Lask & Bryant-Waugh, 1992). Anorexia is about ten times as likely to occur among females as among males (Coupey, 1992; Herzog, 1988). Very little is known about the development of anorexia in males (Hamlett & Curry, 1990).

Three basic symptoms of disordered psychological functioning are central in primary anorexia. First is a disturbance of delusional proportions in body image and body concept (how adolescents view and evaluate their bodies). Even when his or her appearance has become skeletonlike, an adolescent may deny being too thin, and even continue to worry about becoming fat (American Psychiatric Association, 1994; Bruch, 1974; Seebach & Norris, 1989; Steinhauser, 1994). Second is a disturbance in the perception or cognitive interpretation of stimuli arising in the body. Rather than a mere loss of appetite, there is a failure to recognize cues of hunger—a failure similar to that occurring in many obese patients, although the result is very different. Failure to recognize bodily cues indicating fatigue is also likely, and despite severe malnutrition the patient may exhibit hyperactivity (Lask & Bryant-Waugh, 1992; Pope & Hudson, 1989). Finally, there is usually a paralyzing sense of ineffectiveness—a feeling of acting only in response to the demands of others rather than to one's own needs and wishes. This feeling of lack of control is typically masked by a surface negativism and stubborn defiance, making it difficult to treat the disorder effectively (Herzog, 1988; Herzog & Beresin, 1991).

**Factors in the Development of Anorexia.** As noted above, cultural obsessions with thinness as an ideal for females undoubtedly play an important role in the development of anorexia nervosa. Although anorexia was originally identified as a problem of white upperclass girls in the United States, it has become increasingly prevalent among girls in all social classes and ethnic groups, suggesting the pervasiveness of cultural ideals for thinness (Pate et al., 1992). Studies have been consistent in documenting a more negative body image and body dissatisfaction among adolescent girls with eating disorders (Attie & Brooks-Gunn, 1989; Koff & Rierdan, 1993; Leon et al., 1993). Eating disorders may be more prevalent among early maturers (girls who are more

Because of a distorted body image, anorectics may continue to complain of being too fat even when they are severely underweight.

physically developed than most girls and boys of their age) than later maturers (Attie & Brooks-Gunn, 1989; Koff & Rierdan, 1993; Rodin, Striegel-Moore, & Silberstein, 1990). Girls who experience both early maturation and dating at the same time are more at risk than others of developing eating disorders (Smolak, Levine, & Gralen, 1993).

Twin studies suggest that genetic factors may increase the risk of developing anorexia, perhaps by impairing the release of particular hormones (i.e., gonadotropins) from the anterior pituitary gland; another possibility is that there is a defect in the feedback control mechanisms for certain neurotransmitters (e.g., dopamine or norepinephrine) in the brain (Herzog, 1988; Herzog & Beresin, 1991; Pope & Hudson, 1989). However, there is more evidence that psychological influences, such as a negative body image, predominate in the development of eating disorders.

Other risk factors have also been noted, including the presence of depressive symptoms, strong negative emotional reactions to stress, and difficulties in labeling feelings. Combined with cultural pressures for thinness, a negative mood and an inability to identify feelings may produce an eating disorder (Leon et al., 1993).

Although many anorectics are highly achieving, obedient, helpful, and dependable (Bruch, 1973; Herzog & Beresin, 1991), these qualities tend to be associated with an absence of individual initiative and autonomy—a sense of identity as a separate and distinct individual. At least unconsciously, anorectics are likely to have had

feelings of being "enslaved, exploited, and not being permitted to lead a life of their own" (Bruch, 1973, p. 250). They strive for perfection but fear maturity, and lack a clear sense of emerging selfhood, despite their prolonged struggle to be perfect (Hood, Moore, & Garner, 1982; Pike & Rodin, 1991). Also characteristic is an obsessive need to be in control of every aspect of life, particularly one's own body (Larson & Johnson, 1981).

Not surprisingly, parents of female anorectic adolescents are likely to have exerted such rigid control and regulation that the child had difficulty establishing a sense of identity and confidence in his or her ability to make decisions. The parents are likely to display intrusive concern, overinvolvement (enmeshment), and overprotection and to discourage separation and autonomy (Coupey, 1992; Minuchin, Rosman, & Baker, 1978; Russell, 1985). Discomfort at the idea of separation leads the parent (most often the mother) to reinforce the child's reliance on her, thereby hampering the development of a sense of self. Such parents are likely to encourage their children to become perfectionistic overachievers; they also control the child's pleasures. Such a regulated child may become so focused on external cues and controls as determinants of behavior that, like the obese child, he or she may fail to learn to respond appropriately to differential cues—physiological and psychological—originating within him- or herself.

Similar results have been obtained in a study using very rigorous methods to assess family interactions; in addition, the study suggested that the parents of the anorectic are dependent on him or her to nurture them as well as to modulate and inhibit conflict between them (Goldstein, 1981). There is some evidence that improvement in the adolescent as a result of treatment is likely to exacerbate neurotic problems in the parents (Crisp, 1986; Minuchin, Rosman, & Baker, 1978; Russell, 1985).

Finally, a study indicated that adolescent girls with eating disorders were more likely than a comparison group to have mothers who were also eating-disordered (Pike & Rodin, 1991). This study also found that mothers of eating-disordered girls were more likely to want their daughters to be thinner, and thought of their daughters as less attractive than the daughters perceived themselves to be. These results suggest that some girls may develop eating disorders in part because they learn to do so in a family context where there is pressure to be thin.

**Treatment of Anorexia Nervosa.** Estimates are that anorexia will result in death in 3–21 percent of all cases (Leon & Dinklage, 1989). Proper management requires both psychological and medical intervention (Coupey, 1992). As in the case of obesity, psychological approaches to treatment range from intensive psy-

## 13.3 Developing Eating Problems
### A LONGITUDINAL STUDY OF GIRLS

Eating disorders in girls generally develop sometime during adolescence, but few longitudinal studies (following a group of girls across adolescence) have been conducted to chart the emergence of and physical and psychological risk factors for such disorders. A recent study, however, has done just that (Graber et al., 1994). In this study, 116 middle- to upper-middle-class white females were questioned on three occasions across an 8-year-period: once as young adolescents (7th, 8th, or 9th grade); once as middle adolescents two years later; and once as young adults (age 21 to 23). The participants in this study were questioned about their eating habits and thoughts (preoccupation about being thin), physical development, body image (whether they evaluate their bodies negatively), self-image (what they think of themselves), psychological well-being, and family relations.

On the basis of their eating *problems* (not yet full-blown *disorders*) in young and middle adolescence, girls were classified into one of four groups that indicated their risk for development of a clinical eating disorder: low risk (no eating problem as a young or middle adolescent), early transient risk (eating problem as a young adolescent but not as a

middle adolescent); late transient risk (an eating problem in middle but not young adolescence); and chronic (an eating problem both in young and middle adolescence). The chronic group was most at risk for having or developing a clinical eating disorder.

The researchers sought to determine the physical and psychological factors that distinguished the four groups. The results indicated that chronic eating problems were most evident in girls who as adolescents:

- Were early maturers (attained early menarche)
- Had higher percentages of body fat (associated with early puberty)
- Had poorer or more negative body images
- Had higher (clinical) levels of depressed affect (see Figure B13.3)
- Had higher levels of psychopathological behaviors

As young adults, the chronic group was also more depressed than the other groups, suggesting a long-term relationship between eating disorders and depression.

---

chotherapy to behavior modification techniques. The primary psychotherapeutic goal is to help the patient see herself or himself as having a separate identity from parents and the right to self-respect (Bruch, 1974). In behavior modification, patient and therapist may enter into a contract spelling out increasing rewards (such as access to television or visits with other patients and family) as progress in eating and weight gain occurs (Bemis, 1987; Steinhauser, 1994). In instances in which depression is also involved, antidepressant drugs may be helpful as an adjunctive treatment.

The relative long-term success of various treatment approaches is still being evaluated (Herzog, 1988). It appears, however, that long-term success without relapse must include the reorganization of maladaptive patterns of family interaction through family therapy (Lask & Bryant-Waugh, 1992; Minuchin, Rosman, & Baker, 1978; Schwartz, Barnett, & Sabor, 1985).

### Bulimia

During the 1980s there was a dramatic increase in the number of young women who engaged alternatively in binge eating and purging. This disorder is called **bulimia** (or bulimia nervosa) (Barber, 1991; Herzog, 1988; Russell, 1985). It is characterized by frequent binge eating accompanied by an awareness that the eating pattern is abnormal; fear of not being able to stop the pattern voluntarily; self-induced vomiting, use of laxatives or diuretics, or rigorous dieting, fasting, or exercising to prevent weight gain; and persistent concern with body shape and weight (American Psychiatric Association, 1994; Herzog, 1988; Russell, 1985).

A significant number of bulimics also suffer from depression and self-deprecating thoughts. In some cases bulimia appears to be primarily a consequence of depression and can be alleviated by antidepressant drugs

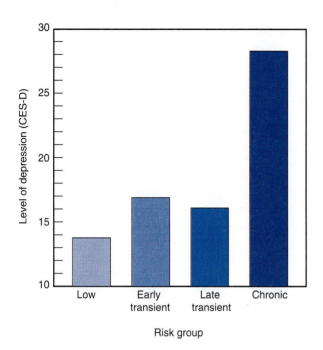

The transient groups (early and late) had some of the risk factors (such as psychopathology) that the chronic group had, but not as severely. Interestingly, though, equal percentages (about 47 percent) of women in the chronic, early transient, and late transient groups were likely to exhibit an eating problem in young adulthood. A much smaller proportion (13 percent) of low-risk girls, on the other hand, indicated an eating problem in young adulthood. These girls had fewer physical and psychological risk factors generally in adolescence and reported positive family relations.

This study points to physical and psychological factors that can set an adolescent female on a path toward significant eating problems that may continue into adulthood (Graber et al., 1994). The authors of this study urged the use of prevention and intervention programs to offset the serious eating problems that begin to develop in early adolescence.

**Figure** B13.3

Higher levels of depression in mid-adolescence among girls who have chronic eating problems and who are at high risk of developing a clinical eating disorder. Adapted from J. A. Graber, J. Brooks-Gunn, R. L. Paikoff, & M. P. Warren (1994). Prediction of eating problems: An 8-year study of adolescent girls. *Developmental Psychology,* **30,** 823–834. Copyright © 1994 by the American Psychological Association. Adapted with permission.

(Barber, 1991; Herzog, 1988). Bulimia is also associated with high rates of anxiety, including generalized anxiety disorder and social phobia (fear of social situations in which embarrassment could occur). One study found that 80 percent of bulimic women had a history of an anxiety disorder, with anxiety preceding the development of bulimia in many cases (Schwalberg et al., 1992).

Typically, bulimics are middle- to upper-middle-class white girls, and they appear to be socially well-adjusted (Boeck, 1992). Either accidentally or through friends the bulimic becomes aware of purging as a method of weight management. Bulimics typically binge on "junk food" that is high in carbohydrates.

In one study almost all of a sample of young women who engaged in binge eating reported doing so at least daily; the average number of calories per binge was estimated at 4800, usually in the form of sweets. Of those who reported purging (71 percent of the respondents),

69 percent vomited, 39 percent used laxatives, and 26 percent used both (Johnson, 1982).

After binging, bulimics characteristically feel depressed and out of control; they report having feelings of guilt, shame, and low self-esteem (Herzog, 1988). A bulimic young person is more likely than an anorectic to be distressed by her symptoms and willing to accept help. Unlike anorectics, who are more likely to be isolated and asexual, bulimics are usually outgoing and report normal heterosexual interest and experience (Herzog, 1988; Johnson, 1982). Some bulimics exhibit a strong need for social approval and for avoiding conflict, and experience difficulty in identifying and assessing their own needs (Boskind-White & White, 1983; Rodin, Silberstein, & Striegel-Moore, 1990). However, most acknowledge that their eating problem has adversely affected their lives in most areas except work, and almost three-quarters report adverse effects on their physical health.

About 10 to 15 percent of bulimics are male (Carlat & Camargo, 1991). Although research is rare, the available evidence suggests that, compared to bulimic females, bulimic males have a later age of onset (18–26 years, compared to 15–18 years for females), a higher prevalence of childhood obesity, a higher likelihood of homosexuality, and less dieting.

## Risk Factors for Bulimia

Why is bulimia primarily a female disorder, why does it appear to be on the increase, and which women are most at risk? Ruth Striegel-Moore, Lisa Silberstein, and Judith Rodin (1986), psychologists at Yale University, explored these questions in an effort to understand better the causes, course, and consequences of bulimia. In addressing the first two questions, they note that contemporary Western society places a high value on thinness, particularly for women (Rodin, Silberstein, & Striegel-Moore, 1990). Adolescent girls are more concerned and more self-critical about their looks than boys, and they are well aware of the premium society places on physical attractiveness in women (Crisp & Kalucy, 1974; Rodin, Silberstein, & Striegel-Moore, 1990; Striegel-Moore, Silberstein, & Rodin, 1986). Adolescent girls also tend to be more interpersonally oriented than boys. They worry more about what other people think of them and are more concerned with popularity and conforming to social expectations (Hill & Lynch, 1983; Simmons & Rosenberg, 1975). Finally, physical maturation is more likely to bring boys closer to the current masculine ideal, whereas for girls it is more likely to mean "development away from what is currently considered beautiful" (Striegel-Moore, Silberstein, & Rodin, 1986, p. 250).

**Which Women Are at Greatest Risk?** Striegel-Moore, Silberstein, and Rodin (1986) hypothesized that the women who are at greatest risk of bulimia are those "who have accepted and internalized most deeply the sociocultural mores of thinness and attractiveness" (p. 247). As predicted, they found that compared to non-bulimic women, bulimic women express substantially greater acceptance of the idea that fat is bad and thin is beautiful and increases the likelihood of success.

Some groups and occupations place a stronger emphasis on thinness than others and appear to place their members at greater risk for bulimia and anorexia. For example, schools in which dating is emphasized have a higher incidence of bulimia than schools that are less oriented toward dating (Rodin, Silberstein, & Striegel-Moore, 1985). Eating disorders, including bulimia, are more common among members of certain professions, such as ballet dancers, gymnasts, models, actresses, and athletes (Crago et al., 1985; Rodin, Silberstein, & Striegel-Moore, 1990; Striegel-Moore, Silberstein, & Rodin, 1986).

It also appears that young women who are genetically programmed "to be heavier than the svelte ideal will be at higher risk for bulimia than those women who are naturally thin" (Striegel-Moore, Silberstein, & Rodin, 1986, p. 254; Rodin, Silberstein, & Striegel-Moore, 1990). Similarly, early-maturing girls, because of their earlier increases in body fat, may be at greatest risk for bulimia as well as anorexia (Striegel-Moore, Silberstein, & Rodin, 1986).

As in the case of anorexia nervosa, some parents may foster bulimia. In addition to being overly involved emotionally (enmeshed), overprotective, and rigid, the families of bulimic patients appear to be unduly conscious of appearance and to attach special meaning to food and eating (Johnson & Flach, 1985; Schwartz, Barnett, & Sabor, 1985). There also may be poorer communication processes and lower family satisfaction in families of adolescent girls at risk for eating disorders (Leon et al., 1994). However, much more research is needed before firm conclusions can be drawn about the role of family variables in bulimia.

Treatment for bulimia may include individual psychotherapy, group therapy (psychodynamically, cognitively, or educationally oriented), family therapy, and cognitive–behavioral therapy, which works on changing the bulimic's beliefs about herself and her eating behaviors (Herzog, 1988; Yates, 1990). Recently, self-help groups have grown rapidly. "These groups usually encourage contact outside the group. Members can develop a sense of self-worth by seeing others who have recovered or improved and can become aware that improvement is possible" (Herzog, 1988, p. 443). Experimental programs in schools also have been tried, with some optimistic evidence for changes in attitudes regarding dieting and weight (Moreno & Thelan, 1993).

# Conduct Disorders

A diagnosis of **conduct disorder** may be made for some adolescents who display "a repetitive and persistent pattern of behavior in which the basic rights of others or major age-appropriate societal norms or rules are violated" (American Psychiatric Association, 1994, p. 90). Conduct disorder may be manifested by aggression to people or animals (such as bullying, physical abuse, and forced sexual activity), the deliberate destruction of property, theft, or serious violations of rules such as school truancy before age 13, or running away from home. The hallmark of conduct disorder is consistent antisocial behavior, infringing on others, that is not a reaction to

immediate environmental circumstances (such as protecting oneself in a threatening context) or to another underlying pathology such as schizophrenia. A diagnosis of conduct disorder should be made extremely judiciously because many of its symptoms overlap with other psychological disturbances, and it is easy to overdiagnose adolescents as having conduct disorders (Lewis, 1991). Although some of the behaviors indicative of conduct disorder may overlap with delinquency (see Chapter 12), *delinquency* is a legal term that refers to illegal offenses carried out by minors (Wenar, 1994).

Conduct disorders may emerge in childhood or adolescence, with a diagnosis of conduct disorder rarely made after age 16 (American Psychiatric Association, 1994; Kazdin, 1995; Lewis, 1991; Wenar, 1994). Its prevalence has increased in the last few decades, particularly in urban areas. Typically, more males than females are diagnosed with conduct disorder, and there is an earlier onset among males (before age 10) than among females (ages 14 to 16). Moreover, males more often show aggressive types of conduct disorder such as fighting, theft, and vandalism, whereas females more often exhibit truancy, running away, and substance use. Some conduct-disordered adolescents will continue to evidence significant problems in adulthood, including other psychological disturbances and the perpetration of criminal acts (Kazdin, 1995; Martin & Hoffman, 1990; Offord & Bennett, 1994).

There is no one effective treatment for conduct disorders, given that it includes a broad variety of behaviors, and there may be multiple sources of the disorder, including a troubled family situation, parental abuse, association with similar friends, and certain types of brain dysfunctions (Earls, 1994; Lewis, 1991). Interventions designed to train parents to manage their children's antisocial behavior, family therapy, and teaching antisocial children problem-solving skills hold some promise in treating conduct disorders, as long as the family situation is not too unstable to benefit from such treatment (Bank et al., 1991; Farrington et al., 1990; Kazdin, 1995; Lewis, 1991).

# Psychoses

The term **psychosis** is applied to disorders that involve severe distortions of cognitive and perceptual functioning. Often, but by no means always, psychotic people are unaware of the nature of their illness (even though they may be painfully aware of their suffering), and their ability to make realistic, rational judgments regarding their own condition or events in the world around them is seriously impaired. As a result, they are usually unable to maintain even minimally adequate personal, social, or work relationships or to take responsibility for their own welfare. Some psychoses, such as those stemming from toxic drug reactions or disease, are clearly organic in origin; others may be primarily psychological in origin. Among adolescents, schizophrenia is by far the most common psychotic disorder.

## Schizophrenia

The incidence of **schizophrenia,** though still relatively rare, increases dramatically from age 15 on and reaches a peak during late adolescence and early adulthood, leveling off toward the end of the third decade (Cancro, 1983; Committee, 1989; Graham & Rutter, 1985; Werry & Taylor, 1994). Schizophrenia affects equal proportions of males and females, but an earlier onset (before age 20) is more common among males than females (Weiner, 1992).

**Symptoms.** Like its adult counterpart, adolescent schizophrenia is characterized by disordered thinking; distortions of, or lack of contact with, reality; limited capacity for establishing meaningful relationships with others; and poor emotional control (Graham & Rutter, 1985; Weiner, 1992). In its fully developed form, adolescent schizophrenia can usually be identified without much difficulty: The young person's speech is likely to be peculiar—stilted, overelaborate, disconnected, or even incoherent. He or she may display odd facial grimaces or movements; appear distracted, withdrawn, or confused; and manifest inappropriate emotional reactions, either failing to respond with appropriate feeling or overreacting in a poorly controlled fashion. Hallucinations—usually auditory and reflecting control by others (such as outside voices telling one what to do)—and intense, bizarre delusions may also be present (Steinberg, 1985; Weiner, 1992).

Proper diagnosis may be difficult in the early stages of this disorder, partly because the symptoms may be far less obvious or dramatic than they tend to be later, and partly because some characteristics that might suggest incipient schizophrenia in adults are likely to occur among nonschizophrenic as well as schizophrenic adolescents. These include circumstantial thinking, abstract preoccupation, and conscious awareness of blatant sexual and aggressive imagery, as well as ideas of reference (belief that others are talking about one), all of which tend to occur more often among nonschizophrenic adolescents than among nonschizophrenic adults (Weiner, 1992).

This kind of thinking, occasionally observed among nonschizophrenic adolescents, is not too surprising when one realizes that adolescence itself is a period of rapid change during which psychological equilibrium may be temporarily disrupted and controls on thought and psychological defense mechanisms are not yet firmly established. Chronically disordered

thinking and impaired emotional integration and control, however, are important clues to schizophrenic disturbance in adolescents and adults.

**Precursors.** Although schizophrenia is most likely to become manifest after middle adolescence, adolescent schizophrenics, along with adolescents suffering from other emotional disorders, are likely to have displayed greater than average psychological vulnerability in earlier periods (Glick & Zigler, 1990; Hellgren, Gillberg, & Enerskog, 1987; Rutter & Garmezy, 1983). Studies of the earlier adjustment of adolescent schizophrenics have found a higher-than-expected incidence of shyness, social withdrawal, poor social relationships, difficulty in making friends, "peculiar" behavior, stubbornness, sensitivity, lack of humor, difficulties in concentration, fear of demanding situations, and problems in managing daily life (Garmezy, 1987; Holzman & Grinker, 1974; Rutter & Garmezy, 1983; Steinberg, 1985). Adolescent schizophrenics are likely to have shown both internalizing (withdrawing) and externalizing (aggressive) behaviors in middle childhood (Ledingham, 1990).

In addition, a number of investigators have found neurodevelopmental problems in the form of poor motor and visual–spatial skills, clumsiness, and attention deficits (including difficulty filtering out relevant stimuli from background noise) (Asarnow, 1988; Harvey, 1991; Holzman, 1990; Nuechterlein et al., 1990; Waldo, Adler, & Freedman, 1988). It should be noted, however, that such characteristics in childhood are not manifested by all young people who become schizophrenic or have schizophrenic episodes during adolescence, nor can we be confident that the presence of these characteristics in childhood or adolescence is necessarily indicative of later development of schizophrenia (Hanson, Gottesman, & Heston, 1990; Rutter & Garmezy, 1983).

**What Causes Schizophrenia?** Several generations ago it was thought that traumatic experiences in childhood were the primary cause of schizophrenia. However, research indicates that biological and hereditary factors play a major role (Hanson, Gottesman, & Heston, 1990; Holzman, 1990; Kety & Matthysse, 1988; Werry & Taylor, 1994). In a number of studies, the incidence of this disorder (or set of disorders with similar symptoms) among the relatives of schizophrenics has been shown to vary according to how closely they are related biologically (Gottesman & Shields, 1982; Plomin, 1986; Tsuang, Gilbertson, & Faraone, 1991). For example, schizophrenia occurs more often in the children of schizophrenics than in their nieces and nephews.

More important from the standpoint of separating genetic from environmental influences, several well-controlled investigations have found that if one identical twin has schizophrenia, the chances that the other twin will also develop it are 25 to 50 percent (O'Rourke et al., 1982; Walker, Davis, & Gottleib, 1991), but if one nonidentical (dizygotic) twin has schizophrenia, the chances of the other twin also developing it are less than 10 percent (Gottesman & Shields, 1982; Kety & Matthysse, 1988). In an interesting twist of the genetic puzzle, the children of identical twins discordant for schizophrenia (one twin has developed schizophrenia and the other has not) have an equal chance of being affected by schizophrenia. The nonschizophrenic twin parent carries the abnormal genotype (Gottesman & Bertelsen, 1989).

Compelling evidence of a genetic contribution to schizophrenia comes from studies of adopted children (Kety & Matthysse, 1988; Vandenberg, Singer, & Pauls, 1986; Werry & Taylor, 1994). In an extensive study conducted in Denmark, two groups of children who had been adopted early in life were studied after they reached adulthood (Kendler, Gruenberg, & Strauss, 1981; Kety et al., 1978). One group consisted of people who had become schizophrenic in the course of their development. The other was a control group that was matched with the first group for age, sex, age at adoption, and socioeconomic status of the adopting family. The incidence of schizophrenia was examined among both the biological and adoptive relatives (parents, siblings, and half-siblings) of each group. There was no significant difference in the prevalence of schizophrenic disorders among the adoptive relatives of the two groups. However, schizophrenia occurred at a rate almost six times higher among the biological relatives of schizophrenics (11 percent) than among their adoptive relatives (about 2 percent). In the control group there was no significant difference in incidence of schizophrenia between biological and adoptive relatives (Kety et al., 1978).

Nongenetic biological factors may also play a part in the development of schizophrenia, as indicated by recent research showing consistent differences in brain structure (e.g., size of cerebral ventricles) between monozygotic twins when one twin has schizophrenia and the other does not (Mesulam, 1990; Suddath et al., 1990).

Having close biological relatives with schizophrenia does not mean that one is likely to develop this disorder; in fact, it is unlikely. In the first place, except in the case of identical twins, relatives do not share all of the same genes. (As we saw earlier, schizophrenia often occurs in one identical twin but not in the other.) Second, the disorder called schizophrenia may in fact be a number of different disorders with similar symptoms (Kety & Matthysse, 1988; Mesulam, 1990; Scarr & Kidd, 1983). Third, an adequate genetic model for

schizophrenia has not yet been developed. Neither a single gene nor a "polygenic" model (representing a complex combination of interacting genes) appears to be adequate to predict the occurrence of schizophrenia (Plomin, 1986; Scarr & Kidd, 1983).

All in all, the current view among most researchers is that the individual inherits an increased *vulnerability to schizophrenia* rather than inheriting schizophrenia per se. In that case, whether or not the disorder is manifested would depend on many factors, including how vulnerable the individual is genetically and how much or what kind of environment he or she is subjected to (Campbell et al., 1991; Holzman, 1990). Longitudinal studies have found that high-risk or vulnerable individuals (those with schizophrenic relatives) are more likely to develop schizophrenia or to suffer relapses after treatment if their families are characterized by high levels of stress, negative expressed emotions, and disturbed communication patterns (Goldstein, 1990; Marcus et al., 1987; Mednick, Parnas, & Schulsinger, 1987; Tienari et al., 1987).

**Prognosis.** Among hospitalized adolescent schizophrenics, about one-quarter recover, about one-quarter improve but suffer residual symptoms or occasional relapses, and about half make little or no progress and require continuing care (Weiner, 1992). Although comparable data are not available for milder cases in which the person is not hospitalized, it is reasonable to expect that the proportions who recover or show improvement would be significantly higher.

In general, the older the adolescent is when schizophrenia appears, the better the prognosis. Other favorable indications include sudden, rather than gradual, onset; clear precipitating factors; above-average intelligence; good personal, academic, and social adjustment before onset; and early response to treatment (Glick & Zigler, 1990; Steinberg, 1985; Weiner, 1992; Wyatt et al., 1988). Finally, the outlook for improvement is better if the family is able to accept the disturbance and if there is adequate planning for future treatment and for school, work, and living arrangements (Doane et al., 1981; Goldstein, 1990).

## Brief Psychotic Disorder

It is important to distinguish between schizophrenia and brief psychotic episodes (American Psychiatric Association, 1994). In **brief psychotic disorder,** the person may exhibit such symptoms as incoherence, disorganized behavior, delusions, or hallucinations that appear suddenly and are short-lived (varying from a few hours to less than a month). Such symptoms typically (but not

necessarily) appear immediately following a severe and recognizable psychosocial stressor such as loss of a loved one or a life-threatening event that would evoke symptoms of distress in almost anyone. Invariably, there is emotional turmoil manifested in rapid, generally depressed and anxious mood swings. This disorder, which usually appears first in adolescence or young adulthood, may be followed by feelings of mild depression or loss of self-esteem. But with psychological assistance and support, the young person may be expected to return fully to his or her previous level of functioning.

# Working With Adolescents

Like other adolescents, those with significant psychological problems are at a unique stage of development. Their treatment therefore presents special challenges as well as special opportunities (Coleman, 1987; Conger, 1991b; Nicholi, 1988). Working with adolescents is more difficult and demanding than working with younger children or adults (Nicholi, 1988; Weiner, 1992). Many adolescent patients, particularly younger adolescents, tend initially to be uncommunicative, skeptical, impatient, uncooperative, and unpredictable, often because they are not seeking help on their own but are sent by someone else (such as a parent) (Weiner, 1992). As a result, the course of adolescent therapy, like that of true love, seldom runs smoothly. Acting-out behaviors or threats of such behavior (such as running away, becoming involved in a sexual adventure, quitting school, taking drugs, committing delinquent acts, and making suicidal gestures) are not uncommon in adolescent therapy and may be a source of considerable concern to the therapist. One discouraged psychotherapist compared adolescent therapy to "running next to an express train" (Anthony, 1974, p. 234).

At the same time, work with adolescents, if it is carried out properly by a skilled and experienced therapist, can be deeply rewarding. Because adolescence itself is a period of change and new beginnings, the young person is less likely than an adult to be already fixed in maladaptive patterns that are resistant to change. Moreover, despite their surface defensiveness and skepticism, at heart many adolescents remain open to experience and eager to learn from it.

Psychotherapy with adolescents is likely to be complicated by the fact that these young people typically are experiencing conflict with their parents over independence and dependence. These conflicts tend to be transferred to the therapist, producing alternating cycles of regressive dependence and unrealistic assertions of independence (Conger, 1977; Lamb, 1986). However, it is important to recognize that problems of dependence and

independence in therapy are not merely a matter of transferring parental conflicts to the therapeutic situation. They also represent important reality problems. The establishment of autonomy is a crucial developmental task for all adolescents, and the therapist must be alert to the dangers of allowing regressive dependence on therapy to become a substitute for the development of autonomy and self-reliance (Conger, 1977; Nicholi, 1988). The adolescent psychotherapist—like the wise parent, only more so—must be on guard against the temptation to try to substitute his or her own identity for that of the young person or to prolong therapy unduly.

## Qualifications of the Therapist

Therapists who work with adolescents need special knowledge of, and experience with, this age group. It also requires personal qualities—of warmth, flexibility, openness and honesty, and a capacity for limit-setting without hostility—that training may be able to foster, but rarely to create. Adolescent therapists "need to be worthy of the adolescent's trust and respect, and, in turn, need to demonstrate basic trust in, and respect for, the adolescent as a unique human being" (Conger, 1977, p. 96). The job is seldom easy, but it is less difficult for those who genuinely like adolescents, which in the last analysis probably means having come to terms with the part of the self that was once an adolescent.

Adolescents, even more than children, have a talent for spotting phoniness and exploiting it. If the therapist is straightforward, neither minimizing his or her qualifications nor retreating into professional pomposity, the adolescent will usually develop a feeling of trust and respect, though outwardly the young person may still need to make it overly clear that he or she isn't awed by "shrinks." The effective adolescent psychotherapist must also be flexible, prepared to move from listening to questioning, reassuring, clarifying reality, interpreting, even arguing and, when necessary, setting limits. As Irene Josselyn succinctly observed,

Adolescents not only need but often want limits imposed. They need externally imposed limits because, as a result of their confused state, they are not able to set their own limits. Many adolescents become frightened when they feel that limits have not been defined. They seek a fence beyond which they cannot go, within which they can experiment and by trial and error and accidental success find a self-concept with which they can feel satisfied (1971, p. 146).

Donald Holmes provides an amusing but significant example of setting limits that did more to meet the patient's needs at the time than either logical reasoning or anxious compliance on the part of the therapist:

A 16-year-old girl says, "I'm-going-to-get-out-of-here-and-get-an-apartment-and-get-married-and-you-can't-stop-me!" Her doctor replies, "No you're not, and yes I can." She acknowledges, quietly enough, "Oh" (1964, p. 110).

Obviously, such directness can be successful only when the young person has basic trust in the therapist and the therapist has already made it clear that he or she respects the individuality and worth of the patient. If the therapist sets limits only when they are necessary for the well-being of the patient, the young person typically will value the therapist because of the security those limits provide. The patient comes to see the therapist not as a restricting parental figure but as an ally of the side of himself or herself that is striving to establish a confident sense of identity. Conversely, in many instances, failure on the therapist's part to set limits when they are essential is likely to be interpreted by the adolescent as a lack of either real concern or understanding on the part of the therapist.

## The Nature of Adolescent Therapy

In most cases psychotherapy with adolescents must be directed toward personality development and synthesis—finding new, more adaptive, and less self-defeating ways of handling problems or relating to others; eliminating unnecessary fears and conflicts; and achieving a more workable integration between the young person's basic needs and values and the demands of reality. In helping the adolescent achieve these goals, the therapist may note distortions in the young person's reactions to people and events in everyday life, including distortions in the relationship with the therapist. For example, the therapist may observe that an adolescent girl is alienating her peers with critical comments not because those peers are basically stupid or hostile, as claimed, but because she fears being rejected if she allows them to come close. Or the therapist may note that an adolescent boy's worry about pleasing a part-time employer appears to stem not from any lack of ability on his own part or from the behavior of the employer (who may have made it clear that he was pleased with the boy's work), but from the fact that nothing he ever did appeared able to satisfy his father.

Similarly, the therapist may wonder whether an adolescent's scornful attitude toward the other sex really reflects a fear of growing up.

In most cases in which such techniques are used to help the adolescent reevaluate unrealistic or self-defeating behavior, the focus is basically on the present (Josselyn, 1971; Kazdin, 1991; Nicholi, 1988; Weiner, 1992). Attempts to achieve deep insights, to strip away psychological defenses, and to reconstruct the past are usually avoided. For one thing, most adolescents have little patience with rehashing the past. The adolescent's main developmental task is to cope with the present while moving toward the future: "For an adolescent in search of an identity, overcoming the fears and failures of the moment is much more important than knowing the events which led up to them" (Miller, 1959, p. 774).

The majority (79 percent) of therapists who work with adolescents prefer to engage in one-on-one psychotherapy, and rate this as the most effective treatment approach generally (Kazdin, Siegel, & Bass, 1990). Most (73 percent) also believe that it is best to bring an eclectic approach to working with adolescents such that different therapies (including individual, family, behavioral, cognitive–behavioral, and group) are considered and used as appropriate.

## Group Therapy

Group therapy with adolescents, either alone or in combination with individual or other therapies, is often an effective way for adolescents to work at overcoming the fears and failures of the moment. It may be conducted in nonresidential settings such as youth centers, mental-health clinics, private offices, or schools, or as part of the treatment program in a residential treatment center (Azima & Richmond, 1989; Coleman, 1987; Lewis, 1991; Wilson & Hersov, 1985).

Group therapy with adolescents has a natural advantage in that the forces of identification with a peer group can be put to work. "The emotional impact of observing one's own experience expressed by someone else in the same situation is usually quite a powerful one and one that facilitates personal involvement and emotional interchanges" (Christ, 1974, p. 350). Group discussions can cover a wide range of topics and will vary according to the nature of the group. For example, some groups may discuss why an adolescent uses drugs, what situations or people tend to provoke this behavior, and its effects on the young person.

Many troubled adolescents, particularly those with more serious disturbances, have had very checkered experiences with parents and other adults. Such experiences may include divorce, death, rejection, exploitation, physical or sexual abuse, and even abandonment (actual or psychological). The adolescent may respond with anxiety, distrust, depression, profound feelings of loss, or anger and resentment. Under the guidance of a skilled group therapist or therapists (sometimes a mixed-sex pair), adolescents can often help each other communicate and deal with such feelings and provide mutual support through shared experiences. This kind of group therapy has been especially effective when combined with behavioral techniques (Kazdin, 1990).

# Summary

Although the rapid physical, psychological, and social changes that occur during adolescence can be a source of stress, most adolescents are able to cope with them successfully. A minority, however, cannot. About 10–15 percent of adolescents suffer from a significant psychological disturbance. Although these disturbances usually have their roots in earlier periods of development, they may emerge or be manifested during adolescence.

Some symptoms of adolescent psychological problems are easy to understand, as in the case of the transient depression of a young person who has recently lost a parent or close friend. Other kinds of symptoms are more puzzling, as in the case of an anorexic adolescent who is wasting away while still worrying about being too fat. In some cases the source of these symptoms may lie in disturbing impulses and feelings that cannot be consciously expressed because they would produce painful anxiety and guilt.

*Anxiety disorders* are one of the more common disturbances diagnosed in adolescence. They fall into two major categories: *separation anxiety* and *generalized anxiety*. Anxiety states can be either acute or, if left untreated, chronic. Acute anxiety may sometimes be so intense that it produces panic and terror. The treatment of panic disorder may sometimes be aided by a combination of psychotherapy, relaxation techniques, and an antidepressant drug.

An intense fear that the person consciously recognizes as unrealistic is called a *phobia*. In general, phobias are learned responses, but they also can be attributed to

fear of some person, object, or event that is too painful and anxiety-producing to be given conscious recognition. Behavioral modification and cognitive strategies can be effective in treating phobias.

*School refusal* or school phobia is a fear (which may approach panic) of leaving home and going to school. Although many problems may be symbolized by school refusal, it usually indicates dread of some aspect of the school situation, concern about leaving home, or, often, both. Many parents (particularly mothers) of children and adolescents who refuse to attend school are overprotective, and encourage a dependent parent–child relationship.

*Adolescent depression* covers a wide spectrum, ranging from mild, temporary states of sadness to severely disturbed conditions. Three categories of adolescent depression have been investigated: depressive mood (which affects a large number of adolescents), depressive syndrome, and clinical depression (usually manifested as a *major depressive disorder* during later adolescence). There are significant sex differences in depression after the age of 13, when girls become significantly more depressed than boys. Explanations for this sex difference include the possibility that girls are exposed to more risk factors both before and during adolescence (such as sexual abuse and early maturation combined with school transitions or dating). Influences on the development of depression include a troubled family environment, exposure to stresses, a nonaggressive coping style, and genetic influences. The development of *bipolar (manic–depressive) disorder,* which is characterized by periods of euphoria alternating with periods of depression, appears to have a strong genetic component.

*Suicide* is rare in childhood and early adolescence. Beginning at about age 15, however, the suicide rate increases rapidly, particularly among white males. In the United States since 1950, the suicide rate among white and nonwhite male adolescents has quadrupled. It has tripled in white female adolescents, and stayed at relatively low levels in nonwhite female adolescents. Adolescent suicide may initially appear to be a response to a particular event, such as the breakup of a romance. On closer examination, however, it becomes clear that the event represents the culmination of a long history of mounting difficulties, often including family instability and discord.

Adolescent *eating disorders* include *obesity, anorexia nervosa* (chronic undereating and consequent severe weight loss), and *bulimia* (alternating episodes of binge eating and purging). Although the psychological and physiological factors involved in these disorders vary and are quite complex, in each case our society's obsession with thinness is likely to contribute to the problem. These disorders also tend to involve a feeling of lack of autonomy and control over one's own life and difficulty in establishing a clear sense of self. Research indicates that adolescent girls most at risk for developing an eating disorder are more likely than low-risk girls to have experienced early maturation, a higher percentage of body fat, a poor body image, depressive affect, and higher levels of psychopathology.

A diagnosis of *conduct disorder* may be made for some adolescents who display consistent antisocial behavior that infringes on the rights of others. Many of its symptoms overlap with other psychological disturbances, and it is easy to overdiagnose adolescents as having conduct disorders. Its prevalence has increased in the last few decades, particularly in urban areas. Typically, more males than females are diagnosed with conduct disorder, and there is an earlier onset among males than among females. Some conduct-disordered adolescents will continue to evidence significant problems in adulthood, including other psychological disturbances and the perpetration of criminal acts.

The most common adolescent psychosis is *adolescent schizophrenia,* which is characterized by disoriented thinking, distortion of reality, difficulty in establishing meaningful relationships, and poor emotional control. Although this disorder is most likely to be manifested after middle adolescence, adolescent schizophrenics are likely to have shown evidence of psychological vulnerability in earlier periods. Twin and adoption studies indicate that genetic influences play a major role in the etiology of schizophrenia. It is important to distinguish between schizophrenia and *brief psychotic disorder* following severe stress.

Therapeutic work with adolescents, whether individually or in groups, demands skill and extensive experience with young people. It also requires personal qualities—warmth, flexibility, openness and honesty, and a capacity to set limits without hostility—that may be fostered but can rarely be created by training. Adolescent therapists need to be worthy of the adolescent's trust and respect, and, in turn, need to demonstrate basic trust in and respect for the adolescent as a unique human being.

# Review Questions

1. What are the two major categories of anxiety disorders in childhood and adolescence? Can these overlap? What is panic disorder?

2. How can phobias be explained? How can they be treated?

3. What are the hallmarks of school refusal (school phobia) and how does school refusal differ from typical truancy? What role do parents, particularly mothers, play in this disorder?

4. What are the three major categories of depression in adolescence? What percentages of adolescents could be placed into these categories?

5. What is the nature of the sex difference in depression during adolescence? What are the possible explanations for this difference?

6. Is it true that a person who talks about committing suicide is unlikely to do so? What warning signals can alert careful observers to the possibility of adolescent suicide?

7. Describe the three eating disorders that are most often encountered among adolescents. What psychological and social factors are involved in each? Why are girls especially at risk?

8. What are the symptoms of conduct disorder? Why is there a risk of overdiagnosing this disorder?

9. What symptoms characterize adolescent schizophrenia, and what do we know about the causes of this disorder? How can a brief psychotic disorder be distinguished from schizophrenia?

10. What personal and professional qualifications should a therapist have in order to work successfully with adolescents? In what ways does adolescent therapy differ from therapy with younger children or with adults? Why?

# Recommended Readings

Ebata, A. T., Petersen, A. C., & Conger, J. J. (1990). The development of psychopathology in adolescence. In J. Rolf, A. S. Masten, D. Cicchetti, K. H. Nuechterlein, & S. Weintraub (Eds.), *Risk and protective factors in the development of psychopathology* (pp. 308–333). New York: Cambridge University Press.

Holinger, P. C., Offer, D., Barter, J. T., & Bell, C. C. (1994). *Suicide and homicide among adolescents.* New York: Guilford Press.

Kazdin, A. E. (1995). *Conduct disorders in childhood and adolescence* (2nd ed.). Thousand Oaks, CA: Sage Publications.

March, J. S. (Ed.). (1995). *Anxiety disorders in children and adolescents.* New York: Guilford Press.

Petersen, A. C., Compas, B. E., Brooks-Gunn, J., Stemmler, M., Ey, S., & Grant, K. E. (1993). Depression in adolescence. *American Psychologist,* **48,** 155–168.

Rodin, J., Striegel-Moore, R. H., & Silberstein, L. R. (1990). Vulnerability and resilience in the age of eating disorders: Risk and protective factors for bulimia nervosa. In J. Rolf, A. S. Masten, D. Cicchetti, K. H. Nuechterlein, & S. Weintraub (Eds.), *Risk and protective factors in the development of psychopathology* (pp. 361–383). New York: Cambridge University Press.

Rutter, M., & Hersov, L. (1994). *Child and adolescent psychiatry* (3rd ed.). London: Blackwell Scientific Publications.

Weiner, I. B. (1992). *Psychological disturbance in adolescence* (2nd ed.). New York: Wiley.

# Epilogue

As we noted at the beginning of this book, our society views the adolescent years and adolescents themselves in varied and often conflicting ways. At this juncture we hope we can view adolescence with a clearer perspective and a greater ability to distinguish myth from reality. Although there is a widespread tendency to exaggerate the extent of adolescent turmoil in our society, adolescence *is* a complex and often difficult period in development, for both adolescents and their families.

It could hardly be otherwise. Confronted by rapid physical, psychological, and cognitive changes and by an accelerating series of societal demands, adolescents face formidable challenges as they attempt to decide who they are, what they are going to be, and how they are going to live their lives.

Moreover, the challenges of this period have been increasing, partly as a consequence of continuing changes in the family and other social institutions and partly because of the accelerated rate of these changes. Much of this book has been devoted to a consideration of the kinds of influences—personal, interpersonal, and societal—that facilitate or hinder the adolescent's struggle toward maturity and a clearly defined sense of identity.

In the course of our discussion we have tried to dispel a number of myths. Among these is the view that today's adolescents and youth are a breed apart, bearing little similarity to previous generations of young people—or, conversely, that apparent generational differences are illusory, a matter of form rather than substance. A related myth is that there is something monolithic about the majority of adolescents and youth, in contrast to adults, whose diversity is more readily recognized.

In reality, there is nothing monolithic or homogeneous about contemporary adolescents. As we have seen throughout this book, in almost any area one chooses to consider—moral and religious values, social concerns and political beliefs, sexual attitudes and behavior, intellectual and educational interests, vocational goals, or emotional maturity—there is at least as much diversity among young people as there is among adults. Moreover, in most matters differences *within*

both the adolescent and adult populations are far wider than differences *between* the average adolescent and the average adult. Consequently, sweeping generalizations about "today's youth" should be treated with caution. It soon becomes clear that what is really being talked about is *some* young people—if indeed the speaker is talking about real people at all, and not simply projecting his or her own hopes and fears.

Nevertheless, there are important differences between contemporary adolescents and adults. As we have seen, some of these differences reflect differences in the positions they occupy in the life cycle. Others are the result of very real differences between the worlds into which today's adolescents and their elders were born and in which they developed, as well as profound differences in the futures they face. Today's

youth are entering an increasingly uncertain world. In an earlier era, young people were more likely to prepare for and enter a particular occupation, and then to pursue it for much, if not all, of their lives, often with the same employer. As a result of the current rapidly changing, knowledge-based technological revolution and the need to compete in a global economy, young people can seldom rely on the security of lifetime employment. Widespread corporate downsizing in pursuit of greater profits and rapid shifts in business goals, resulting in sudden and often unpredictable layoffs, have convinced many youth and young adults that security lies not in traditional company loyalty, but in the quality and diversity of their own skills.

For some, especially educationally advantaged young men and women, this represents an exciting challenge; for others it can be a source of anxiety and resentment. For still others, particularly the growing number of young people who have grown up in poverty, isolated from the mainstream of American society, it is likely to be a source of hopelessness, anger, or despair.

Not entirely coincidentally, these changes in the world of work are occurring at a time when our society is becoming increasingly polarized socially, politically, and economically: a time when violence, exploitive sex, and ruthless pursuit of money and power are being widely condemned, yet simultaneously glorified in movies, television, and computer games; when tabloid sensationalism and voyeurism are no longer confined to the supermarket checkout counter, but now appear regularly on the major television networks; when "family values" are on everyone's lips, but mean vastly different things to the religious right and the liberal left; and when the economic gap between rich and poor is growing ever wider.

Despite public concern about problems of adolescent drug and alcohol use, gang violence, adolescent pregnancy, school failure, and suicide, the kind of broad philosophical fascination with the views of youth that characterized earlier eras—and especially the late sixties and early seventies—is largely absent in the latter half of the nineties. Why? Obviously, there are a variety of reasons, many of which have been addressed in the course of this book: a decline in youthful activism, dissent, and alternative lifestyles; a narrowing of the so-called generation gap; a temporary shift in the population bulge from the baby-bust generation of today's adolescents and youth to the baby-boom generation of their parents; and increased concern among both youth and adults about the economy, the job market, and the costs of housing, education, and health care.

In a number of respects, the lessened preoccupation with youth can be viewed as positive. In the long run, young people and adults alike may benefit from the recognition that the experience of adolescence is not an end in itself, but a challenging and, one hopes, exciting stage in a continuous process of personal and social development. Similarly, a greater sense of generational continuity between parents and children may add meaning to human existence in an unpredictable, often chaotic world.

If this were the full extent of the matter, there would be little cause for concern. Unfortunately, however, the decreased emphasis on youth has an added, more troublesome dimension: a decline in our society's commitment to the well-being of its children and adolescents. The self-preoccupation, materialism, and obsession with "the good life" that characterized much of the 1980s encouraged us to turn our backs on the nation's children, youth, and families. We preferred to "feel good about ourselves," even at the cost of shallowness and self-deception. As a result, we accepted assurances of the existence of a "safety net for the truly needy" at the same time that many important health care, nutrition, child care, housing, education, job training and employment programs were being severely reduced or eliminated, including many programs aimed specifically at adolescents and youth (Conger, 1988; Edelman, 1987; Moynihan, 1986).

Not until the mid-1990s, however, did this trend reach its peak. In 1995, as part of its self-proclaimed "Contract with America," the United States Congress decided that, after nearly six decades of involvement, the federal government would no longer be responsible for the basic survival needs of the nation's children and their families, regardless of where they lived. In order to accomplish this, the "entitlement" status of core federal programs of financial assistance, health care, nutrition, and child care for children and families in demonstrated need were to be repealed, along with programs providing longer-term support of children who are severely disabled, mentally or physically; funding for foster care and adoption assistance; and protection of children from neglect and abuse, among other programs (Children's Defense Fund, 1995).

Substituted were financially capped block grants to the states, with few requirements for their use, and—most importantly—no provision for additional funding in the event of a recession or other emergencies. As Marion Wright Edelman, president of the Children's Defense Fund, has noted, these actions pose a far greater threat than the budget cuts of the 1980s: simple budget cuts can be reversed; elimination of need-based entitlements alters the fundamental structure of the federal government's ability to respond to the needs of children and adolescents, without providing any assurance that

individual states will be able or willing to fill the gap. Yet we are assured by the authors of this legislation—not as yet acted upon because of conflicts between Congress and the Administration—that it will benefit rather than harm needy children, adolescents, and families, by turning a "welfare society" into an "opportunity society." But opportunity for whom?

It appears that self-deception and the language of what George Orwell called doublespeak, once entered into, can erode the capacity for critical judgment, even in matters of ultimate self-interest. When "the bottom line" becomes the ultimate measure of success, it all too often becomes the only measure, and other values are abandoned.

Fortunately, however, there remain significant numbers of young people—and adults—who are actively trying to create a more human and humane world, whether in personal relationships, social-service activities, community involvement, school and work or even (given the current negative climate) politics. They are expressing strong concern about such problems as homelessness, child abuse, AIDS, hunger and malnutrition, and inadequate educational, social, health, and mental health services for poor children and adolescents, as well as about destruction of the environment and violations of human rights at home and abroad. Whether they can herald a significant shift in social values as we prepare to enter a new millennium remains to be seen.

One thing is certain: As a society, we can ill afford to abandon the needs and dreams of youth. No matter what the fads and fashions of the moment, or the state of the economy, or the conflicts between nations and the divisions within them, one central fact is inescapable. For better or worse, the future of our society, and quite possibly of the world itself, rests in the hands of today's young people.

If this book has in any way helped adults to better understand adolescents or helped adolescents gain a deeper understanding of themselves and their peers, it will have served its purpose.

# Glossary

## A

**addiction** Physiological dependence on a habit-forming drug.

**adolescent growth spurt** The accelerated rate of increasing height and weight that accompanies puberty.

**alienation** Profound rejection of the values of society or isolation from other people that goes well beyond the skepticism of the average adolescent.

**androgens** Male sex hormones.

**androgynous** A combination of socially valued "masculine" and "feminine" characteristics in the same individual.

**anorexia nervosa** A severe eating disorder characterized by a pathological loss of interest in eating, accompanied by a debilitating (sometimes life-threatening) weight loss. Typically the individual has a distorted body image and continues to worry about being too fat even when emaciated.

**antecedent–consequent relationships** The idea that the effects of events occurring at any stage of development depend on and proceed from earlier developmental events and will, in turn, influence the person's responses to future events.

**anxiety** A state of apprehension, tension, and worry that has both physiological and cognitive components.

**anxiety disorders** A group of psychological disturbances characterized by intense anxiety or by defensive maladaptive behaviors aimed at relieving anxiety.

**ataxia** An inability to coordinate voluntary muscular movements that is symptomatic of some neurological disorders.

**authoritarian parents** Parents who are unresponsive and highly demanding.

**authoritative (democratic) parents** Parents who are highly responsive and demanding.

**autonomy** Self-directed independence; taking responsibility for one's own life.

## B

**behavior modification (behavior therapy)** Application of the principles of learning to make changes in behavior.

**bidirectionality** The principle that parent–child influences flow both ways, from parent to child and from child to parent.

**bipolar (manic–depressive) disorder** A severe affective disorder characterized by alternating episodes of mania and depression.

**brief psychotic disorder** A short period (less than a month) of incoherence, disorganized behavior, and delusions that follow a severely stressful event.

**bulimia** An eating disorder characterized by alternating episodes of binge eating and inappropriate compensatory methods to prevent weight gain (such as purging and excessive exercise). The person is usually aware that this eating pattern is abnormal but fears being unable to stop it voluntarily.

## C

**classical conditioning** A type of learning process through which a response becomes attached to a previously neutral stimulus.

**clique** A small, tightly knit social group whose members typically are similar in age, sex, and social status.

**cognitive development** The changes and advances that occur in cognitive skills during the course of development.

**concrete operations** According to Piaget, the stage of cognitive development (ages 7–11) when children can reason logically about actual objects but are not yet able to engage in hypothetico-deductive, propositional thinking.

**conduct disorder** A consistent pattern of antisocial behavior that infringes on the rights of others, such as aggression, vandalism, theft.

**conventional level** Kohlberg's second level of moral development, during which the focus is on living up to the expectations of family, friends, and society.

**correlation** A number ranging from $-1.00$ to $+1.00$, which indicates the direction and magnitude of the relationship between two variables.

**crack** An extremely potent and highly addictive form of cocaine.

**crowd** A relatively large group made up of people who share interests, likes, and social ideals. Members meet

on the basis of shared activities, not because of mutual attraction.

**crystallized intelligence** Mental abilities that are influenced primarily by experience and acquired knowledge.

## D

**defense mechanism** A largely unconscious mental process that functions to prevent the emergence into consciousness of anxiety-producing thoughts and feelings.

**delinquency** See *juvenile delinquent.*

**demandingness** A dimension of parenting that indicates the parent's level of control over the adolescent's behavior.

**depression** An affective, or mood, disorder characterized by sadness, decreased motivation and interest in life, low energy level, and negative thoughts. See also *bipolar disorder, major depressive disorder.*

**development** The physical, psychological, and cognitive changes that take place over the life span.

**developmental stage** A period of development characterized by distinctive biological, psychological, or behavioral changes.

**developmental tasks** Challenges in a person's life that are unique to a particular stage of development and that are faced by everyone in that stage in a particular society.

**discrimination** Learning to react to differences. Discrimination is brought about by selective reinforcement of responses that have been appropriately generalized and by the elimination, or extinction, of incorrectly generalized responses.

**dizygotic (DZ) twins** Twins who develop from separate ova ("fraternal" twins).

## E

**ecological psychology** The study of the progressive accommodation that takes place over the life span between the human organism and the environments in which it grows.

**emotion-focused coping** Attempts by a person to reduce anxiety without dealing directly with the anxiety-producing situation. See *defense mechanism.*

**estrogens** Female sex hormones.

**extinction** A principle of learning in which responses or behaviors are eliminated through lack of reinforcement.

## F

**fetal alcohol syndrome** A fetal condition characterized by retarded growth, physical abnormalities, and intellectual defects that results from maternal consumption of alcohol during pregnancy.

**field theory** Kurt Lewin's theory that behavior ($B$) is a function ($f$) of the person ($P$) and his or her environment ($E$); hence, $B = f(PE)$.

**fluid intelligence** Mental abilities that depend largely on flexibility, adaptability, and speed of information processing.

**formal operations** According to Piaget, the stage of cognitive development (about age 12 and up) when the child becomes capable of engaging in abstract reasoning about hypothetical situations.

## G

**gender identity** Awareness and acceptance of one's biological nature as a male or female.

**gender intensification** The hypothesis that behavioral, attitudinal, and psychological differences between boys and girls increase across adolescence and are the result of socialization pressures to conform to sex roles.

**generalization** See *stimulus generalization.*

**generalized anxiety** A type of anxiety disorder characterized by excessive and diffuse anxiety and worry that the person finds difficult to control.

**gradient of generalization** A principle of learning that states that the more similar one stimulus is to another, the greater the likelihood that a response learned to one will generalize to the other, and the stronger the response will be.

## H

**homosexuality** (homosexual orientation) Sexual attraction primarily to members of one's own sex.

**hormones** Secretions of the endocrine glands that circulate in the bloodstream and affect behavior.

## I

**identification** The process by which one is led to think, feel, or behave as though the characteristics of another person belonged to oneself.

**identity** A sense of oneself as a separate, distinct, self-consistent person who has continuity over time.

**identity achievement** An identity status in which the person has established a firm and coherent sense of identity.

**identity confusion** An identity status in which the person has not yet established a firm and coherent sense of identity.

**identity foreclosure** An identity status in which the person has made premature ideological and occupational commitments.

**imaginary audience** The egocentric adolescent belief that others are preoccupied with one's behavior and appearance.

**induction** A non-power-assertive disciplinary technique

in which the parent gives explanations or reasons for requiring certain behaviors of the child. Unlike other disciplinary techniques, induction appeals to the child's pride and striving to be grown up.

**information processing** An approach to cognition that studies the ways in which people mentally represent and process information.

**instrumental conditioning** See *operant conditioning.*

**intelligence** The capacity to learn and use the skills required for successful adaptation to the demands of one's culture and environment.

**intelligence quotient (IQ)** An intelligence test score, originally based on the ratio between mental age and chronological age. The average intelligence quotient for a person of any age is set at 100.

**intimacy** A relationship between two people characterized by closeness, ease of communication, attachment, and affection.

**IQ** See *intelligence quotient.*

## J

**juvenile delinquent** A young person, generally under 18 years of age, who engages in behavior that is punishable by law.

## L

**learning** The process by which behavior (or the potential for behavior) is modified as a result of experience.

**lifelong process** The assumption that people develop from the time they are conceived until their death.

**life-span developmental perspective** A theoretical perspective on human development that assumes lifelong development, reciprocal individual–environment interactions, and the individual as an active organism.

**longitudinal** A research design in which the same people are assessed repeatedly over time.

**love–withdrawal** A non-power-assertive disciplinary technique that relies on fear of the loss of parental love to influence the child's behavior.

## M

**mainlining** Injecting a psychoactive drug into a principal vein.

**major depressive disorder** A clinical depression characterized by severe depressive episodes involving a depressed mood or loss of interest or pleasure along with other symptoms such as changes in sleeping or eating patterns. Key to this disorder is no history of other mood episodes such as a manic episode (a period of extreme elation, irritation, or erratic behavior).

**manic–depressive disorder** See *bipolar disorder.*

**maturation** Growth processes that results in orderly physical and behavioral changes and are relatively

independent of exercise or experience.

**menarche** The time of first menstruation, an indication of sexual maturation in a girl.

**mental age** A person's age as measured by performance on an intelligence test. A person who scores as well as the average 10-year-old has a mental age of 10, regardless of his or her chronological age.

**monozygotic (MZ) twins** Twins who develop from the division of a single fertilized ovum ("identical" twins).

**moral development** The acquisition of increasingly sophisticated internalized standards of right and wrong.

**moral relativism** The belief that there are no absolute standards of right and wrong and that one set of beliefs or values may be no better or worse than another set.

**motivation** The needs, goals, and desires that provoke a person to action.

**multidirectionality** The assumption that the course of individual development may follow any one of multiple paths.

**myelination** The development of a soft, white, somewhat fatty sheath around certain nerve fibers. Nerve impulses travel faster and with less expenditure of energy in myelinated fibers.

## N

**negative life events** Discrete or sudden undesirable occurrences in a person's life that may lead to stress.

**normal achiever** A person whose performance is about what would be anticipated on the basis of his or her IQ score or another measure of ability.

## O

**obesity** Weighing more than 20 percent above normal requirements for one's height and skeletal structure.

**observational learning** Learning by observing the behavior of others.

**ongoing life stressors** Continual undesirable occurrences or strains in a person's life that may lead to stress.

**operant (or instrumental) conditioning** A type of learning in which the subject's own response is instrumental in producing a reward; that is, it operates to bring about the reward.

**overachiever** A person whose performance exceeds what would be anticipated on the basis of his or her IQ score or another measure of ability.

## P

**panic disorder** A disorder characterized by acute and intense anxiety that produces unbearable panic and terror. The person experiences overwhelming and persistent concern about having another "panic

attack," which are brief (usually 10 minutes or less) but are likely to recur.

**permissive–indifferent parents** Parents who are unresponsive and undemanding.

**permissive–indulgent parents** Parents who are highly responsive and undemanding.

**person–environment fit** The degree of match between the person and his or her social (school and family) environment.

**personal fable** The belief that one is somehow special and unique, especially with respect to one's feelings.

**phobia** An intense fear of a person, object, or situation that the person consciously recognizes as unrealistic or excessive.

**Piagetian approach** Jean Piaget's theory of cognitive development based on the person's movement through four stages.

**pituitary gland** An endocrine gland, located immediately below the brain, that helps regulate growth and the action of other endocrine glands.

**political socialization** The way in which adolescents learn about their national government, leaders, the law, and their roles as citizens.

**postconventional level** Kohlberg's third level, during which moral judgments come to be based on broad, abstract principles that are accepted because they are believed to be inherently right rather than because society considers them right.

**power-assertive discipline** A technique that relies on punishment or fear of punishment to influence the child's behavior, rather than on the child's inner resources.

**preconventional level** Kohlberg's first level of moral development, during which children judge right and wrong primarily by the consequences of actions.

**preoperational** According to Piaget, the stage of cognitive development (about ages 2–7) when the child's ability to use language begins to dominate intellectual development but the child does not yet comprehend certain rules or mental operations.

**problem behaviors** Behaviors that depart from familial or social standards and pose some potential risk to the person or to society (such as illegal acts and underage drinking).

**problem-focused coping** Coping in which the person confronts and evaluates a stressful situation and then takes steps to deal with it.

**progestins** Pregnancy-related hormones.

**psychoactive drug** A drug that affects personality, mood, intellectual functioning, or behavior.

**psychometric approach** An approach to intellectual development that relies on intelligence testing.

**psychosis (psychotic disorder)** A severe mental disorder in which cognitive and emotional functioning are so impaired that the person loses touch with reality and cannot meet the demands of everyday living. See *schizophrenia*.

**psychosocial moratorium** A period in which the adolescent actively explores alternatives and searches for an identity.

**pubertal timing** The adolescent's position in terms of pubertal development relative to peers. Pubertal timing is referred to as on-time, early, or late.

**puberty** The initial phase of adolescence, during which the reproductive system matures and secondary sex characteristics develop.

## R

**recapitulation** The theory that during development the person passes through stages similar to those that occurred during the history of the human race (e.g., from primitive to civilized behavior).

**reciprocal interactions** The assumption that people and environments are constantly changing, with changes in one leading to changes in the other.

**regression** The readoption of a response that was characteristic of an earlier phase of development.

**reinforcement** A principle of learning in which a reward is given in order to increase a desired response.

**responsiveness** A dimension of parenting that indicates the parent's level of acceptance, warmth, and affection expressed to the adolescent.

## S

**schizophrenia** A severe mental disorder characterized by disordered thinking; distortions of, or lack of contact with, reality; limited capacity for relating emotionally to others; and poor emotional control.

**school phobia** See *school refusal*.

**school process** What actually goes on in schools, including teacher expectations, amount of teacher time spent interacting with the class, provision of opportunities for responsibility in school life, and use of rewards and incentives.

**school refusal ("school phobia")** A fear, which may approach panic, of leaving home and going to school.

**sensorimotor stage** According to Piaget, the stage of cognitive development (birth to age 2) when the infant discovers relationships between sensory impressions and motor activities.

**separation anxiety** A type of anxiety disorder in which the predominant disturbance is excessive anxiety at separation from major attachment figures or from home or other familiar surroundings.

**serial monogamists** Adolescents and youth who have a relationship with only one partner during a given period.

**sex-role flexibility** The capability of changing one's behavior, regardless of gender, to meet the demands of the context.

**sex role identity** One's perception of oneself as masculine or feminine.

**sex roles** Societal expectations regarding the appropriate behaviors for females (the feminine sex role) and males (the masculine sex role).

**sex-typing** The process by which children attain the attributes that are consistent with sex roles, or societal expectations for their gender.

**sexual adventurers** Adolescents and youth who move freely from one sexual partner to another and feel no obligation to be faithful to any one partner.

**sexual identity** A consistent, enduring self-recognition or self-labeling of one's sexual orientation.

**sexuality** The totality of a person's sexual thoughts, feelings, values, beliefs, and relationships.

**social cognition** The ability of people to interpret the social world about them—to infer what others are thinking and feeling, what their intentions are, what their relations with others are, and how they view the world.

**status offense** An act that is illegal only when it is committed by a legal minor.

**stereotypes** Uncritically assuming that all members of a group share the same personality traits, abilities, or other characteristics.

**stimulus generalization** A learning principle stating that when a particular response has been learned to one stimulus, it is likely to occur in the response to similar stimuli.

**storm and stress** The concept that adolescence is a period of extreme turmoil.

**stress** The psychological, physiological, or physical response (conscious or unconscious) of the person to noxious conditions.

## T

**temperament** Relatively consistent biologically influenced attributes that are present early in life and that are expressed in behaviors such as activity level, emotionality, and sociability.

**testosterone** The primary male sex hormone, produced by the testes.

## U

**underachiever** A person whose performance falls below what would be anticipated on the basis of his or her IQ score or another measure of ability.

**underclass** The growing number of citizens, victims of poverty and discrimination, who feel excluded from society and typically reject commonly accepted values and beliefs.

**unipolar depression** See *major depressive disorder.*

# References

**Abelson, H. I., et al.** (1977). *National survey on drug abuse, 1977: A nationwide study—Youth, young adults and older people.* Rockville, MD: National Institute on drug abuse. DHEW Publication No. (ADM), 78-618.

**Achenbach, T. M.** (1991). *Integrative guide for the 1991 CBCL/4-18, YSR, and TRF Profiles.* Burlington: University of Vermont, Department of Psychiatry.

**Achenbach, T. M., & Edelbrock, C. S.** (1981). Behavioral problems and competencies reported by parents of normal and disturbed children aged four through sixteen. *Monographs of the Society for Research in Child Development,* **46,** (Serial No. 188).

**Adams, G. R.** (1992). Runaways. In S. B. Friedman, M. Fisher, & S. K. Schonberg (Eds.), *Comprehensive adolescent health care* (pp. 795–800). St. Louis, MO: Quality Medical Publishing.

**Adams, G. R., Abraham, K. G., & Markstrom, C. A.** (1987). The relations among identity development, self-consciousness, and self-focusing during middle and late adolescence. *Developmental Psychology,* **23,** 292–297.

**Adams, P. L., Milner, J. R., & Schrepf, N. A.** (1984). *Fatherless children.* New York: Wiley-Interscience.

**Adelson, J.** (1971). The political imagination of the young adolescent. *Daedalus,* **100,** 1013–1050.

**Adelson, J.** (1975). The development of ideology in adolescence. In S. E. Dragastin & G. H. Elder, Jr. (Eds.), *Adolescence in the life cycle: Psychological change and social context* (pp. 63–78). New York: Wiley.

**Adelson, J.** (1982, Summer). Rites of passage: How children learn the principles of community. *American Educator,* 6 ff.

**Adelson, J.** (1986). *Inventing adolescence: The political psychology of everyday schooling.* New Brunswick, NJ: Transaction Books.

**Adelson, J.** (1991). Political development. In R. M. Lerner, A. C. Petersen, & J. Brooks-Gunn (Eds.), *Encyclopedia of adolescence,* **Vol. II.** (pp. 792–793). New York: Garland Publishing.

**Adolescent pregnancy: Testing prevention strategies.** (1986 Summer/Fall). *Carnegie Quarterly,* **31** (3 and 4), 1–7.

**Alan Guttmacher Institute.** (1994). *Sex and America's teenagers.* New York: Author.

**Albert, R. S., & Runco, M. A.** (1989). Independence and the creative potential of gifted and exceptionally gifted boys. *Journal of Youth and Adolescence,* **18,** 221–230.

**Alcohol and health.** (1994). Eight special reports to the U.S. Congress from the Secretary of Health and Human Services. Washington, DC: National Institute on Drug Abuse.

**Alexander, J. F.** (1973). Defensive and supportive communications in normal and deviant families. *Journal of Consulting and Clinical Psychology,* **40,** 223–231.

**Alexander, J. F., & Parsons, B. V.** (1973). Short term behavioral intervention with delinquent families: Impact on family processes and recidivism. *Journal of Abnormal Psychology,* **81,** 219–225.

**Alexander, P. C., Moore, S., & Alexander, E. R., III.** (1991). What is transmitted in the intergenerational transmission of violence? *Journal of Marriage and the Family,* **53,** 657–668.

**Allen, J. P., Hauser, S. T., Bell, K. L., & O'Connor, T. G.** (1994). Longitudinal assessment of autonomy and relatedness in adolescent–family interactions as predictors of adolescent ego development and self-esteem. *Child Development,* **65,** 179–194.

**Allen, J. P., Weissberg, R. P., & Hawkins, J. A.** (1989). The relation between values and social competence in early adolescence. *Developmental Psychology,* **25,** 458–464.

**Allen, K., Moss, A., Giovino, G. A., Shopland, D. R., & Pierce, J. P.** (1993). Teenage tobacco use data: Estimates from the teenage attitudes and practices survey, United States, 1989. *Advance Data,* **224.**

**Allgood-Merten, B., & Stockard, J.** (1991). Sex role identity and self-esteem: A comparison of children and adolescents. *Sex Roles,* **25,** 129–139.

**Allison, P. D., & Furstenberg, F. F.** (1989). How marital dissolution affects children: Variations by age and sex. *Developmental Psychology,* **25,** 540–549.

**Almeida, D. M., & Galambos, N. L.** (1991). Examining father involvement and the quality of father–adolescent relations. *Journal of Research on Adolescence,* **1,** 155–172.

**Almeida, D. M., Maggs, J. L., & Galambos, N. L.** (1993). Wives' employment hours and spousal participation in family work. *Journal of Family Psychology,* **7,** 233–244.

**Almquist, E. M., & Angrist, S. S.** (1971). Role model influences on college women's career aspirations. *Merrill-Palmer Quarterly,* **71,** 263–279.

**Alsaker, F. D.** (1992). Pubertal timing, overweight, and psychological adjustment. *Journal of Early Adolescence,* **12,** 396–419.

**Alton, I. R.** (1982). Nutritional needs and assessment of adolescents. In R. W. Blum (Ed), *Adolescent healthcare.* New York: Academic Press.

**Amato, P. R., & Keith, B.** (1991a). Parental divorce and adult well-being: A meta-analysis. *Journal of Marriage and the Family,* **53,** 43–58.

Amato, P. R., & Keith, B. (1991b). Parental divorce and the well-being of children: A meta-analysis. *Psychological Bulletin,* **110,** 26–46.

Ambert, A. (1994). A qualitative study of peer abuse and its effects: Theoretical and empirical implications. *Journal of Marriage and the Family,* **56,** 119–130.

America 2000. (1991). *Congressional Digest, 70,* 294–295.

*America's youth 1977–1988.* (1988). Princeton, NJ: George Gallup International Institute.

American Psychiatric Association. (1994). *Diagnostic and statistical manual of mental disorders (DSM-IV)* (4th ed.). Washington, DC: American Psychiatric Association.

Andrews, J. A., Hops, H., Ary, D., Tildesley, E., & Harris, J. (1993). Parental influence on early adolescent substance use: Specific and nonspecific effects. *Journal of Early Adolescence, 13,* 285–310.

Aneshensel, C. S., & Rosen, B. C. (1980). Domestic roles and sex differences in occupational expectations. *Journal of Marriage and the Family,* **42,** 121–131.

Anthenelli, R. M., & Schuckit, M. A. (1992). Genetics. In J. H. Lowinson, P. Ruiz, R. B. Millman, & J. G. Langrod (Eds.), *Substance abuse: A comprehensive textbook* (2nd ed., pp. 39–50). Baltimore: Williams & Wilkins.

Anthony, E. J. (1974). Psychotherapy of adolescence. In G. Caplan (Ed.), *American handbook of psychiatry,* **Vol. II:** *Child and adolescent psychiatry, sociocultural and community psychiatry* (pp. 234–249). New York: Basic Books.

Applebee, A. N., Langer, J. A., & Mullis, I. V. S. (1986). *The writing report card: Writing achievement in American schools.* Princeton, NJ: National Assessment of Educational Progress, Educational Testing Service.

Applebome, P. (1996, Jan. 12). Crime fear is seen forcing changes in youth behavior. *The New York Times,* p. A6.

Arafat, I. S., & Cotton, W. L. (1974). Masturbation practices of males and females. *Journal of Sex Research, 10,* 293–307.

Arbuthnot, J., Gordon, D. A., & Jurkovic, G. J. (1987). Personality. In H. C. Quay (Ed.), *Handbook of juvenile delinquency* (pp. 139–183). New York: Wiley.

Archer, S. L. (1985). Career and/or family: The identity process for adolescent girls. *Youth and Society,* **16,** 289–314.

Archer, S. L. (1989). Gender differences in identity development: Issues of process, domain and timing. *Journal of Adolescence,* **12,** 117–138.

Archer, S. L., & Waterman, A. S. (1990). Varieties of identity diffusions and foreclosures: An exploration of subcategories of identity statuses. *Journal of Adolescent Research, 5,* 96–111.

Ariès, E. (1974, Aug. 30–Sept. 3). *Interaction patterns and themes of male, female, and mixed groups.* Paper presented at the annual meeting of the American Psychological Association, New Orleans.

Ariès, P. (1962). *Centuries of childhood: A social history of family life* (R. Baldick, trans.). New York: Random House.

Aristotle. *Ethica Nicomachea.* (1941). In R. McKeon (Ed.), *The basic works of Aristotle* (W. D. Ross, trans.). New York: Random House.

Arnett, J. (1992). Reckless behavior in adolescence: A developmental perspective. *Developmental Review, 12,* 339–373.

Asarnow, J. R. (1988). Children at risk for schizophrenia: Converging lines of evidence. *Schizophrenic Bulletin,* **14,** 613–631.

Asher, S. A., & Renshaw, P. D. (1981). Children without friends: Social knowledge and social skill training. In S. R. Asher & J. M. Gottman (Eds.), *The development of children's friendships.* New York: Cambridge University Press.

Astin, A. W., Green, K. C., Korn, W. S., Schalit, M., & Berz, E. R. (1988). *The American Freshman: National norms for fall 1988.* Los Angeles: Higher Education Research Institute, University of California.

Astin, A. W., Korn, W. S., & Riggs, E. R. (1993). *The American freshman: National norms for fall 1993.* Los Angeles: Higher Education Research Institute, University of California.

Astin, A. W., Korn, W. S., Sax, L. J., & Mahoney, K. M. (1994). *The American freshman: National norms for fall 1994.* Los Angeles: Higher Education Research Institute, University of California.

Astin, A. W., Korn, W. S., Sax, L. J., & Mahoney, K. M. (1995). *The American freshman: National norms for fall 1995.* Los Angeles: Higher Education Research Institute, University of California.

Astone, N. M. (1993). Are adolescent mothers just single mothers? *Journal of Research on Adolescence, 3,* 353–371.

Astone, N. M., & Upchurch, D. M. (1994). Forming a family, leaving school early, and earning a GED: A racial and cohort comparison. *Journal of Marriage and the Family,* **56,** 759–771.

Atkinson, R. L., Atkinson, R. C., Smith, E. E., & Hilgard, E. R. (1987). *Introduction to psychology* (9th ed.). New York: Harcourt Brace Jovanovich.

Attie, I., & Brooks-Gunn, J. (1989). Development of eating problems in adolescent girls. *Developmental Psychology,* **25,** 70–79.

Ausubel, D. P. (1954). *Theory and problems of adolescent development.* New York: Grune & Stratton.

Averch, H. A., et al. (1974). *How effective is schooling? A critical review of research.* Englewood Cliffs, NJ: Educational Technology Publications.

Azima, F. J., & Richmond, L. H. (Eds.). (1989). *Adolescent group psychotherapy.* New York: International Universities Press.

Bacas, H. (1986, Aug.). Where are the teenagers? *Nation's Business,* pp. 18–25.

Bachman, J. G. (1970). *Youth in transition,* **Vol II:** *The impact of family background and intelligence on tenth-grade boys.* Ann Arbor: Institute for Social Research, University of Michigan.

Bachman, J. G., & Johnston, L. D. (1979). *Fewer rebels, fewer causes: A profile of today's college freshmen.* Ann Arbor: Survey Research Center, Institute for Social Research, University of Michigan.

Bachman, J. G., & Johnston, L. D. (1980). *Fewer rebels, fewer causes: A profile of today's college freshmen. Monitoring the future.* Occasional Paper 4. Ann Arbor: Institute of Social Research, University of Michigan.

Bachman, J. G., Green, S., & Wirtanen, I. (1972). *Dropping out—Problem or symptom.* Ann Arbor: Institute for Social Research, University of Michigan.

Bachman, J. G., Johnston, L. D., & O'Malley, P. M. (1981). *Monitoring the future: Questionnaire responses from the nation's high school seniors, 1980.* Ann Arbor: Institute for Social Research, The University of Michigan.

Bachman, J. G., Johnston, L. D., & O'Malley, P. M. (1987). *Monitoring the future: Questionnaire responses from the nation's high school seniors, 1986.* Ann Arbor: Institute for Social Research, University of Michigan.

Bachman, J. G., Johnston, L. D., & O'Malley, P. M. (1993). *Monitoring the future: Questionnaire responses of the nation's high school seniors, 1992.* Ann Arbor: Institute for Social Research, University of Michigan.

Bachman, J. G., Johnston, L. D., & O'Malley, P. M. (in preparation). *Monitoring the future: Questionnaire responses from the nation's high school seniors, 1994.* Ann Arbor: Institute for Social Research, University of Michigan.

Bachman, J. G., & O'Malley, P. M. (1978). *The search for school effects: Some new findings and perspectives.* Unpublished manuscript. Ann Arbor: Institute for Social Research, University of Michigan.

Bachman, J. G., O'Malley, P. M., & Johnston, J. (1978). *Youth in transition,* **Vol. VI:** *Adolescence to adulthood—change and stability in the lives of young men.* Ann Arbor: Institute for Social Research, University of Michigan.

Bachman, J. G., & Schulenberg, J. (1993). How part-time work intensity relates to drug use, problem behavior, time use, and satisfaction among high school seniors: Are these consequences, or merely correlates? *Developmental Psychology, 28,* 210–221.

Bachrach, C. A., Clogg, C. C., & Carver, K. (1993). Outcomes of early childbearing: Summary of a conference. *Journal of Research on Adolescence, 3,* 337–348.

Bailey, J. M., & Pillard, R. C. (1991). A genetic study of male sexual orientation. *Archives of General Psychiatry, 48,* 1089–1096.

Bailey, J. M., Pillard, R. C., Neale, M. C., & Agyei, Y. (1993). Heritable factors influence sexual orientation in women. *Archives of General Psychiatry, 50,* 217–223.

Baldwin, J. D., & Baldwin, J. I. (1989). The socialization of homosexuality and heterosexuality in a non-Western society. *Archives of Sexual Behavior, 18,* 13–29.

Baldwin, W. (1993). The consequences of early childbearing: A perspective. *Journal of Research on Adolescence, 3,* 349–352.

Bales, J. (1986, Nov.). New studies cite drug use dangers. *The American Psychological Association Monitor,* p. 28.

Baltes, P. B. (1987). Theoretical propositions of life-span developmental psychology: On the dynamics between growth and decline. *Developmental Psychology, 23,* 611–626.

Baltes, P. B., Reese, H. W., & Lipsitt, L. P. (1980). Life-span developmental psychology. *Annual Review of Psychology, 31,* 65–110.

Baltes, P. B., & Willis, S. L. (1982). Plasticity and enhancement of intellectual functioning in old age. In F. I. M. Craik & S. E. Trehub (Eds.), *Aging and cognitive processes* (pp. 353–389). New York: Plenum.

Bandura, A. (1964). The stormy decade: Fact or fiction? *Psychology in the Schools, 1,* 224–231.

Bandura, A. (1967). The role of modelling processes in personality development. In W. W. Hartup & N. L. Smothergill (Eds.), *The young child: Reviews of research.* Washington, DC: National Association for the Education of Young Children.

Bandura, A. (1977a). Self-efficacy: Toward a unifying theory of behavioral change. *Psychological Review, 84,* 191–215.

Bandura, A. (1977b). *Social learning theory.* Englewood Cliffs, NJ: Prentice-Hall.

Bank, L., Marlowe, J. H., Reid, L. B., Patterson, G. R., & Weinrott M. R. (1991). A comparative evaluation of parent-training interventions for families of chronic delinquents. *Journal of Abnormal Child Psychology, 19,* 15–33.

Barber, B. K. (1992). Family, personality, and adolescent problem behaviors. *Journal of Marriage and the Family, 54,* 69–79.

Barber, B. L., & Eccles, J. S. (1992). Long-term influence of divorce and single parenting on adolescent family- and work-related values, behaviors, and aspirations. *Psychological Bulletin, 111,* 108–126.

Barber, J. K. (1991). Bulimia nervosa. In J. M. Weiner (Ed.), *Textbook of child and adolescent psychiatry* (pp. 376–381). Washington, DC: American Psychiatric Press.

Barich, B. (1986, Nov. 3). A reporter at large: The crazy life. *The New Yorker,* pp. 97–130.

Barinaga, M. (1995). "Obese" protein slims mice. *Science, 269,* 475–478.

Barker, R. G., & Gump, P. V. (Eds.) (1964). *Big school, small school.* Stanford, CA: Stanford University Press.

Barker, R. G., & Wright, H. F. (1971). *Midwest and its children: The psychological ecology of an American town.* Hamden, CT: Archor Books. (Original work published in 1955 by Harper & Row).

Barling, J. (1991). Father's employment: A neglected influence on children. In J. V. Lerner & N. L. Galambos (Eds.), *Employed others and their children* (pp. 181–209). New York: Garland.

Barlow, D. H. (1988). *Anxiety and its disorders.* New York: Guilford Press.

Barnes, G. M. (1984). Adolescent alcohol abuse and other problem behaviors: Their relationships and common parental influences. *Journal of Adolescence and Youth, 13,* 329–348.

Barnes, H., & Olson, D. H. (1985). Parent–child communication and the circumplex model. *Child Development, 56,* 438–447.

Barnett, R., & Volker, J. M. (1985). *Moral judgment as life experience.* Unpublished manuscript. Minneapolis: University of Minnesota.

Barry, H., III, & Schlegel, A. (1986). Cultural customs that influence sexual freedom in adolescence. *Ethnology, 25,* 151–162.

Baruch, G. K. (1972). Maternal influences upon college women's attitudes toward women and work. *Developmental Psychology, 6,* 32–37.

Bassuk, E. L., & Rubin, L. (1987). Homeless children: A neglected population. *American Journal of Orthopsychiatry, 57,* 279–286.

Baughman, E. E. (1971). *Black Americans.* New York: Academic Press.

Baumrind, D. (1979). *Sex-related socialization effects.* Paper presented at the meeting of the Society for Research in Child Development, San Francisco.

Baumrind, D. (1987). A developmental perspective on adolescent risk taking in contemporary America. In C. E. Irwin

(Ed.), *Adolescent social behavior and health, New Directions for Child Development* (No. 37, pp. 93–125). San Francisco: Jossey-Bass.

**Baumrind, D.** (1989, Aug.). *The influence of parenting style on adolescent competence and problem behavior.* G. Stanley Hall Award address presented at the annual meeting of the American Psychological Association, New Orleans.

**Baumrind, D.** (1991a). The influences of parenting style on adolescent competence and substance use. *Journal of Early Adolescence, 11,* 56–95.

**Baumrind, D.** (1991b). Effective parenting during the early adolescent transition. In P. E. Cowan & E. M. Hetherington (Eds.), *Advances in family research* (**Vol. 2,** pp. 111–163). Hillsdale, NJ: Lawrence Erlbaum Associates.

**Baumrind, D., & Moselle, K. A.** (1985). A developmental perspective on adolescent drug abuse. *Advances in Alcohol and Substance Abuse, 4,* 41–67.

**Baumrind, D., Moselle, K. A., & Martin, J. A.** (1985). Adolescent drug abuse research: A critical examination from a developmental perspective. *Advances in Alcohol and Substance Abuse, 4,* 41–67.

**Bayley, N.** (1949). Consistency and variability in the growth of intelligence from birth to eighteen years. *Journal of Genetic Psychology, 75,* 165–196.

**Bayley, N.** (1966). Learning in adulthood: The role of intelligence. In H. J. Klausmeier & C. W. Harris (Eds.), *Analysis of concept learning* (pp. 117–138). New York: Academic Press.

**Bayley, N.** (1970). Development of mental abilities. In P. H. Mussen (Ed.), *Carmichael's manual of child psychology* (3rd ed., **Vol. 1,** pp. 1163–1209). New York: Wiley.

**Bayley, N.** (1971). Learning in adulthood: The role of intelligence. In M. C. Jones, N. Bayley, J. W. Macfarlane, & M. P. Honzik (Eds.), *The course of human development.* Waltham, MA: Xerox Publishing Co.

**Becker, W. C.** (1964). Consequences of different kinds of parental discipline. In M. L. Hoffman & L. W. Hoffman (Eds.), *Review of child development research* (**Vol. 1,** pp. 169–280). New York: Russell Sage Foundation.

**Behrman, R. E., Vaughn, V. C., & Nelson, W. E.** (1987). *Textbook of pediatrics* (13th ed.). Philadelphia: W.B. Saunders.

**Bell, A. P.** (1969). Role modelling of fathers in adolescence and young adulthood. *Journal of Counseling Psychology, 16,* 30–35.

**Bell, A. P., & Weinberg, M. S.** (1978). *Homosexualities: A study of diversity among men and women.* New York: Simon & Schuster.

**Bell, A. P., Weinberg, M. S., & Hammersmith, S. K.** (1981). *Sexual preference: Its development in men and women.* Bloomington: Indiana University Press.

**Bell, N. J., & Bell, R. W. (Eds.)** (1993). *Adolescent risk taking.* Newbury Park: Sage.

**Bell, N., Avery, A. W., Jenkins, D., Feld, J., & Schoenrock, C. J.** (1985). Family relationships and social competence during late adolescence. *Journal of Youth and Adolescence, 14,* 109–119.

**Bell, R.** (1988). *Changing bodies, changing lives: A book for teens on sex and relationships (rev. ed).* New York: Random House.

**Bell, R., & Wildflower, L. Z.** (1983). *Talking with your teenager: A book for parents.* New York: Random House.

**Bell, R. Q.** (1979). Parent, child, and reciprocal influences. *American Psychologist, 34,* 821–826.

**Belsky, J., Lerner, R. M., & Spanier, G. B.** (1984). *The child in the family.* Reading, MA: Addison-Wesley.

**Belsky, J., Steinberg, L., & Draper, P.** (1991). Childhood experience, interpersonal development, and reproductive strategy: An evolutionary theory of socialization. *Child Development, 62,* 647–670.

**Belsky, J., & Vondra, J.** (1989). Lessons from child abuse: The determinants of parenting. In D. Cicchetti & V. Carlson (Eds.), *Child maltreatment: Theory and research on the causes and consequences of child abuse and neglect* (pp. 153–202). New York: Cambridge University Press.

**Bem, S. L.** (1975). Sex-role adaptability: One consequence of psychological androgyny. *Journal of Personality and Social Psychology, 31,* 634–643.

**Bemis, K. M.** (1987). The present status of operant conditioning for the treatment of anorexia nervosa. *Behavior Modification, 11,* 432–463.

**Benbow, C. P.** (1992). Academic achievement in mathematics and science of students between ages 13 and 23: Are there differences in the top one percent of mathematical ability? *Journal of Educational Psychology, 84,* 51–61.

**Benbow, C. P., & Stanley, J. C.** (1980). Sex differences in mathematical ability. *Science, 210,* 1262–1264.

**Benin, M. H., & Edwards, D. A.** (1990). Adolescents' chores: The difference between dual- and single-earner families. *Journal of Marriage and the Family, 52,* 361–373.

**Benson, M. J., Harris, P. B., & Rogers, C. S.** (1992). Identity consequences of attachment to mothers and fathers among late adolescents. *Journal of Research on Adolescence, 2,* 187–204.

**Berg, C. A.** (1992). Perspectives for viewing intellectual development throughout the life course. In R. J. Sternberg & C. A. Berg (Eds.), *Intellectual development* (pp. 1–15). Cambridge: Cambridge University Press.

**Berg, I.** (1991). School avoidance, school phobia, and truancy. In M. Lewis (Ed.), *Child and adolescent psychiatry: A comprehensive textbook* (pp. 1092–1098). Baltimore: Williams & Wilkins.

**Berg, I., Collins, R., McGuire, R., & O'Melia, J.** (1975). Educational attainment in adolescent school phobia. *Psychological Medicine, 4,* 428–434.

**Berkowitz, M., Oser, F., & Althof, W.** (1987). The development of sociomoral discourse. In W. M. Kurtines & J. L. Gewirtz (Eds.), *Moral development through social interaction* (pp. 322–352). New York: Wiley.

**Berndt, T. J.** (1979). Developmental changes in conformity to peers and parents. *Developmental Psychology, 15,* 606–616.

**Berndt, T. J.** (1982). The features and effects of friendship in early adolescence. *Child Development, 53,* 1447–1460.

**Berndt, T. J.** (1992). Friendship and friends' influence in adolescence. *Current Directions in Psychological Science, 1,* 156–159.

**Berndt, T. J., & Hawkins, J.** (1985, April). *The effects of friendships on students' adjustment after the transition to high school.* Paper presented at the annual meeting of the American Educational Research Association, Chicago.

Berndt, T. J., & Mekos, D. (1995). Adolescents' perceptions of the stressful and desirable aspects of the transition to junior high school. *Journal of Research on Adolescence, 5,* 123–142.

Bernstein, B., & Shkuda, A. N. (1974). *The young drug user: Attitudes and obstacles to treatment.* New York Center for New York City Affairs. New York: New School.

Bernstein, G. A., & Borchardt, C. M. (1991). Anxiety disorders of childhood and adolescence: A critical review. *Journal of the American Academy of Child and Adolescent Psychiatry, 30,* 519–532.

Berretini, W., Ferraro, T. N., Goldin, L. R., et al. (1994). Chromosome 18 DNA markers and manic–depressive illness: Evidence for a susceptibility gene. *Proceedings of the National Academy of Sciences, 91,* 5918–5921.

Berrueta-Clement, J., & Schweinhart, L., Barnett, W., & Weikart, D. (1986). In J. Burchard, & S. Burchard (Eds.), *Prevention of delinquent behavior* (pp. 220–240). Newbury Park, CA: Sage.

Beyth-Marom, R., Austin, L., Fischhoff, B., Palmgren, C., & Jacobs-Quadrel, M. (1993). Perceived consequences of risky behaviors: Adults and adolescents. *Developmental Psychology, 29,* 549–563.

Bianchi, S. M. (1982). Private school enrollment: Trends and debates. In A. C. Kerckhoff (Ed.), *Research in sociology in education and socialization* **(Vol. 3).** Greenwich, CT: JAI Press.

Bibby, R. W., & Posterski, D. C. (1992). *Teen trends: A nation in motion.* Toronto: Stoddart.

Bidwell, C. E., & Quiroz, P. A. (1991). Organizational control in the high school workplace: A theoretical argument. *Journal of Research on Adolescence, 1,* 211–230.

Billy, J. O. G., & Udry, J. R. (1985). Patterns of adolescent friendship and effects on sexual behavior. *Social Psychological Quarterly, 48,* 27–41.

Binder, A. (1988). Juvenile delinquency. *Annual Review of Psychology, 39,* 253–282.

Black, B. (1995). Separation anxiety disorder and panic disorder. In J. S. March (Ed.), *Anxiety disorders in children and adolescents* (pp. 212–234). New York: Guilford Press.

Blanchard, R., Zucker, K. J., Bradley, S. J., & Hume, C. S. (1995). Birth order and sibling ratio in homosexual male adolescents and probably prehomosexual feminine boys. *Developmental Psychology, 31,* 22–30.

Blasi, A. (1980). Bridging moral cognition and moral action: A critical review of the literature. *Psychological Bulletin, 88,* 1–45.

Blasi, A. (1984). Moral identity: Its role in moral functioning. In W. M. Kurtines & J. L. Gewirtz (Eds.), *Morality, moral behavior, and moral development* (pp. 128–139). New York: Academic Press.

Block, J. H. (1973). Conceptions of sex role: Some cross-cultural and longitudinal perspectives. *American Psychologist, 28,* 512–526.

Block, J. H. (1984). *Sex role identity and ego development.* San Fransisco: Jossey-Bass.

Block, J. H., Block, J., & Gjerde, P. F. (1986). The personality of children prior to divorce: A prospective study. *Child Development, 57,* 827–840.

Bloom, B. (1985). *Developing talent in young people.* New York: Ballantine.

Blos, P. (1971a). *On Adolescence.* New York: Free Press.

Blos, P. (1971b). The child analyst looks at the young adolescent. *Daedalus, 100,* 961–978.

Blos, P. (1979a). *The adolescent passage: Developmental issues.* New York: International Universities Press.

Blos, P. (1979b). Modifications in the classical psychoanalytical model of adolescence. *Adolescent Psychiatry, 7,* 6–25.

Blum, R. H., et al. (1972). *Horatio Alger's children.* San Francisco: Jossey-Bass.

Blume, J. (1990, June). Tales of a mother/confessor. *Newsweek Special Issue: The New Teens,* pp. 18, 20.

Blume, S. B. (1992). Alcohol and other drug problems in women. In J. H. Lowinson, P. Ruiz, R. B. Millman, & J. G. Langrod (Eds.), *Substance abuse: A comprehensive textbook* (2nd ed., pp. 794–807). Baltimore: Williams & Wilkins.

Blyth, D. A., Hill, J. P., & Smyth, C. K. (1981). The influence of older adolescents on younger adolescents: Do grade-level arrangements make a difference in behaviors, attitudes, and experiences? *Journal of Early Adolescence, 1,* 85–110.

Blyth, D., Hill, J., & Thiel, K. (1982). Early adolescents' significant others: Grade and gender differences in perceived relationship with familial and non-familial adults and young people. *Journal of Youth and Adolescence, 11,* 425–440.

Blyth, D. A., Simmons, R. G., Bulcroft, R., Felt, D., Van-Cleave, E. F., & Bush, D. M. (1981). The effects of physical development on self-image and satisfaction with body-image for early adolescent males. In R. G. Simmons (Ed.), *Research in Community and Mental Health, 2,* 43–73. Greenwich, CT: JAI Press.

Blyth, D. A., Simmons, R. G., & Carlton-Ford, S. (1983). The adjustment of early adolescents to school transitions. *Journal of Early Adolescence, 3,* 105–120.

Board on Mathematical Sciences/Mathematical Sciences Education Board. (1989). *Everybody counts: A report to the nation on the future of mathematics education.* Washington, DC: National Academy Press.

Bodmer, W. F., & Cavalli-Sforza, L. L. (1970). Intelligence and race. *Scientific American, 4,* 19–29.

Boeck, M. A. (1992). Disorders of appetite. In S. J. Segalowitz & I. Rapin (Eds.), *Handbook of neuropsychology* (Vol. 7, pp. 357–372). Amsterdam, Netherlands: Elsevier Science.

Boehnke, K., Silvereisen, R. K., Eisenberg, N., Reykowski, J., & Palmonari, A. (1989). Developmental pattern of prosocial motivation: A cross-national study. *Journal of Cross-National Psychology, 20,* 219–243.

Bolger, N., Downey, G., Walker, E., & Steininger, P. (1989). The onset of suicidal ideation in childhood and adolescence. *Journal of Youth and Adolescence, 18,* 175–190.

Booth, A., & Amato, P. R. (1994). Parental marital quality, parental divorce, and relations with parents. *Journal of Marriage and the Family, 56,* 21–34.

Borow, H. (1966). Development of occupational motives and roles. *Review of Child Development Research* (Vol. 2, pp. 373–422). Chicago: University of Chicago Press.

**Boskind-White, M., & White, W. C.** (1983). *Bulimarexia: The binge/purge cycle.* New York: Norton.

**Botwinick, J.** (1977). Intellectual abilities. In J. E. Birren, & K. W. Schaie (Eds.), *Handbook of the psychology of aging* (pp. 580–605). New York: Van Nostrand Reinhold.

**Bouchard, C., & Pérusse, L.** (1993). Genetic aspects of obesity. In C. L. Williams & S. Y. S. Kimm (Eds.), *Prevention and treatment of childhood obesity* (pp. 26–35). New York: The New York Academy of Sciences.

**Bouchard, T. J., Jr., & McGee, M.** (1981). Familial studies of intelligence: A review. *Science, 212,* 1055–1059.

**Bower, G. H., & Hilgard, E. R.** (1981). *Theories of learning* (5th ed.). Englewood Cliffs, NJ: Prentice-Hall.

**Bowlby, J.** (1969). *Attachment*: **Vol. 1.** *Attachment and loss.* New York: Basic Books.

**Bowler, S., Sheon, A. R., D'Angelo, L. J., & Vermund, S. H.** (1992). HIV and AIDS among adolescents in the United States: Increasing risk in the 1990s. *Journal of Adolescence, 15,* 345–371.

**Boyer, E. L.** (1983). *High school: A report on secondary education in America.* New York: Harper & Row.

**Boys Clubs of America** (1986, 1987). *Targeted outreach Newsletters,* II–1, III–1.

**Braddock, J. H., & McPartland, J. M.** (1992). *Education of at-risk youth: Recent trends, current status, and future needs.* Commissioned paper for the Panel on High Risk Youth, Commission on Behavioral and Social Sciences and Education, National Research Council, Washington, DC.

**Bradley, R. H., Caldwell, B. M., & Elardo, R.** (1977). Home environment, social status, and mental test performance. *Journal of Educational Psychology, 69,* 697–70l.

**Braithwaite, J.** (1981). The myth of social class and criminality reconsidered. *American Sociological Review, 46,* 36–57.

**Brand, D.** (1987, August 31). The new whiz kids. *Time,* pp. 42–5l.

**Braucht, G. N.** (1980). Psychosocial research on teenage drinking: Past and future. In F. R. Scarapeteti & S. K. Datesman (Eds.), *Sage Annual Review of Drug and Alcohol Abuse, 4,* 109–143.

**Braucht, G. N.** (1984). Problem drinking among adolescents: A review and analysis of psychosocial research. In *National Institute on Alcohol Abuse and Alcoholism, Special Population Issues. Alcohol and Health Monograph No. 4.* Rockville, MD: The Institute.

**Brecher, F. M.** (1971). *The sex researchers.* New York: New American Library.

**Brehm, N. M., & Khantzian, E. J.** (1992). A psychodynamic perspective. In J. H. Lowinson, P. Ruiz, R. B. Millman, & J. G. Langrod (Eds.), *Substance abuse: A comprehensive textbook* (2nd ed., pp. 106–117). Baltimore: Williams & Wilkins.

**Brennan, T., Huizinga, D., & Elliot, D. S.** (1978). *The social psychology of runaways.* Lexington, MA: D.C. Heath.

**Briere, J., & Runtz, M.** (1988). Symptomatology associated with childhood sexual victimization in a nonclinical adult sample. *Child Abuse & Neglect, 12,* 51–59.

**Briere, J., & Runtz, M.** (1990). Differential adult symptomatology associated with three types of child abuse histories. *Child Abuse & Neglect, 14,* 357–364.

**Briere, J., & Runtz, M.** (1991). The long-term effects of sexual abuse: A review and synthesis. In J. Briere (Ed.), *Treating victims of child sexual abuse* (pp. 3–13). New Directions for Mental Health Services (No. 51). San Francisco: Jossey-Bass.

**Briere, J., Evans, D., Runtz, M., & Wall, T.** (1988). Symptomatology in men who were molested as children: A comparison study. *American Journal of Orthopsychiatry, 58,* 457–461.

**Britton, P. O., De Maruo, D., & Gambrell, A. E.** (1992/93). HIV/AIDS education: SIECUS study on HIV/AIDS education for schools finds states make progress but work remains. *SIECUS Report, 21* (2), 1–8.

**Brody, J. E.** (1988, Aug. 30). Widespread abuse of drugs by pregnant women is found. *The New York Times,* p. 16.

**Bronfenbrenner, U.** (1960). Freudian theories of identification and their derivatives. *Child Development, 31,* 15–40.

**Bronfenbrenner, U.** (1970). *Two worlds of childhood: U.S. and U.S.S.R.* New York: Russell Sage Foundation.

**Bronfenbrenner, U.** (1977). Toward an experimental ecology of human development. *American Psychologist, 32,* 513–531.

**Bronfenbrenner, U.** (1979). Contexts of child rearing: Problems and prospects. *American Psychologist, 34,* 844–850.

**Bronfenbrenner, U.** (1985). Freedom and discipline across the decades. In G. Becker, H. Becker, & L. Huber (Eds.), *Ordnung and Unordnung [Order and Disorder]* (pp. 326–339). Weinheim, West Germany: Beltz Berlag.

**Bronfenbrenner, U., Alvarez, W. F., & Henderson, C. R., Jr.** (1984). Working and watching: Maternal employment status and parents' perceptions of their three-year-old children. *Child Development, 55,* 1362–1378.

**Bronfenbrenner, U., & Crouter, A.** (1982). Work and family through time and space. In S. B. Kamerman & C. D. Hayes (Eds.), *Families that work: Children in a changing world* (pp. 39–83). Washington, DC: National Academy Press.

**Bronfenbrenner, U., Moen, P., & Garbarino, J.** (1984). Child, family and community. In R. D. Parke (Ed.), *Review of child development research*: **Vol. 7.** *The family* (pp. 283–328). Chicago: University of Chicago Press.

**Bronstein, P.** (1988). Marital and parenting roles in transition: An overview. In P. Bronstein & C. P. Cowan (Eds.), *Fatherhood today: Men's changing roles in the family* (pp. 66–78). New York: Wiley.

**Brook, J. S., Brook, D. W., Gordon, A. S., Whiteman, M., & Cohen, P.** (1990). The psychosocial etiology of adolescent drug use: A family interactional approach. *Genetic, Social, and General Psychology Monographs, 116.*

**Brooks-Gunn, J.** (1988). *Psychological adaptation to the early adolescent transition: Biological and social contributions.* Paper presented at the annual meeting of the American Psychological Association, New York.

**Brooks-Gunn, J.** (1991). Motivational timing variations in adolescent girls, consequences of. In R. M. Lerner, A. C. Petersen, & J. Brooks-Gunn. *Encyclopedia of adolescence* (**Vol. 2,** pp. 897–926).

**Brooks-Gunn, J., & Furstenberg, F. F., Jr.** (1989). Adolescent sexual behavior. *American Psychologist, 44,* 249–257.

**Brooks-Gunn, J., Guo, G., & Furstenberg, F. F., Jr.** (1993). Who drops out of and who continues beyond high school? A 20-year follow-up of black urban youth. *Journal of Research on Adolescence, 3,* 271–294.

**Brooks-Gunn, J., & Reiter, E. O.** (1990). The role of pubertal processes. In S. S. Feldman & G. R. Elliott (Eds.), *At the threshold: The developing adolescent* (pp. 16–53). Cambridge, MA: Harvard University Press.

**Brooks-Gunn, J., & Ruble, D. N.** (1983). The experience of menarche from a developmental perspective. In J. Brooks-Gunn & A. C. Petersen (Eds.), *Girls at puberty: Biological, psychological, and social perspectives* (pp. 155–178). New York: Plenum.

**Brooks-Gunn, J., & Warren, M. P.** (1985). Effects of delayed menarche in different contexts: Dance and nondance students. *Journal of Youth and Adolescence, 14,* 285–300.

**Brooks-Gunn, J., & Warren, M. P.** (1989). Biological and social contributions to negative affect in young adolescent girls. *Child Development, 60,* 40–55.

**Brophy, J.** (1986). Teacher influences on student achievement. *American Psychologist, 41,* 1069–1077.

**Brown, A. L., Bransford, J. D., Ferrara, R. A., & Campione, J. C.** (1983). Learning, remembering, and understanding. In J. H. Flavell & E. M. Markman (Eds.), *Handbook of child psychology: Cognitive development* (**Vol. 3,** pp. 77–166). New York: Wiley.

**Brown, B. B.** (1989). The role of peer groups in adolescent's adjustment to secondary school. In T. J. Berndt & G. W. Ladd (Eds.), *Peer relationships in child development* (pp. 188–215). New York: Wiley.

**Brown, B. B.** (1990). Peer groups and peer cultures. In S. S. Feldman & G. R. Elliot (Eds.), *At the threshold: The developing adolescent.* (pp. 171–196). Cambridge, MA: Harvard University Press.

**Brown, B. B., Clasen, D. R., & Eicher, S. A.** (1986). Perceptions of peer pressure, peer conformity, dispositions, and self-reported behavior among adolescents. *Developmental Psychology, 22,* 521–530.

**Brown, B. B., Mounts, N., Lamborn, S. D., & Steinberg, L.** (1993). Parenting practices and peer group affiliation in adolescence. *Child Development, 64,* 467–482.

**Browne, A., & Finkelhor, D.** (1986). Impact of child sexual abuse: A review of the research. *Psychological Bulletin, 99,* 66–77.

**Bruch, H.** (1973). *Eating disorders.* New York: Basic Books.

**Bruch, H.** (1974). Eating disturbances in adolescence. In G. Caplan (Ed.), *American handbook of psychiatry:* **Vol. II.** *Child and adolescent psychiatry, sociocultural and community psychiatry* (pp. 275–286). New York: Basic Books.

**Bruch, H.** (1979). Anorexia nervosa: Theory and therapy. *American Journal of Psychiatry, 139,* 1531–1538.

**Bryant, T. E., et al.** (1978). *Report to the President from the President's Commission on Mental Health* **(Vol. I).** Washington, DC: U.S. Government Printing Office.

**Buchanan, C. M., Eccles, J. S., & Becker, J. B.** (1992). Are adolescents the victims of raging hormones? Evidence for activational effects of hormones on moods and behavior at adolescence. *Psychological Bulletin, 111,* 62–107.

**Buchanan, C. M., Maccoby, E. E., & Dornbusch, S. M.** (1991). Caught between parents: Adolescents' experience in divorced homes. *Child Development, 62,* 1008–1029.

**Buhrmester, D.** (1990). Intimacy of friendship, interpersonal competence, and adjustment during preadolescence and adolescence. *Child Development, 61,* 1101–1111.

**Bukowski, W. M., Gauze, C., Hoza, B. & Newcomb, A. F.** (1993). Differences and consistency between same-sex and other-sex peer relationships during early adolescence. *Developmental Psychology, 29,* 255–263.

**Bukowksi, W. M., Newcomb, A. F., & Hartup, W. W. (Eds.).** (1996). *The company they keep: Friendship during childhood and adolescence.* New York: Cambridge University Press.

**Bullough, V. L.** (1981). Age at menarche: A misunderstanding. *Science, 213,* 365–366.

**Burchard, J., & Burchard, S. (Eds.).** (1986). *Prevention of delinquent behavior.* Newbury Park, CA: Sage.

**Burchinal, L. G.** (1965). Trends and prospects for young marriages in the U.S. *Journal of Marriage and the Family, 27,* 243–254.

**Buri, J. R., Louiselle, P. A., Misukanis, T. M., & Mueller, R. A.** (1988). Effects of parental authoritarianism and authoritativeness on self-esteem. *Personality and Social Psychology Bulletin, 14,* 271–282.

**Burke, K. C., Burke, J. D., Regier, D. A., & Rae, D. S.** (1990). Age at onset of selected mental disorders in five community populations. *Archives of General Psychology, 47,* 511–518.

**Buss, A. H., & Plomin, R.** (1984). *Temperament: Early developing personality traits.* Hillsdale, NJ: Erlbaum.

**Camarena, P. M., Sarigiani, P. A., & Petersen, A. C.** (1990). Gender-specific pathways to intimacy in early adolescence. *Journal of Youth and Adolescence, 19,* 19–32.

**Camarena, P. M., Stemmler, M., & Petersen, A. C.** (1994). The gender-differential significance of work and family: An exploration of adolescent experience and expectation. In R. K. Silbereisen & E. Todt (Eds.), *Adolescent in context: The interplay of family, school, peers, and work in adjustment* (pp. 201–221). New York: Springer-Verlag.

**Campbell, M., Spencer, E. K., Kowalik, S. C., & Erlenmeyer-Kimling, L.** (1991). Schizophrenic and psychotic disorder. In J. M. Weiner (Ed.), *Textbook of child and adolescent psychiatry* (pp. 223–239). Washington, DC: American Psychiatric Press.

**Campbell, S. B.** (1986). Developmental issues in childhood anxiety. In R. Gittelman (Ed.), *Anxiety disorders in childhood* (pp. 24–57). New York: Guilford.

**Campione, J. C., Brown, A. L., & Ferrara, R. A.** (1982). Mental retardation and intelligence. In R. J. Sternberg (Ed.), *Handbook of human intelligence* (pp. 392–473). New York: Cambridge University Press.

**Cancro, R.** (1983). History and overview of schizophrenia. In H. I. Kaplan & B. J. Sadock, *Comprehensive textbook of psychiatry* (**Vol. 1,** pp. 631–642). Baltimore: Williams & Wilkins.

**Canter, R. J.** (1982). Family correlates of male and female delinquency. *Criminology, 20,* 149–160.

Carlat, D. J., & Camargo, C. A., Jr. (1991). Review of bulimia nervosa in males. *American Journal of Psychiatry,* **148,** 831–843.

Carlsmith, J. M., Dornbusch, S. M., & Gross, R. T. (1983). Unpublished study cited in Atkinson et al., 1987.

Carnegie Council on Adolescent Development, Task Force on Education of Young Adolescents. (1989). *Turning points: Preparing American youth for the 21st century.* New York: Carnegie Corporation of New York.

Carroll, C. A. (1985). *Drugs in modern society.* Dubuque, IA: Wm. C. Brown.

Carroll, J. B. (1982). The measurement of intelligence. In R. J. Sternberg (Ed.), *Handbook of human intelligence* (pp. 29–122). New York: Cambridge University Press.

Carroll, J. B. (1989). Factor analysis since Spearman: Where do we stand? What do we know? In R. Kanfer, P. L. Ackerman, & R. Cudeck (Eds.), *Abilities, motivation, and methodology: The Minnesota Symposium on Learning and Individual Differences* (pp. 29–122). Hillsdale, NJ: Erlbaum.

Carroll, J. F. X. (1986). Secondary prevention: A pragmatic approach to the problem of substance abuse among adolescents. In G. Beschner & A. S. Friedman (Eds.), *Teen drug use* (pp. 163–184). Lexington, MA: Lexington Books.

Carroll, J. L., & Rest, J. R. (1982). Moral development. In B. B. Wolman (Ed.), *Handbook of developmental psychology.* Englewood Cliffs, NJ: Prentice-Hall.

Caspi, A., Lynam, D., Moffitt, T. E., & Silva, P. A. (1993). Unravelling girls' delinquency: Biological, dispositional, and contextual contributions to adolescent misbehavior. *Developmental Psychology, 29,* 19–30.

Caspi, A., & Moffitt, T. E. (1991). Individual differences are accentuated during periods of social change: The sample case of girls at puberty. *Journal of Personality and Social Psychology, 61,* 157–168.

Cattell, R. B. (1963). Theory of fluid and crystallized intelligence: An initial experiment. *Journal of Educational Psychology, 105,* 105–111.

Cavior, N., & Dokecki, P. R. (1973). Physical attractiveness, perceived attitude similarity, and academic achievement as contributors to interpersonal attraction among adolescents. *Developmental Psychology, 9,* 44–54.

Ceci, S. J., & Bronfenbrenner, U. (1985). "Don't forget to take the cupcakes out of the oven": Prospective memory, strategic time-monitoring, and context. *Child Development, 56,* 152–164.

Centers for Disease Control and Prevention. (1989). *Reducing the health consequences of smoking: 25 years of progress. A report of the Surgeon General.* USDHHS Pub. No. (CDC) 89–8411. Washington, DC: General Accounting Office.

Centers for Disease Control and Prevention. (1994). *Preventing tobacco use among young people: A report of the Surgeon General.* Washington, DC: U.S. Department of Health and Human Services.

Centers for Disease Control. (1995a). Trends in sexual behavior among high school students—United States, 1990, 1991, 1993. *Morbidity and Morality Weekly report, 44,* 124–125, 131–132.

Centers for Disease Control. (1995b). *Adolescent health: State of the nation—pregnancy, sexually transmitted diseases, and related risk behaviors among U.S. adolescents.* Atlanta: U.S. Department of Health and Human Services: DHHS publication no. CDC099-4630.

Cervantes, L. F. (1965). *The dropout: Causes and cures.* Ann Arbor: University of Michigan Press.

Chalmers, J. B., & Townsend, M. A. R. (1990). The effects of training in social perspective taking on socially maladjusted girls. *Child Development, 61,* 178–190.

Chapman, A. H. (1974). *Management of emotional problems of children and adolescents.* Philadelphia: Lippincott.

Chasnoff, I. J. (1987, May). Perinatal effects of cocaine. *Contemporary OB/GYN,* pp. 163–179.

Chasnoff, I. J., Burns, W. J., Schnoll, S. H., & Burns, K. A. (1985). Cocaine use in pregnancy. *New England Journal of Medicine, 313,* 666–669.

Chassin, L., Presson, C. C., Sherman, S. J., Montello, D., & McGrew, J. (1986). Changes in peer and parent influence during adolescence: Longitudinal versus cross-sectional perspectives on smoking initiation. *Developmental Psychology, 22,* 327–334.

Chavez, L. (1987, July 16). 10,000 children in New York welfare hostels. *The New York Times,* p. 24.

Cherlin, A. J., Furstenberg, F., Jr., Chase-Lansdale, P. L., Kiernan, K. E., Robins, P. K., Morrison, D. R., & Teitler, J. O. (1991). Longitudinal studies of effects of divorce on children in Great Britain and the United States. *Science, 252,* 1386–1389.

Children's Defense Fund. (1991). *The state of America's children 1991.* Washington, DC: Author.

Children's Defense Fund. (1992). *The state of America's children 1992.* Washington, DC: Author.

Children's Defense Fund. (1994). *The state of America's children, yearbook 1994.* Washington, DC: Author.

Children's Defense Fund. (1995). *The state of America's children, yearbook 1995.* Washington, DC: Author.

Chilman, C. S. (1968). Families in development at mid-stage of the family life cycle. *Family Coordinator, 17,* 297–331.

Chilman, C. S. (1983). *Adolescent sexuality in a changing American society: Social and psychological perspectives* (2nd ed.). Washington, DC: U.S. Government Printing Office.

Chilman, C. S. (1986). Some psychosocial aspects of adolescent sexual and contraceptive behaviors in a changing American society. In J. B. Lancaster & B. A. Hamburg (Eds.), *School-age pregnancy and parenthood: Biosocial dimensions* (pp. 191–217). New York: Aldine De Gruyter.

Chin, K. (1990). *Chinese subculture and criminality: Nontraditional crime groups in America.* Westport, CT: Greenwood Press.

Christ, J. (1974). Outpatient treatment of adolescents and their families. In G. Caplan (Ed.), *American handbook of psychiatry:* **Vol. II.** *Child and adolescent psychiatry, sociocultural and community psychiatry* (pp. 339–352). New York: Basic Books.

Church, G. (1994, Oct. 24). We're #1 and it hurts. *Time, 144,* 50–56.

Cicchetti, D. (1990). A historical perspective on the discipline of developmental psychopathology. In J. Rolf, A. S. Masten, D. Cicchetti, K. H. Nuechterlein, & S. Weintraub (Eds.), *Risk and protective factors in the development of psychopathology* (pp. 2–28). New York: Cambridge University Press.

**Cicchetti, D., & Carlson, V. (Eds.)** (1989). *Child maltreatment: Theory and research on the causes and consequences of child abuse and neglect.* New York: Cambridge University Press.

**Cismoski, J.** (1994). *Addendum to Michigan Alcohol and Other Drugs School Survey.* Western Michigan University (unpublished data).

**Cismoski, J., & Sheridan, M.** (1994). *Alcohol and Tobacco Survey.* Fond du Lac Public Health Nursing Department (unpublished data).

**Clancy, S. M., & Dollinger, S. J.** (1993). Identity, self, and personality: I. Identity status and the five-factor model of personality. *Journal of Research on Adolescence, 3,* 227–245.

**Clark, M. L. & Ayers, M.** (1992). Friendship similarity during early adolescence: Gender and racial patterns. *Journal of Psychology, 126,* 393–405.

**Clark, W. B., & Midanik, L.** (1984). Alcohol use and alcohol problems among U.S. adults. In National Institute on Alcohol Abuse and Alcoholism, *Alcohol consumption and related problems. Alcohol and Health Monographs, No. 1.* Rockville, MD: The Institute.

**Clarke-Stewart, A., & Friedman, S.** (1987). *Child development: Infancy through adolescence.* New York: Wiley.

**Clary, E. G., & Miller, J.** (1986). Socialization and situational influences on sustained altruism. *Child Development, 57,* 1358–1369.

**Clasen, D. R., & Brown, B. B.** (1985). The multidimensionality of peer pressure in adolescence. *Journal of Youth and Adolescence, 14,* 451–468.

**Clausen, J. A.** (1975). The social meaning of differential physical and sexual maturation. In S. E. Dragastin & G. H. Elder, Jr. (Eds.), *Adolescence in the life cycle: Psychological change and social context.* New York: Wiley.

**Cloninger, C. R., Sigvardsson, S., & Bohman, M.** (1988). Childhood personality predicts alcohol abuse in young adults. *Alcoholism: Clinical Experimental Research, 12,* 495–505.

**Cohen, D. J., Dibble, E., & Grawe, J. M.** (1977). Fathers' and mothers' perceptions of children's personality. *Archives of General Psychiatry, 34,* 261–282.

**Cohen, F.** (1984). Coping. In J. Matarazzo, S. W. Weiss, J. A. Herd, N. Miller, & S. M. Weiss (Eds.), *Behavioral health: A handbook of health enhancement and disease prevention* (pp. 261–274). New York: Wiley.

**Cohen, F.** (1987). Measurement of coping. In S. V. Kasl & C. L. Cooper (Eds.), *Stress and health: Issues in research methodology* (pp. 283–305). New York: Wiley.

**Cohen, J. M.** (1972). *Sources of peer group homogeneity. Socioeconomic background and achievement.* New York: Seminar Press.

**Cohen, P., Brook, J., & Kandel, D. B.** (1991). Predictors and correlates of adolescent drug use. In *Encyclopedia of adolescence* (Vol. I, pp. 268–271). New York: Garland Publishing.

**Colby, A., & Damon, W.** (1992). *Pathways to commitment: Moral leaders in our time.* New York: Free Press.

**Colby, A., & Kohlberg, L.** (1987). *The measurement of moral judgment:* Vol. 1. *Theoretical foundations and research validation.* New York: Cambridge University Press.

**Colby, A., Kohlberg, L., Gibbs, J., & Lieberman, M.** (1980). *A longitudinal study of moral development.* Cambridge, MA: Center for Moral Education.

**Colby, A., Kohlberg, L., Gibbs, J., & Lieberman, M.** (1983). A longitudinal study of moral development. *Monographs of the Society for Research in Child Development, 48,* 124.

**Coleman, J. C.** (1980). *The nature of adolescence.* London: Methuen.

**Coleman, J. C. (Ed.)** (1987). *Working with troubled adolescents: A handbook.* London: Academic Press.

**Coleman, J. S.** (1961). *The adolescent society.* New York: Free Press.

**Coleman, J. S., Campbell, E. Q., Hobson, C. J., McPartland, J., Mead, A. M., Weinfeld, F. D., & York, R. L.** (1966). *Equality of educational opportunity.* Washington, DC: U.S. Government Printing Office.

**College Board.** (1995). *National report: College-bound seniors.* New York: The College Board.

**College Entrance Examination Board.** (1979). *National college-bound seniors.* New York: The College Board.

**College Entrance Examination Board.** (1988). *National college-bound seniors.* New York: The College Board.

**College Entrance Examination Board.** (1989). *National college-bound seniors.* New York: The College Board.

**Collins, W. A. (Ed.)** (1980). *Minnesota symposia on child psychology:* Vol. 13. *Development of cognition, affect, and social relations.* Hillsdale, NJ: Lawrence Erlbaum Associates.

**Collins, W. A., & Russell, G.** (1991). Mother–child and father–child relationships in middle childhood and adolescence: A developmental analysis. *Developmental Review, 11,* 99–136.

**Comer, R. J.** (1992). *Abnormal psychology.* New York: W. H. Freeman & Co.

**Commission on Chapter 1.** (1992). *Making schools work for children in poverty: Summary.* Washington, DC: American Association for Higher Education.

**Committee to study the health-related effects of cannabis and its derivatives. National Academy of Sciences, Institute of Medicine.** (1982). *Marijuana and health.* Washington, DC: National Academy Press.

**Committee for the Study of Research on Child and Adolescent Mental Disorders, Division of Mental Health and Behavioral Medicine, Institute of Medicine.** (1989). *Research on children and adolescents with mental, behavioral, and developmental disorders: Mobilizing a national initiative.* Washington, DC: National Academy Press.

**Committee on Ways and Means, House of Representatives.** (1991). *1991 Green Book.* Washington, DC: U.S. Government Printing Office.

**Compas, B. E., Ey, S., & Grant, K. E.** (1993). Taxonomy, assessment, and diagnosis of depression during adolescence. *Psychological Bulletin, 114,* 323–344.

**Compas, B. E., Howell, D. C., Phares, V., Williams, R. A., & Giunta, C. T.** (1989). Risk factors for emotional/behavioral problems in young adolescents: A prospective analysis of adolescent and parental stress and symptoms. *Journal of Consulting and Clinical Psychology, 57,* 732–740.

**Compas, B. E., Malcarne, V. L., & Fondacaro, K. M.** (1988). Coping with stressful events in older children and young adolescents. *Journal of Consulting and Clinical Psychology, 56,* 405–411.

Compas, B. E., Wagner, B. M., Slavin, L. A., & Vannatta, K. (1986). A prospective study of life events, social support, and psychological symptomatology during the transition from high school to college. *American Journal of Community Psychology, 14,* 241–257.

Condry, J., & Siman, M. L. (1974). Characteristics of peer- and adult-oriented children. *Journal of Marriage and the Family, 36,* 543–554.

Conger, J. J. (1971, Fall). A world they never knew: The family and social change. *Daedalus, 100,* 1105–1138.

Conger, J. J. (1973). *Adolescence and youth: Psychological development in a changing world.* New York: Harper & Row.

Conger, J. J. (1975). Sexual attitudes and behavior of contemporary adolescents. In J. J. Conger (Ed.), *Contemporary issues in adolescent development* (pp. 221–230). New York: Harper & Row.

Conger, J. J. (1976). Roots of alienation. In B. Wolman (Ed.), *International encyclopedia of neurology, psychiatry, psychoanalysis, and psychology.* New York: McGraw-Hill.

Conger, J. J. (1977). Parent–child relationships, social change and adolescent vulnerability. *Journal of Pediatric Psychology, 2,* 93–97.

Conger, J. J. (1979). *Adolescence: Generation under pressure.* New York: Harper & Row.

Conger, J. J. (1980). A new morality: Sexual attitudes and behavior of contemporary adolescents. In P. H. Mussen, J. J. Conger, & J. Kagan (Eds.), *Readings in child and adolescent psychology: Contemporary perspectives.* New York: Harper & Row.

Conger, J. J. (1981). Freedom and commitment: Families, youth and social change. *American Psychologist, 36,* 1475–1484.

Conger, J. J. (1984, Aug.). *Health psychology in a changing world.* Invited address presented at the 92nd Annual Convention of the American Psychological Association, Toronto, Canada.

Conger, J. J. (1987). Behavioral medicine and health psychology in a changing world. *Child Abuse and Neglect, 2,* 443–453.

Conger, J. J. (1988). Hostages to fortune: Youth, values, and the public interest. *American Psychologist, 43,* 291–300.

Conger, J. J. (1991a). *Adolescence and youth* (4th ed.). New York: Harper & Row.

Conger, J. J. (1991b, Oct.). Mental health in adolescence. In *Assessing future research needs: Mental and addictive disorders in women.* Summary of an Institute of Medicine Conference (pp. 51–62). Washington, DC: Institute of Medicine, National Academy of Sciences.

Conger, J. J. (1991c, Nov. 4). Adolescence: Change and challenge. Presented in Smithsonian centennial lecture series, *New psychological findings on the mysteries of the life cycle: From infancy to maturity.* Washington, DC: American Psychological Association.

Conger, J. J. (1993). The neglected mental health problems of adolescents. In D. Jarmul (Ed.), *Headline news, science views II* (pp. 72–74). Washington, DC: National Research Council, National Academy Press.

Conger, R. D., Ge, X., Elder, G. H., Jr., Lorenz, F. O., & Simons, R. L. (1994). Economic stress, coercive family processes, and developmental problems of adolescents. *Child Development, 65,* 541–561.

Conger, R. D., Lorenz, F. O., Elder, G. H., Jr., Melby, J. N., Simons, R. L., & Conger, K. J. (1991). A process model of family economic pressure and early adolescent alcohol use. *Journal of Early Adolescence, 11,* 430–449.

Conger, J. J., & Miller, W. C. (1966). *Personality, social class, and delinquency.* New York: Wiley.

Conger, J. J., & Petersen, A. C. (1984). *Adolescence and youth: Psychological development in a changing world* (3rd ed.). New York: Harper & Row.

Congressional Budget Office. (1987). *Educational achievement: Explanations and implications of recent trends.* Washington, DC: Congressional Budget Office.

Connolly, J. A., & Konarski, R. (1994). Peer self-concept in adolescence: Analysis of factor structure and of associations with peer experience. *Journal of Research on Adolescence, 4,* 385–403.

Conrad, J. (1902). *Youth: A narrative and two other stories.* Edinburgh and London: Blackwood. Cited in J. Bartlett (1968), *Familiar quotations.* (14th ed.) (p. 843). Boston: Little, Brown.

Coontz, S. (1992). *The way we never were: American families and the nostalgia trip.* New York: Basic Books.

Cooper, C. R., & Ayers-Lopez, S. (1985). Family and peer systems in early adolescence: New models of the role of relationships in development. *Journal of Early Adolescence, 5,* 9–21.

Cooper, C. R., & Grotevant, H. D. (1987). Gender issues in interface of family experience and adolescents' friendship and dating identity. *Journal of Youth and Adolescence, 16,* 247–264.

Cooper, C. R., Grotevant, H. D., & Condon, S. M. (1983). Individuality and connectedness in the family as a context for adolescent identity formation and role-taking skill. In H. D. Grotevant & C. R. Cooper (Eds.), *Adolescent development in the family* (pp. 43–60). San Francisco: Jossey-Bass.

Corby, B. (1993). *Child abuse: Towards a knowledge base.* Buckingham, PA: Open University Press.

Costello, E. J., & Angold, A. (1995). Epidemiology. In J. S. March (Ed.), *Anxiety disorders in children and adolescents* (pp. 109–124). New York: Guilford Press.

Côté, J. E. (1992). Was Mead wrong about the coming of age in Samoa? An analysis of the Mead/Freeman controversy for scholars of adolescence and human development. *Journal of Youth and Adolescence, 21,* 499–527.

Côté, J. E. (1994). *Adolescent storm and stress: An evaluation of the Mead-Freeman controversy.* Hillsdale, NJ: Lawrence Erlbaum.

Cotterell, J. L. (1992). School size as a factor in adolescents' adjustment to the transition to secondary school. *Journal of Early Adolescence, 12,* 28–45.

Coupey, S. M. (1992). Anorexia nervosa. In S. B. Friedman, M. Fisher, & S. K. Schonberg (Eds.), *Comprehensive adolescent health care* (pp. 217–231). St. Louis: Quality Medical Publishing.

Cowan, A. L. (1989, Aug. 21). Poll finds women's gains have taken personal toll. *The New York Times,* A1, A8.

Cowen, E. L., Pederson, A., Babijian, H., Izzo, L. D., & Trost, M. A. (1973). Long-term follow-up of early detected vulnerable children. *Journal of Consulting and Clinical Psychology, 41,* 438–446.

**Crago, M., Yates, A., Bentler, L. E., & Arizmendi, T. G.** (1985). Height–weight ratios among female athletes: Are collegiate athletics the precursors to an anorexic syndrome? *International Journal of Eating Disorders,* **4,** 79–87.

**Crisp, A. H.** (1986, April). *Prevention of eating disorders.* Paper presented at the Second International Conference on Eating Disorders, New York.

**Crisp, A. H., & Kalucy, R. S.** (1974). Aspects of the perceptual disorder in anorexia nervosa. *British Journal of Medical Psychology,* **47,** 349–361.

**Crittenden, P. M., & Ainsworth, M. D. S.** (1989). Child maltreatment and attachment theory. In D. Cicchetti & V. Carlson (Eds.), *Child maltreatment: Theory and research on the causes and consequences of child abuse and neglect* (pp. 432–463). New York: Cambridge University Press.

**Crockett, L. J., & Petersen, A. C.** (1987). Pubertal status and psychosocial development: Findings from the early adolescent study. In R. M. Lerner & T. T. Roch (Eds.), *Biological and psychosocial interactions in early adolescence: A life-span perspective* (pp. 173–188). Hillsdale, NJ: Erlbaum.

**Crouter, A. C.** (1984). Participative work as an influence of human development. *Journal of Applied Developmental Psychology,* **5,** 71–90.

**Crouter, A. C., MacDermid, S. M., McHale, S. M., & Perry-Jenkins, M.** (1990). Parental monitoring and perceptions of children's school performance and conduct in dual-earner and single-earner families. *Developmental Psychology,* **26,** 649–657.

**Crouter, A. C., Perry-Jenkins, M., Huston, T. L., & McHale, S. M.** (1987). Processes underlying father involvement in dual-earner and single-earner families. *Developmental Psychology,* **23,** 431–440.

**Crowley, T. J.** (1987). Clinical issues in cocaine abuse. In S. Fisher, A. Raskin, & E. H. Uhlenhuth (Eds.), *Cocaine: Clinical and Behavioral Aspects* (pp. 193–211). New York: Oxford University Press.

**Crowley, T. J., & Rhine, M.** (1985). The substance use disorders. In R. Simons & H. Pardes (Eds.), *Understanding human behavior in health and illness* (3rd ed., pp. 730–746). New York: Williams & Wilkins.

**Crowley, T. J., & Riggs, P. S.** (1995). Adolescent substance use disorder with conduct disorder, the comorbid conditions. *NIDA Research Monograph Series.*

**Crystal, D. S., Chen, C., Fuligni, A. J., Stevenson, H. W., Hsu, C., Ko, H., Kitamura, S., & Kimura, S.** (1994). Psychological maladjustment and academic achievement: A cross-cultural study of Japanese, Chinese, and American high school students. *Child Development,* **65,** 738–753.

**Csikszentmihalyi, M., & Larson, R.** (1984). *Being adolescent: Conflict and growth in the teenage years.* New York: Basic Books.

**Csikszentmihalyi, M., Rathunde, K., & Whalen, S.** (1993). *Talented teenagers: The roots of success and failure.* Cambridge: Cambridge University Press.

**Cumsille, P. E., & Epstein, N.** (1994). Family cohesion, family adaptability, social support, and adolescent depressive symptoms in outpatient clinic families. *Journal of Family Psychology,* **8,** 202–214.

**Curran, D. K.** (1987). *Adolescent suicidal behavior.* Washington, DC: Hemisphere.

**Dacey, J. S.** (1989). Discriminating characteristics of the families of highly creative adolescents. *Journal of Creative Behavior,* **23,** 263–271.

**Damon, W., & Hart, D.** (1988). *Self-understanding in childhood and adolescence.* New York: Cambridge University Press.

**Damon, W., & Hart, D.** (1992). Self-understanding and its role in social and moral development. In M. H. Bornstein & M. E. Lamb (Eds.), *Developmental psychology: An advanced textbook* (pp. 421–464). Hillsdale, NJ: Lawrence Erlbaum.

**Damphousse, K. R., & Crouch, B. M.** (1992). Did the devil make them do it? An examination of the etiology of Satanism among juvenile delinquents. *Youth & Society,* **24,** 204–227.

**Daniels, D., Dunn, J., Furstenberg, F. F., & Plomin, R.** (1985). Environmental differences within the family and adjustment differences within pairs of siblings. *Child Development,* **56,** 764–774.

**Daniels, D., & Moos, R. H.** (1990). Assessing life stressors and social resources among adolescents: Applications to depressed youth. *Journal of Adolescent Research,* **5,** 268–289.

**Darling, C. A., Kallen, D. J., & VanDusen, J. E.** (1984). Sex in transition, 1900–1984. *Journal of Youth and Adolescence,* **13,** 385–399.

**Davidson, P., & Youniss, J.** (1991). Which comes first: Morality or identity? In W. Kurtines & J. Gewirtz (Eds.), *Handbook of moral behavior and development.* Hillsdale, NJ: Lawrence Erlbaum.

**Davidson, P., & Youniss, J.** (1995). Moral development and social construction. In W. M. Kurtines & J. L. Gewirtz (Eds.), *Moral development: An introduction* (pp. 289–310). Boston: Allyn and Bacon.

**Davidson, W., & Redner, R.** (1988). The prevention of juvenile delinquency: Diversion from the juvenile justice system. In R. Price, E. Cowen, R. Lorion, & J. Ramos-McKay (Eds.), *14 ounces of prevention* (pp. 123–138).

**Davies, M., & Kandel, D. B.** (1981). Parental and peer influences on adolescents' educational plans: Some further evidence. *American Journal of Sociology,* **87,** 363–387.

**Dawson, D. A.** (1986). The effects of sex education on adolescent behavior. *Family Planning Perspectives,* **18,** 162–170.

**Deaux, K.** (1985). Sex and gender. *Annual Review of Psychology,* **36,** 49–81.

**DeBaryshe, B. D., Patterson, G. R., & Capaldi, D. M.** (1993). A performance model for academic achievement in early adolescent boys. *Developmental Psychology,* **29,** 795–804.

**Dellas, M., & Jernigan, L. P.** (1990). Affective personality characteristics associated with undergraduate ego identity formation. *Journal of Adolescent Research,* **5,** 306–324.

**DeLongis, A., Coyne, J. C., Dakof, G., Folkman, S., & Lazarus, R. S.** (1982). Relationship of daily hassles, uplifts, and major life events to health status. *Health Psychology,* **1,** 119–136.

**DeLongis, A., Folkman, S., & Lazarus, R. S.** (1988). The impact of daily stress on health and mood: Psychological and social resources as mediators. *Journal of Personality and Social Psychology,* **54,** 486–495.

**Detera-Wadleigh, S. D., Berrettini, W. H., Goldin, L. R., Boorman, D., et al.** (1987). Close linkage of c-Harvey-ras -1 and the insulin gene to affective disorder is ruled out in three North American pedigrees. *Nature, 325,* 806–808.

**Devereux, E.** (1970). The role of peer group experience in moral development. In J. Hill (Ed.), *Minnesota Symposium on Child Psychology, 4,* 94–140.

**Dey, E. L., Astin, A. W., & Korn, W. S.** (1991). *The American freshman: Twenty-five-year trends.* Los Angeles: Higher Education Research Institute, University of California, Los Angeles.

**DiClemente, R. J.** (1993). Confronting the challenge of AIDS among adolescents: Directions for future research. *Journal of Adolescent Research, 8,* 156–166.

**Dishion, T. J., Patterson, G. R., Stoolmiller, M., & Skinner, M. L.** (1991). Family, school, and behavioral antecedents to early adolescent involvement with antisocial peers. *Developmental Psychology, 27,* 172–180.

**Dixon, R. A.** (1992). Contextual approaches to adult intellectual development. In R. J. Sternberg & C. A. Berg (Eds.), *Intellectual development* (pp. 350–380). Cambridge: Cambridge University Press.

**Dixon, R. A., Kramer, D. A., & Baltes, P. B.** (1985). Intelligence: A life-span developmental perspective. In B. B. Wolman (Ed.), *Handbook of intelligence: Theories, measurements, and applications* (pp. 301–350). New York: Wiley.

**Dixson, M. C., & Wright, W. E.** (1975). *Juvenile delinquency prevention programs: An evaluation of policy-related research on the effectiveness of prevention programs.* Nashville, TN: Office of Education Services, Peabody College for Teachers.

**Doane, J. A., West, K. L., Goldstein, M. J., Rodnick, E. H., & Jones, J. E.** (1981). Parental communication deviance and affective style: Predictors of subsequent schizophrenic-spectrum disorders in vulnerable adolescents. *Archives of General Psychiatry, 38,* 679–685.

**Donovan, J. E., & Jessor, R.** (1978). Adolescent problem drinking: Psychosocial correlates in a national study sample. *Quarterly Journal of Studies and Alcohol, 39,* 1506–1524.

**Donovan, J. E., & Jessor, R.** (1983). Problem drinking and the dimension of involvement with drugs: A Guttman scalogram analysis of adolescent drug use. *American Journal of Public Health, 73,* 543–552.

**Donovan, J. E., Jessor, R., & Jessor, L.** (1983). Problem drinking in adolescence and young adulthood. *Journal of Studies on Alcohol, 44,* 109–137.

**Dornbusch, S. M., Carlsmith, J. M., Bushwall, S. J., Ritter, P. L., Leiderman, H., Hastorf, A. H., & Gross, R. T.** (1985). Single parents, extended households, and the control of adolescents. *Child Development, 56,* 326–341.

**Dornbusch, S. M., Carlsmith, L., Gross, R. T., Martin, J. A., Jenning, D., Rosenberg, A., & Duke, D.** (1981). Sexual development, age, and dating: A comparison of biological and social influence upon the set of behaviors. *Child Development, 52,* 179–185.

**Dornbusch, S. M., Ritter, D. L., Leiderman, P. H., Roberts, D. F., & Fraleigh, M. J.** (1987). The relation of parenting style to adolescent school performance. *Child Development, 58,* 1244–1257.

**Dornbusch, S. M., Ritter, D. L., Mont-Reynard, R., & Chen, Z. Y.** (1990). Family decision making and academic performance in a diverse high school setting. *Journal of Adolescent Research, 5,* 143–160.

**Dorval, B., Brannan, J., Duckworth, M., & Smith, P.** (1987, April). *Developmental trends in conceptions of friendship in comparison to the quality of friends' talk and commentary on it.* Paper presented at the biennial meeting of the Society for Research in Child Development, Baltimore.

**Dossey, J. A., Mullis, I. V. S., Lindquist, M. M., & Chambers, D. L.** (1988). *The mathematical report card: Are we measuring up? Trends and achievement based on the 1986 National Assessment.* Princeton, NJ: Educational Testing Service.

**Dougherty, D. M.** (1993). Adolescent health: Reflections on a report to the U.S. Congress. *American Psychologist, 48,* 193–201.

**Douvan, E., & Adelson, J.** (1966). *The adolescent experience.* New York: Wiley.

**Dowaliby, F. J., & Schumer, H.** (1971). Teacher-centered versus student-centered mode of college classroom instruction as related to manifest anxiety. *Proceedings, 79th Annual Convention, American Psychological Association.*

**Dreger, R. M., & Miller, K. S.** (1968). Comparative psychological studies of Negroes and whites in the United States: 1959–1965. *Psychological Bulletin Monograph Supplemental, 70,* No. 3, Part. 2.

**Dryfoos, J. G.** (1988). School-based health clinics: Three years of experience. *Family Planning Perspectives, 20,* 193–200.

**Dryfoos, J. G.** (1990). *Adolescents at risk: Prevalence and prevention.* New York: Oxford University Press.

**Dryfoos, J. G.** (1991). Adolescents at risk: A summation of work in the field: Programs and policies. *Journal of Adolescent Health, 12,* 620–637.

**Dryfoos, J. G.** (1993). Schools as places for health, mental health, and social services. *Teacher's College Record, 94,* 540–567.

**Dryfoos, J. G., & Klerman, L. V.** (1988). School-based clinics: Their role in helping students meet the 1990 objectives. *Health Education Quarterly, 15,* 71–80.

**Dubas, J. S., Graber, J. A., & Petersen, A. C.** (1991). A longitudinal investigation of adolescents' changing perceptions of pubertal timing. *Developmental Psychology, 27,* 580–586.

**DuBois, D. L., & Hirsch, B. J.** (1990). School and neighborhood friendship patterns of blacks and whites in early adolescence. *Child Development, 61,* 524–536.

**DuBois, D. L., & Hirsch, B. J.** (1993). School/nonschool friendship patterns in early adolescence. *Journal of Early Adolescence, 13,* 102–122.

**Dugger, C. W.** (1994, May 17). Youthful, impressionable, and accused of murder. *The New York Times,* A1, A14.

**Duncan, P.** (1971). Parental attitudes and interactions in delinquency. *Child Development, 42,* 1751–1765.

**Dunphy, D. C.** (1963). The social structure of urban adolescent peer groups. *Sociometry, 26,* 230–246.

**Dunphy, D. C.** (1972). Peer group socialisation. In F. J. Hunt (Ed.), *Socialisation in Australia* (pp. 200–217). Sydney: Angus & Robertson.

Dunphy, D. C. (1980). Peer group socialization. In R. Muus (Ed.), *Adolescent behavior and society* (3rd ed.). New York: Random House.

Durbin, D. L., Darling, N., Steinberg, L., & Brown, B. B. (1993). Parenting style and peer group membership among European-American adolescents. *Journal of Research on Adolescence, 3,* 87–100.

Durkheim, E. (1961). (originally published 1925). *Moral education.* New York: Free Press.

Dyk, P. H., & Adams, G. R. (1990). Identity and intimacy: An initial investigation of three theoretical models using cross-lag panel correlations. *Journal of Youth and Adolescence, 19,* 91–110.

Earls, F. (1994). Oppositional-defiant and conduct disorder. In M. Rutter, E. Taylor, & L. Hersov (Eds.), *Child and adolescent psychiatry: Modern approaches* (pp. 308–330). Oxford: Blackwell Scientific Publications.

Earls, F., Robbins, L. N., Stifman, A. R., & Powell, J. (1989). Comprehensive health care for high risk adolescents: An evaluation study. *American Journal of Public Health, 79,* 999–1010.

East, P. L., Felice, M. E., & Morgan, M. C. (1993). Sisters' and girlfriends' sexual and childbearing behavior: Effects on early adolescent girls' sexual outcomes. *Journal of Marriage and the Family, 55,* 953–963.

East, P. L., Lerner, R. M., Lerner, J. V., Soni, R. A., Ohannessian, C. M., & Jacobson, L. P. (1992). Early adolescent–peer group fit, peer relations, and psychosocial competence: A short-term longitudinal study. *Journal of Early Adolescence, 12,* 132–152.

East, P. L., & Rook, K. S. (1992). Compensatory patterns of support among children's peer relationships: A test using school friends, nonschool friends, and siblings. *Developmental Psychology, 28,* 163–172.

Ebata, A. T., & Moos, R. H. (1991). Coping and adjustment in distressed and healthy adolescents. *Journal of Applied Developmental Psychology, 12,* 33–54.

Ebata, A. T., & Moos, R. H. (1994). Personal, situational, and contexual correlates of coping in adolescents. *Journal of Research on Adolescence, 4,* 99–125.

Ebata, A. T., Petersen, A. C., & Conger, J. J. (1990). The development of psychopathology in adolescence. In J. E. Rolf, A. S. Masten, D. Cicchetti, K. H. Nuechterlein, & S. Weintraub (Eds.), *Risk and protective factors in the development of psychopathology* (pp. 308–333). New York: Cambridge University Press.

Eccles, J. S., Buchanan, C. M., Flanagan, C. A., Fuligni, A., Midgley, C., & Yee, D. (1991). Control versus autonomy during early adolescence. *Journal of Social Issues, 47,* 53–68.

Eccles, J. S., Midgley, C., Wigfield, A., Buchanan, C. M., Reuman, D., Flanagan, C., & MacIver, D. (1993). Development during adolescence: The impact of stage–environment fit on young adolescents' experiences in schools and families. *American Psychologist, 48,* 90–101.

Eckholm, E. (1993). Teen-age gangs are inflicting lethal violence on small cities. *The New York Times,* pp. 1, 8.

Edelman, M. W. (1987). *Families in peril: An agenda for social change. Teenage pregnancy: The problem that hasn't gone away.* New York: Alan Guttmacher Institute, 1981.

Edelman, M. W. (1995). Introduction. *The state of America's children, 1995* (pp. 1–5). Washington, DC: Children's Defense Fund.

Edwards, C. P. (1980). The comparative study of the development of moral judgment and reasoning. In R. W. Monroe, R. Monroe, & B. B. Whiting (Eds.), *Handbook of cross-cultural human development.* New York: Garland.

Egeland, J. A., Gerhard, D. S., Pauls, D. L., Sussex, J. N., et al. (1987). Bipolar affective disorders linked to DNA markers on chromosome 11. *Nature, 325,* 783–787.

Ehrhardt, A. A., & Baker, S. W. (1975). Hormonal orientations and their implications for the understanding of normal sex differentiation. In P. H. Mussen, J. J. Conger, & J. Kagan (Eds.), *Basic and contemporary issues in developmental psychology* (pp. 113–121). New York: Harper & Row.

Eichorn, D. H. (1970). Physiological development. In P. H. Mussen (Ed.), *Carmichael's manual of child psychology* (**Vol. 2,** 3rd ed., pp. 152–283). New York: Wiley.

Eichorn, D. H. (1975). Asynchronizations in adolescent development. In S. E. Dragastin & G. H. Elder, Jr. (Eds.), *Adolescence in the life cycle: Psychological change and social context* (pp. 81–96). New York: Wiley.

Eichorn, D. H. (1980). The school. In M. Johnson (Ed.), *Toward adolescence: The middle school years.* 79th Yearbook of the National Society for the Study of Education. Chicago: University of Chicago Press.

Eisenberg, N. (1990). Prosocial development in early and mid-adolescence. In R. Montemayor, G. R. Adams, & T. P. Gullotta (Eds.), *From childhood to adolescence: A transitional period?* (pp. 240–268). Newbury Park, CA: Sage.

Eisenberg, N., & McNally, S. (1993). Socialization and mothers' and adolescents' empathy-related characteristics. *Journal of Research on Adolescence, 3,* 171–191.

Eisenberg, N., Miller, P. A., Shell, R., McNalley, S., & Shea, C. (1991). Prosocial development in adolescence: A longitudinal study. *Developmental Psychology, 27,* 849–857.

Eisenberg-Berg, N., & Mussen, P. H. (1989). *Roots of caring, sharing, and helping* (2nd ed.). Englewood Cliffs, NJ: Prentice-Hall.

Ekstrom, R. B., Goertz, M. E., Pollack, J. M., & Rock, D. A. (1986). Who drops out of school and why? Findings from a national study. *Teacher's College Record, 87,* 356–375.

Elam, S. M., Rose, L. C, & Gallup, A. M. (1993, Oct.). *25th annual Gallup/Phi Delta Kappa Poll of the public's attitude towards the public schools.* Bloomington, IN: Phi Delta Kappa International.

Elder, G. H. (1974). *Children of the Great Depression.* Chicago: University of Chicago Press.

Elder, G. H., Jr. (1980). *Family structure and socialization.* New York: Arno Press.

Elder, G. H., Jr., Caspi, A., & Van Nguyen, T. (1986). Resourceful and vulnerable children: Family influence in hard times. In R. K. Silbereisen, K. Eyferth, & G. Rudinger (Eds.), *Development as action in context* (pp. 167–186). Berlin: Springer-Verlag.

Elder, G. H., Jr., Van Nguyen, T., & Caspi, A. (1985). Linking family hardship to children's lives. *Child Development, 56,* 361–375.

Elkind, D. (1966). Conceptual orientation shifts in children and adolescents. *Child Development, 37,* 493–498

Elkind, D. (1968). Cognitive development in adolescence. In J. F. Adams (Ed.), *Understanding adolescence* (pp. 128–58). Boston: Allyn & Bacon.

Elkind, D. (1970). *Children and adolescents: Interpretive essays on Jean Piaget.* New York: Oxford University Press.

Elkind, D. (1978). *The child's reality: Three developmental themes.* Hillsdale, NJ: Erlbaum.

Elkind, D. (1984). *All grown up and no place to go.* Reading, MA: Addison-Wesley.

Elliott, D. S. (1994a). Serious violent offenders: Onset, developmental onset, and termination—The American Society of Criminology 1993 presidential address. *Criminology, 32,* 1–21.

Elliott, D. S. (1994b). *Youth violence: An overview* (F-693). Boulder, CO: Center for the Study and Prevention of Violence.

Elliott, D. S., & Ageton, S. S. (1980). Reconciling race and class differences in self-reported and official estimates of delinquency. *American Sociological Review, 45,* 95–110.

Elliott, D. S., Ageton, S. S., Huizinga, D., Knowles, B. A., & Canter, R. J. (1983). *The prevalence and incidence of delinquent behavior, 1976–1980.* Boulder, CO: Behavioral Research Institute.

Elliott, D. S., Huizinga, D., & Ageton, S. S. (1985). *Explaining delinquency and drug use.* Beverly Hills, CA: Sage.

Elliott, D. S., Huizinga, D., & Menard, S. (1989). *Multiple-problem youth: Delinquency, substance use, and mental health problems.* New York: Springer-Verlag.

Emery, R. E. (1982). Interparental conflict and the children of discord and divorce. *Psychological Bulletin, 92,* 310–330.

Enright, R. D., Lapsley, D. K., Franklin, C. C., & Steuck, K. (1984). Longitudinal and cross-cultural validation of the belief-discrepancy reasoning construct. *Developmental Psychology, 20,* 143–149.

Ensel, W. M., & Lin, N. (1991). The life stress paradigm and psychological distress. *Journal of Health and Social Behavior, 32,* 321–341.

Ensminger, M. E. (1990). Sexual activity and problem behaviors among black, urban adolescents. *Child Development, 61,* 2032–2046.

Entwisle, D. R. (1990). Schools and the adolescent. In S. S. Feldman & G. R. Elliott (Eds.), *At the threshold: The developing adolescent* (pp. 197–224). Cambridge, MA: Harvard University Press.

Entwisle, D. R., & Hallinan, M. T. (Eds.). (1991). School characteristics and student outcomes [Special issue]. *Journal of Research on Adolescence, 1*(3).

Epstein, J. L. (1989). The selection of friends: Changes across grades and in different school environments. In T. J. Berndt & G. W. Ladd (Eds.), *Peer relationships in child development* (pp. 158–187). New York: Wiley.

Ericksen, K. P., & Trocki, K. F. (1994). Sex, alcohol, and sexually transmitted diseases. *Family Planning Perspectives, 26,* 257–263.

Erikson, E. H. (1956). The problem of ego identity. *Journal of the American Psychoanalytic Association, 4,* 56–121.

Erikson, E. H. (1963). *Childhood and society* (2nd ed.). New York: Norton.

Erikson, E. H. (1968). *Identity: Youth and crisis.* New York: Norton.

Erikson, E. H. (1983). Obstacles and pathways in the journey from adolescence to parenthood. In M. Sugar (Ed.), *Adolescent psychiatry: Developmental and clinical studies* (Vol. XI). Chicago: University of Chicago Press.

Erikson, E. H. (1985). Pseudospeciation in the nuclear age. Annual meeting of the American Psychiatric Association (1984, Anaheim, CA). *Political Psychology, 6,* 213–217.

Esbensen, F. A., & Elliott, D. B. (1994). Continuity and discontinuity in illicit drug use: Patterns and antecedents. *Journal of Drug Issues, 24,* 75–97.

Estes, W. K. (1980). Is human memory obsolete? *American Scientists, 68,* 62–69.

Etaugh, C. (1993). Maternal employment: Effects on children. In J. Frankel (Ed.), *The employed mother and the family context* (pp. 68–88). New York: Springer.

Evangelauf, J. (1988, Sept. 28). Minority groups continue gains on admissions tests. *The Chronicle of Higher Education,* pp. 1, 32.

Evans, R. I. (1984a). A social inoculation strategy to deter smoking in adolescents. In J. D. Matarazzo, S. M. Weiss, J. A. Herd, N. Miller, & S. M. Weiss (Eds.), *Behavioral health: A handbook of health enhancement and disease prevention* (pp. 765–777). New York: Wiley.

Evans, R. I. (1984b). Smoking prevention: Overview. In J. D. Matarazzo, S. M. Weiss, J. A. Herd, N. Miller, & S. M. Weiss (Eds.), *Behavioral health: A handbook of health enhancement and disease prevention* (pp. 693–695). New York: Wiley.

Evans, R. I., Henderson, A., Hill, P., & Raines, B. (1979). Smoking in children and adolescents: Psychosocial determinants and prevention strategies. In *Smoking and health: A report of the Surgeon General.* (DHEW Publication No. (PHS) 79-50066, U. S. Department of Health, Education and Welfare) (Chapter 17, pp. 1–30). Washington, DC: U. S. Government Printing Office (No. 017-000-00218-0).

Evans, R. I., Rozelle, R. M., Mittlemark, M. B., Hansen, W. B., Bane, A. L., & Havis, J. (1978). Deterring the onset of smoking in children: Knowledge of immediate physiological effects and coping with peer pressure, media pressure, and parent modelling. *Journal of Applied Social Psychology, 8,* 126–135.

Evans, R. I., Smith, C. K., & Raines, B. E. (1985). Deterring cigarette smoking in adolescents: A psychosocial behavioral analysis of an intervention strategy. In A. Baum, J. Singer, & S. Taylor (Eds.), *Social psychological aspects of health.* Hillsdale, NJ: Erlbaum.

Evans, R. K., Raines, B. E., & Getz, J. G. (1992). Applying the social inoculation model to a smokeless tobacco use prevention program with Little Leaguers. In *National Cancer Institute, Smokeless tobacco or health: An international perspective.* NIH Pub. No. 92-3461. Washington, DC: NCI.

Eveleth, P., & Tanner, J. (1978). *Worldwide variation in human growth.* Cambridge, MA: Cambridge University Press.

**Eveleth, P. B., & Tanner, J. M.** (1990). *Worldwide variation in human growth* (2nd ed.). Cambridge, MA: Cambridge University Press.

**Everybody counts: A report to the nation on the future of mathematics education.** (1989). National Research Council. Washington, DC: National Academy Press.

**Eysenck, H. J.** (with Kamin, L.) (1981). *The intelligence controversy.* New York: Wiley.

**Farel, A.** (1982). *Early adolescence and religion: A status study.* Carrboro, NC: Center for Early Adolescence.

**Farrell, A. D., & Danish, S. J.** (1993). Peer drug associations and emotional restraint: Causes or consequences of adolescents' drug use? *Journal of Consulting and Clinical Psychology, 61,* 327–334.

**Farrell, A. D., Danish, S. J., & Howard, C. W.** (1992). Relationship between drug use and other problem behaviors in urban adolescents. *Journal of Consulting and Clinical Psychology, 60,* 705–712.

**Farrington, D. P.** (1983). Offending from 10 to 25 years of age. In K. T. Van Dusen & S. A. Mednick (Eds.), *Prospective studies of crime and delinquency* (pp. 17–37). Boston: Kluwer-Nijhoff.

**Farrington, D. P.** (1986). Age and crime. In M. Tonry & N. Morris (Eds.), *Crime and Justice* (**Vol. 7,** pp. 29–60). Chicago: University of Chicago Press.

**Farrington, D. P.** (1987). Epidemiology. In H. C. Quay (Ed.), *Handbook of juvenile delinquency* (pp. 33–61). New York: Wiley.

**Farrington, D. P., Gallagher, B., Morley, L., & St. Ledger, R. J., & West, J. W.** (1986). Unemployment, school leaving, and crime. *British Journal of Criminology, 26,* 335–356.

**Farrington, D. P., Loeber, R., Elliott, D. S., Hawkins, J. D., Kandel, D. B., Klein, M. W., McCord, J., Rowe, D. C., & Tremblay, R. E.** (1990). Advancing knowledge about the onset of delinquency and crime. In B. B. Lahey & A. E. Kazdin (Eds.), *Advances in clinical child psychology* (**Vol. 13,** pp. 283–336). New York: Plenum.

**Faust, M.** (1983). Alternative constructions of adolescent growth. In J. Brooks-Gunn & A. C. Petersen (Eds.), *Girls at puberty: Biological, psychological, and social perspectives* (pp. 105–126). New York: Plenum.

**Faust, M. S.** (1977). Somatic development of adolescent girls. *Monographs of the Society for Research in Child Development, 42*(1), 1–90.

**Fawcett, J.** (1975). Biochemical and neuropharmacological research in the affective disorders. In E. J. Anthony & T. Benedek (Eds.), *Depression and human existence* (pp. 21–52). Boston: Little, Brown.

**Federle, K. H., & Chesney-Lind, M.** (1992). Special issues in juvenile justice: Gender, race, and ethnicity. In I. M. Schwartz (Ed.), *Juvenile justice and public policy: Toward a national agenda* (pp. 165–195). New York: Lexington Books.

**Feigelman, S., Stanton, B. F., & Ricardo, I.** (1993). Perceptions of drug selling and drug use among urban youths. *Journal of Early Adolescence, 13,* 267–284.

**Feinberg, I.** (1987). Adolescence and mental illness. *Science, 236,* 507–508.

**Feinstein, S. C., & Ardon, M. S.** (1973). Trends in dating patterns and adolescent development. *Journal of Youth and Adolescence, 2,* 157–166.

**Feld, B. C.** (1992). Criminalizing the juvenile court: A research agenda for the 1990s. In I. M. Schwartz (Ed.), *Juvenile justice and public policy: Toward a national agenda* (pp. 1–19). New York: Lexington Books.

**Feldman, D. H.** (1989). Creativity: Proof that development occurs. In W. Damon (Ed.), *Child development today and tomorrow* (pp. 240–260). San Francisco: Jossey-Bass.

**Feldman, L. (Ed.)** (1988). *Partnership for youth 2000: A program models manual.* Tulsa: University of Oklahoma, National Resource Center for Youth Services.

**Feldman, N. S., Klosson, E. C., Parsons, J. E., Rholes, W. S., & Ruble, D. N.** (1976). Order of information presentation on children's moral judgments. *Child Development, 47,* 556–559.

**Feldman, S. S., & Weinberger, D. A.** (1994). Self-restraint as a mediator on boys' delinquent behavior: A longitudinal study. *Child Development, 65,* 195–211.

**Feldman, S. S., & Wentzel, K. R.** (1990). The relationship between parenting styles, sons' self-restraint, and peer relations in early adolescence. *Journal of Early Adolescence, 10,* 439–454.

**Feldman, S. S., & Wood, D. N.** (1994). Parents' expectations for preadolescent sons' behavioral autonomy: A longitudinal study of correlates and outcomes. *Journal of Research on Adolescence, 4,* 45–70.

**Fenzel, L. M., Blyth, D. A., & Simmons, R. G.** (1991). School transitions, secondary. In R. M. Lerner, A. C. Petersen, & J. Brooks-Gunn (Eds.), *Encyclopedia of adolescence* (**Vol. 2,** pp. 970–973). New York: Garland Publishing.

**Ferris, B. G., Whittenberger, J. L., & Gallagher, J. R.** (1952). Maximum breathing capacity and vital capacity of male children and adolescents. *Pediatrics, 9,* 659–670.

**Fine, J. T.** (1981). Sex similarities in behavior in a seventh grade classroom. *Journal of Early Adolescence, 1,* 233–243.

**Fine, M.** (1988). Sexuality, schooling, and adolescent females: The missing discourse of desire. *Harvard Educational Review, 58,* 29–55.

**Fingerhut, L. A., Ingram, D. D., & Feldman, J. J.** (1992). Firearm and nonfirearm homicide among persons 15 through 19 years of age: Differences by level of urbanization, United States, 1979 through 1989. *Journal of the American Medical Association, 267,* 3048–3053.

**Finkelhor, D.** (1990). Early and long-term effects of child sexual abuse: An update. *Professional psychology: Research and Practice, 21,* 325–330.

**Finnegan, L. P., & Kandall, S. R.** (1992). Maternal and neonatal effects of alcohol and drugs. In J. H. Lowinson, P. Ruiz, R. B. Millman, & J. G Langrod (Eds.), *Substance abuse: A comprehensive textbook* (2nd ed., pp. 628–656). Baltimore: Williams & Wilkins.

**Fischer, C. S.** (1977). *Networks and places: Social relations in the urban setting.* New York: Free Press.

**Fischer, J.** (1981). Transitions in relationship style from adolescence to young adulthood. *Journal of Youth and Adolescence, 10,* 11–23.

**Fischer, J. L.** (1980). Reciprocity, agreement, and family style in family systems with a disturbed and nondisturbed adolescent. *Journal of Youth and Adolescence,* **9,** 391–406.

**Fischer, K. W., & Silvern, L.** (1985). Stages and individual differences in cognitive development. *Annual Review of Psychology,* **36,** 613–618.

**Fiske, E. B.** (1987a, Jan. 4). Searching for the key to science literacy. *The New York Times,* pp. 20–23.

**Fiske, E. B.** (1987b, Aug. 24). Report warns school reforms may fall short. *The New York Times,* pp. 1, 10.

**Flanagan, C. A.** (1990). Change in family work status: Effects on parent–adolescent decision-making. *Child Development,* **61,** 163–177.

**Flanagan, C. A., & Eccles, J. S.** (1993). Changes in parents' work status and adolescents' adjustment at school. *Child Development,* **64,** 246–257.

**Flanagan, C. A., Schulenberg, J., & Fuligni, A.** (1993). Residential setting and parent–adolescent relationships during the college years. *Journal of Youth and Adolescence,* **22,** 171–189.

**Flannery, D. J., Rowe, D. C., & Gulley, B. L.** (1993). Impact of pubertal status, timing, and age on adolescent sexual experience and delinquency. *Journal of Adolescent Research,* **8,** 21–40.

**Flavell, J. H.** (1963). *The developmental psychology of Jean Piaget.* New York: Van Nostrand.

**Flavell, J. H.** (1985). *Cognitive development* (2nd ed.). Englewood Cliffs, NJ: Prentice-Hall.

**Fleming, J. E., & Offord, D. R.** (1990). Epidemiology of childhood depressive disorders: A critical review. *Journal of the American Academy of Child and Adolescent Psychiatry,* **29,** 571–580.

**Floderus-Myrhed, B., Pedersen, N., & Rasmuson, I.** (1980). Assessment of heritability for personality based on a short form of the Eysenck Personality Inventory: A study of 12,898 twin pairs. *Behavior Genetics,* **10,** 153–162.

**Ford, C. S.** (1961). Culture and sex. In A. Ellis & A. Abarband (Eds.), *The encyclopedia of sexual behavior* (**Vol. 1,** pp. 306–312). New York: Hawthorn Books.

**Ford, C. S. & Beach, F. A.** (1951). *Patterns of sexual behavior.* New York: Harper & Row.

**Ford, D. Y.** (1992). Self-perceptions of underachievement and support for the achievement ideology among early adolescent African-Americans. *Journal of Early Adolescence,* **12,** 228–252.

**Ford, M. E.** (1982). Social cognition and social competence in adolescence. *Developmental Psychology,* **18,** 323–340.

**Forehand, R., Wierson, M., Thomas, A. M., Fauber, R., Armistead, L., Kemptom, T., & Long, N.** (1991). A short-term longitudinal examination of young adolescent functioning following divorce: The role of family factors. *Journal of Abnormal Child Psychology,* **19,** 97–111.

**The forgotten half: Pathways to success for America's youth and families.** (1988). Washington, DC: Youth and America's Future: The William T. Grant Commission on Work, Family, and Citizenship.

**Forrest, J. P., & Singh, S.** (1990). The sexual and reproductive behavior of American women, 1982–1988. *Family Planning Perspectives,* **22,** 206–214.

**Fowler, J. W.** (1981). *Stages of faith: The psychology of human development and the quest for meaning.* San Francisco: Harper & Row.

**Frances, R. J., & Miller, S. I.** (1991). *Clinical textbook of addictive disorders.* New York: Guilford Press.

**Frankel, J. (Ed.)** (1993). *The employed mother and the family context.* New York: Springer.

**Fraser, F. C., & Nora, J. J.** (1986). *Genetics of man* (2nd ed.). Philadelphia: Lea & Febiger.

**Freedland, J., & Dwyer, J.** (1991). Nutrition in adolesent girls. In R. M. Lerner, A. C. Petersen, & J. Brooks-Gunn. *Encyclopedia of adolescence* (**Vol. II,** pp. 714–728). New York: Garland.

**Freedman, J., & Humphrey, R.** (1985). Antecedents of college drinking. *Journal of Youth and Adolescence,* **14,** 11–22.

**Freedman, M.** (1971). *Homosexuality and psychological functioning.* Monterey, CA: Brooks/Cole.

**Freeman, D.** (1983). *Margaret Mead and Samoa: The making and unmaking of an anthropological myth.* Cambridge, MA: Harvard University Press.

**Freeman, R. N.** (1986, July 20). Cutting black youth unemployment. *The New York Times.*

**Freud, A.** (1958). Adolescence. *Psychoanalytic Study of the Child,* **13,** 255–278.

**Freud, A.** (1966). *The ego and the mechanisms of defense* (rev. ed.). New York: International Universities Press.

**Freud, A.** (1968). Adolescence. In A. E. Winder & D. Angus (Eds.), *Adolescence: Contemporary studies* (pp. 13–24). New York: American Book.

**Freud, A.** (1969). Adolescence as a developmental disturbance. In G. Caplan & S. Lebovici (Eds.), *Adolescence: Psychosocial perspectives.* New York: Basic Books.

**Freud, S.** (1953). *A general introduction to psychoanalysis* (Joan Riviere, trans.). New York: Permabooks.

**Freud, S.** (1964). *An outline of psychoanalysis.* Standard edition of the works of Sigmund Freud. London: Hogarth Press.

**Friedman, M. A., & Brownell, K. D.** (1995). Psychological correlates of obesity: Moving to the next research generation. *Psychological Bulletin,* **117,** 3–20.

**Friedman, W. J., Robinson, A. B., & Friedman, B. L.** (1987). Sex differences in moral judgments: A test of Gilligan's theory. *Psychology of Women Quarterly,* **11,** 37–46.

**Friedrich, W., Reams, R., & Jacobs, J.** (1982). Depression and suicidal ideation in early adolescents. *Journal of Youth and Adolescence,* **11,** 403–407.

**Frisch, R. E., Gotz-Welbergen, A. V., McArthur, J. W., Albright, T., Witschi, J., Bullen, B., Birnhelz, J., Reed, R. B., & Hermann, H.** (1981). Delayed menarche and amenorrhea of college athletes in relation to age of onset and training. *Journal of the American Medical Association,* **246,** 1559–1590.

**Fromm, E.** (1941). *Escape from freedom.* New York: Holt, Rinehart & Winston.

**Fromm, E.** (1955). *The sane society.* New York: Holt, Rinehart & Winston.

**Fuligni, A. J., Eccles, J. S., & Barber, B. L.** (1995). The long-term effects of seventh-grade ability grouping in mathematics. *Journal of Early Adolescence,* **15,** 58–89.

**Fullerton, H. N.** (1986). The 1995 labor force: BLS' latest projections. In *Employment projections for 1995: Data and*

*methods* (pp. 16–24). Washington, DC: U.S. Government Printing Office.

Furby, L., & Beyth-Marom, R. (1992). Risk taking in adolescence: A decision-making perspective. *Developmental Review, 12,* 1–44.

Fuhrmann, B. S. (1986). *Adolescence, adolescents.* Boston: Little, Brown.

Furman, W., & Buhrmester, D. (1992). Age and sex differences in perceptions of networks of personal relationships. *Child Development, 63,* 103–115.

Furstenberg, F. F., Brooks-Gunn, J., & Chase-Lansdale, L. (1989). Teenage pregnancy and childbearing. Special issues: Children and their development: Knowledge base, research agenda, and social policy application. *American Psychologist, 44,* 313–320.

Furstenberg, F. I., Jr., Brooks-Gunn, J., & Morgan, S. P. (1987). *Adolescent mothers in later life.* New York: Cambridge University Press.

Gaddis, A., & Brooks-Gunn, J. (1985). The male experience of pubertal change. *Journal of Youth and Adolescence, 14,* 61–69.

Galambos, N. L., & Almeida, D. M. (1992). Does parent–adolescent conflict increase in early adolescence? *Journal of Marriage and the Family, 54,* 737–747.

Galambos, N. L., Almeida, D. M., & Petersen, A. C. (1990). Masculinity, femininity, and sex role attitudes in early adolescence: Exploring gender intensification. *Child Development, 61,* 1905–1914.

Galambos, N. L., & Ehrenberg, M. F. (in press). The family as health risk and opportunity: A focus on divorce and working families. In J. Schulenberg, J. Maggs, & K. Hurrelmann (Eds.), *Health risks and developmental transitions during adolescence.* Cambridge: Cambridge University Press.

Galambos, N. L., & Garbarino, J. (1985). Adjustment of unsupervised children in a rural setting. *Journal of Genetic Psychology, 146,* 227–231.

Galambos, N. L., & Maggs, J. L. (1991). Out-of-school care of young adolescents and self-reported behavior. *Developmental Psychology, 27,* 644–655.

Galambos, N. L., Petersen, A. C., & Lenerz, K. (1988). Maternal employment and sex-typing in adolescence: Contemporaneous and longitudinal relations. In A. E. Gottfried & A. Gottfried (Eds.), *Maternal employment and children's development: Longitudinal research* (pp. 155–189). New York: Plenum.

Galambos, N. L., Sears, H. A., Almeida, D. M., & Kolaric, G. C. (1995). Parents' work overload and problem behavior in young adolescents. *Journal of Research on Adolescence, 5,* 201–223.

Galambos, N. L., & Silbereisen, R. K. (1987). Influence of income change and parental acceptance on adolescent transgression proneness and peer relations. *European Journal of Psychology of Education, 1,* 17–28.

Gallup, G. (1978, Jan. 15). Gallup youth survey. *Denver Post,* p. 50. *The Gallup Report.* (1991, Jan. 10).

Gallup, G. (1979, Nov. 20). Gallup youth survey. *Denver Post,* p. 36.

Galotti, K. M., Kozberg, S. F., & Farmer, M. C. (1991). Gender and developmental differences in adolescents' conceptions of moral reasoning. *Journal of Youth and Adolescence, 20,* 13–30.

Gamoran, A., & Nystrand, M. (1991). Background and instructional effects on achievement in eighth-grade English and social studies. *Journal of Research on Adolescence, 1,* 277–300.

Gantman, C. A. (1978). Family interaction patterns among families with normal, disturbed, and drug-abusing adolescents. *Journal of Youth and Adolescence, 7,* 429–440.

Garbarino, J. (1980). Some thoughts on school size and its effects on adolescent development. *Journal of Youth and Adolescence, 9,* 19–31.

Garbarino, J. (1985). *Adolescent development: An ecological perspective.* Columbus, OH: Charles E. Merrill.

Garbarino, J. (1989). Troubled youth, troubled families: The dynamics of adolescent maltreatment. In D. Cicchetti & V. Carlson (Eds.), *Child maltreatment: Theory and research on the causes and consequences of child abuse and neglect* (pp. 685–706). New York: Cambridge University Press.

Garbarino, J., & Kelly, A. F. (1986). An introduction to troubled youth and troubled families. In J. Garbarino, C. J. Schellenbach, & J. M. Sebes (Eds.), *Troubled youth, troubled families: Understanding families at risk for adolescent maltreatment* (pp. 3–26). New York: Aldine de Gruyter.

Garbarino, J., Schellenbach, C. J., & Sebes, J. M. (1986). *Troubled youth, troubled families: Understanding families at risk for adolescent maltreatment.* New York: Aldine de Gruyter.

Garbarino, J., & Sherman, D. (1980). High-risk neighborhoods and high-risk families: The ecology of child maltreatment. *Child Development, 51,* 188–198.

Gardner, H. (1983). *Frames of mind: The theory of multiple intelligences.* New York: Basic Books.

Gardner, H. (1989). Beyond a modular view of the mind. In W. Damon (Ed.), *Child development today and tomorrow* (pp. 222–230). San Francisco: Jossey-Bass.

Gardner, H. (1993). *Multiple intelligences: The theory in practice.* New York: Basic Books.

Gardner, M. K., & Clark, E. (1992). The psychometric perspective on intellectual development in childhood and adolescence. In R. J. Sternberg & C. A. Berg (Eds.), *Intellectual development* (pp. 16–43). Cambridge: Cambridge University Press.

Garmezy, N. (1987). Stress, competency, and development: Continuities in the study of schizophrenic adults, children vulnerable to psychopathology, and the search for stress-resistant children. *American Journal of Orthopsychiatry, 57,* 159–174.

Garmezy, N., & Masten, A. S. (1994). Chronic adversities. In M. Rutter, E. Taylor, & L. Hersov (Eds.), *Child and adolescent psychiatry: Modern approaches* (pp. 191–208). Oxford: Blackwell Scientific Publications.

Garmezy, N., Masten, A. S., & Tellegen, A. (1984). The study of stress and competence in children: A building block for developmental psychopathology. *Child Development, 55,* 97–111.

Gavazzi, S. M., Anderson, S. A., & Sabatelli, R. M. (1993). Family differentiation, peer differentiation, and adolescent adjustment in a clinical sample. *Journal of Adolescent Research, 8,* 205–224.

Gawronski, D. A., & Mathis, C. (1965). Differences between over-achieving, normal-achieving, and under-achieving high-school students. *Psychology in the Schools,* **2,** 152–155.

Gaylin, J. (1978, March). What boys look for in girls. *Seventeen,* 107–113.

Gaylin, J. (1979, March). What girls really look for in boys. *Seventeen,* 131–137.

Ge, X., Lorenz, F. O., Conger, R. D., Elder, G. H., Jr., & Simons, R. L. (1994). Trajectories of stressful life events and depressive symptoms during adolescence. *Developmental Psychology,* **30,** 467–483.

Gelman, D. (1990, Summer/Fall). A much riskier passage. *Newsweek* (Special Edition), pp. 10–17.

Gerber, R. W., & Norman, I. M. (1989). Predicting future smoking of adolescent experimental smokers. *Journal of Youth and Adolescence,* **18,** 191–201.

Gesell, A., Ilg, F. L., & Ames, L. B. (1956). *Youth: The years from ten to sixteen.* New York: Harper & Row.

Gibbs, J. C., Arnold, K. D., & Burkhart, J. E. (1984). Sex differences in the expression of moral judgment. *Child Development,* **55,** 1040–1043.

Gibbs, N. (1993, May 24). How should we teach our children about sex? *Time,* **141,** 60–66.

Gilligan, C. (1977). In a different voice: Women's conception of the self and of morality. *Harvard Educational Review,* **47,** 481–517.

Gilligan, C. (1979). Woman's place in man's life cycle. *Harvard Educational Review,* **49,** 431–446.

Gilligan, C. (1982). *In a different voice: Psychological theory and women's development.* Cambridge, MA: Harvard University Press.

Gilligan, C., & Attanucci, J. (1988). Two moral orientations: Gender differences and similarities. *Merrill–Palmer Quarterly,* **34,** 223–237.

Gillis, J. R. (1974). *Youth and history.* New York: Academic Press.

Ginsburg, G. S., & Bronstein, P. (1993). Family factors related to children's intrinsic/extrinsic motivational orientation and academic performance. *Child Development,* **64,** 1461–1474.

Ginsburg, H., & Opper, S. (1979). *Piaget's theory of intellectual development* (2nd ed.). Englewood Cliffs, NJ: Prentice-Hall.

Ginzberg, E. (1972). Toward a theory of occupational choice: A restatement. *Vocational Guidance Quarterly,* **20,** 169–176.

Giordano, P. C., Cernkovich, S. A., & DeMaris, A. (1993). The family and peer relations of black adolescents. *Journal of Marriage and the Family,* **55,** 277–287.

Glick, M., & Zigler, E. (1990). Premorbid competence and the courses and outcomes of psychiatric disorders. In J. Rolf, A. S. Masten, D. Cicchetti, K. H. Nuechterlein, & S. Weintraub (Eds.), *Risk and protective factors in the development of psychopathology* (pp. 497–513). Cambridge: Cambridge University Press.

Glick, P. C. (1984). Marriage, divorce, and living arrangements: Prospective changes. *Journal of Family Issues,* **5,** 7–26.

Glynn, T. J. (1981). From family to peer: A review of transitions of influence among drug using youth. *Journal of Youth and Adolescence,* **10,** 363–383.

Glyshaw, K., Cohen, L., & Towbes, L. (1989). Coping strategies and psychological distress: Prospective analysis of early and middle adolescence. *American Journal of Community Psychology,* **17,** 607–623.

Goertz, M. E., Ekstrom, R. B., & Rock, D. A. (1991). High school drop-outs: Issues of race and sex. In R. M. Lerner, A. C. Petersen, & J. Brooks-Gunn (Eds.), *Encyclopedia of adolescence* (pp. 250–253). New York: Garland.

Gold, D., & Andres, D. (1978a). Comparisons of adolescent children with employed and nonemployed mothers. *Merrill–Palmer Quarterly,* **24,** 242–254.

Gold, D., & Andres, D. (1978b). Developmental comparisons between 10-year-old children with employed and nonemployed mothers. *Child Development,* **49,** 75–84.

Gold, M. (1987). Social ecology. In H. C. Quay (Ed), *Handbook of juvenile delinquency* (pp. 62–105). New York: Wiley.

Gold, M. S. (1992). Cocaine (and crack): Clinical aspects. In J. H. Lowinson, P. Ruiz, R. B. Millman, & J. G. Langrod (Eds.), *Substance abuse: A comprehensive textbook* (2nd ed., pp. 205–221). Baltimore: Williams & Wilkins.

Gold, M. S., Miller, N. S., Jonas, J. M. (1992). Cocaine (and crack): Neurobiology. In J. H. Lowinson, P. Ruiz, R. B. Millman, & J. G. Langrod (Eds.), *Substance abuse: A comprehensive textbook* (2nd ed., pp. 222–235). Baltimore: Williams & Wilkins.

Gold, M. S., & Petronio, R. J. (1980). Delinquent behavior in adolescence. In J. Adelson (Ed.), *Handbook of adolescent psychology.* New York: Wiley.

Gold, M. S., & Verebey, K. (1984). The psychopharmacology of cocaine. *Psychiatric Annals,* **14,** 714–723.

Goldfarb, J. L., Mumford, D. M., Schum, D. A., Smith, P. B., Flowers, C., & Schum, D. (1977). An attempt to detect "pregnancy susceptibility" in indigent adolescent girls. *Journal of Youth and Adolescence,* **6,** 127–144.

Goldsen, R., Rosenberg, M., Williams, R., & Suchman, I. (1960). *What college students think.* New York: Van Nostrand.

Goldsmith, H. H. (1984). Continuity of personality: A genetic perspective. In R. N. Emde & R. J. Harmon (Eds.), *The development of attachment and affiliative systems.* New York: Plenum.

Goldsmith, H. H. (1994, Winter). The behavior-genetic approach to development and experience: Contexts and constraints. *SRCD Newsletter,* **1**(6), 10–11.

Goldstein, M. J. (1981). Family factors associated with schizophrenia and anorexia nervosa. *Journal of Youth and Adolescence,* **10,** 385–405.

Goldstein, M. J. (1987). The UCLA high-risk project, 1962–1986. *Schizophrenia Bulletin,* **13,** 505–514.

Goldstein, M. J. (1990). Family relations as risk factors for the onset and course of schizophrenia. In J. Rolf, A. Masten, D. Cicchetti, K. H. Nuechterlein, & S. Weintraub (Eds.), *Risk and protective factors in the development of psychopathology* (pp. 408–423). Cambridge: Cambridge University Press.

Goldstein, M. J., Baker, B. L., & Jamison, K. R. (1980). *Abnormal psychology: Experiences, origins, and interventions.* Boston: Little, Brown.

Goldstein, M. J., Rodnick, E. H., Jones, J. E., McPherson, S. R., & West, K. L. (1978). Familial precursors of

schizophrenia spectrum disorders. In L. D. Wynne, R. L. Cromwell, & S. Matthysse (Eds.), *The nature of schizophrenia.* New York: Wiley.

**Good, T. L., & Weinstein, R. S.** (1986). Schools make a difference: Evidence, criticisms, and new directions. *American Psychologist, 41,* 1090–1097.

*Good Housekeeping.* (1993, June). Parents! What you must know about your teenager's sex life, pp. 144–145, 196–199.

**Goodchilds, J. D., & Zellman, G. L.** (1984). Sexual signalling and sexual aggression in adolescent relationships. In N. M. Malamuth & E. D. Donnerstein (Eds.), *Pornography and sexual aggression.* New York: Academic Press.

**Gordon, D. A., & Arbuthnot, J.** (1987). Individual, group, and family interventions. In H. C. Quay (Ed.), *Handbook of juvenile delinquency* (pp. 290–324). New York: Wiley.

**Gore, S., Aseltine, R. H., Jr., Colten, M. E.** (1993). Gender, social-relational involvement, and depression. *Journal of Research on Adolescence, 3,* 101–125.

**Gose, B.** (1995, March 17). Many freshmen become binge drinkers during their first semester, study finds. *Chronicle of Higher Education,* p 3.

**Gottesman, I. I., & Bertelsen, A.** (1989). Confirming unexpressed genotypes for schizophrenia: Risks in the offspring of Fischer's Danish identical and fraternal discordant pairs. *Archives of General Psychiatry, 46,* 867–872.

**Gottesman, I. I., & Shields, J.** (1982). *Schizophrenia: The enigmatic puzzle.* New York: Cambridge University Press.

**Gottfredson, G. D., Jones, E. M., & Holland, J. L.** (1993). Personality and vocational interests: The relation of Holland's six interest dimensions to five robust dimensions of personality. *Journal of Counselling Psychology, 40,* 518–524.

**Gottfried, A. E., Gottfried, A. W., & Bathhurst, K.** (1988). Maternal employment, family environment and children's development: Infancy through the school years. In A. E. Gottfried & A. W. Gottfried (Eds.), *Maternal employment and children's development: Longitudinal research* (pp. 11–58). New York: Plenum.

**Gove, W., & Peterson, C.** (1980). An update of the literature on personal and marital satisfaction: The effect of children and the employment of wives. *Marriage and Family Review, 3,* 63–96.

**Graber, J. A., Brooks-Gunn, J., Paikoff, R. L., & Warren, M. P.** (1994). Prediction of eating problems: An 8-year study of adolescent girls. *Developmental Psychology, 30,* 823–834.

**Graber, J. A., & Petersen, A. C.** (1991). Cognitive changes at adolescence: Biological perspectives. In K. R. Gibson & A. C. Petersen (Eds.), *Brain maturation and cognitive development: Comparative and cross-cultural perspectives* (pp. 253–279). New York: Aldine de Gruyter.

**Grabowski, J. (Ed.).** (1984). *Cocaine: Pharmacology, effects, and treatment* (NIDA Research Monograph 50.) Washington, DC: U.S. Government Printing Office.

**Grace, W. C., & Sweeney, M. E.** (1986). Comparison of the P>V sign on the WISC-R and WAIS-R in delinquent males. *Journal of Clinical Psychology, 42,* 173–176.

**Graham, P. J.** (1985). Psychosomatic relationships. In M. Rutter & L. Hersov (Eds.), *Child and adolescent psychiatry: Modern approaches* (pp. 599–613). Oxford: Blackwell Scientific Publications.

**Graham, P., & Rutter, M.** (1985). Adolescent disorders. In M. Rutter & L. Hersov (Eds.), *Child and adolescent psychiatry: Modern approaches* (pp. 351–367). Oxford: Blackwell Scientific Publications.

**Grant, J., & Cappel, F.** (1983). *Reducing school crime: A report on the School Team Approach.* Washington, DC: U.S. Government Printing Office.

**Graziano, A. M., & Diament, D. M.** (1992). Parental behavioral training: An examination of the paradigm. *Behavior Modification, 16,* 3–38.

**Green, R.** (1980). Homosexuality. In H. I. Kaplan, A. M. Freedeman, & B. J. Sadock (Eds.), *Comprehensive textbook of psychiatry* (**Vol. 2,** pp. 1762–1770). Baltimore: Williams & Wilkins.

**Green, R.** (1987). *"The sissy boy syndrome" and the development of homosexuality: A 15-year prospective study.* New Haven, CT: Yale University Press.

**Greenberger, E., & Goldberg, W. A.** (1989). Work, parenting, and the socialization of children. *Developmental Psychology, 25,* 22–35.

**Greenberger, E., & Steinberg, L.** (1986). *When teenagers work: The psychological and social costs of adolescent employment.* New York: Basic Books.

**Grinspoon, L., & Bakalar, J. D.** (1992). Marijuana. In J. H. Lowinson, P. Ruiz, R. B. Millman, & J. G. Langrod (Eds.), *Substance abuse: A comprehensive textbook* (2nd ed., pp. 262–264). Baltimore: Williams & Wilkins.

**Grosvenor, G. M.** (1989). Our year in review: Superpowers not so super in geography. *National Geographic, 176,* 816–821.

**Grotevant, H. D., & Cooper, C. R.** (Eds.). (1983). *Adolescent development in the family.* San Francisco: Jossey-Bass.

**Grotevant, H. D., & Cooper, C. R.** (1985). Patterns of interaction in family relationships and the development of identity exploration in adolescence. *Child Development, 56,* 415–428.

**Grotevant, H. D., & Cooper, C. R.** (1988). The role of family experience in career exploration: A life-span perspective. In R. M. Lerner & D. Featherman (Eds.), *Life-span development and behavior* (**Vol. 8**). Hillsdale, NJ: Erlbaum.

**Grusec, J. E., & Goodnow, J. J.** (1994). Impact of parental discipline methods on the child's internalization of values: A reconceptualization of current points of view. *Developmental Psychology, 30,* 4–19.

**Guerin, D. W., Gottfried, A. W., Oliver, P. H., & Thomas, C. W.** (1994). Temperament and school functioning during early adolescence. *Journal of Early Adolescence, 14,* 200–225.

**Guidubaldi, J., & Nastasi, B. K.** (1987, April). *Home environment factors as predictors of child adjustment in mother-employed households: Results of a nationwide study.* Paper presented at the biennial meeting of the Society for Research in Child Development, Baltimore.

**Guidubaldi, J., & Perry, J. D.** (1985). Divorce and mental health sequelae for children: A two-year follow-up of a nationwide sample. *Journal of the American Academy of Child Psychiatry, 24,* 531–537.

**Guilford, J. P.** (1982). Cognitive psychology's ambiguities: Some suggested remedies. *Psychological Review, 89,* 48–49.

Gump, P. V. (1966). *Big schools, small schools.* Moravia, NY: Chronicle Guidance Publications.

Gupta, D., Attanasio, A., & Raaf, S. (1975). Plasma estrogen and androgen concentrations in children during adolescence. *Journal of Clinical Endocrinology and Metabolism,* **40,** 636–643.

Gustafson, S. B., Stattin, H., & Magnusson, D. (1992). Aspects of the development of a career versus homemaking orientation among females: The longitudinal influence of educational motivation and peers. *Journal of Research on Adolescence,* **2,** 241–259.

Guttmacher, A. F., & Kaiser, J. H. (1986). *Pregnancy, birth, and family planning.* New York: New American Library.

Haan, N. (1977). *Coping and defending: Processes of self-environment organization.* New York: Academic Press.

Halaas, J. L., Gajiwala, K. S., Maffei, M., Cohen, S. L., Chait, B. T., Rabinowitz, D., Lallone, R., Burley, S. K., & Friedman, J. M. (1995). Weight-reducing effects of the plasma protein encoded by the *obese* gene. *Science,* **269,** 543–546.

Hale, S. (1990). A global developmental trend in cognitive processing speed. *Child Development,* **61,** 653–663.

Hall, G. S. (1904, 1905). *Adolescence: Its psychology and its relations to physiology, anthropology, sociology, sex, crime, religion, and education* (**Vol. I**) Englewood Cliffs, NJ: Prentice-Hall.

Hall, G. S. (1923). *Life and confessions of a psychologist.* Englewood Cliffs, NJ: Prentice-Hall.

Hallinan, M. (1981). Recent advances in sociometry. In S. Asher & J. Gottman (Eds.), *The development of children's friendships* (pp. 91–115). New York: Cambridge University Press.

Hallinan, M. T. (1991). School differences in tracking structures and track assignments. *Journal of Research on Adolescence,* **1,** 251–276.

Hallinan, M. T. (1994). School differences in tracking effects on achievement. *Social Forces,* **72,** 799–820.

Halmic, K. A., Goldberg, S. C., Casper, R. C., Eckert, E. D., & Davis, J. M. (1979). Pretreatment predictors of outcome in anorexia nervosa. *British Journal of Psychiatry,* **134,** 71–78.

Halter, M. (1995). *Tzedek: The Righteous* (documentary film).

Hamburg, D. A., Elliott, G. R., & Parron, D. L. (1982). *Health and behavior: Frontiers of research in the biobehavioral sciences.* Washington, DC: National Academy Press.

Hamburg, D. A., & Trudeau, M. B. (1981). *Biobehavioral aspects of aggression.* New York: Alan R. Liss.

Hamer, D. H., Hu, S., Magnuson, V. L., Hu, N., & Pattatucci, A. M. L. (1993). A linkage between DNA markers on the X chromosome and male sexual orientation. *Science,* **261,** 321–327.

Hamilton, S. W. (1994). Employment prospects as motivation for school achievement: Links and gaps between school and work in seven countries. In R. K. Silbereisen & E. Todt (Eds.), *Adolescence in context: The interplay of family, school, peers, and work in adjustment* (pp. 267–283). New York: Springer-Verlag.

Hamlett, K. W., & Curry, J. F. (1990). Anorexia nervosa in adolescent males: A review and case study. *Child Psychiatry and Human Development,* **21,** 79–94.

Hammond, W. R., & Yung, B. (1993). Psychology's role in the public health response to assaultive violence among young African-American men. *American Psychologist,* **48,** 142–154.

Hannah, J. S., & Kahn, S. E. (1989). The relationship of socioeconomic status and gender to the occupational choices of grade 12 students. *Journal of Vocational Behavior,* **34,** 161–178.

Hansen, D. J., Christopher, J. S., & Nangle, D. W. (1992). Adolescent heterosexual interactions and dating. In V. B. Van Hasselt & M. Hersen (Eds.), *Handbook of social development: A life-span perspective* (pp. 371–394). New York: Plenum Press.

Hanson, C. L., Cigrang, J., Harris, M., Carle, D., Relyea, G., & Burghen, G. (1989). Coping styles in youths with insulin-dependent diabetes mellitus. *Journal of Consulting and Clinical Psychology,* **57,** 644–651.

Hanson, D. R., Gottesman, I. I., & Heston, L. L. (1990). Long-range schizophrenia forecasting: Many a slip twixt cup and lip. In J. Rolf, A. S. Masten, D. Cicchetti, K. H. Nuechterlein, & S. Weintraub (Eds.), *Risk and protective factors in the development of psychopathology* (pp. 480–496). Cambridge: Cambridge University Press.

Harberg, E. D., Francisco, W., Webster, D. W., Gleiberman, L., & Schork, A. (1990). Familial transmission of alcohol use. II. Initiation of an aversion to parent drinking by adult offspring. *Journal of Studies on Alcohol,* **51,** 133–138.

Harevan, T. K. (1984). Themes in the historical development of the family. In R. D. Parke (Ed.), *Review of child development research* (**Vol. 7,** pp. 137–178). Chicago: University of Chicago Press.

Harlan, W. R. (1993). Epidemiology of childhood obesity: A national perspective. In C. L. Williams & S. Y. S. Kimm (Eds.), *Prevention and treatment of childhood obesity* (pp. 1–5). New York: New York Academy of Sciences.

Harlan, W. R., Harlan, E. A., & Grillo, G. R. (1980). Secondary sex characteristics of girls 12–17 years of age: The U.S. Health Examination Survey. *Journal of Pediatrics,* **96,** 1074–1087.

Harrel, T. W., & Harrel, M. S. (1945). Army General Classification Test scores for civilian occupations. *Educational and Psychological Measurement,* **5,** 229–239.

Harrington, R. (1994). Affective disorders. In M. Rutter, E. Taylor, & L. Hersov (Eds.), *Child and adolescent psychiatry* (3rd ed., pp. 330–350). Boston: Blackwell Scientific Publishers.

Harris, L. (1987). *Inside America.* New York: Vintage Books.

Hart, D. (1988). A longitudinal study of adolescents' socialization and identification as predictors of adult moral judgment development. *Merrill–Palmer Quarterly,* **34,** 245–260.

Hart, D., & Chmiel, S. (1992). Influence of defense mechanisms on moral judgment development: A longitudinal study. *Developmental Psychology,* **28,** 722–730.

Harter, S. (1990). Processes underlying adolescent self-concept formation. In R. Montemayor, G. R. Adams, & T. P. Gullotta (Eds.), *From childhood to adolescence: A transitional period?* (pp. 205–239). Newbury Park, CA: Russell Sage.

Harter, S. (1992). Developmental analysis of conflict caused by opposing attributes in the adolescent self-portrait. *Developmental Psychology,* **28,** 251–260.

Harter, S., Alexander, P. C., & Neimeyer, R. A. (1988). Long-term effects of incestuous child abuse in college women: Social adjustment, social cognition, and family characteristics. *Journal of Consulting and Clinical Psychology*, **56**, 5–8.

Hartley, R. E. (1960). Children's concepts of male and female roles. *Merrill–Palmer Quarterly*, **6**, 83–91.

Hartup, W. W. (1983). Peer relations. In P. H. Mussen (Series Ed.), E. M. Hetherington (Ed.), *Handbook of child psychology: Vol. 4. Socialization, personality, and social development* (4th ed., pp. 103–196). New York: Wiley.

Hartup, W. W. (1989). Social relationships and their significance. *American Psychologist*, **44**, 120–126.

Hartup, W. W., & Overhauser, S. (1991). Friendships. In R. M. Lerner, A. C. Petersen, & J. Brooks-Gunn (Eds.), *Encyclopedia of adolescence* (pp. 378–384). New York: Garland.

Harvey, P. D. (1991). Cognitive and linguistic functions of adolescent children at risk for schizophrenia. In E. F. Walker (Ed.), *Schizophrenia: A life-course developmental perspective* (pp. 139–156). San Diego, CA: Academic Press.

Hass, A. (1979). *Teenage sexuality: A survey of teenage sexual behavior.* New York: Macmillan.

Hauser, S. T., Book, B. K., Houlihan, J., Powers, S., Weiss-Perry, B., Follanshee, D., Jacobson, M., & Noan, G. G. (1987). Sex differences within the family: Studies of adolescent and parent family interactions. *Journal of Youth and Adolescence*, **16**, 199–220.

Havighurst, R. J. (1953). *Human development and education.* New York: Longmans, Green.

Hawkins, J. D., Catalano, R. F., & Miller, J. Y. (1992). Risk and protective factors for alcohol and other drug problems in adolescence and early adulthood: Implications for substance abuse prevention. *Psychological Bulletin*, **112**, 64–105.

Hayes, D. (Ed.) (1987). *Risking the future: Adolescent sexuality, pregnancy, and childbearing* (**Vol. 1**). Washington, DC: National Academy Press.

*Healthy people: The Surgeon General's report on health promotion and disease prevention.* (1979). Washington, DC: U.S. Government Printing Office.

Heath, A. (1983). *The self-concepts of school refusers.* Doctoral dissertation, University of London.

Hefner, R., Rebecca, M., & Oleshansky, B. (1975). Development of sex-role transcendence. *Human Development*, **18**, 143–158.

Hellgren, L., Gillberg, C., Enerskog, I. (1987). Antecedents of adolescent psychosis: A population-based study of school health problems in children who develop psychosis in adolescence. *Journal of the American Academy of Child and Adolescent Psychiatry*, **26**, 351–355.

Herbert, B. (1994, February 6). Kids know the real deal. *The New York Times*, p. 17.

Herrnstein, R. J., & Murray, C. (1994). *The bell curve.* New York: Free Press.

Hersen, M., Eisler, R. M., & Miller, P. M. (Eds.). (1990). *Progress in behavior modification* (**Vol. 25**). Newbury Park, CA: Sage.

Hershberger, S. L., & D'Augelli, A. R. (1995). The impact of victimization on the mental health and suicidality of lesbian, gay, and bisexual youths. *Developmental Psychology*, **31**, 63–74.

Hersov, L. (1985a). Emotional disorders. In M. Rutter & L. Hersov (Eds.), *Child and adolescent psychiatry: Modern approaches* (pp. 368–381). Oxford: Blackwell Scientific Publications.

Hersov, L. (1985b). School refusal. In M. Rutter & L. Hersov (Eds.), *Child and adolescent psychiatry: Modern approaches* (pp. 382–399). Oxford: Blackwell Scientific Publications.

Herzog, D. B., & Beresin, E. V. (1991). Anorexia nervosa. In J. M. Weiner (Ed.), *Textbook of child and adolescent psychiatry* (pp. 362–375). Washington, DC: American Psychiatric Press.

Herzog, D. P. (1988). Eating disorders. In A. M. Nicholi, Jr. (Ed.), *The new Harvard guide to psychiatry* (pp. 434–445). Cambridge, MA: Harvard University Press.

Hess, E. H. (1970). Ethology and developmental psychology. In P. H. Mussen (Ed.), *Carmichael's manual of child psychology* (**Vol. 1**, pp. 1–38). New York: Wiley.

Hess, R. D., & Halloway, S. D. (1984). Family and school as educational institutions. In R. D. Parke (Ed.), *Review of child development research*: **Vol. 7.** *The family* (pp. 179–222). Chicago: University of Chicago Press.

Hetherington, E. M. (1989). Coping with family transitions: Winners, losers, and survivors. Meetings of the Society for Research in Child Development (1987, Baltimore, Maryland). *Child Development*, **60**, 1–14.

Hetherington, E. M. (1993). An overview of the Virginia Longitudinal Study of Divorce and Remarriage with a focus on early adolescence. *Journal of Family Psychology*, **7**, 39–56.

Hetherington, E. M., & Camara, K. A. (1984). Families in transition: The process of dissolution and reconstitution. In R. D. Parke (Ed.), *Review of child development research*: **Vol. 7.** *The family* (pp. 398–439). Chicago: University of Chicago Press.

Hetherington, E. M., Clingempeel, G. W., Anderson, E. R., Deal, J. E., Hagan, M. S., Hollier, E. A., & Lindner, M. S. (1992). Coping with marital transitions: A family systems perspectives. *Monographs of the Society for Research in Child Development*, **57** (2–3, Serial No. 227).

Hetherington, E. M., Cox, M., & Cox, R. (1985). Long-term effects of divorce and remarriage on the adjustment of children. *Journal of the American Academy of Child Psychiatry*, **24**, 518–530.

Hetherington, E. M., Stouwie, R. J., & Redberg, E. H. (1971). Patterns of family interaction and child rearing attitudes related to three dimensions of juvenile delinquency. *Journal of Abnormal Psychology*, **75**, 160–176.

Higgins, E. T., & Bargh, J. A. (1987). Social cognition and social perception. *Annual Review of Psychology*, **38**, 369–425.

Higham, E. (1980). Variations in adolescent psychohormonal development. In J. Adelson (Ed.), *Handbook of Adolescent Psychology.* New York: Wiley.

Hilgard, E. R., Atkinson, R. L., & Atkinson, R. C. (1979). *Introduction to psychology* (7th ed.). New York: Harcourt Brace Jovanovich.

Hill, J., & Palmquist, W. (1978). Social cognition and social relations in early adolescence. *International Journal of Behavioural Development*, **1**, 1–36.

Hill, J. P., & Holmbeck, G. (1987). Disagreement about rules in families with seventh grade boys and girls. *Journal of Youth and Adolescence*, **16**, 221–246.

Hill, J. P., & Lynch, M. E. (1983). The intensification of gender-related role expectations during early adolescence. In J. Brooks-Gunn & A. C. Petersen (Eds.), *Girls at puberty: Biological, psychological, and social perspectives* (pp. 201–228). New York: Plenum.

Hiltes, P. (1995, April 19). Black teenagers are turning away from smoking. *The New York Times*, p. B7.

Hinojosa, M. (1995). *Crews: Gang members talk to Maria Hinojosa.* New York: Harcourt Brace.

Hirsch, B. J., & Rapkin, B. D. (1987). The transition to junior high school: A longitudinal study of self-esteem, psychological symptomatology, school life and social support. *Child Development*, **58**, 1235–1243.

Hirschi, T. (1969). *Causes of delinquency.* Berkeley: University of California Press.

Hirschi, T., & Hindelang, M. J. (1977). Intelligence and delinquency: A revisionist review. *American Sociological Review*, **42**, 571–587.

Hirschman, R. S., Leventhal, H., & Glynn, K. (1984). The development of smoking behavior: Conceptualization and supporting cross-sectional survey data. *Journal of Applied Social Psychology*, **14**, 184–206.

Hirschorn, M. W. (1988, Jan. 27). Coalition of 120 colleges hopes to encourage a million students to tutor "at risk" youths. *The Chronicle of Higher Education*, pp. A35, A38.

Hochschild, A. (1989). *The second shift.* New York: Avon.

Hock, E. (1980). Working and nonworking mothers and their infants: A comparative study of maternal care-giving characteristics and infant social behavior. *Merrill–Palmer Quarterly*, **26**, 79–101.

Hofferth, S. L. (1990). Trends in adolescent sexual activity, contraception, and pregnancy in the United States. In J. Bancroft & J. M. Reinisch (Eds.), *Adolescence and puberty* (pp. 218–233). New York: Oxford University Press.

Hofferth, S. L., Kahn, J. R., & Baldwin, W. (1987). Premarital sexual activity among U.S. teenage women over the past three decades. *Family Planning Perspectives*, **19**, 46–53.

Hoffman, L. W. (1973). The professional woman as mother. *Annals of the New York Academy of Sciences*, **208**, 211–216.

Hoffman, L. W. (1980). The effects of maternal employment on the academic attitudes and performance of school-aged children. *School Psychology Review*, **9**(4), 319–336.

Hoffman, L. W. (1984). Work, family, and socialization of the child. In R. D. Parke et al. (Eds.), *The review of child development research: Vol. 7. The family: An interdisciplinary perspective.* Chicago: University of Chicago Press.

Hoffman, L. W. (1986). Work, family, and the child. In M. Pallak & R. O. Perloff, *Psychology and work: Productivity, change, and employment* (pp. 171–220). Washington, DC: American Psychological Association.

Hoffman, L. W. (1989). Effects of maternal employment in the two-parent family. *American Psychologist*, **44**, 283–292.

Hoffman, M. (1994). Discipline and internalization. *Developmental Psychology*, **30**, 26–28.

Hoffman, M. L. (1970). Moral development. In P. H. Mussen (Ed.), *Carmichael's manual of child psychology* (**Vol. 2,** pp. 261–360). New York: Wiley.

Hoffman, M. L. (1975). Moral internalization, parental power, and the nature of parent–child interaction. *Developmental Psychology*, **11**, 228–239.

Hoffman, M. L. (1980). Moral development in adolescence. In J. Adelson (Ed.), *Handbook of adolescent psychology* (pp. 295–343). New York: Wiley.

Hoffman, M. L. (1983). Affective and cognitive processes in moral internalization. In E. T. Higgins, D. N. Ruble, & W. W. Hartup (Eds.) *Social cognition and social development: A sociocultural perspective* (pp. 236–274). New York: Cambridge University Press.

Hogan, R. (1980). The gifted adolescent. In J. Adelson (Ed.), *Handbook of adolescent psychology* (pp. 536–559). New York: Wiley.

Holahan, C. J., & Moos, R. H. (1987). Risk, resistance, and psychological distress: A longitudinal analysis with adults and children. *Journal of Abnormal Psychology*, **96**, 3–13.

Holinger, P. C., Offer, D., Barter, J. T., & Bell, C. C. (1994). *Suicide and homicide among adolescents.* New York: Guilford.

Holland, J. L. (1963a). Explorations of a theory of vocational choice: Part I. Vocational images and choice. *Vocational Guidance Quarterly*, **11**, 232–239.

Holland, J. L. (1963b). Explorations of a theory of vocational choice: Part II. Self-descriptions and vocational preferences. *Vocational Guidance Quarterly*, **12**, 17–24.

Holland, J. L. (1985). *Making vocational choices: A theory of vocational personalities and work environments.* Englewood Cliffs, NJ: Prentice-Hall.

Hollingworth, L. S. (1928). *The psychology of the adolescent.* Englewood Cliffs, NJ: Prentice-Hall.

Hollister, L. E. (1986). Health aspects of cannabis. *Pharmological Reviews*, **38**, 1–20.

Holmes, C. T. (1989). Grade level retention effects: A meta-analysis of research studies. In L. A. Shepard & M. L. Smith (Eds.), *Flunking grades: Research and policies on retention.* New York: Palmer Press.

Holmes, D. J. (1964). *The adolescent in psychotherapy.* Boston: Little, Brown.

Holmes, J., & Silverman, E. L. (1992). *We're here, listen to us!: A survey of young women in Canada.* Ottawa: Canadian Advisory Council on the Status of Women.

Holms, V. L., & Esses, L. M. (1988). Factors influencing Canadian high school girls' career motivation. *Psychology of Women Quarterly*, **12**, 313–328.

Holstein, C. B. (1976). Irreversible, stepwise sequence in the development of moral judgment: A longitudinal study of males and females. *Child Development*, **47**, 51–61.

Holzman, P. S. (1990). Schizophrenia: A new model for its transmission and its variations. In J. Rolf, A. S. Masten, D. Cicchetti, K. H. Nuechterlein, & S. Weintraub (Eds.), *Risk and protective factors in the development of psychopathology* (pp. 480–496). Cambridge: Cambridge University Press.

Holzman, P. S., & Grinker, R. R., Sr. (1974). Schizophrenia in adolescence. *Journal of Youth and Adolescence*, **3**, 267–279.

Honzik, M. P. (1973). The development of intelligence. In B. B. Wolman (Ed.), *Handbook of general psychology* (pp. 644–655). Englewood Cliffs, NJ: Prentice-Hall.

Honzik, M. P., Macfarlane, J. W., & Allen, L. (1948). The stability of mental test performance between two and eighteen years. *Journal of Experimental Education,* **17,** 309–324.

Hood, J., Moore, T. E., & Garner, D. M. (1982). Locus of control as a measure of ineffectiveness in anorexia nervosa. *Journal of Consulting and Clinical Psychology,* **50,** 3–13.

Horn, J. L., & Hofer, S. M. (1992). Major abilities and development in the adult period. In R. J. Sternberg & C. A. Berg (Eds.), *Intellectual development* (pp. 44–99). Cambridge: Cambridge University Press.

Horney, K. (1937). *The neurotic personality of our time.* New York: Norton.

Horney, K. (1950). *Neurosis and human growth.* New York: Norton.

Hornick, J. P., Doran, L., & Crawford, S. H. (1979). Premarital contraceptives usage among male and female adolescents. *The Family Coordinator,* **28,** 181–190.

Horowitz, F. D., & O'Brien, M. (1985). *The gifted and talented: Developmental perspectives.* Washington, DC: American Psychological Association.

Horowitz, M. J. (1988). *Introduction to psychodynamics.* New York: Basic Books.

Hotvedt, M. E. (1990). Emerging and submerging adolescent sexuality: Culture and sexual orientation. In J. Bancroft & J. M. Reinisch (Eds.), *Adolescence and puberty* (pp. 157–172). New York: Oxford University Press.

Hubble, L. M., & Groff, M. (1982). WISC-R Verbal Performance IQ discrepancies among Quay-classified adolescent male delinquents. *Journal of Youth and Adolescence,* **10,** 179–184.

Hudson Institute, U.S. Department of Labor. (1987). *Workforce 2000: Work and workers for the 21st century.* Washington, DC: U.S. Government Printing Office.

Huff, C. R. (1992). The new youth gangs: Social policies and malign neglect. In I. M. Schwartz (Ed.), *Juvenile justice and public policy: Toward a national agenda* (pp. 20–44). New York: Lexington Books.

Hughes, D., Johnson, K., Rosenbaum, J., & Lin, J. (1989). *The health of America's children: Maternal and child health data book.* Washington, DC: Children's Defense Fund.

Huizinga, D., & Elliott, D. S. (1987). Juvenile offenders: Prevalence, offender incidence, and arrest rates by race. *Crime and Delinquency,* **33,** 206–223.

Hull, J. D. (1995). Running scared. *Time,* **144,** 93–96.

Hunt, M. (1974). *Sexual behavior in the 1970s.* Chicago: Playboy Press.

Hunter, S., Croft, J. B., Vizelber, I. A., & Berenson, G. S. (1987). Psychosocial influences on cigarette smoking among youth in a Southern community: The Bogalusa heart study. *Morbidity and Morality Weekly Report,* **36,** 175–245.

Hurrelmann, K. (1990). Health promotion for adolescents: Preventive and corrective strategies against problem behavior. *Journal of Adolescence,* **13,** 231–250.

Hurrelmann, K., & Losel, F. (Eds.). (1990). *Health hazards in adolescence.* Berlin: Walter de Gruyter.

Huston, A. C. (1983). Sex typing. In E. M. Hetherington (Ed.) & P. H. Mussen (Series Ed.), *Handbook of child psychology:* **Vol. 4.** *Socialization, personality, and social development* (4th ed., pp. 387–467). New York: Wiley.

Huston, A. C., McLoyd, V. C., & Coll, C. G. (1994). Children and poverty: Issues in contemporary research. *Child Development,* **65,** 275–282.

Hyde, J. S. (1981). How large are cognitive gender differences? A meta-analysis using $w^2$ and d. *American Psychologist,* **36,** 892–901.

Hyde, J. S. (1993). Meta-analysis and the psychology of women. In F. L. Denmark & M. A. Paludi (Eds.), *Psychology of women: A handbook of issues and theories* (pp. 67–103). Westport, CT: Greenwood Press.

Illingworth, R. S. (1987). *The development of the infant and young child: Normal and abnormal.* Edinburgh: Churchill Livingstone.

Inhelder, B., & Piaget, J. (1958). *The growth of logical thinking from childhood to adolescence.* New York: Basic Books.

Inoff-Germain, G., Arnold, G. S., Nottelmann, E. D., & Susman, E. J. (1988). Relations between hormone levels and observational measures of aggressive behavior of young adolescents in family interactions. *Developmental Psychology,* **24,** 129–139.

Institute of Medicine (1980). *Smoking and behavior.* Washington, DC: National Academy of Sciences.

Institute of Medicine (1988). *Homelessness, health, and human needs.* Washington, DC: National Academy Press.

International Association for the Evaluation of Educational Achievement. (1988). *Science achievement in 17 countries: A preliminary report.* New York: Teachers College, Columbia University.

Jacobs, J. (1971). *Adolescent suicide.* New York: Wiley.

Jadack, R. A., Hyde, J. S., Moore, C. F., & Keller, M. L. (1995). Moral reasoning about sexually transmitted diseases. *Child Development,* **66,** 167–177.

Jaffe, J. H. (1990). Drug addiction and drug abuse. In A. G. Gilman, T. W. Rall, T. W. Nies, & P. Taylor (Eds.), *The pharmological basis of therapeutics* (9th ed., pp. 522–573). New York: McGraw-Hill.

Jaffe, J. H. (1992). Opiates: Clinical aspects. In J. H. Lowinson, P. Ruiz, R. B. Millman, & J. G. Langrod (Eds.), *Substance abuse: A comprehensive textbook* (2nd ed., pp. 186–194). Baltimore: Williams & Wilkins.

Janos, P. M., & Robinson, N. M. (1985). Psychosocial development in intellectually gifted children. In F. D. Horowitz & M. O'Brien (Eds.), *The gifted and talented: Developmental perspectives* (pp. 149–195). Washington, DC: American Psychological Association.

Janus, M. D., McCormack, A., Burgess, A. W., & Hartman, C. (1987). *Adolescent runaways: Causes and consequences.* Lexington, MA: Lexington Books.

Jargowsky, P., & Bane, M. J. (1990). Ghetto poverty in the United States, 1970–1980. In C. Jencks, & P. E. Petersen (Eds.), *The urban underclass* (pp. 235–273). Washington, DC: The Brookings Institution.

**Jencks, C. S., Smith, M., Acland, H., Bane, M. J., Cohen, D., Gintis, H., Heyns, B., & Michelson, S.** (1972). *Inequality: A reassessment of the effects of family and schooling in America.* New York: Basic Books.

**Jenkins, R. R., & Westney, O. E.** (1990). Initiation of sexual behavior in black adolescents. In R. M. Lerner, A. C. Petersen, & J. Brooks-Gunn (Eds.), *Encyclopedia of adolescence* (pp. 1022–1027). New York: Garland.

**Jensen, A. R.** (1969). How much can we boost IQ and school achievement? *Harvard Educational Review,* **39,** 1–123.

**Jensen, A. R.** (1973). *Educability and group differences.* New York: Harper & Row.

**Jensen, A. R.** (1980). *Bias in mental testing.* New York: Free Press.

**Jepsen, D. A.** (1984). The developmental perspective on vocational behavior: A review of theory and research. In S. D. Brown & R. W. Lent (Eds.), *Handbook of counselling psychology* (pp. 178–215). New York: Wiley.

**Jessor, R.** (1979). Marihuana: A review of recent psychosocial research. In R. I. Dupont, A. Goldstein, & J. O'Donnell (Eds.), *Handbook on drug abuse* (pp. 337–356). Washington, DC: U.S. Government Printing Office.

**Jessor, R.** (1984a). Adolescent development and behavioral health. In J. D. Matarazzo, S. M. Weiss, J. A. Herd, N. Miller, & S. M. Weiss (Eds.), *Behavioral health: A handbook of health enhancement and disease prevention* (pp. 69–90). New York: Wiley.

**Jessor, R.** (1984b, Nov.). *Adolescent problem drinking: Psychosocial aspects and developmental outcomes.* Paper presented at the Carnegie Conference on Unhealthful Risk-Taking Behavior Among Adolescents, Stanford, CA.

**Jessor, R.** (1992). Risk behavior in adolescence: A psychosocial framework for understanding and action. *Developmental Review,* **12,** 374–390.

**Jessor, R., Donovan, J. E., & Widmer, K.** (1980). *Psychosocial factors in adolescent alcohol and drug use: The 1978 national sample study, and the 1974–78 panel study.* Boulder: Institute of Behavioral Sciences, University of Colorado.

**Jessor, R., & Jessor, S. L.** (1973). *Problem drinking in youth: Personality, social and behavioral antecedents and correlates.* Publication 144: Boulder: Institute of Behavioral Sciences, University of Colorado.

**Jessor, R., & Jessor, S. L.** (1977). *Problem behavior and psychosocial development: A longitudinal study of youth.* New York: Academic Press.

**Johnson, A. M.** (1959). Juvenile delinquency. In S. Arieti (Ed.), *American handbook of psychiatry* (pp. 840–856). New York: Basic Books.

**Johnson, B. D., & Muffler, J.** (1992). Sociocultural aspects of drug use and abuse in the 1990s. In J. H. Lowinson, P. Ruiz, R. B. Millman, & J. G. Langrod (Eds.), *Substance abuse: A comprehensive textbook* (2nd ed., pp. 118–137). Baltimore: Williams & Wilkins.

**Johnson, C.** (1982). Anorexia nervosa and bulimia. In T. J. Coates, A. C. Petersen, & C. Perry (Eds.), *Adolescent health: Crossing the barriers.* New York: Academic Press.

**Johnson, C., & Flach, A.** (1985). Family characteristics of 105 patients with bulimia. *American Journal of Psychiatry,* **142,** 1321–1324.

**Johnson, S. S.** (1975). *Update on education: A digest of the National Assessment of Educational Progress.* Denver: Education Commission of the States.

**Johnston, L. D.** (1973). *Drugs and American youth.* Ann Arbor, MI: Institute for Social Research.

**Johnston, L. D.** (1994, Dec. 12). Drug use continues to climb among American teenagers (press release). Ann Arbor: University of Michigan News and Information Service.

**Johnston, L. D., & O'Malley, P. M.** (1986). Why do the nation's students use drugs and alcohol? Self-reported reasons from nine national surveys. *Journal of Drug Issues,* **16,** 29–66.

**Johnston, L. D., O'Malley, P. M., & Bachman, J. G.** (1989). *Drug use, drinking and smoking: National survey results from high school, college and young adults populations, 1975–1988.* Washington, DC: National Institute on Drug Abuse.

**Johnston, L. D., O'Malley, P. M., & Bachman, J. G.** (1990). *Drug use, drinking, and smoking: National survey results from high school, college, and young adults populations, 1975–1989.* Washington, DC: National Institute on Drug Abuse.

**Johnston, L. D.** (1995a, December 15). Drug use rises again in 1995 among American teens. *News release.* News and Information Services. Ann Arbor: The University of Michigan.

**Johnston, L. D.** (1995b, December 15). Cigarette smoking among American teens rises again in 1995. *News release.* News and Information Services. Ann Arbor: The University of Michigan.

**Johnston, L. D., O'Malley, P. M., & Bachman, J. G.** (1995a). *National survey results on drug use from the monitoring the future study, 1975–1994.* **Vol. I,** *Secondary school students.* Washington, DC: National Institute on Drug Abuse.

**Johnston, L. D., O'Malley, P. M., & Bachman, J. G.** (1995b). *National survey results on drug use from the monitoring the future study, 1975–1994.* **Vol. II,** *College students and young adults.* Washington, DC: National Institute on Drug Abuse.

**Johnston, L. D., O'Malley, P. M., & Bachman, J. G.** (in press). *National survey results on drug use from the monitoring the future study, 1975–1995.* **Vol. 1:** *Secondary school students.* Washington, DC: National Institute on Drug Abuse.

**Jones, E. F., Forrest, J. D., Goldman, N., Henshaw, S., Lincoln, R., Rosoff, J. I., Westoff, C. F., & Wulf, D.** (1987). *Teenage pregnancy in industrialized countries.* New Haven, CT: Yale University Press.

**Jones, H. E.** (1946). Environmental influence on moral development. In L. Carmichael (Ed.), *Manual of child psychology.* New York: Wiley.

**Jones, H. E.** (1954). The environment and mental development. In L. Carmichael (Ed.), *Manual of child psychology* (2nd ed.). New York: Wiley.

**Jones, M. C.** (1957). The later careers of boys who were early or late maturing. *Child Development,* **28,** 113–128.

**Jones, M. C., & Mussen, P. H.** (1958). Self-conceptions, motivations, and interpersonal attitudes of early and late maturing girls. *Child Development,* **29,** 491–501.

**Jones, R. B.** (1987). Use of smokeless tobacco in the 1988 World Series. *New England Journal of Medicine,* **316,** 952.

**Josephson, E.** (1974). Indicators of change in adolescent marihuana use. In E. Josephson & E. Carroll (Eds.), *The epidemiology of drug abuse.* Washington, DC: Winston.

**Josephson, E., & Carroll, E. E.** (1974). *Drug use: Epidemiological and sociological approaches.* New York: Wiley.

**Josselyn, I. M.** (1954). The ego in adolescence. *American Journal of Orthopsychiatry,* **24,** 223–227.

**Josselyn, I. M.** (1959). Psychological changes in adolescence. *Children,* **6,** 43–47.

**Josselyn, I. M.** (1968). *Adolescence.* Washington, DC: Joint Commission on Mental Health of Children.

**Josselyn, I. M.** (1971). *Adolescence.* New York: Harper & Row.

**Julian, T. W., McKenry, P. C., & Arnold, K.** (1990). Psychosocial predictors of stress associated with the male midlife transition. *Sex Roles, 22,* 707–722.

**Kacerguis, M., & Adams, G.** (1980). Erikson's stage resolution: The relationship between identity and intimacy. *Journal of Youth and Adolescence, 9,* 117–126.

**Kagan, J.** (1964). Acquisition and consequences of sex-typing and sex-role identity. In M. L. Hoffman & L. W. Hoffman (Eds.), *Review of child development research,* **Vol. II** (pp. 137–167). New York: Russell Sage.

**Kagan, J.** (1989). Temperamental contributions to social behavior. *American Psychologist,* **44,** 668–674.

**Kagan, J., Reznick, J. S., & Snidman, N.** (1988a). Biological bases of childhood shyness. *Science, 240,* 167–171.

**Kagan, J., Reznick, J. S., & Snidman, N.** (1988b). Temperamental influences on reactions to unfamiliarity and challenge. In G. P. Chrousos, D. L. Loriaux, & P. W. Gold (Eds.), *Mechanisms of physical and emotional stress. Advances in experimental medicine and biology* (pp. 319–339). New York: Plenum Press.

**Kagan, J., & Segal, J.** (1988). *Psychology: An introduction* (6th ed.). San Diego, CA: Harcourt Brace Jovanovich.

**Kagan, J., Sontag, L. W., Baker, C. T., & Nelson, V. L.** (1958). Personality and I.Q. change. *Journal of Abnormal and Social Psychology,* **56,** 261–266.

**Kail, R.** (1991). Processing time declines exponentially during childhood and adolescence. *Developmental Psychology,* **27** 259–266.

**Kail, R., & Bisanz, J.** (1992). The information-processing perspective on cognitive development in childhood and adolescence. In R. J. Sternberg & C. A. Berg (Eds.), *Intellectual Development* (pp. 229–260). New York: Cambridge University Press.

**Kamin, L.** (with Eysenck, H. J.) (1981). *The intelligence controversy.* New York: Wiley.

**Kamptner, N. L.** (1988). Identity development in late adolescence: Causal modeling of social and familial influences. *Journal of Youth and Adolescence,* **17,** 493–514.

**Kandel, D.** (1973). The role of parents and peers in adolescent marijuana use. *Science,* **181,** 1067–1070.

**Kandel, D.** (1974). Inter- and intragenerational influences on adolescent marijuana use. *Journal of Social Issues, 30,* 107–135.

**Kandel, D. B.** (1978a). Homophily, selection, and socialization in adolescent friendships. *American Journal of Sociology,* **84,** 427–436.

**Kandel, D. B.** (1978b). Similarity in real-life adolescent friendship pairs. *Journal of Personality and Social Psychology,* **36,** 306–312.

**Kandel, D. B.** (1980). Drug and drinking behavior among youth. *Annual Review of Psychology,* **6,** 235–285.

**Kandel, D. B.** (1985, Spring/Summer). On processes of peer influences in adolescent drug use: A developmental perspective. In J. Brook, D. Lettieri, & D. Brook (Eds.), *Advances in Alcohol and Substance Abuse,* **4,** 139–163.

**Kandel, D. B.** (1991). Drug use epidemiology and developmental stages. In R. M. Lerner, A. C. Petersen, & J. Brooks-Gunn (Eds.), *Encyclopedia of adolescence,* **Vol I.** (pp. 262–264). New York: Garland Publishing.

**Kandel, D. B., & Andrews, K.** (1987). Processes of adolescent socialization by parents and peers. *International Journal of Addictions,* **22,** 319–342.

**Kandel, D. B., Davies, M., Karus, D., & Yamaguchi, K.** (1986). The consequences in young adulthood of adolescent drug involvement: An overview. *Archives of General Psychiatry,* **43,** 746–754.

**Kandel, D. B., & Faust, R.** (1975). Sequence and stages in patterns of adolescent drug use. *Archives of General Psychiatry,* **32,** 923–932.

**Kandel, D. B., Kessler, R. C., & Margulies, R. Z.** (1978). Antecedents of adolescent initiation into stages of drug use: A developmental analysis. In D. B. Kandel (Ed.), *Longitudinal research on drug use: Empirical findings and methodological issues* (pp. 73–99). Washington, DC: Hemisphere Publishing Corporation.

**Kandel, D. B., & Lesser, G. S.** (1969). Parental and peer influences on educational plans of adolescents. *American Sociological Review,* **34,** 213–223.

**Kandel, D. B., & Lesser, G. S.** (1972). *Youth in two worlds.* San Francisco: Jossey-Bass.

**Kandel, D. B., Murphy, D., & Karus, D.** (1985). Cocaine use in young adulthood: Patterns of use and psychosocial correlates. In N. J. Kozel, & E. H. Adam (Eds.), *Cocaine in America: Epidemiologic and clinical perspectives.* (NIDA research monograph No. 61, pp. 76–110). Rockville, MD: National Institute on Drug Abuse.

**Kandel, D. B., Raveis, V. H., & Kandel, P.** (1984). Continuity in discontinuities: Adjustment in young adulthood of former school absentees. *Youth and Society,* **15,** 325–353.

**Kandel, D. B., Rosenbaum, E., & Chen, K.** (1994). Impact of maternal drug use and life experiences on preadolescent children born to teenage mothers. *Journal of Marriage and the Family,* **56,** 325–340.

**Kantner, J., & Zelnik, M.** (1973). Contraception and pregnancy: Experience of young unmarried women in the United States. *Family Planning Perspectives,* **5,** 21–35.

**Kantrowitz, B.** (1986, March 31). A mother's choice. *Newsweek,* pp. 46–51.

**Kaplan, H. S.** (1979). *The new sex therapy: Active treatment of sexual dysfunctions.* New York: Brunner/Mazel.

**Karniol, R.** (1978). Children's use of intention cues in excusing behavior. *Psychological Bulletin,* **85,** 76–86.

Kasarda, J. D., & Janowitz, M. (1974). Community attachment in mass society. *American Sociological Review, 39,* 328–339.

Kashani, J. H., & Eppright, T. D. (1991). Mood disorders in adolescence. In J. M. Weiner (Ed.), *Textbook of child and adolescent psychiatry* (pp. 248–258). Washington, DC: American Psychiatric Press.

Katchadourian, H. A. (1985). *Fundamentals of human sexuality* (4th ed.). New York: Holt, Rinehart, & Wilson.

Katchadourian, H. A. (1989). *Fundamentals of human sexuality* (5th ed.). New York: Holt, Rinehart, & Winston.

Katchadourian, H. A. (1990). In S. S. Feldman & G. R. Elliott (Eds.), *At the threshold: The developing adolescent* (pp. 330–351). Cambridge: Harvard University Press.

Kaufman, I. R. (1979, Oct. 14). Juvenile justice: A plea for reform. *New York Times Magazine,* pp. 42–60.

Kaufman, J., & Zigler, E. (1987). Do abused children become abusive parents? *American Journal of Orthopsychiatry, 57,* 186–192.

Kavrell, S. M., & Petersen, A. C. (1984). Patterns of achievement in early adolescence. In M. L. Maehr & M. W. Steinkamp (Eds.), *Women and science.* Greenwich, CT: JAI Press.

Kawash, G. F., Kerr, E. N., & Clewes, J. L. (1985). Self-esteem in children as a function of perceived parental behavior. *Journal of Psychology, 119,* 235–242.

Kazdin, A. E. (1990). Psychotherapy for children and adolescents. *Annual Review of Psychology, 41,* 21–54.

Kazdin, A. E. (1991). Behavior modification. In J. M. Weiner (Ed.), *Textbook of child and adolescent psychiatry* (pp. 576–593). Washington, DC: American Psychiatric Press.

Kazdin, A. E. (1995). *Conduct disorders in childhood and adolescence* (2nd ed.). Thousand Oaks, CA: Sage Publications.

Kazdin, A. E., Siegel, T. C., & Bass, D. (1990). Drawing on clinical practice to inform research on child and adolescent psychotherapy: Survey of practitioners. *Professional Psychology, 41,* 189–198.

Kearney, C. A. (1993). Depression and school refusal behavior: A review with comments on classification and treatment. *Journal of School Psychology, 31,* 267–279.

Keating, D. P. (1975). Precocious cognitive development at the level of formal operations. *Child Development, 46,* 476–480.

Keating, D. P. (1980). Thinking processes in adolescence. In J. Adelson (Ed.), *Handbook of adolescent psychology* (pp. 211–246). New York: Wiley.

Keating, D. P. (1988, July). Cognitive processes in adolescence. In G. R. Elliott & S. S. Feldman (Eds.), *Volume on Normal Adolescent Development.* Stanford, CA: Stanford University and Carnegie Corporation of New York.

Keating, D. P. (1990). Adolescent thinking. In S. S. Feldman & G. R. Elliot (Eds.), *At the threshold: The developing adolescent* (pp. 54–89). Cambridge, MA: Harvard University Press.

Kelley, K. (1979). Socialization factors in contraceptive attitudes: Roles of affective responses, parental attitudes, and sexual experience. *Journal of Sex Research, 15,* 6–20.

Kelsoe, J. R., Ginns, E. I., Egeland, J. A., et al. (1989). Re-evaluation of the linkage between chromosome 11p loci and the gene for bipolar affective disorders in the Old Order Amish. *Nature, 342,* 238–243.

Kempe, R. S., & Kempe, C. H. (Eds.) (1978). *Child abuse.* Cambridge, MA: Harvard University Press.

Kempe, R. S., & Kempe, C. H. (1984). *The common secret: Sexual abuse of children and adolescents.* New York: W.H. Freeman.

Kendall, P. C., Lerner, R. M., & Craighead, W. E. (1984). Human development and intervention in child psychopathology. *Child Development, 55,* 71–82.

Kendler, K. S., Gruenberg, A. M., & Strauss, J. S. (1981). An independent analysis of the Copenhagen sample of the Danish Adoption Study of Schizophrenia. I. The relationship between anxiety disorder and schizophrenia. *Archives of General Psychiatry, 38,* 937–977.

Keniston, K. (1960). *The uncommitted: Alienated youth in American society.* New York: Dell.

Kerr, M., Lambert, W. W., Stattin, H., & Klackenberg-Larsson, I. (1994). Stability of inhibition in a Swedish longitudinal sample. *Child Development, 65,* 138–146.

Kerr, P. (1986, Nov. 17). Anatomy of an issue: Drugs, the evidence, the reaction. *The New York Times,* pp. 1, 12.

Kessler, R. C., & McRae, J. A., Jr. (1982). The effects of wives' employment on the mental health of married men and women. *American Sociological Review, 47,* 216–227.

Kett, J. F. (1977). *Rites of passage: Adolescence in America, 1790 to the present.* New York: Basic Books.

Ketterlinus, R. L., & Lamb, M. E. (1994). *Adolescent problem behaviors: Issues and research.* Hillsdale, NJ: Erlbaum.

Kety, S., & Matthysse, S. (1988). Genetic and biochemical aspects of schizophrenia. In A. M. Nicholi, Jr. (Ed.), *The new Harvard guide to psychiatry* (pp. 139–151). Cambridge, MA: Harvard University Press.

Kety, S. S., Rosenthal, D., Wender, P. H., Schulsinger, F., & Jacobsen, B. (1978). The biological and adoptive families of adopted individuals who became schizophrenic: Prevalence of mental illness and other characteristics. In L. C. Wynne, R. L. Cromwell, & S. Matthysse (Eds.), *The nature of schizophrenia: New approaches to research and treatment.* New York: Wiley.

Keyes, S., & Block, J. (1984). Prevalence and patterns of substance abuse among early adolescents. *Journal of Youth and Adolescence, 13,* 1–14.

Kiell, N. (1967). *The universal experience of adolescence.* Boston: Beacon Press.

Kifer, E. (1975). Relationships between academic achievement and personality characteristics: A quasi-longitudinal study. *American Educational Research Journal, 12,* 191–210.

King, A. J. C., Beazley, R. P., Warren, W. K., Hankins, C. A., Robertson, A. S., & Radford, J. L. (1988). *Canada Youth & AIDS Study.* Ottawa: Health and Welfare Canada.

King, G. R., & Ellinwood, E. H., Jr. (1992). Amphetamines and other stimulants. In J. H. Lowinson, P. Ruiz, R. B. Millman, & J. G. Langrod (Eds.), *Substance abuse: A comprehensive textbook* (2nd ed., pp. 247–270). Baltimore: Williams & Wilkins.

King, N. J., Ollier, K., Iacuone, R., Schuster, S., Bayes, K., Gullone, E., & Ollendick, T. H. (1989). Fears of children and adolescents: A cross-sectional Australian study using the Revised-Fear Survey Schedule for Children. *Journal of Child Psychology and Psychiatry, 30,* 775–784.

REFERENCES

**Kinsey, A. C., Pomeroy, W. B., & Martin, C. E.** (1948). *Sexual behavior in the human male.* Philadelphia: Saunders.

**Kinsey, A. C., Pomeroy, W. B., Martin, C. E., & Gebhard, P. H.** (1953). *Sexual behavior in the human female.* Philadelphia: Saunders.

**Kisker, E. E.** (1990). Family planning clinics: Efficacy for adolescents. In R. M. Lerner, A. C. Petersen, & J. Brooks-Gunn (Eds.), *Encyclopedia of adolescence* (pp. 345–348). New York: Garland.

**Klatzky, R. L.** (1980). *Human memory: Structures and processes* (2nd ed.). San Francisco: Freeman.

**Klein, J. R., & Litt, I. F.** (1983). Menarche and dysmenorrhea. In J. Brooks-Gunn & A. C. Petersen (Eds.), *Girls at puberty: Biological, psychological and social perspectives.* New York: Plenum.

**Klein, R. G.** (1994). Anxiety disorders. In M. Rutter, E. Taylor, & L. Hersov (Eds.), *Child and adolescent psychiatry* (3rd ed., pp. 351–374). Boston: Blackwell Scientific Publishers.

**Klerman, G. L.** (1988a). Depression and related disorders of mood (affective disorders). In A. M. Nicholi, Jr., (Ed.) *The new Harvard guide to psychiatry* (pp. 309–336). Cambridge, MA: Harvard University Press.

**Klerman, G. L.** (1988b). The current age of youth melancholia: Evidence for increase in depression among adolescents and young adults. *British Journal of Psychiatry, 152,* 4–14.

**Klerman, G. L., & Weissman, M. M.** (1989). Increasing rates of depression. *Journal of the American Medical Association, 261,* 2229–2235.

**Klerman, L. V.** (1991). The health of poor children: Problems and programs. In A. C. Huston (Ed.), *Children in poverty: Child development and public policy* (pp. 136–157). Cambridge: Cambridge University Press.

**Kochanska, G.** (1993). Toward a synthesis of parental socialization and child temperament in early development of conscience. *Child Development, 64,* 325–347.

**Kochanska, G.** (1994). Beyond cognition: Expanding the search for the early roots of internalization and conscience. *Developmental Psychology, 30,* 20–22.

**Koff, E., & Rierdan, J.** (1993). Advanced pubertal development and eating disturbance in early adolescent girls. *Journal of Adolescent Health, 14,* 433–439.

**Kohlberg, L.** (1969). Stage and sequence: The cognitive–developmental approach to socialization. In D. Gostlin (Ed.), *Handbook of socialization theory and research.* Skokie, IL: Rand McNally.

**Kohlberg, L.** (1976). Moral stages and moralization: The cognitive–developmental approach. In T. Lickona (Ed.), *Moral development and behavior.* New York: Holt, Rinehart & Winston.

**Kohlberg, L.** (1979). *The meaning and measurement of moral development.* Clark Lectures, Clark University.

**Kohlberg, L.** (1987). *Child psychology and childhood education: A cognitive developmental view.* New York: Longman.

**Kohlberg, L., Boyd, D. R., & Levine, C.** (1990). The return of Stage 6: Its principle and moral point of view. In T. Wren (Ed.), *The moral domain: Essays in the ongoing discussion between philosophy and the social sciences* (pp. 151–181). Cambridge, MA: MIT Press.

**Kohlberg, L., & Gilligan, C.** (1971, Fall). The adolescent as a philosopher: The discovery of the self in a postconventional world. *Daedalus, 100,* 1051–1086.

**Kohlberg, L. & Kramer, R.** (1969). Continuities and discontinuities in childhood and adult development. *Human Development, 12,* 93–120.

**Kohlberg, L., Levine, C., & Hewer, A.** (1983). *Moral stages: A current formulation and a response to critics.* Basel, Switzerland: S. Karger.

**Kohn, M. L., & Schooler, C.** (1978). The reciprocal effects of the substantive complexity of work and intellectual flexibility: A longitudinal assessment. *American Journal of Sociology, 84,* 24–52.

**Kohn, M. L., & Schooler, C.** (1982). Job conditions and personality: A longitudinal assessment of their reciprocal effects. *American Journal of Sociology, 87,* 1257–1286.

**Kolaric, G. C., & Galambos, N. L.** (1995). Face-to-face interactions in unacquainted female–male dyads: How do girls and boys behave? *Journal of Early Adolescence, 15,* 363–382.

**Kolata, G.** (1989, Aug. 11). In cities, poor families are dying of crack. *The New York Times,* pp. 1, 10.

**Konopka, G.** (1976). *Young girls: A portrait of adolescence.* Englewood Cliffs, NJ: Prentice-Hall.

**Konopka, G.** (1985). *Young girls: A portrait of adolescence.* New York: Harrington Park Press.

**Koski, K. J., & Steinberg, L.** (1990). Parenting satisfaction of mothers during midlife. *Journal of Youth and Adolescence, 19,* 465–474.

**Kovach, J. A., & Glickman, N. W.** (1986). Levels and psychosocial correlates of adolescent drug use. *Journal of Youth and Adolescence, 115,* 61–78.

**Kovacs, M.** (1989). Affective disorders in children and adolescents. *American Psychologist, 44,* 209–215.

**Krisberg, B.** (1992). Youth crime and its prevention: A research agenda. In I. M. Schwartz (Ed.), *Juvenile justice and public policy: Toward a national agenda* (pp. 1–19). New York: Lexington Books.

**Kroupa, S. E.** (1988). Perceived parental acceptance and female juvenile delinquency. *Adolescence, 123,* 171–185.

**Kulin, H. E.** (1991a). Puberty, endocrine changes at. In R. M. Lerner, A. C. Petersen, & J. Brooks-Gunn. *Encyclopedia of adolescence, Vol. II* (pp. 897–899). New York: Garland Publishing.

**Kulin, H. E.** (1991b). Spermarche. In R. M. Lerner, A. C. Petersen, & J. Brooks-Gunn. *Encyclopedia of adolescence, Vol. II* (pp. 1091–1092). New York: Garland Publishing.

**Kupersmidt, J. B., & Coie, J. D.** (1990). Preadolescent peer status, aggression, and school adjustment as predictors of externalizing problems in adolescence. *Child Development, 61,* 1350–1362.

**Kurdek, L. A., & Fine, M. A.** (1993). Parent and nonparent residential family members as providers of warmth and supervision to young adolescents. *Journal of Family Psychology, 7,* 245–249.

**Kurdek, L. A., & Sinclair, R. J.** (1988). Adjustment of young adolescents in two-parent nuclear, stepfather, and mother-custody families. *Journal of Consulting and Clinical Psychology, 56,* 91–96.

Kvaraceus, W. C. (1945). *Juvenile delinquency and the school.* New York: Harcourt Brace Jovanovich.

Kyman, W., Berger, D., & Perez, G. (1987). The making of an adolescent clinic. *Adolescence,* **22,** 879–881.

Laboratory of Comparative Human Cognition. (1983). Culture and cognitive development. In P. H. Mussen (Series Ed.) & W. Kessen (Ed.), *Handbook of child psychology* **(Vol. 1):** *History, theory, and methods* (pp. 295–358). New York: Wiley.

LaFromboise, T. D., & Low, K. G. (1989). American Indian children and adolescents. In J. T. Gibbs & L. N. Hwang (Eds.), *Children of color: Psychological interventions with minority youth* (pp. 114–147). San Francisco: Jossey-Bass.

Lam, M. S., Powers, S. I., Noam, G. G., Hauser, S. T., & Jacobson, A. M. (1993). Parental moral stage and adolescent moral development. In J. Demick, K. Bursik, & R. DiBiase (Eds.), *Parental development* (pp. 75–85). Hillsdale, NJ: Lawrence Erlbaum.

Lamar, J. W., Jr. (1986, June 2). Crack. *Time,* pp. 16–18.

Lamb, D. (1986). *Psychotherapy with adolescent girls* (2nd ed.). New York: Plenum Press.

Lamb, M. E. (1987). *The father's role: Cross-cultural perspectives.* New York: Wiley.

Lambert, N. M. (1988). Adolescent outcomes for hyperactive children: Perspectives on general and specific patterns of childhood risk for adolescent educational, social, and mental health problems. Meeting of the American Psychological Association (1987, New York). *American Psychologist,* **43,** 786–799.

Lamborn, S. D., Mounts, N. S., Steinberg, L., & Dornbusch, S. M. (1991). Patterns of competence and adjustment among adolescents from authoritative, authoritarian, indulgent, and neglectful families. *Child Development,* **61,** 1049–1065.

Lamborn, S. D., & Steinberg, L. (1993). Emotional autonomy redux: Revisiting Ryan and Lynch. *Child Development,* **64,** 483–499.

Lamke, L. K. (1982). The impact on sex-role orientation on self-esteem in early adolescence. *Child Development,* **53,** 1530–1535.

Lao, R. C. (1980). Differential factors affecting male and female academic performance in high school. *The Journal of Psychology,* **104,** 119–127.

Lapointe, A. E., Mead, N. A., & Askew, J. M. (1992). *Learning mathematics.* Princeton, NJ: International Assessment of Educational Progress, Educational Testing Service.

Lapsley, D. K. (1990). Continuity and discontinuity in adolescent social cognitive development. In R. Montemayor, G. R. Adams, & T. P. Gullotta (Eds.), *From childhood to adolescence: A transitional period?* Newbury Park, CA: Sage.

Lapsley, D. K., FitzGerald, D. P., Rice, K. G., & Jackson, S. (1989). Separation-individuation and the "new look" at the imaginary audience and personal fable: A test of an integrative model. *Journal of Adolescent Research,* **4,** 483–505.

Lapsley, D. K., Jackson, S., Rice, K. G., & Shadid, G. E. (1988). Self-monitoring and the "new look" at the imaginary audience and personal fable: An ego-developmental analysis. *Journal of Adolescent Research,* **3,** 17–31.

Lapsley, D. K., Milstead, M., Quintana, S., Flannery, D., & Buss, R. R. (1986). Adolescent egocentrism and formal operations: Tests of a theoretical assumption. *Developmental Psychology,* **22,** 800–807.

Larson, L. E. (1972a). The influence of parents and peers during adolescence. *Journal of Marriage and the Family,* **34,** 67–74.

Larson, L. E. (1972b). The relative influence of parent–adolescent affect in predicting the salience hierarchy among youth. *Pacific Sociological Review,* **15,** 83–102.

Larson, R., Csikszentmihalyi, M., & Graef, R. (1980). Mood variability and the psychosocial adjustment of adolescents. *Journal of Youth and Adolescence,* **9,** 469–490.

Larson, R., & Johnson, C. (1981). Anorexia nervosa in context of daily living. *Journal of Youth and Adolescence,* **10,** 455–471.

Larson, R., & Lampman-Petraitis, C. (1989). Daily emotional states as reported by children and adolescents. *Child Development,* **60,** 1250–1260.

Lask, B., & Bryant-Waugh, R. (1992). Early-onset anorexia nervosa and related eating disorders. *Journal of Child Psychology and Psychiatry,* **33,** 281–300.

Last, C. G., & Perrin, S. (1993). Anxiety disorders in African-American and white children. *Journal of Abnormal Child Psychology,* **21,** 153–164.

Last, C. G., & Strauss, C. C. (1990). School refusals in anxiety-disordered children and adolescents. *Journal of the American Academy of Child and Adolescent Psychiatry,* **29,** 31–35.

Lau, R. R., Quandrel, M. J., & Hartman, K. A. (1990). Development and change of young adult's preventative health beliefs and behavior: Influences from parents and peers. *Journal of Health and Social Behavior,* **31,** 240–259.

Laumann, E. O., Michael, R. T., Michaels, S., & Gagnon, J. H. (1994). *The social organization of sexuality.* Chicago: University of Chicago Press.

Laursen, B. (1993). The perceived impact of conflict on adolescent relationships. *Merrill–Palmer Quarterly,* **39,** 535–550.

Laursen, B. (1996). Closeness and conflict in adolescent peer relationships: Interdependence with friends and romantic partners. In W. M. Bukowksi, A. F. Newcomb, & W. W. Hartup (Eds.), *The company they keep: Friendship during childhood and adolescence.* New York: Cambridge University Press.

Laursen, B., & Ferreira, M. (1994, Feb.). *Does parent–child conflict peak in mid-adolescence?* Paper presented at the meeting of Society for Research on Adolescence, San Diego, CA.

Lavery, B., Siegel, A. W., Cousins, J. H., & Rubovits, D. S. (1993). Adolescent risk-taking: An analysis of problem behaviors in problem children. *Journal of Experimental Child Psychology,* **55,** 277–294.

Lavin, A. T., Shapiro, G. R., & Weill, K. W. (1992). Creating an agenda for school-based health promotion. A review of 25 selected reports. *Journal of School Health,* **62,** 212–228.

Law, D. J., Pellegrino, J. W., & Hunt, E. B. (1993). Comparing the tortoise and the hare: Gender differences and experience in dynamic visual tasks. *Psychological Science,* **4,** 35–40.

Lazar, I., & Darlington, R. (1982). Lasting effects of early education: A report from the Consortium for Longitudinal Studies. *Monographs of the Society for Research in Child Development, 47,* 2–3.

Lazarus, R. S., & Folkman, S. (1984). *Stress, appraisal, and coping.* New York: Springer.

Leahy, R. L. (1981). Parental practices and the development of moral judgment and self-image disparity during adolescence. *Developmental Psychology, 17,* 580–594.

Ledingham, J. E. (1990). Recent developments in high-risk research. In B. B. Lahey & A. E. Kazdin (Eds.), *Advances in clinical child psychology* (Vol. 13, pp. 91–137). New York: Plenum.

Lee, V. E., & Bryk, A. S. (1986). Effects of single-sex secondary schools on student achievement and attitudes. *Journal of Educational Psychology, 78,* 381–395.

Lehmann, P. (1991). *The promised land: The great black migration and how it changed America.* New York: Alfred Knopf.

Leitenberg, H., Detzer, M. J., & Srebnik, D. (1993). Gender differences in masturbation and the relation of masturbation experience in preadolescence and/or early adolescence to sexual behavior and sexual adjustment in young adulthood. *Archives of Sexual Behavior, 22,* 87–98.

Leitenberg, H., & Rosen, J. C. (1988). Cognitive–behavioral treatment of bulimia nervosa. In H. Hersen, R. M. Eisler, & P. M. Miller (Eds.), *Progress in behavior modification* (Vol. 23, pp. 11–35). Newbury Park, CA: Sage.

Leland, N. L., & Barth, R. P. (1993). Characteristics of adolescents who have attempted to avoid HIV and who have communicated with parents about sex. *Journal of Adolescent Research, 8,* 58–76.

Lemann, N. (1986, June). The origins of the underclass. *The Atlantic,* pp. 31–55.

Lempers, J. D., & Clark-Lempers, D. S. (1993). A functional comparison of same-sex and opposite-sex friendships during adolescence. *Journal of Adolescent Research, 8,* 89–108.

Leon, G. R., & Dinklage, D. (1989). Obesity and anorexia nervosa. In T. H. Ollendick & M. Hersen (Eds.), *Handbook of child psychopathology* (pp. 253–276). New York: Plenum.

Leon, G. R., Fulkerson, J. A., Perry, C. L., & Cudeck, R. (1993). Personality and behavioral vulnerabilities associated with risk status for eating disorders in adolescent girls. *Journal of Abnormal Psychology, 102,* 438–444.

Leon, G. R., Fulkerson, J. A., Perry, C. L., & Dube, A. (1994). Family influences, school behaviors, and risk for the later development of an eating disorder. *Journal of Youth and Adolescence, 23,* 499–515.

Lerner, J. V., & Galambos, N. L. (Eds.) (1991). *Employed mothers and their children.* New York: Garland.

Lerner, R. M., & Busch-Rossnagel, N. A. (Eds.). (1981). *Individuals as producers of their development: A life-span perspective.* New York: Academic Press.

Lerner, R. M., Hultsch, D. F., & Dixon, R. A. (1983). Contextualism and the character of developmental psychology in the 1970s. *Annals of the New York Academy of Sciences, 412,* 101–128.

Lerner, R. M., & Knapp, J. R. (1975). Actual and perceived intrafamilial attitudes of late adolescents and their parents.

*Journal of Youth and Adolescence, 4,* 17–36.

Lerner, R. M., & Lerner, J. V. (1983). Temperament and adaption across life: Theoretical and empirical issues. In P. B. Baltes & O. G. Brim, Jr. (Eds.), *Life-span development and behavior* (Vol. 5, pp. 197–231). New York: Academic Press.

Lerner, R. M., Lerner, J. V., Hess, L. E., Schwab, J., Jovanovic, J., Talwar, R., & Kucher, J. S. (1991). Physical attractiveness and psychosocial functioning among early adolescents. *Journal of Early Adolescence, 11,* 300–320.

Lerner, R. M., Sorrell, A. T., & Brackney, B. E. (1981). Sex differences in self-concept and self-esteem in late adolescents: A time-lag analysis. *Sex Roles, 7,* 709–722.

Lesser, G. S., & Kandel, D. (1969). Parent–adolescent relationships and adolescent independence in the United States and Denmark. *Journal of Marriage and the Family, 31,* 348–358.

Lester, B. M., Corwin, M. J., Sepkoski, C., Seifer, R., Peucker, M., McLaughlin, S., & Golub, H. L. (1991). Neurobehavioral syndromes in cocaine-exposed infants. *Child Development, 62,* 694–705.

Letter to the Editor. *Times-Colonist* (Victoria, BC), Aug. 21, 1994.

LeVay, S. (1991). A difference in hypothalamic structure between heterosexual and homosexual men. *Science, 253,* 1034–1037.

Levin, H. M. (1985). The educationally disadvantaged: A national crisis. *The State Youth Initiatives Project, Working paper No. 6.* Philadelphia: Public/Private Ventures.

Lewin, K. (1935). *A dynamic theory of personality.* New York: McGraw-Hill.

Lewin, K, (1939). Field theory and experiment in social psychology: Concepts and methods. *American Journal of Sociology, 44,* 868–897.

Lewin, K. (1951). *Field theory and social science.* New York: Harper & Row.

Lewin, T. (1994, July 11). Traditional family favored by boys, not girls, poll says. *New York Times,* pp. A1, C10.

Lewis, D. O. (1991). Conduct disorder. In M. Lewis (Ed.), *Child and adolescent psychiatry: A comprehensive textbook* (pp. 561–573). Baltimore: Williams & Wilkins.

Lewis, D. O., Mallouh, C., & Webb, V. (1989). Child abuse, delinquency, and violent criminality. In D. Cicchetti & V. Carlson (Eds.), *Child maltreatment: Theory and research on the causes and consequences of child abuse and neglect* (pp. 707–721). New York: Cambridge University Press.

Lewis, T. J., & Sugai, G. (1993). Teaching communicative alternatives to socially withdrawn behavior: An investigation in maintaining treatment effects. *Journal of Behavioral Education, 3,* 61–75.

Liem, J. H., & Liem, G. R. (1990). Understanding the individual and family effects of unemployment. In J. Eckenrode and S. Gore (Eds.), *Stress between work and family* (pp. 175–204). New York: Plenum Press.

Linares, L. O., Leadbeater, B. J., Kato, P. M., & Jaffe, L. (1991). Predicting school outcomes for minority group adolescent mothers: Can subgroups be identified? *Journal of Research on Adolescence, 1,* 379–400.

Lindsay, J. W. (1985). *Teens look at marriage: Rainbows, role, and realities.* Buena Park, CA: Morning Glory Press.

Linn, M. C., & Hyde, J. S. (1991). Cognitive and psychosocial gender differences, trends in. In R. M. Lerner, A. C. Petersen, J. Brooks-Gunn (Eds.), *Encyclopedia of adolescence* (pp. 139–150).

Linn, M., & Petersen, A. C. (1985). Gender differences and spatial ability: Emergence and characterization. *Child Development, 56,* 1479–1498.

Lipsey, M. W. (1992). The effect of treatment on juvenile delinquents: Results from meta-analysis. In F. Losel, D. Bender, & T. Bliesener (Eds.), *Psychology and law: International perspectives* (pp. 131–143). Berlin: Walter de Gruyter.

Lipsitz, J. (1977). *Growing up forgotten.* Lexington, MA: Lexington Books.

Litt, I. F., & Vaughn, V. C., III. (1987). Growth and development during adolescence. In R. E. Behrman, V. C. Vaughn, & W. E. Nelson (Eds.), *Textbook of pediatrics* (13th ed., pp. 20–24). Philadelphia: W.B. Saunders.

Livesley, W. J., & Bromley, D. B. (1973). *Person perception in childhood and adolescence.* New York: Wiley.

Livingston, R. (1991). Anxiety disorders. In M. Lewis (Ed.), *Child and adolescent psychiatry: A comprehensive textbook* (pp. 673–685). Baltimore: Williams & Wilkins.

Livson, N., & Peskin, H. (1980). Perspectives on adolescence from longitudinal research. In J. Adelson (Ed.), *Handbook of adolescent psychology* (pp. 47–98). New York: Wiley.

Lloyd, D. (1978). Prediction of school failure from third-grade data. *Educational Psychological Measurement, 38,* 1193–1200.

Lloyd, M. A. (1985). *Adolescence.* New York: Harper & Row.

Loeber, R., & Dishion, T. (1983). Early predictors of male delinquency: A review. *Psychological Bulletin, 94,* 68–99.

Loeber, R., & Stouthamer-Loeber, M. (1986). Family factors as correlates and predictors of juvenile conduct problems and delinquency. In M. Tonry & N. Morris (Eds.), *Crime and Justice* (**Vol. 7,** pp. 29–149). Chicago: University of Chicago Press.

Loehlin, J. C. (1992). *Genes and environment in personality development.* Newbury Park, CA: Sage.

Loehlin, J. C., Willerman, L., & Horn, J. M. (1988). Human behavior genetics. *Annual Review of Psychology, 39,* 101–133.

Lomax, J. W. (1989). Obesity. In H. I. Kaplan & B. J. Sadock (Eds.), *Comprehensive textbook of psychiatry* (5th ed., pp. 1179–1186). Baltimore: Williams & Wilkins.

London, K. A., Mosher, W. D., Pratt, W. F., & Williams, L. B. (1989, March). *Preliminary findings from the National Survey of Family Growth, Cycle IV.* Paper presented at the annual meeting of the Population Association of America, Baltimore.

London, P. (1970). The resources: Motivational hypotheses about Christians who saved Jews from the Nazis. In J. Macaulay & L. Berkowitz (Eds.), *Altruism and helping behavior.* New York: Academic Press.

Long, N., & Forehand, R. (1987). The effects of parental divorce and parental conflict on children: An overview. *Journal of Developmental and Behavioral Pediatrics, 5,* 292–296.

Lord, S. E., Eccles, J. S., & McCarthy, K. A. (1994). Surviving the junior high school transition: Family processes and self-perceptions as protective and risk factors. *Journal of Early Adolescence, 14,* 162–199.

Lorenz, K. Z. (1981). *The foundations of ethology.* New York: Springer-Verlag.

Lorion, R. P., Tolan, P. H., & Wahler, R. G. (1987). Prevention. In H. C. Quay (Ed.), *Handbook of juvenile delinquency* (pp. 383–416). New York: Wiley.

Lozoff, B. (1989). Nutrition and behavior. Special issue: Children and their development: Knowledge base, research agenda, and social policy application. *American Psychologist, 44,* 231–236.

Lucas, A. R. (1991). Eating disorders. In M. Lewis (Ed.), *Child and adolescent psychiatry: A comprehensive textbook* (pp. 573–582). Baltimore: Williams & Wilkins.

Lueptow, L. B. (1992). Change and stability in the sex typing of adolescent work orientations: 1976–1989. *Perceptual and Motor Skills, 75,* 1114.

Luria, Z., Friedman, S., & Rose, M. D. (1987). *Human sexuality.* New York: Wiley.

Luthar, S. S. (1991). Vulnerability and resilience: A study of high-risk adolescents. *Child Development, 62,* 600–616.

Lynch, B. S., & Bonnie, R. J. (Eds.) (1994). *Growing up tobacco free: Preventing nicotine addiction in children and youths.* Institute of Medicine. Washington, DC: National Academy Press.

Maccoby, E. E. (1990). Gender and relationships: A developmental account. *American Psychologist, 45,* 513–520.

Maccoby, E. E. (1991, Oct.). The social experience of boys and girls. Its relationship to women's health. In *Assessing future research needs: Mental and addictive disorders in women.* Summary of an Institute of Medicine Conference, Washington, DC: Institute of Medicine, National Academy of Sciences.

Maccoby, E., & Jacklin, C. (1974). *The psychology of sex differences.* Stanford, CA: Stanford University Press.

Maccoby, E. E., & Martin, A. (1983). Socialization in the context of the family: Parent–child interaction. In P. H. Mussen (Series Ed.) & E. M. Hetherington (Ed.), *Handbook of child psychology:* **Vol. 4.:** *Socialization, personality and social behavior* (4th ed., pp. 1–102). New York: Wiley.

MacDonald, K. (1992). Warmth as a developmental construct: An evolutionary analysis. *Child Development, 63,* 753–773.

MacKinnon, D. W. (1983). Creative architects. In R. S. Albert (Ed.), *Genius and eminence: The social psychology of creativity and exceptional achievement* (pp. 291–301). Elmsford, NY: Pergamon Press.

Maggs, J. L. (in press). Alcohol use and binge drinking as goal-directed action during the transition to post-secondary education. In J. E. Schulenberg, J. L. Maggs, & K. Hurrelmann (Eds.), *Health risks and developmental transitions during adolescence.* New York: Cambridge University Press.

Maggs, J. L., Almeida, D. M., & Galambos, N. L. (1995). Risky business: The paradoxical meaning of problem behavior for young adolescents. *Journal of Early Adolescence, 15,* 339–357.

Maggs, J. L., & Galambos, N. L. (1993). Alternative structural models for understanding adolescent problem behavior in two-earner families. *Journal of Early Adolescence, 13,* 79–101.

Magnusson, D., Stattin H., & Allen, V. L. (1986). Differential maturation among girls and its relations to social adjustment: A longitudinal perspective. In P. B. Baltes, D. L. Featherman, & R. M. Lerner (Eds.), *Life-span development and behavior* (**Vol. 7**, pp. 135–172). Hillsdale, NJ: Erlbaum.

Malina, R.M. (1991). Growth spurt, adolescent. II. In R.M. Lerner, A.C. Petersen, & J. Brooks-Gunn (Eds.), *Encyclopedia of adolescence* (**Vol. 1**). New York: Garland.

Marantz, S. A., & Mansfield, A. F. (1977). Maternal employment and the development of sex-role stereotyping in five- to eleven-year-old girls. *Child Development,* **48,** 668–673.

March, J. S. (Ed.). (1995). *Anxiety disorders in children and adolescents.* New York: Guilford Press.

Marcia, J. E. (1980). Identity in adolescence. In J. Adelson (Ed.), *Handbook of adolescent psychology.* New York: Wiley.

Marcoen, A., Goosens, L., & Coes, P. (1987). Loneliness in pre- through late adolescence: Exploring the contributions of a multidimensional approach. *Journal of Youth and Adolescence,* **16,** 561–578.

Marcus, J., Hans, S. L., Nagler, S., Auerbach, J. G., Mirsky, A. P., & Aubrey, A. (1987). Review of the NIMH Israel Kibbutz-city study and the Jerusalem infant development study. *Schizophrenia Bulletin,* **13,** 425–438.

*Marihuana and health.* (1980). Eighth annual report to the U.S. Congress from the Secretary of Health, Education, and Welfare. Washington, DC: U.S. Government Printing Office.

Marini, M. M. (1978). Sex differences in the determination of adolescent aspirations: A review of research. *Sex Roles,* **4,** 723–753.

Marino, D. D., & King, J. C. (1980). Nutritional concerns during adolescence. *Pediatric Clinics of North America,* **27,** 125–139.

Markstrom-Adams, C. (1989). Androgyny and its relation to adolescent psychosocial well-being: A review of the literature. *Sex Roles,* **21,** 325–340.

Markward, M. J. (1992). Involvement of workplace superiors in the lives of youths who work. *International Journal of Adolescence and Youth,* **4,** 19–32.

Marsh, H. W. (1991). Employment during high school: Character building or a subversion of academic goals? *Sociology of Education,* **64,** 172–189.

Marshall, D. S. (1971). Sexual behavior on Mangaia. In D. S. Marshall & R. C. Suggs (Eds.), *Human sexual behavior: Variation in the ethnographic spectrum.* New York: Basic Books.

Marshall, W. A., & Tanner, J. M. (1986). Puberty. In F. Falkner & J.M. Tanner (Eds.), *Human growth* (2nd ed., **Vol. 2**, pp. 171–209). New York: Plenum.

Martin, B., & Hoffman, J. A. (1990). Conduct disorders. In M. Lewis & S. Miller (Eds.), *Handbook of developmental psychopathology* (pp. 109–118). New York: Plenum.

Martin, C. S., Arria, A. M., Mezzich, A. C., & Bukstein, O. G. (1993). Patterns of polydrug use in adolescent alcohol abusers. *American Journal of Drug and Alcohol Abuse,* **19,** 511–521.

Martin, J. A. (1984). Neglected fathers: Limitations in diagnostic and treatment resources for violent men. *Child Abuse & Neglect,* **8,** 387–392.

Marzuk, P. M., & Barchas, J. C. (1995). Psychiatry. *Journal of the American Medical Association,* **273,** 1715–1716.

Massad, C. M. (1981). Sex role identity and adjustment during adolescence. *Child Development,* **52,** 1290–1298.

Massey, S. (1993, Sep. 10). Co-ed schools are studying all-girls classes. *Wall Street Journal,* pp. B1, B2.

Masten, A. S., Neemann, J., & Andenas, S. (1994). Life events and adjustment in adolescents: The significance of event independence, desirability, and chronicity. *Journal of Research on Adolescence,* **4,** 71–97.

Masters, W. H., & Johnson, V. E. (1979). *Homosexuality in perspective.* Boston: Little, Brown.

Masters, W. H., Johnson, V. E., & Kolodny, R. C. (1988). *CRISIS: Heterosexual behaviour in the time of AIDS.* New York: Grove.

Masters, W. H., Johnson, V. E., & Kolodny, R. C. (1992). *Human sexuality* (4th ed.). New York: HarperCollins.

Matarazzo, J. D. (1984). Behavioral health: A 1990 challenge for the health services profession. In J. D. Matarazzo, S. N. Weiss, J. A. Herd, N. E. Miller, & S. M. Weiss (Eds.), *Behavioral health: A handbook of health enhancement and disease prevention* (pp. 3–40). New York: Wiley.

Matheny, A. P. (1983). A longitudinal twin study of stability of components from Bayley's Infancy Behavior Record. *Child Development,* **54,** 356–360.

Matyas, M., & Kahle, J. (1986). *Equitable precollege science and mathematics: A discrepancy model.* Paper presented at the Workshop on Underrepresentation and Career Differentials of Women in Science and Engineering. Washington, DC: National Academy of Sciences.

Mawby, R. I., McCulloch, J. W., & Batta, I. D. (1979). Crime amongst Asian juveniles in Bradford. *International Journal of the Sociology of Law,* **7,** 297–306.

McAlister, A. L., Perry, C., Killen, J., Slinkard, L. A., & Maccoby, N. (1980). Pilot study of smoking, alcohol and drug abuse prevention. *American Journal of Public Health,* **70,** 719–721.

McAndrew, G. L. (1981). *Adolescents: Behavior and development.* New York: Holt, Rinehart and Winston.

McCabe, M. P. (1984). Toward a theory of adolescent dating. *Adolescence,* **19,** 159–170.

McCabe, M. P., & Collins, J. K. (1979). Sex role and dating orientation. *Journal of Youth and Adolescence,* **8,** 407–425.

McCall, R. B., Appelbaum, M. I., & Hogarty, P. S. (1973). Developmental changes in mental performance. *Monographs of the Society for Research in Child Development,* **38**(3), 1–84.

McCandless, B. (1970). *Adolescents: Behavior and development.* New York: Holt, Rinehart and Winston.

McCarthy, B. (1994). Youth on the street: Violent offenders and victims. In H. Coward (Ed.), *Anger in our city: Youth seeking meaning* (pp. 69–107). Victoria, BC: Centre for Studies in Religion and Society.

McCarthy, B., & Hagan, J. (1992). Surviving on the street: The experiences on homeless youth. *Journal of Adolescent Research,* **7,** 412–430.

McCartney, K., Harris, M. J., & Bernieri, F. (1990). Growing up and growing apart: A meta-analysis of twin studies. *Psychological Bulletin,* **107,** 226–237.

**McCord, J.** (1990). Problem behaviors. In S. S. Feldman & G. R. Elliott (Eds.), *At the threshold: The developing adolescent* (pp. 414–430). Cambridge, MA: Harvard University Press.

**McCoy, K., & Wibbelsman, C.** (1984). *The teenage body book.* New York: Pocket Books.

**McDonald, G. W.** (1977). Parental identification by the adolescent: A social power approach. *Journal of Marriage and the Family,* **39,** 705–720.

**McDonald, G. W.** (1980). Parental power and adolescents' parental identification: A reexamination. *Journal of Marriage and the Family,* **42,** 289–296.

**McGarrell, E. F., & Flanagan, T. J.** (Eds.) (1985). *Source book of criminal justice statistics, 1984.* Washington, DC: U.S. Department of Justice.

**McGee, M. G.** (1979a). *Human spatial abilities.* New York: Praeger.

**McGee, M. G.** (1979b). Human spatial abilities: Psychometric studies and environmental, genetic, hormonal, and neurological influences. *Psychological Bulletin,* **86,** 889–918.

**McGue, M., Bacon, S., & Lykken, D. T.** (1993). Personality stability and change in early adulthood: A behavioral genetic analysis. *Developmental Psychology,* **29,** 96–109.

**McLoyd, V. C.** (1993). Employment among African-American mothers in dual-earner families: Antecedents and consequences for family life and child development. In J. Frankel (Ed.), *The employed mother and the family context* (pp. 180–226). New York: Springer.

**McLoyd, V. C., Jayaratne, T. E., Ceballo, R., & Borquez, J.** (1994). Unemployment and work interruption among African American single mothers: Effects on parenting and adolescent socioemotional functioning. *Child Development,* **65,** 562–589.

**Mead, M.** (1928). *Coming of age in Samoa: A psychological study of primitive youth for western civilization.* New York: Morrow Quill Paperbacks.

**Mednick, S. A., Parnas, J., & Schulsinger, F.** (1987). The Copenhagen high-risk project. *Schizophrenia Bulletin,* **13,** 485–495.

**Meikle, S., Peitchinis, J. A., & Pearce, K.** (1985). *Teenage sexuality.* San Diego, CA: College-Hill Press.

**Mensch, B. S., & Kandel, D. B.** (1988). Dropping out of high school and drug involvement. *Sociology of Education,* **61,** 95–113.

**Mesulam, M. M.** (1990). Schizophrenia and the brain. *New England Journal of Medicine,* **322,** 842–844.

**Miller, D. C.** (1959). Short-term therapy with adolescents. *American Journal of Orthopsychiatry,* **29,** 772–779.

**Miller, G. A.** (1983). Personal communication. Cited in Kagan and Segal (1988), p. 281.

**Miller, K. E.** (1990). Adolescents' same-sex and opposite-sex peer relations: Sex differences in popularity, perceived social competence, and social cognitive skills. *Journal of Adolescent Research,* **5,** 222–241.

**Miller, M. L., Chiles, J. A., & Barnes, V. E.** (1982). Suicide attempters within a delinquent population. *Journal of Consulting and Clinical Psychology,* **50,** 490–498.

**Miller, N. E.** (1984). Learning: Some facts and needed research relevant to maintaining health. In J. Matarazzo, S. W. Weiss, J. A. Herd, N. Miller, & S. M. Weiss (Eds.), *Behavioral health: A handbook of health enhancement and disease prevention* (pp. 199–208). New York: Wiley.

**Miller, P. Y., & Simon, W.** (1980). The development of sexuality in adolescence. In J. Adelson (Ed.), *Handbook of adolescent psychology* (pp. 383–407). New York: John Wiley & Sons.

**Millstein, S. G., & Litt, I. F.** (1990). Adolescent health. In S. S. Feldman & G. R. Elliot (Eds.), *At the threshold: The developing adolescent* (pp. 16–53). Cambridge, MA: Harvard University Press.

**Millstein, S. G., Petersen, A. C., & Nightingale, E. O. (Eds.).** (1993). *Promoting the health of adolescents: New directions for the twenty-first century.* New York: Oxford University Press.

**Minuchin, P. P., & Shapiro, E. K.** (1983). The school as a context for social development. In P. H. Mussen (Ed.) & E. M. Hetherington (Series Ed.) *Handbook of child psychology* **(Vol. 3,** *Social development; 4th ed.).* New York: Wiley.

**Minuchin, S., Rosman, B. L., & Baker, L.** (1978). *Psychosomatic families: Anorexia nervosa in context.* Cambridge, MA: Harvard University Press.

**Mischel, W., & Mischel, H. N.** (1976). A cognitive social learning approach to morality and self-regulation. In T. Lickona (Ed.), *Moral development and behavior.* New York: Holt, Rinehart & Winston.

**Modell, J., & Goodman, M.** (1990). Historical perspectives. In S. S. Feldman & G. R. Elliott (Eds.), *At the threshold: The developing adolescent* (pp. 93–122). Cambridge, MA: Harvard University Press.

**Moffitt, T. E.** (1990). Juvenile delinquency and attention deficit disorders: Boys' developmental trajectories from age 3 to age 15. *Child Development,* **61,** 893–910.

**Moffitt, T. E., Caspi, A., Belsky, J., & Silva, P. A.** (1992). Childhood experience and the onset of menarche: A test of a sociobiological model. *Child Development,* **63,** 47–58.

**Molotsky, J.** (1986, December 16). Surgeon General, citing risks, urges smoke-free workplace. *The New York Times,* p. 14.

**Money, J.** (1988). *Gay, straight, and in-between: The sexology of erotic orientation.* New York: Oxford University Press.

**Money, J., & Ehrhardt, A.** (1972). *Man and woman, boy and girl: The differentiation and dimorphisms of gender identity from conception to maturity.* Baltimore: Johns Hopkins University Press.

**Montemayor, R.** (1984). Maternal employment and adolescents' relations with parents, siblings, and peers. *Journal of Youth and Adolescence,* **13,** 543–557.

**Montemayor, R., & Brownlee, J. R.** (1987). Fathers, mothers, and adolescents: Gender-based differences in parental roles during adolescence. *Journal of Youth and Adolescence,* **16,** 281–291.

**Montemayor, R., & Clayton, M. D.** (1983). Maternal employment and adolescent development. *Theory Practice,* **22,** 112–118.

**Montemayor, R., Eberly, M., & Flannery, D. J.** (1993). Effects of pubertal status and conversation topic on parent and adolescent affective expression. *Journal of Early Adolescence,* **13,** 431–447.

**Montemayor, R., & Eisen, M.** (1977). The development of self-conceptions from childhood to adolescence. *Developmental Psychology,* **13,** 314–319.

Montemayor, R., & Flannery, D. J. (1990). Making the transition from childhood to early adolescence. In R. Montemayor, G. R. Adams, & T. P. Gullotta (Eds.), *From childhood to adolescence: A transitional period?* (pp. 291–301). Newbury Park, CA: Sage.

Moore, D., & Schultz, N. (1983). Loneliness at adolescence: Correlates, attributions, and coping. *Journal of Youth and Adolescence, 12,* 95–100.

Moore, K. A., Nord, C. W., & Peterson, J. L. (1989). Non-voluntary sexual activity among adolescents. *Family Planning Perspectives, 21,* 110–114.

Moore, T. W. (1975). Exclusive early mothering and its alternatives. *Scandinavian Journal of Psychology, 16,* 256–272.

Moorehouse, M. J. (1991). Linking maternal employment patterns to mother–child activities and children's school competence. *Developmental Psychology, 27,* 295–303.

Moos, R. H., Moos, B. S., & Kulik, J. A. (1976). College-student abstainers, moderate drinkers, and heavy drinkers: A comparative analysis. *Journal of Youth and Adolescence, 5,* 349–360.

Moreno, A. B., & Thelan, M. H. (1993). A preliminary prevention program for eating disorders in a junior high school population. *Journal of Youth and Adolescence, 22,* 109–124.

Morison, P., & Masten, A. S. (1991). Peer reputation in middle childhood as a predictor of adaptation in adolescence: A seven-year follow up. *Child Development, 62,* 991–1007.

Morrison, D. M. (1985). Adolescent contraceptive behavior: A review. *Psychological Bulletin, 98,* 538–568.

Morrow, A. J. (1969). *The practical theorist: The life and work of Kurt Lewin.* New York: Basic Books.

Mortimer, J. T. (1974). Patterns of intergenerational occupational movements: A smallest-space analysis. *American Journal of Sociology, 79,* 1278–1299.

Mortimer, J. T. (1976). Social class, work, and the family: Some implications of the father's occupation for familial relationships and sons' career decisions. *Journal of Marriage and the Family, 38,* 241–256.

Mortimer, J. T., Finch, M. D., Owens, T. J., & Shanahan, M. (1990). Gender and work in adolescence. *Youth and Society, 22,* 201–224.

Mortimer, J. T., Finch, M., Shanahan, M., & Ryu, S. (1992). Work experience, mental health, and behavioral adjustment in adolescence. *Journal of Research on Adolescence, 2,* 25–57.

Mortimer, J. T., & Kumka, D. (1982, Winter). A further examination of the "occupational linkage hypothesis." *The Sociological Quarterly, 23,* 3–16.

Mortimer, J. T., Lorence, J., & Kumka, D. (1986). *Work, family and personality: Transition to adulthood.* Norwood, NJ: Ablex.

Moshman, D., Glover, J. A., & Bruning, R. H. (1987). *Developmental psychology: A topical approach.* Boston: Little, Brown.

Mott, F. L., & Haurin, R. J. (1988). Linkages between sexual activity and drug use among adolescents. *Family Planning Perspectives, 20,* 128–136.

Moynihan, D. P. (1986). *Family and nation.* New York: Harcourt Brace Jovanovich.

Mueller, E., & Silverman, N. (1989). Peer relations in maltreated children. In D. Cicchetti & V. Carlson (Eds.), *Child maltreatment: Theory and research on the causes and consequences of child abuse and neglect* (pp. 569–578). New York: Cambridge University Press.

Mullis, V. S., Dossey, J. A., Campbell, J. R., Gentile, C. A., O'Sullivan, C., & Latham, A. S. (1994). *NAEP 1992 trends in academic progress.* Washington, DC: Office of Educational Research and Improvement, U.S. Department of Education.

Mullis, V. S., Dossey, J. A., Owen, E. H., & Philips, G. W. (1991). *The state of mathematics achievement: Executive summary.* Princeton, NJ: Educational Testing Service, for the U.S. Department of Education, National Center for Education Statistics.

Mullis, V. S., & Jenkins, L. B. (1988). *The science report card: Elements of risk and recovery. Trends and achievement based on the 1986 National Assessment.* Princeton, NJ: Educational Testing Service.

Mullis, R. L., & McKinley, K. (1989). Gender-role orientation of adolescent females: Effects on self-esteem and locus of control. *Journal of Adolescent Research, 4,* 483–505.

Murphy, J., & Gilligan, C. (1980). Moral development in late adolescence and adulthood: A critique and reconstruction of Kohlberg's theory. *Human Development, 23,* 77–104.

Murphy, K., & Schneider, B. (1994). Coaching socially rejected early adolescents regarding behaviors used by peers to infer liking: A dyad-specific intervention. *Journal of Early Adolescence, 14,* 83–95.

Mussen, P. H., Conger, J. J., & Kagan, J. (1979). *Child development and personality* (5th ed.). New York: Harper & Row.

Mussen, P. H., Conger, J. J., Kagan, J., & Huston, A. (1984). *Child development and personality* (6th ed.). New York: Harper & Row.

Mussen, P. H., Conger, J. J., Kagan, J., & Huston, A. (1990). *Child development and personality* (7th ed.). New York: Harper & Row.

Mussen, P. H., & Jones, M. C. (1957). Self-conceptions, motivations, and interpersonal attitudes of late and early maturing boys. *Child Development, 28,* 243–256.

Mussen, P. H., & Rosenzweig, M. R., et al. (1973). *Psychology: An introduction.* Lexington, MA: Heath.

Muus, R. E. (1988). *Theories of adolescence* (5th ed.). New York: Random House.

Nathanson, C. A., & Becker, M. H. (1986). Family and peer influence on obtaining a method of contraception. *Journal of Marriage and the Family, 48,* 513–525.

National Academy of Sciences, National Research Council. (1980). *Recommended dietary allowances* (9th ed.). Washington, DC: Author.

*National adolescent student health survey.* (1988). Reston, VA: American Alliance for Health, Physical Education, Recreation, and Dance.

National Assessment of Educational Progress. (1979). *Changes in mathematical achievement, 1973–1978.* Denver: NAEP/Education Commission of the States.

**National Assessment of Educational Progress.** (1981). *Reading, thinking, and writing: Results from the 1979–80 national assessment of reading and literature.* Denver: Educational Commission of the States.

**National Assessment of Educational Progress.** (1986). *The reading report card: Progress toward excellence in our schools. Trends in reading over four national assessments, 1971–1984.* Princeton, NJ: NAEP/Educational Testing Service.

**National Assessment of Educational Progress (NAEP).** (1994). 1992 Science, Mathematics, Reading, and Writing Trend Assessments. Washington, DC: Office of Educational Research and Improvement, U.S. Department of Education.

**National Cancer Institute.** (1992). *Smokeless tobacco or health. Monograph 2,* NIH Pub. No. 93–3461. Washington, DC: U.S. Department of Health and Human Services.

**National Commission on Children.** (1991). *Speaking of kids: A national survey of children and parents.* Washington, DC: Author.

**National Commission on Excellence in Education.** (1983). *A nation at risk: The imperative for educational reform.* Washington, DC: U.S. Government Printing Office.

**National Educational Goals Panel.** (1994) *National educational goals report: Building a nation of learners.* Washington, DC: U.S. Government Printing Office.

*National excellence: A case for developing America's talent.* (1993). Washington, DC: United States Department of Education.

*National household survey on drug abuse: Main Findings 1992.* (1995). Substance Abuse and Mental Health Services Administration, Office of Applied Studies (Publication No. SMA 94-3012). Rockville, MD: Department of Health and Human Services.

*National household survey on drug abuse: Population estimates of 1993.* (1994). Substance Abuse and Mental Health Services Administration, Office of Applied Studies (Publication No. SMA 94-3017). Rockville, MD: Department of Health and Human Services.

**National Institute on Drug Abuse.** (1989, Aug.). "NIDA Capsules" (press release developed from *1988 National Household Survey on Drug Abuse*). Rockville, MD: National Institute on Drug Abuse.

**Neimark, E. D.** (1975a). Intellectual development during adolescence. In F. D. Horowitz (Ed.), *Review of child development research* (**Vol. 4,** pp. 541–594). Chicago: University of Chicago Press.

**Neimark, E. D.** (1975b). Longitudinal development of formal operations thought. *Genetic Psychology Monographs, 91,* 171–225.

**Neinstein, L. S.** (1984). *Adolescent health care: A practical guide.* Baltimore/Munich: Urban & Schwarzenberg.

**Nelsen, H. M., Potvin, R. H., & Shields, J.** (1977). *The religion of children.* Washington, DC: U.S. Catholic Conference.

**Nemeth, M.** (1994, Oct. 31). An alarming trend: Suicide among the young has quadrupled. *Maclean's,* p. 15.

**Nemiah, J. C.** (1988). Psychoneurotic disorders. In A. M. Nicholi, Jr. (Ed.), *The new Harvard guide to psychiatry* (pp. 234–258). Cambridge, MA: Harvard University Press.

**Newcomb, M. D., & Bentler, P. M.** (1988). *Consequences of adolescent drug use: Impact on the lives of young adults.* Newbury Park, CA: Sage.

**Newcomb, M. D., Huba, G. J., & Bentler, P. M.** (1981). A multidimensional assessment of stressful life events among adolescents: Derivation and correlates. *Journal of Health and Social Behavior, 2,* 400–415.

**Newcombe, N., & Bandura, M. M.** (1983). The effect of age at puberty on spatial ability in girls: A question of mechanism. *Developmental Psychology, 19,* 215–224.

**Newcombe, N., & Dubas, J. S.** (1987). Individual differences in cognitive ability: Are they related to timing of puberty? In R. M. Lerner & T. T. Foch (Eds.), *Biological–psychosocial interactions in early adolescence* (pp. 249–302). Hillsdale, NJ: Lawrence Erlbaum.

**Newcombe, N. S., & Baenninger, M.** (1989). Biological change and cognitive ability in adolescence. In G. R. Adams, R. Montemayor, & T. P. Gullotta (Eds.), *Biology of adolescent behavior and development* (pp. 168–191). Newbury Park, CA: Sage.

**Newcomer, S., & Udry, J. R.** (1987). Parental marital status effects on adolescent sexual behavior. *Journal of Marriage and the Family, 49,* 235–240.

**Newman, B. M.** (1975a). Characteristics of interpersonal behavior among adolescent boys. *Journal of Youth and Adolescence, 4,* 145–153.

**Newman, B. M.** (1975b). Interpersonal behavior and preferences for exploration in adolescent boys: A small group study. In J. G. Kelly (Ed.), *The socialization process in the high school years.* New York: Behavioral Publications.

*New York Times.* (1994, July 20). Perfect score for Americans in world math tourney, p. A16.

**Nicholi, A. M., Jr.** (1988). The adolescent. In A. M. Nicholi, Jr. (Ed.), *The new Harvard guide to psychiatry* (pp. 637–664). Cambridge, MA: Harvard University Press.

**Nichols, P. L.** (1984). Familial mental retardation. *Behavior Genetics, 14,* 161–170.

**Noble, E. P.** (Ed.). (1978). *Alcohol and health: Third special report to the U.S. Congress* (preprint edition). Rockville, MD: National Institute on Alcohol Abuse and Alcoholism.

**Nolen-Hoeksema, S., & Girgus, J. S.** (1994). The emergence of gender differences in depression during adolescence. *Psychological Bulletin, 115,* 424–443.

**Nolin, M. J., & Petersen, K. K.** (1992). Gender differences in parent–child communication about sexuality. *Journal of Adolescent Research, 7,* 59–79.

**Norback, C. (Ed.).** (1980). *The complete book of American surveys.* New York: New American Library.

**Norman, J., & Harris, M.** (1981). *The private life of the American teenager.* New York: Rawson, Wade.

**Norton, A. J., & Moorman, J. E.** (1986, April). *Marriage and divorce patterns of U.S. women in the 1980s.* Paper presented at the annual meeting of the Population Association of America, San Francisco.

**Nuechterlein, K. H., Phipps-Yonas, S., Driscoll, R., & Garmezy, N.** (1990). Vulnerability factors in children at risk: Anomalies in attentional functioning and social behavior. In J. Rolf, A. S. Masten, D. Cicchetti, K. H.

Nuechterlein, & S. Weintraub (Eds.), *Risk and protective factors in the development of psychopathology* (pp. 445–479). Cambridge: Cambridge University Press.

Oakes, J. (1985). *Keeping track.* New Haven, CT: Yale University Press.

O'Connor, B. P., & Nikolic, J. (1990). Identity development and normal operations as sources of adolescent egocentrism. *Journal of Youth and Adolescence, 19,* 149–158.

Offer, D., & Offer, J. (1974). Normal adolescent males: The high school and college years. *Journal of the American College Health Association, 22,* 209–215.

Offer, D., & Offer, J. (1975). *From teenage to young manhood.* New York: Basic Books.

Offer, D., Ostrov, E., & Howard, K. I. (1981). *The adolescent: A psychological self-portrait.* New York: Basic Books.

Offord, D. R., & Bennett, K. J. (1994). Conduct disorder: Long-term outcomes and intervention effectiveness. *Journal of the American Academy of Child and Adolescent Psychiatry, 33,* 1069–1078.

Ohannessian, C. M., & Crockett, L. J. (1993). A longitudinal investigation of the relationship between educational investment and adolescent sexual activity. *Journal of Adolescent Research, 8,* 167–182.

Ollendick, T. H., King, N. J., & Frary, R. B. (1989). Fears in children and adolescents: Reliability and generalizability across gender, age and nationality. *Behavior Research and Therapy, 27,* 19–26.

Olson, L., & Holmes, W. (1983). *Youth at risk: Adolescents and maltreatment.* Boston, MA: Center for Applied Social Research.

Olweus, D. (1980). Familial and temperamental determinants of aggressive behavior in adolescent boys: A causal analysis. *Developmental Psychology, 16,* 644–660.

Olweus, D., Mattsson, A., Schalling, D., & Low, H. (1988). Circulating testosterone levels and aggression in adolescent males: A causal analysis. *Psychosomatic Medicine, 50,* 261–272.

Orlando, F. A., & Crippen, G. L. (1992). The right of children and the juvenile court. In J. M. Schwartz (Ed.), *Juvenile justice and public policy: Toward a national agenda.* New York: Lexington Books.

Orlofsky, J., Marcia, J., & Lesser, I. (1973). Ego identity status and intimacy versus isolation crisis of young adulthood. *Journal of Personality and Social Psychology, 27,* 211–219.

O'Rourke, D. H., Gottesman, I. I., Suarez, B. K., Rice, J., & Reich, T. (1982). Refutation of the general single-locus model for the etiology of schizophrenia. *American Journal of Human Genetics, 34,* 630–649.

Osborn, S. G., & West, D. J. (1979). Conviction records of fathers and sons compared. *British Journal of Criminology, 19,* 120–135.

Osborn, S. G., & West, D. J. (1980). Do young delinquents really reform? *Journal of Adolescence, 3,* 99–114.

Osipow, S. H. (1986). Career issues through the life span. In M. Pallak & R. O. Perloff, *Psychology and work: Productivity, change, and employment* (pp. 141–168). Washington, DC: American Psychological Association.

Osofsky, J. D. (Ed.). (1987). *Handbook of infant development* (2nd ed.). New York: Wiley.

Osofsky, J. D. (1990, Winter). Risk and protective factors for teenage mothers and their infants. *Society for Research in Child Development Newsletter,* pp. 1–2.

Osterrieth, P. A. (1969). Adolescence: Some psychological aspects. In G. Caplin & S. Lebovici (Eds.), *Adolescence: Psychological perspectives.* New York: Basic Books.

Ouston, J., (1984). Delinquency, family background, and educational attainment. British Journal of Criminology, **24,** pp. 2–26.

Padgham, J. J., & Blyth, D. A. (1991). Dating during adolescence. In R. M. Lerner, A. C. Petersen, & J. Brooks-Gunn (Eds.), *Encyclopedia of adolescence* (pp. 196–198). New York: Garland.

Paikoff, R. L., & Brooks-Gunn, J. (1991). Do parent–child relationships change during puberty? *Psychological Bulletin, 110,* 47–66.

Panel on High-Risk Youth. Commission on Behavioral and Social Sciences and Education, National Research Council. (1993). *Losing generations: Adolescents in high-risk settings.* Washington, DC: National Academy Press.

Parcel, G. S., Simons-Morton, G. G., O'Hara, N. M., Baranowski, T., Kolbe, L. J., & Bee, D. E. (1987). School promotion of a healthly diet and exercise behavior: An integration of organizational change and social learning theory interventions. *Journal of School Health, 57,* 150–156.

Parker, G., Tupling, H., & Brown, L. B. (1979). A parental bonding instrument. *British Journal of Medical Psychology, 52,* 1–10.

Parker, J. G., & Asher, S. R. (1987). Peer relations and later adjustment: Are low-accepted children "at risk"? *Psychological Bulletin, 102,* 357–389.

Parker, J. G. & Gottman, J. M. (1989). Social and emotional development in a relational context: Friendship interaction from early childhood to adolescence. In T. J. Berndt & G. W. Ladd (Eds.), *Peer relationships in child development* (pp. 95–132). New York: Wiley.

Parkhurst, J. T., & Asher, S. R. (1992). Peer rejection in middle school: Subgroup differences in behavior, loneliness, and interpersonal concerns. *Developmental Psychology, 28,* 231–241.

Parry-Jones, W. L. (1985). Adolescent disturbance. In M. Rutter & L. Hersov (Eds.), *Child and adolescent psychiatry: Modern approaches* (pp. 584–598). Oxford: Blackwell Scientific Publications.

Parsons, J. E., Adler, T. & Kaczala, C. M. (1982). Socialization of achievement attitudes and beliefs: Parental influences. *Child Development, 53,* 310–321.

Parsons, J. E., Kaczala, C. M., & Meece, J. L. (1982). Socialization of achievement attitudes and beliefs: Classroom influences. *Child Development, 53,* 322–339.

Pascarelli, E. F. (1973). Methaqualone: The quiet epidemic. In R. P. Shafer et al., *Drug use in America: Problem in perspective* (Appendix, **Vol. 1,** pp. 102–105). Second report of the National Commission on Marijuana and Drug Abuse (Publication No. 5266-00004). Washington, DC: U.S. Government Printing Office.

Pascual-Leone, J. (1970). A mathematical model for transition in Piaget's developmental stages. *Acta Psychologica, 32,* 301–345.

Passell, P. (1989, July 16). Forces in society and Reaganism helped dig deep hole for poor. *The New York Times,* pp. 1, 12.

Pate, J. E., Pumariega, A. J., Hester, C., & Garner, D. M. (1992). Cross-cultural patterns in eating disorders: A review. *Journal of the American Academy of Child and Adolescent Psychiatry, 31,* 802–809.

Patterson, G. R. (1982). *Coercive family process.* Eugene, OR: Castalia Press.

Patterson, G. R., DeBarsyshe, B. D., & Ramsey, E. (1989). A developmental perspective on antisocial behavior. *American Psychologist, 44,* 329–335.

Paulson, S. E. (1994). Relations of parenting style and parental involvement with ninth-grade students' achievement. *Journal of Early Adolescence, 14,* 250–267.

Pearlin, L. I., Menaghan, E. G., Lieberman, M. A., & Mullan, J. T. (1981). The stress process. *Journal of Health and Social Behavior, 22,* 337–356.

Pearlin, L. I., & Schooler, C. (1978). The structure of coping. *Journal of Health and Social Behavior, 19,* 2–21.

Pelcovitz, D., Kaplan, S., Samit, C., Krieger, R., & Cornelius, P. (1984). Adolescent abuse: Family structure and implications for treatment. *Journal of Child Psychiatry, 23,* 85–90.

Pelleymounter, M. A., Cullen, J., Baker, M. B., Hecht, R., Winters, D., Boone, T., & Collins, F. (1995). Effects of the *obese* gene product on body weight reduction in ob/ob mice. *Science, 269,* 540–543.

Perlmutter, M. (1988). Cognitive potential throughout life. In J. E. Birren & K. L. Bengtson (Eds.), *Emergent theories of aging.* New York: Springer.

Personick, V. A. (1986). A second look at industry output and employment trends through 1995. In *Employment projections for 1995: Data and methods* (pp. 25–40). Washington, DC: U.S. Government Printing Office.

Peskin, H. (1973). Influence of the developmental schedule of puberty on learning and ego functioning. *Journal of Youth and Adolescence, 2,* 273–290.

Petersen, A. C. (1979). Female pubertal development. In M. Sugar (Ed.), *Female adolescent development* (pp. 23–46). New York: Brunner/Mazel.

Petersen, A. C. (1981). Sex differences in performance on spatial tasks: Biopsychosocial influences. In H. Ansara, N. Geschwind, A. Galaburda, M. Albert, & N. Gertrell (Eds.), *Sex differences in dyslexia* (pp. 41–54). Towson, MD: Orton Society.

Petersen, A. C. (1983). Menarche: Meaning of measures and measuring meaning. In S. Golub (Ed.), *Menarche.* Lexington, MA: D.C. Heath.

Petersen, A. C. (1988). Adolescent development. *Annual Review of Psychology, 39,* 583–608.

Petersen, A. C. (1993). Presidential address: Creating adolescents: The role of context and process in developmental trajectories. *Journal of Research on Adolescence, 3,* 1–18.

Petersen, A. C., & Boxer, A. (1982). Adolescent sexuality. In T. Coates, A. Petersen, & C. Perry (Eds.), *Adolescent health: Crossing the barriers* (pp. 237–253). New York: Academic Press.

Petersen, A. C., Compas, B. E., Brooks-Gunn, J., Stemmler, M., Ey, S., & Grant, K. E. (1993). Depression in adolescence. *American Psychologist, 48,* 155–168.

Petersen, A. C., & Crockett, L. J. (1985). Pubertal timing and grade effects on adjustment. *Journal of Youth and Adolescence, 14,* 191–206.

Petersen, A. C., & Ebata, A. T. (1987). Developmental transitions and adolescent problem behavior: Implications for prevention and intervention. In K. Hurrelmann (Ed.), *Social prevention and intervention.* New York: de Gruyter.

Petersen, A. C., Kennedy, R. E., & Sullivan, P. A. (1991). Coping with adolescence. In M. E. Colton & S. Gore (Eds.), *Adolescent stress: Causes and consequences. Social institutions and social change* (pp. 93–110). New York, NY: Aldine de Gruyter.

Petersen, A. C., Richmond, J. B., & Leffert, N. (1993). Social changes among youth: The United States experience. *Journal of Adolescent Health, 14,* 632–637.

Petersen, A. C., Sarigiani, P. A., & Kennedy, R. E. (1991). Adolescent depression: Why more girls? *Journal of Youth and Adolescence, 20,* 247–271.

Petersen, A. C., & Spiga, R. (1982). Adolescence and stress. In L. Goldwater & S. Breznitz (Eds.), *Handbook of stress: Theoretical and clinical aspects* (pp. 515–528). New York: Free Press.

Petersen, A. C., Susman, E. J., & Beard, J. L. (1989). The development of coping responses during adolescence: Endocrine and behavioral aspects. In D. S. Palermo (Ed.), *Coping with uncertainty: Behavioral and developmental perspectives. The Penn State series on child & adolescent development* (pp. 151–172). Hillsdale, NJ: Lawrence Erlbaum.

Petersen, A. C., & Taylor, B. (1980). The biological approach to adolescence: Biological change and psychological adaptation. In J. Adelson (Ed.), *Handbook of adolescent psychology* (pp. 117–155). New York: Wiley.

Petersen, R. C. (1980). Marijuana research findings: 1980. *NIDA Research Monograph 31* (DHHS Publication No. ADM 80-1001). Washington, DC: U.S. Government Printing Office.

Peterson, J. L., & Zill, N. (1986). Marital disruption, parent–child relationships, and behavior problems in children. *Journal of Marriage and the Family, 48,* 295–307.

Pfeffer, C. R. (1989). Family characteristics and support systems as risk factors for youth suicidal behavior. In *Report of the Secretary's task force on youth suicide,* **Volume 2:** *Risk factors for youth suicide* (pp. 71–87). Washington, DC: U.S. Government Printing Office.

Pfeffer, C. R. (1991). Attempted suicide in children and adolescents. In M. Lewis (Ed.), *Child and adolescent psychiatry: A comprehensive textbook* (pp. 664–672). Baltimore: Williams & Wilkins.

Phares, V., & Compas, B. E. (1992). The role of fathers in child and adolescent psychopathology: Make room for Daddy. *Psychological Bulletin, 111,* 387–412.

Phelps, L., Johnson, L. S., Jimenez, D. P., Wilczenski, F. L., Andrea, R. K., & Healy, R. W. (1993). Figure preference, body dissatisfaction, and body distortion in adolescence. *Journal of Adolescent Research, 8,* 297–310.

Piaget, J. (1948). *The moral judgment of the child.* New York: Free Press.

**Piaget, J.** (1954). *The construction of reality in the child.* New York: Basic Books.

**Piaget, J.** (1970). Piaget's theory. In P. H. Mussen (Ed.), *Carmichael's manual of child psychology,* **Vol. I** (pp. 703–732). New York: Wiley.

**Pianta, R., Egeland, B., & Erickson, M. F.** (1989). The antecedents of maltreatment: Results of the Mother–Child Interaction Research Project. In D. Cicchetti & V. Carlson, (Eds.), *Child maltreatment: Theory and research on the causes and consequences of child abuse and neglect* (pp. 203–253). New York: Cambridge University Press.

**Pike, K. M., & Rodin, J.** (1991). Mothers, daughters, and disordered eating. *Journal of Abnormal Psychology, 100,* 198–204.

**Pillard, R. C., & Weinrich, J. D.** (1987). The periodic table model of the gender transpositions: Part I. A theory based on masculinization and defeminization of the brain. *The Journal of Sex Research, 23,* 425–454.

**Piotrkowski, C. S.** (1979). *Work and the family system.* New York: Macmillan.

**Plato.** (1953) (B. Jewett, trans.). *The dialogues of Plato* (**Vol. 4,** 4th ed.). New York: Oxford University Press (Clarendon Press).

**Plomin, R.** (1986). *Development, genetics, and psychology.* Hillsdale, NJ: Lawrence Erlbaum.

**Plomin, R.** (1990). The role of inheritance in behavior. *Science,* **248,** 183–188.

**Plomin, R., Coon, H., Carey, G., DeFries, J. C., & Fulker, D. W.** (1991). Parent–offspring and sibling adoption analyses of parent ratings of temperament in infancy and childhood. *Journal of Personality,* **59,** 705–732.

**Plomin, R., & Neiderhiser, J. M.** (1992). Quantitative genetics, molecular genetics, and intelligence. *Intelligence,* **15,** 369–387.

**Plomin, R., & Nesselroade, J. R.** (1990). Behavioral genetics and personality change. *Journal of Personality,* **58,** 191–220.

**Pope, H. G., Jr., & Hudson, J. I.** (1989). Eating disorders. In H. I. Kaplan & B. J. Sadock (Eds.), *Comprehensive textbook of psychiatry* (5th ed., pp. 1854–1864). Baltimore: Williams & Wilkins.

**Posterski, D., & Bibby, R.** (1988). *Canada's youth, ready for today: A comprehensive survey of 15–24-year-olds.* Ottawa: Canadian Youth Foundation.

**Potvin, R. H., Hoge, D. R., & Nelsen, H. M.** (1976). *Religion and American youth: With emphasis on Catholic adolescents and young adults.* Washington, DC: Catholic Conference.

**Power, F. C., Higgins, A., & Kohlberg, L.** (1989). *Lawrence Kohlberg's approach to moral education.* New York: Columbia University Press.

**Power, T. G., & Shanks, J. A.** (1989). Parents as socializers: Maternal and paternal view. *Journal of Youth and Adolescence,* **18,** 203–220.

**Prescott, P. S.** (1981). *The child savers.* New York: Knopf.

**Price, J. M., & Dodge, K. A.** (1989). Peers' contribution to children's social maladjustment: Description and intervention. In T. J. Berndt & G. W. Ladd (Eds.) *Peer relationships in child development* (pp. 341–370). New York: Wiley.

**Prinz, R. J., Rosenblum, R. S., & O'Leary, K. D.** (1978). Affective communication differences between distressed and nondistressed mother–adolescent dyads. *Journal of Abnormal Child Psychiatry,* **6,** 373–383.

**Puig-Antich, J.** (1986). Psychobiological markers: Effects of age and puberty. In M. Rutter, C. E. Izard, & P. B. Read (Eds.), *Depression in young people: Developmental and clinical perspectives* (pp. 341–382). New York: Guilford.

**Putka, G.** (1988, Sept. 20). SAT scores fall for first time since '80. *Wall Street Journal,* p. 40.

**Quadrel, M. J., Fischhoff, B., & Davis, W.** (1993). Adolescent (in)vulnerability. *American Psychologist,* **48,** 102–116.

**Quay, H. C.** (Ed.) (1987a). *Handbook of juvenile delinquency.* New York: Wiley.

**Quay, H. C.** (1987b). Intelligence. In H. C. Quay (Ed.). *Handbook of juvenile delinquency* (pp. 106–117). New York: Wiley.

**Quay, H. C.** (1987c). Patterns of delinquent behavior. In H. C. Quay (Ed.), *Handbook of juvenile delinquency* (pp. 118–138). New York: Wiley.

**Rachal, J. V., Maisto, S. A., Guess, L. L., & Hubbard, R. L.** (1984). Alcohol use among adolescents. In National Institute on Alcohol Abuse and Alcoholism, *Alcohol consumption and related problems.* Alcohol and Health Monograph No. 1. Rockville, MD: The Institute.

**Radke-Yarrow, M., & Sherman, T.** (1990). Hard growing. In J. E. Rolf, A. Masten, D. Cicchetti, K. H. Nuechterlein, & S. Weintraub (Eds.), *Risk and protective factors in the development of psychopathology.* New York: Cambridge University Press.

**Ravitch, D. O., & Finn, C. E., Jr.** (1987). *What do our 17-year-olds know? A report on the first national assessment of history and literature.* New York: Harper & Row.

**Ravussin, E., Lillioja, S., Knowler, W. C., Christin, L., Boyce, V., Howard, B. V., & Bogardus, C.** (1988). Reduced rate of energy expenditure as a risk factor for body-weight gain. *New England Journal of Medicine,* **318,** 467–472.

**Reed, S. C., & Rich, S. S.** (1982). Parent–offspring correlations and regressions for IQ. *Behavior Genetics,* **12,** 535–542.

**Reeves, D.** (1984). Parental power and adolescents' drinking. *Psychological Reports,* **55,** 161–162.

**Reich, R.** (1994, Jan. 10). Interview on *Morning Edition.* National Public Radio, Washington, DC.

**Reich, R.** (1995). *Good for business: Making full use of the nation's human capital. V. Environmental scan, a fact finding report of the Federal Glass Ceiling Commission.* Washington, DC: U.S. Government Printing Office.

**Reinherz, H. Z., Frost, A. K., Stewart-Berghauer, G., Pakiz, B., Kennedy, K., & Schille, C.** (1990). The many faces of correlates of depressive symptoms in adolescents. *Journal of Early Adolescence,* **10,** 455–471.

**Reinherz, H. Z., Giaconia, R. M., Lefkowitz, E. S., Pakiz, B., & Frost, A. K.** (1993). Prevalence of psychiatric disorders in a community population of older adolescents. *Journal of the American Academy of Child and Adolescent Psychiatry,* **32,** 369–377.

**Reiss, A. J.** (1952). Social correlates of psychological types of delinquency. *American Sociological Review,* **17,** 710–718.

**Reiss, A. J., Jr., & Roth, J. A.** (1993). *Understanding and preventing violence.* Washington, DC: National Academy Press.

**Remafedi, G.** (1990). Adolescent sexuality. In R. M. Lerner, A. C. Petersen, & J. Brooks-Gunn (Eds.), *Encyclopedia of adolescence* (pp. 504–507). New York: Garland.

*Report of the Secretary's task force on youth suicide, Volume 1: Overview and recommendations.* (1989a). Washington, DC: U.S. Government Printing Office.

*Report of the Secretary's task force on youth suicide, Volume 2: Risk factors for youth suicide.* (1989b). Washington, DC: U.S. Government Printing Office.

Rest, J. R. (1983). Morality. In P. H. Mussen, J. Flavel, & E. Markman (Eds.), *Handbook of child psychology,* **Vol. 3:** *Cognitive development* (4th ed.). New York: Wiley.

Rest, J. R. (1986). *Moral development: Advances in research and theory.* New York: Praeger.

Rich, D. (1985). *The forgotten factor in school success—the family.* Washington, DC: Home and School Institute.

Richards, M. H., Boxer, A. W., Petersen, A. C., & Albrecht, R. (1990). Relation of weight to body image in pubertal girls and boys from two communities. *Developmental Psychology,* **26,** 313–321.

Richards, M. H., & Duckett, E. (1994). The relationship of maternal employment to early adolescent daily experience with and without parents. *Child Development,* **65,** 225–236.

Richards, M. H., & Larson, R. (1993). Pubertal development and the daily subjective states of young adolescents. *Journal of Research on Adolescence,* **3,** 145–169.

Richardson, J. G., & Cranston, J. E. (1981). Social change, parental values, and the salience of sex education. *Journal of Marriage and the Family,* **43,** 547–558.

Richardson, J. L., Dwyer, K., McGuigan, K., Hansen, W. B., Dent, C., Johnson, C. A., Sussman, S. Y., Brannon, B., & Flay, B. (1989). Substance use among eighth-grade students who take care of themselves after school. *Pediatrics,* **84,** 556–566.

Richardson, R. A., Galambos, N. L., Schulenberg, J. E., & Petersen, A. C. (1984). Young adolescents' perceptions of the family environment. *Journal of Early Adolescence,* **4,** 131–153.

Richman, L. C., & Lindgren, S. D. (1981). Verbal mediation deficits: Relation to behavior and achievement in children. *Journal of Abnormal Psychology,* **90,** 99–104.

Richman, N., Stevenson, J., & Graham, P. J. (1982). *Pre-school to school: A behavioural study.* London: Academic Press.

Ricketts, E., & Mincy, R. (1990). Growth of the underclass: 1970–1980. *Journal of Human Resources,* **25,** 137–145.

Riding, A. (1995, Jan. 3). Documenting what motivated those who helped save the Jews. *The New York Times,* pp. B1–2.

Rierdan, J., & Koff, E. (1985a, March). *Depression in adolescent girls.* Poster presented at the biennial meeting of the Society for Research in Child Development.

Rierdan, J., & Koff, E. (1985b). Timing of menarche and initial menstrual experience. *Journal of Youth and Adolescence,* **14,** 237–244.

Rierdan, J., & Koff, E. (1991). Depressive symptomatology among very early maturing girls. *Journal of Youth and Adolescence,* **20,** 415–425.

Rierdan, J., Koff, E., & Stubbs, M. L. (1989). Timing of menarche, preparation, and initial menstrual experience: Replication and further analyses in a prospective study. *Journal of Youth and Adolescence,* **18,** 413–426.

Rimberg, H. M., & Lewis, R. J. (1994). Older adolescents and AIDS: Correlates of self-reported safer sex practices. *Journal of Research on Adolescence,* **4,** 453–464.

Robert Wood Johnson Foundation. (1990). The mental health services program for youth. *Journal of Mental Health Administration,* **17,** 115–121.

Roberts, J. (1971). *Intellectual development of children by demographic and socioeconomic factors.* Washington, DC: Department of Health, Education and Welfare, Publication No. (HSM) 72-1012 (Data from National Health Survey, Series 11, No. 110).

Roberts, L. R., Sarigiani, P. A., Petersen, A. C., & Newman, J. L. (1990). Gender differences in the relationship between achievement and self-image during adolescence. *Journal of Early Adolescence,* **10,** 159–175.

Roberts, S. (1987, April 23). For homeless struggles include getting to school. *The New York Times,* p. B1.

Roberts, S. B. (1993). Energy expenditure and the development of early obesity. In C. L. Williams & S. Y. S. Kimm (Eds.), *Prevention and treatment of childhood obesity* (pp. 18–25). New York: New York Academy of Sciences.

Robertson, M. (1989). False start on manic depression. *Nature,* **342,** 222.

Robins, L. (1978). Sturdy childhood predictors of adult antisocial behavior: Replications from longitudinal studies. *Psychological Medicine,* **8,** 611–622.

Robins, L. N. (1979). Addict careers. In R. I. Dupont, A. Goldstein, & J. O'Donnell (Eds.), *Handbook on drug abuse* (pp. 325–336). Washington, DC: U.S. Government Printing Office.

Robins, L. N., & Mus, J. L. (1993). Effects of in utero exposure to street drugs. *American Journal of Public Health,* (supplement to Volume 83).

Robins, L. N., & Price, R. K. (1991). Adult disorders predicted by childhood conduct problems: Results from the NIMH Epidemiological Catchment Area project. *Psychiatry,* **54,** 116–132.

Robins, L., West, P. A., & Herjanic, B. L. (1975). Arrests and delinquency in two generations: A study of black urban families and their children. *Journal of Child Psychology and Psychiatry,* **76,** 125–140.

Roche, A. F. (1978). Bone growth and maturation. In F. Falkner & J. M. Tanner (Eds.), *Human growth:* **Vol. 2.** *Postnatal growth.* New York: Plenum.

Rodgers, J. L. (1992). Development of sexual behavior. In S. B. Friedman, M. Fisher, S. K. Schonberg (Eds.), *Comprehensive adolescent health care.* St. Louis, MO: Quality Medical Publishing.

Rodin, J. (1985). Insulin levels, hunger, and food intake: An example of feedback loops in body weight regulation. *Health Psychology,* **4,** 1–24.

Rodin, J., Silberstein, L. R., & Striegel-Moore, R. H. (1985). Women and weight: A normative discontent. In T. B. Sonderegger (Eds.), *Nebraska symposium on motivation.* **Vol. 32:** *Psychology and gender* (pp. 267–307). Lincoln: University of Nebraska Press.

Rodin, J., Striegel-Moore, R. H., & Silberstein, L. R. (1990). Vulnerability and resilience in the age of eating

disorders: Risk and protective factors for bulimia nervosa. In J. Rolf, A. S. Masten, D. Cicchetti, K. H. Nuechterlein, & S. Weintraub (Eds.), *Risk and protective factors in the development of psychopathology* (pp. 361–383). New York: Cambridge University Press.

**Rodman, H., Pratto, D., & Nelson, R. S.** (1985). Child care arrangements and children's functioning: A comparison of self-care and adult-care children. *Developmental Psychology, 21,* 413–418.

**Rodriguez, J.** (1990). Childhood injuries in the United States. *American Journal of Diseases of Childhood, 144,* 627–646.

**Rooney, B.** (1992). *A meta-analysis of smoking-prevention programs after adjustment for study design.* Minneapolis–St. Paul: University of Minnesota.

**Roper Center survey.** (1994). Cited in J. Giles (1994, June 6); Generation X. *Newsweek,* 62–72.

**Roscoe, B., Diana, M., & Brooks, R.** (1987). Early, middle, and late adolescents' views on dating and factors influencing selection of a dating partner. *Adolescence, 22,* 59–68.

**Rosenbaum, J. E.** (1991). Are adolescent problems caused by school or society? *Journal of Research on Adolescence, 1,* 301–322.

**Rosenthal, D. A., & Feldman, S. S.** (1991). The influence of perceived family and personal factors on self-reported school performance of Chinese and Western high school students. *Journal of Research on Adolescence, 1,* 135–154.

**Rotheram, M. J.** (1987). Evaluation of imminent danger for suicide among youth. *American Journal of Orthopsychiatry, 57,* 102–110.

**Rotheram-Borus, M. J.** (1993). Suicidal behavior and risk factors among runaway youth. *American Journal of Psychiatry, 150,* 103–107.

**Rotheram-Borus, M. J., & Koopman, C.** (1991). AIDS and adolescents. In R. M. Lerner, A. C. Petersen, & J. Brooks-Gunn (Eds.), *Encyclopedia of adolescence* (pp. 29–36). New York: Garland.

**Rotheram-Borus, M. J., Rosario, M., & Koopman, C.** (1991). Minority youths at high risk: Gay males and runaways. In M. E. Colton, S. Gore, & R. Aseltine (Eds.), *Adolescent stress: Causes and consequences* (pp. 181–200). New York: Aldine de Gruyter.

**Rotheram-Borus, M. J., Rosario, M., Van Rossem, R., Reid, H., & Gillis, R.** (1995). Prevalence, course, and predictors of multiple problem behaviors among gay and bisexual male adolescents. *Developmental Psychology, 31,* 75–85.

**Rowe, I., & Marcia, J. E.** (1980). Ego identity status, formal operations, and moral development. *Journal of Youth and Adolescence, 9,* 87–99.

**Ruble, D. N.** (1977). Premenstrual symptoms. *Science, 197,* 291–292.

**Ruble, D. N., & Brooks, J.** (1977). *Attitudes about menstruation.* Paper presented at the Biennial Meeting of the Society for Research in Child Development, New Orleans, March 17–20.

**Ruble, D. N., & Brooks-Gunn, J.** (1982). The experience of menarche. *Child Development, 53,* 1557–66.

**Rumberger, R. W.** (1983, Summer). Dropping out of high school: The influence of race, sex, and family background. *American Education Research Journal, 201,* 199–200.

**Russell, G. F. M.** (1985). Anorexia and bulimia nervosa. In M. Rutter & L. Hersov (Eds.), *Child and adolescent psychiatry: Modern approaches* (pp. 625–637). Oxford: Blackwell Scientific Publications.

**Rust, J. O., & Troupe, P. A.** (1991). Relationships of treatment of child sexual abuse with school achievement and self-concept. *Journal of Early Adolescence, 11,* 420–429.

**Rutter, M.** (1980). *Changing youth in a changing society: Patterns of adolescent development and disorder.* Cambridge, MA: Harvard University Press.

**Rutter, M.** (1986). Child psychiatry: The interface between clinical and developmental research. *Psychological Medicine, 16,* 151–169.

**Rutter, M.** (1989a). Intergenerational continuities and discontinuities in serious parenting difficulties. In D. Cicchetti & V. Carlson (Eds.), *Child maltreatment: Theory and research on the causes and consequences of child abuse and neglect* (pp. 317–348). New York: Cambridge University Press.

**Rutter, M.** (1989b). Isle of Wight revisited: Twenty-five years of child psychiatric epidemiology. *Journal of the American Academy of Child and Adolescent Psychiatry, 28,* 633–653.

**Rutter, M., & Garmezy, N.** (1983). Developmental psychopathology. In P. H. Mussen (Series Ed.) & E. M. Hetherington (Ed.), *Handbook of child psychology:* **Vol. IV.** *Socialization, personality and social development* (pp. 775–911). New York: Wiley.

**Rutter, M., & Giller, H.** (1984). *Juvenile delinquency: Trends and perspectives.* New York: Guilford.

**Rutter, M., Graham, O. F. D., & Yule, W.** (1976). Adolescent turmoil: Fact or fiction? *Journal of Child Psychology and Psychiatry, 17,* 35–36.

**Rutter, M., Izard, C. E., & Read, P. B.** (1986). *Depression in young people: Developmental and clinical perspectives.* New York: Guilford Press.

**Rutter, M., Maughan, B., Mortimore, P., & Ouston, J.** (1979). *Fifteen thousand hours: Secondary schools and their effects on children.* Cambridge, MA: Harvard University Press.

**Rutter, M., Tizard, J., & Whitmore, K.** (1970/1981). *Education, health and behavior.* Huntington, NY: Krieger (Original work published 1970, London: Longmans).

**Ryan, N. D., Puig-Antich, J., Ambrosini, P., Rabinovich, H., Robinson, D., Nelson, B., Iyengar, S., & Twomey, J.** (1987). The clinical picture of major depression in children and adolescence. *Archives of General Psychiatry, 44,* 854–861.

**Ryan, R. M., & Lynch, J. H.** (1989). Emotional autonomy versus detachment: Revisiting the vicissitudes of adolescence and young adulthood. *Child Development, 60,* 340–356.

**Ryan, R. M., Stiller, J. D., & Lynch, J. H.** (1994). Representations of relationships to teachers, parents, and friends as predictors of academic motivation and self-esteem. *Journal of Early Adolescence, 14,* 226–249.

**St. Lawrence, J. S., Brasfield, T. L., Jefferson, K. W., Allyene, E., & Shirley, A.** (1994). Social support as a factor in African-American adolescents' sexual risk behavior. *Journal of Adolescent Research, 9,* 292–310.

Salzinger, S., Feldman, R. S., Hammer, M., & Rosario, M. (1993). The effects of physical abuse on children's social relationships. *Child Development, 64,* 169–187.

Sameroff, A. J., Seifer, R., Baldwin, A., & Baldwin, C. (1993). Stability of intelligence from preschool to adolescence: The influence of social and family risk factors. *Child Development, 64,* 80–97.

Sampson, R. J., & Lamb, J. H. (1994). Urban poverty and the family context of delinquency: A new look at structure and process in a classic study. *Child Development, 65,* 523–540.

Sanders, B., & Soares, M. P. (1986). Sexual maturation and spatial ability in college students. *Developmental Psychology, 22,* 199–203.

Sanders, B., Soares, M. P., & D'Aquila, J. M. (1982). The sex difference on one test of spatial visualization: A nontrivial difference. *Child Development, 53,* 1106–1110.

Santilli, N. R., & Furth, H. G. (1987). Adolescent work perception: A developmental approach. In J. H. Lewko (Ed.), *How children and adolescents view the world of work* (pp. 33–49). San Francisco: Jossey-Bass.

Santolupo, S., & Pratt, M. W. (1994). Age, gender, and parenting style variations in mother–adolescent dialogues and adolescent reasoning about political issues. *Journal of Adolescent Research, 9,* 241–261.

Santrock, J. W. (1993). *Adolescence: An introduction* (5th ed.). Madison, WI: Brown & Benchmark.

Sarason, S. B. (1983). *Schooling in America: Scapegoat and salvation.* New York: Free Press.

Savin-Williams, R. C. (1980a). Dominance hierarchies in groups of late adolescent males. *Journal of Youth and Adolescence, 9,* 75–83.

Savin-Williams, R. C. (1980b). Social interactions of adolescent females in natural groups. In H. C. Foot, A. J. Chapman, & J. R. Smith (Eds.), *Friendship and social relations in children.* New York: Wiley.

Savin-Williams, R. C. (1989). Gay and lesbian adolescents. *Marriage and Family Review, 14,* 197–216.

Savin-Williams, R. C. (1990). Gay and lesbian youth. In R. M. Lerner, A. C. Petersen, & J. Brooks-Gunn (Eds.), *Encyclopedia of adolescence* (pp. 385–388). New York: Garland.

Savin-Williams, R. C. (1994). Verbal and physical abuse as stressors in the lives of lesbian, gay male, and bisexual youths: Associations with school problems, running away, substance abuse, prostitution, and suicide. *Journal of Consulting and Clinical Psychology, 62,* 261–269.

Savin-Williams, R. C., & Berndt, T. J. (1990). Friendship and peer relations. In S. S. Feldman & G. R. Elliott (Eds.), *At the threshold: The developing adolescent* (pp. 277–307). Cambridge, MA: Harvard University Press.

Scarr, S. (1992). Developmental theories for the 1990s: Development and individual differences. *Child Development, 63,* 1–19.

Scarr, S., & Carter-Saltzman, L. (1979). Twin method: Defense of a critical assumption. *Behavior Genetics, 9,* 527–542.

Scarr, S., & Carter-Saltzman, L. C. (1982). Genetics and intelligence. In R. J. Sternberg (Ed.), *Handbook of human intelligence* (pp. 792–896). New York: Cambridge University Press.

Scarr, S., & Kidd, K. K. (1983). Developmental behavior genetics. In M. Haith & J. Campos (Eds.) & P. H. Mussen (Series Ed.), *Handbook of child psychology:* **Vol. II.** *Infancy and developmental psychobiology* (pp. 345–435). New York: Wiley.

Scarr, S., & McCartney, K. (1983). How people make their own environments: A theory of genotype–environment effects. *Child Development, 54,* 424–435.

Scarr, S., & Weinberg, R. A. (1976, Oct.). IQ test performance of black children adopted by white families. *American Psychologist, 31,* 726–739.

Schacter, S. (1971). *Emotion, obesity, and crime.* New York: Academic Press.

Schaefer, E. S. (1965). A configurational analysis of children's reports of parent behavior. *Journal of Consulting and Clinical Psychology, 29,* 552–557.

Schaie, K. W. (1983). The Seattle Longitudinal Study: A twenty-one year exploration of psychometric intelligence in adulthood. In K. W. Schaie (Ed.), *Longitudinal studies of adult psychological development* (pp. 64–135). New York: Guilford.

Schaie, K. W., & Willis, S. L. (1986). Can decline in adult intellectual functioning be reversed? *Developmental Psychology, 23,* 223–232.

Schiedel, D. G., & Marcia, J. E. (1985). Ego identity, intimacy, sex role orientation, and gender. *Developmental Psychology, 21,* 149–160.

Schiff, M., Duyme, M., Dumaret, A., & Tomkiewicz, S. (1982). How much could we boost scholastic achievement and IQ scores: A direct answer from a French adoption study. *Cognition, 12,* 165–196.

Schlegel, A., & Barry, H., III. (1991). *Adolescence: An anthropological inquiry.* New York: Free Press.

Schmidt, G. (1975). Male–female differences in sexual arousal and behavior during and after exposure to sexually explicit stimuli. *Archives of Sexual Behavior, 1,* 353–364.

Schneider, W., & Pressley, M. (1989). *Memory development between two and twenty.* New York: Springer-Verlag.

Schofield, J. (1981). Complementary and conflicting identities: Images and interaction in an interracial school. In S. Asher & J. Gottman (Eds.), *The development of children's friendships.* Cambridge: Cambridge University Press.

Schorr, A. L. (1988). Other times, other strategies. *Social Work, 33,* 249–250.

Schorr, L. B., with Schorr, D. (1988). *Within our reach: Breaking the cycle of disadvantage.* New York: Harper & Row.

Schuckit, M. A. (1995). *Drug and alcohol abuse: A clinical guide to diagnosis and treatment* (4th ed.). New York: Plenum.

Schuerger, J. M., & Kuna, D. L. (1987). Adolescent personality and school and college performance: A follow-up study. *Psychology in the Schools, 24,* 281–285.

Schulenberg, J., & Bachman, J. G. (1993). *Long hours on the job? Not so bad for some adolescents in some types of jobs: The quality of work and substance use, affect, and stress.* Paper presented at the Biennial Meeting of the Society for Research in Child Development, New Orleans.

Schulenberg, J., Bachman, J. G., Johnston, L. D., & O'Malley, P. M. (1995). American adolescents' views on family and work: Historical trends from 1976–1992. In P. Noack, M. Hofer, & J. Youniss (Eds.), *Psychological responses to social change: Human development in changing environments* (pp. 37–64). Berlin: Walter de Gruyter.

Schulenberg, J., & Ebata, A. T. (1994). The United States. In K. Hurrelmann (Ed.), *International handbook of adolescence* (pp. 414–430). Westport, CT: Greenwood Press.

Schulenberg, J., Goldstein, A. E., & Vondracek, F. W. (1991). Gender differences in adolescents' career interests: Beyond main effects. *Journal of Research on Adolescence, 1,* 37–61.

Schulman, R., & Kende, B. (1988). A study of runaways from a short-term diagnostic center. *Residential treatment for children and youth, 5,* 11–31.

Schultz, T. R., Wright, K., & Schleifer, M. (1986). Assignment of moral responsibility and punishment. *Child Development, 57,* 177–184.

Schwalberg, M. D., Barlow, D. H., Alger, S. A., & Howard, L. J. (1992). Comparison of bulimics, obese binge eaters, social phobics, and individuals with panic disorder on comorbidity across *DSM-III-R* anxiety disorders. *Journal of Abnormal Psychology, 101,* 675–681.

Schwartz, L. A., Barnett, M. J., & Sabor, G. (1985). Family therapy for bulimia. In D. M. Garner & P. E. Garfinkel (Eds.), *Handbook of psychotherapy for anorexia nervosa and bulimia* (pp. 280–307). New York: Guilford Press.

Schwartz, R. H. (1992). Is Holland's theory worthy of so much attention, or should vocational psychology move on? *Journal of Vocational Behavior, 40,* 179–187.

Scott, R. M. (1980). Coordinating services for runaway youth: The case of New York City. *Journal of Family Issues, 1,* 308–312.

Sears, H. A., & Galambos, N. L. (1992). Women's work conditions and marital adjustment in two-earner couples: A structural model. *Journal of Marriage and the Family, 54,* 789–797.

Sears, H. A., & Galambos, N. L. (1993). The employed mother's well-being. In J. Frankel (Ed.), *The employed mother and the family context* (pp. 49–67). New York: Springer.

Sebald, H. (1984). *Adolescence: A social psychological analysis* (3rd ed.). Englewood Cliffs, NJ: Prentice-Hall.

Sebald, H., & White, B. (1980). Teenagers divided reference groups: Uneven alignment with parents and peers. *Adolescence, 15,* 579–984.

Sechrest, L., & Rosenblatt, A. (1987). Research methods. In H. C. Quay (Ed.), *Handbook of juvenile delinquency* (pp. 417–450). New York: Wiley.

Seebach, S. E., & Norris, R. C. (1989). Brunswikian model for body image research. *Journal of Adolescence Research, 4,* 299–318.

Seeman, M. (1975). Alienation studies. In A. Inkeles, J. Coleman, & N. Smelser (Eds.), *Annual review of sociology* (Vol. I). Palo Alto, CA: Annual Reviews.

Segal, N. L. (1985). Monozygotic and dizygotic twins: A comparative analysis of mental ability profiles. *Child Development, 56,* 1051–1058.

Seidman, E., Allen, L., Aber, J. L., Mitchell, C., & Feinman, J. (1994). The impact of school transitions in adolescence on the self-system and perceived social context of poor urban youth. *Child Development, 65,* 507–522.

Seitz, V., & Apfel, N. H. (1994). Effects of a school for pregnant students on the incidence of low-birthweight deliveries. *Child Development, 65,* 666–676.

Seligman, M. E. P., & Peterson, C. (1986). A learned helplessness perspective on childhood depression: Theory and research. In M. Rutter, C. Izard, & P. Read (Eds.), *Depression in young people: Developmental and clinical perspectives* (pp. 223–249). New York: Guilford Press.

Selman, R. L. (1980). *The growth of interpersonal understanding: Developmental and clinical analyses.* New York: Academic Press.

Selman, R. L. (1981). The child as a friendship philosopher: A case study in the growth of interpersonal understanding. In S. R. Asher & J. M. Gottman (Eds.), *The development of children's friendships.* Cambridge, England: Cambridge University Press.

Selman, R. L., & Selman, A. D. (1979). Children's ideas about friendship: A new theory. *Psychology Today, 13,* (4), 71ff.

Senn, M. J. E., & Solnit, A. J. (1968). *Problems in child behavior and development.* Philadelphia: Lea & Febiger.

Setterberg, S. R. (1992). Suicidal behavior and suicide. In S. B. Friedman, M. Fisher, & S. K. Schonberg (Eds.), *Comprehensive adolescent health care* (pp. 862–867). St. Louis, MO: Quality Medical Publishing.

Severson, H., Glasgow, R., Wirt, R., Brozovsky, P., Zoref, L., & Black, C., et al. (1991). Preventing the use of smokeless tobacco and cigarettes by teens: Results of a classroom intervention. *Health Education Research, 6,* 109–120.

Sex education and sex related behavior. (1986). *Family Planning Perspectives, 18,* 150–192.

Shaffer, D. (1988). The epidemiology of teen suicide: An examination of risk factors. *Journal of Clinical Psychiatry, 49,* 36–41.

Shaffer, D., & Piacentini, J. (1994). Suicide and attempted suicide. In M. Rutter, E. Taylor, & L. Hersov (Eds.), *Child and adolescent psychiatry* (3rd ed., pp. 407–424). Boston: Blackwell Scientific Publishers.

Shah, F., & Zelnik, M. (1981). Parent and peer influence on sexual behavior, contraceptive use, and pregnancy experience of young women. *Journal of Marriage and the Family, 43,* 339–348.

Shantz, C. U. (1975). The development of social cognition. In E. M. Hetherington (Ed.), *Review of Child Development Research* (**Vol. 5,** pp. 257–323). Chicago: University of Chicago Press.

Shantz, C. U. (1983). Social cognition. In P. H. Mussen (Series Ed.) & J. H. Flavell & E. M. Markman (Eds.), *Handbook of child psychology.* **Vol. 3:** *Cognitive development* (4th ed., pp. 495–555). New York: Wiley.

Sharabany, R., Gershoni, R., & Hoffman, J. E. (1981). Girlfriend, boyfriend: Age and sex differences in intimate friendship. *Developmental Psychology, 17,* 800–808.

**Sharp, C. W., & Rosenberg, N. L.** (1992). Volatile substances. In J. H. Lowinson, P. Ruiz, R. B. Millman, & J. G. Langrod (Eds.), *Substance abuse: A comprehensive textbook* (2nd ed., pp. 303–327). Baltimore: Williams & Wilkins.

**Shaw, J. A.** (1988). Childhood depression. *Medical Clinics of North America, 72,* 831–845.

**Shea, C.** (1994, Dec. 14). New look at college drinking. *Chronicle of Higher Education,* p. A39.

**Shea, C.** (1995a, January 13). Disengaged freshmen. *Chronicle of Higher Education,* p. A29.

**Shea, C.** (1995b, September 8). SAT scores show biggest increase in 10 years. *Chronicle of Higher Education,* p. A58.

**Shedler, J., & Block, J.** (1990). Adolescent drug use and psychological health. *American Psychologist, 45,* 612–630.

**Shulman, S.** (1993). Close friendships in early and middle adolescence: Typology and friendship reasoning. In B. Laursen (Ed.), *Close friendships in adolescence: New Directions for Child Development.* San Francisco: Jossey-Bass.

**Siegelman, M.** (1974). Parental background of homosexual and heterosexual women. *British Journal of Psychiatry, 124,* 14–21.

**Siegler, R. S., & Richards, D. D.** (1982). The development of intelligence. In R. J. Sternberg (Ed.), *Handbook of human intelligence* (pp. 897–970). Cambridge: Cambridge University Press.

**Sigelman, C. K., & Toebben, J. L.** (1992). Tolerant reactions to advocates of disagreeable ideas in childhood and adolescence. *Merrill–Palmer Quarterly, 38,* 542–557.

**Silbereisen, R. K., & Noack, P.** (1988). On the constructive role of problem behavior in adolescence. In N. Bolger, A. Caspi, G. Downey, & M. Moorehouse (Eds.), *Persons in context: Developmental processes* (pp. 152–179). Cambridge: Cambridge University Press.

**Silbereisen, R. K., Petersen, A. C., Albrecht, H. T., & Kracke, B.** (1989). Maturational timing and the development of problem behavior: Longitudinal studies in adolescence. *Journal of Early Adolescence, 9,* 247–268.

**Silberman, C. E.** (1970). *Crisis in the classroom: The remaking of American education.* New York: Random House.

**Silbert, M., & Pines, A.** (1980). Runaway prostitutes. Unpublished paper. San Francisco: Delancey Street Foundation.

**Silverberg, S. B.** (1992). *Parental well-being and the transition to adolescence.* Paper presented at the Biennial Meeting of the Society for Research on Adolescence, Washington, DC.

**Silverberg, S. B., & Steinberg, L.** (1987). Adolescent autonomy, parent–adolescent conflict, and parental well-being. *Journal of Youth and Adolescence, 16,* 293–312.

**Silverman, W. K., & Ginsburg, G.** (1995). Specific phobias and generalized anxiety disorder. In J. S. March (Ed.), *Anxiety disorders in children and adolescents* (pp. 151–180). New York: Guilford Press.

**Simmons, R. B., Burgeson, R., Carlton-Ford, S., & Blyth, D. A.** (1987). The impact of cumulative change in early adolescence. *Child Development, 58,* 1220–1234.

**Simmons, R. G., & Blyth, D. A.** (1987). *Moving into adolescence: The impact of pubertal change and school context.* New York: Aldine de Gruyter.

**Simmons, R. G., Blyth, D. A., & McKinney, K. L.** (1983). The social and psychological effects of puberty on white females. In J. Brooks-Gunn & A. C. Petersen (Eds.), *Girls at puberty: Biological and psychosocial perspectives* (pp. 229–272). New York: Plenum Press.

**Simmons, R. G., Blyth, D. A., Van Cleave, E. F., & Busch, D. M.** (1979). Entry into early adolescence: The impact of school structure, puberty, and early dating on self-esteem. *American Sociological Review, 44,* 948–967.

**Simmons, R. G., & Rosenberg, F. R.** (1975). Sex, sex roles, and self-image. *Journal of Youth and Adolescence, 4,* 229–258.

**Simons, J. M., Finlay, B., & Yang, A.** (1991). *The adolescent and young adult fact book.* Washington, DC: Children's Defense Fund.

**Simons, R. L., Robertson, J. F., & Downs, W. R.** (1989). The nature of the association between parental rejection and delinquent behavior. *Journal of Youth and Adolescence, 18,* 297–310.

**Simons, R. L., Whitbeck, L. B., Conger, R. D., & Melby, J. N.** (1991). The effect of social skills, values, peers, and depression on adolescent substance use. *Journal of Early Adolescence, 11,* 466–481.

**Singer, M. T.** (1992). Cults. In S. B. Friedman, M. Fisher, & S. K. Schonberg (Eds.), *Comprehensive adolescent health care* (pp. 699–703). St. Louis: Quality Medical Publishing.

**Single, E., Kandel, D., & Faust, R.** (1974). Patterns of multiple drug use in high school. *Journal of Health and Social Behavior, 151,* 344–357.

**Sirles, E. A., Smith, J. A., & Kusama, H.** (1989). Psychiatric status of intrafamilial child sexual abuse victims. *Journal of the American Academy of Child and Adolescent Psychiatry, 28,* 225–229.

**Skoe, E. E., & Diessner, R.** (1994). Ethic of care, justice, identity, and gender: An extension and replication. *Merrill–Palmer Quarterly, 40,* 272–289.

**Slappy, C. A.** (1985). College student drug use: A note on some correlates of cessation. *Youth and Society, 16,* 457–470.

**Small, S. A., Eastman, G., & Cornelius, S.** (1988). Adolescent autonomy and parental stress. *Journal of Youth and Adolescence, 17,* 377–391.

**Small, S. A., & Kerns, D.** (1993). Unwanted sexual activity among peers during early and middle adolescence: Incidence and risk factors. *Journal of Marriage and the Family, 55,* 941–952.

**Small, S. S.** (1988). Parental self-esteem and its relationship to childrearing practices, parent–adolescent interaction, and adolescent behavior. *Journal of Marriage and the Family, 50,* 1063–1072.

**Smetana, J. G.** (1988a). Adolescents' and parents' conceptions of parental authority. *Child Development, 59,* 321–335.

**Smetana, J. G.** (1988b). Concepts of self and social convention: Adolescents' and parents' reasoning about hypothetical and actual family conflicts. In M. R. Gunnar & W. A. Collins (Eds.), *Minnesota symposium on child psychology: Vol. 21. Development during the transition to adolescence* (pp. 79–122). Hillsdale, NJ: Erlbaum.

**Smetana, J. G., Killen, M., & Turiel, E.** (1991). Children's reasoning about interpersonal and moral conflicts. *Child Development, 62,* 629–644.

**Smith, G. M., & Fogg, C. P.** (1978). Psychological predictors of early use, late use, and nonuse of marihuana among teenage students. In D. B. Kandel (Ed.), *Longitudinal research on drug use: Empirical findings and methodological issues.* Washington, DC: Hemisphere.

**Smith, N. W.** (1976). Twin studies and heritability. *Human Development, 19,* 65–68.

**Smith, R. E.** (Ed.). (1979). *The subtle revolution: Women at work.* Washington, DC: Urban Institute.

**Smith, S. R.** (1975). Religion and the conception of youth in seventeenth century England. *History of Childhood Quarterly: The Journal of Psychohistory, 2,* 493–516.

***Smoking and health: A report of the Surgeon General*** (1979). (DHEW Publication No. (PHS) 79-50066, U.S. Department of Health, Education and Welfare) Washington, DC: U.S. Government Printing Office (No. 017-000-00218-0).

**Smolak, L., Levine, M. P., & Gralen, S.** (1993). The impact of puberty and dating on eating problems among middle school girls. *Journal of Youth and Adolescence, 22,* 355–368.

**Snow, R. E.** (1986). Individual differences and the design of educational programs. *American Psychologist, 41,* 1029–1039.

**Snow, R. E., & Yalow, E.** (1988). Education and intelligence. In R. J. Steinberg (Ed.), *Handbook of human intelligence* (pp. 493–585). New York: Cambridge University Press.

**Snyder, J., & Patterson, G.** (1987). Family interaction and delinquent behavior. In H. C. Quay (Ed.), *Handbook of juvenile delinquency* (pp. 216–243). New York: Wiley.

**Soler, M.** (1992). Interagency services in juvenile justice systems. In I. M. Schwartz (Ed.), *Juvenile justice and public policy: Toward a national agenda* (pp. 1–19). New York: Lexington Books.

**Sonenstein, F. S., Pleck, J. H., & Ku, L. C.** (1989). Sexual activity, condom use and AIDS awareness among adolescent males. *Family Planning Perspectives, 21,* 152–158.

**Sontag, L. W., Baker, C. T., & Nelson, V. L.** (1958). Mental growth and personality: A longitudinal study. *Monographs of the Society for Research in Child Development, 23*(68), 1–143.

**Sorensen, R. C.** (1973). *Adolescent sexuality in contemporary America: Personal values and sexual behavior ages 13–19.* New York: Abrams.

**Spacks, P. M.** (1981). *The adolescent idea: Myths of youth and the adult imagination.* New York: Basic Books.

**Spanier, G. B., & Furstenberg, F. F.** (1982). Remarriage after divorce: A longitudinal analysis of well-being. *Journal of Marriage and the Family, 44,* 709–720.

**Spearman, C.** (1927). *The abilities of man.* London: Macmillan.

**Speicher, B.** (1992). Adolescent moral judgment and perceptions of family interaction. *Journal of Family Psychology, 6,* 128–138.

**Speicher, B.** (1994). Family patterns of moral judgment during adolescence and early adulthood. *Developmental Psychology, 30,* 624–632.

**Spence, J. T.** (1985). Gender identity and its implications for concepts of masculinity and femininity. In T. B. Sondrigger (Ed.), *Nebraska symposium on motivation: Psychology and gender* **(Vol. 32).** Lincoln: University of Nebraska Press.

**Spence, J. T., & Helmreich, R. L.** (1978). *Masculinity and femininity: Their psychological dimensions, correlates and antecedents.* Austin: University of Texas Press.

**Speroff, L., & Van de Wiele, R. L.** (1971). Regulation of the human menstrual cycle. *American Journal of Obstetrics and Gynecology, 109,* 234–247.

**Spickelmeier, J. L.** (1983). *College experience and moral judgment development.* Doctoral dissertation. Minneapolis: University of Minnesota

**Spock, B.** (1946). *Baby and child care.* New York: Pocket Books.

**Spreen, O., & Strauss, E.** (1991). *A compendium of neuropsychological tests.* New York: Oxford University Press.

**Sroufe, L. A., & Fleeson, J.** (1986). Attachments and the construction of relationships. In W. W. Hartup & Z. Rubin (Eds.), *Relationships and development.* Hillsdale, NJ: Erlbaum.

**Statistics Canada.** (1994). *Declining female labour force participation* (Cat. 75-001E). Ottawa: Minister of Industry, Science and Technology.

**Steele, B.** (1980). Psychodynamic factors in child abuse. In C. H. Kempe and F. E. Helfer (Eds.), *The battered child* (pp. 49–85). Chicago: University of Chicago Press.

**Steele, B.** (1987). Psychodynamic factors in child abuse. In R. E. Helfer & R. S. Kempe, *The battered child* (4th ed.). Chicago: University of Chicago Press.

**Steinberg, D.** (1985). Psychotic and other severe disorders in adolescence. In M. Rutter & L. Hersov (Eds.), *Child and adolescent psychiatry: Modern approaches* (pp. 567–583). Oxford: Blackwell Scientific Publications.

**Steinberg, D.** (1986). *The adolescent unit: Work and teamwork in adolescent psychiatry.* New York: Wiley.

**Steinberg, L.** (1985). *Adolescence.* New York: Alfred A. Knopf.

**Steinberg, L.** (1986). Latchkey children and susceptibility to peer pressure: An ecological analysis. *Developmental Psychology, 22,* 433–439.

**Steinberg, L.** (1987a). Recent research on the family at adolescence: The extent and nature of sex differences. *Journal of Youth and Adolescence, 16,* 191–197.

**Steinberg, L.** (1987b). Single parents, stepparents, and the susceptibility of adolescents to antisocial peer pressure. *Child Development, 58,* 269–275.

**Steinberg, L.** (1988). Reciprocal relation between parent–child distance and pubertal maturation. *Developmental Psychology, 24,* 122–128.

**Steinberg, L., & Dornbusch, S. M.** (1991). Negative correlates of part-time employment during adolescence: Replication and elaboration. *Developmental Psychology, 27,* 304–313.

**Steinberg, L., Dornbusch, S. M., & Brown, B. B.** (1992). Ethnic differences in adolescent achievement: An ecological perspective. *American Psychologist, 47,* 723–729.

**Steinberg, L., Elmen, J. D., & Mounts, N. S.** (1989). Authoritative parenting, psychosocial maturity, and academic success among adolescents. *Child Development, 60,* 1424–1436.

**Steinberg, L., Fegley, S., & Dornbusch, S. M.** (1993). Negative impact of part-time work on adolescent adjustment: Evidence from a longitudinal study. *Developmental Psychology, 29,* 171–180.

Steinberg, L., Greenberger, E., Vaux, A., & Ruggiero, M. (1981). Effects of early work experience on adolescent occupational socialization. *Youth and Society,* **12,** 403–422.

Steinberg, L., & Hill, J. P. (1978). Patterns of family interaction as a function of age, the onset of puberty, and formal thinking. *Developmental Psychology,* **14,** 683–684.

Steinberg, L., Lamborn, S. D., Dornbusch, S. M., & Darling, N. (1992). Impact of parenting practices on adolescent achievement: Authoritative parenting, school involvement, and encouragement to succeed. *Child Development,* **63,** 1266–1281.

Steinberg, L., Mounts, N. S., Lamborn, S. D., & Dornbusch, S. M. (1991). Authoritative parenting and adolescent adjustment across varied ecological niches. *Journal of Adolescent Research,* **1,** 19–36.

Steinberg, L., & Silverberg, S. B. (1986). The vicissitudes of autonomy in early adolescence. *Child Development,* **57,** 841–851.

Steinhauer, J. (1995, January 4). Teen-age girls talk back on exercise. *The New York Times,* pp. B1, B4.

Steinhauser, H. C. (1994). Anorexia and bulimia nervosa. In M. Rutter, E. Taylor, & L. Hersov (Eds.), *Child and adolescent psychiatry* (3rd ed., pp. 425–440). Boston: Blackwell Scientific Publishers.

Stephan, C. W., & Corder, J. (1985). The effects of dual career families on adolescents' sex-role attitudes, work and family plans, and choices of important others. *Journal of Marriage and the Family,* **47,** 921–929.

Stephenson, S. P. (1979). From school to work: A transition with job-search implications. *Youth and Society,* **11,** 114–133.

Sternberg, R. J. (1982). Reasoning, problem solving, and intelligence. In R. J. Sternberg (Ed.), *Handbook of human intelligence* (pp. 227–351). New York: Cambridge University Press.

Sternberg, R. J. (1985). *Beyond IQ: A triarchic theory of intelligence.* San Diego: Harcourt Brace Jovanovich.

Sternberg, R. J. (Ed.) (1988). *The nature of creativity: Contemporary psychological perspectives.* Cambridge: Cambridge University Press.

Sternberg, R. J. (1990, April). *Academic and practical cognition as different aspects of intelligence.* Paper presented at the Twelfth West Virginia Conference on Life Span Developmental Psychology, Morgantown, WV.

Sternberg, R. J., & Nigro, G. (1980). Developmental patterns in the solution of verbal analogies. *Child Development,* **51,** 27–38.

Sternberg, R. J., & Powell, J. S. (1983). The development of intelligence. In P. H. Mussen (Series Ed.), & J. H. Flavell & E. M. Markman (Eds.), *Handbook of child psychology.* **Vol. 3:** *Cognitive development* (pp. 341–419, 4th ed.). New York: Wiley.

Sternberg, R. J., & Rifkin, B. (1979). The development of analogical reasoning processes. *Journal of Experimental Child Psychology,* **27,** 195–232.

Sternberg, R. J., Wagner, R. K., & Okagaki, L. (1993). Practical intelligence: The nature of tacit knowledge in work and at school. In J. M. Puckett & H. W. Reese (Eds.), *Mechanisms of everyday cognition* (pp. 205–227). Hillsdale, NJ: Lawrence Erlbaum.

Stevenson, H. W., & Lee, S. (1990). *Contexts of achievement: A study of American, Chinese and Japanese children.* Chicago: University of Chicago Press.

Stevenson, H. W., Lee, S., & Stigler, J. W. (1986). Mathematics achievement of Chinese, Japanese, and American children. *Science,* **231,** 693–699.

Stevenson, H. W., & Stigler, J. W. (Eds.). (1992). *The learning gap: Why our schools are failing and what we can learn from Japanese and Chinese education.* New York: Summit Books.

Stevenson, W. (1978). The relationship between early work experience and future employability. In A. Adams & G. Mangum (Eds.), *The lingering crisis of youth unemployment.* Kalamazoo, MI: W.E. Upjohn Institute for Employment Research.

Stice, E., & Barrera, M., Jr. (1995). A longitudinal examination of the reciprocal relations between perceived parenting and adolescents' substance use and externalizing behaviors. *Developmental Psychology,* **31,** 322–334.

Stone, L. J., & Church, J. (1973). *Childhood and adolescence: A psychology of the growing person* (3rd ed.). New York: Random House.

Storr, C. (1975). *Growing up: A practical guide to adolescence for parents and children.* London: Arrow Books.

Striegel-Moore, R. H., Silberstein, L. R., & Rodin, J. (1986). Toward an understanding of risk factors for bulimia. *American Psychologist,* **41,** 246–263.

Student survey, 1971. (1971, Sept.). *Playboy,* 118ff.

Student survey. (1976). What's really happening on campus. *Playboy,* **23,** 128–169.

Stunkard, A. J. (1985). Obesity. In H. I. Kaplan & B. J. Sadock (Eds.), *Comprehensive textbook of psychiatry* (4th ed., pp. 1133–1142). Baltimore: Williams & Wilkins.

Stunkard, A. J., Harris, J. R., Pedersen, N. L., & McClearn, G. E. (1990). The body mass index of twins who have been reared apart. *New England Journal of Medicine,* **322,** 1483–1487.

Suddath, R. L., Christison, G. W., Torry, E. F., Casanova, M. F., & Weinberger, D. R. (1990). Anatomical abnormalities in the brains of monozygotic twins discordant for schizophrenia. *New England Journal of Medicine,* **322,** 789–794.

Sullivan, M. L. (1993). Culture and class as determinants of out-of-wedlock childbearing and poverty during late adolescence. *Journal of Research on Adolescence,* **3,** 295–316.

Super, D. (1967). *The psychology of careers.* New York: Harper & Row.

Super, D. E. (1980). A life-span life-space approach to career development. *Journal of Vocational Behavior,* **16,** 282–298.

Surbey, M. K. (1990). Family composition, stress, and human menarche. In T. E. Ziegler & F. B. Bercovitch (Eds.), *Socioendocrinology of primate reproduction* (pp. 11–32). New York: Wiley-Liss.

Susman, E. J., Inoff-Germaine, G., Loriaux, D. L, Cutler, G. B., Jr., & Chrousos, G. P. (1987). Hormones, emotional dispositions, and aggressive attributes in young adolescents. *Child Development,* **58,** 1114–1134.

Susman, E. J., Nottelman, E. O., Inoff-Germain, G. E., Dorn, L. D., Cutler, G. B., Loriaux, D. L., & Chrensos, G. P. (1985). The relation of relative hormonal levels and physical development and social–emotional behavior in young adolescents. *Journal of Youth and Adolescence, 14,* 245–264.

Sussman, S., Burton, D., Stacy, A. W., & Flay, B. R. (1995). *School-based adolescent tobacco use prevention and cessation research.* Newbury Park, CA: Sage Publications.

Swaab, D. F., Fliers, E., & Partiman, T. S. (1985). The suprachiasmatic nucleus of the human brain in relation to sex, age and senile dementia. *Brain Research, 342,* 37–44.

Swaab, D. F., & Hofman, M. A. (1990). An enlarged suprachiasmatic nucleus in homosexual men. *Brain Research, 537,* 141–148.

Swan, G. E., Creeser, R., & Murray, M. (1990). When and why children first start to smoke. *International Journal of Epidemiology, 19,* 323–330.

Swanson, G. E. (1988). *Ego defenses and the legitimation of behavior.* Cambridge: Cambridge University Press.

Swearingen, E. M., & Cohen, L. H. (1985). Life events and psychological distress: A prospective study of young adolescents. *Developmental Psychology, 21,* 1045–1054.

Takanishi, R. (1993). The opportunities of adolescence—research, interventions, and policy. *American Psychologist, 48,* 85–87.

Tanner, J. M. (1970). Physical growth. In P. H. Mussen (Ed.), *Carmichael's manual of child psychology* (**Vol. 2,** 3rd ed., pp. 77–156). New York: Wiley.

Tanner, J. M. (1971). Sequence, tempo, and individual variation in the growth and development of boys and girls aged twelve to sixteen. *Daedalus, 100*(4), 907–930.

Tanner, J. M. (1975). Growth and endocrinology of the adolescent. In J. J. Gardner (Ed), *Endocrine and genetic diseases of childhood* (2nd ed.). Philadelphia: Saunders.

Tanner, J. M. (1991). Growth spurt, adolescent I. In R. M. Lerner, A. C. Petersen, & J. Brooks-Gunn. *Encyclopedia of adolescence* (**Vol. II,** pp. 419–424). New York: Garland Publishing.

Tanner, J. M., Whitehouse, R. H., & Takaishi, M. (1966). Standards from birth to maturing for height velocity, and weight velocity: British children, 1965. *Archives of Disease in Childhood, 41,* 455–471.

Tapp, J. L., & Levine, F. J. (1972). Compliance from kindergarten to college: A speculative research note. *Journal of Youth and Adolescence, 1,* 233–249.

Task Force on Pediatric AIDS, American Psychological Association. (1989). Pediatric AIDS and human immunodeficiency virus infection. *American Psychologist, 44,* 258–264.

Task Force on Teaching as a Profession. (1986). *A nation prepared: Teachers for the 21st century.* Washington, DC: Carnegie Forum on Education and the Economy.

Taylor, A., III (1986, Aug. 18). Why women managers are bailing out. *Fortune,* pp. 16–23.

Taylor, E. (1994). Syndromes of attention deficit and hyperactivity. In M. Rutter, E. Taylor, & L. Hersov (Eds.), *Child and adolescent psychiatry: Modern approaches* (pp. 308–330). Oxford: Blackwell Scientific Publications.

Taylor, R. D., Casten, R., Flickinger, S. M., Roberts, D., & Fulmore, C. D. (1994). Explaining the school performance of African-American adolescents. *Journal of Research on Adolescence, 4,* 2–44.

Terman, L. M., & Merrill, M. A. (1960). *Stanford–Binet intelligence scale. Manual for 3rd revision.* Boston: Houghton Mifflin.

Tesch, S. (1983). Review of friendship development across the life span. *Human Development, 26,* 266–276.

Tharp, M. (1987, March 10). High schoolers in U.S. lack drive of Japan's but show spontaneity. *The Wall Street Journal,* pp. 1, 14.

Thissen, P., Bock, R. D., Wainer, H., & Roche, A. F. (1976). Individual growth in stature: A comparison of four growth studies in the U.S.A. *Annals of Human Biology, 3,* 529–542.

Thoma, S. J. (1984). *Estimating gender differences in the comprehension and preference of moral issues.* Unpublished manuscript. Minneapolis: University of Minnesota.

Thoma, S. J. (1993). The relationship between political preference and moral judgment development in late adolescence. *Merrill–Palmer Quarterly, 39,* 359–374.

Thoma, S. J., Rest, J. R., & Davison, M. L. (1991). Describing and testing a moderator of the moral judgment and action relationship. *Journal of Personality and Social Psychology, 61,* 659–669.

Thomas, R. M. (1985). *Comparing theories of child development* (3rd ed.). Belmont, CA: Wadsworth.

Thorndike, R. L., Hagen, E. P., & Sattler, J. M. (1986). *Stanford–Binet Intelligence Scale: Guide for administering and scoring the fourth edition.* Chicago: Riverside.

Thornton, A. (1990). The courtship process and adolescent sexuality. *Journal of Family Issues, 11,* 239–273.

Thurstone, L. L. (1938). Primary mental abilities. *Psychometric Monographs* (No. 1). Chicago: University of Chicago Press.

Thurstone, L. L., & Thurstone, T. G. (1941). Factorial studies of intelligence. *Psychometric Monographs* (no. 2). Chicago: University of Chicago Press.

Tienari, P., Sorri, A., Lahti, J., Naarla, M., Wahlberg, J. M., Pohjola, J., & Wynne, L. C. (1987). Genetic and psychosocial factors in schizophrenia: The Finnish adoptive family study. *Schizophrenia Bulletin, 13,* 477–484.

Tifft, S. (1988, Nov. 14). Who's teaching the children? *Time,* pp. 58–64.

*Time,* June 16, 1980. pp. 54–63.

TIME/CNN Poll, April 13–14, 1993.

Tobin-Richards, M., Boxer, A., & Petersen, A. C. (1983). The psychological impact of pubertal change: Sex differences in perceptions of self during early adolescence. In J. Brooks-Gunn & A. C. Petersen (Eds.), *Girls at puberty: Biological, psychological, and social perspectives* (pp. 127–154). New York: Plenum.

Tocci, C. M., & Engelhard, G., Jr. (1991). Achievement, parental support, and gender differences in attitudes toward mathematics. *Journal of Educational Research, 84,* 280–286.

Tolson, J. M., & Urberg, K. A. (1993). Similarity between adolescent best friends. *Journal of Adolescent Research, 8,* 274–288.

Torgersen, A. M., & Kringlen, E. (1978). Genetic aspects of temperamental differences in infants: A study of same-sexed twins. *Journal of the American Academy of Child Psychiatry,* **17,** 433–444.

Torney-Purta, J. (1990). Youth in relation to social institutions. In S. S. Feldman & G. R. Elliott (Eds.), *At the threshold: The developing adolescent* (pp. 457–477). Cambridge: Harvard University Press.

Torrance, E. P., & Dauw, D. C. (1966, Summer). Attitude patterns of creatively gifted high school seniors. *Gifted Child Quarterly,* pp. 53–57.

Trasler, G. (1987). Biogenetic factors. In H. C. Quay (Ed.), *Handbook of juvenile delinquency* (pp. 184–215). New York: Wiley.

Trussell, J. (1988). Teenage pregnancy in the United States. *Family Planning Perspectives,* **20,** 262–272.

Tsuang, M. T., Gilbertson, M. W., & Faraone, S. V. (1991). The genetics of schizophrenia: Current knowledge and future directions. *Schizophrenia Research,* **4,** 157–171.

Tucker, L. A. (1987). Television, teenagers and health. *Journal of Youth and Adolescence,* **16,** 415–425.

Tuma, N. B., & Hallinan, M. T. (1977). *The affects of similarity and status on change in schoolchildren's friendships.* Unpublished manuscript, Stanford University.

Turiel, E. (1983). *The development of social knowledge: Morality and convention.* New York: Cambridge University Press.

Turiel, E., Edwards, C. P., & Kohlberg, L. (1978). Moral development in Turkish children, adolescents and young adults. *Journal of Cross-Cultural Psychology,* **9,** 75–85.

Turiel, E., Hildebrandt, C., & Wainryb, C. (1991). Judging social issues. *Monographs of the Society for Research in Child Development,* **56** (2, Serial No. 224).

Turner, C. F., Miller, H. G., & Moses, L. E. (Eds.). (1989). *AIDS, sexual behavior, and intravenous drug use.* Washington, DC: National Academy Press.

Turner, N. K., & Shaffer, D. (1992). Depression. In S. B. Friedman, M. Fisher, & S. K. Schonberg (Eds.), *Comprehensive adolescent health care* (pp. 853–861). St. Louis: Quality Medical Publishing.

U.S. Bureau of the Census. (1978). *Statistical abstract of the United States: 1977* (99th ed.). Washington, DC: U.S. Government Printing Office.

U.S. Bureau of the Census. (1989). *Statistical abstract of the United States: 1989* (109th ed.). Washington, DC: U.S. Government Printing Office.

U.S. Bureau of the Census. (1993). *Statistical abstract of the United States: 1993* (113th ed.). Washington, DC: U.S. Government Printing Office.

U.S. Bureau of the Census. (1994). *Statistical abstract of the United States: 1994* (114th ed.). Washington, DC: U.S. Government Printing Office.

U.S. Bureau of the Census. (1995). *Statistical abstract of the United States: 1995* (115th ed.). Washington, DC: U.S. Government Printing Office.

U.S. Department of Commerce, Bureau of the Census. (1990). *Current Population Reports,* Series P-20, no. 445, *Marital Status and Living Arrangements: March 1989.* Washington, DC: U.S. Government Printing Office.

U.S. Department of Education, National Center for Education Statistics. (1980). *The condition of education: Statistical report.* Washington, DC: U.S. Government Printing Office.

U.S. Department of Justice. (1994). *Uniform crime reports for the United States, 1993.* Washington, DC: U.S. Government Printing Office.

U.S. Department of Justice. (1995). Data from the Federal Bureau of Investigation, cited in Children's Defense Fund (1995). *The state of America's children 1995.* Washington, DC: Children's Defense Fund.

U.S. Department of Labor. (1994). *Report on the American workforce.* Washington, DC: U.S. Government Printing Office.

U.S. Department of Labor. (1995). Employment situation, July, 1995 (press release). Washington, DC: U.S. Department of Labor, Bureau of Labor Statistics.

U.S. Department of Labor, Bureau of Labor Statistics. (1986). *Occupational projections and training data,* Bulletin 2251. Washington, DC: U.S. Government Printing Office.

U.S. Department of Labor, Bureau of Labor Statistics. (1988). *Occupational outlook handbook,* Bulletin 2300. Washington, DC: U.S. Government Printing Office.

U.S. Department of Labor, Bureau of Labor Statistics. (1991). *Dictionary of occupational titles* **(2 vol.).** Washington, DC: U.S. Government Printing Office.

U.S. Department of Labor, Bureau of Labor Statistics. (1993), *Selected characteristics of occupations defined in the dictionary of occupational titles.* Washington, DC: U.S. Government Printing Office.

U.S. Department of Labor, Bureau of Labor Statistics. (1994a). *The American workforce: 1992–2005,* Bulletin 2452. Washington, DC: U.S. Government Printing Office.

U.S. Department of Labor, Bureau of Labor Statistics. (1994b). *Occupational outlook handbook,* Bulletin 2450. Washington, DC: U.S. Government Printing Office.

U.S. Department of Labor, Bureau of Labor Statistics. (1994c). *Tomorrow's jobs,* Bulletin 2450-1. Washington, DC: U.S. Government Printing Office.

U.S. Department of Labor, Office of the Secretary, Women's Bureau. (1983). *Time of change: 1983 handbook on women workers,* Bulletin 298. Washington, DC: U.S. Government Printing Office.

Udry, J. R. (1988). Biological predispositions and social control in adolescent sexual behavior. *American Sociological Review,* **52,** 841–855.

Udry, J. R. (1990). Hormonal and social determinants of adolescent sexual initiation. In J. Bancroft & J. M. Reinisch (Eds.), *Adolescence and puberty* (pp. 70–87). New York: Oxford University Press.

Udry, J. R., Billy, J. O. G., Morris, N. M., Groff, T. R., & Raj, M. H. (1985). Serum androgenic hormones motivate sexual behavior in adolescent boys. *Fertility and Sterility,* **43,** 129–139.

Udry, J. R., Talbert, L., & Morris, N. M. (1986). Biosocial foundations for adolescent female sexuality. *Demography,* **23,** 217–230.

Ungerleider, J. T., & Pechnick, R. (1992). Hallucinogens. In J. H. Lowinson, P. Ruiz, R. B. Millman, & J. G. Langrod

(Eds.), *Substance abuse: A comprehensive textbook* (2nd ed., pp. 280–289). Baltimore: Williams & Wilkins.

Upchurch, D. M. (1993). Early schooling and childbearing experiences: Implications for postsecondary school attendance. *Journal of Research on Adolescence, 3,* 423–443.

Urberg, K. A. (1992). Locus of peer influence: Social crowd and best friend. *Journal of Youth and Adolescence, 21,* 439–450.

Useem, E. L. (1991). Student selection into course sequences in mathematics: The impact of parental involvement and school policies. *Journal of Research on Adolescence, 1,* 231–250.

Vandell, D. L., & Corasaniti, M. A. (1988). The relation between third graders' after-school care and social, academic, and emotional functioning. *Child Development, 59,* 868–875.

Vandell, D. L., & Ramanan, J. (1991). Children of the National Longitudinal Survey of Youth: Choices in after-school care and child development. *Developmental Psychology, 27,* 637–643.

Vandenberg, S. G., & Kuse, A. R. (1978). Mental rotations: A group test of three-dimensional spatial visualization. *Perceptual and Motor Skills, 47,* 599–604.

Vandenberg, S. G., & Kuse, A. R. (1979). Spatial ability: A critical review of the sex-linked major-gene hypothesis. In M. A. Wittig & A. C. Petersen (Eds.), *Sex-related differences in cognitive functioning* (pp. 67–91). New York: Academic Press.

Vandenberg, S. G., Singer, S. M., & Pauls, D. (1986). *The heredity of behavior disorders in adults and children.* New York: Plenum.

Vandenberg, S. G., & Vogler, G. P. (1985). Genetic determinants of intelligence. In B. B. Wolman (Ed.), *Handbook of intelligence: Theories, measurements, and applications* (pp. 3–57). New York: Wiley.

Vernberg, E. M., Ewell, K. K., Beery, S. H., & Abwender, D. A. (1994). Sophistication of adolescents' interpersonal negotiation strategies and friendship formation after relocation: A naturally occurring experiment. *Journal of Research on Adolescence, 4,* 5–19.

Victor, H. R., Grossman, J. C., & Eisenman, R. (1973). Openness to experience and marijuana use in high school students. *Journal of Consulting and Clinical Psychology, 41,* 78–85.

*Violence and youth* (1993). Washington, DC: U.S. Government Printing Office.

Visher, C. A., & Roth, J. A. (1986). Participation in criminal careers. In A. Blumstein, J. Cohen, J. A. Roth, & C. A. Visher (Eds.), *Criminal careers and "career criminals"* (**Vol. 1,** pp. 211–291). Washington, DC: National Academy Press.

Vogel, S. R., Broverman, I. K., Broverman, D. M., Clarkson, F., & Rosenkrantz, P. (1970). Maternal employment and perception of sex roles among college students. *Developmental Psychology, 3,* 384–391.

Vondracek, F. W. (1994). Vocational identity development in adolescence. In R. K. Silbereisen & E. Todt (Eds.), *Adolescents in context: The interplay of family, school, peers, and work in adjustment* (pp. 284–303). New York: Springer-Verlag.

Vondracek, F. W., Schulenberg, J., Skorikov, V., Gillespie, L. K., & Wahlheim, C. (1995). The relationship of identity status to career indecision during adolescence. *Journal of Adolescence, 18,* 17–29.

Vuchinich, S., Bank, L., & Patterson, G. R. (1992). Parenting, peers, and the stability of antisocial behavior in preadolescent boys. *Developmental Psychology, 28,* 510–521.

Vuchinich, S., Hetherington, E. M., Vuchinich, R. A., & Clingempeel, W. G. (1991). Parent-child interaction and gender differences in early adolescents' adaption to stepfamilies. *Developmental Psychology, 27,* 618–626.

Waber, D. P. (1977). Sex differences in mental abilities, hemispheric lateralization, and rate of physical growth at adolescence. *Developmental Psychology, 13,* 29–38.

Waber, D. P. (1979). Cognitive abilities and sex-related variations in the maturation of cerebral cortical functions. In M. A. Wittig & A. C. Petersen (Eds.), *Sex-related differences in cognitive functioning* (pp. 161–184). New York: Academic Press.

Waber, D. P., Mann, M. B., Merola, J., & Moylan, P. M. (1985). Physical maturation rate and cognitive performance in early adolescence: A longitudinal examination. *Developmental Psychology, 21,* 666–681.

Wadsworth, M. E. J. (1979). *Roots of delinquency: Infancy, adolescence, and crime.* Oxford: M. Robinson.

Wainryb, C. (1993). The application of moral judgments to other cultures: Relativism and universality. *Child Development, 64,* 924–933.

Waldo, M. C., Adler, L. E., & Freedman, R. (1988). Defects in auditory sensory gating and their apparent compensation in relatives of schizophrenics. *Schizophrenic Research, 1,* 19–24.

Walker, E. F., Davis, D. M., & Gottleib, L. A. (1991). Charting the developmental trajectory of schizophrenia. In D. Cicchetti & S. L. Toth (Eds.), *Models and integrations: Rochester symposium on developmental psychopathology* (**Vol. 3,** pp. 185–205). Rochester, NY: University of Rochester Press.

Walker, L. J. (1980). Cognitive and perspective-taking prerequisites for moral development. *Child Development, 51,* 131–139.

Walker, L. J. (1989). A longitudinal study of moral reasoning. *Child Development, 60,* 157–166.

Walker, L. J. (1991). Sex differences in moral reasoning. In W. M. Kurtines & J. L. Gewirtz (Eds.), *Handbook of moral behavior and development: Research* (**Vol. 2,** pp. 333–364). Hillsdale, NJ: Erlbaum.

Walker, L. J., de Vries, B., Trevethan, S. D. (1987). Moral stages and moral orientations in real-life and hypothetical dilemmas. *Child Development, 58,* 842–858.

Walker, L. J., Pitts, R. C., Henning, K. H., & Matsuba, M. K. (1995). Reasoning about morality and real-life moral problems. In M. Killen & D. Hart (Eds.), *Morality in everyday life: Developmental perspectives.* New York: Cambridge University Press.

Walker, L. J., & Taylor, J. H. (1991a). Family interactions and the development of moral reasoning. *Child Development, 62,* 264–283.

Walker, L. J., & Taylor, J. H. (1991b). Stage transitions in moral reasoning: A longitudinal study of developmental processes. *Developmental Psychology, 27,* 330–337.

Wallace-Broscious, A., Serafica, F. C., & Osipow, S. H. (1994). Adolescent career development: Relationships to self-concept and identity status. *Journal of Research on Adolescence, 44,* 127–149.

Wallach, M. A. (1985). Creativity testing and giftedness. In F. D. Horowitz & M. O'Brien (Eds.), *The gifted and talented: Development perspectives* (pp. 99–123). Washington, DC: American Psychological Association.

Wallach, M. A., & Kogan, N. (1965). *Modes of thinking in young children: A study of the creativity–intelligence distinction.* New York: Holt, Rinehart and Winston.

Wallach, M. A., & Kogan, N. (1971). A new look at the creativity–intelligence distinction. In J. P. Hill, & J. Shelton (Eds.), *Readings in adolescent development and behavior.* Englewood Cliffs, NJ: Prentice-Hall.

Wallerstein, J. S. (1985). Children of divorce: Preliminary report of a ten year follow-up of older children and adolescents. *Journal of the American Academy of Child Psychiatry, 24,* 545–553.

Wallerstein, J. S., Corbin, S. B., & Lewis, J. M. (1988). Children of divorce: A ten year study. In E. M. Hetherington & J. D. Arasteh (Eds.), *Impact of divorce, single parenting and stepparenting on children.* Hillsdale, NJ: Lawrence Erlbaum.

Ward, S. L. D., Schuetz, D. E., & Seymore, R. C. (1986). Abnormal sleeping ventilatory patterns in infants of substance-abusing mothers. *American Journal of Diseases of Children, 140,* 1015–1020.

Warr, M. (1993). Parents, peers, and delinquency. *Social Forces, 72,* 247–264.

Washton, A. M., & Gold, M. S. (1984). Chronic cocaine abuse: Evidence for adverse effects on health and functioning. *Psychiatric Annals, 14,* 737–739.

Waterman, A. S. (1982). Identity development from adolescence to adulthood: An extension of theory and a review of research. *Developmental Psychology, 18,* 341–358.

Wechsler, D. (1981). *WAIS-R Manual: Wechsler Intelligence Scale—Revised.* New York: Psychological Corporation.

Wiener, I. B. (1970). *Psychological disturbance in adolescence.* New York: Wiley.

Weiner, I. B. (1982). *Child and adolescent psychopathology.* New York: Wiley.

Weiner, I. B. (1992). *Psychological disturbances in adolescence* (2nd ed.). New York: Wiley.

Weisberg, D. K. (1985). *Children of the night: A study of adolescent prostitution.* Lexington, MA: Heath

Weiss, B., Dodge, K. A., Bates, J. E., & Pettit, G. S. (1992). Some consequences of early harsh discipline: Child aggression and a maladaptive social information processing style. *Child Development, 63,* 1321–1335.

Weiss, R. J. (1982). Understanding moral thought: Effects on moral reasoning and decision-making. *Developmental Psychology, 18,* 852–861.

Weissman, M. M., et al. (1984). The epidemiology of depression: An update on sex differences in rates. *Journal of Affective Disorders, 7,* 179–188.

Weller, E. B., & Weller, R. A. (1991). In M. Lewis (Ed.), *Child and adolescent psychiatry: A comprehensive textbook* (pp. 646–663). Baltimore: Williams & Wilkins.

Wells, G. C. (1983). Language, learning and curriculum. *Early Child Development and Child Care, 12,* 277–302.

Welte, J. W., & Barnes, G. M. (1985). Alcohol: The gateway to other drug use among secondary school students. *Journal of Youth and Adolescence, 14,* 487–488.

Wenar, C. (1994). *Developmental psychopathology: From infancy through adolescence* (3rd ed.). New York: McGraw-Hill.

Wentzel, K. R., Feldman, S. S., & Weinberger, D. A. (1991). Parental child rearing and academic achievement in boys: The mediational role of social–emotional adjustment. *Journal of Early Adolescence, 11,* 321–339.

Werry, J. S., & Taylor, E. (1994). Schizophrenic and allied disorders. In M. Rutter, E. Taylor, & L. Hersov (Eds.), *Child and adolescent psychiatry* (3rd ed., pp. 594–615). Boston: Blackwell Scientific Publishers.

Wessel, D. (1986, Sept. 22). Growing gap: U.S. rich and poor gain in numbers. *The Wall Street Journal,* p. 1, 20.

Wesson, D. R., Smith, D. E., & Seymore, R. C. (1992). Sedative-hypnotics and tricyclics. In J. H. Lowinson, P. Ruiz, R. B. Millman, & J. G. Langrod (Eds.), *Substance abuse: A comprehensive textbook* (2nd ed., pp. 271–279). Baltimore: Williams & Wilkins.

West, D. J., & Farrington, D. (1973). *Who becomes delinquent?* London: Heinemann Educational.

West, D. J., & Farrington, D. (1977). *The delinquent way of life.* London: Heinemann.

West, K. L. (1981). Assessment and treatment of disturbed adolescents and their families: A clinical research perspective. In M. Lansky (Ed.), *Major psychopathology and the family.* New York: Grune & Stratton.

Westerman, P. L., & Davidson, P. M. (1993). Homophobic attitudes and AIDS risk behavior of adolescents. *Journal of Adolescent Health, 14,* 208–213.

Whiting, J. W. M., & Child, I. L. (1953). *Child training and personality.* New Haven, CT: Yale University Press.

Wicker, A. W. (1968). Undermanning, performances, and students' subjective experiences in behavior settings of large and small high schools. *Journal of Personality and Social Psychology, 10,* 255–261.

Wigfield, A., & Eccles, J. S. (1994). Children's competence beliefs, achievement values, and general self-esteem: Change across elementary and middle school. *Journal of Early Adolescence, 14,* 107–138.

Wigfield, A., & Eccles, J. S. (Eds.). (1995). Middle grades schooling and early adolescent development, part 2: Interventions, practices, beliefs, and contexts [Special issue]. *Journal of Early Adolescence, 15*(1).

Wikler, A. (1970). Clinical and social aspects of marihuana intoxication. *Archives of General Psychiatry, 23,* 320–325.

Wilkerson, I. (1995, March 5). Teenager builds life up from crack. *The Denver Post,* pp. 21A, 22A.

Wilkerson, I. (1994, May 16). Two boys, a debt, a gun, a victim: The face of violence. Second report in a periodic series, When Trouble Starts Young. *The New York Times,* p. 1.

**Wilks, J.** (1986). The relative importance of parents and friends in adolescent decision making. *Journal of Youth and Adolescence,* **15,** 323–334.

**Willerman, L.** (1979). Effects of families on intellectual development. *American Psychologist,* **34,** 923–929.

**Williams, C. L., & Kimm, S. Y. S.** (Eds.) (1993). *Prevention and treatment of childhood obesity.* New York: New York Academy of Sciences.

**Wilson, H.** (1980). Parental supervision: A neglected aspect of delinquency. *British Journal of Criminology,* **20,** 203–235.

**Wilson, J. Q., & Herrnstein, D. P.** (1985). *Crime and human nature.* New York: Simon & Schuster.

**Wilson, P., & Hersov, L.** (1985). Individual and group psychotherapy. In M. Rutter & L. Hersov (Eds.), *Child and adolescent psychiatry: Modern approaches* (pp. 826–839). Oxford: Blackwell Scientific Publications.

**Wilson, R. S.** (1975). Twins: Patterns of cognitive development as measured on the Wechsler Preschool and Primary Scale of Intelligence. *Developmental Psychology,* **11,** 126–134.

**Wilson, R. S.** (1977). Twins and siblings: Concordance for school-age mental development. *Child Development,* **48,** 211–216.

**Wilson, R. S.** (1983). The Louisville twin study: Developmental synchronies in behavior. *Child Development,* **54,** 298–316.

**Wilson, R. S., & Harpring, E. B.** (1972). Mental and motor development in infant twins. *Developmental Psychology,* **7,** 277–287.

**Wilson, S. M., Peterson, G. W., & Wilson, P.** (1993). The process of educational and occupational attainment of adolescent females from low-income, rural families. *Journal of Marriage and the Family,* **55,** 158–175.

**Windle, M.** (1992). Temperament and social support in adolescence: Interrelations with depressive symptoms and delinquent behaviors. *Journal of Youth and Adolescence,* **21,** 1–21.

**Winick, C.** (1992). Methoqualone. In J. H. Lowinson, P. Ruiz, R. B. Millman, & J. G. Langrod (Eds.), *Substance abuse: A comprehensive textbook* (2nd ed., pp. 722–732). Baltimore: Williams & Wilkins.

**Winokur, G.** (1975). Heredity in the affective disorders. In E. Anthony & T. Benedek (Eds.), *Depression in human existence.* Boston: Little, Brown.

**Wolensky, R. P.** (1977). College students in the fifties: The silent generation revisited. In S. C. Feinstein & P. L. Giovacchini, *Adolescent psychiatry: Developmental and clinical studies* **(Vol. 5).** New York: Aronson.

*Women and smoking: Report of the Surgeon General* (1980, Jan). Washington, DC: U.S. Public Health Service, Department of Health, Education and Welfare.

**Wooden, K.** (1976). *Weeping in the playtime of others.* New York: McGraw-Hill.

**Woods, P. D., Haskell, W. L., Stern, S. L., & Perry, C.** (1977). Plasma lipoprotein distributions in male and female runners. *Annals of the New York Academy of Sciences,* **301,** 748–763.

**Woolston, J. L.** (1991). Obesity in infancy and childhood. In J. M. Weiner (Ed.), *Textbook of child and adolescent psychiatry* (pp. 382–387). Washington, DC: American Psychiatric Press.

**Worden, J. W.** (1989). Methods as a risk factor in youth suicide. In *Report of the Secretary's task force on youth suicide,* **Volume II:** *Risk factors for youth suicide* (pp. 184–192). Washington, DC: U.S. Government Printing Office.

**Wright, J. D., & Weber, E.** (1987). *Homelessness and health.* New York: McGraw-Hill.

**Wright, S. A., & Piper, E. S.** (1986). Familial factors related to youth leaving or remaining in deviant religious groups. *Journal of Marriage and the Family,* **48,** 15–25.

**Wyatt, G. E.** (1990). Changing influences on adolescent sexuality over the past forty years. In J. Bancroft & J. M. Reinisch (Eds.), *Adolescence and puberty* (pp. 182–206). New York: Oxford University Press.

**Wyatt, R. J., Alexander, R. C., Egan, M. F., & Kirch, D. G.** (1988). Schizophrenia, just the facts: What do we know, how well do we know it? *Schizophrenic Research,* **1,** 3–18.

**Wynne, L. C., Singer, M. T., Bartko, J. J., & Toohey, M.** (1976). Schizophrenics and their families: Recent research on parental communication. In J. M. Tanner (Ed.), *Psychiatric research: The widening perspective.* New York: International Universities Press.

**Yakoler, P. I., & Lecours, A. R.** (1967). The myelogenetic cycles of regional maturation in the brain. In A. Minkowski (Ed.), *Regional development of the brain in early life.* Oxford: Blackwell.

**Yamaguchi, K., & Kandel, D. B.** (1984a). Patterns of drug use from adolescence to young adulthood: I. Sequences of progression. *American Journal of Public Health,* **74,** 658–672.

**Yamaguchi, K., & Kandel, D. B.** (1984b). Patterns of drug use from adolescence to young adulthood: II. Predictors of progression. *American Journal of Public Health,* **74,** 673–681.

**Yanish, D. L., & Battle, J.** (1985). Relationship between self-esteem, depression and alcohol consumption among adolescents. *Psychological Reports,* **57,** 331–334.

**Yankelovich, D.** (1969). *Generations apart.* New York: CBS News.

**Yankelovich, D.** (1974). *The new morality: A profile of American youth in the 1970s.* New York: McGraw-Hill.

**Yankelovich, D.** (1981). *New rules: Searching for fulfillment in a world turned upside down.* New York: Random House.

**Yankelovich Partners TIME/CNN poll.** (1995). Cited in Church, G. J. (1995, Oct. 24), We're #1 and it hurts. *Time,* **144,** 50–56.

**Yates, A.** (1990). Current perspectives on the eating disorders: II. Treatment, outcome, and research directions. *Journal of the American Academy of Child and Adolescent Psychiatry,* **29,** 1–9.

**Yesavage, J. A., Leirer, V. O., Enari, M., & Hollister, L. E.** (1985). Carry-over effects of marijuana intoxication on aircraft pilot performance: A preliminary report. *American Journal of Psychiatry,* **142,** 1325–1329.

**Young, H., & Ferguson, L.** (1979). Developmental changes through adolescence in the spontaneous nomination of reference groups as a function of decision context. *Journal of Youth and Adolescence,* **8,** 239–252.

**Youniss, J.** (1980). *Parents and peers in social development: A Sullivan–Piaget perspective.* Chicago: University of Chicago Press.

Youniss, J. (1981). Moral development through a theory of social construction: An analysis. *Merrill–Palmer Quarterly, 27,* 385–403.

Youniss, J. (1983). Social construction of adolescence by adolescents and parents. In H. D. Grotevant & C. R. Cooper (Eds.), *Adolescent development in the family.* San Francisco: Jossey-Bass.

Youniss, J., & Ketterlinus, R. D. (1987). Communication and connectedness in mother– and father–adolescent relationships. *Journal of Youth and Adolescence, 16,* 762–768.

Youniss, J. & Smollar, J. (1985). *Adolescent relations with mothers, fathers, and friends.* Chicago: University of Chicago Press.

Youniss, J. & Smollar, J. (1989). Adolescents: Interpersonal relationships in social contexts. In T. J. Berndt & G. W. Ladd (Eds.), *Peer relationships in child development* (pp. 300–316). New York: Wiley.

Zabin, L. S. (1992). School-linked health services: The Johns Hopkins program. In B. C. Miller et al. (Eds.), *Preventing adolescent pregnancy* (pp. 156–184). Newbury Park, CA: Sage.

Zabin, L. S., Astone, N. M., & Emerson, M. R. (1993). Do adolescents want babies? The relationship between attitudes and behavior. *Journal of Research on Adolescence, 3,* 67–86.

Zebrowitz, L. A., Kendall-Tackett, K., & Fafel, J. (1991). The influence of children's facial maturity on parental expectations and punishments. *Journal of Experimental Child Psychology, 52,* 221–238.

Zebrowitz, L. A., & Montepare, J. M. (1992). Impressions of babyfaced individuals across the life span. *Developmental Psychology, 28,* 1143–1152.

Zelnik, M., & Kantner, J. (1977). Sexual and contraceptive experience of young unmarried women in the United States, 1976 and 1971. *Family Planning Perspectives, 9,* 55–71.

Zelnik, M., & Kantner, J. F. (1980). Sexual activity, contraceptive use and pregnancy among metropolitan-area teenagers: 1971-1979. *Family Planning Perspectives, 12,* 230–237.

Zigler, E., & Hall, N. W. (1989). Physical child abuse in America: Past, present, and future. In D. Cicchetti & V. Carlson (Eds.), *Child maltreatment: Theory and research on the causes and consequences of child abuse and neglect* (pp. 38–75). New York: Cambridge University Press.

Zill, N., Morrison, D. R., & Coiro, M. J. (1993). Long-term effects of parental divorce on parent–child relationships, adjustment, and achievement in young adulthood. *Journal of Family Psychology, 7,* 91–103.

Zimiles, H., & Lee, E. (1991). Adolescent family structure and educational progress. *Developmental Psychology, 27,* 314–320.

Zuckerman, B., Frank, D. A., Hingson, R., et al. (1989). Effects of maternal marijuana and cocaine use on fetal growth. *New England Journal of Medicine, 320,* 762–768.

Zukin, S. T., & Zukin, R. S. (1992). Phencyclidine. In J. H. Lowinson, P. Ruiz, R. B. Millman, & J. G. Langrod (Eds.), *Substance abuse: A comprehensive textbook* (2nd ed., pp. 290–302). Baltimore: Williams & Wilkins.

# Photo Credits

Unless otherwise acknowledged, all photographs are the property of Scott, Foresman and Company. Page abbreviations are as follows: (T)top, (C)center, (B)bottom, (L)left, (R)right.

## Chapter 1

p. 2, Ronnie Kaufman/Stock Market; p. 3, Richard Hutchings/Photo Researchers; p. 6, Alinari/Art Resource; p. 7(T), New York Historical Society; p. 7(B), Susan Van Etten/Picture Cube, Inc.; p. 8, Library of Congress; p. 10, Clark University Archives; p. 11, David Young-Wolff/PhotoEdit; p. 13, American Museum of Natural History; p. 15, Library of Congress; p. 19(R), The Freud Museum; p. 19(L), The Freud Museum; p. 21, Ronnie Kaufman/Stock Market

## Chapter 2

p. 24, Cleo Photographers/Picture Cube, Inc.; p. 26(T), Tony Freeman/PhotoEdit; p. 26(B), Dr. John J. Conger; p. 27, Esbin-Anderson/Image Works; p. 31, Rick Friedman/Black Star; p. 34, AP/Wide World; p. 37, Dave Schaefer/Picture Cube, Inc.; p. 41, Cleo Photographers/Picture Cube, Inc.; p. 42, Rhoda Sidney/Image Works; p. 43(T), Newsweek; p. 43(B), Michael Newman/PhotoEdit; p. 46(T), Laura Dwight; p. 46(TC), Nancy Sheehan/Picture Cube, Inc.; p. 46(B), Robert Brenner/PhotoEdit; p. 46(BC), David Young-Wolff/PhotoEdit; p. 47(T), Dr. John J. Conger; p. 47(TC), Photograph courtesy of David Hiser, Photographers/Aspen; p. 47(B), D. Wells/Image Works; p. 47(BC), Dr. John J. Conger; p. 49, Billy E. Barnes/PhotoEdit

## Chapter 3

p. 54, Paul Barton/Stock Market; p. 57, Bob Daemmrich/Stock Boston; p. 60, Tony Freeman/PhotoEdit; p. 61, Tom Hannon/Picture Cube, Inc.; p. 68, AP/Wide World; p. 72, Don Mason/Stock Market; p. 77, Larry Lawfer/Picture Cube, Inc.; p. 78, David Bitters/Picture Cube, Inc.

## Chapter 4

p. 82, MugShots/Stock Market; p. 85, Bob Daemmrich/Stock Boston; p. 86, Corbis-Bettmann Archive; p. 98, Mark Antman/Image Works; p. 100, Anderson/Monkmeyer Press Photo Service, Inc.; p. 102, David Powers/Stock Boston; p. 103, Bob Daemmrich/Image Works; p. 106, Richard Hutchings/PhotoEdit; p. 107, Jon Feingersh/Stock Market

## Chapter 5

p. 114, Vince Streano/Stock Market; p. 118, Bruce Davidson/Magnum Photos; p. 121, J. D. Sloan/Picture Cube, Inc.; p. 122, Lew Long/Stock Market; p. 125, Jon Feingersh/Stock Market; p. 129, Michael Newman/PhotoEdit; p. 131, Myrleen Ferguson/PhotoEdit; p. 133, Tony Freeman/PhotoEdit; p. 142, Petersen/Stock Market

## Chapter 6

p. 146, Bob Daemmrich/Stock Boston; p. 148, Jeff I. Greenberg/Photo Researchers; p. 153, Will and Deni McIntyre/Photo Researchers; p. 154, M. Richards/PhotoEdit; p. 157, Bob Daemmrich/Image Works; p. 162, D. Fineman/Sygma

## Chapter 7

p. 176, Ariel Skelly/Stock Market; p. 178, Tony Freeman/PhotoEdit; p. 182, Ken Lax/Photo Researchers; p. 186, Ariel Skelly/Stock Market; p. 191, Richard Hutchings/Photo Researchers; p. 196, Mary Kate Denny/PhotoEdit

## Chapter 8

p. 206, B. Bachmann/PhotoEdit; p. 210, Jonathan Weinstein/New York Times; p. 215, Paul Barton/Stock Market; p. 221, Stephen Ellison/People Weekly, ©1988 The Time Inc. Magazine Company; p. 225, Jeff Persons/Stock Boston; p. 227, David R. Frazier/Photo Researchers

## Chapter 9

p. 238, Sarah Putnam/Picture Cube, Inc.; p. 241, P. McCarten/PhotoEdit; p. 245, Bob Daemmrich/ Image Works; p. 249, Rhoda Sidney/Stock Boston; p. 259, Mark Richards/PhotoEdit; p. 261, David Young-Wolff/PhotoEdit

## Chapter 10

p. 266, Bob Daemmrich/Image Works; p. 274, Michael Newman/PhotoEdit; p. 276, K. Clineff/Picture Cube, Inc.; p. 282, Jonathan Nourok/PhotoEdit; p. 283, Bob Daemmrich; p. 286, Larry Lawfer/Picture Cube, Inc.

## Chapter 11

p. 292, Myrleen Ferguson/PhotoEdit; p. 298, Roy Morsch/Stock Market; p. 304, Gene Peach/Picture Cube, Inc.; p. 306, Michael Newman/PhotoEdit; p. 316, Mark Richards/PhotoEdit; p. 318, Robert Brenner/PhotoEdit

## Chapter 12

p. 326, Dorothy Littell/Stock Boston; p. 328, Jack Spratt/Image Works; p. 331, Brent Peterson/Stock Market; p. 339, AP/Wide World; p. 347, Bob Daemmrich/Image Works

## Chapter 13

p. 354, Jeff Greenberg/Picture Cube, Inc.; p. 356, Tony Freeman/PhotoEdit; p. 362, Carol Lee/Picture Cube, Inc.; p. 365, Chauvel/Sygma; p. 369, Susan Rosenberg/Photo Researchers

## Epilogue

p. 381, Betty Moore Photo

# Author Index

# Subject Index

Note: *b*, *f*, *t* after page numbers refer to information in boxes, figures, and tables.